2016 Shanghai Statistical Yearbook

2016上海统计年鉴

上　海　市　统　计　局
国家统计局上海调查总队
SHANGHAI MUNICIPAL STATISTICS BUREAU
SURVEY OFFICE OF THE NATIONAL BUREAU
OF STATISTICS IN SHANGHAI

中国统计出版社
China Statistics Press

编者说明

一、《上海统计年鉴－2016》是一本信息高度密集的资料工具书。本书收录了2015年上海的经济和社会等各方面的统计数据，以及重要年份和改革开放以来的主要统计数据。

二、全书内容分为23个篇目，即：1. 综合；2. 人口；3. 从业人员和职工工资；4. 国民经济核算；5. 财政收支；6. 能源与环境；7. 固定资产投资；8. 对外经济贸易和旅游；9. 价格水平；10. 人民生活；11. 城市建设；12. 农业；13. 工业；14. 建筑业；15. 交通运输、邮政和信息传输；16. 批发、零售和住宿、餐饮；17. 金融业；18. 房地产业；19. 科学技术；20. 教育；21. 卫生、社会保障和社会福利业；22. 文化和体育；23. 法律、公证和其他。为便于读者正确地使用资料，各篇目还附有简要说明和主要统计指标解释。

三、本年鉴数据除特别说明外，是由上海市统计局和国家统计局上海调查总队通过年报调查收集。

四、资料中所使用的度量衡单位均采用国际统一标准计量单位，金额除特别标明外，均以人民币计量。

五、本年鉴总量指标计算所采用的价格均为现行价格。

六、本年鉴部分数据合计数或相对数由于单位取舍不同产生的计算误差均未作机械调整。

七、本年鉴表中的符号使用说明：

“…”表示数据不足本表最小计量单位数；

“空格”表示该项统计数据不详或无该项数据；

“#”表示其中的主要项。

八、《上海统计年鉴》公开出版以来，受到了国内外广大读者的关心和支持，对本年鉴的内容和编辑工作提出了许多宝贵的意见，对此我们深表谢意。限于我们的水平，欢迎读者继续对年鉴的不足之处给予批评和指正，帮助我们进一步改进年鉴的编辑工作，以期更好地为广大读者服务。

EDITOR'S NOTE

Ⅰ. Shanghai Statistical Yearbook 2016 contains comprehensive statistics of Shanghai's social and economic development in 2015 and selected data of some important years and of the period since China adopted the policy of reform and opening to the outside world.

Ⅱ. The book is composed of 23 parts viz. 1. General Survey; 2. Population; 3. Employment and Wages; 4. National Economic Accounting; 5. Fiscal Revenue and Expenditure; 6. Energy and Environment Protection; 7. Investment in Fixed Assets; 8. Foreign Economic Relations, Trade and Tourism; 9. Prices; 10. Living Standards; 11. Urban Construction; 12. Agriculture; 13. Industry; 14. Construction; 15. Transportation, Posts and Information Transmission; 16. Wholesale and Retail, Hotels and Catering Services; 17. Finance; 18. Real Estate; 19. Science and Technology; 20. Education; 21. Health, Social Security and Social Welfare; 22. Culture, Sports; 23. Laws, Notary and others. In order to make readers using materials correctly, brief introduction and explanations of major statistical indicators are attached after every chapter.

Ⅲ. Main part of the data in this yearbook are investigated and collected by Shanghai Municipal Statistical Bureau and Survey Office of the National Bureau of Statistics in Shanghai, except those with special notes.

Ⅳ. The international standard unit of measurement is applied in this book. All amounts are denominated in RMB, except those with special notes.

Ⅴ. The prices used for calculating of gross indicators in this yearbook are current prices.

Ⅵ. Statistical discrepancies in this book due to rounding are not adjusted.

Ⅶ. Marks in this book: … means not large enough to be rounded into the least unit of measurement; blank space means data are not available; # indicates major item in a category.

Ⅷ. Previous editions of Shanghai Statistical Yearbook have won wide acclaim among the readers. In order to get further improvement in the yearbook editing, we welcome all candid comments and criticism from our readers.

目录 CONTENTS

第一篇 CHAPTER 1 综合 GENERAL SURVEY

目录
CONTENTS

第二篇 CHAPTER 2 人口 POPULATION

第三篇 CHAPTER 3 从业人员和职工工资 EMPLOYMENT AND WAGES

第四篇 CHAPTER 4 国民经济核算 NATIONAL ECONOMIC ACCOUNTING

目录

CONTENTS

第五篇 CHAPTER 5 财政收支 FISCAL REVENUE AND EXPENDITURE

第六篇 CHAPTER 6 能源与环境 ENERGY AND ENVIRONMENT PROTECTION

目录
CONTENTS

第七篇 CHAPTER 7 固定资产投资 INVESTMENT IN FIXED ASSETS

第八篇 CHAPTER 8 对外经济贸易和旅游 FOREIGN ECONOMIC RELATIONS, TRADE AND TOURISM

目录
CONTENTS

第九篇 CHAPTER 9 价格水平 PRICES

第十篇 CHAPTER 10 人民生活 LIVING STANDARDS

目录 CONTENTS

第十一篇 CHAPTER 11 城市建设 URBAN CONSTRUCTION

第十二篇 CHAPTER 12 农 业 AGRICULTURE

目录 CONTENTS

第十三篇 CHAPTER 13 工 业 INDUSTRY

第十四篇 CHAPTER 14 建筑业 CONSTRUCTION

目录
CONTENTS

第十五篇 CHAPTER 15 交通运输、邮政和信息传输 TRANSPORTATION, POSTS AND INFORMATION TRANSMISSION

第十六篇 CHAPTER 16 批发、零售和住宿、餐饮 WHOLESALE AND RETAIL, HOTELS AND CATERING SERVICES

目录
CONTENTS

第十七篇 CHAPTER 17 金融业 FINANCE

第十八篇 CHAPTER 18 房地产业 REAL ESTATE

目录
CONTENTS

第十九篇 CHAPTER 19 科学技术 SCIENCE AND TECHNOLOGY

目录
CONTENTS

第二十篇 CHAPTER 20 教育 EDUCATION

第二十一篇 CHAPTER 21 卫生、社会保障和社会福利业 HEALTH,SOCIAL SECURITY AND SOCIAL WELFARE

目录
CONTENTS

第二十二篇 CHAPTER 22 文化和体育 CULTURE AND SPORTS

目录
CONTENTS

第二十三篇 CHAPTER 23 法律、公证和其他 LAWS,NOTARY AND OTHERS

第一篇
CHAPTER 1

综　合
GENERAL SURVEY

简要说明

本篇章主要内容和资料来源

一、综合资料主要包括上海市行政区划、国民经济和社会发展综合资料两部分。分别由上海市民政局、上海市统计局和国家统计局上海调查总队编辑整理。

二、行政区划资料，由上海市民政局根据上海市政府批准的、截止到上一年末上海市区划变更情况汇总整理并提供。

三、国民经济和社会发展综合资料是抽取全书的精华，通过对各篇章主要统计指标及其速度、结构、比例和效益等的加工计算，来反映国民经济和社会发展的总体情况。

BRIEF INTRODUCTION

Main Contents and Sources of Data

1. This chapter consists of two parts: divisions of Shanghai administrative areas and summary data on the national economy and social development, which are compiled by the Shanghai Municipal Civil Affairs Bureau, Shanghai Municipal Statistics Bureau and the Survey Office of the National Bureau of Statistics in Shanghai.

2. Data on divisions of administrative areas in Shanghai, are prepared and provided by the Shanghai Municipal Civil Affairs Bureau on the basis of the changes in the divisions of administrative areas as approved by the Shanghai municipal government at the end of the previous year.

3. The summary data on the national economy and social development reflect on the overall situation of the economy and social development by presenting further processed statistics including growth, structure, ratio, and efficiency data derived from other chapters.

表 1.1　行政区划（2015）
ADMINISTRATIVE DIVISION

单位：个（unit）

地　区	District	镇 Towns	乡 Township	街道办事处 Urban Sub-district Office	居民委员会 Neighbourhood Committees	村民委员会 Village Committees
全　市	**Total**	**107**	**2**	**104**	**4 154**	**1 593**
浦东新区	Pudong New Area	24		12	876	365
黄 浦 区	Huangpu			10	183	
徐 汇 区	Xuhui	1		12	303	
长 宁 区	Changning	1		9	185	
静 安 区	Jing'an			5	70	
普 陀 区	Putuo	2		8	252	7
闸 北 区	Zhabei	1		8	204	1
虹 口 区	Hongkou			8	212	
杨 浦 区	Yangpu	1		11	308	
闵 行 区	Minhang	9		4	425	132
宝 山 区	Baoshan	9		3	367	104
嘉 定 区	Jiading	7		3	179	143
金 山 区	Jinshan	9		1	99	124
松 江 区	Songjiang	11		6	211	86
青 浦 区	Qingpu	8		3	101	184
奉 贤 区	Fengxian	8		1	111	177
崇 明 县	Chongming	16	2		68	270

注：本表数据由上海市民政局提供。
Note: Data in this table are provided by Shanghai Civil Affairs Bureau.

表 1.2 主要气象指标（2015）
MAIN CLIMATE INDICATORS

指 标	Indicators	2015	指 标	Indicators	2015
平均气温(℃)	Annual Average Temperature(℃)	17.1	蒸发量(毫米)	Evaporation (mm)	984.4
极端最高气温(℃)	Utmost Highest Air Temperature(℃)	38.5	降水量(毫米)	Precipitation(mm)	1 649.1
极端最低气温(℃)	Utmost Lowest Air Temperature(℃)	-4.8	降雨日(天)	Annual Rainy Days(day)	152
日照时间（小时）	Annual Sunshine Time(h)	1 493.8	无霜期(天)	Frost-free Period(day)	269

表 1.3 各月主要气象指标(2015)
MAIN CLIMATE INDICATORS OF EVERY MONTH

月 份	Month	平均气温(℃) Annual Average Temperature (℃)	极端最高气温(℃) Utmost Highest Air Temperature(℃)	极端最低气温(℃) Utmost Lowest Air Temperature(℃)	平均最高气温(℃) Average Maximum temperature(℃)	平均最低气温(℃) Average Minimum temperature(℃)
1月	Jan.	6.0	19.7	-4.8	10.3	2.7
2月	Feb.	6.8	18.4	-4.8	10.1	3.9
3月	Mar.	10.6	29.0	-3.8	14.5	7.3
4月	Apr.	15.9	31.7	-1.2	20.9	11.4
5月	May.	20.5	29.5	3.7	24.4	17.1
6月	Jun.	24.2	35.0	10.6	27.8	21.6
7月	Jul.	26.7	38.1	17.2	30.0	24.0
8月	Aug.	27.8	38.5	16.9	31.3	25.0
9月	Sep.	24.2	30.9	21.9	27.4	21.4
10月	Oct.	19.6	27.1	18.3	23.4	15.8
11月	Nov.	14.0	26.2	10.2	16.8	11.4
12月	Dec.	7.8	17.9	-2.1	11.1	4.6

表 1.3 续表 continued

月 份	Month	日照时间（小时） Annual Sunshine Time(h)	降水量(毫米) Precipitation (mm)	降雨日(天) Annual Rainy Days (day)	蒸发量(毫米) Evaporation (mm)
1月	Jan.	119.0	61.1	9	54.3
2月	Feb.	102.3	81.1	10	50.2
3月	Mar.	130.5	96.4	15	70.9
4月	Apr.	169.8	108.9	12	103.5
5月	May.	169.7	131.4	12	111.5
6月	Jun.	77.0	486.4	18	97.8
7月	Jul.	108.3	173.1	16	107.2
8月	Aug.	162.3	125.6	11	118.4
9月	Sep.	138.3	140.5	9	101.2
10月	Oct.	158.2	49.3	7	77.3
11月	Nov.	62.7	113.9	21	50.1
12月	Dec.	95.7	81.4	12	42.0

注：本页资料由上海市气象局提供。
Note: Data on this page are provided by Shanghai Meteorological Bureau.

表 1.4　中国(上海)自由贸易试验区主要经济指标(2015)
MAIN ECONOMIC INDICATORS OF THE CHINA(SHANGHAI) PILOT FREE TRADE ZONE

指　标	Indicators	单　位	Unit	2015
税收总额	Total Tax Revenue	亿元	100 million yuan	1 022.20
一般公共预算收入	General Budgetary Revenue	亿元	100 million yuan	444.74
外商直接投资合同项目	Foreign Direct Investment Projects	个	unit	3 072
外商直接投资合同金额	Contracted Capital of Foreign Direct Investment	亿美元	100 million USD	396.26
外商直接投资实际到位金额	Foreign Direct Investment Actually Absorbed	亿美元	100 million USD	48.21
新增内资企业注册户数	New Domestic Funded Enterprises Registered	个	unit	10 901
新增内资企业注册资本	Registered Capital of New Domestic Funded Enterprises	亿元	100 million yuan	7 362.79
全社会固定资产投资总额	Total Investment in Fixed Assets	亿元	100 million yuan	563.11
工业总产值	Gross Output Value of Industry	亿元	100 million yuan	3 901.03
社会消费品零售额	Total Retail Sales of Consumer Goods	亿元	100 million yuan	1 051.35
商品销售总额	Commodity Sales	亿元	100 million yuan	26 866.48
服务业营业收入	Revenue of Service Industry	亿元	100 million yuan	3 599.06
外贸进出口总额	Total Value of Imports and Exports	亿元	100 million yuan	7 415.46
#出　口	Exports	亿元	100 million yuan	2 027.02
经认定的企业研发机构	Identified R&D Institutions of Enterprises	个	unit	555
发明专利授权数	Invention Patent Certified	个	unit	2 843
期末监管类金融机构	Regulatory Financial Institutions	个	unit	758
新兴金融机构	Emerging Financial Institutions	个	unit	4 154
跨境人民币结算总额	Total Cross-border Settlement in RMB	亿元	100 million yuan	12 026.40
跨境人民币境外借款金额	Overseas Borrowing of Cross-border RMB	亿元	100 million yuan	69.82

①自贸区按注册地口径统计，统计范围为 120.72 平方公里。
②一般公共预算收入按开发区财力结算口径。
③外贸进出口总额仅包括自贸区保税片区。
❶The statistics of China (shanghai) Pilot Free Trade Zone follow registration place, and statistical range covers 120.72 square kilometers.
❷The statistics of general public budget revenue follow the financial settlement standard of Development Zone.
❸Total Value of Imports and Exports only contains the bonded area of free trade zone.

表 1.5 主要年份社会经济主要指标
MAJOR SOCIAL AND ECONOMIC INDICATORS IN MAIN YEARS

指标	Indicators	1990	2000	2010	2014	2015
人口与就业	**Population and Employment**					
人　口	**Population**					
年末常住人口(万人)	Year-end Resident Population (10 000 persons)	1 334.00	1 608.60	2 302.66	2 425.68	2 415.27
年末户籍人口(万人)	Year-end Registered Population(10 000 persons)	1 283.35	1 321.63	1 412.32	1 438.69	1 442.97
就　业	**Employment**					
城镇登记失业率(%)	Registered Unemployment Rate in Urban Areas (%)	1.5	3.5	4.2	4.2	4.1
宏观经济	**Macro Economy**					
国民经济核算	**National Economic Accounts**					
上海市生产总值(亿元)	Gross Domestic Product(100 million yuan)	781.66	4 771.17	17 165.98	23 567.70	25 123.45
#第一产业	Primary Industry	34.24	76.68	114.15	124.26	109.82
第二产业	Secondary Industry	505.70	2 207.63	7 218.32	8 167.71	7 991.00
第三产业	Tertiary Industry	241.82	2 486.86	9 833.51	15 275.73	17 022.63
#工　业	Industry	469.83	1 998.96	6 536.21	7 362.84	7 162.33
人均生产总值(元)(按常住人口计算)	Per Capita Gross Domestic Product(yuan) (Calculated by Resident Population)	5 911	30 047	76 074	97 370	103 795
经济增长贡献率(%)	Contribution Rate of Economic Growth (%)					
#第一产业	Primary Industry	2.5	0.6	-0.4	…	-1.0
第二产业	Secondary Industry	62.6	55.7	69.2	23.6	6.7
第三产业	Tertiary Industry	37.2	43.7	31.2	76.3	94.3
#工　业	Industry	74.6	54.7	66.6	21.8	2.7
固定资产投资	**Investment in Fixed Assets**					
全社会固定资产投资总额(亿元)	Total Investment in Fixed Assets (100 million yuan)	227.08	1 869.67	5 317.67	6 016.43	6 352.70
#房地产开发	Investment in Real Estate	8.16	566.17	1 980.68	3 206.48	3 468.94

表 1.5 续表 1　continued

指　标	Indicators	1990	2000	2010	2014	2015
财　政	**Public Finance**					
一般公共预算收入(亿元)	General Budgetary Revenue of Local Government (100 million yuan)	166.99	497.96	2 873.58	4 871.76	5 519.50
一般公共预算支出(亿元)	General Budgetary Expenditure of Local Government (100 million yuan)	75.56	622.84	3 302.89	5 182.65	6 191.56
价　格	**Price**					
居民消费价格指数(上年 = 100)	Consumer Price Index(preceding = 100)	106.3	102.5	103.1	102.7	102.4
商品零售价格指数(上年 = 100)	Retail Price Index(preceding = 100)	104.8	96.4	101.7	100.9	101.1
外商直接投资	**Foreign Direct Investment**					
合同项目(个)	Number of Contracts (item)	203	1 814	3 906	4 697	6 007
合同金额(亿美元)	Contractual Foreign Capital(100 million USD)	2.14	63.90	153.07	316.09	589.43
实到金额(亿美元)	Foreign Investment Actually Absorbed (100 million USD)	1.77	31.60	111.21	181.66	184.59
产　业	**Industries**					
农　业	**Agriculture**					
农业总产值(亿元)	Gross Output Value of Agriculture (100 million yuan)	68.16	216.50	287.03	322.22	302.62
工　业	**Industry**					
工业总产值(亿元)	Gross Output Value of Industry (100 million yuan)	1 642.75	7 022.98	31 038.57	34 071.19	33 211.57
建筑业	**Construction**					
建筑业总产值(亿元)	Gross Output Value of Construction (100 million yuan)	75.62	631.64	4 300.19	5 499.94	5 652.47
交通运输、邮政业和信息传输	**Transportation, Post and Information Transmission**					
货物运输量(万吨)	Freight Transportation Volume (10 000tons)	22 848	47 954	81 024	90 341	91 239
旅客发送量(万人次)	Passenger Departures (10 000person-times)	3 835	6 893	13 432	17 208	18 571
港口货物吞吐量(万吨)	Port Cargo Freight Throughput (10 000tons)	13 959	20 440	65 339	75 529	71 740
国际标准集装箱吞吐量(万 TEU)	International Container Throughput Capacity (10 000TEU)	45.60	561.20	2 906.90	3 528.53	3 653.70
邮电业务总量(亿元)	Revenue from Post and Telecommunications Services (100 million yuan)	10.23	171.70	1 016.44	907.52	1 166.07
年末固定电话用户(万户)	Year-end Installed Telephones (10 000 households)	45.69	549.00	935.91	840.18	797.29

表1.5 续表2 continued

指 标	Indicators	1990	2000	2010	2014	2015
批发和零售	**Wholesale and Retail**					
社会消费品零售总额(亿元)	Total Retail Sales of Consumer Goods (100 million yuan)	333.86	1 865.28	6 186.58	9 303.49	10 131.50
批发零售业商品销售总额(亿元)	Sales of Commodities of Wholesale and Retail (100 million yuan)	1 305.41	7 474.81	48 659.55	87 829.31	93 406.57
对外经济贸易	**Foreign Trade**					
上海关区进出口总额(亿美元)	Total Trade Value Through Customs (100 million USD)	172.89	1 093.11	6 846.45	8 634.55	8 187.86
进口额	Imports	86.27	477.39	2 613.05	3 402.43	3 182.06
出口额	Exports	86.62	615.72	4 233.40	5 232.12	5 005.80
上海市进出口总额(亿美元)	Total Value of Foreign Trade Imports and Exports (100 million USD)	74.31	547.10	3 688.69	4 666.22	4 517.33
进口额	Imports	21.10	293.56	1 880.85	2 563.45	2 547.64
出口额	Exports	53.21	253.54	1 807.84	2 102.77	1 969.69
外商直接投资	**Foreign Direct Investment**					
合同项目(个)	Number of Contracts (item)	203	1 814	3 906	4 697	6 007
合同金额(亿美元)	Contractual Foreign Capital (100 million USD)	2.14	63.90	153.07	316.09	589.43
实到金额(亿美元)	Foreign Investment Actually Absorbed (100 million USD)	1.77	31.60	111.21	181.66	184.59
国际旅游	**International Tourism**					
国际旅游入境人数(万人次)	Number of Overseas Tourists Through Shanghai Custom (10 000 persons-times)	89.30	181.40	851.12	791.30	800.16
国际旅游(外汇)收入(亿美元)	Foreign Exchange Earnings from International Tourism (100 million USD)	2.31	16.13	64.05	57.05	59.60
金 融	**Finance**					
金融机构存款余额(亿元)	Saving Deposits Balance of Financial Institutions (100 million yuan)	851.51	9 349.83	52 190.04	73 882.45	103 760.60
金融机构贷款余额(亿元)	Loan Balance of Financial Institutions(100 million yuan)	1 106.80	7 254.26	34 154.17	47 915.81	53 387.21
有价证券成交总额(亿元)	Total Volume of Priced Securities Trading (100 million)		49 901	398 396	1 281 498	2 663 691
#股 票	Stocks		31 374	304 312	377 162	1 330 992
原保险保费收入(亿元)	Premium of Primary Insurance (100 million yuan)	8.99	127.23	883.86	986.75	1 125.16
原保险赔付支出(亿元)	Payment of Primary Insurance (100 million yuan)	2.22	36.44	194.54	378.66	473.59
教育、科技、文化	**Education, Science&Technology and Culture**					
教 育	**Education**					
在校学生数(万人)	Students Enrollment(10 000 persons)					
普通高等学校	Regular Institutions of Higher Education	12.13	22.68	51.57	50.66	51.16
普通中学	Regular Secondary Schools	48.31	79.54	59.44	58.42	57.05
普通小学	Primary Schools	110.19	78.86	70.16	80.30	79.87
每万人拥有大学生(人)	Number of College and University Students Per 10 000 Persons(person)	90	141	224	209	212

表 1.5 续表 3 continued

指 标	Indicators	1990	2000	2010	2014	2015
科 技	**Science and Technology**					
科技成果（项）	Achievements in Science and Technology (item)	2 092	1 102	2 318	2 384	2 356
研究与试验发展经费内部支出（亿元）	Expenditures on R&D (100 million yuan)	10.13	76.73	481.70	861.95	936.14
研究与试验发展经费支出相当于上海市生产总值比例(%)	R&D Expenditure as Percentage of Gross Domestic Product (%)	1.30	1.61	2.81	3.66	3.73
文 化	**Culture**					
出版数量	Number of Publications					
图 书（亿册）	Books (100 million copies)	2.98	2.54	2.89	3.26	3.53
期 刊（亿册）	Periodicals (100 million copies)	1.73	1.85	1.78	1.45	1.28
报 纸（亿份）	Newspapers (100 million copies)	16.16	16.77	15.90	11.45	10.80
故事影片产量（部）	Feature Films Produced(film)	16	10	19	28	34
家庭、生活、环境	**Family, Living and Environment**					
家 庭	**Household**					
家庭总户数（万户）	Total Households (10 000 households)	415.28	475.73	519.27	532.55	536.76
平均每户家庭人口（人）	Average Persons per Household (person)	3.09	2.78	2.72	2.70	2.69
婚 姻	**Marriages and Divorces**					
准予登记结婚（万对）	Marriage Registration Permitted (10 000 couples)	10.77	9.31	13.03	14.19	14.18
离婚件数（万件）	Divorce (10 000 cases)	1.64	3.18	4.67	6.15	6.66
住 宅	**Housing**					
城镇居民人均住房居住面积（平方米）	Dwelling Area per Capita of Urban Residents(sq. m)	6.6	11.8	16.7	17.8	18.1
生 活	**Living**					
全市居民人均可支配收入(元)	Per Capita Annual Disposable Income of Residents(yuan)					49 867
全市居民人均消费支出(元)	Per Capita Annual Consumption Expenditure of Residents(yuan)					34 784
城镇常住居民人均可支配收入(元)	Per Capita Annual Disposable Income of Urban Households(yuan)					52 962
城镇常住居民人均消费支出(元)	Per Capita Annual Consumption Expenditures of Urban Households(yuan)					36 946
农村常住居民人均可支配收入(元)	Per Capita Annual Disposable Income of Rural Households(yuan)					23 205
农村常住居民人均消费支出(元)	Per Capita Annual Consumption Expenditure of Rural Households(yuan)					16 152
个人存款(住户存款)余额（亿元）	Household Deposits(100 million yuan)		2 627.07	16 249.29	24 057.05	23 384.73

注：城镇居民人均住房居住面积由市房地局提供。
Note: Dwelling Area per Capita of Urban Residents data are provided by Shanghai Municipal Housing Land and Resources Administration.

表1.5 续表4 continued

	指 标 Indicators	1990	2000	2010	2014	2015
工 资	**Wages**					
职工工资总额(亿元)	Total Wages of Staff and Workers (100 million yuan)	146.78	614.53	3 018.55	7 643.73	8 318.57
职工平均工资(元)	Average Wages of Staff and Workers (yuan)	2 917	15 420	46 757	65 417	71 268
卫 生	**Health Care**					
医 院(个)	Quantity of Hospitals (unit)	462	459	306	332	338
医 生(万人)	Doctors (10 000 persons)	5.82	4.99	5.13	6.13	6.31
医院床位数(万张)	Quantity of Hospital Beds (10 000 beds)	6.21	7.31	8.48	9.83	10.35
每万人拥有医生(人)	Quantity of Doctors Per 10 000 Persons (person)	44	31	22	25	26
城市建设	**Urban Construction**					
城市基础设施投资额(亿元)	Urban Infrastructure Investment (100 million yuan)	47.22	449.90	1 497.46	1 057.25	1 425.08
自来水售水量(亿立方米)	Total Quantity of Water Supply(100 million cu. m)	12.25	19.75	24.44	24.82	24.58
用电量(亿千瓦时)	Electricity Power Consumption (100 million kwh)	264.74	559.51	1 295.87	1 369.03	1 405.55
天然气销售总量(亿立方米)	Sales of Natural Gas(100 million cu. m)		2.16	42.66	66.39	69.73
年末出租车运营总数(辆)	Year-end Operating Taxi Vehicles(vehicle)	11 298	42 943	50 007	50 738	49 586
运营公交车辆数(辆)	Total Number of Operating Public Transportation Vehicles (vehicle)	6 264	17 939	17 455	16 155	16 531
道路长度(公里)	Length of Roads (km)	1 631	6 641	16 687	17 797	18 184
城市人均公园绿地面积(平方米)	Per Capita Park Green Areas(sq. m)	1.0	4.6	13.0	7.3	7.6
城市绿化覆盖率(%)	Coverage Rate of Urban Green Areas (%)	12.4	22.2	38.2	38.4	38.5
森林覆盖率(%)	Coverage Rate of Forest(%)	5.5	9.2	12.6	14.0	15.0
环境保护投资相当于上海市生产总值比例(%)	Investment on Environment Protection as Percentage of Gross Domestic Product (%)		3.10	2.96	2.97	2.82
环境空气质量优良率(%)	Rate of Good Ambient Air Quality (%)		80.8	92.1	77.0	70.7
火灾、交通事故	**Fires and Traffic Accidents**					
火灾发生数(起)	Quantity of Fires (unit)	2 146	5 164	5 703	5 846	4 606
火灾损失额(万元)	Loss of Fires (10 000 yuan)	1 868	1 919	22 949	7 428	14 000
交通事故发生数(万起)	Quantity of Traffic Accidents(10 000units)	0.76	4.13	0.22	0.12	0.10
交通事故损失额(万元)	Loss of Traffic Accidents (10 000 yuan)	1 345	20 391	967	463	470

注：本表总量指标中的价值量指标均按当年价格计算。
Note: The data in value terms in the table are calculated at current prices.

表 1.6　主要年份社会经济主要指标发展速度
GROWTH RATE OF MAJOR SOCIAL AND ECONOMIC INDICATORS IN MAIN YEARS

单位:%

指　标	Indicators	2015 年比下列各年增长 Indicator's Growth Rate Between 2015 and Year Below			
		1990	2000	2010	2014
年末常住人口	Year-end Residnet Population	81.1	50.1	4.9	-0.4
上海市生产总值	Gross Domestic Product	11.8 倍	3.0 倍	34.0	6.9
第一产业	Primary Industry	9.0	-14.0	-3.4	-13.6
第二产业	Secondary Industry	10.1 倍	2.6 倍	20.9	1.2
第三产业	Tertiary Industry	15.4 倍	3.4 倍	43.8	10.6
全社会固定资产投资总额	Total Investment in Fixed Assets	28.6 倍	2.5 倍	25.7	5.6
一般公共预算收入	General Budgetary Revenue of Local Government		10.1 倍	92.1	13.3
一般公共预算支出	General Budgetary Expenditure of Local Government		8.9 倍	87.5	19.5
农业总产值	Gross Output Value of Agriculture	29.1	-18.4	-9.2	-6.7
工业总产值	Gross Output Value of Industry	18.9 倍	3.9 倍	12.1	-0.5
货物运输量	Freight Transportation Volume	3 倍	90.3	12.6	1.0
旅客发送量	Passenger Departures	3.8 倍	1.7 倍	38.3	7.9
港口货物吞吐量	Port Freight Throughput	4.1 倍	2.5 倍	9.8	-5.0
社会消费品零售总额	Total Retail Sales of Consumer Goods	29.3 倍	4.4 倍	54.9	8.9
上海关区进出口总额	Total Trade Value Through Customs	47.4 倍	7.5 倍	19.6	-5.2
进口额	Imports	36.9 倍	6.7 倍	21.8	-6.5
出口额	Exports	57.8 倍	8.1 倍	18.2	-4.3
上海市进出口总额	Total Value of Foreign Trade Imports and Exports	60.8 倍	8.3 倍	22.5	-3.2
进口额	Imports	120.7 倍	8.7 倍	35.5	-0.6
出口额	Exports	37.0 倍	7.8 倍	9.0	-6.3
外商直接投资	Foreign Direct Investment				
合同项目	Number of Contracts	28.6 倍	2.3 倍	53.8	27.9
合同金额	Contractual Foreign Capital	156.3 倍	8.2 倍	2.9 倍	86.5
实到金额	Foreign Investment Actually Absorbed	103.2 倍	4.8 倍	66.0	1.6
全市居民人均可支配收入	Per Capita Annual Disposable Income of Residents				8.5
全市居民人均消费支出	Per Capita Annual Consumption Expenditures of Residents				5.2
城镇常住居民人均可支配收入	Per Capita Annual Disposable Income of Urban Households				8.4
城镇常住居民人均消费支出	Per Capita Annual Consumption Expenditures of Urban Households				5
农村常住居民人均可支配收入	Per Capita Annual Disposable Income of Rural Households				9.5
农村常住居民人均消费支出	Per Capita Annual Consumption Expenditures of Rural Households				9.0
城市基础设施投资额	Urban Infrastructure Investment	30.9 倍	2.2 倍	2.3	34.8
医　生	Doctors	8.4	26.5	23.0	2.9
普通高等学校在校学生	Student Enrollment of Institutions of Higher Education	3.2 倍	1.3 倍	-0.8	1.0

注：本表速度指标中，上海市生产总值及三次产业、工业总产值、农业总产值均按可比价格计算。
Note: The growth rates of the following indicators are calculated by comparable prices: Gross Domestic Product and three industries, gross output value of agriculture and Industry.

表 1.6 续表 continued

单位:%

指 标	Indicators	平均每年增长 Indicators'Average Annual Growth Rate 1991～2015	2001～2015	2011～2015
年末常住人口	Year-end Resident Population	2.4	2.7	1.0
上海市生产总值	Gross Domestic Product	11.0	10.2	7.5
第一产业	Primary Industry	-0.2	-2.0	-3.5
第二产业	Secondary Industry	10.2	9.1	4.1
第三产业	Tertiary Industry	12.3	11.1	9.7
全社会固定资产投资总额	Total Investment in Fixed Assets	17.4	10.2	3.9
一般公共预算收入	General Budgetary Revenue of Local Government		17.4	13.9
一般公共预算支出	General Budgetary Expenditure of Local Government		16.5	13.4
农业总产值	Gross Output Value of Agriculture	1.4	-1.0	-0.7
工业总产值	Gross Output Value of Industry	12.7	11.1	2.3
货物运输量	Freight Transportation Volume	5.7	4.4	2.4
旅客发送量	Passenger Departures	6.5	6.8	6.7
港口货物吞吐量	Port Freight Throughput	6.8	8.7	1.9
社会消费品零售总额	Total Retail Sales of Consumer Goods	14.0	10.8	7.3
上海关区进出口总额	Total Trade Value Through Customs	16.7	14.4	3.6
进口额	Imports	15.5	13.5	4.0
出口额	Exports	17.6	15.0	3.4
上海市进出口总额	Total Value of Foreign Trade Imports and Exports	17.9	15.1	4.1
进口额	Imports	21.1	15.5	6.3
出口额	Exports	15.5	14.6	1.7
外商直接投资	Foreign Direct Investment			
合同项目	Number of Contracts	96.9	27.1	9.0
合同金额	Contractual Foreign Capital	1.8倍	56.0	31.0
实到金额	Foreign Investment Actually Absorbed	1.5倍	42.3	10.7
医 生	Doctors	0.3	1.6	4.2
普通高等学校在校学生	Student Enrollment of Institutions of Higher Education	5.9	5.6	-0.2
城市基础设施投资额	Urban Infrastructure Investment	18.5	10.8	-6.5

表 1.7 主要年份社会经济发展结构指标
STRUCTURAL INDICATORS OF SOCIAL AND ECONOMIC DEVELOPMENT IN MAIN YEARS

单位：%

指 标	Indicators	1990	2000	2010	2014	2015
人口性别结构	Structure of Sex	100	100	100	100	100
男	Male	50.4	50.4	49.8	49.7	49.6
女	Female	49.6	49.6	50.2	50.3	50.4
上海市生产总值产业结构	Industrial Structure of GDP	100	100	100	100	100
第一产业	Primary Industry	4.4	1.6	0.7	0.5	0.4
第二产业	Secondary Industry	64.7	46.3	42.0	34.7	31.8
第三产业	Tertiary Industry	30.9	52.1	57.3	64.8	67.8
上海市生产总值所有制结构	Ownership Structure of GDP	100	100	100	100	100
公有制经济	Public State-owned	95.4	71.4	50.5	48.3	47.7
国有经济	State-owned	71.2	55.0	45.2	44.5	44.5
集体经济	Collective-owned	24.2	16.4	5.3	3.9	3.2
非公有制经济	Non-state-owned	4.6	28.6	49.5	51.7	52.3
全社会固定资产投资所有制结构	Ownership Structure of Total Investment	100	100	100	100	100
国有经济	State-owned	84.7	44.4	42.0	29.9	31.1
非国有经济	Non-State-owned	15.3	55.6	58.0	70.1	68.9
一般公共预算收入	General Budgetary Revenue of Local Government	100	100	100	100	100
#增值税	Value-added Tax		18.8	13.5	19.9	18.3
营业税	Business Tax		30.9	32.5	20.6	22.0
企业所得税	Enterprise Income Tax		20.7	21.1	19.3	20.0
个人所得税	Personal Income Tax		12.1	9.1	8.4	8.8
农业总产值结构	Structure of Gross Output Value of Agriculture	100	100	100	100	100
#种植业	Planting	42.7	41.5	54.1	52.6	53.6
牧 业	Animal Husbandry	44.4	40.3	21.9	21.7	21.7
渔 业	Fishery	11.8	17.5	18.3	19.4	17.1
货物运输总量结构	Structure of Freight Transportation	100	100	100	100	100
铁 路	Railways	5.5	2.2	1.2	0.6	0.5
公 路	Roadways	38.2	59.1	50.5	47.4	44.5
水 运	Waterways	56.3	38.5	47.9	51.6	54.6
民用航空	Civil Aviation	…	0.2	0.5	0.4	0.4
社会消费品零售总额结构	Structure of Retail Sales of Consumer Goods	100	100	100	100	100
吃	Food	42.6	39.8	25.9	22.2	22.2
穿	Clothing	15.7	13.4	13.6	14.1	15.1
用	Articles	41.1	46.0	51.9	56.0	56.9
烧	Fuels	0.6	0.8	8.6	7.7	5.7
上海市出口总额结构	Structure of Exports		100	100	100	100
#一般贸易	General Trade		40.1	35.0	41.8	42.6
加工贸易	Processing Trade		58.3	55.5	43.7	42.8
外商直接投资实到金额投资方式结构	Foreign Direct Investment Structure of Foreign Investment Actually Absorbed	100	100	100	100	100
#合资企业	Joint Ventures	61.0	40.9	16.0	12.1	21.3
合作企业	Coopratative Enterprises	37.9	9.5	1.5	4.6	2.9
独资企业	Sole-foreign Enterprises	1.1	49.6	81.6	83.2	74.9

表 1.7 续表 continued

单位:%

指 标	Indicators	1990	2000	2010	2014	2015
金融机构境内存款结构	Structure of Domestic Deposits of Financial Institutions					100
住户存款	Household Deposits					23.3
非金融企业存款	Non Financial Enterprise Deposits					38.0
广义政府存款	General Government Deposits					13.4
非银行业金融机构存款	Deposits of Non Banking Financial Institutions					25.3
金融机构境内贷款结构	Structure of Domestic Loans of Financial Institutions					100
住户贷款	Household Loans					22.8
非金融企业及机关团体贷款	Loans of Non Financial Enterprise and Non-profit Institutions					76.6
非银行业金融机构贷款	Loans of Non Banking Financial Institutions					0.6
在校学生结构	Structure of Students Enrollment	100	100	100	100	100
大学生	University and College Students	7.1	12.5	28.5	26.8	27.2
中学生	Secondary Students	28.3	43.9	32.8	30.8	30.3
小学生	Primary Students	64.6	43.6	38.7	42.4	42.5
全市居民消费支出构成	Consumption Structure of Residents					100
#食品烟酒	Food,Cigarettes and Liquors					26.6
衣　着	Clothing					4.7
居　住	Residence					32.5
生活用品及服务	Living Goods and Services					4.3
交通通信	Transportation and Communication					12.1
教育文化娱乐	Education,Culture and Entertainment					10.7
城镇常住居民消费支出构成	Consumption Structure of Urban Residents					100
#食品烟酒	Food,Cigarettes and Liquors					26.2
衣　着	Clothing					4.6
居　住	Residence					32.8
生活用品及服务	Living Goods and Services					4.3
交通通信	Transportation and Communication					12.1
教育文化娱乐	Education,Culture and Entertainment					11.0
农村常住居民消费支出构成	Consumption Structure of Rural Residents					100
#食品烟酒	Food,Cigarettes and Liquors					35
衣　着	Clothing					5.3
居　住	Residence					25.8
生活用品及服务	Living Goods and Services					4.5
交通通信	Transportation and Communication					12.7
教育文化娱乐	Education,Culture and Entertainment					5.5
卫生机构数结构	Structure of Health Care Institutions	100	100	100	100	100
#医　院	Hospitals	6.0	10.4	9.4	6.7	6.7
卫生技术人员结构	Structure of Medical Professionals	100	100	100	100	100
#医　生	Doctors	49.2	46.6	37.9	37.4	37.1
护师、护士	Senior and Junior Nurses	27.6	34.4	41.3	43.9	44.3

①2011 年起，单位存款口径进行了调整，故与往年数据不可比。
②2013 年起，卫生机构数中新增村卫生室数据，故与往年数据不可比。
❶The statistic caliber of unit deposits has been adjusted since 2011, so the data are not comparable with the previous years.
❷The number of Health Care Institutions has contained the data of village health rooms since 2013, so it can not be comparable with the previous years.

表 1.8　各时期社会经济主要指标
MAJOR SOCIAL AND ECONOMIC INDICATORS OF EACH PERIOD

时　期	Period	上海市生产总值（亿元）Gross Domestic Product (100 million yuan)	其中 of which 第一产业 Primary Industry	第二产业 Secondary Industry	第三产业 Tertiary Industry	一般公共预算收入（亿元）General Budgetary Revenue (100 million yuan)
"一五"时期	"First Five-year Plan" Period	293.26	12.56	163.89	116.81	14.93
"二五"时期	"Second Five-year Plan" Period	568.99	21.03	412.70	135.26	304.28
1963 ~ 1965		304.94	17.28	220.81	66.85	172.51
"三五"时期	"Third Five-year Plan" Period	657.06	37.64	487.88	131.54	374.19
"四五"时期	"Fourth Five-year Plan" Period	918.76	42.75	708.84	167.17	633.79
"五五"时期	"Fifth Five-year Plan" Period	1 309.61	49.26	1 004.23	256.12	797.56
"六五"时期	"Sixth Five-year Plan" Period	1 871.24	74.20	1 349.98	447.06	846.92
"七五"时期	"Seventh Five-year Plan" Period	3 162.79	132.52	2 105.23	925.04	846.96
"八五"时期	"Eighth Five-year Plan" Period	8 017.61	213.47	4 698.27	3 105.87	1 006.06
"九五"时期	"Ninth Five-year Plan" Period	19 157.33	365.76	9 434.90	9 356.67	1 962.85
"十五"时期	"Tenth Five-year Plan" Period	34 965.87	412.41	16 507.97	18 045.49	4 792.94
"十一五"时期	"Eleventh Five-year Program " Period	69 348.55	535.42	29 846.95	38 966.18	11 499.22
"十二五"时期	"Twelfth Five-year Program " Period	109 886.71	611.71	39 849.18	69 425.82	21 674.31

表 1.8 续表 continued

时　期	Period	一般公共预算支出（亿元）General Budgetary Expenditure (100 million yuan)	工　业总产值（亿元）Gross Output Value of Industry (100 million yuan)	全社会固定资产投资总额（亿元）Total Investment in Fixed Assets (100 million yuan)	上海市出口总额（亿美元）Total Exports Value (100 million USD)	社会消费品零售总额（亿元）Retail Sales of Consumer Goods (100 million yuan)
"一五"时期	"First Five-year Plan" Period	12.25	512.03	19.29	17.46	121.02
"二五"时期	"Second Five-year Plan" Period	60.79	1 069.50	55.60	31.00	145.82
1963 ~ 1965		19.28	596.63	20.29	20.12	79.50
"三五"时期	"Third Five-year Plan" Period	39.41	1 334.94	34.77	43.08	153.86
"四五"时期	"Fourth Five-year Plan" Period	86.78	1 894.01	95.79	92.86	200.62
"五五"时期	"Fifth Five-year Plan" Period	111.30	2 550.91	151.44	150.33	302.07
"六五"时期	"Sixth Five-year Plan" Period	138.52	3 509.15	412.74	180.08	576.32
"七五"时期	"Seventh Five-year Plan" Period	327.68	6 498.13	1 020.34	226.96	1 383.16
"八五"时期	"Eighth Five-year Plan" Period	775.11	17 308.90	3 994.67	403.31	3 408.52
"九五"时期	"Ninth Five-year Plan" Period	2 421.50	29 776.04	9 620.86	880.57	7 874.26
"十五"时期	"Tenth Five-year Plan" Period	5 762.87	59 716.74	13 261.11	2 724.27	12 261.12
"十一五"时期	"Eleventh Five-year Program " Period	12 925.94	124 634.89	23 804.15	7 495.49	23 225.42
"十二五"时期	"Twelfth Five-year Program " Period	24 001.72	168 202.99	28 338.39	10 280.86	43 456.25

表 1.9 各时期社会经济主要指标平均增长率
GROWTH RATE OF MAJOR SOCIAL AND ECONOMIC INDICATORS OF EACH PERIOD

单位:%

时 期	Period	上海市生产总值 Gross Domestic Product	其中 of which 第一产业 Primary Industry	第二产业 Secondary Industry	第三产业 Tertiary Industry	一般公共预算收入 General Budgetary Revenue
"一五"时期	"First Five-year Plan" Period	13.8	3.3	18.4	8.3	12.6
"二五"时期	"Second Five-year Plan" Period	1.6	1.3	4.1	-3.1	57.2
1963 ~ 1965		17.0	11.6	21.8	5.6	12.3
"三五"时期	"Third Five-year Plan" Period	8.7	3.3	9.7	5.7	9.7
"四五"时期	"Fourth Five-year Plan" Period	6.6	-1.6	7.1	6.2	6.4
"五五"时期	"Fifth Five-year Plan" Period	8.4	0.9	8.6	8.6	5.1
"六五"时期	"Sixth Five-year Plan" Period	9.1	4.3	8.3	12.3	1.1
"七五"时期	"Seventh Five-year Plan" Period	5.7	1.2	5.0	8.0	-1.6
"八五"时期	"Eighth Five-year Plan" Period	13.1	1.4	13.9	12.8	6.0
"九五"时期	"Ninth Five-year Plan" Period	11.5	3.4	9.7	15.5	17.0
"十五"时期	**"Tenth Five-year Plan" Period**	**11.9**	**-1.4**	**13.1**	**11.2**	**23.6**
"十一五"时期	"Eleventh Five-year Program" Period	11.2	-0.9	10.2	12.3	14.9
"十二五"时期	"Twelfth Five-year Program " Period	7.5	-3.5	4.1	9.7	13.9

表 1.9 续表 continued

单位:%

时 期	Period	一般公共预算支出 General Budgetary Expenditure	工 业总产值 Gross Output Value of Industry	全社会固定资产投资总额 Total Investment in Fixed Assets	上海市出口总额 Total Exports Value	社会消费品零售总额 Retail Sales of Consumer Goods
"一五"时期	"First Five-year Plan" Period	12.3	14.5	23.1	30.6	5.6
"二五"时期	"Second Five-year Plan" Period	0.6	4.9	26.5	4.2	1.2
1963 ~ 1965		25.2	18.8	31.4	11.4	-0.1
"三五"时期	"Third Five-year Plan" Period	11.2	10.2	-3.6	2.5	3.3
"四五"时期	"Fourth Five-year Plan" Period	15.5	7.5	19.4	20.7	8.4
"五五"时期	"Fifth Five-year Plan" Period	-6.3	7.6	-2.4	14.0	11.0
"六五"时期	"Sixth Five-year Plan" Period	19.2	7.7	20.6	-4.7	16.6
"七五"时期	"Seventh Five-year Plan" Period	10.4	5.9	18.7	9.6	14.0
"八五"时期	"Eighth Five-year Plan" Period	28.8	18.0	45.4	16.8	25.8
"九五"时期	"Ninth Five-year Plan" Period	18.4	12.3	6.2	17.0	12.2
"十五"时期	**"Tenth Five-year Plan" Period**	**21.7**	**19.2**	**11.9**	**29.0**	**11.6**
"十一五"时期	"Eleventh Five-year Program" Period	14.7	12.6	10.0	14.8	15.7
"十二五"时期	"Twelfth Five-year Program " Period	13.4	2.3	3.9	1.7	10.8

表 1.10　国民经济主要指标比上年增长(1978～2015)
GROWTH RATE OF MAJOR NATIONAL ECONOMIC INDICATORS OVER PRECEDING YEAR

单位:%

年　份 Year	上海市 生产总值 Gross Domestic Product	一般公共 预算收入 General Budgetary Revenue of Local Government	一般公共 预算支出 General Budgetary Expenditure of Local Government	工　业 总产值 Gross Output Value of Industry	全社会固定资产 投资总额 Total Investment in Fixed Assets
1978	15.8	14.6	51.4	12.1	55.1
1979	7.4	2.1	4.0	8.6	27.5
1980	8.4	1.2	-29.1	6.5	27.7
1981	5.6	-0.2	-0.6	3.7	20.2
1982	7.2	-3.6	8.5	4.7	30.7
1983	7.8	-6.9	8.3	7.0	6.5
1984	11.6	4.8	35.4	9.9	21.5
1985	13.4	12.4	51.9	13.5	28.5
1986	4.4	-2.6	28.2	5.5	23.9
1987	7.5	-5.8	-8.9	6.7	26.8
1988	10.1	-4.3	22.3	10.5	31.7
1989	3.0	3.3	11.3	3.0	-12.4
1990	3.5	0.1	3.1	4.0	5.7
1991	7.1	5.1	13.9	14.1	13.7
1992	14.8	5.7	10.4	20.2	38.4
1993	15.1	30.6	36.1	20.0	83.0
1994	14.5	-27.7	52.3	18.2	71.8
1995	14.3	29.6	36.0	17.4	42.6
1996	13.1	26.9	27.9	15.5	21.9
1997	12.8	22.1	25.2	14.5	1.3
1998	10.3	11.3	12.1	7.8	-0.6
1999	10.4	10.1	13.7	10.5	-5.5
2000	11.0	15.3	14.0	13.5	0.7
2001	10.5	24.6	16.6	16.4	6.7
2002	11.3	16.1	20.9	14.6	9.6
2003	12.3	24.9	25.6	31.4	12.1
2004	14.2	24.5	26.6	20.3	25.8
2005	11.4	28.7	19.0	13.9	14.8
2006	12.7	11.6	9.2	13.9	10.8
2007	15.2	31.4	21.4	15.7	13.6
2008	9.7	13.3	18.9	8.1	8.3
2009	8.2	7.7	15.3	3.2	9.2
2010	10.3	13.1	10.5	22.9	0.8
2011	8.2	19.4	18.5	6.6	0.3
2012	7.5	9.2	6.9	-0.3	3.7
2013	7.7	9.8	8.2	4.3	7.5
2014	7.0	11.6	8.7	1.6	6.5
2015	6.9	13.3	19.5	-0.5	5.6

表1.10 续表 continued

单位:%

年份 Year	社会消费品零售总额 Total Retail Sales of Consumer Goods	上海市进出口总额 Total Value of Foreign Trade Import and Export	#出口总额 Export	外商直接投资合同金额 Contracted Foreign Direct Investment	外商直接投资实到金额 Foreign Investment Actually Absorbed	港口货物吞吐量 Port Freight Throughput
1978	9.8	30.4	30.3			30.6
1979	26.2	28.2	27.0			5.0
1980	17.8	16.2	16.1			1.6
1981	10.3	-7.9	-10.8	1.0倍	…	-1.7
1982	1.2	-6.2	-5.3	1.8倍	…	7.7
1983	12.1	6.3	1.2	1.8倍	2.7倍	2.4
1984	22.9	6.3	-1.7	3.1倍	1.5倍	9.5
1985	40.1	17.6	-6.3	56.4	1.2倍	12.2
1986	13.5	0.6	6.6	-68.9	58.1	11.6
1987	14.4	15.2	16.1	35.8	1.2倍	1.8
1988	31.3	20.8	10.7	28.7	71.7	3.8
1989	12.0	8.3	9.3	6.6	15.9	9.6
1990	0.7	-5.3	5.7	20.9	-58.1	-4.4
1991	14.4	8.2	7.9	30.4	-1.1	5.2
1992	21.7	21.3	14.2	5.7倍	6.2倍	11.0
1993	45.4	30.5	12.6	1.0倍	84.1	8.0
1994	23.5	24.6	23.0	42.3	39.4	-5.8
1995	25.9	19.9	27.5	0.2	0.6	-0.1
1996	19.7	17.0	14.3	8.4	45.1	-1.0
1997	14.1	11.2	11.2	-8.4	2.0	…
1998	11.0	26.6	8.4	9.9	-24.3	-0.1
1999	8.1	23.2	17.7	-29.8	-16.2	13.7
2000	8.3	41.7	35.0	55.7	3.7	9.7
2001	8.1	11.3	9.0	15.4	39.0	8.1
2002	9.3	19.3	16.0	43.4	14.5	19.4
2003	9.1	54.7	51.2	23.5	30.1	19.8
2004	10.5	42.4	51.6	12.6	11.8	19.8
2005	12.1	16.5	23.4	18.3	4.7	16.9
2006	13.3	22.1	25.2	5.4	3.8	21.3
2007	14.8	24.4	26.7	2.0	11.4	4.5
2008	18.2	13.8	17.7	15.1	27.3	3.6
2009	13.0	-13.8	-16.2	-22.3	4.5	1.8
2010	17.3	32.8	27.4	15.1	5.5	10.4
2011	12.3	18.6	16.0	31.3	13.3	11.4
2012	8.8	-0.2	-1.4	11.1	20.5	1.1
2013	8.6	1.1	-1.2	11.6	10.5	5.5
2014	8.7	5.6	3.0	26.8	8.3	-2.6
2015	8.9	-3.2	-6.3	86.5	1.6	-5.0

表 1.11　上海社会经济主要指标占全国比重(2015)
PERCENTAGE OF THE NATIONAL TOTAL OF SHANGHAI'S MAJOR SOCIAL AND ECONOMIC INDICATORS

指　标	Indicators	全　国 Country	上　海 Shanghai	上海占全国比重(%) Percentage of the National Total(%)
生产总值(亿元)	Gross Domestic Product (100 million yuan)	676 708.00	25 123.45	3.7
#第一产业	Primary Industry	60 863.00	109.82	0.2
第二产业	Secondary Industry	274 278.00	7 991.00	2.9
第三产业	Tertiary Industry	341 567.00	17 022.63	5.0
#工　业	Industry	228 974.00	7 162.33	3.1
港口货物吞吐量(亿吨)	Port Freight Throughput(100 millions tons)	78.46	7.17	9.1
邮电业务总量(亿元)	Revenue of Post and Telecommunication (100 million yuan)	28 220.40	1 166.07	4.1
全社会固定资产投资总额(亿元)	Total Investment in Fixed Assets (100 million yuan)	561 999.80	6 352.70	1.1
社会消费品零售总额(亿元)	Total Retail Sales of Consumer Goods (100 million yuan)	300 930.80	10 131.50	3.4
上海关区进出口总额(亿美元)	Total Trade Value Through Customs (100 million USD)	39 569.01	8 187.86	20.7
进口额	Imports	16 819.51	3 182.06	18.9
出口额	Exports	22 749.50	5 005.80	22.0
外商直接投资实到金额(亿美元)	Foreign Direct Investment Actually Absorbed (100 million USD)	1 262.70	184.59	14.6
国际旅游入境人数(万人次)	Number of International Tourists (10 000 person-times)	13 382.04	800.16	6.0
研究与试验发展经费支出(亿元)	Expenditures on R&D (100 million yuan)	14 220	936.14	6.6
图书出版量(亿册)	Books Published (100 million copies)	81	3.53	4.4
期　刊(亿册)	Periodicals (100 million copies)	30	1.28	4.3
报纸出版量(亿份)	Newspapers Published (100 million copies)	440	10.8	2.5
医　生(万人)	Doctors (10 000 persons)	300	6.31	2.1
医院床位数(万张)	Beds in Hospitals (10 000 beds)	534	10.35	1.9

注：全国港口货物吞吐量为沿海规模以上主要港口货物吞吐量数据。
Note: National Port freight throughput refers to freight throughput of major coastal ports above the set scale.

表 1.12 主要年份人大情况
BASIC STATISTICS OF SHANGHAI MUNICIPAL PEOPLE'S CONGRESS IN MAIN YEARS

类别	Types	2000	2010	2014	2015
全国人大代表人数(人)	Quantity of National Congress(person)	68	66	60	62
#女性	Female	17	17	15	15
全国人大代表提出议案(件)	Proposals Offered by National Congress Representations (case)		21	22	22
市人大代表人数(人)	Quantity of Municipal CongressRepresentatives (person)	865	864	861	864
#女性	Female	203	244	267	268
市人大常委会组成人员数(人)	Quantity of Municipal Standing Committee(person)	65	64	64	65
#女性	Female	13	9	11	12
市人大代表提出议案(件)	Proposals Offered by Municipal CongressRepresentatives (case)		78	48	31
区县人大代表人数(人)	Quantity of District Level Congress Representatives (person)	4 944	4 667	4 595	4 580
#女性	Female	1 451	1 454	1 551	1 545
区县人大常委人数(人)	Quantity of District Level Standing Committee (person)	432	414	449	444
#女性	Female	67	94	131	128

注：本表数据由市人大代表工作委员会提供。
Note: Data in this Table are provided by Shanghai Committee of People's Congress.

表 1.13 主要年份政协情况
BASIC STATISTICS OF SHANGHAI MUNICIPAL PEOPLE'S POLITICAL CONSULTATIVE CONFERENCE IN MAIN YEARS

类别	Types	2000	2010	2014	2015
全国政协委员人数(人)	Quantity of National Commissary (person)	104	109	106	106
#女性	Female	20	18	17	17
全国政协委员提出提案(件)	Proposals Offered by National Commissary (case)		30	280	281
市政协委员人数(人)	Quantity of Municipal Commissary(person)	729	817	841	826
#女性	Female	120	168	187	186
市政协常委人数(人)	Quantity of Municipal Standing Committee(person)	121	132	161	158
#女性	Female	20	24	32	30
市政协委员提出提案(件)	Proposals Offered by Municipal Commissary (case)	1 197	944	966	963
区县政协委员人数(人)	Quantity of District Level Commissary(person)	4 802	5 280	5 154	5 191
#女性	Female	1 230	1 459	1 566	1 594
区县政协常委人数(人)	Quantity of District Level Standing Committee(person)	707	709	869	861
#女性	Female	174	154	236	235

注：本表数据由市政协提供。
Note: Data in this table are provided by Shanghai Municipal People's Political Consultative Conference.

上 / 海 / 统 / 计 / 年 / 鉴

主要统计指标解释

行政区划

指国家对行政区域的划分。根据宪法规定,我国的行政区域划分如下:(1)全国分为省、自治区、直辖市;(2)省、自治区分为自治州、县、自治县、市;(3)自治州分为县、自治县、市;(4)县、自治县分为乡、民族乡、镇;(5)直辖市和较大的市分为区、县;(6)国家在必要时设立的特别行政区。

气 候

指地球与大气之间长期能量交换与质量交换所形成的一种自然环境状态,它是多种因素综合作用的结果。气候既是人类生活和生产的环境要素之一, 又是供给人类生活和生产的重要资源。气温、降水、湿度等气象要素的多年平均值是用来描述一个地区气候状况的主要参数,而各种气象要素某年、某月的平均值(或总量)则可以反映出该时期天气气候状况的重要特征。

气 温

指空气的温度,一般以摄氏度(℃)为单位表示。气象观测的温度表是放在离地面约 1.5 米处通风良好的百叶箱里测量的,因此,通常说的气温指的是离地面 1.5 米处百叶箱中的温度。其统计计算方法为:

月平均气温是将全月各日的平均气温相加, 除以该月的天数而得。

年平均气温是将 12 个月的月平均气温累加后除以 12 而得。

降水量

指从天空降落到地面的液态或固态(经融化后)水,未经蒸发、渗透、流失而在地面上积聚的深度。其统计计算方法为:

月降水量是将全月各日的降水量累加而得。

年降水量是将 12 个月的月降水量累加而得。

日照时间

指太阳实际照射地面的时间。其统计方法与降水量相同。

国民经济行业分类

《国民经济行业分类》国家标准于 1984 年首次发布,1994 年对其进行了第一次修订,2002 年为第二次修订,2011 年为第三次修订。

本年鉴的行业分类除特别说明外均使用 2011 年修订的行业分类标准。

2011 年新行业分类标准立足我国社会经济发展的实际情况,确保国家经济结构和产业结构的完整性、科学性和可观察性;确保国家统计、核算真实的反映我国的经济结构和产业结构。此次修订不仅坚持行业分类的修订原则和国际惯例, 同时顺应《国务院关于加快培育和发展战略性新兴产业的决定》要求,准确反映一定时期内国民经济行业的构成状况。

此次修订主要调整如下:

1.调整部门门类名称和顺序。如将“信息传输、计算机服务和软件业”更名为“信息传输、软件业和信息技术服务业”,将“科学研究、技术服务和地址勘查业”更名为“科学研究和技术服务业”,将“居民服务和其他服务业”更名为“居民服务、修理和其他服务业”,将“卫生、社会保障和社会福利业”更名为“卫生和社会工作”。但整体行业门类的数目保持不变,保证了行业分类的延续性。

2. 为与联合国分类相对应以及反映我国产业的状况,行业大类由 95 个调整为 96 个,新增了“开采辅助活动”、“汽车制造业”、“金属制造、机械和设备修理业”、“房屋建筑业”、“互联网和相关服务”、“机动车、电子产品和日用品修理业”等 6 大类,减少了“建筑装修业”、“城市公共交通业”、“其他金融活动”、“地址勘查业”等 4 大类,合并“橡胶制品业”和“塑料制品业”为一个大类。

3.为反映我国日益发展的互联网、信息技术、金融、影视娱乐等产业,行业中类新增了“互联网接入及相关服务”、“信息系统集成服务”、“化纤织造及印染精加工”等中类,取消了“猪的饲养”、“纺织制成品制造”等中类。

4. 为与联合国 ISIC Rev.4 的小类进行转换同时反映我国新兴产业,行业小类增加了“稻谷种植”、“食用菌种植”“葡萄的种植”等小类,取消了“常用有色金属压延加工”、“制帽”、“车辆、飞机及工程机械轮胎制造”等小类。

各个计划时期

表内所用各个“时期”代表的年份如下:恢复时期为 1950 到 1952 年;第一个五年计划时期(简称“一五”时期)为 1953 到 1957 年;第二个五年计划时期(简称“二

主要统计指标解释

五”时期)为1958到1962年;第三个五年计划时期(简称“三五”时期)为1966到1970年;第四个五年计划时期(简称“四五”时期)为1971到1975年;第五个五年计划时期(简称“五五”时期)为1976到1980年;第六个五年计划时期(简称“六五”时期)为1981到1985年;第七个五年计划时期(简称“七五”时期)为1986到1990年;第八个五年计划时期(简称“八五”时期)为1991到1995年;第九个五年计划时期(简称“九五”时期)为1996到2000年;第十个五年计划时期(简称“十五”时期)为2001到2005年;第十一个五年规划时期(简称“十一五”时期)为2006到2010年;第十二个五年规划时期(简称“十二五”时期)为2011到2015年。

指　数

指数是一种表明社会经济现象动态的相对数。运用指数可以测定不能直接相加和直接对比的社会经济现象的总动态；可以分析社会经济现象总变动中各因素变动的影响程度；可以研究总平均指标变动中各组标志水平和总体结构变动的作用。它是在把各个年份的产值换算成可比价格的基础上，根据定基指数等于相应各个环比指数的连乘积这个换算关系计算出来的。

本年鉴所列的上海市生产总值、工业总产值、农业总产值等指标增长速度，就是分别使用上海市生产总值指数、工业总产值指数、农业总产值指数直接计算的。

平均每年增长速度

在我国计算平均增长速度有两种方法。一种是习惯上经常使用的“水平法”,又称几何平均法,是以间隔期最后一年的水平同基期水平对比来计算平均每年增长（或下降)速度;另一种是“累计法”,又称代数平均法或方程法，是以间隔期内各年水平的总和同基期水平对比来计算平均每年增长(或下降)速度。

在一般正常情况下，两种方法计算的平均每年增长速度比较接近。但在经济发展不平衡,出现大起大落时,两种方法计算的结果差别较大。

本年鉴内所列的平均每年增长速度，除固定资产投资、直接吸收外资是用“累计法”计算以外,其余均用“水平法”计算。从某年到某年平均增长速度的年份,均不包括基期年在内。如1991-2009年平均增长速度是以1990年为基期计算的,余类推。

SHANGHAI STATISTICAL YEARBOOK

EXPLANATORY NOTES TO MAJOR STATISTICAL INDICATORS

□ Administrative Division

Administrative Division refers to the division of administrative areas by the state. The Constitution of the People's Republic of China stipulates that the administrative areas in China are divided as: 1) The whole country is divided into provinces, autonomous regions and municipalities directly under the central government; 2)Provinces and autonomous regions are divided into autonomous prefectures, counties, autonomous counties and cities; 3) Autonomous prefectures are divided into counties, autonomous counties and cities; 4) Counties and autonomous counties are divided into townships, nationality townships and towns; 5) Municipalities and large cities are divided into districts and counties, 6) The state shall, when necessary, establish special administrative regions.

□ Climate

Climate refers to the natural environmental status formed by the long-term exchange of energy and mass between the earth and the air, and is the results of interaction of many factors. Climate is both one of the environment factors and the important resources for the living and production activities of the human being. The average values across several years of meteorological factors such as temperature, rainfall and humidity are used as important parameters to describe the climate of a region, while the average values (or total values) of a given year or month of meteorological factors reflect the key characteristics of climate for that period of time.

□ Temperature

Temperature refers to the air temperature. It often uses centigrade as the unit. The thermometry used for weather observation is put in a breezy shutter, which is 1.5 meters high from the ground. Therefore, the commonly used temperature refers to the temperature in the breezy shutter 1.5 meters away from the ground. The calculation method is as follows:

Monthly average temperature is the summation of average daily temperature of one month divided by the actual days of that particular month. Annual average temperature is the summation of monthly average of a year divided by 12 months.

□ Volume of Precipitation

Volume of Precipitation refers to the deepness of liquid state or solid state (thawed) water falling from the sky to the ground that has not been evaporated, infiltrated or run off. The calculation method is as follows:

Monthly precipitation is the summation of daily precipitation of a month.

Annual precipitation is the summation of 12 months precipitation of a year.

□ Sunshine Hours

Sunshine Hours refer to the actual hours of sun irradiating the earth. The calculation method is the same as that of the precipitation.

□ Classification of the Sectors of the National Economy

The national standard of <Classification of the Sectors of the National Economy> was first released in 1984, and was revised for the first time in 1994, for the second revision in 2002, and for the third revision in 2011.

Unless otherwise stated, the industry classification used in this yearbook was based on Industrial Classification Standard revised in 2011.

The new industrial classification standard was based on China's social and economic development, to ensure that the national economic structure and industrial structure is integrity, scientific, and observability; to ensure national statistics and accounting reflecting the economic structure and industrial structure integrity. This revision was not only adhere to revision principle of industry classification and international practice, and conformed to the requirement in <State Council on accelerating the cultivation and development of emerging industries of strategic decision>, accurately reflect the composition of national economy industry in a given period.

The revision was mainly adjusted as follows:

1. Adjusting sector category name and order. For example, "information transmission, computer service and software industry" was renamed to "information transmission, software industry and information technology service", "scientific research, techni-

EXPLANATORY NOTES TO MAJOR STATISTICAL INDICATORS

cal service and geological prospecting" was renamed to "scientific research and technical service", "resident service and other services" was renamed to "resident service, repairs and other services", "health, social security and social welfare" was renamed to "health and social work". But the overall number of industry categories remain unchanged, ensuring the continuity of industry classification.

2. In order to correspond with the classification of the United Nations, and reflect the situation of our industry, number of industry categories was adjusted from 95 to 96, six new categories, "mining support activities", "the automotive manufacturing", "metal products, machinery and equipment repair industry", "housing construction", "internet and related services", "motor vehicles, electronics and daily necessities repair industry" were added, and four categories, "building decoration industry", "urban public transport industry", "other financial activities", "geological prospecting" were reduced. "Rubber products manufacturing" and "plastic products manufacturing" were combined into one category.

3. In order to reflect our growing internet, information technology, finance, entertainment and other industries, new medium categories, "internet and related services", "information integration system services", "fiber weaving and dyeing and finishing" were added, "pig breeding", "textile manufactured goods manufacturing" were reduced.

4. In order to convert with ISIC Rev.4 and reflect our emerging industries, new minimal categories, "ice planting", "mushroom cultivation", "grape cultivation" were added, "common non-ferrous metal rolling processing", "hat manufacturing", "vehicles, aircraft and construction machinery tire manufacturing" were reduced.

□ Various Planning Periods

The conventional division of time period in this statistical yearbook is as follows: Rehabilitation Period, 1950-1952; The First Five-Year Plan period (cited as first-five period), 1953-1957; The Second Five-Year Plan period (cited as second-five period), 1958-1962; The Third Five-Year Plan period (cited as third-five period), 1966-1970; The Fourth Five-Year Plan period (cited as fourth-five period), 1971-1975; The Fifth Five-Year Plan period (cited as fifth-five period), 1976-1980; The Sixth Five-Year Plan period (cited as sixth-five period), 1981-1985; The Seventh Five-Year Plan period (cited as seventh-five period), 1986-1990; The Eight Five-Year Plan period (cited as eighth-five period), 1991-1995; The Ninth Five-Year Plan period (cited as ninth-five period),1996-2000;The Tenth Five-Year Plan period (cited as tenth-five period),2001-2005; The eleventh Five-Year Plan period (cited as eleventh-five period),2006-2010; The twelfth Five-Year Plan period (cited as twelfth-five period), 2011-2015.

□ Index

Index refers to the relative figures indicating social and economic phenomena and developments. Index is used to evaluate the overall development of social and economic phenomena which can not be determined by simple addition or direct comparison. It is also used to analyze the outcome of various changes in the general phenomenon movement of social and economic development, and to study the level of each sub-index in the changes of general average index and the role of the changes of the overall structure. It is calculated at the comparable prices conversed from the output value of each year, using the formula of index number with fixed base period equal to the continuous product of its relative chain index .

The increases of Shanghai Gross Domestic Product, industrial output value and agricultural output value compared with the previous year, which are listed in this yearbook, are calculated according to Shanghai GDP index, industrial output value index and agricultural output value index.

□ Average Annual Growth Rate

Two methods for calculating Average Annual Growth Rate are applied in China, one is often called "level approach" or geometry average, which is derived by comparing the growth rate for the last year of the interval with that of the beginning year; the other is called "accumulating approach" or algebraic average or equation method, which is calculated by comparing the total growth rate of each year for the interval with that of base year .

Usually the results calculated by the two methods are fairly close, but they differ sharply when imbalance occurred in economic development with striking fluctuations in growth.

The Average Annual Growth Rates listed in this statistical yearbook are calculated by "level approach" except for the growth rate of investment in fixed assets and foreign capital absorbed. The base years are not listed when the years are listed for average annual growth rates for instance, the average annual growth rate of 1991-2009 is calculated with the base year 1990, and the analogy of this is also for the rest.

第二篇
CHAPTER 2

人　口
POPULATION

简要说明

一、本篇资料的主要内容

本篇资料反映上海市 1978-2015 年人口方面的基本情况，包括全市及各区县的主要人口统计数据，如：1978-2015 年全市常住人口数和户籍人口数；2015 年各区县常住人口数和外省市来沪常住人口数；1990-2015 年户籍人口自然增长和机械增长变动；2015 年各区县户籍人口年龄构成、计划生育情况；主要年份外籍常住人口数等。

二、本篇的资料来源

本篇资料由上海市统计局人口和就业统计处整理。1982、1990、2000、2010 年年末常住人口数据为当年普查数据推算数，其余年份数据为年度人口抽样调查推算数据，部分年份数据根据人口普查数据进行了修订。表 2-1 中除常住人口数据外，其余数据统计范围均为户籍人口，由市公安局提供。表 2-2 中土地面积由市民政局提供，各区县常住人口数和外省市来沪常住人口数根据上海市 2015 年 1%人口抽样调查数据推算。表 2-3 至表 2-7 数据统计范围均为户籍人口，由市公安局提供。表 2-8 数据统计范围为户籍人口，由市卫生和计划生育委员会提供。表 2-11 由市公安局出入境管理局提供。

三、本篇的统计调查方法

目前由上海市统计局人口和就业统计处实施的人口统计调查有：

在逢“0”的年份进行全国人口普查；在逢“5”的年份进行全国 1%人口抽样调查；其余年份进行全国人口变动情况抽样调查，其样本量约占全市总人口的 1.3‰左右。人口抽样调查是以全国为总体，省级单位为次总体，采用分层、多阶段、整群概率比例抽样方法抽取样本。

BRIEF INTRODUCTION

I. Main Contents

Data in this chapter reflect the basic conditions of Shanghai's population between 1978 and 2015, including data of the city as well as districts and counties under it. For example: there are data of the city's permanent residents and registered population between 1978 and 2015; permanent residents and residents from other provinces and cities in districts and counties in 2015; changes of registered population's natural growth and mechanical growth between 1990 and 2015; registered population age structure in districts and counties in 2015 and their conditions of family planning; population of foreign residents in main years.

II. Sources of Data

Data in this chapter are collected, prepared, and provided by the Department of Population and Employment Statistics of the Shanghai Statistics Bureau. Data of permanent residents by the year end for 1982, 1990, 2000 and 2010 are the census year estimates; the rest of the data are estimates from the annual national sample survey on population changes and data for selected years have been revised according to the census results. Data in table 2–1, provided by the Shanghai Public Security Bureau, refer to registered population, with permanent residents in exception. Land area data in table 2–2 are provided by the Shanghai Civil Affairs Bureau, and the data on permanent residents in districts and counties, and residents from other provinces and cities are estimates based on 1% Sample Survey of Population in Shanghai in 2015. Data in table 2–3 to table 2–7, provided by the Shanghai Public Security Bureau, all refer to registered population. Data in table 2–8, provided by the Shanghai Municipal Commission of Health and Family Planning, refer to registered population. Data in table 2–11 are provided by the Shanghai Public Security Bureau Exit–Entry Administration.

III. Survey Methodology

The statistical surveys on population which are conducted by the Department of Population and Employment Statistics of the Shanghai Statistics Bureau are as follows:

The national population census is conducted in the year ending with 0; the national 1 percent population sample survey is conducted in the year ending with 5; sample surveys on population changes are conducted in the rest of the years which cover about 1.3 per thousand of the total population of the city. The sample survey on population change takes the whole nation as the population sample with each province, autonomous region or municipality as sub–populations, and the stratified multi–stage systematic PPS cluster sampling scheme is used.

表2.1 户数、人口、人口密度和户籍人口期望寿命(1978~2015)
TOTAL HOUSEHOLDS, POPULATION, DENSITY OF REGISTERED POPULATION AND LIFE EXPECTANCY

年　份 Year	常住人口 (万人) Year-end Resident Population (10 000 persons)	人口密度 (人/平方公里) Density of Population (person/sq. km)	总户数 (万户) Total Households (10 000 households)	平均每户人口 (人) Average Persons Per Household (person)	年末户籍人口 (万人) Year-end Registered Population (10 000 persons)
1978	1 104.00	1 785	291.69	3.77	1 098.28
1979	1 137.00	1 838	296.71	3.82	1 132.14
1980	1 152.00	1 862	303.87	3.77	1 146.52
1981	1 168.00	1 888	314.56	3.70	1 162.84
1982	1 186.00	1 917	321.71	3.67	1 180.51
1983	1 201.00	1 942	330.60	3.61	1 194.01
1984	1 217.00	1 968	340.78	3.54	1 204.78
1985	1 233.00	1 993	351.72	3.46	1 216.69
1986	1 249.00	1 970	364.92	3.38	1 232.33
1987	1 265.00	1 995	380.19	3.29	1 249.51
1988	1 288.00	2 031	394.95	3.20	1 262.42
1989	1 311.00	2 067	406.82	3.14	1 276.45
1990	1 334.00	2 104	415.28	3.09	1 283.35
1991	1 350.00	2 128	425.84	3.02	1 287.20
1992	1 365.00	2 154	431.67	2.99	1 289.37
1993	1 381.00	2 179	438.69	2.95	1 294.74
1994	1 398.00	2 204	444.38	2.92	1 298.81
1995	1 414.00	2 230	450.76	2.89	1 301.37
1996	1 451.00	2 288	457.49	2.85	1 304.43
1997	1 489.00	2 348	461.40	2.83	1 305.46
1998	1 527.00	2 409	465.72	2.81	1 306.58
1999	1 567.00	2 472	470.11	2.79	1 313.12
2000	1 608.60	2 537	475.73	2.78	1 321.63
2001	1 668.33	2 631	478.92	2.77	1 327.14
2002	1 712.97	2 702	481.77	2.77	1 334.23
2003	1 765.84	2 785	486.06	2.76	1 341.77
2004	1 834.98	2 894	490.58	2.76	1 352.39
2005	1 890.26	2 981	496.69	2.74	1 360.26
2006	1 964.11	3 098	499.54	2.74	1 368.08
2007	2 063.58	3 255	503.29	2.74	1 378.86
2008	2 140.65	3 376	506.64	2.75	1 391.04
2009	2 210.28	3 486	509.79	2.75	1 400.70
2010	2 302.66	3 632	519.27	2.72	1 412.32
2011	2 347.46	3 702	522.01	2.72	1 419.36
2012	2 380.43	3 754	524.31	2.72	1 426.93
2013	2 415.15	3 809	527.52	2.72	1 432.34
2014	2 425.68	3 826	532.55	2.70	1 438.69
2015	2 415.27	3 809	536.76	2.69	1 442.97

①户数和年末户籍人口由市公安局提供，户籍人口期望寿命由市卫生和计划生育委员会提供。
②上海取消农业户口和非农业户口性质区分。
❶The figures of household and year-end registered population are provided by Shanghai Municipal Public Security Bureau, and the figures of life expendency are provided by Shanghai Municipal Health and Family Planning Commission.
❷Shanghai has cancelled the distinction between agricultural and non-agricultural household accounts.

表 2.1 续表 continued

年 份 Year	按性别分 Grouped by Sex 男 性 Male	按性别分 Grouped by Sex 女 性 Female	户籍人口期望寿命（岁）Life Expectancy of Registered Population (year)	其 中 of which 男 性 Male	其 中 of which 女 性 Female
1978	542.70	555.58	73.35	70.69	74.78
1979	560.40	571.74	73.14	70.64	75.48
1980	569.30	577.22	73.33	71.25	75.36
1981	578.76	584.08	73.38	71.28	75.47
1982	588.82	591.69	74.04	71.77	76.25
1983	596.67	597.34	73.23	71.15	75.26
1984	602.59	602.19	73.90	71.73	76.17
1985	609.70	606.99	74.27	72.14	76.37
1986	618.88	613.45	74.71	72.54	76.85
1987	628.78	620.73	74.46	72.32	76.60
1988	635.82	626.60	74.63	72.50	76.77
1989	643.51	632.94	74.98	72.85	77.12
1990	647.13	636.22	75.46	73.16	77.74
1991	649.03	638.17	75.79	73.58	77.95
1992	649.97	639.40	75.97	74.04	77.91
1993	652.92	641.82	75.97	74.04	77.91
1994	655.14	643.67	76.26	74.29	78.23
1995	656.48	644.89	76.03	74.11	77.97
1996	657.86	646.57	76.11	74.07	78.21
1997	657.93	647.53	77.20	75.18	79.21
1998	658.22	648.36	77.03	75.06	79.02
1999	661.19	651.93	78.44	76.38	80.53
2000	665.51	656.12	78.77	76.71	80.81
2001	668.32	658.82	79.66	77.47	81.83
2002	672.05	662.18	79.52	77.36	81.63
2003	675.47	666.30	79.80	77.78	81.81
2004	680.38	672.01	80.29	78.08	82.48
2005	683.51	676.75	80.13	77.89	82.36
2006	686.66	681.42	80.97	78.64	83.29
2007	691.08	687.78	81.08	78.87	83.29
2008	695.57	695.47	81.28	79.06	83.50
2009	699.25	701.45	81.73	79.42	84.06
2010	703.57	708.75	82.13	79.82	84.44
2011	706.37	712.99	82.51	80.23	84.80
2012	709.62	717.31	82.41	80.18	84.67
2013	711.93	720.41	82.47	80.19	84.79
2014	714.71	723.99	82.29	80.04	84.59
2015	716.37	726.60	82.75	80.47	85.09

表2.2 各区、县土地面积、常住人口及人口密度（2015）
LAND AREA, POPULATION AND DENSITY OF POPULATION IN DISTRICTS AND COUNTIES

地 区 District		行政区域面积（平方公里）Land Area (sq. km)	年末常住人口（万人）Year-end Resident Population (10 000 persons)	其 中 of which 外来人口 Floating People	人口密度（人/平方公里）Density of Population (person/sq·km)
全 市	**Total**	**6 340.50**	**2 415.27**	**981.65**	**3 809**
浦东新区	Pudong New Area	1 210.41	547.49	234.32	4 523
黄 浦 区	Huangpu	20.46	65.86	16.52	32 190
徐 汇 区	Xuhui	54.76	108.91	26.82	19 889
长 宁 区	Changning	38.30	69.11	16.71	18 044
静 安 区	Jing'an	7.62	23.69	5.22	31 089
普 陀 区	Putuo	54.83	128.80	34.35	23 491
闸 北 区	Zhabei	29.26	83.71	20.88	28 609
虹 口 区	Hongkou	23.46	80.94	15.65	34 501
杨 浦 区	Yangpu	60.73	131.52	26.09	21 657
闵 行 区	Minhang	370.75	253.79	127.26	6 845
宝 山 区	Baoshan	270.99	202.29	84.57	7 465
嘉 定 区	Jiading	464.20	156.80	90.79	3 378
金 山 区	Jinshan	586.05	79.80	27.34	1 362
松 江 区	Songjiang	605.64	176.02	108.58	2 906
青 浦 区	Qingpu	670.14	120.91	72.05	1 804
奉 贤 区	Fengxian	687.39	115.99	59.93	1 687
崇 明 县	Chongming	1 185.49	69.64	14.57	587

表2.3 主要年份户籍人口出生率、死亡率、自然增长率
BIRTH RATE, DEATH RATE AND NATURAL GROWTH RATE OF REGISTERED POPULATION IN MAIN YEARS

年份 Year	出生 Birth		死亡 Death		自然增长 Natural Growth	
	人数（万人） Population (10 000 persons)	出生率（‰） Birth Rate (‰)	人数（万人） Population (10 000 persons)	死亡率（‰） Death Rate (‰)	人数（万人） Population (10 000 persons)	自然增长率（‰） Natural Growth Rate (‰)
1990	13.12	10.25	8.63	6.74	4.49	3.51
1995	7.11	5.47	9.79	7.53	-2.68	-2.06
1996	6.79	5.21	9.77	7.50	-2.98	-2.29
1997	6.42	4.92	9.57	7.33	-3.15	-2.41
1998	6.17	4.73	10.13	7.75	-3.96	-3.03
1999	6.56	5.01	9.54	7.28	-2.98	-2.27
2000	6.95	5.27	9.45	7.17	-2.50	-1.90
2001	5.76	4.34	9.34	7.05	-3.58	-2.71
2002	6.20	4.66	9.67	7.27	-3.47	-2.61
2003	5.73	4.28	10.07	7.52	-4.34	-3.24
2004	8.09	6.00	9.65	7.16	-1.56	-1.16
2005	8.25	6.08	10.23	7.54	-1.98	-1.46
2006	8.12	5.95	9.80	7.19	-1.68	-1.24
2007	10.08	7.34	10.22	7.44	-0.14	-0.10
2008	9.67	6.98	10.70	7.73	-1.03	-0.75
2009	9.23	6.62	10.67	7.64	-1.44	-1.02
2010	10.02	7.13	10.87	7.73	-0.84	-0.60
2011	10.15	7.17	11.11	7.85	-0.96	-0.68
2012	12.11	8.51	11.74	8.25	0.37	0.26
2013	10.89	7.62	11.67	8.16	-0.78	-0.54
2014	12.41	8.64	11.95	8.32	0.46	0.32
2015	10.59	7.35	12.42	8.62	-1.83	-1.27

表2.4 主要年份户籍人口迁移
MIGRATION OF REGISTERED POPULATION IN MAIN YEARS

年份 Year	迁入 Inflows		迁出 Outflows		机械增长 Mechanical Increase	
	人口（万人） Population (10 000 persons)	迁入率（‰） Rate of Inflows (‰)	人口（万人） Population (10 000 persons)	迁出率（‰） Rate of Outflows (‰)	人口（万人） Population (10 000 persons)	增长率（‰） Growth Rate (‰)
1990	12.18	9.52	10.72	8.38	1.46	1.14
1995	13.12	10.09	6.47	4.98	6.65	5.11
1996	13.01	9.99	6.41	4.92	6.60	5.07
1997	11.47	8.79	5.72	4.38	5.75	4.41
1998	11.73	8.98	5.04	3.86	6.69	5.12
1999	14.06	10.73	5.08	3.88	8.98	6.85
2000	15.16	11.51	5.32	4.04	9.84	7.47
2001	14.63	11.05	5.56	4.20	9.07	6.85
2002	15.41	11.58	4.38	3.29	11.03	8.29
2003	14.92	11.15	3.69	2.76	11.23	8.39
2004	13.93	10.34	2.74	2.03	11.19	8.31
2005	12.96	9.55	3.46	2.55	9.50	7.00
2006	12.86	9.43	3.50	2.57	9.36	6.86
2007	14.69	10.70	3.95	2.88	10.74	7.82
2008	17.28	12.48	4.29	3.10	12.99	9.38
2009	15.72	11.26	4.77	3.42	10.95	7.84
2010	17.22	12.24	4.97	3.53	12.25	8.71
2011	13.15	9.29	5.33	3.76	7.82	5.53
2012	12.96	8.11	5.89	4.14	7.07	3.97
2013	12.12	8.48	6.06	4.24	6.06	4.24
2014	11.55	8.05	5.78	4.02	5.77	4.03
2015	11.61	8.06	5.32	3.69	6.29	4.37

表2.5 各区、县户籍人口迁移(2015)
MIGRATION OF REGISTERED POPULATION IN DISTRICTS AND COUNTIES

地 区 District		迁 入(人) Inflows(person)		迁 出(人) Outflows(person)	
		市内迁入 From Inside of the City	市外迁入 From Outside of the City	迁往市内 To the Inside of the City	迁往市外 To the Outside of the City
全 市	**Total**	**11 345**	**116 069**	**11 396**	**53 229**
浦东新区	Pudong New Area	1 058	25 109	689	9 070
黄 浦 区	Huangpu	63	3 452	139	933
徐 汇 区	Xuhui	187	10 548	128	7 845
长 宁 区	Changning	104	4 491	127	2 304
静 安 区	Jing'an	32	1 314	33	365
普 陀 区	Putuo	247	5 316	228	1 135
闸 北 区	Zhabei	405	3 297	300	845
虹 口 区	Hongkou	254	4 108	267	1 455
杨 浦 区	Yangpu	447	16 378	437	10 527
闵 行 区	Minhang	659	14 081	373	4 819
宝 山 区	Baoshan	3 045	8 420	1 535	3 332
嘉 定 区	Jiading	201	4 587	62	1 594
金 山 区	Jinshan	47	1 216	13	245
松 江 区	Songjiang	117	9 135	60	6 824
青 浦 区	Qingpu	41	1 966	30	1 042
奉 贤 区	Fengxian	49	1 538	28	625
崇 明 县	Chongming	4 389	1 113	6 947	269

表2.6 各区、县户籍人口年龄构成(2015)
AGE STRUCTURE OF REGISTERED POPULATION IN DISTRICTS AND COUNTIES

单位:万人(10 000 persons)

地 区	District	合 计 Total	17岁及以下 17 and below	18~34岁 18~34	35~59岁 35~59	60岁及以上 60 and above
全 市	**Total**	**1 442.97**	**162.05**	**291.40**	**553.57**	**435.95**
浦东新区	Pudong New Area	291.87	36.14	59.89	113.52	82.31
黄浦区	Huangpu	87.39	8.48	18.17	31.85	28.89
徐汇区	Xuhui	91.97	11.36	19.89	32.54	28.18
长宁区	Changning	58.59	6.12	12.40	21.58	18.48
静安区	Jing'an	28.81	3.19	5.69	10.16	9.75
普陀区	Putuo	89.47	9.41	17.50	33.18	29.39
闸北区	Zhabei	67.72	6.81	13.71	25.37	21.82
虹口区	Hongkou	77.25	7.32	15.71	28.28	25.95
杨浦区	Yangpu	108.48	10.60	25.13	39.00	33.75
闵行区	Minhang	106.58	14.74	21.33	40.95	29.55
宝山区	Baoshan	94.80	10.89	18.50	37.06	28.36
嘉定区	Jiading	59.81	6.93	11.14	23.49	18.24
金山区	Jinshan	51.83	5.52	9.33	22.14	14.84
松江区	Songjiang	61.16	7.82	13.11	24.23	16.00
青浦区	Qingpu	47.18	5.22	8.90	19.75	13.31
奉贤区	Fengxian	52.85	5.95	9.45	22.19	15.26
崇明县	Chongming	67.23	5.53	11.54	28.27	21.89

表2.7 各区、县户籍老年人口年龄构成(2015)
AGE STRUCTURE OF REGISTERED AGING POPULATION IN DISTRICTS AND COUNTIES

单位:万人(10 000 persons)

地区	District	合计 Total	60~64岁 60~64	65~79岁 65~79	80岁及以上 80 and above
全 市	**Total**	**435.95**	**152.57**	**205.33**	**78.05**
浦东新区	Pudong New Area	82.31	28.73	39.53	14.05
黄 浦 区	Huangpu	28.89	10.69	12.38	5.82
徐 汇 区	Xuhui	28.18	9.18	13.26	5.74
长 宁 区	Changning	18.48	6.26	8.34	3.88
静 安 区	Jing'an	9.75	3.29	4.44	2.02
普 陀 区	Putuo	29.38	11.08	12.87	5.43
闸 北 区	Zhabei	21.82	8.27	9.50	4.05
虹 口 区	Hongkou	25.94	9.43	11.50	5.01
杨 浦 区	Yangpu	33.75	12.46	14.84	6.45
闵 行 区	Minhang	29.55	9.93	14.60	5.02
宝 山 区	Baoshan	28.36	10.46	13.40	4.50
嘉 定 区	Jiading	18.24	6.14	8.99	3.11
金 山 区	Jinshan	14.84	4.98	7.60	2.26
松 江 区	Songjiang	16.00	5.37	8.04	2.59
青 浦 区	Qingpu	13.31	4.42	6.71	2.18
奉 贤 区	Fengxian	15.26	5.18	7.70	2.38
崇 明 县	Chongming	21.89	6.70	11.63	3.56

表2.8　各区、县计划生育基本情况(2015)
FAMILY PLANNING IN DISTRICTS AND COUNTIES

地　区	District	出生人数 (万人) Birth (10 000 persons)	已婚育龄妇女人数 (万人) Married Women at Childbearing Age (10 000 persons)	计　划 生育率 (%) Family Planning Rate (%)
全　市	**Total**	**10.59**	**204.85**	**99.7**
浦东新区	Pudong New Area	2.35	45.18	99.9
黄 浦 区	Huangpu	0.65	10.72	99.7
徐 汇 区	Xuhui	0.70	11.91	99.7
长 宁 区	Changning	0.43	8.01	99.4
静 安 区	Jing'an	0.22	3.62	99.8
普 陀 区	Putuo	0.66	9.84	99.6
闸 北 区	Zhabei	0.49	8.51	99.9
虹 口 区	Hongkou	0.55	9.40	99.4
杨 浦 区	Yangpu	0.75	13.38	99.7
闵 行 区	Minhang	0.95	15.97	99.9
宝 山 区	Baoshan	0.66	13.19	99.5
嘉 定 区	Jiading	0.40	9.11	99.5
金 山 区	Jinshan	0.31	8.75	99.7
松 江 区	Songjiang	0.52	9.89	99.7
青 浦 区	Qingpu	0.32	8.83	99.4
奉 贤 区	Fengxian	0.33	8.12	99.2
崇 明 县	Chongming	0.31	10.42	99.4

表2.9 主要年份婚姻情况
MARRIAGE STATISTICS IN MAIN YEARS

年 份 Year	准予登记结婚（万对）Marriage Registration Permitted (10 000 couples)	初 婚（万人）First Marriage (10 000 persons)	再 婚（万人）Remarriage (10 000 persons)	其中 of which 女 性 Female	离婚件数（万件）Divorce (10 000 cases)	其中 of which 民政部门批准 Approved by the Civil Administration	其中 of which 法院调判 Mediated by the Court
1990	10.77	19.49	2.04	1.06	1.64	0.73	0.91
1995	8.40	14.61	2.19	1.09	2.27	0.98	1.29
1996	8.96	14.98	2.31	1.24	2.47	1.07	1.40
1997	8.84	15.12	2.57	1.27	2.73	1.19	1.54
1998	8.57	14.48	2.67	1.28	2.96	1.43	1.53
1999	9.05	15.07	2.46	1.24	3.12	1.69	1.43
2000	9.31	15.08	2.89	1.45	3.18	1.76	1.42
2001	9.30	15.23	2.68	1.40	3.15	1.68	1.47
2002	9.10	14.60	3.05	1.40	2.96	1.54	1.42
2003	10.82	17.20	3.97	2.31	3.30	1.98	1.32
2004	12.49	20.27	4.18	2.05	3.63	2.67	0.96
2005	10.27	16.44	4.09	2.05	3.93	3.10	0.83
2006	16.56	27.29	5.83	2.93	4.72	3.78	0.94
2007	12.01	18.10	5.93	2.95	4.69	3.75	0.94
2008	14.16	22.04	6.28	3.17	4.68	3.72	0.96
2009	14.99	23.33	6.65	3.31	4.83	3.92	0.91
2010	13.03	20.10	5.96	2.98	4.67	3.81	0.86
2011	14.89	23.94	5.84	2.90	4.78	3.92	0.86
2012	14.42	22.96	5.88	2.86	5.29	4.42	0.87
2013	14.95	22.17	7.74	3.77	6.96	6.09	0.87
2014	14.19	20.14	8.25	4.06	6.15	5.30	0.85
2015	14.18	19.89	8.47	4.19	6.66	5.83	0.83

表2.10 主要年份涉外婚姻情况
CHINESE-FOREIGN MARRIAGE IN MAIN YEARS

年 份 Year	涉外婚姻（对）Chinese-Foreign Marriage (couple)	在涉外婚姻中的国内公民（人）In Chinese-Foreign Marriage Chinese Citizens (person)	在国内公民中 Among the Chinese Citizens 男 性 Male	在国内公民中 Among the Chinese Citizens 女 性 Female
1990	1 345	1 345	136	1 209
1995	3 033	3 030	274	2 756
1996	3 107	3 105	307	2 798
1997	2 839	2 838	298	2 540
1998	2 926	2 923	293	2 630
1999	2 872	2 869	343	2 526
2000	3 187	3 182	374	2 808
2001	3 447	3 438	399	3 039
2002	2 705	2 690	67	2 623
2003	2 418	2 418	367	2 051
2004	2 636	2 623	417	2 206
2005	2 407	2 385	372	2 013
2006	2 943	2 943	540	2 403
2007	2 495	2 483	109	2 374
2008	2 626	2 553	428	2 125
2009	2 492	2 416	305	2 111
2010	2 231	2 144	414	1 730
2011	2 225	2 125	474	1 651
2012	2 195	2 064	473	1 591
2013	2 054	1 900	430	1 470
2014	1 962	1 817	437	1 380
2015	1 778	1 642	397	1 245

注：本页数据由市民政局和市高级人民法院提供。
Note: This table is provided by Shanghai Civil Affairs Bureau and Shanghai Municipal Senior People's Court.

表2.11　主要年份在沪外国常住人口
RESIDENT FOREIGNERS IN SHANGHAI IN MAIN YEARS

单位：人(person)

	行　业 Sector	2005	2010	2014	2015
总　计	**Total**	**100 011**	**162 481**	**171 874**	**178 335**
居留许可外国人	**Residence Permitted Foreigners**	**95 384**	**159 303**	**169 686**	**175 931**
按国别(地区)分	Grouped by Country and Region				
#日　本	Japan	27 812	35 075	33 948	33 440
韩　国	Republic of Korea	14 047	21 073	19 976	21 178
新加坡	Singapore	5 547	7 545	6 445	6 421
德　国	Germany	4 591	8 023	8 461	8 446
英　国	United Kingdom	2 904	5 591	6 402	6 543
加拿大	Canada	4 279	7 306	7 868	8 012
美　国	United States	14 329	24 358	25 396	25 537
澳大利亚	Australia	3 729	6 165	7 143	7 444
法　国	France	4 181	8 238	9 607	9 993
按类别分	By Types				
#工　作	Work			87 736	91 372
学　习	Study			14 397	16 030
团　聚	Reunit			18 375	17 112
私人事务	Private Transaction			46 911	48 915
新闻从业人员	Journalists			79	98
永久居留外国人	**Permanent Resident Foreigners**		**948**	**2 188**	**2 404**

上 / 海 / 统 / 计 / 年 / 鉴

主要统计指标解释

人口

人口数为每年12月31日的年末总人口。根据统计口径的不同,分为户籍人口和常住人口。户籍人口是指在公安部门办理了户籍登记的人口。常住人口是指实际上经常居住在一个地方(住所)的人口,一般都以在其住所居住半年以上者为常住人口。

出生率

出生率(又称粗出生率)指在一定时期内(通常为一年)一定地区的出生人数与同期平均人数(或期中人数)之比,一般用千分率表示。计算公式:

$$出生率=\frac{年出生人数}{年平均人数}\times1000‰$$

出生人数是指活产婴儿,即胎儿脱离母体时(不管怀孕月数),有过呼吸或其他生命现象。年平均人数是年初、年底人口数的平均数,也可用年中人口数代替。

死亡率

死亡率(又称粗死亡率)指在一定时期内(通常为一年)一定地区的死亡人数与同期平均人数(或期中人数)之比,一般用千分率表示。计算公式:

$$死亡率=\frac{年死亡人数}{年平均人数}\times1000‰$$

人口自然增长率

指在一定时期内(通常为一年)人口自然增加数(出生人数减死亡人数)与该时期内平均人数(或期中人数)之比,一般用千分率表示。计算公式:

$$人口自然增长率=\frac{本年出生人数-本年死亡人数}{年平均人数}\times1000‰$$

$$人口自然增长率=人口出生率-人口死亡率$$

户籍人口期望寿命

指在一定年龄组的死亡率水平下,该年龄组人群日后平均可能继续生存的年(岁)数。通常所说的平均期望寿命是指刚出生的一批人平均一生可能存活的年数。

SHANGHAI STATISTICAL YEARBOOK

EXPLANATORY NOTES TO MAJOR STATISTICAL INDICATORS

□ Population

Population refers to the total population by December 31 every year. According to different statistical approaches, there are two definitions of population named as population with registered residence and population with permanent residence. The former refers to the population with registration in the police while the latter refers to the population that actually reside in a place (residence) permanently, usually longer than half a year.

□ Birth Rate

Birth Rate (or gross birth rate) means the ratio of the number of births in a certain period (usually a year) to the average population in the same period (or mid-year figure). It is usually calculated in terms of permillage and its calculating formula is:

$$\text{Birth Rate} = \frac{\text{Number of Births}}{\text{Average Number of Population}} \times 1000‰$$

Number of Births refers to live births, when babies have showed any vital phenomena regardless of the length of pregnancy.

Average Number of Population is the average of the number of population at the beginning of the year and, at the end of the year and sometimes is substituted for with mid-year population.

□ Death Rate

Death Rate (or Gross Death Rate) refers to the ratio of number of deaths to the average population (or mid-year population) during a certain period of time (usually a year), which is often presented as permillage. Its calculating formula is :

$$\text{Death Rate} = \frac{\text{Number of Deaths}}{\text{Average Number of Population}} \times 1000‰$$

□ Natural Growth Rate of Population

Natural Growth Rate of Population refers to the ratio of natural increase in population (number of births minus number of deaths) in a certain period of time (usually a year) to the average population (or mid-year population) of the same period, which is often presented as permillage. The following formula are applied:

$$\text{Natural Growth Rate of Population} = \frac{\text{Number of Births} - \text{Number of Deaths}}{\text{Average Number of Population}} \times 1000‰$$

Natural Growth Rate of Population = Birth Rate−Death Rate

□ Life Expectancy of Registered Population

Life Expectancy of Registered Population refers to the average age that an age group may possibly live at a certain mortality rate of the group, in the common knowledge, the average age that a group of new-borns may possibly live.

第三篇
CHAPTER 3

从业人员和职工工资
EMPLOYMENT AND WAGES

简要说明

一、本篇资料的主要内容

本篇资料反映上海市劳动经济方面的基本情况。如:从业人员、城镇登记失业人数和城镇登记失业率,新增就业岗位,离退休、退职职工人数,工资总额,平均工资及离退休、退职人员养老金情况等。

二、本篇资料的统计范围

《劳动统计报表制度》的调查范围为上海市国民经济各行业法人单位及其所属的产业活动单位。

上海市人力资源和社会保障局有关统计报表的统计范围为上海市国民经济各行业法人单位及其所属的产业活动单位。

三、本篇的资料来源

1. 从业人员、工资总额等资料是根据《劳动统计报表制度》搜集资料,加工整理汇总取得。

2. 城镇登记失业人数和城镇登记失业率,新增就业岗位,离退休、退职职工人数,离退休、退职人员养老金情况,由上海市人力资源和社会保障局提供。

四、本篇的统计调查方法

本篇资料对规模以上工业、有资质的建筑业、限额以上批发和零售业、限额以上住宿和餐饮业、全部房地产开发经营业、规模以上服务业法人单位采取全面调查;除上述范围以外的法人单位采取抽样调查方法。人力资源社会保障的资料采用全面调查方法,由市人力资源社会保障部门收集相关数据资料加工整理取得。

BRIEF INTRODUCTION

I. Main Contents

Data in this chapter reflect the basic conditions of Shanghai's labor economy, such as number of employed people, the urban registered unemployed people and unemployment rate, the number of new jobs, the number of retired people, total wages, average wages and pension situations.

II. Scope and Coverage of Statistics

The Reporting Form System on Labor Statistics covers various corporate units with legal person status and their subordinated business units in Shanghai's economic and social development.

The reporting forms provided by the Shanghai Human Resources and Social Security Bureau cover various corporate units with legal person status and their subordinated business units in Shanghai's economic and social development.

III. Sources of Data

(1) Data on basic conditions including employment and total wages are collected, prepared and compiled through The Reporting Form System on Labor Statistics.

(2) Data on the urban registered unemployed people and unemployment rate, the number of new jobs, the number of retired people and pension situations are provided by the Shanghai Human Resources and Social Security Bureau.

IV. Methodology of Survey

Data of this chapter are from comprehensive surveys on industry above designated size, the construction industry, the wholesale and retail industry above the set scale, the accommodation and catering industry above the set scale, all real estate development business, service industry corporations above the set scale.

表3.1 全社会各行业从业人员(2014～2015)
QUANTITY OF WHOLE SOCIAL EMPLOYEES IN DIFFERENT SECTORS

单位:万人(10 000 persons)

行业	Sector	2014	2015
总计	**Total**	**1 365.63**	**1 361.51**
按产业分	**Grouped by Industry**		
第一产业	Primary Industry	44.81	46.01
第二产业	Secondary Industry	476.87	459.74
第三产业	Tertiary Industry	843.95	855.76
按行业分	**Grouped by Sector**		
农、林、牧、渔业	Farming, Forestry, Animal Husbandry and Fishery	48.25	49.03
采矿业	Mining	0.04	0.04
制造业	Manufacturing	366.14	351.03
电力、热力、燃气及水的生产和供应业	Electricity, Heat, Gas and Water Production and Supply Industry	4.32	4.76
建筑业	Construction	110.09	108.33
批发和零售业	Retail and Wholesale	235.52	238.31
交通运输、仓储和邮政业	Transportation, Warehousing and Post Industries	87.55	88.20
住宿和餐饮业	Hoteling and Catering	51.47	51.91
信息传输、软件和信息技术服务业	Information Transmission, Software and IT Services	45.72	46.26
金融业	Finance	34.42	35.07
房地产业	Real Estate	48.64	49.84
租赁和商务服务业	Leasing and Business Service Industries	125.88	130.65
科学研究和技术服务业	Scientific and Technical Services	43.92	44.97
水利、环境和公共设施管理业	Water Conservancy, Environment and Public Facility Management	20.08	20.16
居民服务、修理和其他服务业	Resident Services, Repairs and Other Services	34.92	34.98
教育	Education	36.92	36.13
卫生和社会工作	Health and Social Work	27.53	27.71
文化、体育和娱乐业	Culture, Sports and Entertainment	10.77	10.67
公共管理、社会保障和社会组织	Public Administration, Social Security and Social Organizations	33.45	33.46

表 3.2　主要年份城镇登记失业人数和城镇登记失业率
QUANTITY OF URBAN REGISTERED UNEMPLOYED AND URBAN REGISTERED UNEMPLOYMENT RATE IN MAIN YEARS

指　标	Indicators	2000	2010	2014	2015
城镇登记失业人数(万人)	Registered Urban Unemployment (10 000 persons)	20.08	27.73	25.63	24.81
区	District	18.86	26.97	24.90	24.10
县	County	1.22	0.76	0.73	0.71
城镇登记失业率(%)	Registered Urban Unemployment Rate (%)	3.5	4.2	4.2	4.1

表 3.3　主要年份新增就业岗位
NEWLY ADDED WORKING POST IN MAIN YEARS

指　标	Indicators	2003	2010	2014	2015
新增就业岗位(万个)	Newly Added Working Post (10 000 units)	46.20	63.15	59.96	59.66
#农村富余劳动力实现非农就业	Non-agricultural Working Post Gained by Surplus Rural Labor Force	12.50	12.18	10.78	10.33

表 3.4　主要年份离休、退休及退职职工人数
QUANTITY OF RETIRED AND RESIGNED PERSONS IN MAIN YEARS

单位:万人(10 000 persons)

指　标	Indicators	2000	2010	2014	2015
总　计	**Total**	**234.23**	**352.02**	**404.07**	**415.81**
国有单位	State-owned Units	165.55	166.38	163.97	164.25
离　休	Retired Veteran Cadres	3.39	1.82	1.38	1.28
退　休	Retired	161.03	160.53	160.73	161.13
退　职	Resigned	1.13	4.03	1.86	1.84
集体单位	Collective-owned Units	50.22	46.97	47.22	46.92
离　休	Retired Veteran Cadres	0.10	0.04	0.03	0.03
退　休	Retired	48.40	45.15	45.81	45.56
退　职	Resigned	1.72	1.78	1.38	1.33
其他单位	Other Ownership Units	18.46	138.67	192.88	204.64
离　休	Retired Veteran Cadres	0.21	0.68	0.52	0.47
退　休	Retired	18.05	132.29	186.34	197.89
退　职	Resigned	0.20	5.70	6.02	6.28

表 3.5　职工工资总额和平均工资(1978～2015)
TOTAL WAGES AND AVERAGE ANNUAL WAGES OF STAFF AND WORKERS

年份 Year	职工工资总额（亿元）Total Wages of Staff and Workers (100 million yuan)	其中 of which 国有单位 State-owned Units	集体单位 Collective-owned Units	其他单位 Other Ownership Units	职工平均工资（元）Average Annual Wages of Staff and Workers (yuan)	其中 of which 国有单位 State-owned Units	集体单位 Collective-owned Units	其他单位 Other Ownership Units
1978	28.12	23.82	4.30		672	716	500	
1979	32.73	27.63	5.10		784	834	590	
1980	38.10	31.59	6.51		873	918	702	
1981	39.59	32.42	7.17		870	910	727	
1982	41.34	33.71	7.63		883	920	750	
1983	42.91	34.93	7.98		897	935	763	
1984	53.72	43.19	10.08	0.45	1 110	1 160	938	1 149
1985	68.99	55.50	13.00	0.49	1 416	1 467	1 227	1 628
1986	83.35	67.49	15.15	0.71	1 689	1 752	1 443	2 029
1987	94.78	77.19	16.87	0.72	1 893	1 960	1 623	2 510
1988	114.47	93.62	19.55	1.30	2 277	2 354	1 951	2 715
1989	131.10	105.08	23.77	2.25	2 608	2 691	2 259	3 235
1990	146.78	119.26	24.30	3.22	2 917	3 037	2 394	3 611
1991	172.84	139.12	28.51	5.21	3 375	3 487	2 817	4 363
1992	217.21	175.95	32.89	8.37	4 273	4 451	3 363	5 486
1993	279.33	206.12	36.60	36.61	5 650	5 784	4 253	7 043
1994	357.89	259.78	44.73	53.38	7 401	7 529	5 389	9 617
1995	440.75	314.69	51.61	74.45	9 279	9 578	6 309	11 518
1996	492.70	348.96	54.92	88.82	10 663	11 015	7 051	13 186
1997	510.10	353.69	53.69	102.72	11 425	11 733	7 329	14 313
1998	510.35	330.10	44.13	136.12	12 059	12 361	7 138	14 430
1999	583.54	366.21	43.22	174.11	14 147	14 419	7 935	16 736
2000	614.53	371.39	39.35	203.79	15 420	15 737	8 041	17 942
2001	678.29	389.91	35.79	252.59	17 764	17 820	8 525	20 865
2002	733.31	404.44	31.54	297.33	19 473	19 777	8 707	21 886
2003	803.84	430.92	30.52	342.40	22 160	22 541	9 844	24 359
2004	837.39	428.49	29.36	379.53	24 398	24 726	11 539	26 270
2005	1 146.97	463.24	28.44	655.29	26 823	28 803	12 819	26 792
2006	1 475.93	539.88	28.41	907.64	29 569	36 010	15 209	27 459
2007	1 802.17	673.20	32.75	1 096.22	34 707	46 426	19 244	30 687
2008	2 184.20	753.44	31.72	1 399.04	39 502	53 554	21 787	35 180
2009	2 594.20	889.50	34.24	1 670.46	42 789	62 390	25 390	37 104
2010	3 018.55	994.05	33.62	1 990.88	46 757	70 585	28 225	40 397
2011	4 505.57	1 185.91	50.60	3 269.06	51 968	79 541	42 010	46 314
2012	5 347.99	1 245.58	60.73	4 041.68	56 300	86 042	45 990	51 035
2013	6 183.93	1 040.35	56.32	5 087.26	60 435	90 965	48 735	56 694
2014	7 643.73	1 111.15	83.52	6 449.06	65 417	99 279	49 223	62 036
2015	8 318.57	1 225.70	94.02	6 998.85	71 268	105 774	50 852	67 762

①2013 年起，职工工资总额和平均工资包括全部私营企业职工工资。
② 本表“其他单位”包括港澳台及外商企业。
❶Total and average wages of staff and workers has included private enterprises since 2013.
❷“Other Ownership Units” in this table includes foreign invested and HongKong, Macao and Taiwan funded enterprises.

表3.6 职工平均工资(2015)
AVERAGE ANNUAL WAGES OF STAFF AND WORKERS

单位:元(yuan)

行 业	Sectors	合 计 Total	国有单位 State-owned Units	集体单位 Collective-owned Units	港澳台及外商投资单位 Units with Investment from Hong Kong, Macao, Taiwan and Foreign Countries	其他单位 Other Ownership Units
全 市	**Total**	**71 268**	**105 774**	**50 852**	**109 547**	**51 749**
按产业分	**Grouped by Industry**					
第一产业	Primary Industry	38 544	63 933	31 297	52 852	37 015
第二产业	Secondary Industry	56 850	100 599	46 221	78 139	44 771
第三产业	Tertiary Industry	80 509	106 212	53 194	144 006	56 241
按行业分	**Grouped by Sector**					
农、林、牧、渔业	Farming, Forestry, Animal Husbandry and Fishery	39 416	66 393	34 590	51 957	37 707
采矿业	Mining	131 501				131 501
制造业	Manufacturing	58 120	74 739	42 429	77 637	42 860
电力、热力、燃气及水的生产和供应业	Electricity, Heat, Gas and Water Production and Supply Industry and Supply	138 759	170 727	66 675	131 754	119 327
建筑业	Construction	49 213	82 099	60 135	118 416	47 566
批发和零售业	Wholesale and Retail	62 004	62 741	31 571	125 233	33 141
交通运输、仓储和邮政业	Transportation, Warehousing and Post	75 464	96 702	26 355	96 256	64 939
住宿和餐饮业	Hoteling and Catering	41 558	60 376	37 833	52 576	35 869
信息传输、软件和信息技术服务业	Information Transmission, Software and IT Services and Software Industries	115 122	89 604	43 472	190 280	81 847
金融业	Financial Industries	206 679	208 162	42 075	261 346	193 940
房地产业	Real Estate	57 590	59 070	32 309	101 917	50 672
租赁和商务服务业	Leasing and Business Services	70 742	42 459	51 726	206 231	38 752
科学研究和技术服务业	Scientific and Technical Services	104 559	132 993	85 923	197 488	73 598
水利、环境和公共设施管理业	Water Conservancies, Environment and Public Facilities Management	62 920	82 678	42 867	159 056	57 946
居民服务、修理和其他服务业	Resident Service and Other Services	33 720	50 653	35 060	64 880	29 707
教 育	Education	95 957	110 204	77 355	113 029	57 305
卫生和社会工作	Health and Social Work	115 126	141 128	89 104	182 346	60 535
文化、体育和娱乐业	Culture, Sports and Entertainment	69 443	99 808	55 739	83 091	55 684
公共管理、社会保障和社会组织	Public Administration, Social Security and Social Organizations	107 534	117 801	57 160		77 502

表 3.7 主要年份离退休、退职人员养老金
PENSION FOR NONWORKING STAFF AND WORKERS IN MAIN YEARS

单位:亿元(100 million yuan)

指标	Indicators	2000	2010	2014	2015
离退休、退职人员养老金	**Pension for Nonworking Staff and Workers**	**205.14**	**783.42**	**1 377.17**	**1 658.44**
离休职工的离休费	Pensions for Retired Veteran Cadres	7.32	11.41	9.29	10.52
退休职工的退休费	Pensions for Retired	195.90	763.44	1 361.25	1 640.68
退职人员的退职生活费	Living Expenses for the Resigned	1.92	8.57	6.63	7.24

表 3.8 离退休、退职人员养老金(2015)
PENSION FOR NONWORKING STAFF AND WORKERS

单位:亿元(100 million yuan)

指标	Indicators	合计 Total	国有单位 State-owned Units	集体单位 Collective-owned Units	其他单位 Other Ownership Units
离退休、退职人员养老金	**Pension for Nonworking Staff and Workers**	**1 658.44**	**710.16**	**174.11**	**774.17**
离休职工的离休费	Pensions for Retired Veteran Cadres	10.52	7.59	0.17	2.76
退休职工的退休费	Pensions for Retired	1 640.68	700.48	172.18	768.02
退职人员的退职生活费	Living Expenses for the Resigned	7.24	2.09	1.76	3.39

注：本表“其他单位”包括港澳台及外商企业。
Note: “Other Ownership Units” in this table includes foreign invested and HongKong, Macao and Taiwan funded enterprises.

上 / 海 / 统 / 计 / 年 / 鉴

主要统计指标解释

从业人员

指从事一定社会劳动并取得工资或其他形式劳动报酬的人员，包括在岗职工、劳务派遣人员、再就业的离退休人员、私营业主、个体户主、私营和个体从业人员、乡镇企业从业人员、农村从业人员、其他从业人员(包括民办教师、宗教职业者等)。这一指标反映了一定时期内全部劳动力资源的实际利用情况，是研究我国基本国情国力的重要指标。

城镇登记失业人员

指有非农业户口，在一定的劳动年龄内(16 岁以上及男 50 岁以下、女 45 岁以下)，有劳动能力，无业而要求就业，并在当地就业服务机构进行求职登记的人员。

城镇登记失业率

指城镇登记失业人员同城镇单位就业人员、城镇私营企业及个体就业人员(扣除使用的农村劳动力、聘用的离退休人员、港澳台及外方人员)和城镇登记失业人员、城镇单位中的不在岗职工之和的比。计算公式为:

城镇登记失业率 = 城镇登记失业人员 /(城镇单位就业人员 − 使用的农村劳动力 − 聘用的离退休人员 − 聘用的港澳台及外方人员 + 不在岗职工 + 城镇私营企业及个体就业人员 + 城镇登记失业人员) × 100%

职工工资总额

指在报告期内直接支付给本单位职工的劳动报酬或生活费。职工工资总额包括在岗职工工资和离岗职工生活费两部分。

职工平均工资

指企业、事业、机关单位的职工在一定时期内平均每人所得的货币工资额。它表明一定时期职工工资收入的高低程度，是反映职工工资水平的主要指标。计算公式为:

职工平均工资 = 报告期实际支付的全部职工工资总额 / 报告期全部职工平均人数

SHANGHAI STATISTICAL YEARBOOK

EXPLANATORY NOTES TO MAJOR STATISTICAL INDICATORS

□ Employees

Employees refer to the persons who are engaged in social working and receive wages and other forms of remuneration payment, including total staff and workers, labor dispatched personnel, re-employed retirees, employers of private enterprises, self-employed workers, employees in private enterprises and individual economy, employees in township enterprises, employed persons in the rural areas , and other employed persons (including teachers in the schools run by the local people, people engaged in religious profession, etc.). This indicator reflects the actual utilization of total labour force during a certain period of time and is often used for the research on China's economic situation and national power.

□ Registered Urban Unemployment

Registered Urban Unemployment refers to those non-agricultural population within working age (16-50 years for male and 16-45 years for females),who are able and willing to work but unemployed and have registered for job in local employment service agencies.

□ Registered Urban Unemployment Rate

Registered Urban Unemployment Rate refers to the ratio of the number of the registered unemployed to the sum of the number of persons employed in various units (minus the rural labour force, retirees, and Hong Kong, Macao, Taiwan and foreign employees they employ) laid-off workers in urban units, urban self-employed individuals and the registered urban unemployed persons . The formula is as follows:

Registered Urban Unemployment Rate = Number of Registered Urban Unemployed Persons ÷ (Number of Persons Employed in Urban Units - rural labour force employed- retirees employed - Hong Kong, Macao, Taiwan and foreign employees + laid-off workers + Self-employed Individuals in Urban Areas + Number of Registered Urban Unemployed Persons) × 100%.

□ Total Wages of Staff and Workers

Total Wages of Staff and Workers refer to the compensation for services of living cost a unit pays to its employees on the payroll, including the living cost paid to those not on duty.

□ Average Wages of Staff and Workers

Average Wages of Staff and Workers refers to the average wage in money terms per person during a certain period of time for staff and workers in enterprises, institutions, and government agencies, which reflects the general level of wage income during a certain period of time and is calculated as follows:

Average Wages of Staff and Workers = Total Wages of Staff and Workers at Reference Time /Average Number of Staff and Workers at Reference Time.

第四篇
CHAPTER 4

国民经济核算
NATIONAL ECONOMIC ACCOUNTING

简要说明

生产总值(简称 GDP)核算采取国家和地区分级核算制度,上海市生产总值由上海市统计局核算处核算,主要包括:(1)初步核算数。我国按照季度开展 GDP 核算,1-4 季度 GDP 的初步核算数即为年度 GDP 初步核算数,于次年 1 月 20 日左右公布;(2)初步核实数,根据专业统计年报、财政决算资料和行政记录资料计算,在次年《上海市统计年鉴》上公布。由于基础资料和核算方法的不同,年度 GDP 初步核算数和初步核实数会有所差异。除上述核算程序外,在国家开展普查和重点行业调查,或计算方法、分类标准发生变化时,上海市统计局会根据国家统计局的有关要求对 GDP 当期或历史数据进行调整,并在《上海市统计年鉴》上公布。

本年鉴所公布的 GDP 核算数据包括:(1)按照当年价格计算的总量;(2)可比增长及指数。GDP 总量变动受到价格变化和物量变化共同影响,在比较不同时期的 GDP 总量时要剔除价格变化的影响,以反映生产活动成果的实际变动。本年鉴公布的 GDP 及相关指标的增速为剔除价格变动影响的可比增速,并在此基础上计算指数。本篇 GDP 核算行业分类标准采用《国民经济行业分类》(GB/T 4754-2011),产业划分标准采用《三次产业划分规定》(国统字[2012]108 号)。

BRIEF INTRODUCTION

The gross domestic product, or GDP, uses nation–level and city–level classification system for calculation. Shanghai's GDP is produced by the Department of Accounting at the Shanghai Statistics Bureau. It covers (1) Preliminary figure: China calculates quarterly GDP figures, and the yearly preliminary GDP, which is published around January 20 in the following year, equals the preliminary rate for the four quarters combined. (2) Verified figure: it is calculated based on professional statistical report, fiscal accounts data and administrative records, published in the following year's Shanghai Statistical Yearbook. Because of differences in basic information and method of calculation, preliminary figure of the annual GDP and its verified figure may be different. In addition to the above–mentioned calculation procedure, the Shanghai Statistics Bureau modifies related GDP figures when China carries out national census or surveys in key industries, or when calculation methods or classification criteria change. The results should be published on The Shanghai Statistical Yearbook.

GDP data published in this yearbook include: (1) The total output based on the year's prices; (2) Comparable growth and indices. The total output of GDP changes with the prices and volumes, so the comparison of GDP in different periods should exclude the effect of price changes to reflect the actual movement in production activities. Growth of GDP data and related indicators in this yearbook has excluded the effect of price changes and is thus comparable. The indices are based on such comparable data as well. The calculation of GDP on sector classification still uses The Classification of National Economic Sectors (GB/T 4754–2011). Industrial division standard uses Three Industry Classification Regulation (National Statistic Word No.108, 2012)

表 4.1 上海市生产总值(1978～2015)
GROSS DOMESTIC PRODUCT

年 份 Year	上海市生产总值(亿元) Gross Domestic Product (100 million yuan)	按产业分 Grouped by Industry 第一产业 Primary Industry	第二产业 Secondary Industry	第三产业 Tertiary Industry	按行业分 Grouped by Industry #工 业 Industry	建筑业 Construction
1978	272.81	11.00	211.05	50.76	207.47	3.58
1979	286.43	11.39	221.21	53.83	216.62	4.59
1980	311.89	10.10	236.10	65.69	230.87	5.23
1981	324.76	10.58	244.34	69.84	237.12	7.22
1982	337.07	13.31	249.32	74.44	240.75	8.57
1983	351.81	13.52	255.32	82.97	246.26	9.06
1984	390.85	17.26	275.37	98.22	263.19	12.18
1985	466.75	19.53	325.63	121.59	311.12	14.51
1986	490.83	19.69	336.02	135.12	318.89	17.13
1987	545.46	21.60	364.38	159.48	336.54	27.84
1988	648.30	27.36	433.05	187.89	399.53	33.52
1989	696.54	29.63	466.18	200.73	432.92	33.26
1990	781.66	34.24	505.60	241.82	469.83	35.77
1991	893.77	34.06	550.64	309.07	514.79	35.85
1992	1 114.32	34.16	677.39	402.77	636.68	40.71
1993	1 519.23	37.82	902.38	579.03	846.71	55.67
1994	1 990.86	47.61	1 148.45	794.80	1 074.37	74.08
1995	2 499.43	59.82	1 419.41	1 020.20	1 308.20	111.21
1996	2 957.55	68.72	1 596.72	1 292.11	1 452.79	143.93
1997	3 438.79	72.03	1 774.02	1 592.74	1 598.91	175.11
1998	3 801.09	73.84	1 871.89	1 855.36	1 670.19	201.70
1999	4 188.73	74.49	1 984.64	2 129.60	1 787.98	196.66
2000	4 771.17	76.68	2 207.63	2 486.86	1 998.96	208.67
2001	5 210.12	78.00	2 403.18	2 728.94	2 166.74	236.44
2002	5 741.03	79.68	2 622.45	3 038.90	2 368.02	254.43
2003	6 694.23	81.02	3 209.02	3 404.19	2 941.24	267.78
2004	8 072.83	83.45	3 892.12	4 097.26	3 593.25	298.87
2005	9 247.66	90.26	4 381.20	4 776.20	4 036.85	344.35
2006	10 572.24	93.81	4 969.95	5 508.48	4 575.30	394.65
2007	12 494.01	101.84	5 571.06	6 821.11	5 154.42	416.64
2008	14 069.87	111.80	6 085.84	7 872.23	5 576.79	509.05
2009	15 046.45	113.82	6 001.78	8 930.85	5 408.75	593.03
2010	17 165.98	114.15	7 218.32	9 833.51	6 536.21	682.11
2011	19 195.69	124.94	7 927.89	11 142.86	7 208.59	719.30
2012	20 181.72	127.80	7 854.77	12 199.15	7 097.76	757.01
2013	21 818.15	124.89	7 907.81	13 785.45	7 139.18	791.08
2014	23 567.70	124.26	8 167.71	15 275.73	7 362.84	831.86
2015	25 123.45	109.82	7 991.00	17 022.63	7 162.33	855.22

注：2013 年起，三次产业分类执行国家统计局 2012 年制定的《三次产业划分规定》(国统字[2012]108 号)，与 2012 年及以前年度数据不可比(下表同)。
Note: Since 2013, classification of three industrials follows "The Regulation of Industrial Division" (National Statistics (2012) No. 108) formulated by the National Bureau of Statistics in 2012. So the data since 2013 can not be compared with the data of 2012 and previous years (same as follows).

表4.2 上海市生产总值比上年增长(1978~2015)
GROWTH RATE OF GROSS DOMESTIC PRODUCT RAISED PRECEDING YEAR

单位:%

年份 Year	上海市生产总值 Gross Domestic Product	按产业分 Grouped by Industry			按行业分 Grouped by Industry	
		第一产业 Primary Industry	第二产业 Secondary Industry	第三产业 Tertiary Industry	#工业 Industry	建筑业 Construction
1978	15.8	27.0	16.6	10.6	15.8	89.8
1979	7.4	-0.7	8.6	3.1	8.8	-2.2
1980	8.4	-0.6	6.0	22.2	6.1	1.6
1981	5.6	0.3	4.9	8.9	4.1	39.2
1982	7.2	26.2	4.6	13.4	4.2	18.7
1983	7.8	平	7.5	9.8	7.5	8.9
1984	11.6	25.2	10.0	14.7	9.7	19.3
1985	13.4	-22.2	14.9	14.7	15.0	11.1
1986	4.4	-0.2	4.0	6.0	3.7	11.7
1987	7.5	-2.7	7.4	8.9	6.8	22.3
1988	10.1	4.6	9.4	12.6	9.3	12.1
1989	3.0	0.3	1.6	7.1	1.9	-4.4
1990	3.5	4.3	2.8	5.3	2.7	5.1
1991	7.1	0.4	6.9	8.6	8.8	-18.7
1992	14.8	0.4	17.2	12.0	17.7	7.7
1993	15.1	-2.7	16.7	13.7	16.9	13.8
1994	14.5	2.9	14.2	16.2	14.2	14.1
1995	14.3	6.4	14.8	13.7	14.3	25.0
1996	13.1	5.0	11.1	18.1	10.4	24.9
1997	12.8	4.2	10.6	17.9	10.2	16.9
1998	10.3	2.2	8.2	14.8	7.8	14.8
1999	10.4	2.1	9.0	13.4	9.6	-0.6
2000	11.0	3.4	9.8	13.5	10.2	3.0
2001	10.5	3.0	12.0	9.4	12.1	10.9
2002	11.3	3.0	12.1	10.9	12.7	6.4
2003	12.3	2.3	16.1	9.0	17.6	1.3
2004	14.2	-5.0	14.9	14.1	16.1	0.8
2005	11.4	-9.7	10.5	12.8	10.5	10.2
2006	12.7	0.8	12.0	13.6	11.8	14.5
2007	15.2	2.0	11.5	18.8	12.2	4.0
2008	9.7	0.7	7.5	11.7	7.6	5.7
2009	8.2	-1.1	3.5	12.2	2.9	11.7
2010	10.3	-6.6	16.8	5.7	17.5	8.0
2011	8.2	-0.7	6.3	9.6	7.4	-3.5
2012	7.5	0.5	3.1	10.6	2.8	6.1
2013	7.7	-3.3	5.9	9.0	6.1	4.7
2014	7.0	0.1	4.2	8.8	4.3	4.0
2015	6.9	-13.6	1.2	10.6	0.5	8.3

表 4.3 上海市生产总值指数(以 1978 年为 100，1978～2015)
INDEX OF GROSS DOMESTIC PRODUCT (1978 = 100)

年份 Year	上海市生产总值 Gross Domestic Product	按产业分 Grouped by Industry			按行业分 Grouped by Industry	
		第一产业 Primary Industry	第二产业 Secondary Industry	第三产业 Tertiary Industry	#工业 Industry	建筑业 Construction
1978	100.0	100.0	100.0	100.0	100.0	100.0
1979	107.4	99.3	108.6	103.1	108.8	97.8
1980	116.4	98.7	115.1	126.0	115.4	99.4
1981	122.9	99.0	120.7	137.2	120.1	138.4
1982	131.7	124.9	126.3	155.6	125.1	164.3
1983	142.0	124.9	135.8	170.8	134.5	178.9
1984	158.5	156.4	149.4	195.9	147.5	213.4
1985	179.7	121.7	171.7	224.7	169.6	237.1
1986	187.6	121.5	178.6	238.2	175.9	264.8
1987	201.7	118.2	191.8	259.4	187.9	323.9
1988	222.1	123.6	209.8	292.1	205.4	363.1
1989	228.8	124.0	213.2	312.8	209.3	347.1
1990	236.8	129.3	219.2	329.4	215.0	364.8
1991	253.7	129.8	234.3	357.7	233.9	296.6
1992	291.2	130.3	274.6	400.6	275.3	319.4
1993	335.2	126.8	320.5	455.5	321.8	363.5
1994	383.8	130.5	366.0	529.3	367.5	414.8
1995	438.7	138.9	420.2	601.8	420.1	518.5
1996	496.2	145.8	466.8	710.7	463.8	647.6
1997	559.7	151.9	516.3	837.9	511.1	757.0
1998	617.3	155.2	558.6	961.9	551.0	869.0
1999	681.5	158.5	608.9	1 090.8	603.9	863.8
2000	756.5	163.9	668.6	1 238.1	665.5	889.7
2001	835.9	168.8	748.8	1 354.5	746.0	986.7
2002	930.4	173.9	839.4	1 502.1	840.7	1 049.8
2003	1 044.8	177.9	974.5	1 637.3	988.7	1 063.4
2004	1 193.2	169.0	1 119.7	1 868.2	1 147.9	1 071.9
2005	1 329.2	152.6	1 237.3	2 107.3	1 268.4	1 181.2
2006	1 498.0	153.8	1 385.8	2 393.9	1 418.1	1 352.5
2007	1 725.7	156.9	1 545.2	2 844.0	1 591.1	1 406.6
2008	1 893.1	158.0	1 661.1	3 176.7	1 712.0	1 486.8
2009	2 048.3	156.3	1 719.2	3 564.3	1 761.6	1 660.8
2010	2 259.3	146.0	2 008.0	3 767.5	2 069.9	1 793.7
2011	2 444.6	145.0	2 134.5	4 129.2	2 223.1	1 730.9
2012	2 627.9	145.7	2 200.7	4 566.9	2 285.3	1 836.5
2013	2 830.2	140.9	2 330.5	4 977.9	2 424.7	1 922.8
2014	3 028.4	141.0	2 428.4	5 416.0	2 529.0	1 999.7
2015	3 237.3	121.9	2 457.6	5 990.1	2 541.6	2 165.7

表4.4 上海市生产总值构成(1978～2015)
STRUCTURE OF GROSS DOMESTIC PRODUCT

单位:%

年份 Year	上海市生产总值 Gross Domestic Product	按产业分 Grouped by Industry			按行业分 Grouped by Industry	
		第一产业 Primary Industry	第二产业 Secondary Industry	第三产业 Tertiary Industry	#工业 Industry	建筑业 Construction
1978	100	4.0	77.4	18.6	76.1	1.3
1979	100	4.0	77.2	18.8	75.6	1.6
1980	100	3.2	75.7	21.1	74.0	1.7
1981	100	3.3	75.2	21.5	73.0	2.2
1982	100	3.9	74.0	22.1	71.4	2.6
1983	100	3.8	72.6	23.6	70.0	2.6
1984	100	4.4	70.5	25.1	67.4	3.1
1985	100	4.2	69.8	26.0	66.7	3.1
1986	100	4.0	68.5	27.5	65.0	3.5
1987	100	4.0	66.8	29.2	61.7	5.1
1988	100	4.2	66.8	29.0	61.6	5.2
1989	100	4.3	66.9	28.8	62.1	4.8
1990	100	4.4	64.7	30.9	60.1	4.6
1991	100	3.8	61.6	34.6	57.6	4.0
1992	100	3.1	60.8	36.1	57.1	3.7
1993	100	2.5	59.4	38.1	55.7	3.7
1994	100	2.4	57.7	39.9	54.0	3.7
1995	100	2.4	56.8	40.8	52.3	4.5
1996	100	2.3	54.0	43.7	49.1	4.9
1997	100	2.1	51.6	46.3	46.5	5.1
1998	100	1.9	49.3	48.8	44.0	5.3
1999	100	1.8	47.4	50.8	42.7	4.7
2000	100	1.6	46.3	52.1	41.9	4.4
2001	100	1.5	46.1	52.4	41.6	4.5
2002	100	1.4	45.7	52.9	41.3	4.4
2003	100	1.2	47.9	50.9	43.9	4.0
2004	100	1.0	48.2	50.8	44.5	3.7
2005	100	1.0	47.4	51.6	43.7	3.7
2006	100	0.9	47.0	52.1	43.3	3.7
2007	100	0.8	44.6	54.6	41.3	3.3
2008	100	0.8	43.2	56.0	39.6	3.6
2009	100	0.7	39.9	59.4	36.0	3.9
2010	100	0.7	42.0	57.3	38.0	4.0
2011	100	0.7	41.3	58.0	37.6	3.7
2012	100	0.6	39.0	60.4	35.2	3.8
2013	100	0.6	36.2	63.2	32.7	3.6
2014	100	0.5	34.7	64.8	31.2	3.5
2015	100	0.4	31.8	67.8	28.4	3.4

表 4.5 上海市人均生产总值(1978～2015)
PER CAPITA GROSS DOMESTIC PRODUCT

年 份 Year	上海市生产总值(亿元) Gross Domestic Product (100 million yuan)	人均生产总值(按人民币计算)(元) Per Capita Gross Domestic Product (yuan)	人均生产总值指数 Per Capita Gross Domestic Product Index		人均生产总值(按美元计算)(美元) Per Capita Gross Domestic Product (USD)
			以 1978 年为 100 (1978 = 100)	以上年为 100 (preceding year = 100)	
1978	272.81	2 485	100.0	114.9	1 445
1979	286.43	2 556	105.3	105.3	1 787
1980	311.89	2 725	111.8	106.2	1 829
1981	324.76	2 800	116.5	104.2	1 642
1982	337.07	2 864	123.0	105.6	1 513
1983	351.81	2 947	130.7	106.3	1 492
1984	390.85	3 232	144.0	110.2	1 389
1985	466.75	3 811	161.3	112.0	1 298
1986	490.83	3 956	166.1	103.0	1 146
1987	545.46	4 340	176.2	106.1	1 166
1988	648.30	5 080	191.0	108.4	1 365
1989	696.54	5 362	193.3	101.2	1 424
1990	781.66	5 911	196.6	101.7	1 236
1991	893.77	6 661	207.6	105.6	1 251
1992	1 114.32	8 208	235.6	113.5	1 488
1993	1 519.23	11 061	268.1	113.8	1 920
1994	1 990.86	14 328	303.2	113.1	1 662
1995	2 499.43	17 779	342.3	112.9	2 129
1996	2 957.55	20 647	380.0	111.0	2 483
1997	3 438.79	23 397	417.6	109.9	2 822
1998	3 801.09	25 206	448.9	107.5	3 045
1999	4 188.73	27 071	483.0	107.6	3 270
2000	4 771.17	30 047	522.6	108.2	3 630
2001	5 210.12	31 799	559.7	107.1	3 842
2002	5 741.03	33 958	603.9	107.9	4 103
2003	6 694.23	38 486	658.9	109.1	4 650
2004	8 072.83	44 839	727.4	110.4	5 417
2005	9 247.66	49 648	781.2	107.4	6 061
2006	10 572.24	54 858	851.5	109.0	6 882
2007	12 494.01	62 040	939.2	110.3	8 159
2008	14 069.87	66 932	987.1	105.1	9 637
2009	15 046.45	69 165	1 032.5	104.6	10 125
2010	17 165.98	76 074	1 098.6	106.4	11 238
2011	19 195.69	82 560	1 153.5	105.0	12 784
2012	20 181.72	85 373	1 219.3	105.7	13 524
2013	21 818.15	90 993	1 295.7	106.3	14 692
2014	23 567.70	97 370	1 373.5	106.0	15 851
2015	25 123.45	103 795	1 468.7	106.9	16 665

表4.6 主要年份上海市生产总值(按三次产业分)
GROSS DOMESTIC PRODUCT (CLASSIFIED BY THREE INDUSTRIES) IN MAIN YEARS

单位:亿元(100 million yuan)

指 标	Indicators	2013	2014	2015
上海市生产总值	**Gross Domestic Product**	**21 818.15**	**23 567.70**	**25 123.45**
按产业分	Grouped by Industry			
第一产业	Primary Industry	124.89	124.26	109.82
第二产业	Secondary Industry	7 907.81	8 167.71	7 991.00
第三产业	Tertiary Industry	13 785.45	15 275.73	17 022.63
按行业分	Grouped by Sector			
农、林、牧、渔业	Farming, Forestry, Animal Husbandry and Fishery	129.28	128.62	113.99
工 业	Industry	7 139.18	7 362.84	7 162.33
建筑业	Construction	791.08	831.86	855.22
批发和零售业	Retail and Wholesale Industries	3 533.10	3 647.33	3 824.22
交通运输、仓储和邮政业	Transportation, Warehousing and Post	935.91	1 044.46	1 133.17
住宿和餐饮业	Hoteling and Catering	311.81	359.28	374.63
信息传输、软件和信息技术服务业	Information Transmission, Software and IT Services	1 086.06	1 211.83	1 376.69
金融业	Financial Industry	2 823.81	3 400.41	4 162.70
房地产业	Real Estate Industry	1 427.05	1 530.96	1 699.78
租赁和商务服务业	Leasing and Business Services	1 211.96	1 349.74	1 475.72
科学研究和技术服务业	Scientific and Technical Services	601.50	674.60	713.37
水利、环境和公共设施管理业	Water Conservancies, Environment and Public Facilities Management	73.39	88.24	103.62
居民服务、修理和其他服务业	Resident Service and Other Services	252.00	272.83	279.56
教 育	Education	537.58	611.14	684.63
卫生和社会工作	Health and Social Work and Social Welfare	372.19	439.18	478.36
文化、体育和娱乐业	Culture, Sports and Entertainment	136.37	157.58	179.85
公共管理、社会保障和社会组织	Public Administration, Social Security and Social Organizations	455.88	456.79	505.61

表4.7 主要年份上海市生产总值比上年增长(按三次产业分)
GROWTH RATE OF GROSS DOMESTIC PRODUCT IN MAIN YEARS(CLASSIFIED BY THREE INDUSTRIES)

单位:%

指 标	Indicators	2013	2014	2015
上海市生产总值	**Gross Domestic Product**	**7.7**	**7.0**	**6.9**
按产业分	Grouped by Industry			
第一产业	Primary Industry	-3.3	0.1	-13.6
第二产业	Secondary Industry	5.9	4.2	1.2
第三产业	Tertiary Industry	9.0	8.8	10.6
按行业分	**Grouped by Sector**			
农、林、牧、渔业	Farming, Forestry, Animal Husbandry and Fishery	-2.9	0.0	-13.4
工 业	Industry	6.1	4.3	0.5
建筑业	Construction	4.7	4.0	8.3
批发和零售业	Retail and Wholesale Industries	7.1	6.3	3.7
交通运输、仓储和邮政业	Transportation, Warehousing and Post	1.0	9.4	7.0
住宿和餐饮业	Hoteling and Catering	2.3	1.6	-1.2
信息传输、软件和信息技术服务业	Information Transmission, Software and IT Services	13.3	12.5	12.0
金融业	Financial Industry	13.7	14.7	22.6
房地产业	Real Estate Industry	11.6	3.2	9.0
租赁和商务服务业	Leasing and Business Services	9.7	9.0	2.5
科学研究和技术服务业	Scientific and Technical Services	8.3	4.6	6.3
水利、环境和公共设施管理业	Water Conservancies, Environment and Public Facilities Management	6.4	12.1	16.4
居民服务、修理和其他服务业	Resident Service and Other Services	10.6	-0.1	9.9
教 育	Education	13.2	16.5	17.3
卫生和社会工作	Health and Social Work and Social Welfare	8.1	14.0	16.4
文化、体育和娱乐业	Culture, Sports and Entertainment	4.6	9.6	13.6
公共管理、社会保障和社会组织	Public Administration, Social Security and Social Organizations	0.6	-2.4	12.3

表4.8 上海市生产总值收入法项目(1978~2015)
GROSS DOMESTIC PRODUCT(BY INCOME ITEM)

单位:亿元(100 million yuan)

年 份 Year	上海市生产总 值 Gross Domestic Product	劳动者报酬 Compensation of Employees	生产税净额 Net Taxes on Production	固定资产折旧 Depreciation of Fixed Assets	营业盈余 Operating Surplus
1978	272.81	62.03	45.53	10.60	154.65
1979	286.43	68.15	45.61	11.13	161.54
1980	311.89	74.47	49.49	13.05	174.88
1981	324.76	78.99	54.52	14.70	176.55
1982	337.07	85.00	57.09	16.30	178.68
1983	351.81	90.36	57.51	18.73	185.21
1984	390.85	108.79	68.74	20.81	192.51
1985	466.75	125.99	87.36	26.16	227.24
1986	490.83	141.95	86.31	33.42	229.15
1987	545.46	163.88	98.61	40.73	242.24
1988	648.30	197.69	126.95	71.85	251.81
1989	696.54	223.35	136.01	79.79	257.39
1990	781.66	244.03	149.35	92.93	295.35
1991	893.77	302.94	170.42	126.62	293.79
1992	1 114.32	397.72	207.40	160.36	348.84
1993	1 519.23	563.59	257.30	159.93	538.41
1994	1 990.86	692.40	356.32	245.26	696.88
1995	2 499.43	901.83	430.67	339.77	827.16
1996	2 957.55	1 065.85	576.01	376.70	938.99
1997	3 438.79	1 195.63	716.02	425.04	1 102.10
1998	3 801.09	1 341.22	809.04	514.85	1 135.98
1999	4 188.73	1 518.26	902.10	615.28	1 153.09
2000	4 771.17	1 724.29	1 124.30	679.43	1 243.15
2001	5 210.12	1 934.27	1 184.62	769.59	1 321.64
2002	5 741.03	2 205.79	1 219.35	850.69	1 465.20
2003	6 694.23	2 452.32	1 265.89	975.24	2 000.78
2004	8 072.83	2 771.77	1 313.83	1 265.16	2 722.07
2005	9 247.66	3 312.31	1 459.39	1 488.54	2 987.42
2006	10 572.24	3 846.06	1 729.03	1 721.21	3 275.94
2007	12 494.01	4 481.91	2 142.97	1 931.76	3 937.37
2008	14 069.87	5 417.93	2 662.86	2 132.75	3 856.33
2009	15 046.45	5 901.84	2 916.92	2 229.19	3 998.50
2010	17 165.98	6 742.05	3 298.73	2 275.95	4 849.25
2011	19 195.69	7 709.62	3 713.40	2 298.34	5 474.33
2012	20 181.72	8 389.14	4 022.74	2 460.38	5 309.46
2013	21 818.15	9 316.37	4 462.84	2 538.59	5 500.35
2014	23 567.70	10 296.45	4 716.76	2 580.36	5 974.12
2015	25 123.45	11 085.40	4 919.88	2 715.36	6 402.81

表4.9 上海市生产总值收入法项目构成(1978~2015)
STRUCTURE OF GROSS DOMESTIC PRODUCT(BY INCOME ITEM)

单位:%

年 份 Year	上海市生产总值 Gross Domestic Product	劳动者报酬 Compensation of Employees	生产税净额 Net Taxes on Production	固定资产折旧 Depreciation of Fixed Assets	营业盈余 Operating Surplus
1978	100	22.7	16.7	3.9	56.7
1979	100	23.8	15.9	3.9	56.4
1980	100	23.9	15.8	4.2	56.1
1981	100	24.3	16.8	4.5	54.4
1982	100	25.2	17.0	4.8	53.0
1983	100	25.7	16.4	5.3	52.6
1984	100	27.8	17.6	5.3	49.3
1985	100	27.0	18.7	5.6	48.7
1986	100	28.9	17.6	6.8	46.7
1987	100	30.0	18.1	7.5	44.4
1988	100	30.5	19.6	11.1	38.8
1989	100	32.1	19.5	11.5	36.9
1990	100	31.2	19.1	11.9	37.8
1991	100	33.9	19.1	14.1	32.9
1992	100	35.7	18.6	14.4	31.3
1993	100	37.1	16.9	10.5	35.5
1994	100	34.8	17.9	12.3	35.0
1995	100	36.1	17.2	13.6	33.1
1996	100	36.0	19.5	12.7	31.8
1997	100	34.8	20.8	12.4	32.0
1998	100	35.3	21.3	13.5	29.9
1999	100	36.3	21.5	14.7	27.5
2000	100	36.1	23.6	14.2	26.1
2001	100	37.1	22.7	14.8	25.4
2002	100	38.4	21.3	14.8	25.5
2003	100	36.6	18.9	14.6	29.9
2004	100	34.3	16.3	15.7	33.7
2005	100	35.8	15.8	16.1	32.3
2006	100	36.3	16.4	16.3	31.0
2007	100	35.9	17.1	15.5	31.5
2008	100	38.5	18.9	15.2	27.4
2009	100	39.2	19.4	14.8	26.6
2010	100	39.3	19.2	13.3	28.2
2011	100	40.2	19.3	12.0	28.5
2012	100	41.6	19.9	12.2	26.3
2013	100	42.7	20.5	11.6	25.2
2014	100	43.7	20.0	11.0	25.3
2015	100	44.1	19.6	10.8	25.5

表 4.10 主要年份上海市生产总值(按所有制分)
GROSS DOMESTIC PRODUCT(BY OWNERSHIP) IN MAIN YEARS

年 份 Year	上海市生产总值 Gross Domestic Product	其 中 of which				
		公有制经济 Public-owned	其 中 of which		非公有制经济 Non-public-owned	其 中 of which
			国有经济 State-owned	集体经济 Collective-owned		#私营和个体 Private
绝对值(亿元) Absolute Volume(100 million yuan)						
1990	781.66	746.03	556.87	189.16	35.63	22.39
1995	2 499.43	2 047.57	1 489.06	558.51	451.86	192.66
2000	4 771.17	3 409.97	2 626.33	783.64	1 361.20	623.84
2001	5 210.12	3 554.56	2 773.76	780.80	1 655.56	830.27
2002	5 741.03	3 703.46	2 888.57	814.89	2 037.57	1 055.48
2003	6 694.23	4 171.16	3 360.21	810.95	2 523.07	1 258.15
2004	8 072.83	4 810.32	4 069.95	740.37	3 262.51	1 293.56
2005	9 247.66	5 256.49	4 471.92	784.57	3 991.17	1 944.55
2006	10 572.24	5 812.87	4 994.48	818.39	4 759.37	2 281.10
2007	12 494.01	6 674.98	5 852.65	822.33	5 819.03	2 804.01
2008	14 069.87	7 341.75	6 452.92	888.83	6 728.12	3 313.18
2009	15 046.45	7 769.86	6 864.01	905.85	7 276.59	3 571.19
2010	17 165.98	8 662.92	7 755.35	907.57	8 503.06	4 139.07
2011	19 195.69	9 585.12	8 660.23	924.89	9 610.57	4 598.84
2012	20 181.72	9 954.95	9 000.30	954.65	10 226.77	4 887.86
2013	21 818.15	10 634.03	9 727.25	906.78	11 184.12	5 320.27
2014	23 567.70	11 394.46	10 483.78	910.68	12 173.24	5 796.93
2015	25 123.45	12 052.18	11 169.80	882.38	13 071.27	6 279.77
构 成(%) Composition(%)						
1990	100.0	95.4	71.2	24.2	4.6	2.9
1995	100.0	81.9	59.6	22.3	18.1	7.7
2000	100.0	71.4	55.0	16.4	28.6	13.1
2001	100.0	68.2	53.2	15.0	31.8	15.9
2002	100.0	64.5	50.3	14.2	35.5	18.4
2003	100.0	62.3	50.2	12.1	37.7	18.8
2004	100.0	59.6	50.4	9.2	40.4	19.7
2005	100.0	56.9	48.4	8.5	43.1	21.0
2006	100.0	55.0	47.3	7.7	45.0	21.6
2007	100.0	53.4	46.8	6.6	46.6	22.4
2008	100.0	52.2	45.9	6.3	47.8	23.5
2009	100.0	51.6	45.6	6.0	48.4	23.7
2010	100.0	50.5	45.2	5.3	49.5	24.1
2011	100.0	49.9	45.1	4.8	50.1	24.0
2012	100.0	49.3	44.6	4.7	50.7	24.2
2013	100.0	48.7	44.6	4.2	51.3	24.4
2014	100.0	48.3	44.5	3.9	51.7	24.6
2015	100.0	48.0	44.5	3.5	52.0	25.0

表4.11 主要年份非公有制经济增加值(按产业分)
ADDED VALUE OF NON-PUBLIC-OWNED (GROUPED BY INDUSTRY) IN MAIN YEARS

单位:亿元(100 million yuan)

年份 Year	非公有制经济增加值 Added Value of Non-public-owned	其中 of which			其中 of which
		第一产业 Primary Industry	第二产业 Secondary Industry	第三产业 Tertiary Industry	#工业 Industry
1978	2.71	1.64	0.07	0.40	0.40
1990	35.63	9.01	15.22	11.40	13.74
1991	44.72	8.10	22.20	14.41	20.62
1992	73.41	7.65	42.13	23.63	39.85
1993	133.93	8.98	77.02	47.93	72.81
1994	250.63	10.88	154.62	85.13	148.31
1995	451.86	13.29	285.73	152.84	274.64
1996	655.39	14.31	424.30	216.78	407.69
1997	790.60	13.42	503.69	273.49	470.23
1998	940.64	13.25	561.66	365.72	518.25
1999	1 124.96	13.56	635.83	475.57	585.76
2000	1 361.20	14.25	773.50	573.45	715.18
2001	1 655.56	14.77	924.21	716.58	857.62
2002	2 037.57	14.34	1 085.12	938.11	1 004.78
2003	2 523.07	13.04	1 459.67	1 050.36	1 378.21
2004	3 262.51	10.44	1 921.74	1 330.33	1 757.96
2005	3 991.17	11.12	2 228.18	1 751.87	2 054.78
2006	4 759.37	11.41	2 634.01	2 113.95	2 438.40
2007	5 819.03	11.98	3 044.61	2 762.44	2 831.64
2008	6 728.12	13.35	3 294.60	3 420.17	3 039.51
2009	7 276.59	13.09	3 213.99	4 049.50	2 925.50
2010	8 503.06	13.13	3 928.43	4 561.50	3 575.67
2011	9 610.57	14.39	4 338.15	5 258.03	3 960.36
2012	10 226.77	14.72	4 312.21	5 899.84	3 882.90
2013	11 184.12	14.36	4 318.88	6 850.88	3 890.01
2014	12 173.24	14.29	4 498.36	7 660.58	4 049.05
2015	13 071.27	12.63	4 443.21	8 615.43	3 974.84

表 4.12 上海市生产总值(支出法)(1978~2015)
GROSS DOMESTIC PRODUCT(BY EXPENDITURE APPROACH)

年份 Year	上海市生产总值(亿元) Gross Domestic Product (100 million yuan)	其中 of which: 货物和服务净流出 Net Outflows of Goods and Services	其中 of which: 本市使用的生产总值 Gross Domestic Product Used	其中 of which: 最终消费支出 Final Consumption	其中 of which: 资本形成总额 Gross Capital Formation	上海市生产总值构成(%) Composition of GDP(%): #最终消费支出 Final Consumption	上海市生产总值构成(%) Composition of GDP(%): #资本形成总额 Gross Capital Formation
1978	272.81	165.79	107.02	59.06	47.96	21.6	17.6
1979	286.43	171.48	114.95	71.34	43.61	24.9	15.2
1980	311.89	164.13	147.76	81.24	66.52	26.0	21.3
1981	324.76	158.35	166.41	89.73	76.68	27.6	23.6
1982	337.07	153.90	183.17	92.90	90.27	27.6	26.8
1983	351.81	178.76	173.05	101.19	71.86	28.8	20.4
1984	390.85	171.97	218.88	117.25	101.63	30.0	26.0
1985	466.75	122.47	344.28	155.15	189.13	33.2	40.5
1986	490.83	80.97	409.86	181.74	228.12	37.0	46.5
1987	545.46	103.70	441.76	200.74	241.02	36.8	44.2
1988	648.30	57.32	590.98	255.42	335.56	39.4	51.8
1989	696.54	46.24	650.30	298.62	351.68	42.9	50.5
1990	781.66	91.87	689.79	358.45	331.34	45.9	42.4
1991	893.77	167.68	726.09	386.06	340.03	43.2	38.0
1992	1 114.32	150.12	964.20	476.57	487.63	42.7	43.8
1993	1 519.23	75.60	1 443.63	699.52	744.11	46.0	49.0
1994	1 990.86	-90.46	2 081.32	919.83	1 161.49	46.2	58.3
1995	2 499.43	-218.64	2 718.07	1 150.35	1 567.72	46.0	62.7
1996	2 957.55	-348.05	3 305.60	1 348.76	1 956.84	45.6	66.2
1997	3 438.79	-210.99	3 649.78	1 600.83	2 048.95	46.6	59.6
1998	3 801.09	32.25	3 768.84	1 758.09	2 010.75	46.3	52.9
1999	4 188.73	259.37	3 929.36	1 959.12	1 970.24	46.8	47.0
2000	4 771.17	356.93	4 414.24	2 244.52	2 169.72	47.0	45.5
2001	5 210.12	377.21	4 832.91	2 476.20	2 356.71	47.5	45.2
2002	5 741.03	418.68	5 322.35	2 791.06	2 531.29	48.6	44.1
2003	6 694.23	399.96	6 294.27	3 217.59	3 076.68	48.1	46.0
2004	8 072.83	457.99	7 614.84	3 832.59	3 782.25	47.5	46.9
2005	9 247.66	548.33	8 699.33	4 480.34	4 218.99	48.4	45.6
2006	10 572.24	523.75	10 048.49	5 175.15	4 873.34	49.0	46.1
2007	12 494.01	604.04	11 889.97	6 170.38	5 719.59	49.4	45.8
2008	14 069.87	753.38	13 316.49	7 172.67	6 143.82	51.0	43.7
2009	15 046.45	411.80	14 634.65	7 868.64	6 766.01	52.3	45.0
2010	17 165.98	331.91	16 832.07	9 424.29	7 407.78	54.9	43.2
2011	19 195.69	645.45	18 550.24	10 821.18	7 729.06	56.4	40.3
2012	20 181.72	978.32	19 203.40	11 528.58	7 674.82	57.1	38.0
2013	21 818.15	877.01	20 941.14	12 612.33	8 328.81	57.8	38.2
2014	23 567.70	941.78	22 625.92	13 858.14	8 767.78	58.8	37.2
2015	25 123.45	718.11	24 405.34	14 854.50	9 550.84	59.1	38.0

表4.13 最终消费支出及构成(1978~2015)
FINAL CONSUMPTION AND COMPOSITION

年份 Year	最终消费支出(亿元) Final Consumption (100 million yuan)					最终消费支出构成(%) Composition of Final Consumption (%)	
	合计 Total	居民消费支出 Household Consumption	其中 of which 农村居民 Rural Residents	其中 of which 城镇居民 Urban Residents	政府消费支出 Government Consumption	居民消费支出 Household Consumption	政府消费支出 Government Consumption
1978	59.06	48.25	12.82	35.43	10.81	81.7	18.3
1979	71.34	58.80	17.02	41.78	12.54	82.4	17.6
1980	81.24	66.31	19.43	46.88	14.93	81.6	18.4
1981	89.73	73.69	23.25	50.44	16.04	82.1	17.9
1982	92.90	75.02	26.41	48.61	17.88	80.8	19.2
1983	101.19	81.64	26.91	54.73	19.55	80.7	19.3
1984	117.25	94.56	31.10	63.46	22.69	80.6	19.4
1985	155.15	124.78	38.35	86.43	30.37	80.4	19.6
1986	181.74	145.73	42.49	103.24	36.01	80.2	19.8
1987	200.74	161.09	47.23	113.86	39.65	80.2	19.8
1988	255.42	211.04	55.97	155.07	44.38	82.6	17.4
1989	298.62	244.60	61.15	183.45	54.02	81.9	18.1
1990	358.45	284.79	66.15	218.64	73.66	79.5	20.5
1991	386.06	311.09	72.17	238.92	74.97	80.6	19.4
1992	476.57	366.09	84.86	281.23	110.48	76.8	23.2
1993	699.52	555.45	110.30	445.15	144.07	79.4	20.6
1994	919.83	732.71	130.08	602.63	187.12	79.7	20.3
1995	1 150.35	926.54	152.90	773.64	223.81	80.5	19.5
1996	1 348.76	1 080.79	168.13	912.66	267.97	80.1	19.9
1997	1 600.83	1 262.12	176.50	1 085.62	338.71	78.8	21.2
1998	1 758.09	1 379.41	178.52	1 200.89	378.68	78.5	21.5
1999	1 959.12	1 528.95	176.73	1 352.22	430.17	78.0	22.0
2000	2 244.52	1 756.27	176.79	1 579.48	488.25	78.2	21.8
2001	2 476.20	1 910.44	181.22	1 729.22	565.76	77.2	22.8
2002	2 791.06	2 134.79	185.58	1 949.21	656.27	76.5	23.5
2003	3 217.59	2 437.44	187.78	2 249.66	780.15	75.8	24.2
2004	3 832.59	2 869.26	186.78	2 682.48	963.33	74.9	25.1
2005	4 480.34	3 332.99	194.59	3 138.40	1 147.35	74.4	25.6
2006	5 175.15	3 858.54	223.98	3 634.56	1 316.61	74.6	25.4
2007	6 170.38	4 609.59	245.82	4 363.77	1 560.79	74.7	25.3
2008	7 172.67	5 290.40	275.91	5 014.49	1 882.27	73.7	26.3
2009	7 868.64	5 782.88	303.57	5 479.31	2 085.76	73.5	26.5
2010	9 424.29	7 281.88	339.11	6 942.77	2 142.41	77.3	22.7
2011	10 821.18	8 239.76	441.77	7 797.99	2 581.42	76.1	23.9
2012	11 528.58	8 721.25	468.25	8 253.00	2 807.33	75.6	24.4
2013	12 612.33	9 499.01	516.60	8 982.41	3 113.32	75.3	24.7
2014	13 858.14	10 409.36	573.99	9 835.37	3 448.78	75.1	24.9
2015	14 854.50	11 089.56	634.66	10 454.90	3 764.94	74.7	25.3

表 4.14 居民消费水平及指数(1978～2015)
HOUSEHOLD CONSUMPTION LEVEL AND INDEX

年份 Year	居民消费水平(元) Household Consumption Level(yuan)			指数(以1978年为100) Index(1978＝100)		
	全市 Total	其中 of which		全市 Total	其中 of which	
		农村居民 Rural Households	城镇居民 Urban Households		农村居民 Rural Households	城镇居民 Urban Households
1978	440	279	555	100.0	100.0	100.0
1979	525	377	624	117.0	130.1	111.0
1980	579	435	672	122.9	143.0	113.6
1981	635	519	709	132.9	168.3	118.0
1982	637	586	669	133.3	170.0	117.6
1983	684	597	737	142.6	194.7	121.6
1984	782	691	836	159.9	220.4	135.6
1985	1 019	928	1 065	180.5	252.6	150.7
1986	1 174	1 045	1 237	195.5	266.5	164.7
1987	1 282	1 089	1 383	197.7	257.7	170.5
1988	1 654	1 295	1 837	217.3	268.8	190.8
1989	1 883	1 417	2 115	216.6	268.8	189.5
1990	2 154	1 526	2 460	209.5	244.3	186.8
1991	2 318	1 653	2 639	224.8	274.8	197.4
1992	2 697	1 939	3 057	237.4	293.8	207.3
1993	4 044	2 821	4 531	297.2	324.6	263.3
1994	5 273	3 498	5 922	338.5	373.9	296.5
1995	6 591	4 306	7 363	397.4	424.8	347.5
1996	7 545	4 888	8 385	435.9	461.8	379.5
1997	8 587	5 273	9 565	466.4	484.0	404.5
1998	9 147	5 495	10 150	494.9	499.0	428.4
1999	9 881	5 606	10 975	527.6	509.5	456.7
2000	11 060	5 774	12 323	566.1	520.2	490.0
2001	11 660	5 976	12 951	598.4	542.0	516.0
2002	12 627	6 213	14 003	649.3	563.1	558.8
2003	14 013	6 800	15 374	712.3	611.5	606.3
2004	15 937	7 465	17 304	791.4	655.5	666.9
2005	17 894	9 245	18 996	868.2	787.3	715.6
2006	20 022	10 462	21 216	953.3	871.5	785.0
2007	22 889	10 801	24 429	1 050.5	860.2	872.1
2008	25 167	11 563	26 909	1 113.5	880.0	926.2
2009	26 582	12 240	28 428	1 177.0	914.3	979.9
2010	32 271	13 609	34 588	1 293.5	990.2	1 075.0
2011	35 439	17 757	37 558	1 377.6	1 131.8	1 137.4
2012	36 893	18 512	39 095	1 460.3	1 202.0	1 205.6
2013	39 616	20 716	41 809	1 558.1	1 294.6	1 286.4
2014	43 007	22 803	45 352	1 671.8	1 402.1	1 380.3
2015	45 816	23 005	48 750	1 780.5	1 411.9	1 482.4

表4.15 资本形成总额及指数(1978~2015)
GROSS CAPITAL FORMATION AND INDEX

年 份 Year	资本形成总额(亿元) Gross Capital Formation(100 million yuan)			资本形成总额指数(以1978年为100) Index of Gross Capital Formation (1978=100)		
	合 计 Total	固定资本形成总额 Fixed Capital Formation	存货变动 Inventory Change	总指数 Indices	固定资本形成总额 Fixed Capital Formation	存货变动 Inventory Change
1978	47.96	31.69	16.27	100.0	100.0	100.0
1979	43.61	39.05	4.56	90.3	119.7	36.9
1980	66.52	45.57	20.95	134.6	133.5	136.7
1981	76.68	55.10	21.58	156.4	164.4	138.1
1982	90.27	70.49	19.78	178.8	210.5	107.6
1983	71.86	74.51	-2.65	150.7	223.7	-12.5
1984	101.63	90.70	10.93	210.0	262.7	91.9
1985	189.13	116.70	72.43	387.6	308.1	564.0
1986	228.12	144.41	83.71	431.8	352.5	607.4
1987	241.02	183.79	57.23	380.0	415.9	298.8
1988	335.56	236.92	98.64	449.2	474.1	392.1
1989	351.68	232.22	119.46	423.1	419.6	429.7
1990	331.34	248.46	82.88	338.1	430.5	131.1
1991	340.03	276.08	63.95	334.0	447.7	109.0
1992	487.63	382.01	105.62	435.2	561.5	162.1
1993	744.11	624.31	119.80	530.1	731.0	154.5
1994	1 161.49	996.48	165.01	726.8	1 019.1	196.1
1995	1 567.72	1 380.85	186.87	950.6	1 373.7	218.8
1996	1 956.84	1 711.46	245.38	1 158.8	1 660.8	279.5
1997	2 048.95	1 795.83	253.12	1 175.0	1 700.6	268.3
1998	2 010.75	1 804.81	205.94	1 129.2	1 695.5	201.2
1999	1 970.24	1 801.59	168.65	1 098.7	1 683.7	164.0
2000	2 169.72	1 933.01	236.71	1 152.5	1 746.0	191.0
2001	2 356.71	2 099.99	256.72	1 263.2	1 906.6	216.1
2002	2 531.29	2 366.10	165.19	1 387.0	2 192.6	148.9
2003	3 076.68	2 643.07	433.61	1 588.1	2 365.8	299.4
2004	3 782.25	3 239.04	543.21	1 804.1	2 680.5	347.3
2005	4 218.99	3 775.55	443.44	1 962.0	3 024.4	279.9
2006	4 873.34	4 383.33	490.01	2 210.4	3 427.9	299.0
2007	5 719.59	5 192.50	527.09	2 575.3	4 030.2	319.5
2008	6 143.82	5 614.47	529.35	2 708.2	4 235.3	338.4
2009	6 766.01	6 447.52	318.49	2 899.7	4 741.8	199.0
2010	7 407.78	6 380.33	1 027.45	3 094.0	4 533.2	640.2
2011	7 729.06	6 801.78	927.28	3 174.4	4 642.0	666.4
2012	7 674.82	7 012.53	662.29	3 266.5	4 957.7	493.10
2013	8 328.81	7 587.13	741.68	3 554.0	5 379.1	555.7
2014	8 767.78	8 022.49	745.29	3 724.6	5 658.8	559.0
2015	9 550.84	8 999.87	550.97	4 108.2	6 422.7	423.2

表4.16 主要年份旅游产业增加值
VALUE ADDED OF TOURISM INDUSTRY IN MAIN YEARS

指 标	Indicators	2005	2010	2014	2015
增加值(亿元)	**Value Added (100 million yuan)**	**584.26**	**1 360.80**	**1 449.33**	**1 535.64**
按行业分	**Grouped by Sectors**				
#旅行社服务业	Travel Agency	9.02	17.50	24.47	29.16
旅游住宿业	Hotel	91.78	212.34	174.13	186.20
旅游运输业	Travel Transportation	120.86	159.67	171.40	202.65
邮电通讯业	Post and Telecommunication	25.21	38.60	46.41	43.94
旅游商业	Tourism Commerce	96.17	529.28	505.18	500.59
旅游餐饮业	Catering	68.92	67.17	94.00	110.98
城市交通业	Urban Traffic	45.96	93.18	115.00	121.53
园林文化业	Gardening	92.42	169.98	215.01	225.29
旅游产业增加值占上海市生产总值比重(%)	**Ratio of Value Added of Tourism Industry to GDP (%)**	**6.4**	**8.1**	**6.1**	**6.1**

表4.17 主要年份信息产业增加值
VALUE ADDED OF INFORMATION INDUSTRY IN MAIN YEARS

指 标	Indicators	2000	2010	2014	2015
增加值(亿元)	**Value Added (100 million yuan)**	**338.18**	**1 672.14**	**2 460.11**	**2 747.64**
信息产品制造业	Information Products Manufacturing	195.82	690.76	786.36	841.12
信息产品销售业	Information Products Distribution	12.59	54.62	110.66	153.03
信息服务业	Information Services	129.77	926.76	1 563.09	1 753.49
结 构(%)	**Composition(%)**				
信息产品制造业	Information Products Manufacturing	57.9	41.3	32.0	27.9
信息产品销售业	Information Products Distribution	3.7	3.3	4.5	5.6
信息服务业	Information Services	38.4	55.4	63.5	66.5
信息产业增加值占上海市生产总值比重(%)	**Ratio of Value Added of Information Industry to GDP(%).**	**7.1**	**9.7**	**10.4**	**10.9**

上/海/统/计/年/鉴

主要统计指标解释

生产总值(原国内生产总值)

指按市场价格计算的一个国家(或地区)所有常住单位在一定时期内生产活动的最终成果。生产总值有三种表现形态,即价值形态、收入形态和产品形态。从价值形态看，它是所有常住单位在一定时期内所生产的全部货物和服务价值超过同期投入的全部非固定资产货物和服务价值的差额,即所有常住单位的增加值之和;从收入形态看，它是所有常住单位在一定时期内所创造并分配给常住单位和非常住单位的初次收入之和;从产品形态看，它是所有常住单位在一定时期内最终使用的货物和服务减去货物和服务的进口价值。在实际核算中,生产总值有三种计算方法,即生产法、收入法和支出法。三种方法分别从不同的方面反映生产总值及其构成。根据国务院和国家统计局有关我国 GDP 核算和数据发布制度的规定，上海国内生产总值自 2004 年起更名为“上海市生产总值”,简称“上海市 GDP”。

三次产业

三次产业的划分是国际上常用的产业结构分类。第一产业是指产品直接取自自然界的部门，第二产业是指对初级产品进行再加工的部门，第三产业是指为生产和消费提供各种服务的部门。

第一产业是指农、林、牧、渔业(不含农、林、牧、渔服务业)。

第二产业是指采矿业(不含开采辅助活动),制造业(不含金属制品、机械和设备修理业),电力、热力、燃气及水生产和供应业,建筑业。

第三产业即服务业,是指除第一产业、第二产业以外的其他行业。

劳动者报酬

指劳动者因从事生产活动所获得的全部报酬。包括劳动者获得的各种形式的工资、奖金和津贴,既包括货币形式的,也包括实物形式的,还包括劳动者所享受的公费医疗和医药卫生费、上下班交通补贴、单位支付的社会保险费、住房公积金等。对于个体经济来说,其所有者所获得的劳动报酬和经营利润不易区分，这两部分统一作为劳动者报酬处理。

生产税净额

指生产税减生产补贴后的余额。生产税指政府对生产单位从事生产、销售和经营活动以及因从事生产活动使用某些生产要素(如固定资产、土地、劳动力)所征收的各种税、附加费和规费。生产补贴与生产税相反,指政府对生产单位的单方面转移支出,因此视为负生产税,包括政策亏损补贴、价格补贴等。

固定资产折旧

指一定时期内为弥补固定资产损耗按照规定的固定资产折旧率提取的固定资产折旧，或按国民经济核算统一规定的折旧率虚拟计算的固定资产折旧。它反映了固定资产在当期生产中的转移价值。各类企业和企业化管理的事业单位的固定资产折旧是指实际计提的折旧费;不计提折旧的政府机关、非企业化管理的事业单位和居民住房的固定资产折旧是按照统一规定的折旧率和固定资产原值计算的虚拟折旧。原则上,固定资产折旧应按固定资产当期的重置价值计算，但是目前我国尚不具备对全社会固定资产进行重估价的基础，所以暂时只能采用上述办法。

营业盈余

指常住单位创造的增加值扣除劳动者报酬、生产税净额和固定资产折旧后的余额。它相当于企业的营业利润(不包括投资收益)加上生产补贴,但要扣除从利润中开支的工资和福利等。

支出法生产总值

是从最终使用的角度反映一个国家(或地区)一定时期内生产活动最终成果的一种方法，包括最终消费支出、资本形成总额及货物和服务净出口三部分。计算公式为：

支出法生产总值 = 最终消费支出 + 资本形成总额 + 货物和服务净出口

最终消费支出

指常住单位在一定时期内对于货物和服务的全部最终消费支出,也就是常住单位为满足物质、文化和精神生活的需要，从本国经济领土和国外购买的货物和

主要统计指标解释

服务的支出；不包括非常住单位在本国经济领土内的消费支出。最终消费支出分为居民消费支出和政府消费支出。

居民消费支出

指常住住户在一定时期内对货物和服务的全部最终消费支出。居民消费按市场价格计算，即按居民支付的购买者价格计算。购买者价格是购买者取得货物所支付的价格，包括购买者支付的运输和商业费用。居民消费除了直接以货币形式购买货物和服务的消费之外，还包括以其他方式获得的货物和服务的消费支出，即所谓的虚拟消费支出。居民虚拟消费支出包括以下几种类型：单位以实物报酬及实物转移的形式提供给劳动者的货物和服务；住户生产并由本住户消费了的货物和服务，其中的服务仅指住户的自有住房服务；金融机构提供的金融媒介服务；保险公司提供的保险服务。

政府消费支出

指一定时期内政府部门为全社会提供公共服务的消费支出和免费或以较低价格向住户提供的货物和服务的净支出。前者等于政府服务的产出价值减去政府单位所获得的经营收入的价值，政府服务的产出价值等于它的经常性业务支出加上固定资产折旧；后者等于政府部门免费或以较低价格向住户提供的货物和服务的市场价值减去向住户收取的价值。

资本形成总额

指常住单位在一定时期内获得的，并减去处置的固定资产，加上存货的变动，包括固定资本形成总额和存货增加。

固定资本形成总额

指生产者在一定时期内获得的固定资产减处置的固定资产的价值总额。固定资产是通过生产活动生产出来的，且其使用年限在一年以上、单位价值在规定标准以上的资产，不包括自然资产。可分为有形固定资本形成总额和无形固定资本形成总额。有形固定资本形成总额包括一定时期内完成的建筑工程、安装工程和设备工器具购置(减处置)价值，以及土地改良、新增役、种、奶、毛、娱乐用牲畜和新增经济林木价值。无形固定资本形成总额包括矿藏的勘探、计算机软件等获得减处置。

存货增加

指常住单位在一定时期内存货实物量变动的市场价值，即期末价值减期初价值的差额，再扣除当期由于价格变动而产生的持有收益。存货增加可以是正值，也可以是负值，正值表示存货上升，负值表示存货下降。存货包括生产单位购进的原材料、燃料和储备物资等存货，以及生产单位生产的产成品、在制品和半成品等存货。

货物和服务净流出

指货物和服务流出减货物和服务流入的差额。流出包括常住单位向非常住单位出售或无偿转让的各种货物和服务的价值；流入包括常住单位从非常住单位购买或无偿得到的各种货物和服务的价值。地区核算净流出，除包括本地区对外贸易及国外非贸易往来的净出口额，还包括地区间货物和服务流出减流入后的净额。

信息产业

是指与电子信息相关联的各种活动的集合，包括信息产品的制造、销售和信息服务等活动。由于信息产业增加值是依据若干行业的有关资料进行跨行业核算的，因此不宜将其与上海市生产总值中其他行业的增加值进行加总，否则会造成重复计算。

旅游产业

指本市与旅游相关的各行业，为境内外旅游者提供旅游服务的产业。这些服务包括：旅行社服务、交通运输服务、住宿服务、电讯服务、娱乐服务、餐饮服务、商品零售服务等。由于旅游产业增加值是依据相关行业的有关资料进行跨行业核算的，因此不宜将其与上海市生产总值中其他行业的增加值进行加总，否则会造成重复计算。

SHANGHAI STATISTICAL YEARBOOK

EXPLANATORY NOTES TO MAJOR STATISTICAL INDICATORS

□ Gross Regional Product(former Gross Domestic Product)

Gross Regional Product refers to the final products at market prices by (of) all resident units of a country (or region) during a certain period of time. Gross product is expressed in three different forms, i.e value, income, and products respectively. The form of value refers to the total value of all products and services produced by all resident units during a certain period of time minus the total value of input of non-fixed-assets products and services or the summation of the value-added of all resident units; the form of income includes all the income items produced by all resident units and distributed primarily to all resident and non-resident units; the form of product refers to all final goods and services minus the value of imports of goods and services. In the practice of national accounting, it is calculated by three approaches, i.e. product approach, income approach, and expenditure approach, respectively, to reflect Gross Product and its composition of different aspects. According to the regulations of GDP national accounting and data release issued by the State Council and National Bureau of Statistics, since 2004 Shanghai Gross Domestic Product has been renamed as Shanghai Gross Product Value, for short Shanghai GDP.

□ Three Industries

Classification of economic activities into three strata of industry is a common practice in the world. Primary industry refers to extraction of natural resources; secondary industry involves processing of primary products; and tertiary industry provides services of various kinds for production and consumption.

Primary industry includes farming, forestry, animal husbandry, fishery industry (not including the service industry for farming, forestry, animal husbandry and fishery).

Secondary industry includes mining (not including mining auxiliary activities), manufacturing (not including metal products, machinery and equipment repair industry), electricity, gas and water production and supply industry and construction.

Tertiary industry refers to all other industries not included in primary or secondary industries.

□ Labourers Remuneration

Labourers Remuneration refers to the whole payment of various forms earned by the labourers from the productive activities they are engaged in. It includes wages, bonuses and allowances the labourers earned in monetary form and in kind. It also includes the free medical services provided to the labourers and the medicine expenses, traffic subsidies and social insurance, housing fund paid by the employers. As the individual economy is concerned, since the labourers remuneration is not easily distinguished from the operating profit, both are treated as labourers remuneration.

□ Net Taxes on Production

Net Taxes on Production refers to the difference of the taxes on production minus the subsidies on production. The taxes on production refers to the various taxes, extra charges and fees levied on the production units on their production, sale and business activities as well as on the use of some factors of production, such as fixed assets, land and labour force in the production activities they are engaged in. In contrast to the taxes on production, the subsidies on production refer to the unilateral government transfer to the production units and are therefore regarded as negative taxes on production. They include subsidies on the loss due to implementation of government policies, price subsidies, etc.

□ Depreciation of Fixed Assets

Depreciation of Fixed Assets refers to the depreciation of fixed assets of a given period, drawn in accordance with the stipulated depreciation rate for the purpose of compensating the wear loss of the fixed assets or the depreciation of fixed assets calculated in a fictitious way in accordance with the stipulated unified depreciation rate in the national economic accounting system. It reflects the value of transfer of the fixed assets in the production of the current period. The depreciation of fixed assets in various enterprises and institutions managed as enterprises refers to the depreciation expenses actually drawn. In government agencies and institutions not managed as enterprises which do not draw the depreciation expenses, as well as for the houses of residents, the depreciation of fixed assets is the imputed depreciation, which is calculated in accordance with the stipulated unified depreciation rate. In principle, the depreciation of fixed assets should be calculated on the basis of the re-purchased value of the fixed assets. However, there is no actual condition to re-evaluate all the fixed

EXPLANATORY NOTES TO MAJOR STATISTICAL INDICATORS

assets in China. Therefore, the above-mentioned methods are temporarily adopted at present.

□ Operating Surplus

Operating Surplus refers to the balance of the value added created by the resident units deducting the labourers remuneration, net taxes on production and the depreciation of fixed assets. It is equivalent to the business profit (excluding income from investment) of the enterprises plus subsidies on production, but the wages and welfare expenses paid from the profits should be deducted.

□ GDP by Expenditure Approach

GDP by Expenditure Approach refers to the method of measuring the final results of production activities of a country (region) during a given period from the perspective of final use. It includes final consumption, total capital formation and net export of goods and services, i.e.:

GDP by expenditure approach = final consumption + total capital formation + net export of goods and services

□ Final Consumption

Final Consumption refers to the total expenditure of resident units on final consumption of goods and services in a certain period, namely the expenditure of the resident units for purchases of goods and services from domestic economic territory and abroad to meet the requirements of material, cultural and spiritual life. It excludes the expenditure of non-resident units on consumption in the economic territory of the country. The final consumption is classified into household consumption and government consumption.

□ Household Consumption

Household Consumption refers to the total expenditure of resident households on the final consumption of goods and services in a certain period of time. The households consumption is calculated at market prices, namely the purchasers prices which the households pay; the purchasers prices of goods are the prices the households pay when they obtain the goods, including the transport and commercial expenses paid by the households. In addition to the consumption of goods and services bought by the households directly with money, the expenditure on goods and services obtained by the households in other ways, i.e. the so-called imputed expenditure on consumption, is also included in the households consumption. The imputation expenditure of the households on consumption includes the following types: (a) the goods and services provided to the households by the units in the form of payment in kind and transfer in kind; (b) the goods and services produced and consumed by the households themselves, in which the services refer only to the services provided by the residential buildings owned by the households; (c) the services of financial intermediary provided by the financial institutions; (d) the insurance services provided by the insurance companies.

□ Government Consumption

Government Consumption refers to the expenditure on the consumption of the public services provided by the government to the whole society and the net expenditure on the goods and services provided by the government to the households at free charge or lower prices in a certain period of time. The former equals to the output value of the government services minus the value of operating income obtained by the government departments. (The output value of the government services equals to its current operating expenditure plus depreciation of fixed assets). The latter equals to the market value of the goods and services provided by the government free of charge or at low prices to the households minus the value received by the government from the households.

□ Total Capital Formation

Total Capital Formation refers to the fixed assets acquired minus those disposed and the change in inventory, including the total fixed capital assets formation and the increase in inventory.

□ Total Fixed Capital Formation

Total Fixed Capital Formation refers to the value of fixed assets acquired minus those disposed of during a given period. Fixed assets are the assets produced through production activities with specified unit value which could be used for over one year, excluding natural assets. Total fixed capital formation can be categorized into total tangible capital formation and total intangible capital formation. The total tangible capital formation include the value of the construction projects, installation projects completed and the equipment, apparatus and instruments purchased as well as the value of land improved, the value of draught animals, breeding stock, animals for milk, wool and for recreational purpose, and the newly increased forest with economic value during a given period. The total intangible capital formation includes the prospecting of minerals, the acquisition of computer software mi-

EXPLANATORY NOTES TO MAJOR STATISTICAL INDICATORS

nus the disposal of them.

□ Increase in Inventory

Increase in Inventory refers to the market value of the change in inventory of resident units during a given period, i.e. the difference of value between the beginning and the end of the period minus the current gains due to the change in prices. The increase in inventory can be positive or negative. A positive value indicates the increase in inventory while a negative value indicates the decrease in stock. The inventory includes the raw materials, fuels and reserve materials purchased by the production units as well as the inventory of finished products, semi–finished products, work–in–progress, etc.

□ Net Outflow of Goods and Services

Net Outflow of Goods and Service refers to difference of outflow of goods and service minus inflow of goods and service. The outflow includes the value of various goods and service sold or gratuitously transferred by resident unit to non–resident unit, and the inflow includes the value of various goods and service sold or gratuitously transferred by non–resident unit to resident unit. The net outflow of district, include the net outflow of foreign trade or non–trade of local district, and also the difference of outflow minus inflow of goods and service between domestic districts.

□ Information Industry

Information Industry refers to the aggregation of all kinds of activities related to electronic information, including manufactory and distribution of information–related products and information service. As accounted by referring to relevant documents of several industries, the value added of the information industry shall not be counted together with that of other industries in the Shanghai GDP to avoid repetitive computation.

□ Tourism Industry

Tourism Industry refers to those tourism–related industries that provide tourism services to domestic and overseas tourists, including: travel agency service, transportation service, hostelling service, telecommunication service, entertainment service, catering service and retailing service, etc.. As accounted by referring to relevant cross–industry data of several industries, the value added of the tourism industry shall not be counted together with that of other industries in the Shanghai GDP to avoid repetitive computation.

第五篇
CHAPTER 5

财政收支
FISCAL REVENUE AND EXPENDITURE

简要说明

本篇反映上海市地方财政收支和税收收入情况，资料来源于上海市财政局、上海市国家税务局和上海市地方税务局。

有关财政收支方面的资料，根据财政收支总表、财政收入明细表、财政支出明细表和区县财政收支完成情况表等的数据加工整理编制，其中，地方财政收支由市本级财政收支和区县级财政收支组成。有关税收收入方面的资料，根据全市税收收入情况表的数据加工整理编制。

BRIEF INTRODUCTION

The data in this chapter reflect government revenue, expenditure, and tax income situations. The data are collected, provided and complied by the Shanghai Finance Bureau and the Shanghai State Tax Bureau as well as the Shanghai Local Taxation Bureau.

Data on government revenue and expenditure are prepared, collected and compiled on the basis of information from the city's balance sheet of government revenue and expenditures, tables of government revenue and expenditure at city level, and tables of government revenue and expenditure at district and county level. Among them, local fiscal revenue and expenditure is comprised by revenue and expenditure in the city as well as in districts and counties. The data on tax income is prepared, collected and compiled on the base of information on Shanghai's tax income table.

表5.1 一般公共预算收支(1978～2015)
GENERAL BUDGETARY REVENUE AND EXPENDITURE

单位:亿元 (100 million yuan)

年 份 Year	一般公共预算收入 General Budgetary Revenue	其 中 of which 税收收入 Taxes	非税收入 Non-taxes	一般公共预算支出 General Budgetary Expenditure
1978	169.22	51.51	117.71	26.01
1979	172.69	53.73	118.96	27.06
1980	174.73	57.59	117.14	19.18
1981	174.35	62.93	111.42	19.06
1982	167.99	65.79	102.20	20.68
1983	156.39	110.05	46.34	22.39
1984	163.96	137.67	26.29	30.32
1985	184.23	185.76	-1.53	46.07
1986	179.46	177.90	1.56	59.08
1987	168.97	167.26	1.71	53.85
1988	161.62	182.42	-20.80	65.88
1989	166.88	190.21	-23.33	73.31
1990	166.99	183.31	-16.32	75.56
1991	175.53	182.88	-7.35	86.05
1992	185.56	188.61	-3.05	94.99
1993	242.34	252.99	-10.65	129.26
1994	175.33	196.60	-21.27	196.98
1995	227.30	240.06	-12.76	267.89
1996	288.49	308.26	-19.77	342.66
1997	352.33	369.23	-16.90	428.92
1998	392.22	406.73	-14.51	480.70
1999	431.85	427.23	4.62	546.38
2000	497.96	484.00	13.96	622.84
2001	620.24	589.91	30.33	726.38
2002	719.79	657.70	62.09	877.84
2003	899.29	796.87	102.42	1 102.64
2004	1 119.72	1 036.23	83.49	1 395.69
2005	1 433.90	1 238.40	195.50	1 660.32
2006	1 600.37	1 393.97	206.40	1 813.80
2007	2 102.63	1 975.48	127.15	2 201.92
2008	2 382.34	2 223.43	158.91	2 617.68
2009	2 540.30	2 368.45	171.85	2 989.65
2010	2 873.58	2 707.80	165.78	3 302.89
2011	3 429.83	3 172.72	257.11	3 914.88
2012	3 743.71	3 426.79	316.92	4 184.02
2013	4 109.51	3 797.16	312.35	4 528.61
2014	4 871.76	4 219.05	652.71	5 182.65
2015	5 519.50	4 858.16	661.34	6 191.56

注：自2015年1月起，本市7项政府性基金收支和新增机动车额度拍卖收支纳入一般公共预算管理。
Note: Since January 2015, the city's revenue and expenditure of seven governmental funds and the new motor vehicle auction are under the general public budget management.

表5.2 主要年份一般公共预算收入
GENERAL BUDGETARY REVENUE IN MAIN YEARS

	指 标 Indicators	2000	2010	2014	2015
一般公共预算收入(亿元)	**General Budgetary Revenue (100 million yuan)**	**497.96**	**2 873.58**	**4 871.76**	**5 519.50**
#增值税	Value-added Tax	93.55	388.62	969.14	1 012.80
营业税	Business Tax	153.81	933.91	1 001.92	1 215.49
企业所得税	Enterprise Income Tax	103.03	606.05	942.46	1 104.08
个人所得税	Personal Income Tax	60.24	261.20	408.61	487.61
契 税	Deed	14.37	173.58	214.33	270.99
#市级收入	Revenue at Municipal Level	215.81	1 393.23	2 443.32	2 806.13
区县级收入	Revenue at District (County) Level	282.15	1 480.35	2 428.44	2 713.37
一般公共预算收入构成(%)	**Compostion of General Budgetary Revenue (%)**	**100**	**100**	**100**	**100**
#增值税	Value-added Tax	18.8	13.5	19.9	18.3
营业税	Business Tax	30.9	32.5	20.6	22.0
企业所得税	Enterprise Income Tax	20.7	21.1	19.3	20.0
个人所得税	Personal Income Tax	12.1	9.1	8.4	8.8
契 税	Deed	2.9	6.0	4.4	4.9
#市级收入	Revenue at Municipal Level	43.3	48.5	50.2	50.8
区县级收入	Revenue at District (County) Level	56.7	51.5	49.8	49.2

表 5.3 主要年份区县级一般公共预算收支
GENERAL BUDGETARY REVENUE AND EXPENDITURE OF DISTRICTS AND COUNTIES IN MAIN YEARS

单位：亿元（100 million yuan）

地区	District	一般公共预算收入 General Budgetary Revenue				一般公共预算支出 General Budgetary Expenditure			
		2000	2010	2014	2015	2000	2010	2014	2015
总　计	**Total**	**282.15**	**1 480.35**	**2 428.44**	**2 713.37**	**331.15**	**2 024.13**	**3 312.51**	**3 858.09**
浦东新区	Pudong New Area	64.53	425.40	693.25	788.19	79.45	524.06	837.11	920.22
黄浦区	Huangpu	21.91	64.36	164.12	180.88	22.80	80.73	192.48	207.41
卢湾区	Luwan	11.37	51.30			11.32	56.69		
徐汇区	Xuhui	15.40	90.43	133.84	151.08	19.10	99.29	153.57	173.32
长宁区	Changning	13.74	72.08	118.24	129.94	14.80	85.50	130.32	143.80
静安区	Jing'an	11.00	65.96	93.19	106.24	11.27	71.43	107.85	124.41
普陀区	Putuo	12.70	51.97	86.03	96.36	14.56	78.57	134.54	158.52
闸北区	Zhabei	11.89	46.30	79.59	88.13	13.95	68.55	115.38	129.16
虹口区	Hongkou	14.20	48.36	79.47	90.14	16.35	74.52	118.83	126.82
杨浦区	Yangpu	11.52	50.07	86.11	95.77	14.70	82.65	140.60	162.76
闵行区	Minhang	18.98	125.30	191.45	214.40	20.65	156.60	247.67	344.25
宝山区	Baoshan	16.17	70.35	115.45	127.08	17.60	114.43	178.74	219.23
嘉定区	Jiading	13.33	82.96	171.05	191.36	16.12	112.84	205.49	297.24
金山区	Jinshan	8.16	30.75	59.12	65.50	13.61	70.98	127.58	145.18
松江区	Songjiang	12.12	77.33	113.98	123.11	13.34	103.55	170.67	194.30
青浦区	Qingpu	13.24	58.95	117.99	125.33	15.36	88.40	157.26	179.89
奉贤区	Fengxian	6.53	40.43	76.56	84.89	8.04	77.12	156.31	168.18
崇明县	Chongming	5.36	28.04	49.00	54.98	8.13	78.21	138.11	163.39

注：2012 年起，原卢湾区并入黄浦区。
Note: Former Luwan District has been merged into Huangpu District since 2012.

表 5.4 主要年份一般公共预算支出
GENERAL BUDGETARY EXPENDITURE IN MAIN YEARS

指　标	Indicators	2010	2013	2014	2015
一般公共预算支出(亿元)	**General Budgetary Expenditure(100 million yuan)**	**3 302.89**	**4 528.61**	**5 182.65**	**6 191.56**
#一般公共服务	General Public Services	226.02	246.57	248.84	259.84
公共安全	Public Security	187.25	226.51	250.91	269.20
教　育	Education	417.28	679.54	763.95	767.32
社会保障和就业	Social Security and Jobs	362.56	468.01	514.22	543.16
医疗卫生与计划生育	Medical and Health Care, Family Planning	160.07	228.45	264.75	303.46
城乡社区	Urban and Country Community Affairs	475.47	712.92	801.39	1 173.88
#市级支出	Expenditure at Municipal Level	1 278.76	1 590.55	1 870.14	2 333.47
区县级支出	Expenditure at District (County) Level	2 024.13	2 938.06	3 312.51	3 858.09
一般公共预算支出比重(%)	**Percentage of the General Budgetary Expenditure (%)**	**100**	**100**	**100**	**100**
#一般公共服务	General Public Services	6.8	5.4	4.8	4.2
公共安全	Public Security	5.7	5.0	4.8	4.3
教　育	Education	12.6	15.0	14.7	12.4
社会保障和就业	Social Security and Jobs	11.0	10.3	9.9	8.8
医疗卫生与计划生育	Medical and Health Care, Family Planning	4.8	5.0	5.1	4.9
城乡社区	Urban and Country Community Affairs	14.4	15.7	15.5	19.0
#市级支出	Expenditure at Municipal Level	38.7	35.1	36.1	37.7
区县级支出	Expenditure at District (County) Level	61.3	64.9	63.9	62.3

注：自 2014 年开始，计划生育支出从一般公共服务支出中转出，并入原医疗卫生支出，改名为医疗卫生与计划生育支出。
Note: The government takes the expenditure of faminly planning from the expenditure of general public services to the expenditure of medical and health care Since 2014. The name of the item has been changed into the expditure of medical and health care, family planning.

表 5.5 主要年份全市税收总收入
TAXATION IN MAIN YEARS

单位:亿元(100 million yuan)

指　标	Indicators	2000	2010	2014	2015
全市税收总收入	**Taxation**	**1 479.21**	**8 003.43**	**12 083.95**	**13 989.51**
#证券交易印花税	Stamp Tax of Stock Transaction	245.49	305.26	323.45	1 344.31
海关代征	Custom Taxation	313.04	2 082.92	2 876.01	2 759.11
国内增值税	Domestic Value Added Tax	380.21	1 575.00	2 654.29	2 676.46
国内消费税	Domestic Excise	69.71	499.58	775.77	825.26
营业税	Business Tax	171.42	933.93	1 001.76	1 215.49
企业所得税	Enterprise Income Tax	142.47	1 567.31	2 460.06	2 857.32
个人所得税	Personal Income Tax	67.79	653.01	1 021.52	1 219.01

上 / 海 / 统 / 计 / 年 / 鉴

主要统计指标解释

一般公共预算收入

一般公共预算收入是指根据现行财政管理体制规定，划归地方财政的税收收入和非税收入。

税收收入

一般公共预算收入中的税收收入主要包括营业税、房产税、城镇土地使用税、车船税、土地增值税、耕地占用税、契税等固定收入，以及增值税、企业所得税、个人所得税等共享收入部分。

一般公共预算支出

一般公共预算支出是指按照现行中央政府与地方政府事权的划分，经地方人大批准，用于保障地方经济社会发展的各项财政支出。主要包括一般公共服务，公共安全，教育，科学技术，文化体育与传媒，社会保障和就业，医疗卫生与计划生育，环境保护，城乡社区，农林水事务，交通运输等支出。

SHANGHAI STATISTICAL YEARBOOK

EXPLANATORY NOTES TO MAJOR STATISTICAL INDICATORS

□ General Budgetary Revenue

General Budgetary Revenue refers to the tax revenue and non-tax revenue collected by the local government as defined by the finance management system.

□ Tax Revenue

Tax Revenue of general budgetary revenue mainly includes business tax, house property tax, urban land use tax, tax on vehicles and boat operation, land appreciation tax, farm land occupation tax, deed tax, etc and the share part of value added tax, corporate income tax, individual income tax, etc.

□ General Budgetary Expenditure

General Budgetary Expenditure refers to the fiscal expenditure demarcated on the basis of the classification of the affairs administration rights between the central government and local government. It is approved by the local people's congress and used for the development of local economy and society. Local fiscal expenditure mainly includes the expenditure for general public services, public security, education, science and technology, culture, sport and media, social safety and employment, medical and health care, family planning, environment protection, urban and rural community affairs, agriculture, forestry and water conservancy and transportation, etc.

第六篇
CHAPTER 6

能源与环境
ENERGY AND ENVIRONMENT PROTECTION

简 要 说 明

一、本篇资料的主要内容

本篇主要包含两部分内容:能源生产、消费和环境保护治理。

能源生产、消费的主要内容有能源消耗基本情况,能源消费弹性系数,人均、日均能源消费量,分行业、分主要能源品种的时间序列能源消费量,综合能源平衡表和主要能源品种的单项平衡表,电力建设情况等。

环境保护治理的主要内容有环保投入,工业固体废弃物防治,水环境保护,大气环境保护,环境空气状况、声环境及治理和城市环境卫生情况等。

二、本篇资料的统计范围

本篇资料的统计范围为全社会。

三、本篇的资料来源

能源生产、消费的资料来源:电力建设情况由市电力公司提供,其他表的数据均来自历年能源平衡表。

环境保护治理的资料来源:环保投入、工业固体废弃物防治、大气环境保护、环境空气状况和声环境及治理由上海市环境保护局提供;水环境保护由上海市水务局和上海市环境保护局提供;城市环境卫生情况是由上海市绿化和市容管理局提供。

四、关于数据口径与计算方法的说明

(一)能源生产、消费

1. 根据第三次经济普查结果,1995~2013 年份能源消费量作相应调整。

2.单位 GDP 能耗和单位 GDP 电耗所需的 2005~2010 年 GDP 和工业增加值数据按 2005 年可比价计算,2011~2015 年按 2010 年可比价计算。

(二)环境保护治理

1. 2008 年起,工业废气排放量按新排放系数计算。

2. 2011 年起,烟尘排放总量统计口径变更为烟(粉)尘排放量。

3. 2011 年起,废水排放总量中增加了农业源和集中式治理设施排放的废水。

4. 2013 年起,环境空气质量优良率以 AQI 评价。

BRIEF INTRODUCTION

I. Main Contents

Data in this chapter cover mainly energy production, energy consumption, and environment protection and governance.

Energy production and consumption include basic energy consumption situations, elasticity coefficient of energy consumption, average energy consumption per capita, average daily energy consumption, energy consumption in time series by industry and main energy categories, comprehensive energy balance sheet, single balance sheet of main energy categories and electric power construction.

Environment protection and governance include investment in environment protection, prevention of industrial solid waste, water environment protection, air protection, governance of air and acoustic environment, and management of urban sanitation situations.

II. The Scope of Data

The scope of data in this chapter covers the whole city.

III. Sources of Data

Sources of data on energy production and consumption: Data on electric power construction are provided by the Shanghai Electric Power Company, and the rest are collected from the energy balance sheets over the years.

Sources of data on environment protection and governance: Data on investment in environment protection, prevention of industrial solid waste, air protection, and governance of air and acoustic environment are provided by the Shanghai Environmental Protection Bureau; data on water environment protection are provided by the Shanghai Water Authority and Shanghai Environmental Protection Brueau; data on urban sanitation situations are provided by the Shanghai Greening & City Appearance Bureau.

IV. Notes on Coverage and Compilation of Data

(1) Energy production and consumption

(a) According to the results of the third economic census, energy consumption data of 1995–2013 have taken corresponding adjustment.

(b) The GDP and industrial production data between 2005 and 2010 required by unit energy consumption and unit power consumption are calculated on comparable prices in 2005, and the data between 2011 and 2015 are calculated on comparable prices in 2010.

(2)Environment protection and governance

(a)Industrial emission is calculated on new emission coefficient since 2008.

(b)Coverage of dust discharge changes to dust (smoke) discharge since 2011.

(c)Coverage of wastewater discharge started to include agricultural wastewater and wastewater from centralized treatment facilities from 2011.

(d)Ambient air quality is evaluated by AQI since 2013.

表 6.1　主要年份能源消耗基本情况
ENERGY CONSUMPTION IN MAIN YEARS

年　份 Year	能源消费量 (万吨标准煤) Energy Consumption (10 000 tons SCE)	其　中 of which #工　业 Industry	电力消费 (亿千瓦时) Electricity Power Consumption (100 million kwh)	其　中 of which #工　业 Industry
1990	3 191.06	2 462.21	264.74	220.97
1995	4 392.48	3 439.11	403.27	307.01
2000	5 413.45	3 687.90	559.42	393.13
2001	5 819.91	3 851.75	592.99	413.33
2002	6 168.31	3 901.44	645.71	447.46
2003	6 722.27	4 220.50	745.97	507.00
2004	7 303.35	4 406.80	821.44	555.12
2005	7 974.24	4 863.17	921.97	617.59
2006	8 604.89	5 152.05	990.15	656.10
2007	9 374.60	5 452.95	1 072.38	705.90
2008	9 894.52	5 598.41	1 138.22	727.13
2009	10 050.06	5 465.53	1 153.38	701.59
2010	10 671.40	5 996.48	1 295.87	786.61
2011	10 927.62	5 991.37	1 339.62	805.76
2012	11 015.28	5 841.59	1 353.45	786.25
2013	11 345.69	6 009.41	1 410.61	799.45
2014	11 084.63	5 785.41	1 369.02	785.64
2015	11 387.44	5 815.60	1 405.56	787.03

表 6.1 续表 1 continued

年　份 Year	单位生产总值能耗 (吨标准煤/万元) Energy Consumption of GDP (ton SCE/10 000 yuan)	单位生产总值电耗 (千瓦时/万元) Electricity Power Consumption of GDP (kwh/10 000 yuan)	工业增加值能耗 (吨标准煤/万元) Energy Consumption of Value Added in Industry (ton SCE/10 000 yuan)	工业增加值电耗 (千瓦时/万元) Electricity Power Consumption of Value Added in Industry (kwh/10 000 yuan)
1990	4.082	3 386.89	5.241	4 703.19
1995	1.757	1 613.45	2.629	2 346.81
2000	1.135	1 172.50	1.845	1 966.67
2001	1.117	1 138.15	1.778	1 907.61
2002	1.074	1 124.73	1.648	1 889.60
2003	1.004	1 114.35	1.435	1 723.76
2004	0.905	1 017.54	1.226	1 544.90
2005	0.862	996.98	1.205	1 529.88
2006	0.825	949.69	1.142	1 453.81
2007	0.780	892.62	1.077	1 394.24
2008	0.751	863.64	1.027	1 334.46
2009	0.704	808.49	0.975	1 251.82
2010	0.678	823.18	0.910	1 194.02
2011	0.589	721.53	0.853	1 146.70
2012	0.552	678.39	0.809	1 089.46
2013	0.528	656.24	0.785	1 044.47
2014	0.482	595.23	0.725	984.30
2015	0.463	571.45	0.725	980.71

注：单位能耗和单位电耗 2005～2010 按 2005 年可比价计算，2011～2015 年按 2010 年可比价计算。
Note: Note:Energy Intensity and Electricity Intensity by GDP or value added is calculated by comparable prices of 2005 from 2005 to 2010, it is calculated by comparable prices of 2010 from 2011 to 2015.

表6.2 能源消费弹性系数(1978～2015)
ELASTICITY OF ENERGY CONSUMPTION

年 份 Year	能源消费比上年增长(%) Growth Rate of Energy Consumption over Preceding Year(%)	电力消费比上年增长(%) Growth Rate of Electric Power Consumption over Preceding Year(%)	能源消费弹性系数 Elasticity of Energy Consumption	电力消费弹性系数 Elasticity of Electric Power Consumption
1978	6.6	10.8	0.42	0.68
1979	1.5	3.0	0.20	0.41
1980	-0.6	3.4		0.40
1981	1.0	6.4	0.18	1.14
1982	2.6	4.4	0.36	0.61
1983	2.5	4.2	0.32	0.54
1984	2.5	4.1	0.22	0.35
1985	4.9	3.9	0.37	0.29
1986	9.0	6.8	2.05	1.55
1987	5.7	4.1	0.76	0.55
1988	1.3	2.5	0.13	0.25
1989	4.4	1.3	1.47	0.43
1990	2.6	5.8	0.74	1.66
1991	8.6	9.0	1.21	1.27
1992	5.5	10.0	0.37	0.68
1993	7.9	9.0	0.52	0.60
1994	5.8	9.1	0.40	0.63
1995	6.9	6.9	0.48	0.48
1996	3.7	6.7	0.28	0.51
1997	3.6	5.5	0.28	0.43
1998	2.5	6.3	0.25	0.61
1999	4.7	3.8	0.46	0.37
2000	6.9	11.6	0.62	1.05
2001	7.5	6.0	0.72	0.57
2002	6.0	8.9	0.53	0.79
2003	9.0	15.5	0.73	1.26
2004	8.6	10.1	0.61	0.71
2005	9.2	12.2	0.81	1.07
2006	7.9	7.4	0.62	0.58
2007	8.9	8.3	0.59	0.55
2008	5.5	6.1	0.57	0.63
2009	1.6	1.3	0.19	0.16
2010	6.2	12.4	0.60	1.20
2011	2.4	3.4	0.29	0.41
2012	0.8	1.0	0.11	0.13
2013	3.0	4.2	0.39	0.55
2014	-2.3	-3.0		
2015	2.7	2.7	0.39	0.39

表6.3 主要年份能源消费总量
FINAL CONSUMPTION OF ENERGY IN MAIN YEARS

单位：万吨标准煤(10 000 tons SCE)

年 份 Year	能源消费总 量 Energy Consumption	能源终端消费量 Final Consumption of Energy	加工转换投入(－)产出(＋)量 Processing Conversion Input (－) and Output (＋)	损失量 Loss Volume
1990	3 191.06	3 098.82	－52.20	40.04
1995	4 392.48	4 250.44	－1.29	140.75
2000	5 413.45	5 226.81	－3.15	183.49
2001	5 819.91	5 548.53	－60.23	211.16
2002	6 168.31	5 897.19	－52.50	218.62
2003	6 722.27	6 396.66	－82.06	243.55
2004	7 303.35	7 057.01	－27.63	218.71
2005	7 974.24	7 796.90	10.37	187.72
2006	8 604.89	8 375.26	－37.67	191.96
2007	9 374.60	9 193.58	25.43	206.45
2008	9 894.52	9 639.54	－28.02	226.96
2009	10 050.06	9 846.97	29.36	232.44
2010	10 671.40	10 501.04	78.09	248.44
2011	10 927.62	11 131.41	453.85	250.07
2012	11 015.28	11 183.99	428.89	260.18
2013	11 345.69	11 456.08	383.63	273.24
2014	11 084.63	11 281.72	458.96	261.87
2015	11 387.44	11 549.55	433.36	271.25

表6.4 平均每人生活用能源(2012～2015)
ANNUAL RESIDENT ENERGY CONSUMPTION PER CAPITA

品 名	Items	2012	2013	2014	2015
生活消费能源总计(千克标准煤)	**Total Resident Energy Consumption(kg of SCE)**	**476.92**	**508.19**	**474.16**	**505.70**
煤 炭(千克)	Coal (kg)	17.42	14.21	13.87	12.48
天然气(立方米)	Natural Gas (cu. m)	42.01	46.08	48.46	55.77
液化石油气(千克)	Liquefied Petroleum Gas (kg)	14.92	16.28	14.49	10.42
煤 气(立方米)	Gas (cu. m)	16.54	11.14	4.83	0.83
电 力(千瓦时)	Electric Power (kwh)	792.66	855.12	718.43	766.34

注：本表按年平均人口数计算。
Note: Data in this table are calculated by average annual population.

表6.5 平均每天各种能源消费量(2012～2015)
AVERAGE DAILY ENERGY CONSUMPTION BY VARIETY

能源品种	Items	2012	2013	2014	2015
合计(万吨标准煤)	**Total(10 000 tons of SCE)**	**30.18**	**31.08**	**30.37**	**31.20**
煤 炭(万吨)	Coal(10 000 tons)	12.73	13.24	11.31	10.58
焦 炭(万吨)	Coke(10 000 tons)	1.84	1.75	1.79	1.73
燃料油(万吨)	Fuel Oil(10 000 tons)	1.75	1.65	1.52	1.48
汽 油(万吨)	Gasoline(10 000 tons)	1.42	1.46	1.58	1.66
煤 油(万吨)	Kerosene(10 000 tons)	1.10	1.20	1.23	1.40
柴 油(万吨)	Diesel Oil(10 000 tons)	1.56	1.52	1.50	1.54
天然气(亿立方米)	Natural Gas(100 million cu. m)	0.18	0.20	0.20	0.21
电 力(亿千瓦时)	Electricity(100 million kwh)	3.71	3.86	3.75	3.85

表6.6 主要年份能源终端消费量
FINAL CONSUMPTION OF ENERGY IN MAIN YEARS

单位:万吨标准煤(10 000 tons SCE)

年 份 Year	能源终端消费量 Final Consumption of Energy	其 中 of which			
		第一产业 Primary Industry	第二产业 Secondary Industry	第三产业 Tertiary Industry	生活消费 Living Consumption
1980	2 130.56	71.04	1 655.92	194.64	208.96
1990	3 098.82	58.49	2 387.88	403.47	248.98
1995	4 250.44	77.12	3 339.75	517.06	316.51
1996	4 376.40	102.18	3 291.04	626.39	356.79
1997	4 505.70	90.53	3 312.13	715.32	387.72
1998	4 608.14	91.06	3 261.23	828.86	426.99
1999	4 899.57	98.01	3 467.49	915.45	418.62
2000	5 226.81	103.37	3 593.64	1 068.85	460.94
2001	5 548.53	113.84	3 698.17	1 281.30	455.21
2002	5 897.19	109.13	3 802.13	1 507.47	478.45
2003	6 396.66	111.83	4 064.61	1 692.12	528.09
2004	7 057.01	108.35	4 339.05	2 018.63	590.98
2005	7 796.90	61.09	4 864.56	2 231.99	639.26
2006	8 375.26	58.88	5 107.48	2 497.63	711.26
2007	9 193.58	60.44	5 464.98	2 872.14	796.02
2008	9 639.54	62.54	5 548.04	3 139.36	889.60
2009	9 846.97	62.57	5 501.33	3 339.46	943.62
2010	10 501.04	63.19	6 072.25	3 367.65	997.94
2011	11 131.41	64.88	6 442.28	3 575.33	1 048.92
2012	11 183.99	68.25	6 262.81	3 725.52	1 127.41
2013	11 456.08	72.94	6 374.75	3 789.85	1 218.54
2014	11 281.72	70.40	6 227.77	3 835.88	1 147.67
2015	11 549.55	69.99	6 243.33	4 012.19	1 224.03

表6.7 主要年份工业能源终端消费量
FINAL CONSUMPTION OF ENERGY OF INDUSTRY IN MAIN YEARS

年 份 Year	工业能源终端消费量(万吨标准煤) Final Consumption Energy of Industry (10 000 tons SCE)	原 煤(万吨) Coal (10 000 tons)	焦 炭(万吨) Coke (10 000 tons)	燃料油(万吨) Fuel Oil (10 000 tons)	电 力(亿千瓦时) Electric power (100 million kwh)
1980	1 645.20	535.03	211.52	122.41	136.85
1990	2 369.99	596.14	419.24	136.09	209.21
1991	2 591.11	641.71	516.28	140.06	226.69
1992	2 731.13	630.83	651.49	112.47	247.75
1993	2 988.03	700.97	617.24	170.97	262.75
1994	3 053.73	661.10	625.62	165.55	270.54
1995	3 297.07	694.31	687.98	154.76	282.87
1996	3 234.63	726.24	637.73	149.69	293.04
1997	3 245.71	698.14	653.75	147.70	309.74
1998	3 186.98	723.59	660.40	132.93	318.12
1999	3 389.09	792.14	658.28	120.21	335.01
2000	3 506.07	733.65	676.06	139.67	362.94
2001	3 586.48	790.51	654.79	136.93	381.64
2002	3 637.34	676.60	571.92	112.19	413.61
2003	3 903.86	675.58	573.94	117.11	464.74
2004	4 168.26	731.30	552.68	118.77	510.67
2005	4 701.47	843.73	603.16	130.94	568.29
2006	4 935.76	869.58	617.92	118.85	604.59
2007	5 285.71	790.10	691.38	91.99	649.82
2008	5 362.99	787.01	684.92	74.98	667.59
2009	5 290.80	825.59	658.32	71.92	641.58
2010	5 855.55	854.71	705.21	63.12	718.63
2011	6 231.19	813.06	706.34	62.86	735.27
2012	6 049.77	730.71	673.17	40.23	714.46
2013	6 161.00	800.15	640.30	35.36	723.07
2014	6 021.57	862.92	654.84	21.22	710.70
2015	6 025.63	709.70	630.75	11.86	711.54

表6.8 能源平衡表(标准量)(2012～2015)
BALANCE SHEET OF ENERGY (STANDARD EQUIVALENT)

单位:万吨标准煤(10 000 tons SCE)

指 标	Indicators	2012	2013	2014	2015
可供本地区消费的能源量	**Volume of Energy Available for Local Consumption**	**11 016.50**	**11 345.39**	**11 084.22**	**11 385.57**
库存差	Inventory Change	-10.12	67.70	-47.31	-106.24
一次能源生产量	Primary Energy Production	65.54	64.21	57.66	69.04
外省(市)调入量	Inflow from Other Provinces (Autonomous Region and Municipalities)	13 729.77	13 333.12	15 150.41	18 729.61
进口量	Imports	4 111.44	5 365.82	2 864.98	3 561.76
我轮、机在外国加油量	China Airplanes&ships Refueling in Abroad	709.76	643.84	576.48	713.89
本市调出量(-)	Outflow from Shanghai (Autonomous Region of Municipality)	-7 289.39	-7 789.98	-7 061.01	-11 035.50
出口量(-)	Exports	-77.31	-108.93	-204.42	-296.46
外轮、机在我国加油量(-)	Foreign Airplanes&ships Refueling in China	-223.18	-230.39	-252.57	-250.52
加工转换投入(-)产出(+)量	**Processing Conversion Input (-) and Output (+)**	**428.89**	**383.63**	**458.96**	**433.36**
#火力发电	Fuel Power Generation				
供 热	Heating Supply	-32.85	-30.56	-28.23	-31.55
炼 焦	Coke Making	-28.49	-13.24	-7.26	-24.90
炼 油	Oil Refining	-7.69	-5.78	24.93	4.90
制 气	Gas Making	-6.88	-3.39	-1.15	-0.12
回收能	Recovery of Energy	521.15	477.11	502.35	515.42
损失量	**Loss Volume**	**260.18**	**273.24**	**261.87**	**271.25**
#运输和输配损失	Loss in Transportation and Distribution	260.18	273.24	273.69	271.25
终端消费量	**Final Consumption**	**11 183.99**	**11 456.08**	**11 281.72**	**11 549.55**
第一产业	Primary Industry	68.25	72.94	70.40	69.99
第二产业	Secondary Industry	6 262.81	6 374.75	6 227.77	6 243.33
工 业	Industry	6 049.77	6 161.00	6 021.57	6 025.63
建筑业	Construction	213.04	213.75	206.21	217.70
第三产业	Tertiary Industry	3 725.52	3 789.85	3 835.88	4 012.19
#交通运输、仓储和邮政业	Transportation, Storage and Post	2 045.01	2 044.15	2 045.35	2 140.87
批发、零售贸易业和住宿、餐饮业	Wholesale, Retail Sales and Hotel, Restaurants	523.77	533.29	537.68	524.35
生活消费	Living Consumption	1 127.41	1 218.54	1 147.67	1 224.03
城 镇	Urban	957.31	1 059.96	994.54	1 072.69
乡 村	Rural	170.10	158.58	153.13	151.34
平衡差额	**Balance**	**1.22**	**-0.30**	**-0.40**	**-1.87**
能源消费总量	**Total Energy Consumption**	**11 015.28**	**11 345.69**	**11 084.63**	**11 387.44**

表 6.9 能源终端消费量(2015)
FINAL CONSUMPTION OF ENERGY (QUANTITY EQUIVALENT)

单位:万吨(10 000 tons)

行 业	Sectors	原 煤 Coal	焦 炭 Coke	燃料油 Fuel Oil
总 计	**Total**	**811.48**	**630.75**	**536.87**
生产消费	**Production Consumption**	**781.27**	**630.75**	**536.87**
第一产业	Primary Industry	1.10		
第二产业	Secondary Industry	720.38	630.75	16.72
#工 业	Industry	709.70	630.75	11.86
第三产业	Tertiary Industry	59.79		520.15
#交通运输、仓储和邮政业	Transportation, Storage and Post	0.80		515.11
批发、零售贸易业和住宿、餐饮业	Wholesale, Retail Sales and Hotel, Restaurants	27.42		3.26
生活消费	**Living Consumption**	**30.21**		

表 6.9 续表 1 continued

单位:万吨(10 000 tons)

行 业	Sectors	汽 油 Gasoline	煤 油 Kerosene	柴 油 Diesel Oil
总 计	**Total**	**607.69**	**511.45**	**560.84**
生产消费	**Production Consumption**	**371.94**	**511.45**	**518.11**
第一产业	Primary Industry	19.08		13.10
第二产业	Secondary Industry	69.59	1.42	95.31
#工 业	Industry	43.60	0.75	73.38
第三产业	Tertiary Industry	283.27	510.03	409.70
#交通运输、仓储和邮政业	Transportation, Storage and Post	120.63	510.01	201.47
批发、零售贸易业和住宿、餐饮业	Wholesale, Retail Sales and Hotel, Restaurants	65.54		67.37
生活消费	**Living Consumption**	**235.75**		**42.73**

表 6.9 续表 2 continued

行 业	Sectors	其他石油制品(万吨) Other Petroleum Products (10 000 tons)	热 力(万百万千焦) Thermopower (10 000 million K.J)	电 力(亿千瓦时) Electric Power (100 million kwh)
总 计	**Total**	**213.08**	**10 439.19**	**1 330.07**
生产消费	**Production Consumption**	**213.08**	**10 438.86**	**1 144.58**
第一产业	Primary Industry			7.35
第二产业	Secondary Industry	213.08	10 266.70	747.58
#工 业	Industry	213.08	10 248.84	711.54
第三产业	Tertiary Industry		172.16	389.65
#交通运输、仓储和邮政业	Transportation, Storage and Post		55.65	42.12
批发、零售贸易业和住宿、餐饮业	Wholesale, Retail Sales and Hotel, Restaurants		32.56	78.29
生活消费	**Living Consumption**		**0.33**	**185.49**

表6.10 煤炭、石油、电力平衡表（2015）
COAL,PETROLEUM,ELECTRICITY BALANCE SHEET

指标	Indicators	煤炭（万吨）Coal (10 000 tons)	石油（万吨）Crude Oil (10 000 tons)	电力（亿千瓦时）Electricity (100 million kwh)
可供本地区消费的能源量	**Total Energy Available for Consumption**	**4 728.43**	**3 458.51**	**1 405.55**
库存差	Inventory Changes in the Year	-15.23	-73.06	
生产量	Energy Production		9.36	821.19
外省(市)调入量	Inflow from Other Provinces	5 994.19	8 282.92	647.30
进口量	Imports	445.55	1 949.05	
我轮、机在外国加油量	China Airplanes&ships Refueling in Abroad		496.53	
本市调出量(-)	Outflow from Shanghai	-1 696.08	-6 833.85	-62.94
出口量(-)	Exports		-202.17	
外轮、机在我国加油量(-)	Foreign Airplanes&ships Refueling in China		-170.26	
消费量	**Total Energy Consumption**	**4 728.13**	**3 460.19**	**1 405.56**
按行业分	**Consumption by Sectors**			
农、林、牧、渔业	Farming,Forestry,Animal Husbandry,Fishery and Water Conservancy	1.10	32.60	7.35
工业	Industry	4 626.35	1 156.56	787.03
建筑业	Construction	10.68	72.36	36.04
交通运输.仓储和邮政业	Transport,Storage and Post	0.80	1 380.83	42.12
批发、零售业和住宿、餐饮业	Wholesale,Retail Trade and Hotel,Restaurants	27.42	163.52	78.29
其他	Others	31.57	320.92	269.24
生活消费	Residential Consumption	30.21	333.40	185.49
按用途分	**Consumption by Usage**			
终端消费	Final Consumption	848.51	3 432.91	1 330.07
#工业	Industry	746.73	1 129.28	711.54
用于加工转换	Processing and Conversion	3 871.68	27.28	
损失量	Others Losses	7.94		75.49
平衡差额	**Balanced Difference**	**0.30**	**-1.68**	**-0.01**

表6.11 电力建设情况(2012～2015)
STATISTICS OF ELECTRIC POWER COUSTRUCTION

指标	Indicators	2012	2013	2014	2015
发电量(亿千瓦时)	**Electric Power Generated(100 million kwh)**	**973.02**	**971.61**	**808.14**	**821.19**
线损率(%)	Electricity Loss Rate on Lines(%)	6.15	6.20	6.24	6.12
年末发电设备容量(万千瓦)	Power Generating Equipment Capacity (year-end)(10 000kw)	2 145.99	2 162.01	2 183.68	2 343.68
架空线长度(公里)	Length of Overhead Lines(km)	9 426.75	9 431.27	9 142.67	9 928.78
1000KV(公里)	1 000KV(km)		33.97	33.97	33.97
750KV(公里)	750KV(km)	106.13	106.13	106.14	106.14
500KV(公里)	500KV(km)	1 231.34	1 231.34	1 233.40	1 504.48
220KV(公里)	220KV(km)	3 475.20	3 444.67	3 448.61	3 467.13
110KV(公里)	110KV(km)	800.29	796.18	840.91	917.68
35KV(公里)	35KV(km)	3 813.79	3 818.98	3 479.64	3 899.37
电缆长度(公里)	**Length of Cable(km)**	**8 327.17**	**9 076.02**	**9 986.33**	**10 719.90**
500KV(万千伏安)	500KV(10 000kva)	31.25	31.25	31.24	31.26
220KV(万千伏安)	220KV(10 000kva)	550.30	595.35	597.06	655.14
110KV(万千伏安)	110KV(10 000kva)	1 011.86	1 225.86	1 485.67	1 595.09
35KV(万千伏安)	35KV(10 000kva)	6 733.36	7 223.56	7 872.36	8 438.49
公用变电容量(万千伏安)	**Public Transformer Capacity(10 000kva)**	**13 051.90**	**13 936.01**	**15 228.85**	**15 860.69**
500KV(万千伏安)	500KV(10 000kva)	4 537.88	5 174.84	5 580.44	5 680.44
220KV～35KV(万千伏安)	220KV－35KV(10 000kva)	8 514.02	8 761.17	9 648.41	10 180.25
用电最高负荷(万千瓦)	**Peak Electric Power Consumption Load (10 000kw)**	**2 591.50**	**2 940.30**	**2 680.20**	**2 981.90**

注：本表数据由市电力公司提供。
Note: Data in this table is provided by Shanghai Electric Power Corporation.

表6.12 主要年份环保投入
INVESTMENT ON ENVIRONMENT PROTECTION IN MAIN YEARS

单位:亿元(100 million yuan)

年份 Year	环境保护投资 Investment on Environment Protection	其中 of which: #城市环境基础设施建设投资 Urban Environment Infrastructure Investment	环境保护投资相当于GDP(%) Investment on Environment Protection as Percentage of Gross Domestic Product(%)	自然保护区覆盖率(%) Coverage Rate of Natural Preservation Areas(%)
1990			2.06	
1995	46.49		1.86	
1996	68.83		2.33	
1997	82.35		2.39	
1998	102.13		2.69	
1999	111.57		2.66	
2000	141.91		2.97	7.8
2001	152.93		2.94	10.5
2002	162.39	126.99	2.83	11.8
2003	191.53	144.05	2.86	11.8
2004	225.37	166.90	2.79	11.8
2005	281.18	201.01	3.04	11.8
2006	310.85	177.81	2.94	11.8
2007	366.12	233.22	2.93	12.1
2008	422.37	284.30	3.00	12.1
2009	460.42	282.74	3.06	12.1
2010	507.54	294.73	2.96	12.1
2011	557.92	316.79	2.91	12.1
2012	570.49	286.26	2.83	11.8
2013	607.88	284.18	2.81	11.8
2014	699.89	271.79	2.97	11.8
2015	708.83	246.65	2.82	11.8

表6.13 主要年份工业固体废弃物防治
PREVENTION AND CURE OF INDUSTRIAL SOLID WASTES IN MAIN YEARS

指标	Indicators	2000	2010	2014	2015
工业固体废弃物产生量(万吨)	Volume of Industrial Solid Wastes Produced (10 000 tons)	1 354.74	2 448.36	1 924.79	1 868.07
#危险废物	Dangerous Wastes	28.32	51.25	62.84	56.97
工业废弃物综合利用量(万吨)	Volume of Industrial Wastes Treated and Utilized (10 000 tons)	1 515.90	2 366.90	1 876.86	1 796.18
#危险废物	Dangerous Wastes	27.05	28.47	26.79	25.77
工业废弃物综合利用率(%)	Ratio of Industrial Wastes Treated and Utilized (%)	93.26	96.16	97.51	96.15
工业固体废物处置量(万吨)	Volume of Industrial Solid Wastes Disposed (10 000 tons)	90.96	93.86	47.01	72.23
#危险废物	Dangerous Wastes	1.08	23.44	35.73	30.44

注:本页数据由上海市环境保护局提供。
Note: Data on this page are provided by Shanghai Environmental Protection Bureau.

表6.14 水环境保护(1995～2015)
WATER ENVIRONMENT PROTECTION

年 份 Year	废水排放总量(亿吨) Total Waste Water Discharged (100 million tons)	其中 of which 工业 Industrial Waste Water	废水化学需氧量排放总量(万吨) Total Emission of Oxygen of Waste Water Needed by Chemistry (10 000 tons)	其中 of which 工业 Industrial Waste Water	工业重复用水量(万吨) Volume of Interative Used Water by Industry (10 000 tons)	污水处理厂数(座) Quantity Sewage Disposal Plants(unit)	污水处理厂污水处理量(万吨) Volume of Sewage Disposed by Sewage Disposal Plants (10 000 tons)
1995	22.45	11.61		12.29	445 391	17	14 665
1996	22.85	11.41	27.46	12.16	486 278	20	12 876
1997	21.10	9.99	38.55	11.70	495 622	22	14 790
1998	20.81	9.00	36.55	9.63	475 656	22	15 605
1999	20.28	8.52	34.98	8.92	605 772	22	17 479
2000	19.37	7.25	31.87	6.93	592 055	27	23 028
2001	19.50	6.80	30.48	5.27	709 913	26	29 487
2002	19.21	6.49	32.96	4.78	654 133	27	30 658
2003	18.22	6.11	28.38	4.38	690 068	30	39 891
2004	19.34	5.64	29.38	3.76	750 803	37	95 301
2005	19.97	5.11	30.44	3.66	886 503	42	117 833
2006	22.37	4.83	30.20	3.53	843 970	43	155 726
2007	22.66	4.76	29.44	3.38	899 098	45	152 886
2008	22.60	4.41	26.67	2.76	946 198	47	177 090
2009	23.05	4.12	24.34	2.90	1 004 672	51	171 609
2010	24.82	3.67	21.98	2.16	1 047 970	52	189 654
2011	19.86	4.46	24.90	2.74	747 893	53	193 354
2012	22.05	4.77	24.26	2.62	778 841	53	200 685
2013	22.30	4.54	23.56	2.55	727 088	53	203 222
2014	22.12	4.39	22.44	2.48	708 921	53	208 145
2015	22.41	4.69	19.88	2.27	671 466	53	213 944

注：2011年起，废水排放总量中增加了农业源和集中式治理设施排放的废水。
Note: Since 2011, waste water discharged from the agricultural source and centralized treatment facilities has been added in Total Waste Water Discharged.

表6.15 大气环境保护（1995～2015）
ATMOSPHERE ENVIRONMENT PROTECTION

年 份 Year	工业废气排放总量（亿标立方米）Industrial Waste Gas Emission (100 million cu. m)	烟尘排放总量（万吨）Total Emission of Smoke and Dust (10 000 tons)	其中 of which		废气二氧化硫排放总量（万吨）Total Emission of SO_2 (10 000 tons)	其中 of which	
			工 业 Industrial Sector	生活及其他 Residential Sector and Others		工 业 Industrial Sector	生活及其他 Residential Sector and Others
1995	4 625	20.78	13.33	7.45	53.41	38.15	15.26
1996	4 757	15.78	14.77	1.01	51.00	43.30	7.70
1997	4 755	17.08	13.38	3.70	50.85	43.62	7.23
1998	4 912	15.63	10.74	4.89	48.89	39.09	9.80
1999	4 947	13.57	9.00	4.57	40.31	31.09	9.22
2000	5 755	14.12	8.32	5.80	46.49	32.68	13.81
2001	6 964	13.52	6.23	7.29	47.26	30.00	17.26
2002	7 440	10.74	5.60	5.14	44.66	32.49	12.17
2003	7 799	11.54	4.97	6.57	43.54	30.07	13.47
2004	8 834	12.27	5.25	7.02	47.31	34.95	12.36
2005	8 482	11.52	4.95	6.57	51.28	37.52	13.76
2006	9 428	11.29	4.73	6.56	50.80	37.43	13.37
2007	9 591	10.60	4.04	6.56	49.78	36.44	13.34
2008	10 436	10.63	4.06	6.57	44.61	29.80	14.81
2009	10 059	10.18	3.64	6.54	37.89	23.93	13.96
2010	12 969	10.21	4.18	6.03	35.81	26.32	9.49
2011	13 692	8.98	6.64	2.34	24.01	21.01	3.00
2012	13 361	8.71	6.37	2.34	22.82	19.34	3.48
2013	13 344	8.09	6.72	1.37	21.58	17.29	4.29
2014	13 007	14.17	13.14	1.03	18.81	15.54	3.27
2015	12 802	12.07	11.14	0.93	17.08	10.49	6.59

①2008 年起工业废气排放量按新排放系数计算。
②2011 年起，烟尘排放总量统计口径变更为烟(粉)尘排放量。
③2014 年工业粉尘排放量统计口径包括无组织排放量。
❶The Volume of Industrial Exhaust Emission in 2008 was calculated by new emission coefficient.
❷Since 2011, the statistics caliber of Total Emission of Smoke and Dust has been changed to Total Emission of Smoke(Powder) and Dust.
❸The statistics of industrial dust emissions include inorganization emissions in 2014.

表6.16　主要年份环境空气状况
AMBIENT AIR CONDITION IN MAIN YEARS

指　标	Indicators	2000	2010	2014	2015
中心城区二氧化硫年日平均值（毫克/立方米）	Annual Daily Mean Concentration of SO_2 in Urban Area（mg/m^3）	0.045	0.029	0.018	0.017
中心城区二氧化氮年日平均值（毫克/立方米）	Annual Daily Mean Concentration of NO_2 in Urban Area（mg/m^3）	0.090	0.050	0.045	0.046
中心城区可吸入颗粒平均浓度（毫克/立方米）	Mean Concentration of Inhalable Particulate in Urban Area（mg/m^3）		0.079	0.071	0.069
降水 PH 平均值	Rain PH Value	5.19	4.66	4.90	5.07
酸雨频率(%)	Frequency of Acid Rain（%）	26.0	73.9	72.4	60.8
环境空气质量优良天数(天)	Quantity of Days with Good Ambient Air Quality（day）	295	336	281	258
环境空气质量优良率(%)	Rate of Good Ambient Air Quality（%）	80.8	92.1	77.0	70.7

注：2013 年起，环境空气质量优良率以 AQI 评价。
Note：Since 2013, rate of ambient air quality is evaluated by AQI.

表6.17　主要年份声环境及治理
ENVIRONMENTAL NOISE AND TREATMENT IN MAIN YEARS

指　标	Indicators	2000	2010	2014	2015
区域环境噪声平均等效声级	**Average Equivalent Sound Level of Area Ambient Noise**				
昼间时段(LeqdB(A))	Daytime（LeqdB(A)）	56.6	55.8	55.6	56.2
夜间时段(LeqdB(A))	Nighttime（LeqdB(A)）	49.2	48.3	48.1	47.9
交通环境噪声平均等效声级	**Average Equivalent Sound Level of Traffic Noise**				
昼间时段(LeqdB(A))	Daytime（LeqdB(A)）	70.5	69.8	69.8	69.8
夜间时段(LeqdB(A))	Nighttime（LeqdB(A)）	64.1	64.3	65.6	65.5

注：本页数据由上海市环境保护局提供。
Note：Data on this page are provided by Shanghai Environmental Protection Bureau.

表6.18 城市环境卫生情况(1978～2015)
URBAN ENVIRONMENTAL SITUATION

年 份 Year	垃圾产生量 (万吨) Garbage Produced (10 000 tons)	其 中 of which		清运粪便 (万吨) Night Soil Disposal Cleared (10 000 tons)
		生活垃圾 Residential Garbage	建筑垃圾 Construction Garbage	
1978	214	108	106	418
1979	250	125	126	374
1980	272	131	141	331
1981	272	146	126	329
1982	296	169	127	325
1983	280	166	113	311
1984	308	185	123	272
1985	305	196	109	252
1986	328	226	102	263
1987	325	229	97	262
1988	329	240	89	249
1989	344	250	94	246
1990	382	279	103	243
1991	393	296	97	229
1992	428	301	127	242
1993	488	335	152	234
1994	558	358	200	240
1995	668	372	296	216
1996	736	419	317	217
1997	755	454	301	227
1998	824	470	353	218
1999	767	500	267	172
2000	858	641	217	256
2001	901	644	257	219
2002	760	467	293	238
2003	800	585	215	251
2004	802	610	192	258
2005	777	622	155	254
2006	805	658	146	247
2007	852	702	150	232
2008	841	678	153	220
2009	870	710	160	221
2010	890	732	158	201
2011	1 142	704	438	207
2012	11 728	716	11 012	200
2013	13 716	735	12 981	222
2014	15 135	743	14 392	200
2015	10 755	790	9 965	173

①2012 年起，建筑垃圾中增加了工程渣土清运量。
②本页数据由市绿化和市容管理局提供。
❶Since 2012, Construction Garbage Contains Volume of Construction Dregs Clearance.
❷Data on this page are provided by Shanghai Municipal Virescence and Appearance Administration Bureau.

表6.19 环境卫生设施（1978～2015）
URBAN ENVIRONMENTAL SANITATION

年份 Year	公共厕所（座） Public lawatories(unit)	生活垃圾收集点(处) Collection Points of Residential Garbage(unit)	废物箱（只） Trash Cans(unit)	倒粪站（座） Excrements Stations(unit)	化粪池（只） Septic Tanks(unit)
1978	706	13 840	2 333	3 303	25 540
1979	696	12 695	3 151	3 382	25 915
1980	713	15 707	3 402	3 445	26 754
1981	740	17 905	2 546	3 464	27 407
1982	760	18 824	2 821	3 484	28 652
1983	778	17 859	2 733	3 467	29 977
1984	798	20 384	3 890	3 481	30 943
1985	952	22 870	5 700	3 470	33 477
1986	950	31 142	5 983	3 537	39 175
1987	978	37 751	6 341	3 587	40 042
1988	992	42 802	5 117	3 342	41 171
1989	1 057	46 149	5 276	3 107	41 349
1990	1 016	46 368	4 921	2 973	43 655
1991	1 033	40 309	4 980	3 006	43 089
1992	1 048	44 752	4 961	2 655	43 694
1993	1 104	46 741	5 756	2 732	43 323
1994	1 100	50 292	6 993	2 739	43 125
1995	1 100	48 563	9 019	2 532	43 151
1996	1 112	51 456	9 522	2 412	38 657
1997	1 120	53 643	12 735	2 207	44 440
1998	1 203	59 498	15 968	2 127	41 760
1999	1 311	66 067	17 326	2 192	44 694
2000	2 215	22 470	23 189	2 045	46 921
2001	2 406	17 694	24 672	1 890	47 500
2002	3 776	26 787	29 517	1 846	49 220
2003	3 468	27 814	31 272	1 709	48 831
2004	3 640	28 649	34 571	1 611	47 579
2005	3 640	28 388	39 539	1 689	47 424
2006	3 746	29 812	44 888	2 253	46 217
2007	5 415	29 538	47 739	2 158	45 841
2008	5 866	29 965	56 485	2 064	45 537
2009	5 633	30 584	67 465	2 257	43 775
2010	6 026	30 645	74 658	1 900	43 170
2011	5 768	30 648	78 213	1 868	42 652
2012	6 340	31 625	82 454	1 837	42 306
2013	6 224	32 018	98 266	1 800	43 887
2014	6 168	32 122	98 857	1 756	43 629
2015	6 197	32 209	94 310	1 729	43 582

上/海/统/计/年/鉴

主要统计指标解释

能源消费总量

能源消费总量指一定时期内全国(地区)物质生产部门、非物质生产部门和生活消费的各种能源的总和,是观察能源消费水平、构成和增长速度的总量指标。能源消费总量包括原煤和原油及其制品、天然气、电力,但不包括低热值燃料、生物质能和太阳能等的利用。能源消费总量分为三部分,即终端能源消费量、能源加工转换损失量和能源损失量。

(1) 终端能源消费量指一定时期内全国(地区)物质生产部门、非物质生产部门和生活消费的各种能源在扣除了用于加工转换二次能源消费量和损失量以后的数量。

(2) 能源加工转换损失量指一定时期内全国(地区)投入加工转换的各种能源数量之和与产出各种能源产品之和的差额。它是观察能源在加工转换过程中损失量变化的指标。

(3) 能源损失量指一定时期内能源在输送、分配、储存过程中发生的损失和由客观原因造成的各种损失量。不包括各种气体能源放空、放散量。

能源消费弹性系数

能源消费弹性系数反映能源消费增长速度与国民经济增长速度之间比例关系的指标:

$$能源消费弹性系数=\frac{能源消费量年平均增长速度}{国民经济年平均增长速度}$$

电力消费弹性系数

电力消费弹性系数反映电力消费增长速度与国民经济增长速度之间比例关系的指标。计算公式为:

$$电力消费弹性系数=\frac{电力消费量年平均增长速度}{国民经济年平均增长速度}$$

能源加工转换效率

能源加工转换效率指一定时期内能源经过加工转换后，产出的各种能源产品的数量与投入加工转换的各种能源数量的比率。它是观察能源加工转换装置和生产工艺先进与落后、管理水平高低等的重要指标。计算公式为:

$$能源加工转换效率=\frac{加工转换产出量}{加工转换投入量}\times 100\%$$

自然保护区

指对有代表性的自然生态系统、珍稀濒危野生动植物物种的天然分布区、水源涵养区、有特殊意义的自然历史遗迹等保护对象所在的陆地、陆地水体或海域,依法划出一定面积进行特殊保护和管理的区域。以县及县以上各级人民政府正式批准建立的自然保护区为准(包括"六五"以前由部门或"革委会"批准且现仍存在的自然保护区)。风景名胜区、文物保护区不计在内。自然保护区分国家级、省级、地市级和县级。按主管部门分属: 环保、林业、农业、地矿、海洋、水利和其他部门。

工业固体废弃物产生量

指报告期内企业在生产过程中产生的固体状、半固体状和高浓度液体状废弃物的总量,包括危险废物、冶炼废渣、粉煤灰、炉渣、煤矸石、尾矿、放射性废物和其他废物等;不包括矿山开采的剥离废石和掘进废石(煤矸石和呈酸性或碱性的废石除外)。酸性或碱性废石指采掘的废石其流经水、雨淋水的 pH 值小于 4 或 pH 值大于 10.5 者。

危险废物

指列入国家危险废物名录或根据国家规定的危险废物鉴别标准和鉴别方法认定的,具有爆炸性、易燃性、易氧化性、毒性、腐蚀性、易传染疾病等危险特性之一的废物。

工业废弃物综合利用量

指报告期内企业通过回收、加工、循环、交换等方式，从废弃物中提取或者使其转化为可以利用的资源、能源和其他原材料的废弃物量(包括当年利用往年的工业废弃物贮存量),如用作农业肥料、生产建筑材料、筑路等。综合利用量由原产生废弃物的单位统计。

上 / 海 / 统 / 计 / 年 / 鉴

工业废弃物综合利用率

指工业废弃物综合利用量占工业废弃物产生量（包括综合利用往年贮存量）的百分率。计算公式为：

$$工业废弃物综合利用率=\frac{工业废弃物综合利用量}{工业废弃物产生量+综合利用往年贮存量}\times 100\%$$

工业固体废物处置量

指报告期内企业将固体废物焚烧或者最终置于符合环境保护规定要求的场所，并不再回取的工业固体废物量(包括当年处置往年的工业固体废物贮存量)。处置方式有填埋(其中危险废物应安全填埋)、焚烧、专业贮存场(库)封场处理、深层灌注、回填矿井及海洋处置(经海洋管理部门同意投海处置)等。

工业废水排放量

指经过企业厂区所有排放口排到企业外部的工业废水量。包括生产废水、外排的直接冷却水、超标排放的矿井地下水和与工业废水混排的厂区生活污水，不包括外排的间接冷却水(清污不分流的间接冷却水应计算在内)。

工业废水排放达标量

指报告期内废水中各项污染物指标都达到国家或地方排放标准的外排工业废水量，包括未经处理外排达标的，经废水处理设施处理后达标排放的，以及经污水处理厂处理后达标排放的。

工业废水排放达标率

指工业废水排放达标量占工业废水排放量的百分率，计算公式为:

$$工业废水排放达标率=\frac{工业废水排放达标量}{工业废水排放量}\times 100\%$$

工业废气排放量

指企业厂区内燃料燃烧和生产工艺过程中产生的各种排入空气的含有污染物的气体总量，按标准状态〔273K，101 325Pa〕计算。测算公式为：

工业废气排放量 = 燃料燃烧过程中废气排放量 + 生产工艺过程中废气排放量

工业二氧化硫排放总量

指报告期内企业在燃料燃烧和生产工艺过程中排入大气的 SO_2 总量，计算公式为：

工业二氧化硫排放量 = 燃料燃烧过程中二氧化硫排放量 + 生产工艺过程中二氧化硫排放量

工业烟尘排放量

指企业厂区内燃料燃烧过程中产生的烟气中夹带的颗粒物排放量。

酸雨频率

指酸雨出现的次数占降水出现次数的比例，通常称PH 值小于 5.6 的降水为酸雨。

SHANGHAI STATISTICAL YEARBOOK

EXPLANATORY NOTES TO MAJOR STATISTICAL INDICATORS

□ Total Energy Consumption

Total Energy Consumption refers to the total energy consumption of various forms by material production departments, non-material production departments and households in the country (region) in a given period of time. It is a comprehensive indicator to observe the scale, composition and development of energy consumption. The total energy consumption includes raw coal, crude petroleum and their products, natural gas and electricity, but excludes fuel of low calorific value, bioenergy and solar energy. Total domestic energy consumption can be divided into three parts:

(1) Final Energy Consumption refers to the total energy consumption by material production departments, non-material production departments and households in the country (region) in a given period of time, after deducting the secondary energy consumption and loss during the process of energy conversion.

(2) Loss During the Process of Energy Conversion refers to the total input of various forms for conversion, minus the total output of energy of various forms in the country in a given period of time. It is an indicator to observe the loss that occurs during the process of energy conversion.

(3) Loss refers to the total loss of energy due to mistakes or any objective reasons during the course of energy transport, distribution and storage in a given period of time. The loss of various kinds of gas due to gas discharges and stocktaking is excluded.

□ Elasticity of Energy Consumption

Elasticity Ratio of Energy Consumption is an indicator to show the relationship between the growth rate of energy consumption and the growth rate of the national economy. The formula is:

$$\text{Elasticity of Energy Consumption} = \frac{\text{average annual growth rate of energy consumption}}{\text{average annual growth rate of national economy}}$$

□ Elasticity of Electricity Consumption

Elasticity Ratio of Electricity Consumption is an indicator to show the relationship between the growth rate of electricity consumption and the growth rate of the national economy. The formula is:

$$\text{Elasticity of Electricity Consumption} = \frac{\text{average annual growth rate of electricity consumption}}{\text{average annual growth rate of national economy}}$$

□ Efficiency of Energy Transformation

Efficiency of Energy Transformation refers to the ratio of the total output of energy products after transformation and the total input of energy for transformation in the same reference period .It is an indicator to show the current conditions of energy processing and conversion equipment, production technique and management. The formula is:

$$\text{Efficiency of Energy Transformation} = \frac{\text{output of enery from transformation}}{\text{Input of energy for transformation}} \times 100\%$$

□ Natural Reserves

Natural Reserves refer to all the land, water areas on land and sea areas are under special protection or management due to the possess ion of representative natural ecological system, natural distribution of rare and dying out animal zones, water-resource conservation areas, and natural historical relics. Also included are natural reserves formally approved by people's governments at various levels at and above county level (including those approved before the Sixth-five-year Program and still active natural reserves).Scenic spots and historical sites and zones for preservation of cultural relics are not included. Natural reserves are classified as national level, provincial level, prefecture level and county level ones. They are under the jurisdiction of different departments, such as: environment protection, forestry, agriculture, geological and mining, oceanic and water conservancy and so on.

□ Industrial Solid Wastes Produced

Industrial Solid Wastes Produced refers to total volume of solid, semi-solid and high concentration liquid residues produced by industrial enterprises from production process in a given period of time, including hazardous wastes, slag, coal ash, gangue, tailings, radioactive residues and other wastes, but excluding stones stripped or dug out in mining (gangue and acid or alkaline stones not included). A stone is acid or alkaline depending on the pH value of the water below 4 or above 10.5 when the stone is in, or soaked by, the water.

□ Hazardous Wastes

Hazardous Wastes refers to those included in the national

EXPLANATORY NOTES TO MAJOR STATISTICAL INDICATORS

hazardous wastes catalogue or specified as any one of the following properties in the national hazardous wastes identification standards: explosive, ignitable, oxidizable, toxic, corrosive or liable to cause infectious diseases or lead to other dangers.

□ Industrial Wastes Utilized

Industrial Wastes Utilized refers to volume of wastes from which useful materials can be extracted or which can be converted into usable resources, energy or other materials by means of reclamation, processing, recycling and exchange (including utilizing in the year the stocks of industrial wastes of the previous year). Examples of such utilizations include fertilizers, building materials and road materials. The information shall be collected by the producing units of the wastes.

□ Ratio of Industrial Wastes Utilized

Ratio of Industrial Wastes Utilized refers to the percentage of industrial wastes utilized over industrial wastes produced (including stocks of the previous years). It is calculated as:

Ratio of industrial wastes utilized = volume of industrial wastes utilized / (industrial wastes produced + stock of previous years) × 100%

□ Industrial Solid Wastes Disposed

Industrial Solid Wastes Disposed refers to quantity of industrial solid wastes which are burnt or placed ultimately in the sites meeting the requirements for environmental protection and not salvaged or recycled (including disposition in the year of those wastes of previous years). The disposition includes landfill (Safe landfills should be conducted for hazardous wastes), incineration, containment spaces, deep underground disposal, backfill in mining pits and disposal at sea.

□ Volume of Industrial Waste Water Discharged

Volume of Industrial Waste Water Discharged refers to the volume of industrial waste water discharged, through all outlets, to the outside of industrial enterprises, including waste water produced, direct-cooling water, underground water from mines that does not meet the standard of discharge, and the domestic sewage mixed up with industrial waste water when discharged, but excluding discharged indirect-cooling water.

□ Industrial Waste Water Meeting Discharge Standards

Industrial Waste Water Meeting Discharge Standards refers to volume of industrial waste water discharge which, with or without treatment, reaches national or local standards with regard to all pollutants.

□ Ratio of Standard Waste Water Discharged to the Total Discharge

Ratio of Standard Waste Water Discharged to the Total Discharge refers to the share of the volume of waste water up to the standard for discharge of the total volume. The formula is as follows:

$$\text{Ratio of Standard Waste Water Discharged to the Total Discharge} = \frac{\text{average annual growth rate of electricity consumption}}{\text{average annual growth rate of national economy}} \times 100\%$$

□ Volume of Waste Industrial Gas Emission

Industrial Waste Air Emission refers to discharge into atmosphere of waste air containing pollutants generated from fuel burning and production process in enterprises within a given period of time. It is calculated at standard status (273K, 101325Pa) as:

Industrial waste air emission = emission through fuel burning + emission through production process

□ SO_2 Emission through Industrial Activities

SO_2 Emission through Industrial Activities refers to volume of sulphur dioxide emission from fuel burning and production process by enterprises during a given period of time. It is calculated as:

SO_2 emission through industrial activities = SO_2 emission from fuel burning + SO_2 emission from production process

□ Industrial Soot Emission

Industrial Soot Emission refers to volume of soot in smoke emitted in process of fuel burning in premises of enterprises.

□ Acid Rain Frequency

Acid Rain Frequency refers to the proportion of frequencies of acid rainfall to the total rainfall times. Rainfall is defined as acid rain when the PH value of its rainwater is smaller than 5.6.

第七篇
CHAPTER 7

固定资产投资
INVESTMENT IN FIXED ASSETS

简要说明

一、本篇资料的主要内容

本篇资料通过对一定时期全社会建造和购置固定资产活动的数量方面的描述，反映报告期内固定资产投资的规模、速度和内部结构情况，固定资产投资的资金来源及房屋施、竣工面积情况等。

二、本篇资料的统计范围

固定资产投资统计的范围包括：城镇和农村非农户建设项目投资，房地产开发投资及农户投资。

三、本篇的资料来源

城镇和农村非农户建设项目投资的统计资料来自上海市统计局投资建设统计处的固定资产投资统计调查；房地产开发投资的统计资料来自上海市统计局投资建设统计处的房地产开发、经营统计调查；农户投资的统计资料来自国家统计局上海调查总队居民收支调查处的农村住户固定资产投资抽样调查。

四、本篇的统计调查方法

除农户固定资产投资统计采用抽样调查方法外，其他均为全面统计报表。

五、统计口径的变化

自 1997 年起，固定资产投资的统计起点由 5 万元及以上提高到 50 万元及以上。

自 2011 年起，固定资产投资项目的统计起点由计划总投资 50 万元及以上提高到 500 万元及以上。

BRIEF INTRODUCTION

I. Main Contents

Statistics in this chapter describe activities on the construction and purchase of fixed assets of the whole society during a given period of time, and reflect the size, growth, internal structure, source of funds of fixed asset investment and floor space of buildings under construction or completed.

II. Scope of Statistics

Statistics on the investment in fixed assets cover investments in construction projects of urban and rural non–farm households, investments in real estate development, and investment of farm households.

III. Sources of Data

Data on the investments in construction projects of urban and rural non–farm households are from the surveys of investment in fixed assets from Department of Investment and Construction Statistics of the Shanghai Municipal Bureau of Statistics. Data on the real estate investments are from surveys of real estate development and management conducted by Department of Investment and Construction Statistics of the Shanghai Municipal Bureau of Statistics. Data on the investment of farm households are from Sample surveys of fixed assets investment in rural households conducted by Department of Residents Income and Expenditure Survey of the Survey Office of NBS in Shanghai

IV. Methodology of Data Collection

All data on investment in fixed assets are collected by the system of reporting form with complete enumeration, except data on individual investments in fixed assets in rural areas, which are collected through sample surveys.

V. Changes in Statistical Scope

Since 1997, the cut–off point of statistics of investment in fixed assets is raised from 50000 yuan to 500000 yuan.

Since 2011, the cut–off point of projects covered by statistics of investment in fixed assets is raised from an investment of 500000 yuan to 5000000 yuan.

表 7.1 全社会固定资产投资总额(按投资类别分)(1978～2015)
TOTAL INVESTMENT IN FIXED ASSETS(GROUPED BY TYPE OF INVESTMENT)

单位:亿元(100 million yuan)

年 份 Year	本年完成投资合计 Investment Completed Total	其 中 of which 建设项目 Construction Project	其 中 of which 城 镇 Town	农村非农户 Rural Non-agricultural	房地产开发 Investment in Real Estate	农户投资 Farmers' Investment
1978	27.91	26.88	23.92	2.96		0.79
1979	35.58	34.39	32.22	2.17		0.94
1980	45.43	43.45	40.44	3.01		1.41
1981	54.60	49.85	45.20	4.65		3.97
1982	71.34	65.97	61.91	4.06		4.32
1983	75.94	70.21	65.26	4.95		4.48
1984	92.30	83.11	76.04	7.07		7.28
1985	118.56	103.16	96.12	7.04		12.00
1986	146.93	132.44	122.64	9.80		10.30
1987	186.30	167.88	154.04	13.84	0.97	12.66
1988	245.27	219.90	197.71	22.19	1.68	16.90
1989	214.76	194.64	177.70	16.94	1.85	14.32
1990	227.08	199.05	184.67	14.38	8.16	15.96
1991	258.30	232.34	208.72	23.62	7.59	14.17
1992	357.38	318.93	263.51	55.42	12.71	17.00
1993	653.91	610.80	505.98	104.82	22.04	5.33
1994	1 123.29	971.68	830.45	141.23	117.43	10.40
1995	1 601.79	1 097.68	958.11	139.57	466.20	13.10
1996	1 952.05	1 238.85	1 080.53	158.32	657.79	20.00
1997	1 977.59	1 322.92	1 156.76	166.16	614.23	16.80
1998	1 964.83	1 361.41	1 224.01	137.40	577.12	12.76
1999	1 856.72	1 325.84	1 191.51	134.33	514.83	5.54
2000	1 869.67	1 284.08	1 122.47	161.61	566.17	10.36
2001	1 994.73	1 354.22	1 181.09	173.13	630.73	9.28
2002	2 187.06	1 430.69	1 262.77	167.92	748.89	6.87
2003	2 452.11	1 544.38	1 374.38	170.00	901.24	6.49
2004	3 084.66	1 903.33	1 722.51	180.82	1 175.46	5.86
2005	3 542.55	2 288.61	1 984.61	304.00	1 246.86	7.08
2006	3 925.09	2 643.53	2 246.93	396.60	1 275.59	5.96
2007	4 458.61	3 145.87	2 775.81	370.06	1 307.53	5.21
2008	4 829.45	3 459.38	3 044.46	414.92	1 366.87	3.20
2009	5 273.33	3 807.62	3 384.31	423.31	1 464.18	1.53
2010	5 317.67	3 334.95	2 858.56	476.39	1 980.68	2.03
2011	5 067.09	2 893.95	2 519.48	374.47	2 170.31	2.83
2012	5 254.38	2 870.04	2 559.12	310.92	2 381.36	2.98
2013	5 647.79	2 824.54	2 544.99	279.55	2 819.59	3.66
2014	6 016.43	2 806.49			3 206.48	3.46
2015	6 352.70	2 880.45			3 468.94	3.31

注：自 2011 年起，全社会固定资产投资由建设项目投资、房地产开发投资和农户投资三部分组成；建设项目投资由城镇投资和农村非农户投资两部分组成，其中城镇投资包括原来的基本建设、更新改造、其他投资和城镇私人建房投资；从 2014 年起建设项目取消"城乡分组"。

Note: Since 2011, total investment in fixed assets was composed of construction project investment, investment in real estate development and investment of rural households; construction project investment was composed of investment in urban areas and rural non-agricultural investment, in which investment in urban areas was composed of fundamental construction, renovation, other investments and urban private housing investment. Group of urban and rural construction projects was canceled since 2014.

表 7.2 全社会固定资产投资总额(按经济类型分)(1978～2015)
TOTAL INVESTMENT IN FIXED ASSETS (GROUPED BY ECONOMIC TYPES)

单位:亿元(100 million yuan)

年 份 Year	本年完成投资合 计 Investment Completed Total	其 中 of which # 国 有 经 济 State-owned	# 集 体 经 济 Collective-owned	# 股份制 经 济 Share-holding	# 外商、港澳台 经 济 Hong Kong, Macao, Taiwan and Foreign Funded
1978	27.91	23.83	3.20		
1979	35.58	32.08	2.42		
1980	45.43	40.27	3.58		
1981	54.60	45.00	5.43		
1982	71.34	61.62	5.11		
1983	75.94	65.01	6.20		
1984	92.30	75.80	8.98		
1985	118.56	95.92	10.44		
1986	146.93	122.46	13.99		
1987	186.30	154.45	18.65		
1988	245.27	198.68	29.03		
1989	214.76	178.81	21.00		
1990	227.08	192.24	18.29		
1991	258.30	215.61	27.82		
1992	357.38	275.67	64.16		
1993	653.91	419.22	124.18	32.83	61.61
1994	1 123.29	721.37	189.75	76.99	101.78
1995	1 601.79	935.92	247.11	150.17	208.30
1996	1 952.05	1 048.27	239.47	165.57	340.18
1997	1 977.59	1 148.69	257.10	118.80	367.50
1998	1 964.83	1 087.94	208.84	203.81	405.17
1999	1 856.72	986.82	227.19	268.68	325.58
2000	1 869.67	829.98	156.34	421.53	319.05
2001	1 994.73	760.58	136.81	580.75	362.25
2002	2 187.06	742.72	101.33	631.70	369.96
2003	2 452.11	811.85	116.63	647.27	468.20
2004	3 084.66	955.12	146.58	667.52	851.39
2005	3 542.55	1 240.27	131.07	916.27	640.31
2006	3 925.09	1 460.09	159.31	910.31	725.85
2007	4 458.61	1 779.43	121.51	1 169.49	711.35
2008	4 829.45	2 295.74	104.86	1 026.67	748.14
2009	5 273.33	2 618.61	132.30	1 174.81	617.90
2010	5 317.67	2 234.12	183.07	1 200.26	686.95
2011	5 067.09	1 875.48	133.33	1 349.65	726.57
2012	5 254.38	1 855.24	112.41	1 417.80	758.08
2013	5 647.79	1 926.89	102.81	1 601.33	894.47
2014	6 016.43	1 796.22	55.07	1 812.77	1 103.04
2015	6 352.70	1 974.08	53.62	2 124.52	1 164.72

表7.3 主要年份全社会固定资产投资主要指标
MAJOR INDICATORS OF TOTAL INVESTMENT IN FIXED ASSETS IN MAIN YEARS

单位:亿元(100 million yuan)

指 标	Indicators	2000	2010	2013	2014	2015
本年完成投资合计	**Investment Completed Total**	**1 869.67**	**5 317.67**	**5 647.79**	**6 016.43**	**6 352.70**
按隶属关系分	**Grouped by Administrative Relationship**					
中央项目	Central Government Projects	257.67	761.06	553.26	538.44	593.78
地方项目	Local Projects	1 612.00	4 556.61	5 094.53	5 477.99	5 758.92
按构成分	**Grouped by Use of Funds**					
建筑安装工程	Construction and Installation	882.91	2 820.17	3 440.47	3 713.25	3 787.88
设备、工器具购置	Purchase of Equipment and Instruments	482.47	991.10	787.55	624.83	761.20
其他费用	Others	504.29	1 506.40	1 419.77	1 678.35	1 803.63
按建设性质分	**Grouped by Type of Construction**					
#新 建	New Construction	730.76	2 052.69	1 739.51	1 913.30	1 837.92
扩 建	Expansion	216.71	368.07	310.61	303.63	289.65
改建和技术改造	Reconstruction and Technical Transformation	216.40	513.80	428.57	335.59	345.03
单纯购置	Simply Purchase	39.02	373.43	324.92	220.62	391.54
按产业分	**Grouped by Type of Industry**					
第一产业	Primary Industry	7.87	16.40	18.45	11.86	3.95
第二产业	Secondary Industry	615.94	1 435.37	1 242.02	1 157.27	958.84
第三产业	Tertiary Industry	1 245.86	3 865.90	4 387.32	4 847.30	5 389.91
按经济类型分	**Grouped by Economic Types**					
国有经济	State-owned	829.98	2 234.12	1 926.89	1 796.22	1 974.08
非国有经济	Non-state-owned	1 039.69	3 083.55	3 720.90	4 220.21	4 378.62
集体经济	Collective-owned	156.34	183.07	102.81	55.07	53.62
私营经济	Private	83.29	992.16	1 070.65	1 219.43	1 017.10
联营经济	Joint Owned	41.20	11.52	13.99	6.11	5.55
股份制经济	Share-holding	421.53	1 200.26	1 601.33	1 812.77	2 124.52
港澳台商投资	Hong Kong, Macao and Taiwan Funded	96.19	247.67	291.96	465.14	630.61
外商投资	Foreign Funded	222.86	439.28	602.50	637.90	534.11
其他经济	Others	18.28	9.58	37.66	23.79	13.11
新增固定资产	**Newly Increased Fixed Assets**	**1 493.35**	**3 179.40**	**2 664.81**	**2 739.79**	**3 281.26**
固定资产交付使用率(%)	Rate of Fixed Assets Transfered and in Use(%)	79.9	59.8	47.2	45.5	51.7
房屋建筑面积(万平方米)	**Floor Space of Buildings (10 000sq. m)**					
施工面积	Floor Space Under Construction	8 636.31	15 020.76	17 180.27	18 010.06	17 885.94
#住 宅	Residential Housing	4 804.12	7 344.07	8 188.56	8 573.04	8 443.82
竣工面积	Floor Space Completed	3 266.52	2 776.21	2 698.35	2 682.42	2 923.42
#住 宅	Residential Housing	1 724.02	1 415.44	1 439.20	1 549.64	1 617.86

表7.4 地方固定资产投资主要指标(2013~2015)
MAJOR INDICATORS OF LOCAL INVESTMENT IN FIXED ASSETS

单位:亿元(100 million yuan)

指 标	Indicators	2013	2014	2015
本年完成投资合计	**Investment Completed Total**	**5 094.53**	**5 477.99**	**5 758.92**
按构成分	**Grouped by Use of Funds**			
建筑安装工程	Construction and Installation	3 213.79	3 463.74	3 552.66
设备、工器具购置	Purchase of Equipment and Instruments	542.84	430.24	475.11
其他费用	Others	1 337.90	1 584.01	1 731.15
按建设性质分	**Grouped by Type of Construction**			
#新 建	New Construction	1 568.69	1 725.93	1 700.55
扩 建	Expansion	208.30	190.65	179.92
改建和技术改造	Reconstruction and Technical Transformation	352.06	259.60	270.90
单纯购置	Simply Purchase	189.48	155.10	202.28
按产业分	**Grouped by Type of Industry**			
第一产业	Primary Industry	18.45	11.86	3.95
第二产业	Secondary Industry	1 031.27	943.93	796.72
第三产业	Tertiary Industry	4 044.81	4 522.20	4 958.25
按行业分	**Grouped by Sectors**			
#工 业	Industry	1 025.60	943.42	795.20
批发和零售业	Wholesale and Retail	51.78	31.82	34.80
交通运输、仓储和邮政业	Transportation, Storage, Postal and Telecommunications	366.11	383.33	585.36
住宿和餐饮业	Hotel and Catering	34.06	33.35	28.30
信息传输、软件和信息技术服务业	Transmission of Information, Software and Information Technology Services	31.79	36.42	44.99
金融业	Finance	1.36	3.49	13.74
房地产业	Real Estate	2 765.15	3 125.18	3 400.91
租赁和商务服务业	Leasing and Business Service	134.61	153.72	92.03
科学研究和技术服务业	Scientific Research and Technology Service and Geological Prospecting	32.75	39.39	40.65
水利、环境和公共设施管理业	Water Conservancy, Environment and Public Facility Management	421.46	465.73	474.15
居民服务、修理和其他服务业	Residents Service, Repair and Other Services	4.92	5.27	2.75
教 育	Education	63.72	103.42	79.86
卫生和社会工作	Health and Social Work	39.18	30.30	41.62
文化、体育和娱乐业	Culture, Sports and Entertainment	85.89	104.32	107.55
公共管理、社会保障和社会组织	Public Administration and Social Organizations	12.00	6.45	11.54
新增固定资产	**Newly Increased Fixed Assets**	**2 374.17**	**2 459.53**	**2 818.51**
固定资产交付使用率(%)	Rate of Fixed Assets Transfered and in Use(%)	46.6	44.9	48.9
房屋建筑面积(万平方米)	**Floor Space of Buildings (10 000sq. m)**			
施工面积	Floor Space Under Construction	16 579.88	17 292.07	17 252.68
#住 宅	Residential Housing	7 942.34	8 193.08	8 179.35
竣工面积	Floor Space Completed	2 641.90	2 616.90	2 825.65
#住 宅	Residential Housing	1 413.89	1 501.56	1 563.93

表7.5 建设项目固定资产投资主要指标(2015)
MAJOR INDICATORS OF INVESTMENT IN FIXED ASSETS OF THE CONSTRUCTION PROJECT

单位:亿元(100 million yuan)

指标	Indicators	全市 Total	#地方 Local Projects
本年完成投资合计	**Investment Completed Total**	**2 880.45**	**2 364.62**
按建设性质分	**Grouped by Type of Construction**		
#新　建	New Construction	1 837.92	1 700.55
扩　建	Expansion	289.65	179.92
改建和技术改造	Reconstruction and Technical Transformation	345.03	270.90
单纯购置	Simply Purchase	391.54	202.28
按产业分	**Grouped by Type of Industry**		
第一产业	Primary Industry	3.41	3.95
第二产业	Secondary Industry	958.84	796.72
第三产业	Tertiary Industry	1 918.20	1 569.83
按行业分	**Grouped by Economic Sectors**		
#工　业	Industry	957.17	795.20
批发和零售业	Wholesale and Retail	34.80	34.80
交通运输、仓储和邮政业	Transportation, Storage, Postal and Telecommunications	794.56	585.36
住宿和餐饮业	Hotel and Catering	28.30	28.30
信息传输、软件和信息技术服务业	Transmission of Information, Software and Information Technology Services	127.27	44.99
金融业	Finance	24.49	13.74
房地产业	Real Estate	15.01	12.50
租赁和商务服务业	Leasing and Business Service	116.16	92.03
科学研究和技术服务业	Scientific Research and Technology Service	46.12	40.65
水利、环境和公共设施管理业	Water Conservancy, Environment and Public Facility Management	474.38	474.15
居民服务、修理和其他服务业	Residents Service, Repair and Other Services	2.74	2.75
教　育	Education	89.22	79.86
卫生和社会工作	Health and Social Work	45.56	41.62
文化、体育和娱乐业	Culture, Sports and Entertainment	108.04	107.55
公共管理、社会保障和社会组织	Public Administration and Social Organizations	11.56	11.54
新增固定资产	**Newly Increased Fixed Assets**	**1 388.10**	**1 008.94**
固定资产交付使用率(%)	Rate of Fixed Assets Transfered and in Use(%)	48.2	42.7
房屋建筑面积(万平方米)	**Floor Space of Buildings (10 000sq. m)**		
施工面积	Floor Space Under Construction	2 773.21	2 567.11
#住　宅	Residential Housing	54.79	54.79
竣工面积	Floor Space Completed	260.84	260.84
#住　宅	Residential Housing	13.90	13.90

表7.6 工业各行业固定资产投资主要指标(2015)
MAIN INDICATORS OF INVESTMENT IN FIXED ASSETS OF VARIOUS INDUSTRIES

行业	Sectors	施工项目(个) Projects Under Construction (unit)	本年投产项目(个) Projects Completed and Put into Production (unit)	建成投产率(%) Rate of Projects Completed and Put into Use(%)	本年完成投资合计(亿元) Construction Transformation Investment (100 million yuan)
总计	**Total**	**1 743**	**558**	**32.0**	**957.17**
采矿业	**Excavation**	**1**			**0.24**
开采辅助活动	Mining Support Activities	1			0.24
制造业	**Manufacturing**	**1 287**	**377**	**29.3**	**757.77**
农副食品加工业	Farm and Sideline Products Processing	12	1	8.3	8.49
食品制造业	Food Manufacturing	23	9	39.1	10.43
酒、饮料和精制茶制造业	Wine, Drinks and Purified Tea Manufacturing	13	5	38.5	5.29
烟草制品业	Tabacco Manufacturing	2	1	50.0	8.23
纺织业	Textile	12	4	33.3	3.04
纺织服装、服饰业	Textiles and Clothing Industry	22	3	13.6	8.13
皮革、毛皮、羽毛及其制品和制鞋业	Leather, Fur, Wool Products, and Shoes Manufacturing	4	1	25.0	1.88
木材加工和木、竹、藤、棕、草制品业	Timber Processing and Timber, Bamboo,Rattan, Coir and Straw Products Manufacturing	2	1	50.0	0.62
家具制造业	Furniture Manufacturing	11	5	45.5	3.56
造纸和纸制品业	Paper-making and Paper Products Manufacturing	10	2	20.0	2.82
印刷业和记录媒介复制业	Printing and Record Duplicating	19	8	42.1	9.54
文教、工美、体育和娱乐用品制造业	Culture, Education, Industrial Arts, Sports and Entertainment Goods Manufacturing	7			2.50
石油加工、炼焦和核燃料加工业	Oil Processing,Coking and Nuclear Fuel Processing	15	13	86.7	4.46
化学原料和化学制品制造业	Raw Chemical Materials and Chemical Products Manufacturing	131	24	18.3	77.31
医药制造业	Medicine Manufacturing	69	15	21.7	44.43
化学纤维制造业	Chemical Fiber Manufacturing	8	2	25.0	1.32
橡胶和塑料制品业	Rubber and Plastic Products Manufacturing	36	8	22.2	16.15
非金属矿物制品业	Non-metallic Mineral Products Manufacturing	14	6	42.9	6.64
黑色金属冶炼和压延加工业	Ferrous Metal Smelting and Rolling Processing Industry	175	79	45.1	40.37
有色金属冶炼和压延加工业	Nonferrous Metal Smelting and Rolling Processing Industry	7	2	28.6	2.16
金属制品业	Metal Products Manufacturing	54	20	37.0	23.68
通用设备制造业	General Equipment Manufacturing	109	32	29.4	45.28
专用设备制造业	Special Purpose Equipment Manufacturing	99	21	21.2	49.89
汽车制造业	The Automotive Manufacturing	148	26	17.6	118.10
铁路、船舶、航空航天和其他运输设备制造业	The Railroad, Marine, Aerospace and Other Transportation Equipment Manufacturing	33	8	24.2	26.57
电气机械和器材制造业	Electric Machinery Equipments and Manufacturing	92	27	29.3	37.50
计算机、通信和其他电子设备制造业	Computer, Communications and Other Electronic Equipment Manufacturing	76	28	36.8	155.70
仪器仪表制造业	Instrumentation Manufacturing	18	8	44.4	8.03
其他制造业	Other Manufacturing	61	16	26.2	33.79
废弃资源综合利用业	Comprehensive Utilization of Waste Resources	2			0.46
金属制品、机械和设备修理业	Metal Products, Machinery and Equipment Repair Industry	3	2	66.7	1.39
电力、热力、燃气及水生产和供应业	**Electricity, Heat, Gas and Water Production and Supply Industry**	**455**	**181**	**39.8**	**199.17**
电力、热力生产和供应业	Power and Heat Production and Supply	407	158	38.8	132.44
燃气生产和供应业	Gas Production and Supply	15	11	73.3	8.10
水的生产和供应业	Water Production and Supply	33	12	36.4	58.63

注：单纯购置项目和筹建项目固定资产投资不计算施工项目和本年投产项目个数。
Note: The investment in fixed assets of purchasing and preparatory project doesnt be calculated in projects under construction or projects completed and put into production in this year.

表7.7 主要年份六大重点工业行业固定资产投资额
FIXED ASSETS INVESTMENT IN SIX KEY INDUSTRIES IN MAIN YEARS

单位：亿元(100 million yuan)

指 标	Indicators	2000	2010	2014	2015
工业六大重点行业	**Six Key Industries**	**283.73**	**730.68**	**690.16**	**556.33**
电子信息产品制造业	Electronic Information Product Manufacturing	99.30	219.65	163.08	173.28
汽车制造业	Automobile Manufacturing	45.40	109.68	142.67	118.10
石油化工及精细化工制造业	Petrochemical and Fine Chemical Products Manufacturing	37.74	85.03	120.58	67.09
精品钢材制造业	Fine Steel Manufacturing	62.23	113.79	55.94	40.35
成套设备制造业	Equipment Complex Manufacturing	26.71	176.31	132.31	98.30
生物医药制造业	Bio-medicine Manufacturing	12.34	26.21	75.59	59.21

注：自2012年起固定资产投资项目行业代码采用新的分类标准(GB/T 4754-2011)，本表中的数据参照新行业标准进行相应调整。由于个别投资项目同时属于六大重点发展工业行业中的两类，故各分类投资数直接相加大于合计数。

Note: The industry code of fixed asset investment projects use the new classification standard(GB/T 4754-2011) since 2012, the data in this table was adjusted by the new standard. Individual investment projects belong to two types in Six Key Industries, so the sum of each segment is greater than the total number.

表7.8 主要年份新增固定资产
NEWLY INCREASED FIXED ASSETS IN MAIN YEARS

年 份 Year	新增固定资产(亿元) Newly Increased Fixed Assets(100 million yuan)	其 中 of which # 房地产开发 Investment in Real Estate Development	固定资产交付使用率(%) Rate of Fixed Assets Transferred and in Use(%)
1990	222.99	4.97	98.2
1995	826.94	127.08	51.6
2000	1 493.35	477.39	79.9
2005	2 547.02	1 054.02	71.9
2006	2 680.85	1 058.94	68.3
2007	2 466.68	1 048.47	55.3
2008	2 773.14	994.10	57.4
2009	2 686.43	932.24	50.9
2010	3 179.40	964.27	59.8
2011	2 816.59	1 250.88	55.6
2012	2 911.34	1 388.45	55.4
2013	2 664.81	1 354.75	47.2
2014	2 739.79	1 583.93	45.5
2015	3 281.26	1 890.67	51.7

表7.9 主要年份固定资产投资资金来源
CAPITAL SOURCES OF FIXED ASSETS INVESTMENT IN MAIN YEARS

单位：亿元(100 million yuan)

指 标	Indicators	2000	2010	2014	2015
本年实际到位资金合计	**Total Actual Funds This Year**	**2 061.66**	**7 997.62**	**10 524.10**	**10 652.67**
上年末结余资金	Balance at End of Previous Year	241.05	1 440.57	2 562.48	2 472.70
本年实际到位资金小计	Sub-total Actual Funds this Year	1 820.61	6 557.05	7 961.62	8 179.97
国家预算资金	State Budgetary Funds	206.17	624.91	417.89	501.61
国内贷款	Domestic Loans	379.21	1 568.79	2 068.08	2 050.79
债 券	Bonds	4.85	10.06	0.50	
利用外资	Foreign Investment	161.83	239.18	205.05	130.13
# 外商直接投资	Foreign Direct Investment	73.71	139.72	174.16	85.36
自筹资金	Self-Financed Capital	747.59	2 764.91	3 243.55	3 010.99
其他资金	Other Capital	320.96	1 349.21	2 027.05	2 485.96
本年各项应付款合计	The Total Payment of This Year	310.42	997.93	1 329.65	1 661.63
# 工程款	Project Funds	76.52	438.19	724.52	867.08

注：自2012年起，国家预算资金和自筹资金统计口径调整，历年指标数据已做相应调整。

Note: The Statistical caliber of state budget funds and self-financing was adjusted Since 2012, and data over the years have been adjusted accordingly.

表7.10 全社会房屋施工面积、竣工面积(1985~2015)
TOTAL FLOOR SPACE OF CONSTRUCTION AND COMPLETED BUILDINGS

年份 Year	施工面积(万平方米) Floor Area of Construction (10 000 sq. m)	其中 of which #住宅 Residential Housing	其中 of which 占全社会房屋施工面积比重(%) As Percentage of Total Floor Space Of Construction	竣工面积(万平方米) Floor Area Completed (10 000 sq. m)	房屋建筑面积竣工率(%) Construction Completion Rate (%)
1985	4 162.15	2 651.52	63.71	2 909.58	69.9
1986	4 874.44	2 469.27	50.66	2 493.93	51.2
1987	4 382.40	2 658.05	60.65	2 700.96	61.6
1988	4 369.20	2 667.00	61.04	2 457.34	56.2
1989	3 683.77	2 048.20	55.60	1 941.80	52.7
1990	3 801.46	2 269.06	59.69	2 138.44	56.3
1991	3 611.53	2 157.46	59.74	1 923.92	53.3
1992	4 709.52	2 463.79	52.32	2 608.20	55.4
1993	4 724.30	2 142.39	45.35	2 031.76	43.0
1994	6 720.70	3 520.27	52.38	2 519.09	37.5
1995	10 566.42	6 195.12	58.63	3 093.93	29.3
1996	10 730.85	5 874.26	54.74	3 254.57	30.3
1997	9 955.21	5 450.13	54.75	3 614.19	36.3
1998	9 364.36	5 113.52	54.61	3 364.43	35.9
1999	8 364.48	4 608.49	55.10	3 257.57	38.9
2000	8 636.31	4 804.12	55.63	3 266.52	37.8
2001	8 588.49	5 236.93	60.98	3 215.12	37.4
2002	9 425.42	5 994.70	63.60	3 102.54	32.9
2003	11 023.24	6 974.27	63.27	3 582.34	32.5
2004	12 291.81	7 873.44	64.05	4 932.57	40.1
2005	14 477.85	8 267.24	57.10	4 873.82	33.7
2006	14 596.49	8 085.28	55.39	4 901.46	33.6
2007	14 979.37	7 789.91	52.00	5 068.46	33.8
2008	14 083.52	7 060.19	50.13	3 828.79	27.2
2009	13 553.64	6 581.16	48.56	2 970.92	21.9
2010	15 020.76	7 344.07	48.89	2 776.21	18.5
2011	16 553.86	8 423.11	50.90	2 913.78	17.6
2012	16 874.72	8 350.83	49.50	2 838.97	16.8
2013	17 180.27	8 188.56	47.70	2 698.35	15.7
2014	18 010.06	8 573.04	47.60	2 682.42	14.9
2015	17 885.94	8 443.82	47.20	2 923.42	16.3

表7.11 住宅投资和竣工建筑面积(1978～2015)
INVESTMENT IN RESIDENTIAL HOUSING AND FLOOR SPACE OF BUILDINGS COMPLETED

年份 Year	住宅投资额(亿元) Investment in Residential Housing (100 million yuan)	其中 of which #房地产 Real Estate	占全社会固定资产投资总额比重(%) As Percentage of Total Floor Space Of Construction	住宅竣工建筑面积(万平方米) Floor Area of Residence Building Completed (10 000 sq. m)	住宅建筑面积竣工率(%) Construction Completion Rate
1978	2.67		9.6	199.61	
1979	3.31		9.3	215.99	
1980	5.82		12.8	304.32	
1981	10.02		18.4	1 380.70	78.3
1982	11.03		15.5	1 363.63	77.7
1983	11.18		14.7	1 347.79	77.2
1984	15.88		17.2	1 788.44	80.9
1985	25.47		21.5	2 112.04	79.7
1986	28.24		19.2	1 790.01	72.5
1987	36.28		19.5	1 874.90	70.5
1988	44.84		18.3	1 758.29	65.9
1989	35.82	1.85	16.7	1 246.58	60.9
1990	42.94	7.26	18.9	1 339.02	59.0
1991	48.92	7.31	18.9	1 160.61	53.8
1992	61.23	11.73	17.1	1 379.18	56.0
1993	77.14	13.96	11.8	1 017.54	47.5
1994	300.65	106.31	26.8	1 349.24	38.3
1995	433.76	280.38	27.1	1 746.82	28.2
1996	466.99	356.01	23.9	1 872.65	31.9
1997	458.22	334.07	23.2	2 179.68	40.0
1998	404.96	320.66	20.6	1 963.51	38.4
1999	378.82	324.49	20.4	1 731.55	37.6
2000	443.90	408.82	23.7	1 724.02	35.9
2001	466.71	439.17	23.4	1 743.90	33.3
2002	584.51	567.76	26.7	1 880.50	31.4
2003	694.30	676.28	28.3	2 280.79	32.7
2004	922.61	900.67	29.9	3 270.43	41.5
2005	936.36	920.84	26.4	2 819.35	34.1
2006	854.15	835.65	21.8	2 746.80	34.0
2007	853.13	837.53	19.1	2 843.62	36.5
2008	871.52	843.63	18.0	1 899.40	26.9
2009	922.81	918.68	17.5	1 522.07	23.1
2010	1 232.96	1 229.83	23.2	1 415.44	19.3
2011	1 403.13	1 398.75	27.7	1 568.83	18.6
2012	1 457.64	1 451.94	27.7	1 626.73	19.5
2013	1 626.95	1 615.51	28.8	1 439.20	17.6
2014	1 730.81	1 724.65	28.8	1 549.64	18.1
2015	1 822.73	1 813.32	28.7	1 617.86	19.2

注：1981 年以前住宅投资额和住宅竣工建筑面积数据不包括城乡私人建房和农村投资，从 1981 年开始为全社会口径。

Note: Before 1981, investments and floor area of residential housing completed in this table didn't cover private-built houses in urban and rural areas and rural investment, the whole society is covered since 1981.

上 / 海 / 统 / 计 / 年 / 鉴

主要统计指标解释

全社会固定资产投资

固定资产投资是国民经济再生产活动的一个重要部分。固定资产投资额是以货币形式表现的在一定时期内建造和购置固定资产的工作量以及与此有关的费用总称。它是反映固定资产投资规模、结构和发展速度的综合性指标。按照现行国家统计制度,全社会固定资产投资包括建设项目投资、房地产开发投资和农户投资。

自 1997 年起,固定资产投资统计起点为 50 万元(含 50 万元)以上项目;自 2011 年起,固定资产投资统计起点为 500 万元(含 500 万元)以上项目。

固定资产投资按国民经济行业分

固定资产投资按国民经济行业分是根据建设项目建成投产后的主要产品或主要用途及社会经济活动性质来确定国民经济行业。一般情况下,一个建设项目或一个企业、事业单位只能属于一种国民经济行业。

固定资产投资按隶属关系分

固定资产投资按隶属关系分是按建设单位或企业、事业、行政单位的主管上级机关确定的。

(1)中央:是指中共中央、人大常委会和国务院各部、委、局、总公司以及直属机构直接领导的建设项目和企业、事业、行政单位。这些单位的固定资产投资计划由国务院各部门直接编制和下达,建设中所需物资、主要设备以及建设中的问题都由中央有关部门安排和解决。

(2)地方:是由省(自治区、直辖市)、地区(州、盟、省辖市)、县(旗、县级市)三级政府及业务主管部门直接领导和管理的建设项目、企业、事业、行政单位。地方项目还包括不隶属以上各级政府及主管部门的建设项目和企业、事业单位,如外商投资企业和无主管部门的企业等。

固定资产投资按构成分

固定资产投资按构成分是按其工作内容和实现方式来划分的,主要分为建筑安装工程,设备、工具、器具购置,其他费用三个部分。

(1)建筑安装工程(建筑安装工作量):指各种房屋、建筑物的建造工程和各种设备、装置的安装工程。包括各种房屋建造工程;各种用途设备基础和各种工业窑炉的砌筑工程及金属结构工程;为施工而进行的各种准备工作和临时工程以及完工后的清理工作等;铁路、道路的铺设,矿井的开凿及石油管道的架设等;水利工程;防空地下建筑等特殊工程;列入房屋工程预算内的暖气、卫生、通风、照明、煤气等设备的价值及装设油饰工程;列入建筑工程预算内的各种管道(蒸汽、压缩空气、石油、给排水等管道)、电力、电讯电缆导线等的敷设工程;以及各种机械设备的安装工程;为测定安装工程质量,对设备进行的试运工作;房地产开发单位进行的商品房屋开发建设工程、土地开发工程。

在安装工程中,不包括被安装设备本身的价值。

(2)设备、工具、器具购置:指建设单位或企、事业单位购置或自制的,达到固定资产标准的设备、工具、器具的价值。新建单位及扩建单位的新建车间,按照设计或计划要求购置或自制的全部设备、工具、器具,不论是否达到固定资产标准均计入"设备、工具、器具购置"中。

(3)其他费用:指在固定资产建造和购置过程中发生的,除上述几项内容以外的各种应分摊计入固定资产的费用。

固定资产投资的资金来源

固定资产投资的资金来源是根据固定资产投资的资金来源不同,分为国家预算资金、国内贷款、债券、利用外资、自筹资金和其他资金来源。

(1)国家预算资金:自 2011 年起,按照全国人大和国务院的要求,各级财政的所有资金,包括税收和非税收入,均必须纳入预算管理,我国已不存在预算外资金的概念,因此各级政府用于固定资产投资的财政资金均为预算资金。旧的国家预算内资金的内容和现中央预算资金的内容基本一致。国家预算包括一般预算、政府性基金预算、国有资本经营预算和社保基金预算。各类预算中用于固定资产投资的资金全部作为国家预算资金填报。

(2)国内贷款:指报告期内企、事业单位向银行及非银行金融机构借入的用于固定资产投资的各种国内借款。包括银行利用自有资金及吸收的存款发放的贷款、上级主管部门拨入的国内贷款、国家专项贷款(包括煤代油贷款、劳改煤矿专项贷款等)、地方财政专项资金安排的贷款、国内储备贷款、周转贷款等。

(3)债券:是企业(公司)或金融机构通过发行各种债券,筹集用于固定资产投资的资金。包括由银行代理国家

主要统计指标解释

专业投资公司发行的重点企业债券和基本建设债券。

（4）利用外资：指报告期内收到的用于固定资产投资的国外资金，包括统借统还、自借自还的国外贷款，中外合资项目中的外资，以及对外发行债券和股票等。国家统借统还的外资指由我国政府出面同外国政府、团体或金融组织签订贷款协议、并负责偿还本息的国外贷款。

（5）自筹资金：指固定资产投资单位在报告期收到的，由各企事业单位筹集用于固定资产投资的资金，包括各类企事业单位的自有资金和从其他单位筹集的用于固定资产投资的资金，但不包括各类财政性资金、从各类金融机构借入资金和国外资金。

（6）其他资金来源：指在报告期收到的除以上各种资金之外的用于固定资产投资的资金。包括社会集资、个人资金、无偿捐赠的资金及其他单位拨入的资金等。

固定资产投资按建设性质分

建设项目的性质一般分为新建、改建、扩建和单纯建造生活设施。

（1）新建：一般指从无到有"平地起家"开始建设的企业、事业和行政单位或独立的工程。现有企业、事业、行政单位一般不属于新建。但如有的单位原有基础很小，经过建设后新增的固定资产价值超过该企、事业、行政单位原有固定资产价值(原值)三倍以上的也应作为新建。

（2）改建和技术改造：是指现有企业、事业单位对原有设施进行技术改造或更新（包括相应配套的辅助性生产、生活福利设施）的建设项目。改建项目包括现有企业、事业单位为适应市场变化的需要，而改变企业的主要产品种类（如军工企业转民用品等）的建设项目，原有产品生产作业线由于各工序（车间）之间能力不平衡，为填平补齐充分发挥原有生产能力而增建不增加本企业主要产品设计能力的车间的建设项目。技术改造是指企业、事业单位在现有基础上，用先进的技术代替落后的技术，用先进的工艺和装备代替落后的工艺和装备，以改变企业落后的技术经济面貌，实现以内涵为主的扩大再生产，达到提高产品质量、促进产品更新换代、节约能源、降低消耗、扩大生产规模、全面提高社会经效益的目的。技术改造具体包括以下内容：机器设备和工具的更新改造；生产工艺改革、节约能源和原材料的改造；厂房建筑和公共设施的改造；保护环境进行的"三废"治理改造；劳动条件和生产环境的改造等。

（3）扩建：指在厂内或其他地点，为扩大原有产品的生产能力（或效益）或增加新的产品生产能力，而增建主要的生产车间（或主要工程）、分厂、独立的生产线。行政、事业单位在原单位增建业务用房（如学校增建教学用房、医院增建门诊部、病房等）也作为扩建。

现有企、事业单位为扩大原有主要产品生产能力或增加新的产品生产能力，增建一个或几个主要生产车间(或主要工程)、分厂，同时进行一些更新改造工程的，也应作为扩建。

（4）单纯建造生活设施：是指企（事）业及行政单位在不扩建、改建生产性工程和业务用房的情况下，单纯建造职工住宅、托儿所、子弟学校、医务室、浴室、食堂等生活福利设施。

新增固定资产

新增固定资产又称交付使用的固定资产，是指已经完成建造和购置过程，并已交付生产或使用单位的固定资产价值。新增固定资产是表示固定资产投资成果的价值量指标，也是反映建设进度、计算固定资产投资效果的必要数据。

固定资产交付使用率

指一定时期新增固定资产与同期完成投资额的比率。该指标是反映固定资产动用速度，衡量建设过程中宏观投资效果的综合指标。由于新增固定资产是较长时期内形成的结果，而投资额则是当年完成的，因此，该指标一般适宜于反映较长时期内固定资产的动用情况。

施工项目

指报告期内正式进行过建筑或安装施工活动的建设项目。凡是报告期内施过工的建设项目，不论施工时间长短，均作为施工项目统计。施工项目个数可以反映一定时期固定资产投资的实际规模，与同期建成投产的建设项目个数相比，可以从建设速度的角度反映固定资产投资的效果。根据建设项目施工活动的不同性质，施工项目又分为：本年新开工项目，以前年度开工跨入本年继续施工项目，本年全部投产项目，以前年度全部停缓建在本年恢复施工的项目和本年进行过施工又在本年内全部停缓建的项目。

全部投产项目

指报告期内按设计文件规定建成主体工程和相应配套的辅助设施，形成生产能力或工程效益，经过验收合格，并且已正式投入生产或交付使用的建设项目。

全部投产的工业项目是指设计文件规定形成生产能力的主体工程及其相应配套的辅助设施全部建成，经负荷试运转，证明具备生产设计规定合格产品的条件，并经过验收鉴定合格或达到竣工验收标准，与生产性工程配套的

主要统计指标解释

生活福利设施可以满足近期正常生产的需要，正式移交生产的建设项目。

建成投产率

指一定时期内全部投产项目个数与同期施工项目个数的比率。该指标是从建设单位建设速度的角度反映投资效果的指标。

房屋建筑面积竣工率

指一定时期内房屋竣工面积占同期房屋施工面积的比率。该指标从房屋建筑施工速度的角度反映投资效果的指标。

SHANGHAI STATISTICAL YEARBOOK

EXPLANATORY NOTES TO MAJOR STATISTICAL INDICATORS

□ Total Investment in Fixed Assets

Investment in Fixed Assets constitutes an important portion of the national economic reproduction. Fixed assets investment is a general term for both the work volume of production and purchase of fixed assets and relevant expenditure, in the form of currency, during a certain period. It is a comprehensive indicator of scale, structure and development speed of fixed assets investment. As stipulated in the current national statistics regulations, the social fixed assets investment includes infrastructure project investment, real estate development investment and farmers' investment. From 1997, the fixed assets items only include those with investment of 0.5 million yuan and above. From 2011, the fixed assets items only include those with investment of 5 million yuan and above.

□ Investment in Fixed Assets by Sector

Investment in Fixed Assets by Sector refers to determining the classification of construction projects by the major products or the purpose of the projects when they are put into production or use, and by the nature of their social economic activities. In general, one project or one enterprise or institution can only be classified into one sector.

□ Investment in Fixed Assets by Jurisdiction of Management

Investment in Fixed Assets by Jurisdiction of Management refers to the classification of investment by the competent authorities under which investment is made by construction units, enterprises, institutions or administrative units.

(1) Central investment refers to the investment in projects or by enterprises, institutions or administrative units which are under the direct leadership and management of the CPC Central Committee, the NPC Standing Committee, the State Council and of the national commissions, ministries, agencies and state-owned large corporations. Various ministries and departments of the State Council prepare and implement plans for investment in fixed assets by those departments, and arrange and ensure the supply of materials and key equipment required for the projects.

(2) Local investment refers to the investment in projects or by enterprises, institutions or administrative units which are under the direct leadership and management of departments under the provincial, prefecture and county governments. Also included are projects by foreign-invested enterprises and enterprises without competent managing authorities.

□ Investment in Fixed Assets by Structure

Investment in Fixed Assets by Structure is classified by their contents. It is mainly classified into 3 categories, i.e. construction and installation, purchase of equipment and instrument, and other expenses.

(1) Construction and installation (work volume of construction and installation) refers to the construction of various houses and buildings and installation of various kinds of equipment and instruments. They include construction of various houses; equipment foundations, industrial kilns and stoves, and metal structure work; preparation works for project construction, and clearing up works post project construction; pavement of railways and roads, drilling of mines and putting up of oil pipes; construction of projects of water conservancy; construction of underground air-raid shelters and construction of other special projects; value of equipment for heating, sanitation, ventilation, lighting, gas, painting, etc. that are covered by the budget of housing projects; laying out of various pipelines (for steam, compressed air, petroleum, tap water and sewage) and lines for electric power and for communications; installation of various machinery equipment, testing operation for pre-testing the quality of installation projects, and land and other development work conducted by real estate developers for commercial housing. The value of equipment installed is not included in the value of installation projects.

(2) Purchase of equipment and instruments refers to the total value of equipment, tools, and instruments purchased or self-produced which come up to standards for fixed assets by the construction units or investing enterprises or institutions. Equipment, tools and instruments purchased or self-produced for new workshops by newly established or expanded units are categorized as "purchase of equipment and instruments" no matter whether they come up to the standards for fixed assets.

(3) Other expenses refer to expenses occurring during the construction or purchase of fixed assets other than those mentioned above.

EXPLANATORY NOTES TO MAJOR STATISTICAL INDICATORS

□ Sources of Capital for Investment in Fixed Assets

Sources of capital for Investment in Fixed Assets include state budget funds, domestic loans, bond, foreign investment, self-raised funds, and others.

(1)State state budget funds. Since 2011, according to the requirement of the NPC and the State Council, all levels of financial resources, including tax and non-tax revenue, must be included in the budget management, extra-budgetary didn't exist any longer, all levels of government for fixing asset investment funds are budget funds. The old state budget funds were basically the same with the central budget funds. State budget includes the general budget, the government fund budget, the state capital budget and the social security fund budget. All kinds of budgets for all funds invested in fixed assets were reported as state budget funds.

(2)Domestic loans refers to various funds borrowed by enterprises and institutions from banks and non-bank financial institutions during the reference period for the purpose of investment in fixed assets, including loans issued by banks from their self-owned funds and deposit, loans appropriated by higher responsible authorities, special loans by government (including loan for replacing petroleum with coal, special loan for reform-through-labour coal mines), loans arranged by local government from special funds, domestic reserve loan, and working loan, etc.

(3) Bond refers to company and finance institutions raising funds for investment in fixed assets by issuing various bond, including keystone enterprise bond and infrastructure bond issued by banks as agency of national professional investment company.

(4) Foreign Investment refers to foreign funds received during the reference period for the purpose of investment in fixed assets, including foreign funds borrowed and managed by the government, by individual units, foreign fund in joint venture program, and issue of bonds and stocks at the international financial markets. The foreign funds borrowed and managed by the government refer to foreign loans borrowed by the government from foreign governments, organizations, or financial institutions under official agreements signed by both parties, under which government is responsible for the repayment of both the principal and interests of the foreign loans.

(5)Self-raised funds refers to the fixed asset investment units received during the reporting period, by the enterprises and institutions to raise funds for investment in fixed assets, including various types of enterprises and institutions of its own funds and from other units raised funds for investment in fixed assets, but does not include all kinds of financial funds, borrowed funds from various financial institutions and foreign capital.

(6) Other sources of funding refers to the reporting period, in addition to all of these funds received outside funding for investment in fixed assets. Including social funds raised from individuals, donations, funds and funds transferred from other units.

□ Investment in Fixed Assets by Type of Construction

The construction projects in general can be classified, by the type of construction, into new construction, expansion, reconstruction and construction of living facilities.

(1) New construction in general refers to newly constructed enterprises, institutions, administrative agencies or independent projects from scratch. Construction in the existing enterprises, institutions or agencies is not considered as new construction. In case the asset of the existing unit is quite small, and the value of newly added fixed assets exceeds the original value of assets by three times, the expansion will be considered as new construction.

(2)Reconstruction and technical transformation refers to construction projects by existing enterprises or institutions in innovation or technical transformation of the old facilities (including auxiliary production equipment and welfare facilities). Also considered as Reconstruction and Technical Transformation is the construction of new workshops by the existing enterprises or institutions to change the variety of products to meet the market demand (such as the production of civil products by defense industries), or to bring the designed production capacity into full play through a more balanced production process on production lines. Technical transformation refers to replacement of old technology and equipment by new technology and equipment, in order to expand the reproduction through improvement of technology contents in production, to improve product quality, to promote new products, to save energy, to reduce consumption, to expand the production scale and to improve overall social-economic efficiency. Technical transformation contains the following contents: updating of machinery, equipment and tools; reforming production process by using energy or material saving technology; construction of workshops and transformation of public facilities; improvement of working conditions and environment, etc.

(3) Expansion refers to construction of new major production

EXPLANATORY NOTES TO MAJOR STATISTICAL INDICATORS

workshop, branch factory or independent production line within a factory or in other locations, for the purpose of increasing the production capacity (or improving efficiency) of the original products. Newly constructed houses for the operation of institutions and administrative organizations (such as the newly constructed buildings for teaching in schools, buildings for clinics or wards in hospitals, etc.) are also classified as expansion.

Also included in the expansion are investments by existing enterprises or institutions in building major production line(s) or branch factory (ies) along with some work on innovation, for the purpose of expending the production capacity of original products or producing new products.

(4) Simply constructing establishment for life refers to enterprises and administrative unit simply construct the employee's residence, nursery, children school, infirmary, bathroom and eatery, without expanding or rebuilding the productive engineering and operation houses.

□ Newly Increased Fixed Assets

Newly Increased Fixed Assets, also called fixed assets put into operation, refers to the value of fixed assets that has been put into production or handed over to the production units after the completion of the process of construction and purchase. The newly increased fixed asset is an value indicator of the result of investment. It is also the necessary data for reflecting the construction process and the result of investment in fixed assets.

□ Rate of Projects of Fixed Assets Completed and Put into Operation

Rate of Projects of Fixed Assets Completed and Put into Operation refers to the ratio of the newly increased fixed assets to the total investment made in the same period. This is a comprehensive indicator reflecting the speed of the employment of fixed assets and the investment efficiency at the macro-level. As the newly increase fixed assets is the result of a long period while the investment is completed in the current year, this indicator is expected to be used to reflect the employment of fixed assets over a long period of time.

□ Projects under Construction

Projects under Construction refer to projects with construction and installation activities undertaken in the reference period. All projects that have construction activities undertaken during the reference period are reported as projects under construction irrespective of the length of construction work. The number of projects under construction can reflect the actual size of investment in fixed assets during a given period, and when compared with the number of projects completed and put into use during the same period, it demonstrates the results of investment in fixed assets. Depending on the nature of construction activities, projects under construction can also be classified into projects under construction in current year, winding-up projects in current year and stopped or suspended projects in previous years (with preservation work in current year).

□ Projects Completed and Put into Use

Projects Completed and Put into Use Industrial projects refer to the major projects and accessory facilities completed which result in forming production capacity and have been checked and accepted while the living and welfare facilities have been completed and can ensure normal production and formally put into production. Non-industrial projects refer to the major projects and accessory facilities completed which possess the designed capacity and have been checked, accepted and formally put into production.

□ Rate of Construction Projects Completed and Put into Use

Rate of Construction Projects Completed and Put into Use refers to the ratio of the number of construction projects completed and put into use in certain period of time to the number of projects under construction in the same period. This reflects the investment efficiency from the perspective of the speed of projects construction.

□ Completion Rate of Floor Space of Buildings

Completion Rate of Floor Space of Buildings refers to the ratio of the floor space of buildings completed in certain period of time to the floor space of buildings under construction in the same period. This indicator reflects the investment result from the perspective of the speed of construction.

第八篇
CHAPTER 8

2016上海统计年鉴 SHANGHAI STATISTICAL YEARBOOK

对外经济贸易和旅游
FOREIGN ECONOMIC RELATIONS, TRADE AND TOURISM

简要说明

本篇资料综合反映主要年份上海市对外贸易、进出口商品检验、外商直接投资、对外直接投资、对外经济合作和旅游等方面的概况。

一、对外贸易部分

对外贸易统计范围是按照联合国国际贸易统计原则,采用专门贸易记录制,对凡能引起区域内物质资源存量增加或减少的进出口货物,除制度另有规定外,均列入统计。

主要内容包括:上海关区和上海市货物进出口的金额、国别、贸易方式、企业性质、产品类别等项目。

在按国别(地区)分的进、出口总额表中,出口货物按中华人民共和国关境外最终目的国(地区)统计,进口货物按中华人民共和国关境外原产国(地区)统计。

统计资料来源于上海海关,调查方法是全面调查。

二、进出口商品检验部分

进出口商品检验统计范围是涉及安全、卫生和环境保护等检验、检疫进出口商品目录范围内的所有商品。

主要内容包括:进口和出口商品检验批数、金额,不合格商品检验批数、金额等。

资料来源于上海出入境检验检疫局,调查方法是全面调查。

三、外商直接投资部分

外商直接投资统计范围是经上海工商行政管理机关注册登记，经各级商务部门批准和备案（中国(上海)自由贸易试验区)设立的中外合资经营企业、合作经营企业、外资企业、外商投资股份制企业、合作开发项目等具有法人资格的独立核算企业(包括港澳台地区投资企业),在上海从事经营活动的外国及港澳台地区企业及外国公司在中国境内设立的分支机构。

主要内容包括:外商直接投资方式、投资产业和国别地区等情况。

资料来源于上海市商务委员会,调查方法是全面调查。

四、对外直接投资部分

对外直接投资统计范围是境内投资主体通过直接投资在境外设立的各类公司型企业和非公司型企业。

主要内容包括:境内投资主体的单位数、核准投资额。

资料来源于上海市商务委员会,调查方法是全面调查。

五、对外经济合作部分

对外经济合作统计范围是经各级商务主管部门批准的从事对外承包和劳务合作业务并具有法人地位的对外承包、劳务合作企业。

主要内容包括:对外承包工程合同金额、完成营业额和对外劳务合作派出人员等。

资料来源于上海市商务委员会,调查方法是全面调查。

六、旅游部分

旅游统计范围是旅行社、星级饭店和旅游者。

主要内容包括:旅行社接待经营情况、旅游景点和星级饭店基本情况、国际旅游入境人数、国内旅游来沪人数和人均消费支出等。

统计调查方法:国内旅游者来沪人数和人均消费支出指标采取抽样调查方法,其余数据均为全面调查。

资料来源于上海市旅游局、上海出入境边防检查总站。

BRIEF INTRODUCTION

Data in this chapter reflect Shanghai's foreign trade, inspection of imports and exports, foreign direct investment, outbound direct investment, economic cooperation with foreign countries or territories as well as tourism in main years.

I. Foreign Trade

The scope of foreign trade statistics is in accordance with the United Nations' principles on international trade statistics, i.e.: all imports or exports that will lead to stock changes of material resources with the monitored territory; excluding goods by escape clause.

Data on foreign trade include: value of imports and exports through Shanghai ports, imports and exports by countries (regions), mode of trade, nature of trading companies, and product categories.

In the table on the total imports and exports classified by countries and regions, the exports are calculated at the Customs of the countries (regions) of destination and the imports are calculated at the Customs of the countries (regions) of origin.

Sources of data on foreign trade are complied from the Shanghai Customs through a comprehensive reporting system.

II. Inspection of Imports and Exports

The scope of imports and exports inspection includes all commodities that are under the catalog of imports and exports quarantine, related to safety, sanitation and environment protection issues.

Data on inspection of imports and exports include: lot number and value of imports and exports, lot number of ineligible commodities and their value.

Sources of data are from the Shanghai Entry–Exit Inspection and Quarantine Bureau through a comprehensive reporting system.

III. Foreign Direct Investment

The statistics of foreign direct investment cover all the Sino–foreign joint ventures, Sino–foreign cooperative enterprises, wholly–owned foreign enterprise, foreign–funded stock companies, Sino–foreign cooperative development projects (including the enterprises funded by the entrepreneurs from Hong Kong, Macao and Taiwan) with independent accounting system and legal person status, and all foreign enterprises or enterprises funded by the entrepreneurs from Hong Kong Macao and Taiwan which engaged in business activities in Shanghai, and branches of foreign companies which have been approved to be set up within the boundaries of the People's Republic of China after verification and registration through Shanghai's administrative authorities for industry and commerce, and approval and kept on record by the department of commerce at various levels.

Foreign direct investment includes: mode of foreign direct investment, investment by industry and countries (regions).

Sources of data are from the Shanghai Commission of Commerce through a comprehensive reporting system.

IV. Outbound Direct Investment

Outbound direct investment covers all types of overseas corporate and non–corporate enterprises set up by domes–

tic investors through direct investment.

It includes numbers of domestic investors and approved investment capital.

Data are from the Shanghai Commission of Commerce through comprehensive survey.

V. Foreign Economic Cooperationt

The scope of foreign economic cooperation covers enterprises engaged in contracted projects and labor services cooperation with foreign countries with approvals from the department of commerce at various levels.

Data on foreign economic cooperation include: contracted value of project, its revenue and labor services cooperation.

Data on foreign economic cooperation are from the Shanghai Commission of Commerce through a comprehensive reporting system.

VI. Tourism

The scope of tourism covers travel agencies, star–rated hotels and tourists.

Data on tourism include: operating conditions of the travel agencies, tourist attractions and star–rated hotels, the number of international tourists, the number of domestic tourists to Shanghai and consumption expenditure per capita.

Methodologies: sample survey method is used for domestic tourists to Shanghai and consumption expenditure per capita, and the rest are through a comprehensive reporting system.

Data are from the Shanghai Tourism Bureau and the Shanghai Entry–Exit Frontier Inspection Station.

表8.1 主要年份上海关区出口总额
TOTAL EXPORT TRADE VOLUME THROUGH CUSTOMS IN MAIN YEARS

单位:亿美元(100 million USD)

年份 Year	关区出口总额 Export Trade Volume Through Customs	其中 of which				
		#一般贸易 Ordinary Trade	来料加工装配贸易 Processing and Assembly Trade with Customers' Materials	进料加工贸易 Processing Trade with Imported Materials	对外承包工程货物 Construction Projects in Foreign Countries	出料加工贸易 Outward Processing Trade
1990	86.62	51.39	3.20	30.67	0.41	0.45
1995	256.07	149.16	14.31	90.12	0.63	0.06
2000	615.72	341.02	64.21	205.13	1.25	
2001	680.07	380.43	61.09	228.43	1.26	0.13
2002	818.03	473.13	66.88	266.72	1.44	0.13
2003	1 123.06	618.90	78.81	408.79	1.18	0.12
2004	1 612.68	824.92	126.99	623.27	3.18	0.14
2005	2 124.30	1 057.68	195.83	813.26	6.37	0.16
2006	2 665.65	1 319.56	212.77	1 058.07	9.45	0.14
2007	3 284.80	1 659.44	228.77	1 273.71	20.55	0.17
2008	3 936.50	2 050.49	240.91	1 467.78	53.92	0.23
2009	3 251.28	1 647.82	175.38	1 252.87	69.78	0.13
2010	4 233.40	2 183.98	178.52	1 639.70	60.55	0.09
2011	4 999.64	2 691.93	151.78	1 846.59	77.70	0.11
2012	4 911.56	2 722.62	137.52	1 718.06	72.14	0.12
2013	4 991.29	2 857.73	130.46	1 642.18	80.16	0.11
2014	5 232.12	3 112.37	126.18	1 601.78	85.04	0.05
2015	5 005.80	3 016.20	133.26	1 497.66	67.43	0.04

表8.2 主要年份上海关区进口总额
TOTAL IMPORT TRADE VOLUME THROUGH CUSTOMS IN MAIN YEARS

单位:亿美元(100 million USD)

年份 Year	关区进口总额 Import Trade Volume Through Customs	其中 of which				
		#一般贸易 Oridinary Trade	来料加工装配贸易 Processing and Assembly Trade with Customers' Materials	进料加工贸易 Processing Trade with Imported Materials	外商投资企业进口设备 Imported Equipment of Foreign Funded Enterprise	租赁贸易 Leasing Trade
1990	86.27	51.79	2.40	19.70	6.11	
1995	225.30	93.79	13.49	65.96	45.16	0.11
2000	477.39	212.65	44.87	125.13	40.26	2.47
2001	524.81	245.94	47.38	123.39	47.46	2.45
2002	606.98	267.66	48.12	160.91	54.95	1.89
2003	888.95	377.21	54.47	243.24	66.32	2.36
2004	1 213.07	472.16	89.47	338.57	99.72	4.70
2005	1 382.48	502.49	133.69	409.30	74.76	7.85
2006	1 621.89	574.40	122.52	497.41	73.72	23.74
2007	1 924.29	719.30	154.88	528.03	75.22	24.46
2008	2 129.07	848.23	174.86	525.68	76.91	22.21
2009	1 903.61	883.20	121.40	428.62	38.92	4.36
2010	2 613.05	1 209.42	169.36	552.83	43.81	18.56
2011	3 123.50	1 558.35	135.68	610.32	51.18	13.69
2012	3 101.54	1 516.96	123.06	553.38	33.00	10.79
2013	3 130.08	1 628.68	135.19	524.14	23.58	23.68
2014	3 402.43	1 777.08	164.31	568.61	26.63	40.52
2015	3 182.06	1 616.79	155.92	502.04	13.89	23.12

注：自2009年起，原口岸进出口商品总额改为上海关区进出口总额。
Note: Since 2009, Total Value of Port Imports and Exports have been changed to Total Trade Volume through Customs.

表8.3 主要年份按国别(地区)分的上海关区出口总额
TOTAL EXPORT TRADE VOLUME THROUGH CUSTOMS BY COUNTRIES AND REGIONS IN MAIN YEARS

单位:亿美元 (100 million USD)

国别(地区)	Country (Region)	2005	2010	2014	2015
总 计	**Total**	**2 124.30**	**4 233.40**	**5 232.12**	**5 005.80**
亚 洲	**Asia**	**898.90**	**1 653.96**	**2 196.84**	**2 145.10**
#中国香港	Hong Kong, China	160.72	210.46	259.82	260.67
中国台湾	Taiwan, China	59.81	112.52	150.85	137.00
日 本	Japan	298.78	442.82	526.67	474.49
韩 国	Republic of Korea	78.66	138.83	191.83	212.30
新加坡	Singapore	48.69	94.80	119.58	117.74
马来西亚	Malaysia	38.27	73.08	91.68	78.47
泰 国	Thailand	22.39	61.18	93.13	99.26
菲律宾	Philippines	16.58	29.43	47.19	49.70
巴基斯坦	Pakistan	8.07	16.12	28.68	32.55
科威特	Kuwait	1.40	4.05	5.73	5.48
沙特阿拉伯	Saudi Arabia	8.84	19.92	32.94	34.23
阿联酋	United Arab Emirates	23.24	44.97	54.21	49.20
非 洲	**Africa**	**53.42**	**130.79**	**178.39**	**168.00**
#埃 及	Egypt	5.89	12.11	15.08	16.43
苏 丹	Sudan	2.35	4.39	3.04	3.20
欧 洲	**Europe**	**505.52**	**1 095.67**	**1 134.42**	**1 033.36**
#德 国	Germany	99.69	214.67	197.06	186.34
法 国	France	44.84	110.42	81.86	75.35
意大利	Italy	42.81	118.34	91.32	84.83
荷 兰	Netherlands	75.62	154.89	173.80	167.30
英 国	United Kingdoms	59.10	117.88	141.10	142.14
瑞 典	Sweden	9.42	20.26	21.28	19.52
俄罗斯	Russia	18.60	59.95	88.47	55.68
美 洲	**America**	**618.05**	**1 234.11**	**1 574.53**	**1 510.83**
#美 国	United States	501.11	910.54	1 152.02	1 127.24
加拿大	Canada	42.58	74.81	84.63	75.11
巴 西	Brazil	14.61	75.44	96.42	76.11
智 利	Chile	7.26	20.47	27.78	25.89
大洋洲及太平洋岛屿	**Oceanic and Pacific Island**	**48.41**	**118.87**	**147.94**	**148.52**
#澳大利亚	Australia	41.94	95.45	126.26	118.27
新西兰	New Zealand	5.50	9.87	14.58	13.50

表8.4 主要年份按国别(地区)分的上海关区进口总额
TOTAL IMPORT TRADE VOLUME THROUGH CUSTOMS BY COUNTRIES AND REGIONS IN MAIN YEARS

单位:亿美元 (100 million USD)

国别(地区)	Country (Region)	2005	2010	2014	2015
总 计	**Total**	**1 382.48**	**2 613.05**	**3 402.43**	**3 182.06**
亚 洲	**Asia**	**873.45**	**1 477.09**	**1 691.70**	**1 599.12**
#中国香港	Hong Kong, China	17.41	17.05	14.88	8.97
中国台湾	Taiwan, China	155.56	210.86	245.69	225.94
日 本	Japan	267.91	473.84	447.71	393.87
韩 国	Republic of Korea	163.95	279.87	336.61	346.03
新加坡	Singapore	44.30	51.61	69.77	73.92
马来西亚	Malaysia	43.88	117.63	124.64	120.27
泰 国	Thailand	36.53	63.19	64.28	62.99
菲律宾	Philippines	36.08	36.47	37.83	33.81
巴基斯坦	Pakistan	2.15	3.24	4.85	3.81
科威特	Kuwait	0.23	0.71	0.71	0.47
沙特阿拉伯	Saudi Arabia	4.01	8.28	16.21	14.08
阿联酋	United Arab Emirates	0.95	1.85	5.32	5.38
非 洲	**Africa**	**13.76**	**41.85**	**53.62**	**37.10**
#埃 及	Egypt	0.44	1.31	0.96	0.94
南 非	South Africa	6.62	16.60	19.17	14.04
欧 洲	**Europe**	**264.89**	**619.42**	**994.57**	**924.88**
德 国	Germany	103.93	248.28	347.93	297.18
法 国	France	28.81	53.72	89.53	80.22
意大利	Italy	23.91	51.07	79.69	70.69
荷 兰	Netherlands	8.17	15.19	22.80	24.85
英 国	United Kingdoms	15.62	37.69	86.32	70.31
瑞 典	Sweden	11.94	28.75	36.14	34.62
俄罗斯	Russia	8.30	22.93	26.07	34.56
美 洲	**America**	**202.70**	**420.66**	**545.25**	**509.48**
#美 国	United States	139.52	268.76	341.85	344.59
加拿大	Canada	14.89	27.89	27.82	25.09
巴 西	Brazil	13.08	19.03	23.52	21.62
智 利	Chile	18.42	63.82	78.95	57.45
大洋洲及太平洋岛屿	**Oceanic and Pacific Island**	**27.50**	**53.73**	**116.22**	**110.72**
#澳大利亚	Australia	23.79	45.35	97.03	96.07
新西兰	New Zealand	3.04	8.33	18.94	14.40
其 他	**Others**	**0.18**	**0.30**	**1.06**	**0.74**

注:其他为无国别数(以下同)。
Note: Others refer to regions without sovereignty(Same as follows).

表8.5 主要年份上海市进出口总额
TOTAL VALUE OF FOREIGN TRADE IMPORTS AND EXPORTS IN MAIN YEARS

年份 Year	上海市进出口总额（亿美元）Total Value of Foreign Trade Imports and Exports (100 million USD)	上海市进口总额（亿美元）Total Value of Foreign Trade Imports (100 million USD)	上海市出口总额（亿美元）Total Value of Foreign Trade Exports (100 million USD)	进出口差额（亿美元）Balance (100 million USD)	进出口总额相当于生产总值的比例(%) Foreign Trade Imports and Export as Percentage of Gross Domestic Product(%)	出口总额相当于生产总值的比例(%) Foreign Trade Export as Percentage of Gross Domestic Product(%)
1990	74.31	21.10	53.21	32.11	47.0	33.6
1995	190.25	74.48	115.77	41.29	63.6	38.7
1996	222.63	90.25	132.38	42.13	62.6	37.2
1997	247.64	100.40	147.24	46.84	59.7	35.5
1998	313.44	153.88	159.56	5.68	68.3	34.8
1999	386.04	198.19	187.85	-10.34	76.3	37.1
2000	547.10	293.56	253.54	-40.02	94.9	44.0
2001	608.98	332.70	276.28	-56.42	96.7	43.9
2002	726.64	406.09	320.55	-85.54	104.8	46.2
2003	1 123.97	639.15	484.82	-154.33	139.0	59.9
2004	1 600.26	865.06	735.20	-129.86	164.1	75.4
2005	1 863.65	956.23	907.42	-48.81	166.6	81.1
2006	2 274.89	1 139.16	1 135.73	-3.43	174.9	87.3
2007	2 829.73	1 390.45	1 439.28	48.83	179.3	91.2
2008	3 221.38	1 527.88	1 693.50	165.62	163.3	85.9
2009	2 777.31	1 358.17	1 419.14	60.97	127.3	65.1
2010	3 688.69	1 880.85	1 807.84	-73.01	148.0	72.5
2011	4 374.36	2 276.47	2 097.89	-178.58	147.2	70.6
2012	4 367.58	2 299.51	2 068.07	-231.44	136.6	64.7
2013	4 413.98	2 371.54	2 042.44	-329.10	126.6	58.6
2014	4 666.22	2 563.45	2 102.77	-460.68	121.6	54.8
2015	4 517.33	2 547.64	1 969.69	-577.95	111.7	48.7

注：1999 年以前外贸进口、出口商品总额为外经贸委统计口径，1999 年以后为海关统计的上海企业进口、出口总额（以下同）。
Note: Before 1999, the figures of Shanghai's foreign trade imports and exports were based on statistics from Shanghai Foreign Trade and Economic Cooperation Commission. Since 1999, the figures representing imports and exports are made by Shanghai enterprises through Shanghai Custom. Same as follows.

表8.6 主要年份上海市出口总额
TOTAL VALUE OF FOREIGN TRADE EXPORTS IN MAIN YEARS

单位：亿美元（100 million USD）

指标	Indicators	2000	2010	2014	2015
出口总额	**Total Value of Exports**	**253.54**	**1 807.84**	**2 102.77**	**1 969.69**
按企业性质分	**Grouped by Different Enterprises**				
#国有企业	State-owned Enterprises	106.78	307.67	279.17	254.26
外商投资企业	Foreign-funded Enterprises	142.61	1 259.74	1 415.62	1 320.55
按贸易方式分	**Grouped by Trade Modes**				
#一般贸易	Original Trade	101.72	632.74	879.73	838.98
加工贸易	Processing Trade	147.83	1 003.74	919.88	842.59
按产品类别分	**Grouped by Different Products**				
#机电产品	Electrical and Mechanical Products	121.43	1 311.14	1 456.08	1 380.30
#高新技术产品	High-tech Products		841.11	890.63	861.55

表8.7 主要年份按国别(地区)分的上海市出口总额
TOTAL VALUE OF FOREIGN TRADE EXPORTS BY COUNTRIES AND REGIONS IN MAIN YEARS

单位:亿美元 (100 million USD)

国别(地区)	Country (Region)	2000	2010	2014	2015
总　计	**Total**	**253.54**	**1 807.84**	**2 102.77**	**1 969.69**
亚　洲	**Asia**	**129.10**	**725.93**	**934.53**	**911.33**
#中国香港	Hong Kong, China	23.02	134.09	184.65	193.43
中国台湾	Taiwan, China	5.67	56.54	66.82	61.23
日　本	Japan	60.81	196.46	233.13	213.22
韩　国	Republic of Korea	10.59	58.92	71.62	84.80
新加坡	Singapore	7.88	59.01	78.64	70.17
马来西亚	Malaysia	2.59	42.52	44.27	35.78
泰　国	Thailand	2.48	24.14	33.24	34.93
巴基斯坦	Pakistan	0.55	3.08	5.53	6.91
科威特	Kuwait	0.20	1.53	1.81	1.86
沙特阿拉伯	Saudi Arabia	1.14	5.72	9.94	8.60
阿拉伯联合酋长国	United Arab Emirates	1.79	20.67	21.31	18.16
非　洲	**Africa**	**5.63**	**40.98**	**44.86**	**41.80**
#埃　及	Egypt	0.44	3.28	4.52	4.10
苏　丹	Sudan	0.22	1.21	0.93	0.80
阿尔及利亚	Algeria	0.09	1.29	1.65	2.42
摩洛哥	Morocco	0.20	0.97	0.86	1.00
欧　洲	**Europe**	**45.62**	**450.72**	**428.66**	**387.61**
#德　国	Germany	9.48	86.05	73.93	69.52
法　国	France	4.50	60.97	27.81	24.64
意大利	Italy	4.98	36.99	29.87	27.40
荷　兰	Netherlands	6.16	77.61	92.49	90.69
比利时	Belgium	2.95	16.70	13.62	12.41
英　国	United Kingdoms	7.07	43.11	51.81	56.45
俄罗斯	Russia	0.37	21.15	30.17	17.08
美　洲	**America**	**67.82**	**532.30**	**626.66**	**559.97**
#美　国	United States	56.25	409.91	498.45	455.79
加拿大	Canada	4.04	27.80	28.23	20.99
巴　西	Brazil	1.06	26.95	25.59	18.98
古　巴	Cuba	0.07	0.90	0.62	0.97
大洋洲及太平洋岛屿	**Oceanic and Pacific Island**	**5.37**	**57.91**	**68.07**	**68.99**
#澳大利亚	Australia	4.74	45.59	58.27	50.18

表8.8 主要年份按国别(地区)分的上海市进口总额
TOTAL VALUE OF FOREIGN TRADE IMPORTS BY COUNTRIES AND REGIONS IN MAIN YEARS

单位:亿美元 (100 million USD)

国别(地区)	Country (Region)	2000	2010	2014	2015
总　计	**Total**	**293.56**	**1 880.85**	**2 563.45**	**2 547.64**
亚　洲	**Asia**	**161.59**	**1 041.98**	**1 196.76**	**1 185.14**
#中国香港	Hong Kong, China	16.68	12.61	7.90	21.26
中国台湾	Taiwan, China	19.44	150.05	164.75	155.65
日　本	Japan	70.43	308.71	311.75	285.39
韩　国	Republic of Korea	20.63	146.41	190.84	202.03
新加坡	Singapore	9.39	39.42	49.21	57.95
马来西亚	Malaysia	6.49	107.75	111.93	111.38
泰　国	Thailand	4.35	53.09	46.23	44.71
菲律宾	Philippines	1.83	33.44	32.68	28.14
科威特	Kuwait	0.22	0.94	0.92	0.43
沙特阿拉伯	Saudi Arabia	0.78	7.23	11.19	6.98
阿拉伯联合酋长国	United Arab Emirates	0.40	2.11	9.21	9.44
非　洲	**Africa**	**1.89**	**28.19**	**42.63**	**35.47**
欧　洲	**Europe**	**63.36**	**400.75**	**766.61**	**755.13**
#德　国	Germany	26.59	140.61	249.39	224.72
法　国	France	7.95	42.54	74.94	69.21
意大利	Italy	4.81	36.46	60.35	55.14
荷　兰	Netherlands	2.43	11.06	16.91	20.50
比利时	Belgium	2.83	25.08	39.61	21.17
英　国	United Kingdoms	3.76	23.43	94.57	64.38
瑞　士	Switzerland	2.22	29.87	81.75	146.27
瑞　典	Sweden	4.53	15.77	18.90	18.81
美　洲	**America**	**58.60**	**344.63**	**432.46**	**445.44**
#美　国	United States	40.11	202.75	265.53	285.31
加拿大	Canada	7.03	20.90	25.85	28.89
巴　西	Brazil	4.11	40.89	35.94	43.31
大洋洲及太平洋岛屿	**Oceanic and Pacific Island**	**8.07**	**65.13**	**124.17**	**125.91**
#澳大利亚	Australia	6.68	56.25	106.37	113.29
新西兰	New Zealand	1.25	7.48	17.27	11.81
其　他	**Others**	**0.05**	**0.17**	**0.82**	**0.55**

表8.9 主要年份进出口商品检验情况
IMPORTS AND EXPORTS INSPECTION IN MAIN YEARS

指标	Indicators	2000	2010	2014	2015
进口商品检验	**Imports Inspection**				
检验批数(批)	Groups of Inspection(group)	51 940	1 205 446	1 492 507	1 576 130
检验金额(亿美元)	Values of Inspection(100 million USD)	76.16	1 326.68	1 586.40	1 402.54
不合格批数(批)	Unqualified Groups (group)	1 539	5 562	43 495	81 641
占检验批数比重(%)	Percentage in Total (%)	3.0	0.5	2.9	5.2
不合格金额(亿美元)	Unqualified Values (100 million USD)	0.99	9.75	53.21	52.05
占检验金额比重(%)	Percentage in Total (%)	1.3	0.7	3.4	3.7
出口商品检验	**Exports Inspection**				
检验批数(批)	Groups of Inspection(group)	344 138	728 946	166 582	157 015
检验金额(亿美元)	Values of Inspection(100 million USD)	100.86	238.80	93.84	70.64
不合格批数(批)	Unqualified Groups (group)	564	202	360	1 558
不合格金额(亿美元)	Unqualified Values (100 million USD)	0.11	0.06	0.09	0.72

表8.10 主要年份外商直接投资情况
FOREIGN DIRECT INVESTMENT IN MAIN YEARS

指标	Indicators	2000	2010	2014	2015
合同项目(个)	**Number of Contracts (item)**	**1 814**	**3 906**	**4 697**	**6 007**
#合资企业	Joint Ventures	441	445	887	1 391
合作企业	Cooperative Ventures	226	14	7	6
独资企业	Sole-foreign Funded Enterprises	1 146	3 443	3 796	4 600
合同金额(亿美元)	**Contracted Foreign Capital (100 million USD)**	**63.90**	**153.07**	**316.09**	**589.43**
#合资企业	Joint Ventures	13.86	21.54	70.13	101.76
合作企业	Cooperative Ventures	5.86	1.11	1.91	2.71
独资企业	Sole-foreign Funded Enterprises	44.14	128.17	230.19	457.41
实到金额(亿美元)	**Foreign Investment Actually Absorbed (100 million USD)**	**31.60**	**111.21**	**181.66**	**184.59**
#合资企业	Joint Ventures	12.94	17.84	21.92	39.27
合作企业	Cooperative Ventures	2.99	1.69	8.29	5.37
独资企业	Sole-foreign Funded Enterprises	15.67	90.71	151.15	138.34

表8.11 外商直接投资合同项目和金额（2015）
NUMBER OF CONTRACTS SIGNED AND VALUES OF FOREIGN DIRECT INVESTMENT PROJECTS

类别	Types	合同项目（个）Number of Contracts (item)		合同金额（亿美元）Contracted Foreign Capital (100 million USD)		实到金额（亿美元）Foreign Investment Actually Absorbed (100 million USD)	
		2015	至2015年底累计 Total by the End of 2015	2015	至2015年底累计 Total by the End of 2015	2015	至2015年底累计 Total by the End of 2015
总　计	**Total**	**6 007**	**82 415**	**589.43**	**3 330.53**	**184.59**	**1 876.18**
#1 000万美元以上项目	**Projects of Over 10 Million USD**	**1 233**		**525.97**			
按投资方式分	**Grouped by Investment Mode**						
#合资企业	Joint Ventures	1 391	20 620	101.76	686.75	39.27	450.80
合作企业	Cooperative Ventures	6	5 130	2.71	168.40	5.37	119.79
独资企业	Sole-foreign Funded Enterprises	4 600	56 453	457.41	2 381.23	138.34	1 270.73
按产业分	**Grouped by Industry**						
第一产业	Primary Industry	4	318	0.61	6.92	0.21	4.21
第二产业	Secondary Industry	89	26 470	19.59	937.17	25.00	566.34
#工　业	Industry	71	25 517	18.95	913.64	24.90	558.94
第三产业	Tertiary Industry	5 914	55 627	545.00	2 350.47	159.38	1 305.63
按主要国别（地区）分	**Grouped by Country and Region**						
#中国香港	Hong Kong, China	2 589	26 565	409.36	1 575.94	112.95	748.31
中国澳门	Macao, China	12	298	0.93	6.39	0.04	2.19
中国台湾	Taiwan, China	627	8 803	6.56	77.49	0.57	48.38
日　本	Japan	232	10 086	4.45	252.43	4.89	195.89
韩　国	Republic of Korea	375	3 327	5.68	38.71	1.58	20.97
新加坡	Singapore	282	4 186	27.76	196.44	21.70	119.51
泰　国	Thailand	18	274	0.35	4.36	0.02	2.81
德　国	Germany	153	2 059	10.99	97.31	4.30	64.88
英　国	United Kingdoms	123	1 432	4.09	36.15	0.48	25.02
法　国	France	105	948	1.79	38.08	1.26	24.12
意大利	Italy	73	1 021	0.85	11.91	0.88	7.35
美　国	United States	382	8 158	15.95	194.44	10.02	132.06
加拿大	Canada	110	1 367	1.33	12.52	0.13	5.66
澳大利亚	Australia	112	1 451	1.05	15.17	0.05	6.89

表8.12 主要年份引进技术设备实际到货金额
ARRIVED CAPITAL THROUGH IMPORTED TECHNOLOGY AND EQUIPMENT IN MAIN YEARS

单位:万美元(10 000 USD)

国　别(地区)	Country(Region)	2000	2010	2014	2015
总　计	**Total**	**104 558**	**3 903 807**	**6 049 362**	**5 340 179**
#中国香港	Hong Kong, China	10 746	17 414	9 973	7 246
日　本	Japan	10 069	886 132	898 478	792 788
德　国	Germany	16 314	814 006	1 366 323	1 227 568
意大利	Italy	622	123 823	193 662	156 763
美　国	United States	49 431	427 275	629 645	670 077
瑞　士	Switzerland	1 862	126 605	164 335	146 838
英　国	United Kingdoms	712	85 649	726 648	424 994
瑞　典	Sweden	639	72 594	75 138	91 175
奥地利	Austria	1 162	31 804	44 764	39 621
法　国	France	1 926	98 172	128 215	177 119

表8.13 对外承包工程和劳务合作(2012~2015)
OVERSEAS CONTRACTED PROJECTS AND LABOR SERVICES COOPERATION

指　标	Indicators	2012	2013	2014	2015
对外承包工程	**Overseas Contracted Projects**				
签订合同金额(亿美元)	Value of Contract (100 million USD)	103.11	108.16	108.90	111.00
实际营业额(亿美元)	Actual Business Volume (100 million USD)	68.12	80.69	74.00	74.55
派出人员(人次)	Dispatched Persons (person-time)	3 477	4 337	8 532	5 866
对外劳务合作	**Overseas Labor Services Cooperation**				
派出人员(人次)	Dispatched Persons (person-time)	17 767	13 695	18 163	14 369

表8.14 海外企业情况(2014～2015)
ENTERPRISES ABROAD

指　标	Indicators	2014年新增 Established in 2014	至2014年底累计 Total by the End of 2014	2015年新增 Established in 2015	至2015年底累计 Total by the End of 2015
项　目(个)	Number of Projects (unit)	594	2 870	1 338	4 208
投资额(万美元)	Investment Value (10 000 USD)	1 229 253	3 018 278	5 732 462	8 750 470

表8.15 国际会展(2012～2015)
INTERNATIONAL CONFERENCE AND EXHIBITION

指　标	Indicators	2012	2013	2014	2015
举办国际会展个数(个)	International Exhibit(time)	265	247	258	292
国际会展展出总面积(万平方米)	Total Square of International Exhibit (10 000 sq. m)	826.90	874.50	930.20	1 124.06

注：2015年前，本表数据由上海市会展行业协会提供，2015年起本表数据由上海市商务委提供。
Note: Data in this table before 2015 are provided by Shanghai Convention & Exibition Industries Association. Since 2015, data in this table are providede by Shanghai Commossion of Comnerce.

表8.16 主要年份旅行社接待经营情况
TOURISTS RECEIVED BY TOUR AGENCIES IN MAIN YEARS

指　标	Indicators	2005	2010	2014	2015
接待境内外来沪旅游者(万人次)	**Overseas and Domestic Tourists (10 000 person-times)**	**750.89**	**1 239.28**	**763.08**	**816.00**
境外旅游者	Overseas Tourists	95.11	158.25	78.51	64.16
#外国人	Foreigners	90.01	147.79	68.27	56.15
中国香港	Tourists from Hong Kong, China	1.48	4.47	3.62	3.23
中国澳门	Tourists from Macao, China	0.01	0.08	2.68	1.79
中国台湾	Tourists from Taiwan, China	3.51	5.91	3.95	2.98
境内旅游者	Domestic Tourists	655.88	1 081.03	684.57	751.85
出境旅游者(万人次)	**Tourists Going Abroad (10 000 person-times)**	**51.71**	**116.86**	**242.30**	**393.34**
经营和财务状况	**Operation and Financial Status**				
营业收入(亿元)	Operational Revenues(100 million yuan)	132.43	341.88	723.73	826.72
利润总额(亿元)	Total Profits(100 million yuan)	1.61	4.02	0.51	0.31

表8.17 主要年份旅游景点基本情况
BASIC STATISTICS OF SCENIC SPOTS IN MAIN YEARS

指 标	Indicators	2005	2010	2014	2015
A级旅游景点数(家)	Scenic Spots of A Level and above(unit)	18	61	89	98
#5A级景点	AAAAA-Level		3	3	3
4A级景点	AAAA-Level	17	28	46	51
红色旅游基地数(个)	**Red Travelling Base(unit)**		**30**	**34**	**34**
#全国红色旅游基地	National Red Travelling Base		8	9	9

表8.18 主要年份国内旅游者来沪人数和人均消费支出
NUMBER OF DOMESTIC TOURISTS VISITING SHANGHAI AND PER CAPITA CONSUMPTION EXPENDITURES IN MAIN YEARS

指 标	Indicators	2005	2010	2014	2015
国内旅游者来沪人数(万人次)	**Number of Domestic Tourists Visiting Shanghai(10 000 person-times)**	**9 012**	**22 432**	**26 818**	**27 569**
外省市来沪旅游人数	Number of Tourists from other Provinces Visiting Shanghai	6 805	11 255	13 041	13 924
本市市民在本地旅游人数	Number of Local Tourists	2 207	11 177	13 777	13 645
国内旅游者人均消费支出(元)	**Consumption Expenditure Per Person (yuan)**	**1 452**	**1 175**	**1 099**	**1 087**
#长途交通费	Long-distance Traffic Expenditure	176	139	132	143
住宿费	Accommodation Expenditure	219	168	148	152
餐饮费	Food Expenditure	220	153	148	154
购物费	**Shopping Expenditure**	**553**	**453**	**406**	**383**
门票费	Ticket Expenditure	96	131	131	125
娱乐费	Entertainment Expenditure	30	42	39	34
市内交通费	**Local Traffic Expenditure**	**88**	**53**	**47**	**48**
邮电通信费	Post and Telecommunications Expenditure	37	14	7	6

注：本表为抽样调查资料。
Note: Data in this table are from the sampling survey.

表8.19　旅游星级饭店基本情况(2015)
BASIC STATISTICS OF STAR-RATED TOURISM HOTELS

	指　标 Indicators	合　计 Total	五星级 Five-Star	四星级 Four-Star	三星级 Three-Star	二星级 Two-Star	一星级 One-Star
饭店数(个)	Number of Hotels(unit)	247	68	66	82	30	1
客房数(万间)	Number of Rooms (10 000 rooms)	6.12	2.79	1.86	1.20	0.26	0.01
床位数(万张)	Number of Beds (10 000 beds)	9.23	3.89	2.88	2.01	0.43	0.01
客房平均出租率(%)	Average Occupancy Rate (%)	65.5	65.4	68.3	60.2	69.4	54.9
营业收入(亿元)	Business Revenues (100 million yuan)	198.15	125.90	53.07	16.73	2.47	0.03
平均房价 (元/间天)	Average Room Rates (yuan/room. day)	686	970	514	334	240	157

表8.20　主要年份国际旅游入境人数
NUMBER OF OVERSEAS TOURISTS THROUGH SHANGHAI CUSTOM IN MAIN YEARS

	指　标 Indicators	2000	2010	2014	2015
国际旅游入境人数 (万人次)	**Number of Overseas Tourists Through Shanghai Custom(10 000 person-times)**	**181.40**	**851.12**	**791.30**	**800.16**
#外国人	Foreigner	139.14	665.63	611.14	614.64
#日　本	Japanese	53.76	152.47	101.28	92.93
新加坡	Singaporean	5.29	23.50	21.72	19.85
德　国	German	7.11	29.52	31.93	29.97
法　国	French	5.39	24.86	21.81	20.42
英　国	Briton	1.69	20.94	22.77	21.70
意大利	Italian	1.88	11.49	12.20	11.92
加拿大	Canadian	2.25	20.97	17.19	18.90
美　国	American	13.78	80.79	77.42	77.08
澳大利亚	Australian	3.23	21.33	20.59	19.05
港澳同胞	Hong Kong and Macao Chinese	17.62	77.47	66.94	67.53
台湾同胞	Taiwanese	19.88	108.02	113.22	117.99
平均每天来沪旅游人数 (人次/天)	**Average Number of Tourists Visiting Shanghai Everyday (person-time/day)**	**4 970**	**23 382**	**21 679**	**21 922**
来沪旅游者平均逗留天数 (天/人)	**Average Time Tourists Staying in Shanghai (day/person)**	**3.92**	**3.51**	**3.24**	**3.30**
国际旅游(外汇)收入 (亿美元)	**Foreign Exchange Earnings from International Tourism(100 million USD)**	**16.13**	**64.05**	**57.05**	**59.60**

上/海/统/计/年/鉴

主要统计指标解释

关区进出口总额

指在上海海关办理进出口申报手续的进出口商品总额。统计方法依据联合国的国际贸易统计原则,反映进出上海而引起物质资源储备增加或减少的商品运动。按上述原则应具备条件:实际进出上海(海关关境),不仅包括经商业交易行为的进出口货品,也包括援助、捐赠等未发生买卖关系的货品价值。出口按离岸价(FOB)统计,进口按到岸价(CIF)统计。

上海市进出口总额

指海关统计中按经营单位即进出口企业在海关注册地的行政区域口径统计的数据,它反映的是上海行政辖区内各类具有进出口经营权企业(外贸企业)的进出口。它不包含外省市外贸企业途经上海口岸由上海海关结关放行及统计的进出口商品,但包含上海外贸企业经由非上海口岸进出口结关放行及统计的商品。

外商直接投资

指外国企业和经济组织或个人(包括华侨、港澳台胞以及我国在境外注册的企业)按我国有关政策、法规,用现汇、实物、技术等在我国境内开办外商独资企业、与我国境内的企业或经济组织共同举办中外合资经营企业、合作经营企业或合作开发资源的投资(包括外商投资收益的再投资)以及企业投资总额内直接投资者对企业的贷款,即外方股东贷款。

反映外商直接投资状况的指标主要有三个:外商直接投资合同项目、外商直接投资合同金额、外商直接投资实际到位金额。

引进技术

指通过贸易途径从国外获得发展我国国民经济和提高技术水平所需要的技术装备。引进方式有:许可证贸易(技术贸易)、生产线(包括成套设备)、单机(包括关键设备)、软硬件结合(同时引进技术和设备)和其他。

对外承包工程

对外承包工程包括各对外承包公司以招标议标承包方式承揽的下列业务:(1)承包国外工程建设项目。(2)承包我国对外经济援助项目。(3)承包我国驻外机构的工程建设项目。(4)承包我国境内利用外资进行建设的工程项目。(5)与外国承包公司合营或联合承包工程项目时我国公司分包部分。(6)以服务成果向业主收费的技术服务项目(包括承担地形地貌测绘;地质资源勘探与普查;建设区域规划;提供设计文件、图纸、生产工艺技术资料和工程技术经济咨询;工程项目的可行性考察、研究和评估;进行技术指导和培训人员等)。(7)对外承包兼营的房屋开发业务。对外承包工程的营业额是以货币表现的本期内完成的对外承包工程的工作量,包括以前年度签订的合同和本年度新签订的合同在报告期完成的工作量。

对外劳务合作

指以收取工资的形式向业主或承包商提供技术和劳动服务的活动。上海对外承包公司在境外开办的合营企业,上海公司同时又提供劳务的,其劳务部分也纳入劳务合作统计。劳务合作营业额按报告期内向雇主提交的结算数(包括工资、加班费和奖金等)统计。

国际旅游入境人数

指来上海参观、访问、旅行、探亲、访友、休养、考察、参加会议或从事经济、科技、文化、教育、体育、宗教等活动的外国人、华侨、港澳和台湾同胞的人数。不包括来上海常住1年以上的外国专家、留学生等。上海入境的境外旅游人数包括从上海口岸入境的境外旅游人数和从我国其他口岸入境来沪的境外旅游人数。

国际旅游(外汇)收入

指入境旅游的外国人和华侨港澳台同胞在上海旅游过程中发生的一切旅游支出。

EXPLANATORY NOTES TO MAJOR STATISTICAL INDICATORS

□ Total Trade Volume Through Customs

Total Trade Volume through Customes refers to the aggregate volume of commodities that are conducted declaration procedure through Shanghai's ports. The statistics method follows the international trade statistics principles set by the United Nations. It reflects the fluctuation of Shanghai's material reserves caused by export or import. Requirements involved in the principle is: the commodities refer to those enter or leave Shanghai's ports, including not only the business trading activities but also the commodities value of the aid and donations that haven't been involved in sales . Exports are calculated according to FOB price, and imports are calculated according to CIF.

□ Total Value of Foreign Trade Imports and Exports of Shanghai

Total Value of Foreign Trade Imports and Exports of Shanghai is offered by Customs authorities, covering the operation units, or the enterprises involved in import and export, that have registered in the administrative regions where the Customs operate. It reflects the import and export of all the enterprises with import and export rights (foreign trade enterprises) under the administration of Shanghai Municipality. It excludes those commodities of foreign trade enterprises from out of town that underwent customs clearance at Shanghai ports but includes commodities of foreign trade enterprises of Shanghai that underwent customs clearance in non-Shanghai ports.

□ Foreign Direct Investment

Foreign Direct Investment refers to the investments made inside China by foreign enterprises and economic organizations or individuals (including overseas Chinese, compatriots in Hong Kong, Macao and Chinese enterprises registered abroad), in line with the relevant policies and laws of China, for the establishment of wholly foreign-owned enterprises, and joint ventures or development projects launched in China (including re-investment of profits from foreign businesses), and the funds that enterprises borrow from abroad in the total investment of projects which are approved by the relevant departments of the governments and the loans from the direct investors within the total investment of the projects, i.e., foreign shareholders' loans.

There are three main indicators that reflect the status of foreign direct investment: signed contracts of foreign direct investment, contracted foreign capital and foreign investment actually absorbed.

□ Import of Technology

Import of Technology refers to technology and equipments obtained through the trade channel from other countries which are needed for advancing China's national economy and improving its technological level. The import form includes: licensing (technological trade), production lines (including complete plant), single machine (including key equipments), combination of hardware and software (importing technology and equipments simultaneously) and others.

□ Overseas Contracted Projects

Overseas Contracted Projects refer to projects undertaken by Chinese contractors (project contracting companies) through bidding process. They include: (1) overseas civil engineering construction projects financed by foreign investors. (2) overseas projects financed by the Chinese government through its foreign-aid programs. (3) construction projects of Chinese diplomatic missions, trade offices and other institutions stationed abroad. (4) construction projects in China financed by foreign investment. (5) sub-contracted projects to be taken by Chinese contractors through a joint umbrella project with foreign contractor (s). (6) technical assistance projects in the form of service results and chargeable to the owners (such as topographic surveying, geological prospecting, development zone programming, provision of documents, blueprint, materials on production process, technical consultation, project feasibility studies and evaluation, personnel training, etc.). and (7) housing development projects. The business turnover from international contracting is the work of contracted projects completed during the reporting period, expressed in monetary terms, including completed work on project contracts signed in previous years.

□ Overseas Labor Service Cooperation

Overseas Labor Service Cooperation refers to activities of providing technology and labor services to employers or contrac-

EXPLANATORY NOTES TO MAJOR STATISTICAL INDICATORS

tors by collecting salaries and wages. Labor services provided by Shanghai's international contrasting corporations to their overseas joint ventures shall be included into the statistics of overseas services. The business turn over of overseas labor services is the settlement price (including salaries, overtime pay and bonuses) submitted to the employers during the reporting period.

□ Number of Overseas Tourists to Shanghai

Number of Overseas Tourists to Shanghai refers to the number of foreigners, overseas Chinese, and compatriots from Hong Kong, Macao and Taiwan coming to Shanghai for sightseeing, visits, tours, family reunions, meeting friends, vacations, study tours, attending meetings and other activities of an economic, scientific and technological, cultural, physical culture and religious nature. This does not include foreign experts and students residing in Shanghai for over 1 year. The number of overseas tourists to Shanghai includes those overseas tourists entering China through Shanghai customs and through customs other than Shanghai.

□ Foreign Exchange Earnings from International Tourism

Foreign Exchange Earnings from International Tourism refer to the total expenditures of foreigners, overseas Chinese, Chinese compatriots from Hong Kong, Macao and Taiwan during their stay in Shanghai.

第九篇
CHAPTER 9

价格水平
PRICES

简要说明

一、本篇资料的主要内容

本篇价格指数资料,反映生产、流通、消费、投资与交易等环节的价格变动趋势和变动幅度。主要包括居民消费价格指数、商品零售价格指数、工业生产者出厂价格指数、工业生产者购进价格指数、固定资产投资价格指数。

二、本篇的资料来源

价格指数编制由国家统计局上海调查总队组织实施，依据国家统计局统一制定的价格统计调查制度,由上海调查总队直接或通过区县调查队从基层采集原始价格数据汇总后上报。

三、居民消费、商品零售价格指数

编制居民消费、商品零售价格指数的资料采用抽样调查和重点调查相结合的方法取得,即在全市选择不同经济区域和分布合理的商品销售或服务网点,以及有代表性的商品或服务作为样本,对其市场价格进行定期调查,以样本推断总体。目前,居民消费、商品零售价格调查已涉及全市全部 16 个区县。

1. 价格调查网点的抽选方法:对全市消费市场进行摸底调查、掌握市场的基本情况(经营品种、销售额等指标)基础上,将各种类型的商场(店)、超市、农贸市场、服务网点以销售额(成交额或经营规模)为标志，从高到低排队，依据所需调查网点的数量进行等距抽样。选择经营品种齐全、销售额大的商场(店)、超市、农贸市场、服务网点作为价格调查网点。

2. 代表规格品根据全市的消费情况确定,必须遵循以下原则:⑴选择消费量较大的消费项目;⑵价格变动趋势和变动程度有较强的代表性,即选中规格品与未选中规格品的价格变动特征愈相关愈好;⑶在市场销售份额大体相等的情况下,同一基本分类的规格品之间,性质差异愈大愈好,价格变动特征的相关性愈低愈好;⑷生产和销售前景较好;⑸选中的工业消费品必须是合格产品,工业产品包装上必须有注册商标、产地、规格等级等标识。

目前,居民消费价格调查分为 8 大类,262 个基本分类,全市每月共调查 1300 种以上的规格品价格;商品零售价格分为 16 个大类,229 个基本分类,全市每月调查 1000 种以上的规格品价格。

3. 价格调查方法:居民消费、商品零售价格调查是非全面调查,主要方法是定人、定点、定时直接调查。

4. 权数的确定:居民消费价格指数的权数主要根据全市城镇居民家庭消费支出构成确定;商品零售价格指数的权数主要根据全市社会商品零售额资料确定。

5. 指数计算方法:使用链式拉氏公式计算,固定基期为 2010 年。

四、工业生产者出厂价格指数

工业生产者出厂价格是工业品第一次出售时的出厂价格。该项调查采用重点调查与典型调查相结合的调查方法。重点调查对象为规模以上工业法人企业;典型调查对象为规模以下工业法人企业。

1. 选择代表企业的原则:(1)按工业行业选择调查企业,主要中类行业原则上都要有调查企业;(2)大型企业应尽量都选上(或占相当大比重);(3)选择生产正常、稳定的企业作为调查对象;(4)选择企业时要兼顾不同所有制形式。不仅选择国有企业,也要选择非国有企业。根据以上原则上海共选择 1000 家工业企业进行工业生产者价格调查。

2. 选择代表产品的原则:(1)按工业行业选择基本分类和代表产品;(2)选择对国计民生影响大的产品;(3)选择生产较为稳定的产品;(4)选择有发展前景的产品;(5)选择具有地方特色的产品。

根据《工业生产者出厂价格调查目录》,上海编制工业生产者出厂价格指数选用近 500 余个基本分类(1000 余种产品),工业生产者购进价格指数选用了 400 余个基本分类 (近 1000 种产品)。

3. 价格调查方式采用企业网上直报形式。

五、固定资产投资价格指数

固定资产投资价格调查采用重点调查与典型调查相结合的方法。固定资产投资价格调查所涉及的价格是构成固定资产投资额实体的实际购进价格或结算价格。调查的内容包括构成当年建筑工程实体的钢材、木材、水泥、地方材料(如砖、瓦、灰、沙、石等)、化工材料(如油漆等)等主要建筑材料价格;作为活劳动投入的劳动力价格(单位工资)和各种施工机械使用价格;设备、工器具购置和其他费用投资价格。

1. 选择建筑安装工程调查点的原则:(1)样本单位应具有一定覆盖面;(2)投资经济活动代表性强;(3)兼顾不同登记注册类型;(4)选择重点工程;(5)兼顾国民经济各门类及不同工程类别。

2. 选择其他费用调查点的原则:在选择其他费用调查点时,所遵循的原则与建筑安装工程调查点的原则基本相同,特别是要注意选择那些投资额大的工程。但由于其他费用不易取得,所以在实际操作过程中,应同时在建设单位、施工单位开展重点调查,并辅以典型调查(从管理部门取得资料)。

3. 价格调查方式采用企业报表形式,每季度 120 余家调查企业上报数据资料。

BRIEF INTRODUCTION

I. Main Contents

Data on price indices in this chapter show the changing trends and the changing rates in the prices of production, trade, consumption, investment and transaction, mainly including consumer price indices, retail price indices, producer price indices, producer purchasing price indices, price indices for investment in fixed assets.

II. Sources of Data

Statistics on price indices, organized and compiled by the Survey Office of the National Bureau of Statistics in Shanghai, are collected from the grassroots units or survey offices in districts and counties in accordance with the scheme of price survey system stipulated by the National Bureau of Statistics, and then statistics are tabulated and reported to the higher agencies.

III. Consumer Price Indices and Retail Price Indices

Data for compilation of the consumer price indices and the retail price indices in Shanghai are collected through a combination of sample surveys and surveys of key units. Areas distributed in the city's economic regions, representative commodities and representative services are selected as samples. Regular surveys are conducted to collect data on their market prices. Population parameters are inferred on the basis of the sample data. At present, 16 districts and counties in Shanghai are all included in the survey of the consumer price indices and the retail price indices.

(1) The selection of sample survey areas: Based on the basic conditions (including product varieties, their sales and etc) the city's consumer market, the city's consumer market, shops, supermarkets, wet markets and service outlets of different varieties are ranked by sales (turnover or scales) and then selected on the number of survey areas needed via systematic sampling method schemes. The price survey areas should be shops, supermarkets, wet markets and service outlets with a wide range of products and big sales.

(2) The goods are selected on the city's consumption conditions, following these principles: (a) goods sold in large quantities (b) Representative for the price changing trends and the changing rates, which means selected goods are highly relevant with those unselected (c) Under the conditions of similar market shares, the bigger the differences in nature among goods and the lower the price relevance, the better (d) Good production and sales outlook (e) Qualified industrial goods, with registered trademark, origin and grade printed on the packaging.

At present, data are collected on more than 1,300 specifications each month in the city under 262 basic headings in 8 categories in the consumer price surveys. For the retail price surveys, data are collected on more than 1,000 specifications each month under 229 basic headings in 16 categories.

(3) Method of data collection: Sample surveys are used for the consumer price indices and the retail price indices, with method of direct survey with fixed people, fixed location and fixed time period.

(4) Determination of the weights: The weights of the consumer price indices are determined according to the composition of the consumption expenditures of Shanghai's urban and rural households. The weights of the retail price indices are determined mainly according to the total retail sales of commodities in the city.

(5) Method of calculation: the approach of the chain Laspyres with 2010 being a base period.

IV. Producer Price Indices for industrial products

Producer prices for industrial products refer to the ex–factory price of manufactured goods when they are first sold. The survey program is a combined use of the key units' survey and typical units' survey methods. Key units refer to those industrial enterprises above designated sizes. Typical units refer to the industrial enterprises below designated sizes.

(1) Principles for selecting the representative enterprises: (a) Enterprises to be covered in the survey are selected by industrial sectors. In principle, every major second level classifacation should have representative enterprises; (b) All (or a majority of) large–scale enterprises should be selected; (c) Enterprises selected should be those with normal and stable production. (d) Enterprises selected should include both state–owned and private companies to cover owner–ship of different nature.

(2) Principle for the selection of representative goods:

(a) The goods are selected by industrial sectors; (b) The selected goods should have great impact on the national e–conomy and people's living conditions; (c) The production of the goods selected are relatively stable; (d) The prospects of the goods selected are promising; (e) The goods selected are local specialties.

According to The survey catalog of Producer Prices for Industrial Products, more than 1,000 goods in more than 500 basic categories are selected to compile the city's producer price indices, and about 1000 goods in more than 400 basic categories are chose to compile the city's purchasing price for industrial goods.

V. Price Indices for Investment in Fixed Assets

Data on prices of investment in fixed assets are collected by a program involving the combined use of surveys on key units and surveys on typical units. The prices collected in the surveys of investment in fixed assets are the actual purchasing prices or settlement prices of entities of investment in fixed assets. The survey content includes the prices of main construction materials that constitute the architectural engineering entity in the year, such as steel, timber, cement, local construction materials (such as brick, tile, calcareous ashes, sand, stone, and etc.), chemical materials (such as oil paint, and etc.), the price of labor cost (wages), using price of various construction machinery the purchasing price of equipment, tools and instruments and the prices of others investments.

1. Principles for selecting the survey points of construction and installation: (1) Sample units should have a good coverage; (2) The economic activity of investment should have strong representativeness; (3) Different types of registration should be considered; (4) Key projects should be selected; (5) Inclusion of various sectors of the national economy and types of projects.

2. Principles for selecting price survey points of other charges or cost: The principles for selecting survey points of others charges or cost is in general the same as that of construction and installation, with special attention to include projects with huge investment value. Since it is not easy to obtain the other charges or cost, during the actual data gathering operations, survey on key construction owner units and building units should be conducted concurrently with survey on typical units (with information from administration units)

3. Enterprises reporting system is used as the method for the price survey. More than 120 enterprises should report their data in each quarter.

表 9.1 居民消费价格和商品零售价格指数(1978~2015)
OVERALL RESIDENTS CONSUMER PRICE INDEX AND RETAIL PRICE INDEX

年 份 Year	居民消费价格指数 Overall Residents Consumer Price Index		年 份 Year	商品零售价格指数 Retail Price Index	
	以上年价格为 100 preceding year = 100	以 1978 年价格为 100 1978 = 100		以上年价格为 100 preceding year = 100	以 1978 年价格为 100 1978 = 100
1978	100.5	100.0	1978	100.1	100.0
1979	100.9	100.9	1979	101.0	101.0
1980	105.9	106.9	1980	106.5	107.6
1981	101.4	108.3	1981	101.5	109.2
1982	100.3	108.7	1982	100.3	109.5
1983	100.2	108.9	1983	100.1	109.6
1984	102.2	111.3	1984	102.2	112.0
1985	115.2	128.2	1985	116.4	130.4
1986	106.3	136.3	1986	106.7	139.1
1987	108.1	147.3	1987	108.8	151.4
1988	120.1	176.9	1988	121.3	183.6
1989	115.9	205.1	1989	116.7	214.3
1990	106.3	218.0	1990	104.8	224.6
1991	110.5	240.9	1991	109.5	245.9
1992	110.0	265.0	1992	109.7	269.8
1993	120.2	318.5	1993	117.5	317.0
1994	123.9	394.6	1994	117.5	372.4
1995	118.7	468.4	1995	113.0	420.9
1996	109.2	511.5	1996	105.0	441.9
1997	102.8	525.8	1997	98.8	436.6
1998	100.0	525.8	1998	95.1	415.2
1999	101.5	533.7	1999	97.3	404.0
2000	102.5	547.0	2000	96.4	389.5
2001	100.0	547.0	2001	98.6	384.0
2002	100.5	549.7	2002	98.7	379.0
2003	100.1	550.1	2003	99.0	375.4
2004	102.2	561.9	2004	100.9	378.8
2005	101.0	567.3	2005	99.4	376.7
2006	101.2	574.2	2006	100.2	377.3
2007	103.2	592.3	2007	102.4	386.5
2008	105.8	626.5	2008	105.3	407.1
2009	99.6	624.0	2009	99.4	404.8
2010	103.1	643.4	2010	101.7	411.7
2011	105.2	676.7	2011	104.1	428.4
2012	102.8	695.9	2012	101.2	433.6
2013	102.3	711.9	2013	100.2	434.3
2014	102.7	730.7	2014	100.9	438.0
2015	102.4	748.4	2015	101.1	442.8

表9.2 居民消费价格指数(1991 ~2015,以上年价格为100)
OVERALL RESIDENTS CONSUMER PRICE INDEX (PRECEDING YEAR = 100)

年 份 Year	居民消费价格指数 Overall Residents Consumer Price Index	食 品 Food	烟 酒 Cigarettes and Liquors	衣 着 Clothing
1991	110.5	113.5	103.0	105.7
1992	110.0	113.4	109.7	109.5
1993	120.2	122.1	110.2	118.6
1994	123.9	131.8	112.0	115.7
1995	118.7	126.1	106.9	108.8
1996	109.2	110.5	100.0	108.7
1997	102.8	100.0	90.3	101.1
1998	100.0	97.8	96.0	94.0
1999	101.5	97.4	100.4	98.3
2000	**102.5**	**98.2**	**97.2**	**95.3**
2001	100.0	100.3	98.9	98.9
2002	100.5	102.9	98.9	97.5
2003	100.1	101.3	99.8	97.5
2004	102.2	108.3	98.3	94.2
2005	101.0	104.5	99.7	92.1
2006	101.2	102.5	100.2	106.4
2007	103.2	109.4	100.7	101.3
2008	105.8	115.3	101.7	101.6
2009	99.6	102.1	100.8	99.3
2010	**103.1**	**107.7**	**101.1**	**98.6**
2011	105.2	110.8	101.3	104.3
2012	102.8	105.8	101.4	103.0
2013	102.3	104.4	100.1	100.0
2014	102.7	103.2	101.0	103.7
2015	102.4	102.9	104.2	107.8

表9.2 续表 continued

年 份 Year	家庭设备用品及维修服务 Home Appliances and Repair Service	医疗保健和个人用品 Medicine, Medical Services and Personal Aricles	交通和通信 Transportation and Communication	娱乐教育文化用品及服务 Recreation, Education and Culture Articles	居 住 Residence
1991	112.5	113.1	108.5	96.9	129.3
1992	102.6	117.3	100.4	96.8	119.0
1993	109.5	114.4	117.0	123.4	134.4
1994	110.9	119.2	117.3	117.6	120.6
1995	103.8	110.0	114.7	116.2	120.3
1996	99.1	106.0	106.1	118.6	109.7
1997	91.4	102.1	115.6	109.6	120.6
1998	92.5	101.9	103.7	106.3	113.6
1999	96.4	101.9	112.4	111.7	105.9
2000	**95.7**	**99.9**	**110.9**	**121.5**	**103.3**
2001	97.2	97.4	98.1	102.1	102.3
2002	97.7	97.6	96.9	100.8	100.0
2003	98.4	100.0	96.3	100.3	101.1
2004	97.8	100.0	96.5	99.9	101.6
2005	100.8	100.3	97.5	98.3	102.9
2006	102.7	101.1	97.3	98.2	102.9
2007	103.3	100.2	96.9	97.3	104.5
2008	108.3	103.1	97.5	98.2	102.5
2009	101.5	99.4	97.5	98.0	96.6
2010	**101.1**	**103.7**	**97.4**	**100.9**	**103.5**
2011	107.1	104.1	100.2	99.2	105.4
2012	103.5	100.6	100.8	99.3	102.8
2013	101.3	100.0	100.4	100.1	103.9
2014	101.8	100.4	100.1	101.8	104.6
2015	102.9	99.3	97.6	100.3	104.6

表 9.3 主要年份居民消费价格指数（以上年价格为 100）
CLASSIFIED RESIDENTS CONSUMER PRICE INDEX IN MAIN YEARS(PRECEDING YEAR = 100)

类 别	Types	2001	2010	2014	2015
居民消费价格指数	**Overall Residents Consumer Price Index**	**100.0**	**103.1**	**102.7**	**102.4**
#消费品价格指数	Consumer Goods Price Indices	98.6	103.5	101.9	102.0
服务项目价格指数	Services Items Price Indices	105.4	102.0	104.0	103.2
食 品	**Food**	**100.3**	**107.7**	**103.2**	**102.9**
粮 食	Grain	102.9	112.0	102.4	103.0
淀粉及制品	Starch and Its Products	103.6	95.5	102.5	103.9
干豆类及豆制品	Dry Beans and Bean Products	95.6	108.7	100.4	101.2
油 脂	Oil or Fat	84.5	105.6	95.5	98.5
肉禽及其制品	Meat Poultry and Their Products	99.3	104.3	101.4	105.3
蛋	Eggs	102.4	106.1	106.0	98.0
水产品	Aquatic Products	100.1	116.4	102.7	101.3
菜	Vegetables	108.9	111.0	101.5	107.5
调味品	Flavoring	99.2	106.5	103.1	104.9
糖	Sugars	101.4	103.8	102.0	102.2
茶及饮料	Tea and Beverages	98.4	103.9	103.2	103.9
干鲜瓜果	Dried and Fresh Fruits	104.3	112.0	111.6	96.8
糕点饼干面包	Cakes,Biscuits and Bread	100.5	100.5	102.6	101.8
液体乳及乳制品	Milk and Its Products	100.8	102.3	110.1	99.2
在外用膳食品	Dining Out	98.0	105.6	101.9	104.1
其他食品	Other Food	99.2	105.0	103.4	104.2
烟 酒	**Cigarettes and Liquors**	**98.9**	**101.1**	**101.0**	**104.2**
烟 草	Tobacco	99.2	101.0	101.2	104.9
酒	Liquors	98.2	101.6	100.7	102.5
衣 着	**Clothing**	**98.9**	**98.6**	**103.7**	**107.8**
服 装	Garments	96.4	99.9	102.4	107.3
衣着材料	Clothing Materials	98.7	102.9	103.1	106.3
鞋袜帽	Shoes, Socks and Hats	106.2	93.6	108.5	109.8
衣着加工服务	Garment Processing Service	100.0	107.2	110.0	105.5

表9.3 续表 continued

类 别	Types	2001	2010	2014	2015
家庭设备用品及维修服务	**Home Appliances and Repair Service**	**97.2**	**101.1**	**101.8**	**102.9**
耐用消费品	Durable Consumer Goods	94.7	99.6	100.9	101.8
室内装饰品	Interior Decorations	101.0	99.2	93.6	102.2
床上用品	Bed Articles	100.5	104.2	98.4	103.4
家庭日用杂品	Daily Use Household Articles	98.6	99.4	100.5	101.4
家庭服务及加工维修服务	Other Daily Use Articles	100.0	108.8	110.7	108.5
医疗保健和个人用品	**Medicine, Medical Services and Personal Aricles**	**97.4**	**103.7**	**100.4**	**99.3**
医疗保健	Medicine and Medical Services	96.5	100.8	101.7	100.7
个人用品及服务	Personal Articles and Service	99.8	107.1	99.2	98.0
交通和通信	**Transportation and Communication**	**98.1**	**97.4**	**100.1**	**97.6**
交 通	Transportation	102.3	98.7	100.6	97.3
通 信	Communications	94.4	95.3	98.7	98.2
娱乐教育文化用品及服务	**Recreation, Education and Culture Articles**	**102.1**	**100.9**	**101.8**	**100.3**
文娱用耐用消费品及服务	Durable Consumer Goods for Recreational Use	91.2	89.4	93.7	95.9
教 育	Education	109.6	101.2	102.4	102.5
文化娱乐类	Recreation and Culture Articles	105.2	101.0	101.0	100.7
旅 游	Tourism	96.2	115.9	107.9	97.9
居 住	**Residence**	**102.3**	**103.5**	**104.6**	**104.6**
建房及装修材料	Construction and Decoration Materials	97.5	102.1	99.8	101.4
住房租金	Rents	111.0	106.8	105.2	107.3
自有住房	Self-owned House	99.8	103.0	105.3	105.5
水、电、燃料	Water, Electricity and Fuels	101.7	103.8	105.9	102.4

表9.4 主要年份商品零售价格指数(以上年价格为100)
CLASSIFIED RETAIL PRICE INDEX IN MAIN YEARS(PRECEDING YEAR =100)

类别	Types	2001	2010	2014	2015
商品零售价格指数	**Overall Retail Price Index**	**98.6**	**101.7**	**100.9**	**101.1**
食　品	Food	98.4	107.6	103.2	102.8
粮　食	Grain	100.1	112.0	102.0	103.0
淀粉及制品	Starch and Its Products	100.4	95.5	102.5	103.9
干豆类及豆制品	Dry Beans and Bean Products	111.3	108.7	100.4	101.2
油　脂	Oil or Fat	81.4	105.6	95.0	98.0
肉禽及其制品	Meat Poultry and Their Products	100.4	104.2	101.4	105.3
蛋	Eggs	110.7	106.1	106.0	98.0
水产品	Aquatic Products	90.1	116.1	102.7	101.3
菜	Vegetables	107.1	111.0	101.5	107.5
调味品	Flavoring	99.5	106.5	103.1	104.8
糖	Sugars	104.4	103.8	102.0	102.2
干鲜瓜果	Dried and Fresh Fruits	107.3	112.1	111.6	96.8
糕点饼干面包	Cakes, Biscuits and Bread	99.8	100.5	102.6	101.8
液体乳及乳制品	Milk and Its Products	99.8	102.3	110.1	99.2
在外用膳食品	Dining Out	100.7	105.6	101.9	104.1
其他食品	Other Food	99.5	105.0	103.4	104.2
饮料、烟酒	Beverages, Tobacco and Liquor	98.4	101.9	101.4	103.9
服装、鞋帽	Garments, Shoes and Hats	107.7	98.4	103.6	107.9
纺织品	Textiles	98.8	103.9	99.1	104.1
家用电器及音像器材	Household Appliances and Audio-video Appliances	95.0	92.4	96.5	99.3
文化办公用品	Cultural Office Articles	98.7	97.7	98.2	99.2
日用品	Daily Use Articles	99.0	100.3	99.9	101.5
体育娱乐用品	Sports and Recreation Goods	99.1	95.9	98.6	99.4
交通、通信用品	Transportation and Communication Goods	97.4	94.0	98.8	97.8
家　具	Furniture	90.4	101.1	102.6	101.8
化妆品	Cosmetics	100.7	101.0	102.3	100.1
金银珠宝	Jewelry	87.2	111.7	93.7	95.2
中西药品及医疗保健用品	Traditional Chinese and Western Medicines	98.7	99.8	101.7	100.6
书报杂志及电子出版物	Newspapers and Magazines and Electronic Publications	99.5	103.2	100.6	101.7
燃　料	Fuels	111.4	112.8	99.8	91.2
建筑材料及五金电料	Building Materials and Hardwares	101.8	103.3	99.3	99.6

表9.5 工业生产者出厂价格指数 (2008～2015,以2000年价格为100)
PRODUCER PRICE INDEX FOR INDUSTRIAL PRODUCTS (2000 = 100)

类 别	Types	2008	2009	2010	2011
工业生产者出厂价格指数	**Producer Price Index for Industrial Products**	**103.6**	**97.2**	**99.4**	**102.3**
按轻重工业分	**Grouped by Light or Heavy Industries**				
轻工业	Light Industry	93.6	88.7	86.1	89.5
以农产品为原料	Using Farm Products as Raw Materials	111.0	112.2	115.1	120.4
以非农产品为原料	Using Non-farm Products as Raw Materials	85.2	79.3	75.8	78.3
重工业	Heavy Industry	112.7	104.7	111.9	114.8
采 掘	Mining and Guarrying	246.1	203.0	237.3	272.9
原 料	Raw Material	161.5	148.3	173.2	191.0
加 工	Manufacturing	97.4	91.1	93.7	94.3
按用途分	**Grouped by Use**				
生产资料	Means of Production	109.7	101.0	103.7	106.6
生活资料	Consumer Goods	90.9	91.4	92.0	94.7
#食 品	Food	119.1	121.5	126.8	133.8
衣 着	Clothing	107.5	107.8	108.4	110.5
一般日用品	Non-Durable Consumer Goods	99.6	101.5	103.2	108.5
耐用消费品	Durable Consumer Goods	69.5	68.5	66.9	67.0

表9.5 续表 continued

类 别	Types	2012	2013	2014	2015
工业生产者出厂价格指数	**Producer Price Index for Industrial Products**	**100.7**	**98.9**	**97.8**	**94.0**
按轻重工业分	**Grouped by Light or Heavy Industries**				
轻工业	Light Industry	90.1	89.4	88.6	87.4
以农产品为原料	Using Farm Products as Raw Materials	122.6	122.5	122.3	120.8
以非农产品为原料	Using Non-farm Products as Raw Materials	78.1	76.9	75.8	74.7
重工业	Heavy Industry	112.4	110.2	108.9	104.0
采 掘	Mining and Guarrying	273.2	283.9	290.1	247.2
原 料	Raw Material	189.3	184.8	181.5	157.5
加 工	Manufacturing	92.0	90.3	89.4	87.3
按用途分	**Grouped by Use**				
生产资料	Means of Production	104.6	102.4	101.1	96.1
生活资料	Consumer Goods	94.2	93.4	92.8	92.2
#食 品	Food	138.2	138.1	138.7	137.7
衣 着	Clothing	110.1	110.3	110.7	110.7
一般日用品	Non-Durable Consumer Goods	109.5	106.8	105.9	104.5
耐用消费品	Durable Consumer Goods	64.5	64.3	63.6	63.3

表9.6 工业生产者出厂价格指数(2008～2015,以2000年价格为100)(按国民经济行业分)
PRODUCER PRICE INDEX FOR INDUSTRIAL PRODUCTS(GROUPED BY NATIONAL INDUSTRIES, 2000 = 100)

类别	Types	2008	2009	2010	2011
工业生产者出厂价格指数	**Producer Price Index for Industrial Products**	**103.6**	**97.2**	**99.4**	**102.3**
按国民经济行业分	Grouped by National Economy Industries				
石油和天然气开采业	Petroleum and Natural Gas Exploiting	246.1	203.0	237.3	272.9
农副食品加工业	Farm and Sideline Products Processing	183.6	160.3	171.4	205.0
食品制造业	Food Manufacturing	114.3	119.2	124.9	133.3
酒、饮料和精制茶制造业	Wine, Beverage and Refined Tea Manufacturing	103.9	105.1	109.7	113.2
烟草制品业	Tabacco Mannfacturing	129.5	136.2	141.2	141.2
纺织业	Textile	101.5	101.9	104.1	108.6
纺织服装、服饰业	Textile and Garment, Apparel Industry	107.8	108.6	109.6	112.2
皮革、毛皮、羽毛及其制品和制鞋业	Leather, Fur, Feather and Its Products and Shoemaking Industry	101.9	100.9	100.9	101.0
木材加工和木、竹、藤、棕、草制品业	Timber Processing and Timber, Bamboo, Rattan, Coir and Straw Products Manufacturing	100.9	104.4	104.2	110.7
家具制造业	Furniture Manufacturing	98.7	97.1	90.4	92.9
造纸和纸制品业	Paper-making and Paper Products Manufacturing	89.6	94.7	95.2	100.0
印刷和记录媒介复制业	Printing and Record Duplicating Industry	91.0	90.8	90.6	91.9
文教、工美、体育和娱乐用品制造业	Stationary, Education ,Industrial Art, Sport and Entertainment Products Manufacturing	100.8	100.3	101.7	108.8
石油加工、炼焦和核燃料加工业	Oil Processing, Coking and Nuclear Fual Processing	242.1	230.2	279.0	325.6
化学原料和化学制品制造业	Raw Chemical Materials and Chemical Products Manufacturing	140.8	122.5	143.6	159.3
医药制造业	Medicine Manufacturing	93.5	94.2	94.5	97.4
化学纤维制造业	Chemical Fiber Manufacturing	114.3	100.8	116.6	132.5
橡胶和塑料制品业	Rubber and Plastic Products Manufacturing	101.8	103.9	105.5	113.5
非金属矿物制品业	Nonmetal Mineral Products	103.5	101.3	103.9	112.2
黑色金属冶炼和压延加工业	Smelting and Pressing of Ferrous Metals	188.9	150.4	173.1	190.6
有色金属冶炼和压延加工业	Smelting and Pressing of Nonferrous Metals	188.3	156.7	200.3	225.9
金属制品业	Metal Products Manufacturing	125.2	119.1	127.8	131.9
通用设备制造业	General Equipment Manufacturing	97.6	96.2	95.7	94.6
专用设备制造业	Special Purpose Equipment Manufacturing	93.1	94.9	94.6	95.1
汽车制造业	Automotive Industry				
铁路、船舶、航空航天和其他运输设备制造业	Railroads, Ships, Aerospace and other Transportation Equipment Manufacturing Industry				
电气机械和器材制造业	Electric Machinery Equipments and Manufacturing	96.4	93.1	93.9	94.7
计算机、通信和其他电子设备制造业	Computers, Cmmunications and Oher Electronic Equipment Manufacturing Industry	62.4	55.2	50.5	49.5
仪器仪表制造业	Instruments and Meters Manufacturing	83.3	81.6	81.3	82.4
其他制造业	Other manufacturing	126.5	126.2	141.5	164.6
废弃资源综合利用业	Comprehensive Utilization of Waste Resources	160.6	120.5	136.2	167.8
金属制品、机械和设备修理业	Metal Products, Machinery and Equipment Repair				
电力、热力生产和供应业	Production and Supply of Electricity and Thermal Power	106.0	109.9	111.7	112.7
燃气生产和供应业	Production and Supply of Gas	132.2	145.6	151.7	165.4
水的生产和供应业	Production and Supply of Water	119.4	144.4	162.7	179.1

注：废弃资源和废旧材料回收加工业以2002年价格为100。
Note: The price index of Waste Resources and Materials Recycling and Processing was 100 in 2002.

表9.6 续表 continued

	类 别 Types	2012	2013	2014	2015
工业生产者出厂价格指数	**Producer Price Index for Industrial Products**	**100.7**	**98.9**	**97.8**	**94.0**
按国民经济行业分	**Grouped by National Economy Industries**				
石油和天然气开采业	Petroleum and Natural Gas Exploiting	273.2	283.9	290.1	247.2
农副食品加工业	Farm and Sideline Products Processing	213.2	211.1	203.3	187.4
食品制造业	Food Manufacturing	138.2	140.8	143.8	144.8
酒、饮料和精制茶制造业	Wine, Beverage and Refined Tea Manufacturing	119.2	114.3	112.6	110.0
烟草制品业	Tabacco Manufacture	145.4	146.3	146.3	146.3
纺织业	Textile	106.8	105.5	103.9	101.7
纺织服装、服饰业	Textile and Garment, Apparel Industry	111.5	111.6	111.9	111.5
皮革、毛皮、羽毛及其制品和制鞋业	Leather, Fur, Feather and Its Products and Shoemaking Industry	100.4	102.1	103.7	104.1
木材加工和木、竹、藤、棕、草制品业	Timber Processing and Timber, Bamboo, Rattan, Coir and Straw Products Manufacturing	114.6	114.9	118.0	119.7
家具制造业	Furniture Manufacturing	93.2	93.0	93.0	93.2
造纸和纸制品业	Paper-making and Paper Products Manufacturing	101.1	98.9	97.9	96.9
印刷和记录媒介复制业	Printing and Record Duplicating Industry	91.3	89.5	89.6	88.5
文教、工美、体育和娱乐用品制造业	Stationary, Education ,Industrial Art, Sport and Entertainment Products Manufacturing	111.8	104.0	98.8	96.3
石油加工、炼焦和核燃料加工业	Oil Processing, Coking and Nuclear Fual Processing	333.1	327.1	311.7	230.3
化学原料和化学制品制造业	Raw Chemical Materials and Chemical Products Manufacturing	154.2	149.3	147.8	129.0
医药制造业	Medicine Manufacturing	99.2	96.5	96.7	98.2
化学纤维制造业	Chemical Fiber Manufacturing	120.8	118.5	114.9	105.4
橡胶和塑料制品业	Rubber and Plastic Products Manufacturing	113.4	112.6	110.3	105.2
非金属矿物制品业	Nonmetal Mineral Products	107.0	103.9	104.4	99.8
黑色金属冶炼和压延加工业	Smelting and Pressing of Ferrous Metals	167.7	165.0	161.2	138.6
有色金属冶炼和压延加工业	Smelting and Pressing of Nonferrous Metals	205.6	192.9	185.0	168.4
金属制品业	Metal Products Manufacturing	130.1	125.2	120.8	115.6
通用设备制造业	General Equipment Manufacturing	94.0	92.2	91.2	90.8
专用设备制造业	Special Purpose Equipment Manufacturing	95.7	95.2	96.2	98.0
汽车制造业 *	Automotive Industry	96.3	94.9	94.6	93.7
铁路、船舶、航空航天和其他运输设备制造业 *	Railroads, Ships, Aerospace and other Transportation Equipment Manufacturing Industry	98.5	96.5	95.8	95.3
电气机械和器材制造业	Electric Machinery Equipments and Manufacturing	92.9	90.5	89.1	87.2
计算机、通信和其他电子设备制造业	Computers, Cmmunications and Oher Electronic Equipment Manufacturing Industry	49.2	48.4	47.7	47.4
仪器仪表制造业	Instruments and Meters Manufacturing	81.4	81.2	81.0	80.7
其他制造业	Other manufacturing	165.4	165.2	165.4	168.0
废弃资源综合利用业	Comprehensive Utilization of Waste Resources	145.3	132.5	125.9	93.7
金属制品、机械和设备修理业 *	Metal Products, Machinery and Equipment Repair	97.3	96.4	97.6	95.2
电力、热力生产和供应业	Production and Supply of Electricity and Thermal Power	115.4	115.2	116.8	115.4
燃气生产和供应业	Production and Supply of Gas	160.4	150.5	148.7	149.0
水的生产和供应业	Production and Supply of Water	180.5	189.0	223.0	225.7

注：* 为以2011年价格为100。
Note: The price index symbled " * " was 100 in 2011.

表9.7 工业生产者出厂价格指数（2008～2015，以上年价格为100）
PRODUCER PRICE INDEX FOR INDUSTRIAL PRODUCTS(PRECEDING YEAR =100)

类别	Types	2008	2009	2010	2011
工业生产者出厂价格指数	**Producer Price Index for Industrial Products**	**102.2**	**93.8**	**102.3**	**102.9**
按轻重工业分	**Grouped by Light or Heavy Industries**				
轻工业	Light Industry	99.1	94.8	97.1	103.9
以农产品为原料	Using Farm Products as Raw Materials	103.6	101.1	102.6	104.6
以非农产品为原料	Using Non-farm Products as Raw Materials	97.9	93.1	95.6	103.3
重工业	Heavy Industry	105.2	92.9	106.9	102.6
采掘	Mining and Guarrying	125.8	82.5	116.9	115.0
原料	Raw Material	110.7	91.8	116.8	110.3
加工	Manufacturing	102.8	93.5	102.9	100.6
按用途分	**Grouped by Use**				
生产资料	Means of Production	102.5	92.1	102.7	102.8
生活资料	Consumer Goods	101.3	100.6	100.7	102.9
#食品	Food	105.3	102.0	104.4	105.5
衣着	Clothing	102.2	100.3	100.6	101.9
一般日用品	Non-Durable Consumer Goods	102.2	101.9	101.7	105.1
耐用消费品	Durable Consumer Goods	97.2	98.5	97.6	100.2

表9.7 续表 continued

类别	Types	2012	2013	2014	2015
工业生产者出厂价格指数	**Producer Price Index for Industrial Products**	**98.4**	**98.2**	**98.9**	**96.1**
按轻重工业分	**Grouped by Light or Heavy Industries**				
轻工业	Light Industry	100.7	99.2	99.1	98.6
以农产品为原料	Using Farm Products as Raw Materials	101.8	99.9	99.8	98.8
以非农产品为原料	Using Non-farm Products as Raw Materials	99.8	98.5	98.6	98.5
重工业	Heavy Industry	97.9	98.0	98.8	95.5
采掘	Mining and Guarrying	100.1	103.9	102.2	85.2
原料	Raw Material	99.1	97.6	98.2	86.8
加工	Manufacturing	97.6	98.1	99.0	97.7
按用途分	**Grouped by Use**				
生产资料	Means of Production	98.1	97.9	98.7	95.1
生活资料	Consumer Goods	99.5	99.2	99.4	99.3
#食品	Food	103.3	99.9	100.4	99.3
衣着	Clothing	99.6	100.2	100.4	100.0
一般日用品	Non-Durable Consumer Goods	100.9	97.5	99.2	98.7
耐用消费品	Durable Consumer Goods	96.2	99.7	98.9	99.6

表9.8 工业生产者出厂价格指数 (2008～2015,以上年价格为100)(按国民经济行业分)
PRODUCER PRICE INDEX FOR INDUSTRIAL PRODUCTS(GROUPED BY NATIONAL INDUSTRIES, PRECEDING YEAR = 100)

类别	Types	2008	2009	2010	2011
工业生产者出厂价格指数	**Producer Ex-factory Price Index**	**102.2**	**93.8**	**102.3**	**102.9**
按国民经济行业分	**Grouped by National Economy Industries**				
石油和天然气开采业	Petroleum and Natural Gas Exploiting	125.8	82.5	116.9	115.0
农副食品加工业	Farm and Sideline Products Processing	120.7	87.3	106.9	119.6
食品制造业	Food Manufacturing	106.8	104.3	104.8	106.7
酒、饮料和精制茶制造业	Wine, Beverage and Refined Tea Manufacturing	100.7	101.2	104.4	103.2
烟草制品业	Tabacco Manufacture	100.0	105.2	103.7	100.0
纺织业	Textile	100.7	100.4	102.2	104.3
纺织服装、服饰业	Textile and Garment, Apparel Industry	102.3	100.7	100.9	102.4
皮革、毛皮、羽毛及其制品和制鞋业	Leather, Fur, Feather and Its Products and Shoemaking Industry	100.3	99.0	100.0	100.1
木材加工和木、竹、藤、棕、草制品业	Timber Processing and Timber, Bamboo, Rattan, Coir and Straw Products Manufacturing	104.6	103.5	99.8	106.2
家具制造业	Furniture Manufacturing	100.1	98.4	93.1	102.8
造纸和纸制品业	Paper-making and Paper Products Manufacturing	103.8	105.7	100.5	105.0
印刷和记录媒介复制业	Printing and Record Duplicating Industry	102.2	99.8	99.8	101.4
文教、工美、体育和娱乐用品制造业	Stationary, Education ,Industrial Art, Sport and Entertainment Products Manufacturing	100.3	99.5	101.4	107.0
石油加工、炼焦和核燃料加工业	Oil Processing, Coking and Nuclear Fual Processing	122.4	95.1	121.2	116.7
化学原料和化学制品制造业	Raw Chemical Materials and Chemical Products Manufacturing	104.9	87.0	117.2	110.9
医药制造业	Medicine Manufacturing	105.6	100.8	100.3	103.1
化学纤维制造业	Chemical Fiber Manufacturing	100.4	88.2	115.7	113.6
橡胶和塑料制品业	Rubber and Plastic Products Manufacturing	100.1	102.1	101.5	107.6
非金属矿物制品业	Nonmetal Mineral Products	105.7	97.9	102.6	108.0
黑色金属冶炼和压延加工业	Smelting and Pressing of Ferrous Metals	114.1	79.6	115.1	110.1
有色金属冶炼和压延加工业	Smelting and Pressing of Nonferrous Metals	92.2	83.2	127.8	112.8
金属制品业	Metal Products Manufacturing	101.9	95.1	107.3	103.2
通用设备制造业	General Equipment Manufacturing	101.6	98.6	99.5	98.9
专用设备制造业	Special Purpose Equipment Manufacturing	101.1	101.9	99.7	100.5
汽车制造业	Automotive Industry				
铁路、船舶、航空航天和其他运输设备制造业	Railroads, Ships, Aerospace and other Transportation Equipment Manufacturing Industry				
电气机械和器材制造业	Electric Machinery Equipments and Manufacturing	101.4	96.6	100.9	100.8
计算机、通信和其他电子设备制造业	Computers, Cmmunications and Oher Electronic Equipment Manufacturing Industry	94.5	88.4	91.5	98.1
仪器仪表制造业	Instruments and Meters Manufacturing	100.1	98.0	99.6	101.4
其他制造业	Other manufacturing	111.2	99.8	112.1	116.3
废弃资源综合利用业	Comprehensive Utilization of Waste Resources	133.2	75.0	113.0	123.2
金属制品、机械和设备修理业	Metal Products, Machinery and Equipment Repair				
电力、热力生产和供应业	Production and Supply of Electricity and Thermal Power	102.0	103.7	101.6	100.9
燃气生产和供应业	Production and Supply of Gas	104.8	110.1	104.2	109.0
水的生产和供应业	Production and Supply of Water	101.3	120.9	112.7	110.1

表9.8 续表 continued

类 别	Types	2012	2013	2014	2015
工业生产者出厂价格指数	**Producer Price Index for Industrial Products**	**98.4**	**98.2**	**98.9**	**96.1**
按国民经济行业分	**Grouped by National Economy Industries**				
石油和天然气开采业	Petroleum and Natural Gas Exploiting	100.1	103.9	102.2	85.2
农副食品加工业	Farm and Sideline Products Processing	104.0	99.0	96.3	92.2
食品制造业	Food Manufacturing	103.7	101.9	102.1	100.7
酒、饮料和精制茶制造业	Wine, Beverage and Refined Tea Manufacturing	105.3	95.9	98.5	97.7
烟草制品业	Tabacco Manufacture	103.0	100.6	100.0	100.0
纺织业	Textile	98.3	98.8	98.5	97.9
纺织服装、服饰业	Textile and Garment, Apparel Industry	99.4	100.1	100.3	99.6
皮革、毛皮、羽毛及其制品和制鞋业	Leather, Fur, Feather and Its Products and Shoemaking Industry	99.4	101.7	101.6	100.4
木材加工和木、竹、藤、棕、草制品业	Timber Processing and Timber, Bamboo, Rattan, Coir and Straw Products Manufacturing	103.5	100.3	102.7	101.4
家具制造业	Furniture Manufacturing	100.3	99.8	100.0	100.2
造纸和纸制品业	Paper-making and Paper Products Manufacturing	101.1	97.8	99.0	99.0
印刷和记录媒介复制业	Printing and Record Duplicating Industry	99.3	98.0	100.1	98.8
文教、工美、体育和娱乐用品制造业	Stationary, Education ,Industrial Art, Sport and Entertainment Products Manufacturing	102.8	93.0	95.0	97.5
石油加工、炼焦和核燃料加工业	Oil Processing, Coking and Nuclear Fual Processing	102.3	98.2	95.3	73.9
化学原料和化学制品制造业	Raw Chemical Materials and Chemical Products Manufacturing	96.8	96.8	99.0	87.3
医药制造业	Medicine Manufacturing	101.8	97.3	100.2	101.5
化学纤维制造业	Chemical Fiber Manufacturing	91.2	98.1	97.0	91.7
橡胶和塑料制品业	Rubber and Plastic Products Manufacturing	99.9	99.3	98.0	95.4
非金属矿物制品业	Nonmetal Mineral Products	95.4	97.1	100.5	95.6
黑色金属冶炼和压延加工业	Smelting and Pressing of Ferrous Metals	88.0	98.4	97.7	86.0
有色金属冶炼和压延加工业	Smelting and Pressing of Nonferrous Metals	91.0	93.8	95.9	91.0
金属制品业	Metal Products Manufacturing	98.6	96.2	96.5	95.7
通用设备制造业	General Equipment Manufacturing	99.4	98.1	98.9	99.6
专用设备制造业	Special Purpose Equipment Manufacturing	100.6	99.5	101.0	101.9
汽车制造业	Automotive Industry	96.3	98.5	99.7	99.0
铁路、船舶、航空航天和其他运输设备制造业	Railroads, Ships, Aerospace and other Transportation Equipment Manufacturing Industry	98.5	98.0	99.3	99.5
电气机械和器材制造业	Electric Machinery Equipments and Manufacturing	98.1	97.4	98.4	97.9
计算机、通信和其他电子设备制造业	Computers, Cmmunications and Oher Electronic Equipment Manufacturing Industry	99.4	98.3	98.5	99.3
仪器仪表制造业	Instruments and Meters Manufacturing	98.8	99.8	99.8	99.6
其他制造业	Other manufacturing	100.5	99.9	100.1	101.6
废弃资源综合利用业	Comprehensive Utilization of Waste Resources	86.6	91.2	95.0	74.4
金属制品、机械和设备修理业	Metal Products, Machinery and Equipment Repair	97.3	99.1	101.2	97.5
电力、热力生产和供应业	Production and Supply of Electricity and Thermal Power	102.4	99.8	101.4	98.8
燃气生产和供应业	Production and Supply of Gas	97.0	93.8	98.8	100.2
水的生产和供应业	Production and Supply of Water	100.8	104.7	118.0	101.2

表9.9 工业生产者购进价格指数(2008~2015,以2000年价格为100)
PRODUCER PURCHASING PRCIE INDEX (2000 = 100)

类别	Types	2008	2009	2010	2011
工业生产者购进价格指数	**Producer Purchasing Price Index**	**153.4**	**137.8**	**153.2**	**164.7**
燃料、动力类	Fuels and Power	265.6	201.9	260.5	307.1
黑色金属材料类	Ferrous Metals	190.8	165.4	188.4	208.9
#钢 材	Rolled-steel	162.7	142.9	150.0	158.9
有色金属材料类	Nonferrous Metals	175.6	151.5	196.0	223.0
化工原料类	Chemical Raw Materials	131.3	114.9	133.3	147.3
木材及纸浆类	Wood and Paper Pulps	98.9	95.2	98.4	101.9
建筑材料类及非金属矿类	Building Materials and Nonmetal Minerals	115.1	113.5	119.6	138.7
其他工业原材料及半成品类	Other Industrial Raw and Processed Materials	107.7	104.1	106.5	107.5
农副产品类	Farm and Sideline Products	141.0	141.0	152.6	170.5
纺织原料类	Textile Raw Material	105.3	104.5	111.2	123.0

表9.9 续表 continued

类别	Types	2012	2013	2014	2015
工业生产者购进价格指数	**Producer Purchasing Price Index**	**156.0**	**150.5**	**144.3**	**130.7**
燃料、动力类	Fuels and Power	303.7	274.5	257.8	176.1
黑色金属材料类	Ferrous Metals	178.0	171.4	153.7	125.6
#钢 材	Rolled-steel	148.7	141.6	135.2	121.0
有色金属材料类	Nonferrous Metals	202.9	188.7	176.2	156.5
化工原料类	Chemical Raw Materials	142.0	138.0	133.6	119.4
木材及纸浆类	Wood and Paper Pulps	100.1	99.6	98.9	98.2
建筑材料类及非金属矿类	Building Materials and Nonmetal Minerals	130.0	128.6	131.6	124.0
其他工业原材料及半成品类	Other Industrial Raw and Processed Materials	104.4	101.6	99.6	96.6
农副产品类	Farm and Sideline Products	174.8	173.9	168.9	158.9
纺织原料类	Textile Raw Material	121.9	122.0	121.9	122.1

表9.10 工业生产者购进价格指数(2008~2015,以上年价格为100)
PRODUCER PURCHASING PRICE INDEX(PRECEDING YEAR =100)

类别	Types	2008	2009	2010	2011
工业生产者购进价格指数	**Producer Purchasing Price Index**	**110.3**	**89.8**	**111.2**	**107.5**
燃料、动力类	Fuels and Power	135.6	76.0	129.0	117.9
黑色金属材料类	Ferrous Metals	117.0	86.7	113.9	110.9
#钢材	Rolled-steel	114.1	87.8	105.0	105.9
有色金属材料类	Nonferrous Metals	96.4	86.3	129.4	113.8
化工原料类	Chemical Raw Materials	105.9	87.5	116.0	110.5
木材及纸浆类	Wood and Paper Pulps	102.6	96.3	103.4	103.6
建筑材料类及非金属矿类	Building Materials and Nonmetal Minerals	109.0	98.6	105.4	116.0
其他工业原材料及半成品类	Other Industrial Raw and Processed Materials	102.3	96.7	102.3	100.9
农副产品类	Farm and Sideline Products	107.6	100.0	108.2	111.7
纺织原料类	Textile Raw Material	103.2	99.2	106.4	110.6

表9.10 续表 continued

类别	Types	2012	2013	2014	2015
工业生产者购进价格指数	**Producer Purchasing Price Index**	**94.7**	**96.5**	**95.9**	**90.6**
燃料、动力类	Fuels and Power	98.9	90.4	93.9	68.3
黑色金属材料类	Ferrous Metals	85.2	96.3	89.7	81.7
#钢材	Rolled-steel	93.6	95.2	95.5	89.5
有色金属材料类	Nonferrous Metals	91.0	93.0	93.4	88.8
化工原料类	Chemical Raw Materials	96.4	97.2	96.8	89.4
木材及纸浆类	Wood and Paper Pulps	98.2	99.5	99.3	99.3
建筑材料类及非金属矿类	Building Materials and Nonmetal Minerals	93.7	98.9	102.3	94.2
其他工业原材料及半成品类	Other Industrial Raw and Processed Materials	97.1	97.3	98.0	97.0
农副产品类	Farm and Sideline Products	102.5	99.5	97.1	94.1
纺织原料类	Textile Raw Material	99.1	100.1	99.9	100.2

表9.11　固定资产投资价格指数（2001～2015，以2000年价格为100）
PRICE INDEX OF INVESTMENT IN FIXED ASSETS (2000 = 100)

年　份 Year	固定资产投资价格指数 Price Index of Fixed Asset Investment	建筑安装工程 Building Project Price Index	#人工费 Manpower Cost Price Index	材料费 Material Price Index	机械使用费 Machinery Used Price Index	设备、工器具购置 Equipment and Instrument Price Index	其他费用投资 Other Investment Price Index
2001	100.7	102.4	109.0	101.2	99.7	96.5	101.3
2002	101.0	104.3	120.4	101.0	102.5	93.3	101.6
2003	103.4	109.7	125.8	106.6	107.5	91.0	103.0
2004	110.3	121.3	133.0	119.4	116.9	90.5	107.8
2005	111.2	122.4	139.4	118.7	123.4	88.1	111.2
2006	111.3	122.5	146.1	117.0	127.0	85.7	113.4
2007	115.2	128.1	156.8	122.0	130.0	85.2	118.0
2008	124.3	143.6	170.6	139.0	136.4	84.8	124.4
2009	120.6	136.1	181.2	126.6	138.9	81.5	127.1
2010	125.2	144.4	193.7	134.8	142.2	80.4	130.2
2011	133.3	159.7	213.5	150.4	148.0	80.2	133.7
2012	132.5	157.6	230.8	144.1	152.9	79.1	135.8
2013	132.8	157.3	250.2	140.2	158.1	77.9	138.8
2014	133.5	157.8	271.0	137.5	162.5	77.5	140.9
2015	129.5	149.8	286.7	125.8	164.0	77.3	141.7

表9.12　固定资产投资价格指数（1995～2015，以上年价格为100）
PRICE INDEX OF INVESTMENT IN FIXED ASSETS (PRECEDING YEAR = 100)

年　份 Year	固定资产投资价格指数 Price Index of Fixed Asset Investment	建筑安装工程 Building Project Price Index	#人工费 Manpower Cost Price Index	材料费 Material Price Index	机械使用费 Machinery Used Price Index	设备、工器具购置 Equipment and Instrument Price Index	其他费用投资 Other Investment Price Index
1995	103.1	101.9	108.7	99.5		104.8	107.0
1996	107.0	108.9	114.2	97.4	118.5	101.7	107.7
1997	100.5	101.4	109.0	98.7	104.5	97.8	100.8
1998	98.4	98.9	96.0	98.3	99.7	96.1	99.6
1999	98.1	97.8	103.4	96.1	100.5	96.9	99.8
2000	100.0	101.5	100.6	101.8	99.8	97.0	99.9
2001	100.7	102.4	109.0	101.2	99.7	96.5	101.3
2002	100.3	101.9	110.5	99.8	102.8	96.7	100.3
2003	102.4	105.2	104.5	105.5	104.9	97.5	101.4
2004	106.7	110.6	105.7	112.0	108.7	99.4	104.7
2005	100.8	100.9	104.8	99.4	105.6	97.4	103.2
2006	100.1	100.1	104.8	98.6	102.9	97.3	102.0
2007	103.5	104.6	107.3	104.3	102.4	99.4	104.1
2008	107.9	112.1	108.8	113.9	104.9	99.5	105.4
2009	97.0	94.8	106.2	91.1	101.8	96.1	102.2
2010	103.8	106.1	106.9	106.5	102.4	98.6	102.4
2011	106.5	110.6	110.2	111.6	104.1	99.7	102.7
2012	99.4	98.7	108.1	95.8	103.3	98.6	101.6
2013	100.2	99.8	108.4	97.3	103.4	98.5	102.2
2014	100.5	100.3	108.3	98.1	102.8	99.5	101.5
2015	97.0	94.9	105.8	91.5	100.9	99.8	100.6

上/海/统/计/年/鉴

主要统计指标解释

居民消费价格指数

居民消费价格指数是度量一组代表性消费商品及服务项目价格水平随着时间而变动的相对数，反映居民家庭购买的消费品及服务价格水平的变动情况。它是宏观经济分析和决策、价格总水平监测和调控以及国民经济核算的重要指标。其按年度计算的变动率通常被用来作为反映通货膨胀或紧缩程度的指标。

现行的居民消费价格指数按用途分为八个大类，包括食品、烟酒、衣着、家庭设备用品及维修服务、医疗保健和个人用品、交通和通信、娱乐教育文化用品及服务、居住。

商品零售价格指数

商品零售价格指数是反映一定时期内城乡商品零售价格变动趋势和程度的相对数。商品零售价格的变动直接影响城乡居民的生活支出和国家的财政收入，影响居民购买力和市场供需的平衡，影响消费与积累的比例关系。因此，该指数可以从一个侧面对上述经济活动进行观察和分析。

工业生产者出厂价格指数

从2011年起工业品出厂价格指数改为工业生产者出厂价格指数，它是反映一定时期内全部工业产品出厂价格总水平的变动趋势和程度的相对数，包括工业企业售给本企业以外所有单位的各种产品和直接售给居民用于生活消费的产品。该指数可以观察出厂价格变动对工业总产值及增加值的影响。

工业生产者购进价格指数

从2011年起原材料、燃料和动力购进价格指数改为工业生产者购进价格指数，它是反映工业企业作为生产投入，从物资交易市场和能源、原材料生产企业购买原材料、燃料和动力产品时，所支付的价格水平变动趋势和程度的统计指标，是扣除工业企业物质消耗成本中的价格变动影响的重要依据。

目前，上海编制的工业生产者购进价格指数所调查的产品包括燃料动力、黑色金属、有色金属、化工、建材等九大类的约900种产品。

固定资产投资价格指数

固定资产投资价格指数是反映一定时期内固定资产投资品及项目的价格变动趋势和程度的相对数。固定资产投资额是由建筑安装工程投资完成额、设备工器具购置投资完成额和其他费用投资完成额三部分组成的。编制固定资产投资价格指数应首先分别编制上述三部分投资的价格指数，然后采用加权算术平均法求出固定资产投资价格总指数。

该指数可以准确地反映固定资产投资中涉及的各类投资品和收费项目价格变动趋势和变动幅度，消除按现价计算的固定资产投资指标中的价格变动因素，真实地反映固定资产投资的规模、速度、结构和效益，为国家科学地制定、检查固定资产投资计划并提高宏观调控水平，为完善国民经济核算体系提供科学的、可靠的依据。

SHANGHAI STATISTICAL YEARBOOK

EXPLANATORY NOTES TO MAJOR STATISTICAL INDICATORS

□ Consumer Price Index

The Consumer Price Index is an index that reflects the time-based change of prices of a group of representative consumption commodities and services. It is an important reference factor for macro-economic analysis and strategy, monitoring and adjustment of overall price level and the national economic budgeting. The year-on-year change of the index is often a norm reflecting the inflation or deflation.

The current CPI covers eight categories of goods and services: food; tobacco and liquor; garments; household facilities, articles and repair services; medical and health care and personal items; traffic and telecommunications; education, culture and recreation articles and services and residence.

□ Retail Price Index

Retail Price Index reflects the trend and degree of change in retail prices of commodities during a given period. The change in retail prices of commodities directly affect the living expenditure of urban and rural residents, government revenue, purchasing power of residents and the equilibrium of market supply and demand, and the ratio of consumption to accumulation. Therefore, the retail price index is useful to analyze the changes of the above economic activities.

□ Producer Ex-factory Price Index

Since 2011, Ex-factory Price Index of Industrial Products has been changed into Producer Ex-factory Price Index. Producer Ex-factory Price Index reflects the trend and degree of changes in general ex-factory prices of all industrial products during a given period, including sales of industrial products by an industrial enterprise to all units outside the enterprise, as well as sales of consumer goods to residents. It can be used to analyze the impact of ex-factory prices on gross output value and value-added of the industrial sector.

□ Producer Purchasing Price Index

Since 2011, Index of Purchasing Prices of Raw Materials, Fuels and Power has been changed into Producer Purchasing Price Index which reflects changes in the level and degree of prices paid by industrial enterprises when they purchase production input such as raw materials, fuels and power from the market or from other energy or raw materials producing enterprises. This index provides important basis for measuring the material consumption of industrial enterprises after removing influence of price changes.

At present, close to 900 products in 9 categories, including fuels and power, ferrous metals, non-ferrous metals, chemicals, building materials, are covered in Shanghai for the survey to producer purchasing prices index.

□ Price Index of Investment in Fixed Assets

Price Index of Investment in Fixed Assets reflects the trend and degree of changes in prices of investment goods and projects in fixed assets during a given period. The investment in fixed assets consists of three components, namely the investment in construction and installation, the investment in purchases of equipment and instrument, and the investment in other items. Price Index of investment in fixed assets is calculated as the weighted arithmetic mean of the price Index of the three components of investment in fixed assets.

Removing the factor of price change in the aggregates of investment at current prices, this indicator shows the changes in the prices of commodities and fees involved in the investment of fixed assets, and can be used to observe the actual size, growth, structure, and efficiency of investment in fixed assets and provides reliable and scientific data for government planning, management, decision-making, and further improving the current national accounting system.

第十篇
CHAPTER 10

人民生活
LIVING STANDARDS

简要说明

第一部分　2015 年上海居民收支与生活状况调查主要数据(新口径)(见表 10.1　到表 10.10)

一、主要内容

第一部分资料反映 2015 年上海常住居民生活收入、消费及其他生活状况。

二、资料来源

上海常住居民生活状况数据来源于国家统计局上海调查总队居民收支与生活状况抽样调查。

三、住户调查对象

上海居民收支与生活状况调查(简称住户调查,下同)对象为“本市常住居民”,既包括本地户籍,也包括外地户籍;既包括以家庭形式居住的户,也包括以集体形式居住的户,即在本市常住的外来务工人员也被纳入调查对象。调查区域扩展到全市 16 个区县的城镇、农村地区。全市城镇、农村调查样本量分别扩大到 4600 户和 1400 户,合计为 6000 户。

四、调查内容

调查主要内容包括居民现金和实物收支情况、住户成员及劳动力从业情况、居民家庭食品和能源消费情况、住房和耐用消费拥有情况、家庭经营和生产投资情况、收入分配影响因素情况、社区基本情况以及其他民生状况等。

五、指标发布的变化

根据国家统计局要求,国家统计局上海调查总队从 2015 年 1 季度起,发布城乡一体化住户调查新口径调查数据。主要指标包括:上海居民人均可支配收入、城镇常住居民人均可支配收入、农村常住居民人均可支配收入;上海居民人均消费支出、城镇常住居民人均消费支出、农村常住居民人均消费支出等。

六、数据主要变化情况

根据城乡一体化住户调查改革,2015 年起,遵照 " 统计上的城乡划分标准 ",新口径城镇常住居民收入、消费等数据覆盖范围在原有基础上扩大,包括城乡结合部,而农村常住居民范围缩小,不再以行政村划分; 新口径城镇常住居民 " 人均可支配收入 " 指标加入了自有住房折算净租金,扣除了财产性支出和转移性支出等。计算城镇和农村常住居民消费支出时,包括了自有住房折算租金。

第二部分 历年城镇和农村住户调查主要数据(老口径)(见表 10.11 到表 10.20)

一、主要内容

第二部分资料反映 1980—2014 年上海市居民生活现状及变化情况,分为城市居民生活和农村居民生活两部分。

二、城镇住户调查资料来源

城镇居民生活状况的数据来源于国家统计局上海调查总队的城镇住户抽样调查。主要内容包括城市居民生活基本情况、收入、生活消费支出、主要消费品消费量等。

三、城镇住户调查方法

上海城镇住户调查以城市常住户为调查对象,2003 年及之前, 调查样本为 500 户,2004 年至 2014 年,调查样本增至 1000 户,分布于黄浦、卢湾、徐汇、长宁、静安、普陀、闸北、虹口、杨浦、闵行、宝山、浦东等 12 个区。

城镇住户调查采用分层、多阶段与大小成比例(pps)、随机等距等方法抽选调查样本户,采用日记账与问卷调查相结合的方法取得数据。首先,每月向抽中的调查户发放帐本,由调查户采用日记帐方式对本住户及每个成员的收支情况进行记录;然后由调查人员每月在规定的时间将帐本回收并进行审核、编码和录入;最后由国家统计局上海调查总队进行数据汇总得出人均可支配收入等数据资料。另外,家庭和个人基本情况以及部分调查户的收支情况通过问卷的形式取得数据。

四、农村住户调查资料来源

农村居民生活状况的数据来源于国家统计局上海调查总队的住户收支与生活状况调查。主要内容包括农村居民生活基本情况、收入、生活消费支出、主要消费品消费量等。

五、农村住户调查方法

农村住户调查是以农村常住户为调查对象,农村常住户指长期(半年以上)居住在农村范围内的住户。户口不在本地而在本地居住半年及以上的住户也包括在本地农村常住户范围内。按国家统计局住户收支与生活状况调查方案, 采用抽样调查方法在全市郊区县抽取约 1200 户农村居民家庭作为调查样本,分布于浦东、闵行、宝山、嘉定、金山、松江、青浦、奉贤、崇明 9 个区县。

为保证农村住户调查资料的准确性, 住户收支与生活状况调查在 95%的概率把握程度下要求抽样误差不得超过 ± 3%。调查数据采用农村居民记账与一次性调查相结合的方法取得,调查户按照国家统计局上海调查总队统一编制的帐本和要求记账,现金收支帐、实物收支帐发生一笔记一笔,由区县调查员每月收取调查户的帐本,录入计算机,通过乡镇、区县、总队多级审核确保调查数据真实可靠。

BRIEF INTRODUCTION

Part 1 Main Data from Survey of Income and Expenditure and Living Conditions of Residents in Shanghai (New Statistical Standard)

I. Main Contents

The data of first part reflect the income and consumption and other living conditions of residents in Shanghai in 2015.

Ⅱ. Sources of Data

Data on the living conditions of Shanghai residents come from the sample survey on residents revenue and expenditure and living conditions, which is conducted by Survey Office of the National Bureau of Statistics in Shanghai.

Ⅲ.Objects of Household Survey

The objects of survey on Shanghai residents revenue and expenditure and living conditions (abbreviated as household survey, the same below) are residents in Shanghai with residence registration or non-residence registration, including both households living in the form of family and households living in the form of groups, that is, resident migrant workers in the city are also included in the survey. The survey area is extended to urban and rural areas of 16 districts in the whole city. The survey samples of urban and rural are expanded to 4600 households and 1400 households respectively, which amount to 6000 households.

Ⅳ. Contents of the Survey

The main contents of the survey include income and expenditure of residents in cash and in kind, employment situation of household members and labor force, food and energy consumption of households, possession of housing and durable goods consumption, situation of household business and production investment, influencing factors of income distribution, basic situation of the community and other livelihood of people, etc.

Ⅴ.Changes of Index Releasing

According to the requirements of the National Bureau of Statistics, Survey Office of the National Bureau of Statistics in Shanghai releases the data of household survey of urban and rural integration according to new statistic standard since the first quarter of 2015. The main indicators include: per capita disposable income of Shanghai residents, per capita disposable income of urban residents, per capita disposable income of rural residents; per capita consumption expenditure of Shanghai residents, per capita consumption expenditure of urban residents, and per capita consumption expenditure of rural residents

Ⅵ. Main Changes of Data

According to the household survey reform of urban and rural integration, since 2015,following the Statistical Classification of Urban and Rural Areas, coverage of data of new standard on urban resident income and consumption is expanded on the original basis , including the Urban-Rural Binding Region. But Coverage of rural residents is reduced, and is no longer divided by administrative village. The indicator of Per Capita Disposable Income includes self-owned housing converted net rent, and excludes property expenditure and transfer expenditure, etc. The calculation of con-

Part 2 Main Data from Urban and Rural Household Survey Over the Years (Old Statistical Standard)

I. Main Contents

Data in the second part of this chapter reflect the Shanghai people's living conditions and changes from 1980 to 2014, consisting of two parts, on the life of urban and rural households respectively.

II. Sources of Data on the Living Conditions of Urban Residents

Data on the living conditions of urban residents come from the data collected through a sample survey on the urban households conducted by the Survey Office of the National Bureau of Statistics in Shanghai. The main contents of the survey include basic situation of urban residents living, income, consumer spending and the main consumption of consumer goods, etc.

III. Methodology for Urban Household Survey

Data on the survey of urban residents cover long-term residents in urban areas. Shanghai's sample included 500 households before 2003; it increased to 1,000 households between 2004 and 2014, covering 12 districts of Huangpu, Luwan, Xuhui, Changning, Jing'an, Putuo, Zhabei, Hongkou, Yangpu, Minhang, Baoshan and Pudong.

Samples in urban household survey are selected by systematic sampling method schemes, such as stratifying method, multi -stage method and probability proportional to size (PPS) method, and the data are obtained by method of journal combined with questionnaire. Selected households receive account books each month and keep diaries to record income and expenditure of the household and its individual members. Professional inspectors will then collect, encode and audit the data at fixed time each month, deliver them to the Survey Office of the National Bureau of Statistics to calculate data such as the average disposable income per capita. In addition, data of household and personal basic situation as well as the balance of the selected households are obtained through the form of questionnaire.

IV. Sources of Data on the Living of Rural Residents

Data on the living conditions of rural residents come from data collected through the survey on household revenue and expenditure and living condition, which is organized by the Survey Office of the National Bureau of Statistics in Shanghai. The main contents of the survey include the basic condition of rural households, income, consumption expenditure and consumption of major consumer goods.

V. Methodology for Rural Household Survey

Data on the survey of income and expenditure of rural residents cover long–term residents in rural areas. Long–term residents refer to people living within the administered villages for more than half a year. Households without local registered residence are included given they have lived in the area for more than half a year. According to the scheme of the survey on rural household revenue, expenditure and living condition, the sampling approach is used to select about 1,200 rural households as samples through 9 districts and counties of Pudong, Minhang, Baoshan, Jiading, Jinshan, Songjiang, Qingpu, Fengxian, and Chongming.

To guarantee accuracy of the data on the revenue, expenditure and living condition of rural household, it is required that the sampling error should not exceed ±3%, with a confidence probability as 95%. A combination of diaries kept by rural households and the one–time survey is used for collecting data. The households are keeping diaries on unified requirements compiled by the Survey Office of the National Bureau of Statistics in Shanghai. Income and expenditure of cash and real goods are recorded case by case. Data are collected by inspectors from districts and counties and compiled into computers. Inspectors from townships, counties, districts and the headquarters office will audit the data to make them accurate and reliable.

表 10.1 全市居民家庭生活基本情况(2015)
BASIC STATISTICS OF WHOLE CITY HOUSEHOLDS

	指 标 Indicators	全 市 Whole City	城 镇 Urban	农 村 Rural
基本情况(人)	**Basic Statistics(person)**			
户均人口	Population per Household	2.62	2.64	2.47
户均从业人口	Employees per Household	1.29	1.26	1.54
平均每一从业人口负担人数(包括从业者本人)	Persons Supported by Each Employee(person)	2.03	2.09	1.60
从业人员文化程度(%)	**Educational Level of Employees(%)**	**100**	**100**	**100**
未上过学	Not been to school	0.3	0.1	1.4
小 学	Primary School	5.7	4.0	17.1
初 中	Junior Middle School	29.6	25.3	57.6
高中(含职高和中专)	Senior Secondary School(Including Specialized Secondary School and Secondary Vocational School)	24.0	25.3	15.3
大学专科	College	18.1	20.0	6.1
大学本科及以上	Bachelor's Degree and above	22.3	25.3	2.5
常住户家庭收入与支出(元)	Income and Expenditure of Resident Household(yuan)			
人均可支配收入	Per Capita Disposable Income	49 867	52 962	23 205
人均消费支出	Per Capita Consumption Expenditure	34 784	36 946	16 152

注：2012 年起，国家统计局实施了城乡一体化住户调查改革，统一了城乡居民收入名称、分类和统计标准，在上海选取 6000 宅(户)城乡居民家庭，直接开展调查。2015 年起，发布城乡可比的新口径全市居民人均可支配收入以及分城乡常住居民人均可支配收入。

Note: Since 2012, the National Bureau of Statistics has implemented the integrated household survey reform of urban and rural integration with unifying the urban and rural income name, classification and statistical standards, and selected 6000 house (households) of urban and rural resident families in Shanghai for direct investigation. Since 2015, the per capita disposable income of city's residents and per capita disposable income of urban and rural residents which can be compared by new statistical coverage have been released.

表 10.2 个人存款(住户存款)年末余额(1997 ~2015)
HOUSEHOLD DEPOSITS AT YEAR-END

年 份 Year	个人存款(住户存款)余额 (亿元) Household Deposits (100 million yuan)	其 中 of which 活期存款 Current Deposits	定期及其他存款 Time Deposits and Other Deposits	人均个人存款余额 (元) Average Deposits (yuan)
1997	2 109.18	265.93	1 843.25	14 165
1998	2 372.94	355.78	2 017.16	15 540
1999	2 597.12	477.30	2 119.82	16 574
2000	2 627.07	542.86	2 084.21	16 331
2001	3 109.50	808.17	2 301.33	19 266
2002	4 915.54	1 312.49	3 603.05	30 249
2003	6 054.60	1 793.73	4 260.87	35 386
2004	6 960.99	2 056.06	4 904.93	39 956
2005	8 432.49	2 360.66	6 071.83	47 416
2006	9 480.28	2 778.31	6 701.97	52 223
2007	9 326.45	3 140.60	6 185.85	50 194
2008	12 083.66	3 528.02	8 555.64	63 987
2009	14 357.65	4 624.53	9 733.13	74 728
2010	16 249.29	5 396.19	10 853.11	70 918
2011	18 920.43	5 925.39	12 995.04	82 168
2012	21 512.01	6 644.11	14 867.90	90 370
2013	23 097.35	7 251.30	15 846.05	95 635
2014	24 057.05	7 409.90	16 647.15	99 177
2015	23 384.73	8 184.76	15 199.97	96 612

注：本表数据由中国人民银行上海总部提供。1997 年 ~1999 年，个人存款余额为中资金融机构人民币储蓄存款余额；2000 年 ~2010 年，个人存款余额为中外资金融机构本外币储蓄存款余额；2011 年 ~2015 年，个人存款余额含中外资金融机构本外币活期存款余额、定期存款余额、结构性存款余额、保证金存款余额等。

Note: Data in this table are provided by Shanghai Headquarters of the People's Bank of China. From 1997 to 1999, the household deposits refer to RMB savings deposits in domestic funded financial institutions. From 2000 to 2010, the household deposits refer to all personal savings deposits in foreign and domestic funded financial institutions. From 2011 to 2015, the household deposits include current deposits、time deposits、structured deposits、margin deposit for security and so on.

表 10.3 居民收支情况(2015)
BASIC STATISTICS OF INCOME AND EXPENDITURE OF RESIDENTS

单位:元

	指 标 Indicators	全 市 Whole City	城 镇 Urban	农 村 Rural
居民人均可支配收入	**Per Capita Disposable Income of Residents**	**49 867**	**52 962**	**23 205**
工资性收入	Wages	30 499	32 010	17 483
经营净收入	Net Business Income	1 319	1 303	1 462
财产净收入	Net Property Income	7 173	7 915	775
转移净收入	Net Transferred Income	10 876	11 734	3 485
居民人均消费支出	**Per Capita Consumption Expenditure of Residents**	**34 784**	**36 946**	**16 152**
食品烟酒	Food, Cigarettes and Liquors	9 272	9 691	5 660
衣 着	Clothing	1 623	1 711	857
居 住	Residence	11 308	12 137	4 161
生活用品及服务	Living Goods and Services	1 485	1 573	723
交通通信	Transportation	4 206	4 457	2 046
教育文化娱乐	Education, Culture and Entertainment	3 718	4 046	893
医疗保健	Medicine and Medical Services	2 268	2 362	1 464
其他用品及服务	Other Goods and Services	904	969	348

表 10.4 居民收支比上年增长(2015)
GROWTH RATE OF INCOME AND EXPENDITURE OF RESIDENTS ON PRECEDING YEAR

单位:%

	指 标 Indicators	全 市 Whole City	城 镇 Urban	农 村 Rural
居民人均可支配收入	**Per Capita Disposable Income of Residents**	**8.5**	**8.4**	**9.5**
工资性收入	Wages	6.1	6.0	8.1
经营净收入	Net Business Income	-4.2	-4.9	1.5
财产净收入	Net Property Income	10.3	10.3	13.0
转移净收入	Net Transferred Income	16.5	16.4	20.7
居民人均消费支出	**Per Capita Consumption Expenditure of Residents**	**5.2**	**5.0**	**9.0**
食品烟酒	Food, Cigarettes and Liquors	2.9	2.7	6.1
衣 着	Clothing	0.6	0.7	-0.4
居 住	Residence	4.8	4.4	15.1
生活用品及服务	Living Goods and Services	-3.1	-3.5	4.8
交通通信	Transportation and Communication	17.0	17.2	11.8
教育文化娱乐	Education, Culture and Entertainment	12.3	12.2	14.1
医疗保健	Medicine and Medical Services	2.0	1.5	10.1
其他用品及服务	Other Goods and Services	-8.4	-8.4	-8.1

表 10.5 全市居民可支配收入及构成(2015)
DISPOSABLE INCOME AND ITS COMPOSITION OF WHOLE CITY RESIDENTS

	指 标 Indicators	全 市 Whole City	城 镇 Urban	农 村 Rural
可支配收入(元/人)	Disposable Income(yuan/person)	49 867	52 962	23 205
工资性收入	Wages	30 499	32 010	17 483
经营净收入	Net Business Income	1 319	1 303	1 462
财产净收入	Net Property Income	7 173	7 915	775
转移净收入	Net Transferred Income	10 876	11 734	3 485
#养老金或离退休金	Pension or Retirement Pension	12 823	13 795	4 445
可支配收入构成(%)	Composition of Disposable Income	100.0	100.0	100.0
工资性收入	Wages	61.2	60.4	75.3
经营净收入	Net Business Income	2.6	2.5	6.3
财产净收入	Net Property Income	14.4	14.9	3.3
转移净收入	Net Transferred Income	21.8	22.2	15.1
#养老金或离退休金	Pension or Retirement Pension	25.7	26.0	19.2

表 10.6 全市居民可支配收入(2015,按收入水平分组)
DISPOSABLE INCOME OF WHOLE CITY RESIDENTS(CLASSIFIED BY INCOME LEVELS)

	指 标 Indicators	全 市 Whole City	城 镇 Urban	农 村 Rural
可支配收入(元/人)	**Disposable Income(yuan/person)**	**49 867**	**52 962**	**23 205**
低收入户	Low Income	21 086	24 841	11 766
中低收入户	Medium-low Income	34 370	38 060	18 015
中等收入户	Medium Income	45 454	48 710	22 848
中高收入户	Medium-high Income	59 403	62 423	27 905
高收入户	Hign Income	97 276	100 688	39 005
比上年增长(%)	**Growth Rate over the Previous Year(%)**	**8.5**	**8.4**	**9.5**
低收入户	Low Income	9.7	9.5	12.1
中低收入户	Medium-low Income	9.1	9.4	9.8
中等收入户	Medium Income	8.8	9.0	8.4
中高收入户	Medium-high Income	9.3	9.3	4.9
高收入户	Hign Income	8.2	8.1	8.0

表 10.7 全市居民消费支出(2015)
CONSUMPTION EXPENDITURE OF WHOLE CITY RESIDENTS

单位:元/人

指 标	Indicators	全 市 Whole City	城 镇 Urban	农 村 Rural
消费支出	Consumption Expenditure	34 784	36 946	16 152
食品烟酒	Food, Cigarettes and Liquors	9 272	9 691	5 660
#食 品	Food	5 905	6 129	3 972
在外饮食(不含食堂用餐)	Dining Out(excluding the canteen)	2 191	2 387	504
衣 着	Clothing	1 623	1 711	857
衣 类	Garments	1 270	1 343	637
鞋 类	Shoes	353	368	220
居 住	Residence	11 308	12 137	4 161
#租赁房房租	Rents	829	870	476
水电燃料及其他	Water, Electricity, Fuel and Others	951	973	762
生活用品及服务	Living Goods and Services	1 485	1 573	723
#家用器具	Home Appliances	335	355	162
家庭日用杂品	Household Daily Groceries	341	354	230
交通通信	Transportation and Communication	4 206	4 457	2 046
交 通	Transportation	2 913	3 113	1 190
通 信	Communication	1 293	1 344	856
教育文化娱乐	Education, Culture and Entertainment	3 718	4 046	893
教 育	Education	1 345	1 453	419
文化和娱乐	Culture and Entertainment	2 373	2 593	474
医疗保健	Medicine and Medical Services	2 268	2 362	1 464
医疗器具及药品	Medical Devices and Drugs	400	425	187
医疗服务	Medical Service	1 868	1 937	1 277
其他用品及服务	Other Goods and Services	904	969	348

表 10.8 全市居民消费支出及构成(2015)
CONSUMPTION EXPENDITURE AND ITS COMPOSITION OF WHOLE CITY RESIDENTS

指 标	Indicators	全 市 Whole City	城 镇 Urban	农 村 Rural
消费支出(元/人)	Consumption Expenditure(yuan/person)	34 784	36 946	16 152
食品烟酒	Food,Cigarettes and Liquors	9 272	9 691	5 660
衣 着	Clothing	1 623	1 711	857
居 住	Residence	11 308	12 137	4 161
生活用品及服务	Living Goods and Services	1 485	1 573	723
交通通信	Transportation and Communication	4 206	4 457	2 046
教育文化娱乐	Education,Culture and Entertainment	3 718	4 046	893
医疗保健	Medicine and Medical Services	2 268	2 362	1 464
其他用品及服务	Other Goods and Services	904	969	348
消费支出构成(%)	Composition of Consumption Expenditure(%)	100	100	100
食品烟酒	Food,Cigarettes and Liquors	26.6	26.2	35.0
衣 着	Clothing	4.7	4.6	5.3
居 住	Residence	32.5	32.8	25.8
生活用品及服务	Living Goods and Services	4.3	4.3	4.5
交通通信	Transportation and Communication	12.1	12.1	12.7
教育文化娱乐	Education,Culture and Entertainment	10.7	11.0	5.5
医疗保健	Medicine and Medical Services	6.5	6.4	9.1
其他用品及服务	Other Goods and Services	2.6	2.6	2.1

注：因指标口径调整,“食品烟酒”占“消费支出”比重与历史数据不可比。
Note: Because of the adjustment of statistical coverage,the proportion of "food,cigarettes and liquors" in the "consumption expenditure" cannot be compared with the historical data.

表 10.9 全市居民人均消费支出及增长(2015,按收入水平分组)
PER CAPITA CONSUMPTION AND ITS GROWTH OF WHOLE CITY RESIDENTS(CLASSIFIED BY INCOME LEVELS)

	指 标 Indicators	全 市 Whole City	城 镇 Urban	农 村 Rural
消费支出(元/人)	**Consumption Expenditure(yuan/person)**	**34 784**	**36 946**	**16 152**
低收入户	Low Income	15 877	18 261	11 191
中低收入户	Medium-low Income	23 209	25 579	14 273
中等收入户	Medium Income	31 267	33 913	16 030
中高收入户	Medium-high Income	41 126	43 587	18 487
高收入户	Hign Income	68 124	70 218	22 045
比上年增长(%)	**Growth Rate over the Previous Year(%)**	**5.2**	**5.0**	**9.0**
低收入户	Low Income	5.2	6.2	5.9
中低收入户	Medium-low Income	6.6	4.3	7.6
中等收入户	Medium Income	4.7	3.0	10.6
中高收入户	Medium-high Income	0.4	3.2	10.5
高收入户	Hign Income	9.1	8.6	5.3

表 10.10 每百户居民家庭年末耐用消费品拥有量(2015)
DURABLE CONSUMER GOODS OWNED BY EACH HUNDRED HOUSEHOLDS AT END OF THE YEAR

	指 标 Indicators	全 市 Whole City	城 镇 Urban	农 村 Rural
家用汽车(辆)	Family Cars(vehicle)	24	26	14
电动助力车(辆)	Electric Booster Vehicles(vehicle)	58	51	121
洗衣机(台)	Washing Machine (unit)	89	92	70
电冰箱(柜)(台)	Refrigerators or Freezers(unit)	96	97	84
微波炉(台)	Microwave Ovens (unit)	84	87	65
彩色电视机(台)	Colour Televisions(unit)	174	177	148
空调(台)	Air-conditioner(unit)	181	191	101
热水器(台)	Water Heaters(unit)	88	91	66
排油烟机(台)	Range Hoods(unit)	74	79	38
固定电话(线)	Fixed Telephones(line)	75	77	61
移动电话(部)	Mobile Phones(unit)	217	221	187
#接入互联网	Access to the Internet	153	161	94
计算机(台)	Computers(unit)	117	126	47
#接入互联网	Access to the Internet	111	120	40

表 10.11 主要年份城乡居民家庭人均收入及消费支出
PER CAPITA INCOME AND CONSUMPTION EXPENDITURE OF URBAN AND RURAL HOUSEHOLDS IN MAIN YEARS

年份 Year	城市居民家庭人均可支配收入（元）Per Capita Disposable Income of Urban Households	农村居民家庭人均可支配收入（元）Per Capita Disposable Income of Rural Households	城市居民家庭人均消费支出（元）Per Capita Consumption Expenditure of Urban Households	农村居民家庭人均消费支出（元）Per Capita Consumption Expenditure of Rural Households
1980	637	401	553	323
1985	1 075	806	992	778
1990	2 183	1 665	1 937	1 262
1995	7 172	4 246	5 868	3 368
1996	8 159	4 846	6 763	3 868
1997	8 439	5 277	6 820	4 228
1998	8 773	5 407	6 866	4 207
1999	10 932	5 481	8 248	3 867
2000	11 718	5 565	8 868	4 138
2001	12 883	5 850	9 336	4 753
2002	13 250	6 212	10 464	5 311
2003	14 867	6 658	11 040	5 670
2004	16 683	7 337	12 631	6 329
2005	18 645	8 342	13 773	7 265
2006	20 668	9 213	14 762	8 006
2007	23 623	10 222	17 255	8 845
2008	26 675	11 385	19 398	9 115
2009	28 838	12 324	20 992	9 804
2010	31 838	13 746	23 200	10 225
2011	36 230	15 644	25 102	11 272
2012	40 188	17 401	26 253	12 096
2013	43 851	19 208	28 155	13 425
2014	47 710	21 192	30 520	15 291

表10.12 城市居民家庭生活基本情况(1980~2014)
BASIC STATISTICS OF URBAN HOUSEHOLDS

年 份 Year	调查户数 (户) Number of Households Surveyed (household)	平均每人 可支配收入 (元) Per Capita Disposable Income (yuan)	平均每人 消费支出 (元) Per Capita Consumption Expenditures (yuan)	可支配收入 比上年增长(%) (按当年价格) Growth Rate of Disposable Income on Preceding Year(%) (at Current Price)	消费支出 比上年增长(%) (按当年价格) Growth Rate of Consumption Expenditure on Preceding Year(%) (at Current Price)	恩格尔 系数(%) Engel Coefficient (%)
1980	500	637	553	32.5	28.8	56.0
1981	500	637	585	平	5.7	56.8
1982	500	659	576	3.5	-1.5	58.9
1983	500	686	615	4.0	6.9	58.5
1984	500	834	726	21.6	18.0	56.5
1985	500	1 075	992	28.9	36.6	52.1
1986	500	1 293	1 170	20.3	18.0	52.7
1987	500	1 437	1 282	11.1	9.6	54.4
1988	500	1 723	1 648	19.9	28.6	52.7
1989	500	1 976	1 812	14.6	9.9	55.8
1990	500	2 183	1 937	10.5	6.9	56.5
1991	500	2 486	2 167	13.9	11.9	56.9
1992	500	3 009	2 509	21.1	15.8	55.9
1993	500	4 277	3 530	42.2	40.7	53.1
1994	500	5 868	4 669	37.2	32.3	53.5
1995	500	7 172	5 868	22.2	25.7	53.4
1996	500	8 159	6 763	13.8	15.3	50.7
1997	500	8 439	6 820	3.4	0.8	51.7
1998	500	8 773	6 866	4.0	0.7	50.6
1999	500	10 932	8 248	24.6	20.1	45.2
2000	500	11 718	8 868	7.2	7.5	44.5
2001	500	12 883	9 336	9.9	5.3	43.4
2002	500	13 250	10 464	11.5	11.4	39.4
2003	500	14 867	11 040	12.2	5.5	37.2
2004	1 000	16 683	12 631	12.2	14.4	36.4
2005	1 000	18 645	13 773	11.8	9.0	35.9
2006	1 000	20 668	14 762	10.8	7.2	35.6
2007	1 000	23 623	17 255	14.3	16.9	35.5
2008	1 000	26 675	19 398	12.9	12.4	36.6
2009	1 000	28 838	20 992	8.1	8.2	35.0
2010	1 000	31 838	23 200	10.4	10.5	33.5
2011	1 000	36 230	25 102	13.8	8.2	35.5
2012	1 000	40 188	26 253	10.9	4.6	36.8
2013	1 000	43 851	28 155	9.1	7.2	34.9
2014	1 000	47 710	30 520	8.8	8.4	35.0

①本表数据为城市居民家庭收支抽样调查资料，由国家统计局上海调查总队提供。
②2002 年起，人均可支配收入不包括出售财物收入和个人交纳的社会保障支出。其他年份按原口径计算。
③平均每人可支配收入和平均每人消费支出增长按同口径计算的。
④城镇居民人均住房居住面积不是由收支处抽样数据所得，而是由房地局提供。
❶Data in this table are obtained from the sample survey of urban households and provided by Survey Office of the National Bureau of Statistics in Shanghai.
❷Incomes from selling properties and social security expenditure are excluded from disposable income since 2002. Other years follow the original caliber.
❸Growth of per Capita Disposable Income and growth of per Capita Consumption Expenditures are calculatedby the same caliber.
❹The per capita housing area of urban residents is not the data from sampling survey conducted by Revenue and Expenditure Department of Survey Office of the National Bureau of Statisitics in Shanghai, but is provided by Shanghai Municipal Housing Security and Building Administration Bureau.

表 10.13 主要年份城市居民家庭人均可支配收入
PER CAPITA DISPOSABLE INCOME OF URBAN HOUSEHOLDS IN MAIN YEARS

单位:元(yuan)

年 份 Year	人均可支配收入 Average per Capita Disposable Income	工资性收入 Salaries	经营净收入 Net Income from Household Business	财产性收入 Property Income	转移性收入 Transferred Income
1980	637	551			86
1985	1 075	794	1		280
1990	2 183	1 548	1	21	613
1991	2 486	1 780		29	677
1992	3 009	2 138	3	44	824
1993	4 277	3 099	4	37	1 137
1994	5 868	4 224	28	54	1 562
1995	7 172	5 002	69	92	2 009
1996	8 159	5 889	87	61	2 122
1997	8 439	5 969	150	69	2 251
1998	8 773	6 004	98	57	2 614
1999	10 932	7 326	156	68	3 382
2000	11 718	7 832	120	65	3 701
2001	12 883	7 975	119	39	4 750
2002	13 250	7 915	436	94	4 805
2003	14 867	10 097	377	130	4 263
2004	16 683	11 422	507	215	4 539
2005	18 645	12 409	798	292	5 146
2006	20 668	13 962	959	300	5 447
2007	23 623	16 598	1 158	369	5 498
2008	26 675	18 909	1 399	369	5 998
2009	28 838	19 811	1 435	474	7 118
2010	31 838	21 745	1 628	511	7 954
2011	36 230	24 454	1 994	633	9 149
2012	40 188	26 752	2 267	576	10 593
2013	43 851	28 518	2 317	788	12 228
2014	47 710	30 629	2 345	846	13 890

表 10.14 主要年份城市居民家庭人均可支配收入与消费支出
PER CAPITA ANNUAL DISPOSABLE INCOME AND CONSUMPTION EXPENDITURES OF URBAN HOUSEHOLDS IN MAIN YEARS

单位:元(yuan)

指 标	Indicators	2000	2005	2010	2014
人均可支配收入	**Per Capita Disposable Income**	**11 718**	**18 645**	**31 838**	**47 710**
低收入户	Low Income	6 840	7 851	14 996	24 317
中低收入户	Medium-low Income	8 815	11 800	21 780	34 120
中等收入户	Medium Income	10 529	15 668	27 484	40 799
中高收入户	Medium-high Income	12 892	21 313	35 120	52 089
高收入户	High Income	19 959	37 722	62 465	93 901
人均消费支出	**Per Capita Consumption Expenditures**	**8 868**	**13 773**	**23 200**	**30 520**
低收入户	Low Income	6 272	7 698	12 555	17 879
中低收入户	Medium-low Income	7 516	9 807	15 970	20 881
中等收入户	Medium Income	8 555	11 524	21 611	27 974
中高收入户	Medium-high Income	9 445	15 024	26 773	35 904
高收入户	High Income	12 763	25 470	40 744	53 734

表 10.15 主要年份城市居民家庭人均消费支出
PER CAPITA CONSUMPTION EXPENDITURES OF URBAN HOUSEHOLDS IN MAIN YEARS

单位:元

年份 Year	消费支出 Total Consumption Expenditures	食品 Food	衣着 Clothing	居住 Residence	家庭设备用品及服务 Household Facilities, Articles and Services	医疗保健 Medicines and Medical Services	交通和通信 Traffic and Communi-cations	教育文化娱乐服务 Education, Culture and Recreation Services	其他商品和服务 Other Commodities and Services
1980	553	310	79	26	50	7	20	49	12
1985	992	517	148	43	131	5	30	91	27
1990	1 937	1 095	208	90	196	11	58	231	48
1995	5 868	3 131	561	401	637	113	321	508	196
1996	6 763	3 429	590	416	614	148	496	827	243
1997	6 820	3 526	552	605	525	197	397	828	190
1998	6 866	3 477	472	674	453	261	406	893	230
1999	8 248	3 731	551	842	772	347	583	1 094	328
2000	8 868	3 947	567	794	683	501	759	1 287	330
2001	9 336	4 056	577	796	579	558	958	1 422	390
2002	10 464	4 120	613	1 189	653	734	1 115	1 668	372
2003	11 040	4 102	751	1 280	792	603	1 259	1 834	419
2004	12 631	4 593	797	1 327	780	762	1 703	2 195	474
2005	13 773	4 940	940	1 412	800	797	1 984	2 273	627
2006	14 762	5 249	1 027	1 436	877	763	2 333	2 432	645
2007	17 255	6 125	1 330	1 412	959	857	3 154	2 654	764
2008	19 398	7 109	1 521	1 646	1 182	755	3 373	2 875	937
2009	20 992	7 345	1 593	1 913	1 365	1 002	3 499	3 139	1 136
2010	23 200	7 777	1 794	2 166	1 800	1 006	4 076	3 363	1 218
2011	25 102	8 906	2 054	2 226	1 826	1 141	3 808	3 746	1 395
2012	26 253	9 656	2 111	1 790	1 906	1 017	4 564	3 724	1 485
2013	28 155	9 823	2 032	2 848	1 706	1 350	4 736	4 122	1 538
2014	30 520	10 677	2 038	3 031	1 779	1 449	4 885	4 931	1 730

表 10.16 主要年份城市居民家庭人均消费支出构成
COMPOSITION OF PER CAPITA CONSUMPTION EXPENDITURES OF URBAN HOUSEHOLDS IN MAIN YEARS

单位:%

年份 Year	消费支出 Total Consumption Expenditures	食品 Food	衣着 Clothing	居住 Residence	家庭设备用品及服务 Household Facilities, Articles and Services	医疗保健 Medicines and Medical Services	交通和通信 Traffic and Communi-cations	教育文化娱乐服务 Education, Culture and Recreation Services	其他商品和服务 Other Commodities and Services
1980	100	56.0	14.3	4.7	9.0	1.3	3.6	8.9	2.2
1985	100	52.1	14.9	4.4	13.2	0.5	3.0	9.2	2.7
1990	100	56.5	10.7	4.7	10.1	0.6	3.0	11.9	2.5
1995	100	53.4	9.6	6.8	10.8	1.9	5.5	8.7	3.3
1996	100	50.7	8.7	6.2	9.1	2.2	7.3	12.2	3.6
1997	100	51.7	8.1	8.9	7.7	2.9	5.8	12.1	2.8
1998	100	50.6	6.9	9.8	6.6	3.8	5.9	13.0	3.4
1999	100	45.2	6.7	10.2	9.3	4.2	7.1	13.3	4.0
2000	100	44.5	6.4	9.0	7.7	5.6	8.6	14.5	3.7
2001	100	43.4	6.2	8.5	6.2	6.0	10.3	15.2	4.2
2002	100	39.4	5.9	11.4	6.2	7.0	10.7	15.9	3.5
2003	100	37.2	6.8	11.6	7.2	5.4	11.4	16.6	3.8
2004	100	36.4	6.3	10.5	6.2	6.0	13.5	17.4	3.7
2005	100	35.9	6.8	10.2	5.8	5.8	14.4	16.5	4.6
2006	100	35.6	6.9	9.7	5.9	5.2	15.8	16.5	4.4
2007	100	35.5	7.7	8.2	5.5	5.0	18.3	15.4	4.4
2008	100	36.6	7.9	8.5	6.1	3.9	17.4	14.8	4.8
2009	100	35.0	7.6	9.1	6.5	4.8	16.7	14.9	5.4
2010	100	33.5	7.7	9.3	7.8	4.3	17.6	14.5	5.3
2011	100	35.5	8.2	8.9	7.3	4.5	15.2	14.9	5.5
2012	100	36.8	8.0	6.8	7.3	3.9	17.4	14.2	5.6
2013	100	34.9	7.2	10.1	6.1	4.8	16.8	14.6	5.5
2014	100	35.0	6.7	9.9	5.8	4.7	16.0	16.2	5.7

表 10.17 农村居民家庭生活基本情况(1990~2014)
BASIC STATISTICS OF RURAL HOUSEHOLDS

年 份 Year	调查户数 (户) Number of Households Surveyed (household)	平均每人可支配收入 (元) Disposable Income Per Capita (yuan)	平均每人生活消费支出 (元) Per Capita Consumption Expenditures (yuan)	平均每人可支配收入指数 (以1990年为100) Index of Per Capita Disposable Income (1990=100)	平均每人生活消费支出指数 (以1990年为100) Index of Per Capita Consumption Expenditures (1990=100)	平均每人年底居住房屋面积 (平方米) Per Capita Living Space Year-lend (sq. m)
1990	1 000	1 665	1 262	100.0	100.0	37.08
1991	600	2 003	1 540	120.3	122.0	39.60
1992	600	2 226	1 967	133.7	155.9	42.07
1993	600	2 727	2 200	163.8	174.3	44.22
1994	600	3 437	2 715	206.4	215.1	44.15
1995	600	4 246	3 368	255.0	266.9	43.08
1996	600	4 846	3 868	291.1	306.5	45.47
1997	600	5 277	4 228	316.9	335.0	46.44
1998	600	5 407	4 207	324.7	333.4	47.24
1999	600	5 481	3 867	329.2	306.4	49.00
2000	600	5 565	4 138	334.2	327.9	53.58
2001	600	5 850	4 753	351.4	376.6	54.70
2002	600	6 212	5 311	373.1	420.8	57.08
2003	600	6 658	5 670	399.9	449.3	59.03
2004	600	7 337	6 329	440.7	501.5	59.84
2005	600	8 342	7 265	501.0	575.7	56.56
2006	600	9 213	8 006	553.3	634.4	59.99
2007	600	10 222	8 845	613.9	700.9	61.22
2008	600	11 385	9 115	683.8	722.3	62.30
2009	600	12 324	9 804	740.2	776.9	60.18
2010	600	13 746	10 225	825.6	810.2	59.68
2011	1 200	15 644	11 272	939.6	893.2	58.90
2012	1 200	17 401	12 096	1 045.1	958.5	60.42
2013	1 200	19 208	13 425	1 153.6	1 063.8	58.48
2014	1 200	21 192	15 291	1 272.8	1 211.6	58.92

表 10.18 主要年份农村居民家庭人均可支配收入
PER CAPITA DISPOSABLE INCOME OF RURAL HOUSEHOLDS IN MAIN YEARS

指标 Indicators	人均可支配收入(元) Per Capita Disposable Income (yuan)	工资性收入 Wages	家庭经营纯收入 Household Business Income	转移性和财产性收入 Property and Transferred Income	比重(以人均可支配收入为100) Proportion Per Capita Disposable Income =100)		
					工资性收入 Wages	家庭经营纯收入 Household Business Income	转移性和财产性收入 Property and Transferred Income
1990	1 665	1 066	539	60	64.0	32.4	3.6
1995	4 246	2 734	1 183	329	64.4	27.9	7.7
2000	5 565	4 310	934	321	77.4	16.8	5.8
2005	8 342	6 364	811	1 167	76.3	9.7	14.0
2006	9 213	6 892	766	1 555	74.8	8.3	16.9
2007	10 222	7 498	754	1 970	73.3	7.4	19.3
2008	11 385	8 182	711	2 492	71.9	6.2	21.9
2009	12 324	8 721	590	3 013	70.8	4.8	24.4
2010	13 746	9 606	589	3 551	69.9	4.3	25.8
2011	15 644	10 493	877	4 274	67.1	5.6	27.3
2012	17 401	11 496	905	5 000	66.1	5.2	28.7
2013	19 208	12 378	920	5 910	64.4	4.8	30.8
2014	21 192	13 430	1 035	6 727	63.4	4.9	31.7

注：2000 年前平均每人可支配收入按纯收入口径计算。2011 年起，按可比口径计算，全年家庭经营纯收入增长为 22%；“土地征用补偿收入”不再列入财产性收入中。

Note: The per Capita Annual Disposable Income before 2000 refers to the Net Income. Since 2011, according to the calculation with comparable caliber, the growth rate of annual Household Business Income is 22%. Land Requisition Compensation Income is no longer included in the property income.

表 10.19 主要年份农村居民家庭人均可支配收入和人均生活消费支出
PER CAPITA DISPOSABLE INCOME AND LIVING EXPENDITURES FOR CONSUMPTION OF RURAL HOUSEHOLDS IN MAIN YEARS

单位:元(yuan)

年份 Year	总平均 Average	低收入户 Low Income	中低收入户 Medium-low Income	中等收入户 Medium Income	中高收入户 Medium-high Income	高收入户 High Income
人均可支配收入	**Average per Capita Disposable Income**					
2000	5 565	2 330	3 906	5 264	6 725	10 405
2005	8 342	3 347	5 594	7 612	9 755	15 309
2006	9 213	3 830	6 194	8 412	10 714	16 843
2007	10 222	4 321	7 098	9 442	11 807	18 443
2008	11 385	4 690	8 065	10 487	13 094	20 748
2009	12 324	5 279	8 785	11 184	14 039	22 465
2010	13 746	5 968	10 107	12 929	16 327	24 536
2011	15 644	7 018	11 772	14 568	18 145	27 227
2012	17 401	7 707	13 071	16 490	20 340	29 180
2013	19 208	8 708	14 415	18 152	22 618	31 196
2014	21 192	10 476	16 375	20 693	25 129	32 631
人均生活消费支出	**Average per Capita Consumption Expenditures**					
2000	4 138	2 390	3 387	3 887	5 487	5 880
2005	7 265	4 618	5 690	6 317	7 059	12 975
2006	8 006	4 788	6 001	6 951	8 015	15 058
2007	8 845	4 890	6 077	7 305	9 541	17 317
2008	9 115	5 024	6 280	9 555	10 700	14 517
2009	9 804	5 472	6 266	9 026	12 843	16 035
2010	10 225	5 026	7 881	8 739	15 103	15 187
2011	11 272	6 979	9 881	11 701	11 654	16 531
2012	12 096	7 784	8 813	10 802	13 725	19 773
2013	13 425	8 011	10 048	12 150	15 793	20 775
2014	15 291	9 629	12 208	13 487	17 909	22 645

表10.20 主要年份农村居民家庭人均生活消费支出
PER CAPITA CONSUMPTION EXPENDITURES OF RURAL HOUSEHOLDS IN MAIN YEARS

单位:元(yuan)

年　份 Year	生活消费支出 Total Consumption Expenditures	食　品 Food	衣　着 Clothing	居　住 Residence	家庭设备用品及服务 Household Facilities, Articles and Services	交通和通　信 Traffic and Communi-cations	文教娱乐用品及服务 Education, Culture and Recreation Articles and Services	医　疗保　健 Medicines and Medical Services	其他商品和服务 Other Commodities and Services
1990	1 262	586	107	272	129	6	59	33	70
1995	3 368	1 491	233	761	284	159	256	73	111
2000	4 138	1 823	201	724	225	279	559	209	118
2001	4 753	1 915	226	890	294	340	673	265	150
2002	5 311	1 872	226	1 392	281	462	661	280	137
2003	5 670	2 004	250	1 437	297	587	676	333	86
2004	6 329	2 191	280	1 446	344	720	806	425	117
2005	7 265	2 676	367	1 323	458	739	936	562	204
2006	8 006	3 024	418	1 658	481	780	920	549	176
2007	8 845	3 259	476	2 097	452	884	857	571	249
2008	9 115	3 732	467	1 806	504	880	850	697	179
2009	9 804	3 639	496	2 103	481	1 212	943	739	191
2010	10 225	3 807	554	2 070	528	1 459	1 012	585	210
2011	11 272	4 517	644	1 806	649	1 309	1 139	909	299
2012	12 096	4 837	704	1 834	646	1 705	1 088	1 029	253
2013	13 425	5 334	771	2 260	694	1 719	964	1 181	502
2014	15 291	6 188	801	2 747	712	1 891	1 069	1 308	575

表10.21 主要年份农村居民家庭人均生活消费支出构成
COMPOSITION OF PER CAPITA CONSUMER EXPENDITURES OF RURAL HOUSEHOLDS IN MAIN YEARS

单位:%

年　份 Year	生活消费支出 Total Consumption Expenditures	食　品 Food	衣　着 Clothing	居　住 Residence	家庭设备用品及服务 Household Facilities, Articles and Services	交通和通　信 Traffic and Communi-cations	文教娱乐用品及服务 Education, Culture and Recreation Articles and Services	医　疗保　健 Medicines and Medical Services	其他商品和服务 Other Commodities and Services
1990	100	46.4	8.5	21.6	10.2	0.5	4.7	2.6	5.5
1995	100	44.3	6.9	22.6	8.4	4.7	7.6	2.2	3.3
2000	100	44.0	4.9	17.5	5.4	6.7	13.5	5.1	2.9
2001	100	40.3	4.7	18.7	6.2	7.1	14.2	5.6	3.2
2002	100	35.2	4.3	26.2	5.3	8.7	12.4	5.3	2.6
2003	100	35.4	4.4	25.3	5.2	10.4	11.9	5.9	1.5
2004	100	34.6	4.4	22.9	5.4	11.4	12.7	6.7	1.9
2005	100	36.8	5.1	18.2	6.3	10.2	12.9	7.7	2.8
2006	100	37.8	5.2	20.7	6.0	9.7	11.5	6.9	2.2
2007	100	36.8	5.4	23.7	5.1	10.0	9.7	6.5	2.8
2008	100	40.9	5.1	19.8	5.5	9.7	9.3	7.7	2.0
2009	100	37.1	5.1	21.5	4.9	12.4	9.6	7.5	1.9
2010	100	37.2	5.4	20.2	5.2	14.3	9.9	5.7	2.1
2011	100	40.1	5.7	16.0	5.8	11.6	10.1	8.1	2.6
2012	100	40.0	5.8	15.2	5.3	14.1	9.0	8.5	2.1
2013	100	39.7	5.8	16.8	5.2	12.8	7.2	8.8	3.7
2014	100	40.5	5.2	17.9	4.7	12.4	7.0	8.5	3.8

上 / 海 / 统 / 计 / 年 / 鉴

主要统计指标解释

第一部分　2015 年上海居民收支与生活状况调查主要数据（新口径）（适用表 10.1 到表 10.10）

居民可支配收入（城镇 / 农村常住居民）

指居民可用于最终消费支出和储蓄的总和，即居民可用于自由支配的收入。既包括现金收入，也包括实物收入。按照收入的来源，可支配收入包含四项，分别为：工资性收入、经营净收入、财产净收入和转移净收入。

居民消费支出(城镇 / 农村常住居民)

是指居民用于满足家庭日常生活消费需要的全部支出，既包括现金消费支出，也包括实物消费支出。消费支出可划分为食品烟酒、衣着、居住、生活用品及服务、交通通信、教育文化娱乐、医疗保健以及其他用品及服务八大类。

第二部分　历年城镇和农村住户调查主要数据（老口径）（适用表 10.11 到表 10.20）

城镇居民家庭可支配收入

指居民家庭可用于最终消费支出和其他非义务性支出以及储蓄的总和，即居民家庭可以用来自由支配的收入。它是家庭总收入扣除交纳的所得税、个人交纳的社会保障费以及调查户的记账补贴后的收入。

城镇居民家庭消费支出

指居民家庭用于满足家庭日常生活消费需要的全部支出，包括食品、衣着、居住、家庭设备及用品、交通通信、文教娱乐、医疗保健、其他等八大类。消费支出构成是按照商品或服务的用途进行分类，如果消费支出的目的与用途不一致时，必须按照用途归入相应类内。

农村居民家庭可支配收入

指农村居民家庭获得的经过初次分配与再分配后的收入。可支配收入可用于住户的最终消费、非义务性支出以及储蓄。

农村居民家庭可支配收入＝总收入 － 家庭经营费用支出 － 税费支出 － 生产性固定资产折旧 － 财产性支出 － 转移性支出。

农村居民家庭生活消费支出

指农村住户用于物质生活和精神生活方面的支出。包括食品，衣着，居住，家庭设备用品及服务，医疗保健，交通和通信，文化教育娱乐用品及服务，其他商品和服务等消费支出。

SHANGHAI STATISTICAL YEARBOOK

EXPLANATORY NOTES TO MAJOR STATISTICAL INDICATORS

Part I Main Data from Survey of Income and Expenditure and Living Conditions of Residents in Shanghai (New Statistical Standard appliable for table 10.1 to 10.10)

□ Disposable Income of Residents (urban / rural residents)

Refers to the sum of final consumption expenditure and savings of residents, which can be freely allocated by residents. It includes income in cash and in kind. In accordance with the source of income, disposable income includes four parts: wage income, operating income, net income from property and net transfer income.

□ Consumption Expenditures of Residents (urban / rural resident)

Refers to all the expenses that are used to meet the needs of the daily life of the household, including consumption in cash and in kind. Consumption spending can be divided into eight categories: food, alcohol and tobacco, clothing, housing, daily necessities and services, transportation and communication, education culture and entertainment, health care and other goods and services.

Part II Main Data from Urban and Rural Household Survey Over the Years(Old Statistical Standard, appliable for table 10.11 to 10.20)

□ Disposable Income of Urban Households

refers to the actual income at the disposal of members of the households which can be used for final consumption, other non-compulsory expenditure and savings, which is part of the urban households' income that can be disposed by the urban households themselves. It is the income after deducting personal income tax, social insurance paid by individuals and investigation allowance from the total income of the households. The income from selling properties and borrowing are not included.

□ Consumption Expenditures of Urban Households

refers to all the expenditure paid by household for consumption in daily life, including 8 categories as follows: food; clothing; housing; household facilities and articles; traffic and communication; culture, education, and recreation; medical and health care; the others. Consumption expenditure is classified according to the use of goods or services. If the purpose and use of consumption expenditure are inconsistent, it should be included in the appropriate class according to the use.

□ Disposable Income of Rural Households

refers to the actual income at the disposal of rural households after initial distribution and reallocation. Disposal Income can be used for final consumption, non-compulsory expenditure and savings.

Disposal Income of Rural Households=total household income–expenditure for household operations–taxes and fees–depreciation of productive fixed assets–expenses on properties–expenses on transfers.

□ Living Expenditures for Consumption of Rural Households

refers to expenditures of material and culture life of rural household, including expenses on food, clothing, housing, household appliances and service, medical and health care, traffic and communication items, cultural, education and recreation items and service and other commodities and service.

第十一篇
CHAPTER 11

城市建设
URBAN CONSTRUCTION

简要说明

一、本篇资料的主要内容

本篇资料反映上海市城市建设的规模、速度及综合水平等基本情况，主要内容包括：市政道路、房屋建筑、供水排水、供气、城市绿化等城市建设情况。

二、本篇资料的来源

城市基础设施建设、公共事业和市政建设投资统计资料依据上海市统计局制定的《固定资产投资统计报表制度》收集整理提供。

房屋建筑统计资料由上海市住房保障和房屋管理局汇总整理提供。

市政工程部分统计资料和供气统计资料由上海市城乡建设和管理委员会、上海市交通委员会汇总整理提供。

供水排水统计资料由上海市水务局汇总整理提供。

城市绿化统计资料由上海市绿化和市容管理局汇总整理提供。

三、本篇资料的统计范围

城市基础设施建设、公共事业和市政建设投资的统计资料执行范围同《固定资产投资篇》的执行范围。房屋建筑、市政工程、供水排水、供气、城市绿化的统计资料范围均是全市范围。

BRIEF INTRODUCTION

I. Main Contents

The data in this chapter reflect the basic conditions of the scale, growth rate, and overall level of urban construction of Shanghai. The main contents include municipal roads, house construction, water supply, drainage, gas supply, and urban afforestation.

II. Sources of data

Data on infrastructure construction, public facilities, urban construction investment are collected, prepared and provided by Shanghai Municipal Statistics Bureau in accordance with the Statistics Reporting Form System on the Fixed Asset Investment, which is stipulated by the Shanghai Municipal Statistics Bureau.

Data on house construction are collected, prepared, and provided by Shanghai Municipal Housing Security and Building Administration Bureau.

Data on urban construction projects and gas supply are collected, prepared, and provided by Shanghai Urban and Rural Construction and Management Commission and Shanghai Municiplal Transportaton Commission.

Data on water supply and drainage are collected, prepared, and provided by Shanghai Water Authority.

Data on urban afforestation are collected, prepared, and provided by Shanghai Municipal Afforestation & City Appearance and Environmental Sanitation Administration.

III. Scope and Coverage of Statistics

Coverage of data on urban infrastructure construction, public facilities, and urban construction investment is the same with that in the chapter of Fixed Assets Investment. Data on house construction, urban construction projects, water supply, drainage, gas supply, and urban afforestation cover the whole city.

表 11.1 主要年份城市基础设施投资额
URBAN INFRASTRUCTURE INVESTMENT IN MAIN YEARS

单位:亿元(100 million yuan)

年份 Year	合计 Total	其中 of which: 电力建设 Power Generation	运输邮电 Transportation, Postal and Telecommunications	其中 of which: 交通运输 Transportation	邮电通信 Postal and Telecommunications	公用设施 Facilities for Public Use	其中 of which: 公用事业 Public Utilities	市政建设 Civil Construction
1950～1978	60.08	19.71	23.25	19.41	3.84	17.12	6.85	10.27
1980	9.55	5.31	2.91	2.31	0.60	1.33	0.64	0.69
1985	23.49	3.97	6.75	5.52	1.23	12.77	7.88	4.89
1986	24.78	5.68	8.40	6.56	1.84	10.70	5.67	5.03
1987	32.64	9.31	12.39	10.02	2.37	10.94	5.36	5.58
1988	37.08	14.18	12.35	8.80	3.55	10.55	4.01	6.54
1989	36.09	11.69	9.96	6.16	3.80	14.44	6.84	7.60
1990	47.22	17.53	10.06	7.17	2.90	19.63	10.83	8.80
1991	61.38	19.79	19.07	14.49	4.58	22.52	9.15	13.37
1992	84.35	19.70	21.44	15.01	6.43	43.21	12.58	30.63
1993	167.94	25.77	46.44	31.75	14.69	95.73	37.91	57.82
1994	238.16	41.57	72.68	36.83	35.85	123.91	26.77	97.14
1995	273.78	57.33	79.36	25.94	53.42	137.09	35.03	102.06
1996	378.78	77.61	147.21	69.66	77.55	153.96	48.31	105.65
1997	412.85	80.24	146.10	85.06	61.04	186.51	52.24	134.27
1998	531.38	89.58	181.46	108.79	72.67	260.34	58.37	201.97
1999	501.39	83.05	166.16	102.24	63.92	252.18	64.20	187.98
2000	449.90	64.61	117.52	48.83	68.69	267.77	104.43	163.34
2001	510.78	72.22	168.42	60.72	107.70	270.14	92.25	177.89
2002	583.49	62.14	171.24	63.01	108.23	350.11	148.42	201.69
2003	604.62	66.00	350.35	273.77	76.58	188.28	36.91	151.36
2004	672.58	89.52	371.35	316.96	54.39	211.71	26.92	184.80
2005	885.74	124.22	443.90	385.58	58.32	317.62	41.33	276.28
2006	1 125.54	116.23	703.24	589.52	113.72	306.07	56.23	249.84
2007	1 466.33	163.30	942.03	840.46	101.57	361.01	60.90	300.11
2008	1 733.18	129.53	947.49	838.91	108.59	656.15	112.81	543.34
2009	2 113.45	253.39	1 100.90	978.24	122.66	759.16	135.95	623.21
2010	1 497.46	148.50	866.20	754.66	111.54	482.76	86.58	396.18
2011	1 157.34	118.81	668.52	595.75	72.76	370.01	54.22	315.80
2012	1 038.61	110.06	570.37	473.43	96.94	358.18	56.45	301.74
2013	1 043.31	110.35	550.42	458.70	91.72	382.54	47.57	334.97
2014	1 057.25	134.22	510.42	422.48	87.94	412.61	32.80	379.81
2015	1 425.08	129.36	854.89	759.23	95.67	440.83	66.73	374.10

注：本表各项投资额均不包括住宅建设投资。从2003年起，交通运输投资包括公用设施中市内公共交通投资。2011年起，固定资产投资统计起点为500万元以上(含500万元)项目(下表同)。

Note: All items in this table exclude investment in residential housing. Since 2003, public traffic investment, which is belong to facilities for public use has been included in Transportation Investment. Since 2011, statistics of Investment in Fixed Assets only contain the projects with investment of 5 million yuan and above (same as follows).

表 11.2 用于公用事业和市政建设的投资额(1985 ~ 2015)
INVESTMENT IN PUBLIC UTILITIES AND CIVIL CONSTRUCTION

单位:亿元(100 million yuan)

年 份 Year	公用事业 Public Utilities	其中 of which 自来水 Tap Water	煤气 Gas	市政建设 Civil Construction	其中 of which 园林绿化 Parks and Green Areas	环境卫生 Environmental Sanitation	市政设施 Municipal Facilities	其他 Others
1985	7.88			4.89				
1986	5.67	2.74	1.78	5.03	0.43	0.71	3.84	0.05
1987	5.36	2.53	1.79	5.58	0.30	0.34	4.94	…
1988	4.01	0.72	1.25	6.54	0.24	0.58	5.72	…
1989	6.84	1.52	0.90	7.60	0.01	0.52	7.02	0.05
1990	10.83	1.06	1.81	8.80	0.11	0.37	8.31	0.01
1991	9.15	2.34	2.35	13.37	0.15	0.45	12.77	…
1992	12.58	3.20	3.24	30.63	0.32	0.79	28.45	1.07
1993	37.91	6.90	16.72	57.82	0.52	1.06	56.24	…
1994	26.77	11.49	7.80	97.14	2.42	1.01	93.47	0.24
1995	35.03	13.12	12.97	102.06	4.27	1.26	96.21	0.32
1996	48.31	22.12	14.61	105.65	2.66	1.14	101.80	0.05
1997	52.24	27.08	10.03	134.27	5.11	1.62	127.41	0.13
1998	58.37	14.59	13.15	201.97	9.10	3.35	189.41	0.11
1999	64.20	6.41	9.89	187.98	28.62	2.97	155.73	0.66
2000	104.43	5.35	6.88	163.34	38.76	19.34	102.36	2.88
2001	92.25	5.97	5.83	177.89	32.92	2.97	140.63	1.37
2002	148.42	8.62	6.83	201.69	38.83	1.47	160.64	0.75
2003	36.91	22.89	14.02	151.36	33.85	9.25	107.73	0.53
2004	26.92	16.66	10.26	184.80	16.69	7.01	160.22	0.88
2005	41.33	29.66	11.67	276.28	13.88	15.36	246.58	0.46
2006	56.23	43.79	12.44	249.84	26.41	10.17	213.26	
2007	60.90	50.12	10.78	300.11	34.66	11.26	254.19	
2008	112.81	93.24	19.57	543.34	29.01	20.04	494.29	
2009	135.95	109.79	26.16	623.21	27.96	21.91	573.19	0.15
2010	86.58	61.63	24.95	396.18	35.87	10.80	349.27	0.25
2011	54.22	41.85	12.37	315.80	44.71	23.91	247.15	0.03
2012	56.45	40.75	15.70	301.74	20.99	23.74	256.73	0.26
2013	47.57	24.83	22.74	334.97	27.16	12.52	292.48	2.82
2014	32.80	20.00	12.80	379.81	56.46	9.41	313.94	
2015	66.73	58.63	8.10	374.10	34.84	18.49	320.77	

表 11.3 主要年份各类房屋构成情况
COMPOSITION OF BUILDING IN MAIN YEARS

单位：万平方米(10 000 sq. m)

指 标	Indicators	2000	2010	2014	2015
总 计	**Total**	**34 206**	**93 591**	**115 344**	**120 390**
居住房屋	Residential Buildings	20 865	52 639	61 094	63 007
花园住宅	Villas	250	2 064	1 790	1 790
公 寓	Apartments	206	492	56 429	58 308
职工住宅	Staff Dwellings	17 939	47 951		
联列住宅	United Columns Residences			1 241	1 400
新式里弄	Improved Residential Blocks	428	527	311	308
旧式里弄	Old Residential Blocks	1 896	1 237	1 312	1 190
简 屋	Simple Housings	84	29	11	11
其 他	Others	62	339		
非居住房屋	Non-Residential Buildings	13 341	40 952	54 250	57 383
工 厂	Plants	5 739	18 524	23 964	25 103
学 校	Schools	1 417	3 172	3 226	3 366
仓库堆栈	Warehouses	650	1 654	1 762	1 868
办公楼	Offices	2 416	6 365	6 860	7 343
商场店铺	Stores	1 191	5 497	6 469	6 773
医 院	Hospitals	367	754	615	631
旅 馆	Hotels	376	931	1 233	1 265
影剧院	Theatres and Cinemas	47	75	58	65
其 他	Others	1 138	3 979	10 063	10 970

注：根据市住房保障和房屋管理局提供居住房屋分类的调整，2011 年起公寓数据包含职工住宅数据，2012 年起取消其他分类。随着近年城中村建设改造的推进，2013 年将城中村纳入旧式里弄的统计范围。

Note: According to the adjustment of residential houses classification provided by Shanghai Municipal Housing Security and Building Administration Bureau, since 2011, the apartment data contains data of the staff housing, and since 2012, other classifications are canceled. With the promotion of construction and renovation of urban villages in recent years, urban villages will be included in the statistical range of the old residential blocks in 2013.

表 11.4 主要年份八层以上房屋情况
BUILDINGS OVER EIGHT STOREYS IN MAIN YEARS

类 别	Types	单 位 Unit	2000	2010	2014	2015
总 计	**Total**	**幢 (building)**	**3 529**	**20 579**	**38 171**	**40 822**
		万平方米 (10 000 sq. m)	6 180	21 911	36 918	39 652
8～10 层	8～10 Storeys	幢 (building)	536	2 744	5 333	5 568
		万平方米 (10 000 sq. m)	451	2 430	3 708	3 903
11～15 层	11～15 Storeys	幢 (building)	684	9 672	17 372	18 302
		万平方米 (10 000 sq. m)	875	6 320	11 905	12 712
16～19 层	16～19 Storeys	幢 (building)	831	4 247	9 005	10 046
		万平方米 (10 000 sq. m)	1 100	4 449	8 691	9 640
20～29 层	20～29 Storeys	幢 (building)	1 266	2 936	4 951	5 337
		万平方米 (10 000 sq. m)	2 695	5 504	8 342	8 917
30 层以上	Over 30 Storeys	幢 (building)	212	980	1 510	1 569
		万平方米 (10 000 sq. m)	1 059	3 208	4 272	4 481

注：本页数据按建筑面积计算。

Note: Data on this page are calculated according to floor space of builings.

表 11.5 各区、县房屋建筑分布情况(2015)
DISTRIBUTION OF BUILDINGS IN DIFFERENT DISTRICTS AND COUNTIES

单位：万平方米(10 000 sq. m)

地 区	District	建筑面积合 计 Total	其 中 of which 居住房屋 Residential	非居住房屋 Non-Residential
总 计	**Total**	**120 390**	**63 007**	**57 383**
浦东新区	Pudong New Area	27 512	14 601	12 911
黄 浦 区	Huangpu	3 709	1 740	1 969
徐 汇 区	Xuhui	6 056	3 431	2 625
长 宁 区	Changning	4 026	2 415	1 611
静 安 区	Jing'an	1 773	817	956
普 陀 区	Putuo	5 910	3 640	2 270
闸 北 区	Zhabei	3 768	2 214	1 554
虹 口 区	Hongkou	3 526	2 217	1 309
杨 浦 区	Yangpu	5 818	3 381	2 437
闵 行 区	Minhang	13 413	7 655	5 758
宝 山 区	Baoshan	9 512	5 609	3 903
嘉 定 区	Jiading	8 028	3 648	4 380
金 山 区	Jinshan	4 319	1 554	2 765
松 江 区	Songjiang	9 442	4 119	5 323
青 浦 区	Qingpu	5 692	2 317	3 375
奉 贤 区	Fengxian	5 510	2 250	3 259
崇 明 县	Chongming	2 376	1 399	978

表11.6 各区、县各类房屋分布情况(2015)
DISTRIBUTION OF VARIOUS BUILDINGS IN DIFFERENT DISTRICTS AND COUNTIES

单位：万平方米(10 000 sq. m)

地 区	District	居住房屋 Residential Buildings	其 中 of which 花园住宅 Villas	公 寓 Apartments	联列住宅 United Columns Residences
总 计	**Total**	**63 007**	**1 790**	**58 308**	**1 400**
浦东新区	Pudong New Area	14 601	369	13 871	246
黄浦区	Huangpu	1 740	8	1 355	…
徐汇区	Xuhui	3 431	52	3 286	9
长宁区	Changning	2 415	57	2 338	1
静安区	Jing'an	817	21	691	1
普陀区	Putuo	3 640	13	3 570	23
闸北区	Zhabei	2 214	…	2 139	3
虹口区	Hongkou	2 217	7	1 968	…
杨浦区	Yangpu	3 381	3	3 207	18
闵行区	Minhang	7 655	304	7 121	181
宝山区	Baoshan	5 609	29	5 414	116
嘉定区	Jiading	3 648	91	3 387	146
金山区	Jinshan	1 554	17	1 459	42
松江区	Songjiang	4 119	381	3 369	331
青浦区	Qingpu	2 317	301	1 808	171
奉贤区	Fengxian	2 250	98	2 031	87
崇明县	Chongming	1 399	37	1 293	26

表 11.6 续表 1 continued

单位：万平方米(10 000 sq. m)

地 区	District	其 中 of which 新式里弄 Improved Residential Blocks	旧式里弄 Old Residential Blocks	简 屋 Simple Housings
总 计	**Total**	**308**	**1 190**	**11**
浦东新区	Pudong New Area	3	112	1
黄 浦 区	Huangpu	87	288	1
徐 汇 区	Xuhui	52	28	2
长 宁 区	Changning	18	1	…
静 安 区	Jing'an	76	28	…
普 陀 区	Putuo	4	30	…
闸 北 区	Zhabei	1	71	
虹 口 区	Hongkou	60	179	2
杨 浦 区	Yangpu	5	146	1
闵 行 区	Minhang	1	48	…
宝 山 区	Baoshan	…	49	…
嘉 定 区	Jiading		24	…
金 山 区	Jinshan	…	36	…
松 江 区	Songjiang	…	39	…
青 浦 区	Qingpu		36	…
奉 贤 区	Fengxian	1	34	…
崇 明 县	Chongming		41	2

表 11.6 续表2 continued

单位：万平方米(10 000 sq. m)

地 区	District	非居住房屋 Non-Residential Buildings	其 中 of which 工 厂 Plants	学 校 Schools	仓库堆栈 Warehouses	办公楼 Offices
总 计	**Total**	**57 383**	**25 103**	**3 366**	**1 868**	**7 343**
浦东新区	Pudong New Area	12 911	5 189	620	545	1 591
黄 浦 区	Huangpu	1 969	128	105	22	735
徐 汇 区	Xuhui	2 625	512	331	63	738
长 宁 区	Changning	1 611	202	121	34	529
静 安 区	Jing'an	956	62	49	5	363
普 陀 区	Putuo	2 270	435	192	181	494
闸 北 区	Zhabei	1 554	394	103	48	321
虹 口 区	Hongkou	1 309	170	113	30	414
杨 浦 区	Yangpu	2 437	753	374	78	447
闵 行 区	Minhang	5 758	2 921	346	238	342
宝 山 区	Baoshan	3 903	1 658	185	303	257
嘉 定 区	Jiading	4 380	2 217	209	87	402
金 山 区	Jinshan	2 765	1 866	100	50	149
松 江 区	Songjiang	5 323	3 734	205	43	185
青 浦 区	Qingpu	3 375	2 265	85	51	131
奉 贤 区	Fengxian	3 259	2 168	146	44	171
崇 明 县	Chongming	978	429	81	45	74

表11.6 续表3 continued

单位：万平方米(10 000 sq. m)

地 区 District		其 中 of which 商场店铺 Stores	医 院 Hospitals	旅 馆 Hotels	影剧院 Theatres and Cinemas	其 他 Others
总 计	**Total**	**6 773**	**631**	**1 265**	**65**	**10 970**
浦东新区	Pudong New Area	1 427	88	320	4	3 127
黄 浦 区	Huangpu	358	64	143	12	402
徐 汇 区	Xuhui	274	89	92	3	521
长 宁 区	Changning	211	35	106	2	371
静 安 区	Jing'an	118	26	86	2	244
普 陀 区	Putuo	382	26	69	3	487
闸 北 区	Zhabei	234	31	61	4	357
虹 口 区	Hongkou	197	28	67	6	284
杨 浦 区	Yangpu	254	43	33	3	453
闵 行 区	Minhang	668	52	42	5	1 144
宝 山 区	Baoshan	477	25	32	2	962
嘉 定 区	Jiading	562	27	57	7	811
金 山 区	Jinshan	348	30	22	1	198
松 江 区	Songjiang	496	23	39	1	595
青 浦 区	Qingpu	348	16	31	3	446
奉 贤 区	Fengxian	327	10	30	2	361
崇 明 县	Chongming	91	17	33	2	205

表 11.7 各区、县八层以上房屋分布(2015)
DISTRIBUTION OF BUILDINGS OVER EIGHT STOREYS BY DISTRICTS AND COUNTIES

单位：万平方米(10 000 sq. m)

地 区 District		合 计 Total		8～10 层 8～10 Storeys		11～15 层 11～15 Storeys	
		幢 Building	面 积 Floor Space	幢 Building	面 积 Floor Space	幢 Building	面 积 Floor Space
总 计	**Total**	**40 822**	**39 652**	**5 568**	**3 903**	**18 302**	**12 712**
浦东新区	Pudong New Area	9 448	9 233	1 124	869	4 900	3 434
黄 浦 区	Huangpu	1 253	2 278	153	155	163	177
徐 汇 区	Xuhui	2 090	2 853	287	239	579	504
长 宁 区	Changning	1 539	2 029	310	206	436	373
静 安 区	Jing'an	703	1 214	91	60	71	64
普 陀 区	Putuo	2 448	2 783	247	150	772	566
闸 北 区	Zhabei	1 500	1 588	220	134	570	424
虹 口 区	Hongkou	1 379	1 617	207	123	346	241
杨 浦 区	Yangpu	2 020	2 101	287	235	807	637
闵 行 区	Minhang	5 641	4 302	905	713	3 565	2 333
宝 山 区	Baoshan	3 457	2 546	498	264	1 820	1 144
嘉 定 区	Jiading	2 887	2 411	306	222	1 107	761
金 山 区	Jinshan	888	599	155	86	519	311
松 江 区	Songjiang	2 822	2 039	374	231	1 514	994
青 浦 区	Qingpu	1 374	1 017	197	104	543	357
奉 贤 区	Fengxian	1 126	908	110	78	452	302
崇 明 县	Chongming	247	135	97	35	138	91

表 11.7 续表 continued

单位：万平方米(10 000 sq. m)

地 区 District		16～19 层 16～19 Storeys		20～29 层 20～29 Storeys		30 层以上 Over 30 Storeys	
		幢 Building	面 积 Floor Space	幢 Building	面 积 Floor Space	幢 Building	面 积 Floor Space
总 计	**Total**	**10 046**	**9 640**	**5 337**	**8 917**	**1 569**	**4 481**
浦东新区	Pudong New Area	2 185	2 072	949	1 678	290	1 180
黄 浦 区	Huangpu	242	322	455	919	240	705
徐 汇 区	Xuhui	510	616	535	1 029	179	465
长 宁 区	Changning	282	308	380	693	131	448
静 安 区	Jing'an	129	138	298	554	114	398
普 陀 区	Putuo	568	618	668	1 009	193	440
闸 北 区	Zhabei	284	278	298	507	128	244
虹 口 区	Hongkou	353	377	343	581	130	294
杨 浦 区	Yangpu	548	571	327	555	51	103
闵 行 区	Minhang	960	940	188	260	23	56
宝 山 区	Baoshan	940	848	167	238	32	53
嘉 定 区	Jiading	1 021	910	425	480	28	39
金 山 区	Jinshan	175	143	30	45	9	15
松 江 区	Songjiang	789	620	140	191	5	3
青 浦 区	Qingpu	567	476	66	79	1	1
奉 贤 区	Fengxian	482	397	67	96	15	35
崇 明 县	Chongming	11	6	1	2		

表 11.8 主要年份市政工程设施情况
CIVIL FACILITIES IN MAIN YEARS

指 标	Indicators	2000	2010	2014	2015
道路长度(公里)	Length of Roads(km)	6 641	16 687	17 797	18 184
道路面积(万平方米)	Area of Roads (10 000 sq. m)	8 147	25 607	27 918	28 567
城市桥梁(座)	Bridges (bridge)	4 432	11 849	13 304	13 677
防洪堤长度(公里)	Length of Floodwalls (km)	335	1 009	1 159	1 159
城市排水管道长度(公里)	Length of Sewage Pipelines (km)	3 920	11 483	20 972	21 316
污水处理厂污水处理能力(万吨/日)	Capacity of Sewage Treatment(10 000 tons/day)	463	684	788	795
城镇污水处理率(%)	Urban Sewage Treatment Rate(%)	46.8	81.9	89.8	92.8

表 11.9 主要年份自来水情况
TAP WATER SUPPLY IN MAIN YEARS

指 标	Indicators	2000	2010	2014	2015
水厂个数(个)	Number of Water Treatment Works (unit)	218	105	67	37
供水能力(万立方米/日)	Water Supply Capacity (10 000 cu. m/day)	1 048	1 131	1 137	1 137
供水管道长度(公里)	Length of Water Supply Mainss (km)	15 943	31 182	35 068	36 383
供水总量(亿立方米)	Total Quantity of Water Supply (100 million cu. m)	24.00	30.90	31.73	31.22
售水总量(亿立方米)	Total Quantity of Water Sales (100 million cu. m)	19.75	24.44	24.82	24.58
工业用水	Industrial Water Consumption	5.49	5.80	5.16	4.94
生活用水	Comprehensive Domestic Water Consumption	14.26	18.64	19.66	19.64
#居民生活用水	Domestic Water Consumption	6.82	9.80	10.02	9.88
人均日居民生活用水量(升)	Per Capita Daily Domestic Water Consumption(liter)	114	117	113	112

表 11.10 主要年份用电量
ELECTRICITY POWER CONSUMPTION IN MAIN YEARS

指 标	Indicators	2000	2010	2014	2015
用电量（亿千瓦时）	Power Consumption（100 million kwh）	559.51	1 295.87	1 369.03	1 405.55
#农业用电	Agricultural Consumption	9.10	6.07	7.26	7.35
工业用电	Industrial Consumption	392.97	786.61	785.64	787.02
交通运输、仓储、邮政业	Transportation, Storage and Post Industry	5.94	34.11	41.26	42.12
商业、住宿和餐饮业	Commercial, Hotel and Eateries	41.81	69.44	76.45	78.29
金融、房地产、商务及居民服务业	Finance, Real Estate, Commerce and Residential Service	25.00	130.82	164.95	179.54
公共事业及管理组织	Public Affairs and Administrative Organization	23.18	76.64	88.00	93.21
城乡居民生活用电	Urban Residential Consumption	53.20	168.95	173.89	185.49

表 11.11 主要年份电力建设情况
ELECTRICITY POWER CONSTRUCTION IN MAIN YEARS

指 标	Indicators	2001	2010	2014	2015
年末发电设备容量(万千瓦)	Year-end Capacity of Electricity Generating Equipment(10000 KW)	1 121.09	1 855.38	2 183.68	2 343.68
架空线长度(公里)	Length of Trolly Wire(k. m.)	6 480.72	8 549.5	9 142.67	9 928.78
#220KV	220KV	1 756.74	2 956.08	3 448.61	3 467.13
电缆长度(公里)	Length of Cable(k. m.)	3 633.00	7 846.98	9 986.33	10 719.90
#220KV	220KV	145.00	516.44	597.06	655.14
公用变电容量(万千伏安)	Public Power Transformation Capacity(10 000 KVA)	4 601.08	11 657.19	15 228.85	15 860.69
#220KB－35KV	220KB－35KV	3 716.68	7 827.75	9 648.41	10 180.25

注：本页数据由市电力公司提供
Note: Data on this page are provided by Shanghai Electric Power Corporation.

表 11.12 主要年份煤气、液化石油气、天然气情况
GAS,LIQUEFIED PETROLEUM GAS AND NATURAL GAS IN MAIN YEARS

指 标	Indicators	2000	2010	2014	2015
煤 气	**Gas**				
煤气生产能力(万立方米/日)	Production Capacity (10 000 cu. m/day)	984.30	817.4	146.60	
煤气管线长度(公里)	Length of Gas Pipelines (km)	6 606	5 517	2 109	
煤气销售总量(亿立方米)	Total Sales Volume (100 million cu. m)	18.40	12.85	3.01	0.52
#家庭用量	Household Consumption	11.46	6.28	1.35	0.2
家庭煤气用户数 (万户)	Households Users (10 000 households)	255.89	132.89	13.82	
液化石油气	**Liquefied Petroleum Gas (LPG)**				
液化石油气销售总量(万吨)	Sales of LPG (10 000 tons)	45.94	40.05	41.81	42.41
#家庭用量	Household Consumption	20.47	23.62	25.22	25.23
家庭液化石油气用户数(万户)	Household Users (10 000 households)	239.30	316.37	334.68	33.55
天然气	**Natural Gas**				
天然气销售总量(亿立方米)	Sales of Natural Gas (100 million cu. m)	2.16	42.66	66.39	69.73
#家庭用量	Household Consumption	0.45	7.79	12.44	13.50
天然气管线长度(公里)	Length of Natural Gas Pipelines (km)	1 742	17 316	26 057	28 601
家庭天然气用户数 (万户)	Household Users of Natural Gas (10 000 households)	38.10	405.89	614.00	651.32

表 11.13 主要年份公共交通和轮渡情况
PUBLIC TRANSPORTATION AND FERRY IN MAIN YEARS

指 标	Indicators	2000	2010	2014	2015
公共汽电车	**Buses and Trolley Buses**				
公交线路长度(公里)	Length of Public Bus Lines (km)	23 260	23 131	23 897	24 027
公交线路条数(条)	Number of Public Bus Lines (line)	978	1 165	1 377	1 429
运营公交车辆数(辆)	Operating Public Transportation Vehicles (vehicle)	17 939	17 455	16 155	16 531
#公共汽车	Buses	17 358	17 038	15 454	15 056
公交客运总量(亿人次)	Passenger Volume of Pubilc Bus (100million person-times)	26.49	28.08	26.65	25.49
出租汽车	**Taxi**				
运营车辆(辆)	Operating Vehicles (vehicle)	42 943	50 007	50 738	49 586
#小客车	Small Passenger Car	40 806	49 016	49 966	48 840
载客车次(万次)	Number of Carryings(10 000 times)	37 599.00	63 306.89	57 238.00	53 974.00
运营里程(亿公里)	Operation Length (100 million km)	46.48	64.85	62.79	60.85
#载客里程	Transport Lengths of Passengers	24.35	39.79	40.58	39.27
运营收入(亿元)	Operation Revenues(100 million yuan)	76.68	154.72	170.41	166.30
运营单位(个)	Operation Unit (unit)	1 178	3 301	3 146	3 113
轮 渡	**Ferry**				
年末轮渡船数(艘)	Year-end Number of Ferry Boats (ship)	95	42	50	44
乘客人数(亿人次)	Passenger Volume (100 million person-times)	1.85	0.89	0.58	0.53

表 11.14 轨道交通、城市快速路、黄浦江大桥和隧道基本情况（2012～2015）
BASIC FACTS OF RAILWAY COMMUNICATION, URBAN EXPRESSWAYS, BRIDGES ACROSS HUANGPU RIVER AND TUNNELS

指　标	Indicators	2012	2013	2014	2015
轨道交通	**Urban Metro**				
运营车辆(节)	Operating Vehicles(car)	3 130	3 490	3 677	3 797
轨道交通线路条数(条)	Number of Operation Lines(line)	13	15	15	15
运营线路长度(公里)	Length of Operation Lines(km)	468.19	567.42	577.55	617.53
运营里程(万列·公里)	Operation Mileage(10 000 vehicle-km)	5 570	5 872	7 007	7 574
客运总量(万人次)	Volume of Passenger Traffic (10 000 person-times)	227 573	250 628	282 727	306 798
年末从业人数(人)	Year-end Number of Staff and Workers (person)	28 155	28 783	28 987	29 315
城市快速路、大桥和隧道	**Urban Expressways, Bridges and Tunnels**				
城市快速路长度(公里)	Length of Urban Expressways(km)	199	199	187	197
越江大桥数(座)	Number of Bridges Across Huangpu River (bridge)	10	10	11	11
越江隧道数(条)	Tunnels Across Huangpu River (tunnel)	13	13	13	13

注：越江大桥、越江隧道是指跨越长江、黄浦江的桥梁和隧道，不含东海大桥和外滩隧道。
Note: River-Crossing Bridges and River-Crossing Tunnels refer to the bridges and tunnels which cross the Yangtze River and Huangpu River, and exclude the East China Sea Bridge and the the Bund Tunnel.

表 11.15 主要年份城市设施水平
LEVEL OF URBAN FACILITIES IN MAIN YEARS

指　标	Indicators	2000	2010	2014	2015
人均日综合生活用水量(升)	Per Capita Daily Consumption of Water for Life (liter)	241	223	223	224
人均日居民生活用水量(升)	Per Capita Daily Consumption of Water (liter)	114	117	113	112
自来水普及率(%)	Percentage of Population with Access to Tap Water (%)	99.97	99.99	99.99	99.99
拥有道路长度(公里/万人)	Per Capita Length of Roads (km/10 000 persons)	5.84	7.25	7.34	7.53
人均拥有道路面积(平方米)	Per Capita Area of Roads (sq. m)	7.17	11.12	11.51	11.83
每万人拥有城市排水管道长度(公里)	Length of Sewage Pipelines Per 10 000 Persons (km)	2.96	8.13	14.75	14.77
每万人拥有公共交通车辆(标台)	Number of Public Transportation Vehicles Per 10 000 Persons (vehicle)	12.08	12.46	11.97	12.36
每万人拥有出租汽车(辆)	Number of Taxi Per 10 000 Persons (vehicle)	25.61	21.72	20.92	20.53
人均公园绿地面积(平方米)	Per Capita Park Green Areas (sq. m)	4.6	13.0	7.3	7.6
每万人拥有公共厕所(座)	Number of Public Lavatories Per 10 000 Persons (unit)	1.67	4.27	4.31	4.32

注：2010 年起，拥有道路长度和人均拥有道路面积由原先的根据户籍人口计算调整为根据常住人口计算，2014 年起，人均公园绿地面积(平方米)由原先的根据非农户籍人口计算调整为根据常住人口计算。
Note: The indicators of Per Capita Length of Roads and Per Capita Area of Roads are caculated by resident population since 2010. The indicators of Per Capita Park Green Areas are caculated by resident population since 2014.

表 11.16 主要年份城市绿地情况
URBAN GREEN SPACE IN MAIN YEARS

单位：公顷（hectare）

年 份 Year	城市绿地面积 Urban Green Space	其中 of which 公园绿地 Public Green Space	生产绿地 Production Green Space	防护绿地 Environmental Protection Green Space	附属绿地 Sub Green Space	其他绿地 Other Green Space
1990	3 570	983	294	37	2 255	
1995	6 561	1 793	309	30	4 429	
2000	12 601	4 812	388	55	7 346	
2001	14 771	5 820	248	78	8 624	
2002	18 758	7 810	267	178	9 591	912
2003	24 426	9 450	335	2 675	10 631	1 335
2004	26 689	10 979	335	2 669	11 397	1 309
2005	28 865	12 038	336	2 743	12 464	1 284
2006	30 609	13 307	331	2 869	13 218	884
2007	31 795	13 899	204	2 025	14 784	884
2008	34 256	14 777	189	2 039	16 120	1 131
2009	116 929	15 406	230	1 877	17 376	82 040
2010	120 148	16 053	230	1 936	18 589	83 340
2011	122 283	16 446	213	2 081	19 442	84 102
2012	124 204	16 848	269	2 087	20 084	84 917
2013	124 295	17 142	267	2 089	20 645	84 152
2014	125 741	17 789	417	2 152	23 020	82 363
2015	127 332	18 395	417	2 108	23 711	82 701

注：根据《城市和村镇建设统计报表制度》，2009 年对绿地分类进行了调整。城市绿地由公园绿地、生产绿地、防护绿地、附属绿地和其他绿地五大类构成。

Note: The Categories of Urban Green include Public Green Area, Production Green Area, Protection Green Area, Sub Green Area and Other Green Area, which have been adjusted by the Statistical Reporting Regulation of City and Town Construction since 2009.

表 11.16 续表 continued

年 份 Year	公园数 （个） Parks (unit)	游园人数 （万人次） Visitors to Parks and Zooes (10 000 person-times)	行道树实有数 （万株） Roadside Trees (10 000 trees)	新辟绿地面积（公顷） Greenlands Newly Created (hectare)	绿化覆盖率 （%） Coverage Rate of Urban Green Areas(%)
1990	83	8 474	23	186	12.4
1995	100	9 064	33	516	16.0
2000	122	8 184	57	1 458	22.2
2001	125	8 561	65	1 374	23.8
2002	133	8 796	68	2 600	30.0
2003	136	9 629	74	4 904	35.2
2004	136	13 381	80	2 434	36.0
2005	144	13 656	83	2 116	37.0
2006	144	16 652	86	1 691	37.3
2007	146	18 342	69	1 629	37.6
2008	147	22 119	73	1 190	38.0
2009	147	21 671	76	1 096	38.1
2010	148	21 794	81	1 223	38.2
2011	153	20 481	93	1 063	38.2
2012	157	22 231	98	1 038	38.3
2013	158	20 574	99	1 050	38.4
2014	161	22 286	103	1 105	38.4
2015	165	22 208	110	1 190	38.5

表 11.17 各区、县绿化面积(2015)
URBAN GREEN AREA IN DIFFERENT DISTRICTS AND COUNTIES

地 区 District		城市绿地面积 (公顷) Urban Green Space (hectare)	其 中 of which #公园绿地面积 Park Green Areas	公园数 (个) Quantity of Parks (unit)	公园面积 (公顷) Park Area (Hectare)	公园游园人数 (万人次) Visitors to Parks and Zoos (10 000 person-times)
总 计	**Total**	**127 332.22**	**18 395.27**	**165**	**2 407.24**	**22 208.00**
浦东新区	Pudong New Area	27 200.13	6 392.00	26	560.44	2 169.70
黄 浦 区	Huangpu	270.22	170.41	12	65.69	3 092.80
徐 汇 区	Xuhui	1 317.39	531.06	11	136.88	3 049.40
长 宁 区	Changning	1 049.96	461.08	13	135.38	1 611.30
静 安 区	Jing'an	111.51	50.11	3	9.52	399.80
普 陀 区	Putuo	1 285.37	608.93	18	81.16	3 057.90
闸 北 区	Zhabei	643.60	238.88	7	86.88	1 377.50
虹 口 区	Hongkou	410.08	154.69	9	62.24	2 461.10
杨 浦 区	Yangpu	1 386.97	471.66	15	218.80	1 828.30
闵 行 区	Minhang	8 509.81	2 362.17	10	119.02	473.80
宝 山 区	Baoshan	6 700.32	2 306.11	15	374.39	1 426.20
嘉 定 区	Jiading	8 510.47	1 333.33	6	106.06	379.50
金 山 区	Jinshan	8 888.56	633.88	7	13.89	134.40
松 江 区	Songjiang	12 498.07	1 093.48	5	239.09	410.60
青 浦 区	Qingpu	10 368.68	795.92	3	143.09	134.70
奉 贤 区	Fengxian	10 208.58	455.82	2	29.09	149.10
崇 明 县	Chongming	27 972.53	335.74	3	25.61	51.90

上/海/统/计/年/鉴

主要统计指标解释

城市基础设施

城市基础设施包括电力建设、交通运输、邮电通信、公用事业和市政建设等。

道路长度

指道路长度和与道路相通的桥梁、隧道的长度，按车行道中心线计算。

城市绿地

指以自然植被和人工植被为主要存在形态的城市用地。它包含两个层次的内容：一是城市建设用地范围内用于绿化的土地；二是城市建设用地之外，对城市生态、景观和居民休闲生活具有积极作用、绿化环境较好的区域。

绿地面积

指报告期末用作园林和绿化的各种绿地面积。包括公园绿地、生产绿地、防护绿地、附属绿地和其他绿地面积。

其中，公园绿地：指向公众开放的、以游憩为主要功能，有一定的游憩设施和服务设施，同时兼有健全生态、美化景观、防灾减灾等综合作用的绿化用地。它是城市建设用地、城市绿地系统和城市市政公用设施的重要组成部分。

供水管道长度

指从送水泵至用户水表之间所有管道的长度。不包括新安装尚未使用的管道。

供水总量

指报告期供水企业(单位)供出的全部水量。包括有效供水量和漏损水量。

生活用水

生活用水包括城市公共用水和居民家庭用水。城市公共用水包括建筑业用水、公共服务用水及生态环境用水。建筑业用水指土木工程建筑业、线路管道和设备安装业、建筑安装业、建筑装饰业和其他建筑业用水。生态环境用水主要包括城镇绿化、环卫用水及深井回灌用水。公共服务用水指为城市社会公共生活服务的用水。包括行政事业单位、部队营区和公共设施服务、社会服务业、批发零售贸易业、旅馆饮食业以及其他公共服务业等单位的用水。居民家庭用水指城市范围内所有居民家庭的日常生活用水。包括城市居民、农民家庭、公共供水站用水。

煤气生产能力

指报告期末煤气生产厂制气、净化、输送等环节的综合生产能力，不包括备用设备能力。一般按设计能力计算，如果实际生产能力大于设计能力时，应按实际测定的生产能力计算。测定时应以制气、净化、输送三个环节中最薄弱的环节为主。

排水管道长度

指所有排水总管、干管、支管、检查井及连接井进出口等长度之和。

运营公交车辆数

指年末公交企业(单位)用于运营业务的全部车辆数。以企业(单位)固定资产台帐中已投入运营的车辆数为准。

污水日处理能力

指城镇污水处理厂(或处理装置)每昼夜处理污水量的设计能力。

SHANGHAI STATISTICAL YEARBOOK

EXPLANATORY NOTES TO MAJOR STATISTICAL INDICATORS

□ Urban Infrastructure Facilities

Urban Infrastructure Facilities include facilities for power generating, transportation, post and telecommunication, public u-tilities, development of municipal engineering.

□ Length of Roads

The length of roads refers to the length of roads and of the bridges and tunnels connected to the roads, calculated by the center line of the roads.

□ Urban Green

Urban Green refers the urban land mainly used as natural vegetation and artificial vegetation. First, it includes the area of urban construction land for greening. Except the urban construc-tion land, the green area which is beneficial for urban ecology, landscape and residents leisure is also included.

□ Green Space

Green Space includes all kinds of gardens and green at the end of reporting period. Park green area, production green area, protection green area, sub green area and other green area are all included.

Park green area refers to green areas open to the public for amusement and rest with the facilities of amusement, rest and ser-vices. Its function includes perfecting ecology, beautifying land-scape, and preventing and reducing disaster. It is an important part of urban construction land, urban green and municipal public infrastructure in city.

□ Length of Water Supply Pipelines

Length of Water Supply Pipelines refers to the total length of all the pipelines between the water pumps and the user's water meters, excluding pipelines newly installed but not used yet.

□ Volume of Water Supply

Volume of Water Supply refers to the total volume of water supplied by water-works (units) during the reference period, in-cluding both the effective water supply and loss during the water supply.

□ Consumption of Water for Living Use

Consumption of Water for Linvin Use refers to the water consumption for city public and the water consumption of households for daily life. The water consumption for city public includes the water consumption of construction, the water con-sumption of public service facilities and the water consumption of city ecology. The water consumption of construction refers to the water consumption of civil engineering, line pipe and e-quipment installation, construction installation, construction decoration and other construction. The water consumption of city ecology mainly includes the consumption of urban green, urban Sanitation and deep well re-irrigation. The water con-sumption of public service facilities refers to the water con-sumption for urban public services, including the consumption of government agencies and public institutions, military bar-racks, public facilities, wholesale and retail outlets, restaurants, hotels, and other units providing public services. Household water consumption refers to consumption of water for daily life of all households in the boundary of cities, including households of urban residents and farmers, and public water supply sta-tions.

□ Production Capacity of Gas

Production Capacity of Gas refers to the comprehensive production capacity of the urban gasworks in gas generation, purification and delivery at the end of the reference period, ex-cluding capacity of the reserved facilities. In general, it is de-termined by the designed capacity, and when actual production capacity is larger than the designed capacity, the capacity is determined by the actual measurement on the weakest link in the production, purification and delivery.

□ Length of Sewage Pipes

Length of Sewage Pipes refers to the total length of general drainage, trunks, branch and inspection wells, connection wells, inlets and outlets, etc.

EXPLANATORY NOTES TO MAJOR STATISTICAL INDICATORS

□ Number of Operating Public Transportation Vehicles

Number of Operating Public Transportation Vehicles refers to the total number of vehicles under operation by public transport enterprises (units) at the end of the year, based on the records of operational vehicles by the enterprises (units).

□ Daily Disposal Capacity of Urban Sewage

Daily Disposal Capacity of Urban Sewage refers to the designed 24 hour capacity of sewage disposal by the sewage treatment works or urban facilities.

第十二篇
CHAPTER 12

农 业
AGRICULTURE

简要说明

一、本篇资料的主要内容

本篇资料反映本市农业生产和农村经济的基本情况，内容主要包括农林牧渔业产值、农村户数和人口、农作物播种面积、主要农产品产量、农产品出口、农业机械拥有量、农业技术应用等方面的统计资料。

二、本篇资料的统计范围

农业统计范围为上海市，包括闵行区、宝山区、嘉定区、松江区、金山区、青浦区、奉贤区、崇明县和浦东新区（农村）行政区域范围内所有建制乡镇、行政村和涉农街道、居委会辖区内的生产经营单位和农户；上海光明食品（集团）、上海水产（集团）总公司、青东农场、前卫农场、上实现代农业园区以及其他中央属、市属和军委系统的农业生产（经营）活动单位。

1. 种植业:指对各种农作物的种植活动。包括谷物、豆类、薯类、棉花、油料、糖料、麻类、烟叶、蔬菜、园艺作物、水果、坚果、饮料和香料作物、中草药及其他作物的种植。

2. 林业:包括林木的栽培(不包括茶园、桑园和果园的栽培、管理和收获等活动),木材和竹材的采运，林产品的采集。

3. 牧业:包括牲畜饲养和放牧, 家禽饲养以及野生动物的捕猎和饲养。

4. 渔业:包括水生动物和海藻类植物的养殖和捕捞。

5. 农林牧渔服务业:指对种植业、林业、牧业、渔业生产活动进行的各种支持性服务。但不包括各种科学技术和专业性技术服务活动。

农村社会经济统计范围包括除城关镇以外所有乡镇的社会经济活动。

三、本篇的资料来源及统计调查方法

主要由国家统计局上海调查总队根据《农村统计报表制度》的有关资料整理提供。

《农村统计报表制度》包括三部分内容：

一是农林牧渔业统计调查。包括农作物播种面积、主要农作物产量、农产量抽样调查等内容，调查方法由统计部门确定。其中，水果、林业、渔业、农业机械和部分畜牧业数据来源为农委相关部门，调查方法由资料来源相关部门确定。

二是农业产值综合统计。包括农业总产值、农林牧渔业中间消耗、农产品出口、种源农业等内容，调查方法由统计部门确定。

三是农村社会经济基本情况统计。包括乡镇社会经济基本情况、行政村基本情况等内容。上海参照国家统计局《县域社会经济基本情况统计报表制度》充实部分指标进行调查。

BRIEF INTRODUCTION

I. Main Contents

The data in this chapter reflect the basic conditions of agricultural production and rural economy in Shanghai. The main contents include output of agriculture, forestry, animal husbandry and fishery, number of rural households, rural population, sown area of farm crops, output of major agricultural products, agricultural products export, investment in facilities of water conservancy, electricity consumption in rural areas, ownership of agricultural machinery, application and comprehensive development of rural technology.

II. Scope and Coverage of Statistics

Data on agriculture cover the whole Shanghai Municipality including Minhang, Baoshan, Jiading, Songjiang, Jinshan, Qingpu, Fengxian districts, Chongming County, and Pudong New Area (rural area). Included in agriculture statistics are production activities in agriculture by rural production units and by rural households; production activities of farms in counties, villages and rural communities; production activities in agriculture undertaken by Shanghai Bright Food (Group), Shanghai Fisheries (Group) Corporation, the Qingdong Farm, the Qianwei Farm, SIIC Modern Agriculture Park and agricultural production units owned by the central government, municipal government and military agencies.

(1) Agriculture: it refers to cultivation of farm crops, including cereals, beans, tuber crops, cotton, oil-bearing crops, sugar crops, hemp, tobacco leaves, vegetables, gardening plants, fruits, nuts, crops for beverages and spices, medicinal herbs and other farm crops.

(2) Forestry: it includes the planting of trees (excluding activities of planting, managing and harvesting of tea, mulberry fields and fruits), cutting and transport of timber and bamboo and collection of forest products.

(3) Animal husbandry: it includes the raising and grazing of domestic animals and poultry, and the hunting and raising of wild animals.

(4) Fishery: it includes cultivation and catching of aquatic animals and seaweed.

(5) Services in support of agriculture, forestry, animal husbandry and fishery: they include supporting services to production activities in agriculture, forestry, animal husbandry and fishery but do not include activities of science and technology and professional services.

Rural social and economic statistics cover social and economic activities in all townships except towns, where county governments are located.

III. Data Sources and Survey Methodology

Data in this chapter are provided by the Survey Office of the National Bureau of Statistics in Shanghai using data from the Statistical Survey System on Rural Areas.

Statistical Survey System on Rural Areas consists of three parts:

First, it includes statistics on agriculture, forestry, animal husbandry and fishery, including agricultural production area, main crop output and sampling survey of agricultural products, whose survey methodologies are determined by the statistics department. Fruit, forestry, fishery, agricultural machinery and part of animal husbandry data are provided by Shanghai Municipal Agriculture Commission, and survey methodologies are determined by relevant providers of the data.

Second, it includes comprehensive statistics on value of agricultural output, including output of agriculture, intermediate consumption of agriculture, forestry, animal husbandry, and fishery, export of agricultural products, and seed industries. Survey methodologies are determined by the statistics department.

Third, it includes comprehensive statistics on rural areas. The data include basic conditions of social and economic activities at county, township and rural administrations, and municipal agricultural zones. Data are provided according to Statistical Reporting System on the Basic Condition of Social and Economic Activities of Counties with additional standards supplemented by Shanghai authorities.

表 12.1　农业总产值(1978 ~ 2015)
GROSS OUTPUT VALUE OF AGRICULTURE

单位:亿元(100millionyuan)

年份 Year	农业总产值 Gross Output Value of Agriculture	其中 ofwhich 种植业 Planting	林业 Forestry	牧业 Husbandry	渔业 Fishery	农林牧渔服务业 Service Industry for Agriculture
1978	18.26	13.49	0.06	3.67	0.86	
1979	20.41	15.10	0.04	4.22	0.90	
1980	18.90	11.40	0.06	6.27	0.97	
1981	20.33	11.91	0.21	6.38	1.23	
1982	23.97	13.80	0.23	7.81	1.56	
1983	22.68	12.59	0.20	7.80	1.29	
1984	26.59	16.41	0.21	8.06	1.40	
1985	31.38	15.63	0.21	12.25	2.82	
1986	33.76	16.83	0.24	12.75	3.45	
1987	38.84	17.69	0.34	15.48	4.79	
1988	53.07	22.47	0.45	22.18	7.43	
1989	60.63	25.53	0.39	26.41	7.88	
1990	68.16	29.09	0.37	30.25	8.04	
1991	73.65	30.51	0.39	33.38	8.97	
1992	80.01	32.80	0.43	37.19	9.18	
1993	96.20	40.52	0.41	42.95	12.31	
1994	140.24	60.19	0.49	62.04	17.52	
1995	182.47	77.71	0.45	81.48	22.83	
1996	200.95	87.64	0.67	85.46	27.18	
1997	204.41	85.20	0.47	88.37	30.37	
1998	206.75	89.10	0.84	87.27	29.54	
1999	206.90	87.86	0.98	86.35	31.71	
2000	216.50	89.81	1.41	87.35	37.92	
2001	227.61	95.53	3.52	88.43	40.13	
2002	233.57	97.21	7.75	83.48	45.13	
2003	247.29	98.17	13.05	81.13	49.21	5.73
2004	248.89	109.32	13.14	70.77	49.90	5.76
2005	233.39	111.25	11.11	54.34	51.64	5.05
2006	237.01	119.99	10.43	46.29	55.25	5.05
2007	255.98	126.74	10.05	58.00	54.19	7.00
2008	280.35	137.52	9.12	68.40	57.11	8.20
2009	283.15	147.53	8.99	64.61	53.53	8.49
2010	287.03	155.27	7.53	62.90	52.62	8.71
2011	314.58	165.07	7.62	77.44	54.72	9.73
2012	321.73	171.48	9.55	72.59	57.45	10.66
2013	323.48	172.28	9.65	69.97	59.89	11.69
2014	322.22	169.51	8.78	69.93	62.50	11.50
2015	302.62	162.04	12.15	65.61	51.79	11.03

注：2003 年以前，农业总产值不包括农林牧渔服务业。
Note：The Gross Output Value of Agriculture did not include the output value of service industry for planting, forestry, animal husbandary and fishery before 2003.

表 12.2 农业总产值指数(以1978年为100，1978～2015)
GROSS OUTPUT VALUE INDEX OF AGRICULTURE (1978 = 100)

年 份 Year	农业总产值指数 Index of Gross Output Value of Agriculture	其中 ofwhich 种植业 Planting	林 业 Forestry	牧 业 Animal Husbandry	渔 业 Fishery	农林牧渔服务业 Service Industry for Agriculture
1978	100.0	100.0	100.0	100.0	100.0	
1979	101.4	92.9	121.9	128.1	101.6	
1980	92.1	78.6	152.9	115.8	104.1	
1981	100.0	83.9	144.0	140.2	97.3	
1982	117.4	97.4	161.1	170.1	107.3	
1983	109.9	86.0	116.1	167.3	123.6	
1984	124.5	109.0	98.4	167.5	114.7	
1985	113.0	88.2	107.2	181.4	127.6	
1986	119.7	89.5	134.5	201.2	149.5	
1987	122.5	90.6	138.9	206.7	158.1	
1988	130.3	95.3	166.0	227.0	160.0	
1989	132.0	92.3	134.9	245.6	171.8	
1990	139.5	96.3	139.7	271.2	164.3	
1991	146.2	95.6	153.7	299.0	172.7	
1992	154.7	101.3	144.0	322.9	168.8	
1993	147.9	94.1	129.4	313.8	166.8	
1994	159.4	96.0	130.5	336.7	215.0	
1995	177.0	104.0	125.2	363.0	252.4	
1996	191.6	114.5	168.6	389.1	269.6	
1997	202.5	123.1	133.0	404.3	288.4	
1998	207.3	129.4	185.2	412.1	278.6	
1999	212.6	133.2	258.3	418.0	289.2	
2000	220.9	141.2	414.9	414.6	321.9	
2001	236.5	145.2	629.7	433.7	392.0	
2002	243.6	145.7	1 546.0	416.4	442.6	100.0
2003	246.3	135.3	2 062.4	395.5	544.4	102.6
2004	229.6	144.0	2 070.6	306.5	526.4	103.2
2005	205.5	136.7	1 613.0	221.6	555.4	91.4
2006	206.9	141.1	1 514.6	205.0	587.6	90.3
2007	210.0	142.9	1 458.6	214.2	573.5	121.6
2008	210.2	147.2	1 185.8	223.6	520.2	134.6
2009	209.1	145.1	1 147.9	238.6	481.7	140.0
2010	198.4	138.3	960.8	231.9	443.2	139.2
2011	197.2	139.1	914.7	237.2	407.3	147.8
2012	198.2	139.7	1 032.7	233.2	411.0	157.6
2013	192.5	186.0	1 075.0	220.6	400.7	169.1
2014	193.1	187.9	1 001.9	220.8	400.7	161.8
2015	180.2	177.6	1 217.3	199.8	359.0	150.5

注：根据国家统计局方法制度规定，从2006年起，农业总产值指数按可比价计算，2006年以前按不变价计算。
Note: According to the regulation of National Bureau of Statistics, since 2006, index of gross output value of agriculture has been calculated by comparable price, and before 2006, it was calculated by constant price.

表 12.3　主要年份农村户数、人口和从业人员
RURAL HOUSEHOLDS, POPULATION AND EMPLOYEES IN MAIN YEARS

指　标	Indicators	2000	2010	2014	2015
户　数(万户)	**Households (10 000 households)**	**115.17**	**114.22**	**98.54**	**99.20**
人　口(万人)	**Population (10 000 persons)**	**360.71**	**305.68**	**271.56**	**260.09**
农村从业人员(万人)	**Rural Employees(10 000 persons)**	**253.45**	**188.70**	**168.45**	**160.07**
第一产业	Primary Industry	81.45	34.06	37.84	38.61
第二产业	Secondary Industry	119.89	109.84	98.13	92.37
第三产业	Tertiary Industry	52.11	44.80	32.48	29.09

注：根据国家统计制度规定，本表中 2010～2012 年第一产业从业人员中包括农林牧渔服务业从业人员；从 2013 年起，农林牧渔服务业从业人员从第一产业中划出，归入第三产业。

Note: According to the provisions of the national statistical system, the first industry employees of 2010－2012 in this table contained the employees in the service industries of farming, forestry, animal husbandry and fishery. Since 2013, employees in the service industries of farming, forestry, animal husbandry and fishery are separated from first industry and merged into third industry.

表 12.4　主要年份农作物总播种面积
TOTAL SOWN AREA OF PLANTING IN MAIN YEARS

年　份 Year	总播种面积 (万公顷) Total Sown Area (10 000 hectare)	粮食作物 Grain Crops		经济作物 Cash Crops	
		播种面积 Sown Area	占总播种面积(%) Percentage (%)	播种面积 Sown Area	占总播种面积(%) Percentage (%)
1990	63.11	41.71	66.1	21.40	33.9
1995	54.22	34.40	63.5	19.82	36.5
1996	57.01	35.38	62.1	21.63	37.9
1997	55.23	36.58	66.2	18.65	33.8
1998	55.64	35.25	63.4	20.39	36.6
1999	55.17	33.50	60.7	21.67	39.3
2000	52.15	25.88	49.6	26.27	50.4
2001	49.09	21.12	43.0	27.97	57.0
2002	47.67	18.77	39.4	28.90	60.6
2003	41.92	14.83	35.4	27.09	64.6
2004	40.44	15.47	38.3	24.97	61.7
2005	40.36	16.61	41.1	23.75	58.9
2006	40.14	16.55	41.2	23.59	58.8
2007	39.07	16.96	43.4	22.11	56.6
2008	38.84	17.45	44.9	21.39	55.1
2009	39.61	19.33	48.8	20.28	51.2
2010	40.12	17.92	44.7	22.20	55.3
2011	40.06	18.63	46.5	21.43	53.5
2012	39.00	18.76	48.1	20.24	51.9
2013	37.81	16.85	44.6	20.96	55.4
2014	35.89	16.49	45.9	19.40	54.1
2015	34.16	16.19	47.4	17.97	52.6

表 12.5 主要年份农产品产量
OUTPUT OF MAJOR FARM PRODUCTS IN MAIN YEARS

指 标	Indicators	2000	2010	2014	2015
农产品	**Farm Products**				
粮 食(万吨)(包括大豆)	Grain (10 000 tons) (Including Soybean)	174.00	118.40	112.89	112.08
棉 花(万吨)	Cotton (10 000 tons)	0.12	0.35	0.12	0.04
油 料(万吨)	Oil Plants (10 000 tons)	16.37	2.29	1.28	1.18
#油菜籽	Rapeseed	15.71	2.04	1.05	0.96
蔬 菜(万吨)	Vegetables (10 000 tons)	377.00	380.35	377.95	349.35
食用菌(万吨)	Edible Fungus(10 000 tons)		8.73	15.23	15.12
西甜瓜(万吨)	Watermelons and Muskmelons (10 000 tons)	49.88	55.44	38.32	26.57
园林水果(万吨)	Garden Fruits (10 000 tons)	22.54	44.16	45.85	32.76
#生 梨	Pear	1.74	3.84	3.71	2.87
柑 橘	Citrus Fruits	10.18	20.16	23.42	11.44
畜禽产品	**Livestock and Poultry**				
生猪出栏量(万头)	Quantity of Sold Hogs(10 000 heads)	471.46	265.98	243.13	201.37
生猪年末圈存量(万头)	Hogs In Pens By Year-end (10 000 heads)	241.60	171.87	171.68	143.86
奶牛年末头数(万头)	Cows In Pens By Year-end (10 000 heads)	5.83	6.72	5.79	5.82
羊年末头数(万头)	Sheep In Pens By Year-end (10 000 heads)	55.44	24.46	28.08	30.53
兔年末圈存量(万头)	Rabbits In Pens By Year-end (10 000 heads)	88.90	12.17	3.75	3.76
猪 肉(万吨)	Pork (10 000 tons)	25.96	17.87	18.83	16.12
牛羊肉(万吨)	Beef and Mutton (10 000 tons)	0.79	0.54	0.59	0.61
家禽出栏量(万羽)	Quantity of Poultry Sold Birds (10 000 fowls)	17 213	4 084	2 166	1 944
生牛奶(万吨)	Raw Milk (10 000 tons)	25.95	24.71	27.05	27.69
禽 蛋(万吨)	Poultry Eggs (10 000 tons)	16.64	6.28	5.23	4.89
水产品	**Aquatic Products**				
海水产品(万吨)	Seawater Aquatic Products (10 000 tons)	12.23	12.15	17.87	16.95
淡水产品(万吨)	Freshwater Aquatic Products (10 000 tons)	16.64	16.82	13.03	12.21

表 12.6 农牧业特色种养产品产量(2014 ~ 2015)
OUTPUT OF SPECIAL PRODUCTS IN FARMING AND ANIMAL HUSBANDRY

指 标	Indicators	2014	2015	指 标	Indicators	2014	2015
桃(万吨)	Peach (10 000 tons)	8.27	7.89	野 鸡(万只)	Pheasant(10 000 fowls)	19.56	9.95
葡 萄(万吨)	Graper (10 000 tons)	9.73	9.84	野 鸭(万只)	Mallard(10 000 fowls)	80.65	54.20
草 莓(万吨)	Strawberry (10 000 tons)	1.93	2.21	肉 鸽(万只)	Meat Dove(10 000 fowls)	891.52	869.28
枣(吨)	Date(ton)	969	981	鳖(吨)	Soft-shelled Turtle(ton)	535	301
弥猴桃(吨)	Kiwi (ton)	1 996	1 720	中华绒毛蟹(万吨)	Chinese Hairy Crab(10 000 tons)	0.93	1.26

表 12.7 主要农副产品产量与建国以来最高年产量的比较 (2015)
OUTPUT OF MAJOR FARM AND SIDELINE PRODUCTS IN COMPARISON WITH THE PEAK YEAR SINCE 1949

指 标	Indicators	2015	建国以来最高年 Peak Year Since 1949		2015 年为建国以来最高年份(%) 2015/Peak Year Since 1949
			年 份 Year	产 量 Output	
农产品	**Farm products**				
粮 食(万吨)	Grain (10 000 tons)	112.08	1978	260.88	43.0
棉 花(万吨)	Cotton (10 000 tons)	0.04	1978	12.10	0.3
油菜籽(万吨)	Rapeseed (10 000 tons)	0.96	1992	21.84	4.4
蔬 菜(万吨)	Vegetables (10 000 tons)	349.35	2002	476.60	73.3
西甜瓜(万吨)	Watermelons and Muskmelons (10 000 tons)	26.57	2003	76.50	34.7
园林水果(万吨)	Garden Fruits (10 000 tons)	32.76	2008	46.12	71.0
畜禽产品	**Animal Husbandry Products**				
猪年末圈存数(万头)	Quantity of Hogs in Pens (year-end) (10 000 heads)	143.86	1978	365.74	39.3
猪 肉(万吨)	Pork (10 000 tons)	16.12	2001	26.40	61.1
奶牛年末头数(万头)	Quantity of Milk Cow (year-end) (10 000 heads)	5.82	1991	7.31	79.6
生牛奶(万吨)	Raw Milk (10 000 tons)	27.69	2002	27.98	99.0
家禽出栏量(万只)	Quantity of Poultry Sold(10 000 fowls)	1 944	1997	17 851	10.9
禽 蛋(万吨)	Poultry Eggs (10 000 tons)	4.89	2001	16.87	29.0
水产品	**Aquatic Products**				
海水产品(万吨)	Seawater Aquatic Products (10 000 tons)	16.95	2006	19.44	87.2
淡水产品(万吨)	Freshwater Aquatic Products (10 000 tons)	12.21	2003	22.13	55.2

注：建国以来最高年年份和产量均是指 2014 年及以前的年份和产量，不包括 2015 年在内。
Note: Peak year and output of peak year since 1949 refer to the years before 2014, excluding 2015.

表 12.8 主要年份农业商品产值和商品率
OUTPUT VALUE OF AGRICULTURAL COMMODITY AND COMMODITY RATE IN MAIN YEARS

指 标	Indicators	2000	2010	2014	2015
农业商品产值(亿元)	**Output Value of Agricultural Commodity (100 million yuan)**	**179.79**	**236.15**	**278.07**	**255.10**
#种植业	Planting	61.84	120.22	139.82	134.40
#粮食作物	Grain Crops	10.15	16.43	21.96	21.69
牧 业	Animal Husbandry	80.75	58.01	65.01	61.18
#生 猪	Hogs	29.82	30.38	34.91	34.24
家 禽	Poultry	33.41	8.95	5.57	4.54
禽 蛋	Eggs	7.94	5.10	5.21	4.31
渔 业	Fishery	36.53	50.42	60.57	49.47
#淡水产品	Freshwater Aquatic Products	25.14	36.62	37.84	34.10
农业商品率(%)	**Agricultural Commodity Rate (%)**	**83.0**	**82.3**	**86.3**	**84.3**
#种植业	Planting	68.8	77.4	82.5	82.9
#粮食作物	Grain Crops	45.4	53.8	64.7	64.9
牧 业	Animal Husbandry	92.4	92.2	93.0	93.3
#生 猪	Hogs	95.8	94.7	96.2	95.8
家 禽	Poultry	91.9	86.5	86.3	85.1
禽 蛋	Poultry Eggs	82.3	93.3	94.2	94.9
渔 业	Fishery	96.3	95.8	96.9	95.5
#淡水产品	Freshwater Aquatic Products	95.9	95.0	95.6	95.5

表 12.9 主要年份农产品出口情况
EXPORTS OF AGRICULTURAL PRODUCTS IN MAIN YEARS

单位:亿元(100 million yuan)

指 标	Indicators	2000	2010	2014	2015
农产品出口总额	**Output Value of Exports of Agricultural Products**	**7.88**	**11.28**	**11.81**	**10.77**
#种植业产品	Planting Products	0.63	2.30	1.90	1.23
牧业产品	Animal Husbardry Products	1.71	0.16	0.16	0.13
渔业产品	Fishery Products	5.55	8.41	9.64	9.29
农产品直接出口总额	**Output Value of Direct Exports of Agricultural Products**	**6.82**	**9.50**	**10.35**	**9.33**
#种植业产品	Planting Products	0.47	1.27	1.05	0.43
牧业产品	Animal Husbardry Products	0.99	0.07	0.16	0.13
渔业产品	Fishery Products	5.37	7.79	9.02	8.64
主要出口产品	**Main Products of Exports**				
蔬 菜	Vegetables	0.19	2.03	0.22	0.22
生 猪	Hogs	0.63	0.16	0.16	0.13
水产品	Aquatic Products	5.55	8.41	9.64	9.29
海水产品	Seawater Aquatic Products	5.29	7.37	8.48	8.12
淡水产品	Freshwater Aquatic Products	0.26	1.04	1.16	1.17

表 12.10　主要年份农业机械拥有量
POSSESSION OF AGRICULTURAL MACHINERY IN MAIN YEARS

机械名称	Name of Machinery	2000	2010	2014	2015
农业机械总动力（万千瓦）	**Total Power of Agricultural Machinery (10 000 kw)**	**142.50**	**104.15**	**117.76**	**119.01**
耕作机械动力合计（万千瓦）	Total Power of Farming Machinery (10 000 kw)	37.60	29.54	34.38	36.07
#大、中型拖拉机（台）	Large and Medium Tractors (set)	7 844	5 796	7 177	7 468
（万千瓦）	(10 000 kw)	29.30	24.21	31.43	33.44
小型拖拉机（台）	Small Tractors (set)	9 253	5 788	3 279	2 999
（万千瓦）	(10 000 kw)	8.30	5.34	2.96	2.63
排灌机械动力合计（万千瓦）	Total Power of Drainage and Irrigation Machinery (10 000 kw)	25.92	21.80	25.01	24.88
收获机械动力合计（万千瓦）	Total Power of Harvest Machinery (10 000 kw)	33.30	12.19	16.26	17.29
#联合收割机（台）	Combined Harvesters (set)	4 991	2 230	2 778	2 746
（万千瓦）	(10 000 kw)	2.70	8.52	13.16	13.93
植物保护机械动力合计（万千瓦）	Total Power of Plant Protecting Machine (10 000 kw)	3.07	5.34	5.29	5.39
#机动喷雾器（万台）	Motorized Nebulizers (10 000 sets)	2.07	2.11	2.22	2.26
（万千瓦）	(10 000 kw)	3.07	4.72	5.10	5.18
渔业机械动力合计（万千瓦）	Total Power of Fishery Machinery (10 000 kw)	23.40	23.23	26.19	23.61
#机动渔船（艘）	Motorized Fishing Boats (ship)	2 905	1 788	1 329	1 209
（万千瓦）	(10 000 kw)	20.50	18.74	19.27	16.23
其他农业机械动力合计（万千瓦）	Total Power of Other Agricultural Machine (10 000 kw)	11.13	11.05	10.63	11.77
#推土机(辆)	Bulldozers (automobile)	45	41	39	38
（万千瓦）	(10 000 kw)	0.25	0.24	0.20	0.19

表 12.11 主要年份农业技术应用和综合开发情况
TECHNOLOGY APPLICATIONS AND INTEGRATIVE EXPLOITATION IN AGRICULTURE IN MAIN YEARS

指 标	Indicators	2000	2010	2014	2015
机耕面积（万公顷）	Areas of Motorized Cultivation (10 000 hectares)	23.46	39.47	35.74	33.97
机电排灌总控制面积（万公顷）	Total Area with Motorized Drainage and Irrigation Facilities (10 000 hectares)	28.59	17.61	14.30	18.65
粮食机种面积（万公顷）	Areas of Motorized Planting (10 000 hectares)	6.08	5.30	6.11	6.10
占粮食播种面积（%）	Percentage in Total Planting Area of Grain (%)	23.5	29.6	37.1	37.7
粮食机收面积（万公顷）	Areas of Motorized Harvesting (10 000 hectares)	16.42	16.57	15.36	15.28
占粮食收获面积（%）	Percentage in Total Harvesting Area of Grain (%)	63.4	92.5	93.1	94.4
喷、滴管灌面积（万公顷）	Areas of Irrigating by Insufflantion and Dripping Pipeline (10 000 hectares)	0.43	0.80	1.04	1.07
机械植保面积（万公顷）	Areas of Mechancial Protecting (10 000 hectares)	41.10	30.41	33.46	32.46
化肥施用量（实物量）（万吨）	Chemical Fertilizer Consumption (real) (10 000 tons)	82.54	44.89	35.37	33.66
化肥施用量（折纯量）（万吨）	Chemical Fertilizer Consumption (convert to pure amount) (10 000 tons)	19.33	11.84	10.15	9.92
农药施用量(万吨)	Farm Pesticides Consumption (10 000 tons)	1.10	0.70	0.47	0.44
农用塑料薄膜使用量（万吨）	Agricultural Plastic Film Consumption (10 000 tons)	2.13	2.11	1.93	1.80
地膜覆盖面积（万公顷）	Areas Covered by Plastic Film (10 000 hectares)	2.05	2.62	2.13	1.96

表 12.12　域外市属农场农业生产情况(2012～2015)
AGRICULTURAL PRODUCTION OF EXTERNAL MUNICIPAL FARM

指　标	Indicators	2012	2013	2014	2015
农业总产值(亿元)	**Gross Output Value of Agriculture(100 million yuan)**	**16.08**	**18.81**	**21.56**	**25.09**
#种植业	Planting	5.32	5.65	5.95	5.82
林　业	Forestry	0.22	0.15	0.05	0.15
牧　业	Animal Husbandry	7.15	9.55	12.04	15.23
渔　业	Fishery	3.39	3.46	3.52	3.89
主要农产品产量	**Output of Major Farm Products**				
粮　食(万吨)	Grain(10 000 tons)	17.50	18.75	19.01	17.87
夏　粮	Summer Grain Crops	6.82	7.29	7.35	6.77
秋　粮	Autumn Grain Crops	10.68	11.46	11.66	11.10
棉　花(吨)	Cotton(ton)	135		270	
油菜籽(吨)	Rapeseed(ton)	540	550	110	4 103
蔬　菜(吨)	Vegetables(ton)	10 140			155
园林水果(吨)	Fruits(ton)	300	381	424	604
西　瓜(吨)	Watermelon(ton)	515		1 275	7 298
茶　叶(吨)	Tea-leaves(ton)	12	3	6.06	2.43
生猪出栏(万头)	Quantity of Sold Hogs(10 000 heads)	30.70	41.67	54.72	63.27
生牛奶(万吨)	Raw Milk(10 000 tons)	5.66	6.56	7.62	5.97
水产品(万吨)	Aquatic Products(10 000 tons)	2.65	2.75	3.06	3.23

注：域外市属农场是指上海光明食品(集团)有限公司所属的外地农场，其产量和产值不包括在全市总量中。
Note: External municipal farm refers to the nonlocal farms owned to Shanghai bright food (Group) Co., Ltd., whose output and gross output value are not included in the total of the city.

上 / 海 / 统 / 计 / 年 / 鉴

主要统计指标解释

农村从业人员

乡村人口中16岁以上实际参加生产经营活动并取得实物或货币收入的人员，既包括劳动年龄内实际参加劳动人员，也包括超过劳动年龄但实际参加劳动的人员，但不包括户口在家的在外学生、现役军人和丧失劳动能力的人，也不包括待业人员和家务劳动者。劳动者年龄为16岁以上。

农业总产值

农业总产值是以货币表现的农、林、牧、渔业全部产品的总量和对农林牧渔生产活动进行的各种支持性服务活动的价值。它反映一定时期内农业生产的总规模和总成果。

农、林、牧、渔业的统计范围是：

(1)种植业　包括谷物、豆类、薯类、棉、油料、糖料、麻类、烟叶、蔬菜、药材、瓜类和其他农作物的种植，以及茶园、桑园、果园的生产经营。

(2)林业　包括林木的栽培(不包括茶园、桑园和果园的栽培、管理和收获等活动)、林产品的采集和村及村以下合作经济组织和农户的竹木采伐。

(3)牧业　包括除渔业养殖以外的一切动物饲养和放牧，以及野生动物的捕猎和饲养。

(4)渔业　包括水生动物和海藻类植物的养殖和捕捞。

(5)农林牧渔服务业 包括农林牧渔业生产活动进行的各种支持性服务活动。但不包括各种科学技术和专业技术服务活动。

农业总产值的计算方法通常是按农林牧渔业产品及其副产品的产量分别乘以各自单位产品价格求得，少数生产周期较长、当年没有产品或产品产量不易统计的，则采用间接方法匡算其产值，然后将四业产品产值和服务业产值相加即为农业总产值。

1957年以前的农业总产值中包括了厩肥和农民自给性手工业(如农民自制衣服、鞋、袜，自己从事粮食初步加工等)。1958年及以后的农业总产值，林业中增加了村及村以下竹木采伐产值；牧业中取消了厩肥产值；副业中取消了农民自给性手工业产值，增加了村及村以下办的工业产值；渔业中增加了海洋捕捞水产品产值。1980年及以后的农业总产值，在副业中增加了农民家庭兼营工业商品部分的产值。从1984年起村及村以下办工业产值划归工业。从1993年起，取消副业。将野生动物的捕猎划入牧业，野生植物采集和农民家庭兼营商品性工业划归农业。从2003年起，农业总产值中包括了农林牧渔服务业产值。

农业机械总动力

指用于农、林、牧、渔业生产的各种动力机械的动力总和。动力机械包括耕作、排灌、种植、植物保护、收获、农产品加工、运输、畜牧、渔业、农田水利等各种机械。不包括专门用于乡办工业、基本建设、非农业运输、科学试验和教学等非农业生产方面用的动力机械与作业机械的数量。

农作物播种面积

指报告期内收获农产品的作物的实际播种或移植有农作物的面积。凡是实际种植农作物的面积，不论种植在耕地上还是种植在非耕地上，均包括在农作物播种面积中。在播种季节基本结束后，因遭灾而重新改种和补种的农作物面积，也包括在内。

粮食产量

指全社会的产量。包括国有经济经营的、集体统一经营的和农民家庭经营的粮食产量，还包括工矿企业办的农场和其他生产单位的产量。粮食除包括稻谷、小麦、玉米、高粱、谷子及其他杂粮外，还包括薯类和豆类。其产量计算方法，豆类按去豆荚后的干豆计算；薯类(包括甘薯和马铃薯，不包括芋头和木薯)1963年以前按每4公斤鲜薯折1公斤粮食计算，从1964年开始改为按5公斤鲜薯折1公斤粮食计算。城市郊区作为蔬菜的薯类(如马铃薯等)按鲜品计算，并且不作粮食统计。其他粮食一律按脱粒后的原粮计算。1989年以前粮食产量数据主要靠全面报表取得，1989年开始使用抽样调查数据。

棉花产量

指全社会的产量。包括春播棉和夏播棉。产量按皮棉计算。3公斤籽棉折1公斤皮棉，不包括木棉。

油料产量

指全部油料作物的生产量。包括花生、油菜籽、芝麻、

主要统计指标解释

向日葵籽、胡麻籽(亚麻籽)和其他油料。不包括大豆、木本油料和野生油料。花生以带壳干花生计算。

水产品产量

指人工养殖的水产品和天然生长的水产品的捕捞量。包括海水的鱼类、虾蟹类、贝类和藻类以及内陆水域的鱼类、虾蟹类和贝类,不包括淡水生植物。水产品产量是通过各级水产和统计部门逐级上报取得数据。1995 年及以前,贝类中牡蛎按鲜肉计算;蚶、蛤、蛙按 5 斤鲜品折 1 斤计算。1996 年以后则统一按鲜品计算。

猪、牛、羊肉产量

指当年出栏并已屠宰、除去头蹄下水后带骨肉(即胴体重)的重量。包括全社会范围内的产量。1996 年前为各级逐级上报数据。1996 年第一次农业普查以后,由于畜牧业产品年报数据与普查数据之间存在一定的差距,国家统计局农调总队对畜牧业年报数据与普查数据进行衔接。上海仍使用各级统计部门逐级上报数据。

SHANGHAI STATISTICAL YEARBOOK

EXPLANATORY NOTES TO MAJOR STATISTICAL INDICATORS

□ Employees in Rural Areas

Employees in Rural Areas refers to people in rural areas who are older than 16 years and engaged in production and business activities that generate incomes in cash or in practicality. It includes all working laborers, no matter whether they are within the working age or not, whereas students studying outside but with their registered residence at home, active serviceman, people who lost their ability to work, unemployed people, and those engaged in housework are not included. The working age is defined as older than 16 years.

□ Gross Output Value of Agriculture

Gross Output Value of Agriculture refers to the total volume of products of farming, forestry, animal husbandry and fishery expressed in the monetary terms and output value of all kinds of service activities that support farming, forestry, animal husbandry and fishery production. It reflects the overall scale and achievements of agricultural production during a given period of time.

The scope of statistics on farming, forestry, animal husbandry, and fishery are as follows:

(1)Farming includes cultivation of grain crops, legume crops, tuber-crops, cotton, oil-bearing crops, sugar crops, bastfiber plants, tobacco, vegetables, medicinal herbs, melon crops, and cultivation and management of tea plantations, mulberry fields and orchards.

(2)Forestry refers to planting trees of various kinds (excluding tea plantations, mulberry fields and orchards), collection of forestry products and cutting and felling of bamboo and trees by villages and other cooperative organizations under village level.

(3)Animal husbandry refers to raising and grazing of all kinds of farm animals except fishing and aquatic cultivating, and hunting and rising of wild animals.

(4)Fishery refers to cultivation and catching of fish and other aquatic products and cultivation and collection of seaweed and other aquatic plants.

(5)Service Industry for Farming, Forestry, Animal Husbandry and Fishery refers to all kinds of service activities that support farming, forestry, animal husbandry and fishery production, whereas activities of science, technology and professional service are not included.

Gross output value of agriculture is obtained by first multiplying the output of products or by-products by their unit price. For a small number of products, annual output of which is not available or difficult to get due to the long production/growing process involved, the output value will be estimated through an indirect approach. The sum of output value of all products of farming, forestry, animal husbandry and fishery and output value of service activities will then and together to form gross output value of agriculture.

Before 1957, China's gross agricultural output value included the value of barnyard manure and handicraft products for self-consumption (clothes, shoes, stockings, and initial grain processing under-taken by peasants). After 1958, the output value of cutting and felling of bamboo and trees by villages and other cooperative organizations under villages have been included in forestry; value of barnyard manure has been excluded from animal husbandry; the value of self-consumed handicrafts has been excluded from sideline occupations, while output value of industries run by villages and cooperative organizations under village level has been included in sideline occupations and output value of fish catches by motor fishing boats has been added to fishery. Since 1980, the output value of handicraft products made for sale by farmer households has been added to sideline occupations. From 1984, industries run by villages and cooperative organizations under village level have been included in the sector of industry. After 1993, the category of sideline occupations has been canceled and hunting of wild animals has been classified into husbandry, and harvesting of wild vegetation and commodity industry run by rural households have been grouped into the category of agriculture. Since 2003, the output value of service industry for farming, forestry, animal husbandry and fishery is included in the gross output value of agriculture.

□ Total Power of Agricultural Machinery

Total Power of Agricultural Machinery refers to the total mechanical power of machinery used in farming, forestry animal husbandry and fishery, including machines used for ploughing, irrigation and drainage, crop growing, plant protection, harvesting, farm product processing, transport, stock breeding, fishery and water conservancy. Machinery employed for non-agricultural purposes such as township industry, capital construction, non-a-

EXPLANATORY NOTES TO MAJOR STATISTICAL INDICATORS

gricultural transport, scientific experiments and for teaching is excluded.

□ Sown Area of Planting

Sown Area of Planting refers to area of land sown or transplanted with crops that have been harvested during report period, regardless of being in cultivated area or non-cultivated area. Area of land re-sown due to natural disasters is also included.

□ Grain Output

Grain Output refers to the total output in the whole country including grains produced by state farms, collective units, rural households, as well as by farms affiliated to industrial and mining enterprises and other production units. Grain includes rice, wheat, corn, sorghum, millet and other miscellaneous grains as well as tubers and bean. Output of beans refers to dry beans without pods. The output of tubers (sweet potatoes and potatoes, not including taros and cassava) was converted into that of grain at the ratio 4:1, i.e. 4 kilograms of fresh tubers was equivalent to 1 kilogram of grain up to 1963. Since 1964 the ratio for conversion has been 5:1. Tubers supplied as vegetables (such as potatoes) in cities and suburbs are calculated as fresh vegetables and their output is not included in the output of grain. Output of all other grains refers to husked grain. Data on grain production before 1989 were obtained through Comprehensive Statistical Reporting System. Since 1989, data from sample surveys are used.

□ Cotton Output

Cotton Output refers to the cotton production in the whole country including cotton sown in spring and in autumn. Output is measured as the weight of ginned cotton. Three kilograms of seed-cotton are equivalent to 1 kilogram of ginned cotton, excluding ceiba.

□ Output of Oil-bearing Crops

Output of Oil-bearing Crops refers to the total production of oil-bearing crops of various kinds, including peanuts, (dry, in shell) rapeseeds, sesame, sunflower seeds, flax seeds, and other oil-bearing crops. Soybeans, oil-bearing woody plants, and wild oil-bearing crops are not included.

□ Output of Aquatic Products

Output of Aquatic Products refers to catches of both artificially cultured and naturally grown aquatic products, including fish, shrimps, crabs and shellfish in sea and inland water as well as seaweed. Freshwater plants are not included. Data on output of aquatic products are reported by aquatic product and statistical agencies level by level. Before 1995, among the shellfish, the oyster was counted as fresh meat; 5 kilograms of ark shell, clams and frogs are equivalent to 1 kilogram of fresh aquatic products; they are all counted as fresh aquatic products since 1996.

□ Output of Pork, Beef, and Mutton

Output of Pork, Beef, and Mutton refers to the meat of slaughtered hogs, cattle, sheep and goats with head, feet, and offal taken away. Data refers to the production of the whole country. The first agriculture census of China in 1996 revealed some discrepancy between the production of animal products from the annual reports and that from the census. Efforts were made by the Rural Socio-economic Survey Organization of NBS to adjust the output value of animal husbandry to make the figures from the annual reports consistent with the census data. Datao of Shanghai are still reported by statistical agencies level by level.

第十三篇
CHAPTER 13

2016上海统计年鉴 SHANGHAI STATISTICAL YEARBOOK

工　业
INDUSTRY

简要说明

一、本章资料的主要内容

本本篇资料反映上海市工业经济方面的基本情况,主要内容包括:

1. 上海工业经济概况。规模以上工业企业主要经济指标,以及按地区、隶属关系、企业登记注册类型、企业规模和工业行业大类分组的主要经济指标;按隶属关系、企业规模分组和国有控股的主要经济效益指标。

2. 国有控股主要经济指标及其占全市比重。

3. 六个重点工业行业及信息产品制造业主要经济指标。

4.高技术产业(制造业)按登记注册类型和技术领域分组的主要经济指标。

5. 都市型工业按企业规模、登记注册类型和行业分组的主要经济指标。

6. 历年主要工业产品产量及 2015 年主要工业产品产、销量。

7. 大中小型工业企业按隶属关系、从业人员、工业总产值、行业分组的主要经济指标。

8. 国家级、市级工业园区主要经济指标。

二、本篇资料的统计范围

本篇资料除表 14.1 为全市工业企业以外,其余工业数据的统计范围如下:1998 年至 2006 年为全部国有和年主营业务收入 500 万元及以上的非国有工业企业;2007 至 2010 年为年主营业务收入 500 万元及以上的工业企业(即规模以上工业企业);从 2011 年开始,为年主营业务收入 2000 万元及以上的工业企业(即规模以上工业企业)。

本篇资料中工业行业分类按 2011 年《国民经济行业分类》标准划分;企业大中小微型划分按 2011 年《统计上大中小微型企业划分办法》标准执行。

本篇资料中税金总额包含的应交增值税指标从 2015 年年报起,负数不做替零处理。

三、本篇的资料来源和统计调查方法

本篇工业企业统计数据主要是根据工业统计年度报表中有关资料整理汇总的。

BRIEF INTRODUCTION

I. Major Contents

The Data in this chapter reflect the basic conditions of the industrial sector in Shanghai. Major contents include:

(1) Basic conditions of industrial sectors in Shanghai; major economic indicators of industrial enterprises above designated sizes; as well as major economic indicators classified by regions, by subordination, by types of registration, by size of enterprise, and by branch of industry; and major economic efficiency indicators classified by subordination, by sizes of enterprise, and on state–controlled industrial enterprises.

(2) Major economic indicators of state–controlled industrial enterprises and their proportions of the city's total.

(3) Major economic indicators of six key industrial sectors and information technology manufacturing sector.

(4) Major economic indicators of high technology industries (manufacturing) classified by types of registration and by technology areas.

(5) Major economic indicators of urban industries classified by sizes of enterprise, by type of registration, and by industrial sectors.

(6) Output of major industrial products in recent years, as well as output and sales of major industrial products in 2015.

(7)Major economic indicators of large–, medium–, and small–size industrial enterprises classified by subordination, by number of employees, by gross output value of industry, and byindustrial sectors.

(8) Major economic indicators of municipal and national industrial zones.

II. Scope and Coverage of Statistics

Except for table 14.1, which covers all industrial enterprises in the city, the scopes of industrial statistics were all state–owned industrial enterprises and non–state–owned industrial enterprises whose annual revenue from principal business was more than 5 million yuan from 1998 to 2006. For 2007 to 2010, the scopes of industrial statistics were all industrial enterprises whose annual revenue from principal business was more than 5 million yuan, (i.e., the industrial enterprises above designated size). Since 2011, the scope is adjusted to all industrial enterprises whose annual revenue from principal business was more than 20 million yuan (i.e. industrial enterprises above designated size).

Branches of industry in this chapter are based on the 2011's National Industrial Classification of all Economic Activities, and data by size of enterprise are based on 2011 Standards of Enterprises by Size.

In this chapter, the negative numbers of value added tax payable included in the total amount of tax needn't do zero treatment since annual report of 2015.

Ⅲ. Sources of Data and Methodology of Survey

The data of industrial enterprises statistics in this Chapter are collected mainly from the relevant data in the annual industrial statistics reporting forms.

表 13.1 工业总产值及指数 (1978 ~2015)
GROSS OUTPUT VALUE OF INDUSTRY AND INDEX

年 份 Year	工业总产值 (亿元) Gross Output Value of Industry (100 million yuan)	工业总产值指数 (以1978年为100) Indices of Gross Output Value of Industry (1978 = 100)	年 份 Year	工业总产值 (亿元) Gross Output Value of Industry (100 million yuan)	工业总产值指数 (以1978年为100) Indices of Gross Output Value of Industry (1978 = 100)
1978	514.01	100.0	1996	5 126.22	590.1
1979	556.30	108.6	1997	5 649.93	675.7
1980	598.75	115.7	1998	5 763.67	728.5
1981	620.12	120.0	1999	6 213.24	805.1
1982	634.65	125.6	2000	7 022.98	913.7
1983	663.53	134.4	2001	7 806.18	1 063.8
1984	728.12	147.7	2002	8 730.00	1 219.1
1985	862.73	167.7	2003	11 708.49	1 601.9
1986	952.21	177.0	2004	14 595.29	1 927.1
1987	1 073.84	188.9	2005	16 876.78	2 195.0
1988	1 304.66	208.8	2006	19 631.23	2 500.1
1989	1 524.67	215.0	2007	23 108.63	2 892.6
1990	1 642.75	223.6	2008	25 968.38	3 126.9
1991	1 947.18	255.2	2009	24 888.08	3 227.0
1992	2 429.96	306.7	2010	31 038.57	3 966.0
1993	3 327.04	368.2	2011	33 834.44	4 227.8
1994	4 255.19	435.3	2012	33 186.41	4 215.1
1995	5 349.53	510.9	2013	33 899.38	4 396.3
(1995)	(4 547.47)		2014	34 071.19	4 466.7
			2015	33 211.57	4 444.3

注：从1996年开始，工业总产值按新规定计算，括号内数为1995年新规定数(以下同)。
Note: Since 1996, new regulations have been adopted in calculating total industrial gross output value of industry. The figures of 1995 in brackets are calculated in line with the new regulations (same as follows).

表 13.2 各区、县工业企业主要指标(2015)
MAJOR INDICATIORS OF INDUSTRIAL ENTERPRISES IN DISTRICTS AND COUNTIES

地 区	District	单位数 (个) Number of Enterprises (unit)	从业人员 (万人) Employees (10 000 persons)	工业总产值 (亿元) Gross Output Value of Industry (100 million yuan)	年末资产总计 (亿元) Total Assets (year-end) (100 million yuan)	主营业务收入 (亿元) Prime Operating Revenue (100 million yuan)	利润总额 (亿元) Total Pre-tax Profits (100 million yuan)
总 计	**Total**	**8 994**	**224.65**	**31 322.62**	**37 306.95**	**34 172.22**	**2 680.53**
浦东新区	Pudong New Area	1 718	59.11	9 177.80	12 398.01	10 872.94	898.09
黄 浦 区	Huangpu	17	0.86	89.07	116.33	175.73	8.88
徐 汇 区	Xuhui	112	3.00	550.43	615.09	644.79	111.57
长 宁 区	Changning	31	1.83	111.96	209.64	111.32	3.07
静 安 区	Jing'an	4	0.12	10.45	36.75	10.32	-1.48
普 陀 区	Putuo	112	2.26	192.91	294.52	240.14	22.34
闸 北 区	Zhabei	52	1.72	243.69	428.31	254.90	7.99
虹 口 区	Hongkou	22	0.77	104.88	374.39	108.21	33.30
杨 浦 区	Yangpu	71	2.04	1 166.75	1 586.17	1 147.84	253.04
闵 行 区	Minhang	996	26.74	3 168.16	3 808.86	3 413.61	251.99
宝 山 区	Baoshan	494	11.02	1 903.17	3 126.73	2 196.08	75.62
嘉 定 区	Jiading	1 241	29.91	4 944.44	3 980.95	5 126.10	566.16
金 山 区	Jinshan	740	13.52	1 643.56	1 482.36	1 653.64	85.11
松 江 区	Songjiang	1 280	31.36	3 604.84	2 800.26	3 683.89	136.31
青 浦 区	Qingpu	864	17.87	1 510.29	1 640.11	1 550.85	96.93
奉 贤 区	Fengxian	1 075	17.24	1 512.74	1 992.49	1 536.50	97.08
崇 明 县	Chongming	124	3.54	341.57	621.57	306.38	-4.93
其 他	Others	41	1.75	1 045.89	1 794.42	1 139.00	39.47

表 13.3 规模以上工业企业主要指标(2015)
MAJOR INDICATORS OF INDUSTRIAL ENTERPRISES ABOVE THE SET SCALE

类　别	Types	单位数（个）Quantity of Enterprises (unit)
总　计	**Total**	**8 994**
按隶属关系分	**Grouped by Subordination**	
中央工业	Central Government	152
地方工业	Local Government	8 842
按登记注册类型分	**Grouped by Registration Categories**	
内　资	Domestic Funded	5 177
#国　有	State-owned	59
集　体	Collective-owned	73
有限责任公司	Companies with Limited Liabilities	976
股份有限公司	Share-holding Companies with Limited Liabilities	170
私　营	Private	3 840
港澳台商投资	Hong Kong, Macao and Taiwan Funded	1 081
#港澳台商独资	Sole Funded	685
港澳台商投资股份有限公司	Share-holding Companies Ltd.	32
外商投资	Foreign Funded	2 736
#中外合资经营	Joint-venture	628
外资企业	Sole Funded	1 959
外商投资股份有限公司	Share-holding Companies Ltd.	31
按企业规模分	**Grouped by Size of Enterprises**	
大　型	Large	272
中　型	Medium	1 248
小　型	Small	7 474
按工业行业分	**Grouped by Sectors**	
采矿业	**Mining Industry**	**1**
石油和天然气开采业	Petroleum and Natural Gas Exploiting	1
制造业	**Manufacture Industry**	**8 921**
农副食品加工业	Farm and Sideline Products Processing	142
食品制造业	Food Manufacturing	218
酒、饮料和精制茶制造业	Wine, Beverage and Refined Tea Manufacturing	37
烟草制品业	Tabacco Manufacturing	2

从业人员（万人）Employees (10 000 persons)	工业总产值（亿元）Gross Output Value of Industry (100 million yuan)	年末资产总计（亿元）Total Assets (year-end) (100 million yuan)	流动资产合计（亿元）Current Assets (100 million yuan)
224.65	**31 322.62**	**37 306.95**	**21 374.44**
17.51	5 963.89	9 440.85	4 026.40
207.14	25 358.73	27 866.10	17 348.04
97.46	12 295.92	20 578.43	10 533.40
3.00	947.64	2 106.37	316.16
0.87	60.33	59.15	46.38
32.43	5 577.10	8 620.94	5 057.59
10.10	1 926.82	5 469.73	2 090.28
50.29	3 730.96	4 273.90	2 988.00
34.82	4 561.15	3 970.37	2 478.46
21.78	2 869.31	2 199.14	1 575.84
2.72	842.23	653.59	259.98
92.37	14 465.55	12 758.15	8 362.58
23.81	6 354.12	5 231.84	3 349.79
61.29	7 280.66	6 143.30	4 155.15
3.37	502.13	1 067.14	614.86
80.49	16 735.42	19 997.96	10 159.64
65.03	6 556.84	7 896.06	5 034.50
79.14	8 030.37	9 412.93	6 180.29
0.02	**6.56**	**34.24**	**21.85**
0.02	6.56	34.24	21.85
221.05	**29 808.12**	**33 579.17**	**20 796.93**
2.72	333.82	263.44	174.34
7.29	597.87	689.57	442.39
1.25	109.73	130.21	77.46
0.39	1 027.26	1 232.39	945.37

表 13.3 续表 1 continued

类 别	Types	单位数（个）Quantity of Enterprises (unit)
纺织业	Textile	187
纺织服装、服饰业	Textiles and Clothing Industry	357
皮革、毛皮、羽毛及其制品和制鞋业	Leather, Fur, Wool Products and Shoes Manufacturing	116
木材加工和木、竹、藤、棕、草制品业	Timber Processing and Timber, Bamboo, Rattan, Coir and Straw Products Manufacturing	69
家具制造业	Furniture Manufacturing	169
造纸和纸制品业	Paper-making and Paper Products Manufacturing	188
印刷和记录媒介复制业	Printing and Record Duplicating	163
文教、工美、体育和娱乐用品制造业	Culture, Education, Industrial Arts, Sports and Entertainment Goods Manufacturing	127
石油加工、炼焦和核燃料加工业	Oil Processing, Coking and Nuclear Fuel	37
化学原料和化学制品制造业	Raw Chemical Materials and Chemical Products Manufacturing	738
医药制造业	Medicine Manufacturing	199
化学纤维制造业	Chemical Fiber Manufacturing	27
橡胶和塑料制品业	Rubber and Plastic Products Manufacturing	713
非金属矿物制品业	Non-metallic Mineral Products Manufacturing	381
黑色金属冶炼和压延加工业	Ferrous Metal Smelting and Rolling Processing Industry	108
有色金属冶炼和压延加工业	Nonferrous Metal Smelting and Rolling Processing Industry	130
金属制品业	Metal Products Manufacturing	732
通用设备制造业	General Equipment Manufacturing	1 171
专用设备制造业	Special Purpose Equipment Manufacturing	622
汽车制造业	The Automotive Manufacturing	522
铁路、船舶、航空航天和其他运输设备制造业	The Railroad, Marine, Aerospace and Other Transportation Equipment Manufacturing	123
电气机械和器材制造业	Electric Machinery Equipments and Manufacturing	860
计算机、通信和其他电子设备制造业	Computer, Communications and Other Electronic Equipment Manufacturing	475
仪器仪表制造业	Instrumentation Manufacturing	199
其他制造业	Other Manufacturing	42
废弃资源综合利用业	Comprehensive Utilization of Waste Resources	27
金属制品、机械和设备修理业	Metal Products, Machinery and Equipment Repair Industry	40
电力、热力、燃气及水生产和供应业	**Electricity, Heat, Gas and Water Production and Supply Industry**	**72**
电力、热力生产和供应业	Production and Supply of Electricity and Thermal Power	36
燃气生产和供应业	Production and Supply of Gas	13
水的生产和供应业	Production and Supply of Water	23

从业人员 (万人) Employees (10 000 persons)	工业总产值 (亿元) Gross Output Value of Industry (100 million yuan)	年末资产总计 (亿元) Total Assets (year-end) (100 million yuan)	流动资产合计 (亿元) Current Assets (100 million yuan)
3.17	220.21	217.03	153.23
7.85	347.87	347.13	253.92
2.71	178.12	224.24	192.49
0.86	66.96	76.32	51.34
3.63	284.40	271.51	199.37
2.57	240.30	283.15	171.82
2.75	181.77	224.52	131.40
3.19	392.18	246.13	171.71
1.73	1 156.47	420.75	138.37
11.49	2 467.06	2 661.52	1 419.95
5.99	**655.99**	**1 036.23**	**620.15**
0.34	31.91	48.48	31.46
11.34	860.39	1 178.97	648.00
5.33	542.94	728.75	519.15
3.68	1 186.70	2 224.19	800.28
2.01	387.45	300.57	193.74
13.48	896.37	999.05	683.92
22.61	2 515.04	3 496.83	2 400.37
11.28	1 041.77	1 619.40	1 147.00
22.71	5 223.80	6 033.16	3 226.30
6.24	811.45	1 560.82	1 050.31
19.45	2 150.84	2 329.55	1 717.79
37.35	5 323.39	3 835.42	2 626.96
3.87	331.98	380.49	293.90
1.05	53.58	62.30	39.16
0.16	25.67	29.49	15.42
2.54	164.85	427.56	259.85
3.59	**1 507.95**	**3 693.54**	**555.65**
1.96	1 102.86	2 605.43	316.05
0.58	335.97	375.49	125.41
1.05	69.11	712.62	114.19

表13.3 续表2 continued

类别	Types	年末负债合计 Total Liabilities (year-end)	年末所有者权益 Owners' Equity (year-end)
总计	**Total**	**18 111.05**	**19 088.40**
按隶属关系分	**Grouped by Subordination**		
中央工业	Central Government	4 132.46	5 298.90
地方工业	Local Government	13 978.59	13 789.51
按登记注册类型分	**Grouped by Registration Categories**		
内资	Domestic Funded	9 219.44	11 316.87
#国有	State-owned	634.19	1 471.20
集体	Collective-owned	30.61	28.48
有限责任公司	Companies with Limited Liabilities	4 485.60	4 110.92
股份有限公司	Share-holding Companies with Limited Liabilities	1 661.62	3 806.26
私营	Private	2 382.34	1 877.75
港澳台商投资	Hong Kong, Macao and Taiwan Funded	1 939.60	2 023.08
#港澳台商独资	Sole Funded	1 207.60	984.23
港澳台商投资股份有限公司	Share-holding Companies Ltd.	170.84	482.74
外商投资	Foreign Funded	6 952.01	5 748.45
#中外合资经营	Joint-venture	2 980.43	2 233.44
外资企业	Sole Funded	3 171.98	2 942.97
外商投资股份有限公司	Share-holding Companies Ltd.	665.95	391.59
按企业规模分	**Grouped by Size of Enterprises**		
大型	Large	9 276.34	10 680.80
中型	Medium	3 982.70	3 904.17
小型	Small	4 852.01	4 503.44
按工业行业分	**Grouped by Sectors**		
采矿业	**Mining Industry**	**7.70**	**26.55**
石油和天然气开采业	Petroleum and Natural Gas Exploiting	7.70	26.55
制造业	**Manufacture Industry**	**16 769.10**	**16 702.56**
农副食品加工业	Farm and Sideline Products Processing	135.12	128.07
食品制造业	Food Manufacturing	411.55	276.73
酒、饮料和精制茶制造业	Wine, Beverage and Refined Tea Manufacturing	63.53	66.44
烟草制品业	Tabacco Manufacturing	156.84	1 075.56

单位:亿元(100 million yuan)

主营业务收入 Prime Operating Revenue	利润总额 Total Pre-tax Profits	税金总额 Total Tax and Duties	成本费用总额 Total Cost and Expenses
34 172.22	**2 680.53**	**2 009.73**	**31 273.92**
6 195.15	450.27	1 171.26	4 964.52
27 977.06	2 230.26	838.47	26 309.40
13 247.38	1 138.59	1 236.28	12 004.53
961.61	43.71	34.75	923.47
59.29	2.43	2.30	57.76
6 032.72	465.94	892.53	5 128.15
2 336.37	403.87	189.24	2 219.36
3 804.60	220.68	114.51	3 623.74
4 821.60	267.57	228.17	4 448.85
3 083.49	117.09	28.57	2 942.43
841.71	74.75	177.07	655.26
16 103.24	1 274.37	545.28	14 820.54
7 518.25	839.38	407.18	6 621.16
7 731.34	400.64	127.48	7 358.92
508.42	21.74	1.83	510.91
18 776.75	1 709.19	1 562.58	16 672.99
6 933.27	535.70	203.38	6 484.89
8 462.21	435.64	243.77	8 116.03
6.42	**-1.96**	**0.71**	**8.39**
6.42	-1.96	0.71	8.39
32 572.16	**2 574.33**	**1 950.63**	**29 751.51**
378.42	12.41	6.87	374.54
706.29	44.26	40.52	666.27
135.52	16.23	10.99	120.94
999.37	246.49	784.06	141.50

表 13.3 续表 3 continued

类别	Types	年末负债合计 Total Liabilities (year-end)
纺织业	Textile	94.26
纺织服装、服饰业	Textiles and Clothing Industry	195.38
皮革、毛皮、羽毛及其制品和制鞋业	Leather, Fur, Wool Products and Shoes Manufacturing	64.76
木材加工和木、竹、藤、棕、草制品业	Timber Processing and Timber, Bamboo, Rattan, Coir and Straw Products Manufacturing	42.36
家具制造业	Furniture Manufacturing	169.60
造纸和纸制品业	Paper-making and Paper Products Manufacturing	137.49
印刷和记录媒介复制业	Printing and Record Duplicating	89.40
文教、工美、体育和娱乐用品制造业	Culture, Education, Industrial Arts, Sports and Entertainment Goods Manufacturing	127.84
石油加工、炼焦和核燃料加工业	Oil Processing, Coking and Nuclear Fuel	169.81
化学原料和化学制品制造业	Raw Chemical Materials and Chemical Products Manufacturing	1 210.68
医药制造业	Medicine Manufacturing	387.43
化学纤维制造业	Chemical Fiber Manufacturing	21.17
橡胶和塑料制品业	Rubber and Plastic Products Manufacturing	497.61
非金属矿物制品业	Non-metallic Mineral Products Manufacturing	417.99
黑色金属冶炼和压延加工业	Ferrous Metal Smelting and Rolling Processing Industry	929.99
有色金属冶炼和压延加工业	Nonferrous Metal Smelting and Rolling Processing Industry	170.92
金属制品业	Metal Products Manufacturing	516.07
通用设备制造业	General Equipment Manufacturing	2 049.04
专用设备制造业	Special Purpose Equipment Manufacturing	914.73
汽车制造业	The Automotive Manufacturing	2 644.70
铁路、船舶、航空航天和其他运输设备制造业	The Railroad, Marine, Aerospace and Other Transportation Equipment Manufacturing	1 187.50
电气机械和器材制造业	Electric Machinery Equipments and Manufacturing	1 271.43
计算机、通信和其他电子设备制造业	Computer, Communications and Other Electronic Equipment Manufacturing	2 222.97
仪器仪表制造业	Instrumentation Manufacturing	165.77
其他制造业	Other Manufacturing	23.62
废弃资源综合利用业	Comprehensive Utilization of Waste Resources	14.64
金属制品、机械和设备修理业	Metal Products, Machinery and Equipment Repair Industry	264.92
电力、热力、燃气及水生产和供应业	**Electricity, Heat, Gas and Water Production and Supply Industry**	**1 334.26**
电力、热力生产和供应业	Production and Supply of Electricity and Thermal Power	919.38
燃气生产和供应业	Production and Supply of Gas	179.04
水的生产和供应业	Production and Supply of Water	235.85

单位：亿元(100 million yuan)

年末所有者权益 Owners' Equity (year-end)	主营业务收入 Prime Operating Revenue	利润总额 Total Pre-tax Profits	税金总额 Total Tax and Duties	成本费用总额 Total Cost and Expenses
119.79	232.24	14.06	6.54	219.43
151.69	373.90	6.76	6.23	380.20
158.93	179.43	11.89	7.68	167.45
34.01	72.39	1.64	2.18	70.60
101.47	284.15	31.56	8.32	268.69
147.16	262.24	7.78	10.51	254.77
135.02	187.47	18.62	8.32	176.25
118.13	500.65	30.31	7.04	481.56
250.94	1 166.06	50.29	307.86	877.52
1 414.21	2 652.47	178.05	84.32	2 477.79
651.09	**659.35**	**108.39**	**44.93**	**574.26**
27.78	32.04	0.77	0.44	32.82
677.44	880.85	61.12	27.27	832.76
307.99	569.60	29.30	16.87	547.68
1 287.30	1 423.86	16.61	27.54	1 421.34
127.58	398.02	9.12	2.68	391.10
480.87	926.53	52.90	27.13	881.10
1 429.41	2 586.71	161.54	73.55	2 433.93
699.15	1 084.52	60.60	29.84	1 027.43
3 379.91	6 574.19	1 078.11	365.41	5 868.57
372.14	783.17	3.86	-4.03	785.34
1 042.78	2 215.65	151.84	46.31	2 081.77
1 612.01	5 706.66	121.27	-14.30	5 637.47
212.82	354.44	37.73	8.33	322.80
38.69	54.18	3.36	2.82	50.86
14.84	25.48	2.27	0.82	24.49
162.64	166.30	5.19	3.58	160.29
2 359.29	**1 593.65**	**108.16**	**58.39**	**1 514.02**
1 686.06	1 126.70	93.85	51.39	1 051.59
197.12	385.13	7.81	3.49	379.62
476.11	81.82	6.51	3.51	82.81

表 13.4 工业企业销售产值(2015)
SALES VALUE OF INDUSTRIAL ENTERPRISES

单位:亿元(100 million yuan)

类 别	Types	工业销售产值 Sales Value of Industry	其中 of which #出口交货值 Delivery Value of Industry Export
总 计	**Total**	**31 214.32**	**7 595.16**
按隶属关系分	**Grouped by Subordination**		
中央工业	Central Government	5 920.84	739.94
地方工业	Local Government	25 293.48	6 855.22
按登记注册类型分	**Grouped by Registration Categories**		
内 资	Domestic Funded	12 200.04	1 136.77
#国 有	State-owned	948.39	6.70
集 体	Collective-owned	57.32	2.57
有限责任公司	Companies with Limited Liabilities	5 533.58	589.34
股份有限公司	Share-holding Companies with Limited Liabilities	1 917.57	203.90
私 营	Private	3 690.83	330.53
港澳台商投资	Hong Kong, Macao and Taiwan Funded	4 524.61	2 252.30
#港澳台商独资	Sole Funded	2 839.17	1 925.52
港澳台商投资股份有限公司	Share-holding Companies Ltd.	839.77	108.65
外商投资	Foreign Funded	14 489.67	4 206.08
#中外合资经营	Joint-venture	6 326.34	523.13
外资企业	Sole Funded	7 332.43	3 387.72
外商投资股份有限公司	Share-holding Companies Ltd.	500.07	222.10
按企业规模分	**Grouped by Size of Enterprises**		
大 型	Large	16 674.77	5 149.08
中 型	Medium	6 542.37	1 297.08
小 型	Small	7 997.18	1 148.99
按工业行业分	**Grouped by Sectors**		
采矿业	**Mining Industry**	**6.42**	
石油和天然气开采业	Petroleum and Natural Gas Exploiting	6.42	
制造业	**Manufacture Industry**	**29 700.41**	**7 595.16**
农副食品加工业	Farm and Sideline Products Processing	335.46	7.48
食品制造业	Food Manufacturing	598.65	31.00
酒、饮料和精制茶制造业	Wine, Beverage and Refined Tea Manufacturing	108.74	7.14
烟草制品业	Tabacco Manufacturing	1 001.53	11.70

表 13.4 续表 continued

单位：亿元(100 million yuan)

类 别	Types	工业销售产值 Sales Value of Industry	其中 of which #出口交货值 Delivery Value of Industry Export
纺织业	Textile	219.66	40.89
纺织服装、服饰业	Textiles and Clothing Industry	343.65	105.52
皮革、毛皮、羽毛及其制品和制鞋业	Leather, Fur, Wool Products and Shoes Manufacturing	179.67	37.74
木材加工和木、竹、藤、棕、草制品业	Timber Processing and Timber, Bamboo, Rattan, Coir and Straw Products Manufacturing	69.42	6.98
家具制造业	Furniture Manufacturing	282.09	73.54
造纸和纸制品业	Paper-making and Paper Products Manufacturing	245.04	19.24
印刷和记录媒介复制业	Printing and Record Duplicating	179.07	19.90
文教、工美、体育和娱乐用品制造业	Culture, Education, Industrial Arts, Sports and Entertainment Goods Manufacturing	395.79	61.44
石油加工、炼焦和核燃料加工业	Oil Processing, Coking and Nuclear Fuel	1 147.07	52.56
化学原料和化学制品制造业	Raw Chemical Materials and Chemical Products Manufacturing	2 500.57	270.23
医药制造业	Medicine Manufacturing	623.80	50.56
化学纤维制造业	Chemical Fiber Manufacturing	31.03	11.27
橡胶和塑料制品业	Rubber and Plastic Products Manufacturing	855.05	185.90
非金属矿物制品业	Non-metallic Mineral Products Manufacturing	543.90	61.68
黑色金属冶炼和压延加工业	Ferrous Metal Smelting and Rolling Processing Industry	1 182.83	110.53
有色金属冶炼和压延加工业	Nonferrous Metal Smelting and Rolling Processing Industry	379.49	49.87
金属制品业	Metal Products Manufacturing	889.75	217.02
通用设备制造业	General Equipment Manufacturing	2 491.97	498.71
专用设备制造业	Special Purpose Equipment Manufacturing	1 039.54	277.64
汽车制造业	The Automotive Manufacturing	5 203.41	222.99
铁路、船舶、航空航天和其他运输设备制造业	The Railroad, Marine, Aerospace and Other Transportation Equipment Manufacturing	794.92	384.66
电气机械和器材制造业	Electric Machinery Equipments and Manufacturing	2 147.24	456.93
计算机、通信和其他电子设备制造业	Computer, Communications and Other Electronic Equipment Manufacturing	5 335.03	4 160.38
仪器仪表制造业	Instrumentation Manufacturing	331.04	106.18
其他制造业	Other Manufacturing	53.57	8.96
废弃资源综合利用业	Comprehensive Utilization of Waste Resources	26.22	
金属制品、机械和设备修理业	Metal Products, Machinery and Equipment Repair Industry	165.22	46.51
电力、热力、燃气及水生产和供应业	**Electricity, Heat, Gas and Water Production and Supply Industry**	**1 507.49**	
电力、热力生产和供应业	Production and Supply of Electricity and Thermal Power	1 105.79	
燃气生产和供应业	Production and Supply of Gas	335.96	
水的生产和供应业	Production and Supply of Water	65.74	

表 13.5 工业企业经济效益指标(2015)
ECONOMIC EFFICIENCY INDICATORS OF INDUSTRIAL ENTERPRISES

类别	Types	总资产贡献率(%) Total Assets Contribution Ratio (%)	资产保值增值率(%) Ratio of Capital Hold and Rise (%)	资产负债率(%) Asset-debt Ratio (%)
总计	**Total**	**12.84**	**111.06**	**48.55**
#国有控股企业	Enterprises with the State Holding Major Shares	17.59	111.32	43.97
按隶属关系分	**Grouped by Subordination**			
中央工业	Central Government	17.40	104.17	43.77
地方工业	Local Government	11.29	113.94	50.16
按企业规模分	**Grouped by Size of Enterprise**			
大型	Large	16.36	112.31	46.39
中型	Medium	9.87	110.19	50.44
小型	Small	7.83	108.93	51.55

表 13.5 续表 continued

类别	Types	流动资产周转次数(次) Turnover of Current Assets (time)	成本费用利润率(%) Ratio of pre-tax Profits to Cost and Expenses(%)	工业产品销售率(%) Sales Rate of Industrial Products(%)
总计	**Total**	**1.65**	**8.32**	**99.65**
#国有控股企业	Enterprises with the State Holding Major Shares	1.80	12.23	99.25
按隶属关系分	**Grouped by Subordination**			
中央工业	Central Government	1.57	8.88	99.28
地方工业	Local Government	1.67	8.22	99.74
按企业规模分	**Grouped by Size of Enterprise**			
大型	Large	1.90	9.94	99.64
中型	Medium	1.44	7.97	99.78
小型	Small	1.40	5.26	99.59

表13.6　国有控股企业主要指标占全市比重(2015)
PROPORTION OF THE MAJOR INDICATORS OF ENTERPRISES WITH THE STATE HOLDING MAJOR SHARES

指　标	Indicators	合　计 Total	国有控股企业 Enterprises with the State Holding Major Shares	占全市比重(%) Proportion of City(%)
企业单位数(个)	Number of Enterprises (unit)	8 994	689	7.7
从业人员(万人)	Year-end Employees (10 000 persons)	224.65	40.74	18.1
工业总产值(亿元)	Gross Output Value of Industry (100 million yuan)	31 322.62	11 536.58	36.8
年末资产总计(亿元)	**Total Assets (year-end) (100 million yuan)**	**37 306.95**	**17 437.33**	**46.7**
流动资产合计(亿元)	Current Assets(100 million yuan)	21 374.44	7 788.31	36.4
年末负债合计(亿元)	Total Liabilities (year-end) (100 million yuan)	18 111.05	7 666.60	42.3
年末所有者权益(亿元)	Owners Equity (year-end) (100 million yuan)	19 088.40	9 748.79	51.1
主营业务收入(亿元)	Prime Operating Revenue(100 million yuan)	34 172.22	13 430.02	39.3
主营业务税金及附加(亿元)	Product Sales Tax and Addition (100 million yuan)	1 096.79	1 042.13	95.0
利润总额(亿元)	**Total Pre-Tax Profits (100 million yuan)**	**2 680.53**	**1 475.16**	**55.0**
税金总额(亿元)	Total Tax and Duty (100 million yuan)	2 009.73	1 572.52	78.2
亏损企业数(个)	Number of Loss-making Enterprises (unit)	1 925	147	7.6
亏损企业亏损额(亿元)	Total Losses Made by Enterprises-in-red (100 million yuan)	320.60	103.86	32.4

表 13.7 六个重点工业行业主要指标(2015)
MAJOR INDICATORS OF SIX KEY INDUSTRIES ABOVE THE SET SCALE

行业	Sectors	单位数(个) Quantity of Enterprises (unit)	平均从业人员(万人) Average Employees (10 000 persons)	工业总产值(亿元) Gross Output Value of Industry (100 million yuan)
总 计	**Total**	**3 957**	**132.79**	**20 964.36**
电子信息产品制造业	Electronic Information Product Manufacturing	981	52.09	6 285.13
汽车制造业	Automobile Manufacturing	522	22.88	5 223.80
石油化工及精细化工制造业	Petrochemical and Fine Chemical Products Manufacturing	658	12.08	3 359.12
精品钢材制造业	Fine Steel Manufacturing	82	3.26	1 152.91
成套设备制造业	Equipment Complex Manufacturing	1 349	33.22	4 031.83
生物医药制造业	Bio-medicine Manufacturing	365	9.26	911.56
六个重点工业行业占全市比重(%)	Percentage of the Six Key Industries in Shanghai (%)	44.0	56.9	66.9

表 13.7 续表 1 continued

行业	Sectors	工业销售产值(亿元) Sales Value of Industry (100 million yuan)	年末资产总计(亿元) Total Propertry (year-end) (100 million yuan)
总 计	**Total**	**20 898.44**	**23 646.18**
电子信息产品制造业	Electronic Information Product Manufacturing	6 284.70	4 810.18
汽车制造业	Automobile Manufacturing	5 203.41	6 033.16
石油化工及精细化工制造业	Petrochemical and Fine Chemical Products Manufacturing	3 378.42	2 770.29
精品钢材制造业	Fine Steel Manufacturing	1 151.23	2 189.90
成套设备制造业	Equipment Complex Manufacturing	4 002.87	6 365.48
生物医药制造业	Bio-medicine Manufacturing	877.80	1 477.17
六个重点工业行业占全市比重(%)	Percentage of the Six Key Industries in Shanghai (%)	67.0	63.4

表 13.7 续表 2 continued

行业	Sectors	主营业务收入(亿元) Prime Operating Revenue (100 million yuan)	利润总额(亿元) Total Pre-tax Profits (100 million yuan)	税金总额(亿元) Total Tax and Duties (100 million yuan)
总 计	**Total**	**23 181.66**	**1 832.48**	**912.33**
电子信息产品制造业	Electronic Information Product Manufacturing	6 692.13	191.89	5.32
汽车制造业	Automobile Manufacturing	6 574.19	1 078.11	365.41
石油化工及精细化工制造业	Petrochemical and Fine Chemical Products Manufacturing	3 520.91	204.36	380.91
精品钢材制造业	Fine Steel Manufacturing	1 391.77	14.87	26.15
成套设备制造业	Equipment Complex Manufacturing	4 070.74	208.93	80.92
生物医药制造业	Bio-medicine Manufacturing	931.92	134.32	53.60
六个重点工业行业占全市比重(%)	Percentage of the Six Key Industries in Shanghai (%)	67.8	68.4	45.4

表13.8 信息产品制造业主要指标(2015)
MAJOR INDICATORS OF INFORMATION PRODUCTS MANUFACTURING INDUSTRY

单位:亿元(100 million yuan)

行 业	Sectors	平均从业人员(万人) Average Employees (10 000 persons)	工业总产值 Gross Output Value of Industry	工业销售产值 Sales Value of Industry
总 计	**Total**	**52.09**	**6 285.13**	**6 284.70**
通信设备制造	Communications Equipment	12.50	1 833.06	1 878.18
雷达及配套产品制造	Radar ane Supported Product	0.03	1.60	1.60
广播电视设备制造	Broadcast and Television Equipment	0.24	18.49	17.88
电子计算机制造	Computer	9.93	1 895.67	1 866.11
家用视听设备制造	Household Seeing and Hearing Equipment	0.75	158.47	160.69
电子测量仪器制造	Geodesic Equipment of Electron	1.99	173.89	172.65
电子专用设备制造	Special Equipment of Electron	3.22	234.47	232.32
电子元件制造	Electronic Component	9.89	636.21	629.86
电子器件制造	Electronic Equipment	8.56	767.47	768.73
#集成电路制造	Integrated Circuit	4.30	371.95	372.97
电子机电产品制造	Machinery and Electronic Products of Electron	4.77	540.81	532.18
电子专用材料制造	Special Materials of Electron	0.20	25.00	24.51

表13.8 续表 continued

单位:亿元(100 million yuan)

行 业	Sectors	年末资产总计 Total Assets (year-end)	主营业务收入 Prime Operating Revenue	利润总额 Total Pre-tax Profits	税金总额 Total Tax and Duty
总 计	**Total**	**4 810.18**	**6 692.13**	**191.89**	**5.32**
通信设备制造	Communications Equipment	938.72	1 940.28	39.98	-21.06
雷达及配套产品制造	Radar ane Supported Product	1.90	1.60	0.39	0.13
广播电视设备制造	Broadcast and Television Equipment	14.97	21.87	1.18	0.51
电子计算机制造	Computer	899.06	2 148.83	-1.13	2.49
家用视听设备制造	Household Seeing and Hearing Equipment	72.71	159.28	4.47	0.74
电子测量仪器制造	Geodesic Equipment of Electron	190.07	182.37	22.80	3.83
电子专用设备制造	Special Equipment of Electron	273.06	249.51	11.90	4.40
电子元件制造	Electronic Component	646.35	641.84	50.87	8.38
电子器件制造	Electronic Equipment	1 257.49	780.94	32.23	-2.78
#集成电路制造	Integrated Circuit	828.29	374.26	22.39	-0.18
电子机电产品制造	Machinery and Electronic Products of Electron	485.22	540.86	28.32	8.25
电子专用材料制造	Special Materials of Electron	30.61	24.74	0.88	0.43

表 13.9 高技术产业(制造业)主要指标 (2014 ~2015)
MAIN FACT ABOUT HIGH TECHNOLOGY INDUSTRY

类别	Types	单位数(个) Qiantity of Enterprises (unit)		平均从业人员(万人) Average Employees (10 000 persons)	
		2014	2015	2014	2015
总 计	**Total**	**1 013**	**1 020**	**58.27**	**57.12**
占全市比重(%)	**Proportion (%)**	**10.7**	**11.3**	**23.6**	**24.5**
按登记注册类型分	**Grouped by Registration Categories**				
国 有	State-owned	9	8	0.50	0.47
集 体	Collective-owned	3	1	0.05	0.01
股份合作企业	Cooperative	3	3	0.03	0.03
股份制企业	Share Holding	408	431	10.77	12.39
外商投资企业	Foreign Funded	581	565	46.82	44.06
其 他	Others	9	12	0.10	0.16
按技术领域分	**Grouped by Technology Areas**				
医药制造业	Medical and Pharmaceutical Product	198	199	6.20	6.07
航空航天器制造	Aviation and Aircraft Manufaturing	16	17	1.31	2.36
电子及通信设备制造业	Electron and Communicate Equipments	475	473	27.31	32.93
电子计算机及办公设备制造业	Electronic Computers and Office Equipments	58	60	18.03	10.38
医疗设备及仪器仪表制造业	Medical Treatment Instrument and Meter	256	261	5.21	5.20
信息化学品制造	Information Chemical Product	10	10	0.21	0.18

表 13.9 续表 1 continued

类别	Types	工业总产值(亿元) Gross Output Value of Industry (100 million yuan)		工业销售产值(亿元) Sales Value of Industry (100 million yuan)	
		2014	2015	2014	2015
总 计	**Total**	**6 648.34**	**6 809.93**	**6 603.47**	**6 776.66**
占全市比重(%)	**Proportion(%)**	**20.4**	**21.7**	**20.3**	**21.7**
按登记注册类型分	**Grouped by Registration Categories**				
国 有	State-owned	45.03	47.28	44.84	47.67
集 体	Collective-owned	3.43	0.43	3.43	0.37
股份合作企业	Cooperative	1.28	1.10	1.23	1.11
股份制企业	Share Holding	801.66	952.68	767.84	923.77
外商投资企业	Foreign Funded	5 792.15	5 798.19	5 781.26	5 793.75
其 他	Others	4.79	10.25	4.86	10.00
按技术领域分	**Grouped by Technology Areas**				
医药制造业	Medical and Pharmaceutical Product	622.72	655.99	584.83	623.80
航空航天器制造	Aviation and Aircraft Manufaturing	121.55	198.30	119.99	187.79
电子及通信设备制造业	Electron and Communicate Equipments	2 370.22	3 543.15	2 353.27	3 582.01
电子计算机及办公设备制造业	Electronic Computers and Office Equipments	3 089.36	1 951.06	3 104.47	1 926.77
医疗设备及仪器仪表制造业	Medical Treatment Instrument and Meter	419.20	438.03	416.59	433.38
信息化学品制造	Information Chemical Product	25.28	23.39	24.32	22.92

表 13.9 续表 2　continued

类　别	Types	年末资产总计(亿元) Total Property (year-end) (100 million yuan)		主营业务收入(亿元) Prime Operating Revenue (100 million yuan)	
		2014	2015	2014	2015
总　计	**Total**	**5 601.27**	**5 996.53**	**7 081.32**	**7 213.01**
占全市比重(%)	**Proportion (%)**	**15.8**	**16.1**	**20.0**	**21.1**
按登记注册类型分	**Grouped by Registration Categories**				
国　有	State-owned	61.28	75.37	44.85	47.73
集　体	Collective-owned	5.28	0.32	3.27	0.37
股份合作企业	Cooperative	1.84	1.82	1.23	1.11
股份制企业	Share Holding	1 337.51	1 752.79	834.86	998.82
外商投资企业	Foreign Funded	4 192.09	4 155.92	6 191.86	6 155.11
其　他	Others	3.27	10.30	5.25	9.88
按技术领域分	**Grouped by Technology Areas**				
医药制造业	Medical and Pharmaceutical Product	932.47	1 036.23	616.07	659.35
航空航天器制造	Aviation and Aircraft Manufaturing	243.80	397.70	123.45	192.90
电子及通信设备制造业	Electron and Communicate Equipments	2 606.65	3 070.34	2 467.13	3 677.60
电子计算机及办公设备制造业	Electronic Computers and Office Equipments	1 339.84	939.19	3 414.04	2 208.01
医疗设备及仪器仪表制造业	Medical Treatment Instrument and Meter	446.57	523.49	436.20	452.00
信息化学品制造	Information Chemical Product	31.94	29.58	24.43	23.15

表 13.9 续表 3　continued

类　别	Types	利润总额(亿元) Total Pre-tax Profits (100 million yuan)		税金总额(亿元) Total Tax and Duties (100 million yuan)	
		2014	2015	2014	2015
总　计	**Total**	**304.13**	**284.99**	**68.26**	**42.32**
占全市比重(%)	**Proportion (%)**	**11.5**	**10.6**	**3.6**	**2.1**
按登记注册类型分	**Grouped by Registration Categories**				
国　有	State-owned	7.27	7.82	1.51	1.48
集　体	Collective-owned	0.55	0.06	0.10	0.03
股份合作企业	Cooperative	0.13	0.14	0.08	0.10
股份制企业	Share Holding	63.59	42.18	30.15	29.89
外商投资企业	Foreign Funded	231.71	232.80	36.04	8.94
其　他	Others	0.88	1.99	0.39	1.89
按技术领域分	**Grouped by Technology Areas**				
医药制造业	Medical and Pharmaceutical Product	82.64	108.39	36.65	44.93
航空航天器制造	Aviation and Aircraft Manufaturing	6.03	6.16	0.69	0.54
电子及通信设备制造业	Electron and Communicate Equipments	125.87	121.88	18.42	-15.98
电子计算机及办公设备制造业	Electronic Computers and Office Equipments	39.53	2.24	0.71	2.34
医疗设备及仪器仪表制造业	Medical Treatment Instrument and Meter	48.27	45.44	11.36	10.08
信息化学品制造	Information Chemical Product	1.80	0.88	0.41	0.42

表 13.10 都市型工业主要指标(2014 ~2015)
MAIN STATISTICS OF URBAN INDUSTRIES

类别	Types	单位数(个) Quantity of Enterprises (unit)		从业人员(万人) Employees (10 000 persons)		工业总产值(亿元) Gross Output Value of Industry(100 million yuan)	
		2014	2015	2014	2015	2014	2015
总 计	**Total**	**1 923**	**1 808**	**47.90**	**42.96**	**3 636.38**	**3 526.79**
按企业规模分	**Grouped by Size of Enterprises**						
大 型	Large	55	50	12.24	10.83	907.31	926.89
中 型	Medium	323	299	17.32	15.34	1 436.15	1 267.86
小 型	Small	1 545	1 459	18.34	16.79	1 292.93	1 332.04
按登记注册类型分	**Grouped by Registration Categories**						
内 资	Domestic Funded	1 049	999	19.52	18.38	1 484.80	1 442.26
#国 有	State-owned	14	11	0.23	0.12	9.82	7.38
集 体	Collective-owned	11	9	0.15	0.12	4.51	3.67
有限责任公司	Companies with Limited Liabilities	180	163	4.84	4.20	596.58	573.51
股份有限公司	Share-holding Companies with Limited Liabilities	24	29	1.95	2.75	223.24	240.03
私 营	Private	800	771	12.11	10.98	638.82	607.43
港澳台商投资	Hong Kong, Macao and Taiwan Funded	303	277	10.08	8.98	653.86	678.22
#与港澳台商合资经营	Joint-venture	78	67	2.99	2.35	182.87	154.97
港澳台商独资	Sole Funded	191	176	5.93	5.44	349.91	382.05
外商投资	Foreign Funded	571	532	18.30	15.60	1 497.72	1 406.31
#中外合资经营	Joint-venture	133	119	3.58	2.92	348.81	343.97
外资企业	Sole Funded	398	374	12.74	10.84	1 032.82	943.94
按行业分	**Grouped by Sectors**						
服装服饰业	Garment and Trappings	421	374	9.38	7.83	420.31	379.34
食品加工制造业	Food Processing	361	356	11.14	10.68	1 033.84	982.86
包装、印刷业	Packaging and Printing	263	246	4.31	3.88	276.08	264.19
室内装饰用品制造业	Indoor Decoration Materials and Equipments Manufacturing	411	394	8.72	7.58	683.61	654.06
化妆品及清洁洗涤用品制造业	Cosmetics and Cleaning Manufacturing	134	124	3.17	2.99	329.24	353.21
工艺美术品、旅游用品制造业	Art Crafts and Tourism Equipments Manufacturing	171	155	4.54	4.40	458.71	444.14
小型电子信息产品制造业	Small Electronic Information Products Manufacturing	162	159	6.63	5.59	434.59	448.98

表13.10 续表1 continued

单位:亿元(100 million yuan)

类别	Types	工业销售产值 Sales Value of Industry 2014	2015	年末资产总计 Total Assets (year-end) 2014	2015	主营业务收入 Prime Operating Revenue 2014	2015
总　计	**Total**	**3 602.01**	**3 522.41**	**3 437.76**	**3 572.86**	**3 945.31**	**3 893.98**
按企业规模分	**Grouped by Size of Enterprises**						
大　型	Large	890.01	921.14	921.56	970.51	997.92	1 041.91
中　型	Medium	1 424.91	1 271.35	1 255.67	1 261.23	1 563.80	1 428.18
小　型	Small	1 287.09	1 329.92	1 260.53	1 341.13	1 383.59	1 423.89
按登记注册类型分	**Grouped by Registration Categories**						
内　资	Domestic Funded	1 476.81	1 444.51	1 385.50	1 486.11	1 668.99	1 652.36
#国　有	State-owned	9.74	7.46	13.83	11.19	10.27	7.57
集　体	Collective-owned	4.22	3.19	5.86	5.64	5.15	4.62
有限责任公司	Companies with Limited Liabilities	598.64	571.69	452.12	451.76	707.28	703.86
股份有限公司	Share-holding Companies with Limited Liabilities	222.61	251.22	336.04	399.03	291.80	311.42
私　营	Private	629.88	600.54	568.27	610.17	642.75	614.71
港澳台商投资	Hong Kong, Macao and Taiwan Funded	650.09	677.29	697.61	740.80	674.65	715.72
#与港澳台商合资经营	Joint-venture	182.10	155.95	182.90	186.34	177.67	158.23
港澳台商独资	Sole Funded	347.88	384.14	360.98	394.45	377.00	417.20
外商投资	Foreign Funded	1 475.12	1 400.61	1 354.66	1 345.95	1 601.67	1 525.90
#中外合资经营	Joint-venture	349.22	350.81	277.20	283.72	395.96	383.34
外资企业	Sole Funded	1 010.06	932.56	956.67	936.62	1 077.80	1 014.16
按行业分	**Grouped by Sectors**						
服装服饰业	Garment and Trappings	419.96	381.74	403.53	387.27	440.84	412.94
食品加工制造业	Food Processing	1 024.16	984.62	993.73	1 032.53	1 211.15	1 157.03
包装、印刷业	Packaging and Printing	273.21	261.27	319.70	323.70	282.65	270.14
室内装饰用品制造业	Indoor Decoration Materials and Equipments Manufacturing	681.25	638.94	599.81	612.04	688.10	659.31
化妆品及清洁洗涤用品制造业	Cosmetics and Cleaning Manufacturing	321.88	358.70	379.78	468.35	337.39	379.41
工艺美术品、旅游用品制造业	Art Crafts and Tourism Equipments Manufacturing	449.51	447.38	325.00	319.07	537.64	561.10
小型电子信息产品制造业	Small Electronic Information Products Manufacturing	432.04	449.76	416.21	429.90	447.54	454.04

表13.10 续表2 continued

单位:亿元(100 million yuan)

类 别	Types	利润总额 Total Pre-tax Profits 2014	2015	税金总额 Total Tax and Duties 2014	2015
总 计	**Total**	**250.39**	**295.97**	**119.90**	**129.26**
按企业规模分	**Grouped by Size of Enterprises**				
大 型	Large	69.26	104.90	35.67	38.56
中 型	Medium	111.65	105.45	50.05	49.81
小 型	Small	69.48	85.62	34.18	40.89
按登记注册类型分	**Grouped by Registration Categories**				
内 资	Domestic Funded	101.46	135.35	50.83	51.83
#国 有	State-owned	0.12	0.07	0.50	0.28
集 体	Collective-owned	0.32	0.15	0.27	0.33
有限责任公司	Companies with Limited Liabilities	42.12	45.10	16.51	15.97
股份有限公司	Share-holding Companies with Limited Liabilities	26.74	48.93	13.58	14.78
私 营	Private	31.85	40.59	19.61	20.19
港澳台商投资	Hong Kong, Macao and Taiwan Funded	56.03	69.47	17.48	22.93
#与港澳台商合资经营	Joint-venture	20.26	20.27	3.97	5.85
港澳台商独资	Sole Funded	25.58	37.01	11.98	15.77
外商投资	Foreign Funded	92.90	91.15	51.59	54.51
#中外合资经营	Joint-venture	30.77	25.68	7.39	7.27
外资企业	Sole Funded	54.15	59.17	39.24	41.33
按行业分	**Grouped by Sectors**				
服装服饰业	Garment and Trappings	7.74	8.65	9.53	7.76
食品加工制造业	Food Processing	56.43	68.53	49.89	55.61
包装、印刷业	Packaging and Printing	20.93	21.37	11.13	10.99
室内装饰用品制造业	Indoor Decoration Materials and Equipments Manufacturing	53.19	56.98	15.25	17.63
化妆品及清洁洗涤用品制造业	Cosmetics and Cleaning Manufacturing	42.06	69.29	19.80	22.45
工艺美术品、旅游用品制造业	Art Crafts and Tourism Equipments Manufacturing	31.85	37.29	8.94	9.80
小型电子信息产品制造业	Small Electronic Information Products Manufacturing	38.20	33.86	5.36	5.01

表13.11　主要年份工业产品产量
OUTPUT OF INDUSTRIAL PRODUCTS IN MAIN YEARS

年　份 Year	化学纤维（万吨）Chemical Fibers (10 000 tons)	食用植物油（万吨）Vegetable Oil (10 000 tons)	啤　酒（亿升）Beer (100 million litres)	罐　头（万吨）Can (10 000 tons)	彩色电视机（万部）Color TV Set (10 000 units)
1978	11.59	7.32	0.50	4.75	0.24
1980	15.15	6.77	0.66	5.46	0.55
1985	22.49	11.13	0.83	6.84	71.75
1990	25.74	13.42	1.66	4.97	81.48
1995	37.83	39.94	2.16	3.50	111.77
2000	47.15	11.55	3.04	3.26	147.97
2001	45.46	10.32	3.33	3.70	108.30
2002	51.67	9.65	3.62	3.79	137.02
2003	54.17	8.64	3.99	4.02	158.15
2004	48.45	3.51	5.92	4.51	135.08
2005	49.78	45.11	7.05	4.99	145.46
2006	50.60	72.86	7.17	5.78	251.67
2007	51.48	85.24	7.30	7.20	158.37
2008	43.00	96.88	7.27	4.96	185.78
2009	37.91	92.27	6.74	3.71	195.51
2010	49.00	85.31	6.54	4.06	254.03
2011	51.34	84.56	5.09	3.90	224.63
2012	48.24	101.70	5.95	4.29	142.87
2013	47.76	104.24	4.92	4.27	99.38
2014	45.35	109.85	6.11	4.00	155.28
2015	45.85	111.45	6.11	3.98	135.39

表13.11 续表1　continued

年　份 Year	家用洗衣机（万台）Household Washing Machines (10 000 units)	家用电冰箱（万台）Household Refrigerators (10 000 units)	房间空气调节器（万台）Household Airconditioners (10 000 units)	燃气热水器（万台）Water Heaters (10 000 units)	服　装（亿件）Garments (100 million cases)
1978					0.73
1980	0.81	0.42	0.10		1.19
1985	113.85	20.49	0.74		2.33
1990	101.29	53.36	1.83		2.43
1995	144.80	128.72	62.46		6.30
2000	62.11	43.12	186.08	32.27	4.45
2001	70.79	43.44	223.57	27.86	4.35
2002	95.92	35.97	217.57	36.32	4.84
2003	134.27	34.46	239.72	37.24	4.91
2004	165.67	33.14	399.16	51.86	4.63
2005	183.26	42.68	358.57	65.64	6.72
2006	288.74	101.08	410.60	69.89	6.73
2007	289.68	100.66	395.21	80.46	6.60
2008	234.63	123.21	387.12	67.89	6.10
2009	207.79	189.15	317.78	59.35	3.91
2010	216.57	218.55	400.41	103.70	5.72
2011	218.96	185.19	619.91	104.44	5.06
2012	197.12	151.63	584.10	106.49	5.04
2013	184.23	153.93	410.00	126.22	4.78
2014	181.93	153.98	403.53	171.47	5.00
2015	160.27	148.18	327.33	173.62	4.49

表 13.11 续表 2 continued

年 份 Year	机制纸及纸板(万吨) Machine-Made Paper and Paperboards (10 000 tons)	粗 钢 (万吨) Steel (10 000 tons)	成品钢材 (万吨) Rolled-Steel Products (10 000 tons)	生 铁 (万吨) Pig Iron (10 000 tons)
1978	27.34	476.52	360.08	149.86
1980	29.57	521.61	412.63	171.12
1985	41.29	570.16	451.18	215.37
1990	46.49	914.62	609.59	526.90
1995	47.08	1 006.92	738.08	664.04
2000	43.54	1 778.70	1 544.46	1 473.00
2001	41.35	1 874.71	1 641.11	1 468.91
2002	42.61	1 719.42	1 626.98	1 276.12
2003	44.40	1 726.65	1 710.80	1 300.24
2004	35.96	1 823.65	1 818.41	1 356.47
2005	35.73	1 927.96	1 964.16	1 582.89
2006	85.87	1 902.82	2 129.78	1 639.13
2007	83.76	2 081.58	2 144.16	1 790.00
2008	80.46	1 992.09	2 074.95	1 735.87
2009	71.03	2 032.24	2 181.37	1 787.48
2010	86.94	2 214.27	2 475.95	1 901.39
2011	87.28	2 225.48	2 482.81	1 947.48
2012	91.46	1 970.91	2 340.76	1 800.44
2013	85.30	1 811.08	2 322.76	1 637.58
2014	92.14	1 774.55	2 309.14	1 643.29
2015	65.79	1 783.77	2 202.72	1 686.66

表 13.11 续表 3 continued

年 份 Year	轮胎外胎 (万条) Tires (10 000 tires)	水 泥 (万吨) Cement (10 000 tons)	乙 烯 (万吨) Ethylene (10 000 tons)	发电设备 (万千瓦) Power Generating Equipments (10 000 kw)
1978	149.59	139.47	12.69	109.80
1980	174.85	161.28	13.59	58.20
1985	219.00	219.31	14.02	133.00
1990	318.78	230.30	21.95	210.20
1995	375.31	433.22	8.20	496.50
2000	830.66	311.69	59.05	179.00
2001	545.97	334.75	63.10	336.20
2002	704.80	351.58	80.00	461.90
2003	846.92	568.24	94.83	1 013.70
2004	927.17	665.01	95.60	1 520.30
2005	932.27	719.97	160.44	2 138.05
2006	1 055.47	818.28	193.83	2 944.71
2007	932.54	786.24	187.24	2 845.59
2008	866.65	765.46	182.03	2 831.10
2009	849.07	754.19	180.30	2 440.70
2010	915.22	670.80	226.72	2 555.60
2011	908.26	805.56	197.53	2 889.59
2012	1 004.37	794.71	195.57	2 886.30
2013	1 079.57	750.31	212.00	2 538.84
2014	1 045.49	685.97	188.53	3 632.46
2015	971.00	433.59	210.76	2 080.69

表 13.11 续表 4　continued

年　份 Year	发电量 (亿千瓦时) Electric Power Generation (100 million kwh)	硫　酸 (万吨) Sulfuric (10 000 tons)	金属切削机床(台) Metal-cutting Machines (unit)	微型计算机设备(万部) Personal Computers (10 000 units)
1978	199.32	34.49	17 384	
1980	206.41	38.76	16 949	
1985	256.25	35.22	19 408	
1990	284.10	40.04	13 796	0.77
1995	403.42	31.03	15 833	4.07
1996	428.64	36.24	15 379	6.20
1997	458.48	36.79	18 700	40.39
1998	482.16	32.59	11 916	21.16
1999	498.01	38.38	17 822	40.09
2000	553.09	34.22	22 346	42.04
2001	572.86	36.15	21 839	47.13
2002	608.92	30.41	27 252	75.25
2003	684.99	31.41	33 497	734.68
2004	766.15	33.67	13 975	996.09
2005	728.74	33.32	13 158	2 176.17
2006	710.96	30.37	13 372	2 670.09
2007	737.80	30.46	14 440	4 478.78
2008	773.54	26.06	16 430	5 767.97
2009	778.20	27.02	5 641	7 320.15
2010	876.19	28.66	13 386	9 388.44
2011	946.96	27.98	14 813	10 162.53
2012	886.19	18.15	29 012	9 804.83
2013	959.51	19.47	19 051	8 101.30
2014	792.30	18.10	47 036	6 295.42
2015	792.70	19.38	36 371	3 651.98

表 13.11 续表 5　continued

年　份 Year	移动通信基站设备(万信道) Mobile Communication Facilities (10 000 channels)	集成电路 (万块) Semi-conduct IC (10 000 units)	汽　车 (万辆) Motor Vehicles (10 000 vehicles)	其中 of which #轿　车 Cars
1978			1.04	0.26
1980			1.47	0.53
1985			1.22	0.86
1990		1 167	2.81	2.46
1995		15 290	16.27	16.07
1996		11 624	20.17	20.02
1997		88 098	23.30	23.15
1998		92 908	23.64	23.50
1999		170 001	25.58	25.42
2000	1.60	239 330	25.29	25.15
2001	39.49	225 315	29.00	28.88
2002	24.82	339 494	39.19	39.05
2003	28.20	397 313	59.58	58.84
2004	57.67	548 727	55.96	54.99
2005	115.03	677 003	48.45	48.09
2006	174.16	640 483	65.28	64.47
2007	307.46	891 138	82.12	81.15
2008	343.58	830 487	80.65	80.00
2009	198.76	722 883	125.03	122.46
2010	299.44	1 134 629	169.89	159.77
2011	490.40	1 663 143	191.57	174.20
2012	148.75	1 602 978	202.43	180.68
2013	89.73	1 613 762	226.89	201.03
2014	37.18	2 233 261	247.45	214.22
2015	26.24	2 173 552	242.97	203.91

注：2000 年开始移动通信基站设备不包括手机。
Note: The figure of mobile communication facilities has excluded mobile phones since 2000.

表13.12 主要工业产品生产、销售总量(2015)
OUTPUT AND SALES OF MAIN INDUSTRIAL PRODUCTS

产品名称	Product	单 位 Unit	生产量 Output	销售量 Sales
啤 酒	Beer	亿升 (100 million liters)	6.11	6.11
无酒精饮料(软饮料)	Non-alcoholic Beverage	万吨 (10 000 tons)	262.29	260.31
卷 烟	Cigarettes	亿支(100 million pieces)	991.79	971.40
化学纤维	Chemical Fibers	万吨 (10 000 tons)	45.85	44.81
纱	Yarn	万吨 (10 000 tons)	3.11	3.03
布	Cloth	亿米 (100 million m)	0.94	0.73
蚕丝及交织机织物	Silk Products	万米 (10 000 m)	2.72	94.22
服 装	Garments	亿件 (100 million cases)	4.49	4.34
皮革鞋靴	Leather Shoes	万双 (10 000 pairs)	1 864.71	1 867.10
机制纸及纸版	Paperboard	万吨 (10 000 tons)	65.79	65.76
汽 油	Gasoline	万吨 (10 000 tons)	537.31	540.36
柴 油	Diesel Oil	万吨 (10 000 tons)	761.00	763.16
焦 炭	Coke	万吨 (10 000 tons)	534.48	
硫 酸	Sulphuric Acid	万吨 (10 000 tons)	19.38	15.29
烧 碱	Caustic Soda	万吨 (10 000 tons)	68.78	49.43
化学农药原药	Chemical Pesticides	万吨 (10 000 tons)	1.04	1.10
乙 烯	Ethylene	万吨 (10 000 tons)	210.76	31.08
合成橡胶	Synthetic Rubber	万吨 (10 000 tons)	20.49	18.18
合成洗涤剂	Synthetic Detergents	万吨 (10 000 tons)	38.73	38.07
轮胎外胎	Tires	万条 (10 000 tires)	971.00	951.85
水 泥	Cement	万吨 (10 000 tons)	433.59	437.22
铜 材	Copper Materials	万吨 (10 000 tons)	29.70	29.68
生 铁	Pig Iron	万吨 (10 000 tons)	1 686.66	0.95
粗 钢	Steel	万吨 (10 000 tons)	1 783.77	29.53
金属切削机床	Metal-cutting Machines	台(unit)	36 371	36 349
#数控金属切削机床	Digital Machine Tools	台(unit)	2 455	2 463
金属集装箱	Metal Container	万立方米 (10 000 cu. m)	462.97	476.80
卫生陶瓷	Sanitary Ceramics	万件 (10 000 pieces)	87.26	88.24
涂 料	Coating	万吨 (10 000 tons)	190.96	192.63
#建筑涂料	Construction Coating	万吨 (10 000 tons)	102.78	104.68
集成电路	Integrated Circuits	亿块 (100 million units)	217.36	215.27
乳制品	Dairy Product	万吨 (10 000 tons)	49.97	50.01

表 13.12 续表 continued

产品名称	Product	单 位 Unit	生产量 Output	销售量 Sales
成品钢材	Rolled-steel Products	万吨 (10 000 tons)	2 202.72	2 176.99
发动机	Engines	万千瓦 (10 000 kw)	24 816.94	15 470.77
缝纫机	Sewing Machines	万台 (10 000 units)	77.03	80.03
汽 车	**Motor Vehicles**	**万辆 (10 000 vehicles)**	**242.97**	**242.87**
#轿 车	Cars	万辆 (10 000 vehicles)	203.91	204.19
摩托车	Motorcycles	万辆 (10 000 vehicles)	73.86	70.52
两轮脚踏自行车	Bicycles	万辆 (10 000 vehicles)	331.82	330.90
民用钢质船舶	Civil Steel Ships	万载重吨 (10 000 syn-tons)	739.84	739.84
发电设备	Power Generating Equipments	万千瓦 (10 000 kw)	2 080.69	2 697.91
电力电缆	Electric Cable	万公里 (10 000 km)	187.31	176.79
家用洗衣机	Household Washing Machines	万台 (10 000 units)	160.27	161.21
家用电冰箱	Household Refrigerators	万台 (10 000 units)	148.18	146.71
房间空气调节器	Household Air-conditioners	万台 (10 000 units)	327.33	328.76
家用吸排油烟机	Range Hoods	万台 (10 000 units)	7.92	7.60
微波炉	Microwave Oven	万台 (10 000 units)	345.82	345.42
电饭锅	Electric Rice Cookers	万个 (10 000 units)	201.89	206.75
家用吸尘器	Vacuum Cleaners	万台 (10 000 units)	49.43	48.29
燃气热水器	Water Heaters	万台 (10 000 units)	173.62	171.23
程控交换机	Program-controlled Exchanges	万线 (10 000 lines)	95.35	96.59
集成电路圆片	Wafer	万片 (10 000 units)	442.59	439.90
微型计算机设备	**Personal Computers**	**万部 (10 000 units)**	**3 651.98**	**3 659.82**
彩色电视机	Color Television Sets	万部 (10 000 units)	135.39	135.31
移动通信基站设备	Mobile Communication Base Station Facilities	万信道 (10 000 channels)	26.24	26.24
糖 果	Candy	万吨 (10 000 tons)	17.82	17.78
实木木地板	Solid Wood Flooring	万平方米 (10 000 sq. m)	686.72	698.02
复合木地板	Flooring	万平方米 (10 000 sq. m)	2 102.77	2 139.28

表13.13 大型工业企业主要指标(2015)
MAJOR INDICATORS OF LARGE SIZED INDUSTRIAL ENTERPRISES

类别	Types	单位数(个) Quantity of Enterprises (unit)	从业人员(万人) Employees (10 000 persons)	工业总产值(亿元) Gross Output Value of Industry (100 million yuan)
总计	**Total**	**272**	**80.49**	**16 735.42**
按隶属关系分	**Grouped by Subordination**			
中央工业	Central Government	33	14.05	5 254.08
地方工业	Local Government	239	66.44	11 481.34
按从业人员分	**Grouped by Number of Employees**			
1万人及以上	10 000 persons and above	9	19.57	6 700.72
5000~9999人	5000~9999 persons	18	11.96	2 177.79
3000~4999人	3000~4999 persons	40	15.09	2 978.55
3000人以下	Below 3000 persons	205	33.87	4 878.35
按工业总产值分	**Grouped by Gross Output Value of Industry**			
10亿元及以上	1 000 million yuan and above	210	70.91	16 315.80
5~9.99亿元	500~999 million yuan	47	7.05	357.37
5亿元以下	Below 500 million yuan	15	2.53	62.25
按工业行业分	**Grouped by Sectors**			
制造业	**Manufacture Industry**	**267**	**78.34**	**15 868.68**
#农副食品加工业	Farm and Sideline Products Processing	2	0.45	20.94
食品制造业	Food Manufacturing	9	2.77	191.94
酒、饮料和精制茶制造业	Wine, Beverage and Refined Tea Manufacturing	3	0.57	37.68
烟草制品业	Tabacco Manufacturing	1	0.36	1 005.10
纺织业	Textile	3	0.46	45.06
纺织服装、服饰业	Textiles and Clothing Industry	5	1.16	81.44
皮革、毛皮、羽毛及其制品和制鞋业	Leather, Fur, Wool Products and Shoes Manufacturing	3	0.86	108.68
家具制造业	Furniture Manufacturing	5	0.89	83.75

工业销售产值（亿元）Sales Value of Industry Products (100 million yuan)	年末资产总计（亿元）Total Assets (year-end) (100 million yuan)	年末负债合计（亿元）Total Liabilities (year-end) (100 million yuan)	主营业务收 入（亿元）Prime Operation Revenue (100 million yuan)	利润总额（亿元）Total Pre-tax Profits (100 million yuan)	税金总额（亿元）Total Tax and Duties (100 million yuan)	成本费用总额（亿元）Total Costs and Expenses (100 million yuan)
16 674.77	**19 997.96**	**9 276.34**	**18 776.75**	**1 709.19**	**1 562.58**	**16 672.99**
5 223.13	8 033.50	3 375.58	5 405.75	389.60	1 128.33	4 224.29
11 451.64	11 964.46	5 900.76	13 371.00	1 319.59	434.25	12 448.71
6 714.03	6 128.05	2 835.72	6 967.99	434.66	413.37	6 327.20
2 153.99	4 286.92	1 828.29	3 327.36	495.13	101.05	3 186.99
2 918.73	3 749.19	1 535.66	3 054.89	319.05	905.58	2 057.79
4 888.02	5 833.80	3 076.68	5 426.51	460.36	142.58	5 101.01
16 253.65	19 284.78	8 926.00	18 256.60	1 685.91	1 548.42	16 173.94
357.36	582.96	287.69	433.55	18.60	9.81	414.00
63.76	130.23	62.65	86.60	4.69	4.35	85.06
15 809.44	**17 573.23**	**8 564.72**	**17 867.70**	**1 677.97**	**1 529.37**	**15 790.92**
20.94	12.24	5.61	19.53	0.63	0.40	19.05
192.41	221.27	121.01	291.95	17.48	14.58	276.83
37.01	44.19	14.99	45.83	3.80	3.18	41.90
980.69	1 223.16	151.61	978.52	243.23	769.65	135.50
44.15	47.61	11.63	44.15	6.27	1.61	37.82
81.86	109.07	55.23	81.89	1.51	0.58	86.58
109.47	164.87	30.41	108.80	11.11	5.87	97.46
81.22	97.62	61.54	81.23	16.46	2.93	80.48

表 13.13 续表 continued

	类 别 Types	单位数（个）Quantity of Enterprises (unit)	从业人员（万人）Employees (10 000 persons)
造纸和纸制品业	Paper-making and Paper Products Manufacturing	2	0.22
印刷和记录媒介复制业	Printing and Record Duplicating	2	0.31
文教、工美、体育和娱乐用品制造业	Culture, Education, Industrial Arts, Sports and Entertainment Goods Manufacturing	4	1.09
石油加工、炼焦和核燃料加工业	Oil Processing, Coking and Nuclear Fuel Processing	2	1.46
化学原料和化学制品制造业	Raw Chemical Materials and Chemical Products Manufacturing	17	2.61
医药制造业	Medicine Manufacturing	10	1.81
橡胶和塑料制品业	Rubber and Plastic Products Manufacturing	8	1.35
非金属矿物制品业	Non-metallic Mineral Products Manufacturing	5	0.72
黑色金属冶炼和压延加工业	Ferrous Metal Smelting and Rolling Processing Industry	4	2.50
有色金属冶炼和压延加工业	Nonferrous Metal Smelting and Rolling Processing Industry	1	0.17
金属制品业	Metal Products Manufacturing	8	2.54
通用设备制造业	General Equipment Manufacturing	21	5.82
专用设备制造业	Special Purpose Equipment Manufacturing	10	1.60
汽车制造业	The Automotive Manufacturing	36	10.69
铁路、船舶、航空航天和其他运输设备制造业	The Railroad, Marine, Aerospace and Other Transportation Equipment Manufacturing	12	4.32
电气机械和器材制造业	Electric Machinery Equipments and Manufacturing	26	5.03
计算机、通信和其他电子设备制造业	Computer, Communications and Other Electronic Equipment Manufacturing	58	25.99
仪器仪表制造业	Instrumentation Manufacturing	5	0.78
其他制造业	Other Manufacturing	1	0.27
金属制品、机械和设备修理业	Metal Products, Machinery and Equipment Repair Industry	4	1.55
电力、热力、燃气及水生产和供应业	**Electricity, Heat, Gas and Water Production and Supply Industry**	**5**	**2.14**
电力、热力生产和供应业	Production and Supply of Electricity and Thermal Power	1	1.29
燃气生产和供应业	Production and Supply of Gas	2	0.30
水的生产和供应业	Production and Supply of Water	2	0.55

工业总产值(亿元) Gross Output Value of Industry (100 million yuan)	工业销售产值(亿元) Sales Value of Industry Products (100 million yuan)	年末资产总计(亿元) Total Assets (year-end) (100 million yuan)	年末负债合计(亿元) Total Liabilities (year-end) (100 million yuan)	主营业务收　入(亿元) Prime Operation Revenue (100 million yuan)	利润总额(亿元) Total Pre-tax Profits (100 million yuan)	税金总额(亿元) Total Tax and Duties (100 million yuan)	成本费用总额(亿元) Total Costs and Expenses (100 million yuan)
45.64	51.30	64.88	15.59	63.73	5.52	6.33	58.03
27.15	27.13	30.08	4.08	27.22	1.74	1.39	25.78
58.45	57.69	54.14	19.18	61.57	6.51	1.78	55.49
1 067.13	1 070.62	374.14	150.41	1 070.29	41.11	303.51	791.38
805.18	834.27	855.13	385.89	890.45	67.43	25.69	807.69
222.81	206.13	296.24	165.34	236.64	24.51	15.91	216.93
136.98	135.63	336.64	110.58	135.88	10.86	6.28	128.25
85.48	84.85	105.97	61.45	88.26	12.82	2.91	79.71
924.46	918.84	1 965.65	773.28	1 121.09	13.66	22.78	1 120.06
25.55	27.17	24.75	17.12	28.63	2.27	1.37	26.31
141.23	139.97	142.43	66.47	149.62	22.14	4.36	129.00
1 009.78	996.15	1 664.85	1 141.25	1 019.44	61.48	25.22	956.28
229.05	229.49	304.04	223.48	239.87	-0.15	4.65	235.14
3 627.27	3 607.62	4 583.53	1 795.97	4 879.97	946.16	323.80	4 282.29
653.62	638.76	1 341.72	1 072.46	621.10	1.56	-8.65	628.56
646.07	636.66	501.94	273.79	645.48	63.80	12.37	589.12
4 392.38	4 405.04	2 726.51	1 663.91	4 729.85	84.83	-21.60	4 690.03
85.77	84.83	74.41	42.75	97.24	7.70	0.34	90.92
19.21	19.21	23.99	3.23	19.21	2.49	1.49	16.64
90.90	90.34	182.15	126.45	90.23	1.02	0.64	87.69
866.74	**865.33**	**2 424.73**	**711.62**	**909.04**	**31.22**	**33.21**	**882.08**
793.50	793.50	1 812.95	513.39	793.55	28.15	29.64	766.43
34.96	34.96	81.45	60.28	70.39	0.61	1.89	68.42
38.27	36.86	530.33	137.95	45.10	2.46	1.68	47.23

表 13.14 中型工业企业主要指标(2015)
MAJOR INDICATORS OF MEDIUM SIZED INDUSTRIAL ENTERPRISES

类 别	Types	单位数(个) Quantity of Enterprises (unit)	从业人员(万人) Employees (10 000 persons)	工业总产值(亿元) Gross Output Value of Industry (100 million yuan)
总 计	**Total**	**1 248**	**65.03**	**6 556.84**
按隶属关系分	**Grouped by Subordination**			
中央工业	Central Government	40	2.50	438.87
地方工业	Local Government	1 208	62.52	6 117.96
按从业人员分	**Grouped by Number of Employees**			
1 000 人及以上	1 000 persons and above	28	3.68	71.01
500~999 人	500~999 persons	489	33.60	3 606.27
500 人以下	Below 500 persons	731	27.74	2 879.56
按工业总产值分	**Grouped by Gross Output Value of Industry**			
10 亿元及以上	1 billion yuan and above	147	9.26	2 945.85
5~9.99 亿元	500~999 million yuan	229	13.00	1 606.36
1~4.99 亿元	100~499 million yuan	743	37.61	1 914.38
5000~9999 万元	50~99.99 million yuan	105	4.19	81.42
5000 万元以下	Below 50 million yuan	24	0.97	8.83
按工业行业分	**Grouped by Sectors**			
制造业	**Manufacture Industry**	**1 235**	**64.21**	**6 434.40**
#农副食品加工业	Farm and Sideline Products Processing	24	1.17	106.61
食品制造业	Food Manufacturing	44	2.42	250.89
酒、饮料和精制茶制造业	Wine, Beverage and Refined Tea Manufacturing	8	0.40	30.66
烟草制品业	Tabacco Manufacturing	1	0.04	22.16
纺织业	Textile	19	1.09	67.30
纺织服装、服饰业	Textiles and Clothing Industry	63	3.35	96.37
皮革、毛皮、羽毛及其制品和制鞋业	Leather, Fur, Wool Products and Shoes Manufacturing	17	0.76	26.10
木材加工和木、竹、藤、棕、草制品业	Timber Processing and Timber, Bamboo, Rattan, Coir and Straw Products Manufacturing	6	0.29	19.23

工业销售产值（亿元） Sales Value of Industry Products (100 million yuan)	年末资产总计（亿元） Total Assets (year-end) (100 million yuan)	年末负债合计（亿元） Total Liabilities (year-end) (100 million yuan)	主营业务收　入（亿元） Prime Operation Revenue (100 million yuan)	利润总额（亿元） Total Pre-tax Profits (100 million yuan)	税金总额（亿元） Total Tax and Duties (100 million yuan)	成本费用总额（亿元） Total Costs and Expenses (100 million yuan)
6 542.37	**7 896.06**	**3 982.70**	**6 933.27**	**535.70**	**203.38**	**6 484.89**
435.26	1 053.24	567.24	477.05	32.05	29.87	455.06
6 107.11	6 842.83	3 415.46	6 456.21	503.66	173.51	6 029.84
66.93	198.72	125.08	72.01	-2.23	0.05	77.96
3 599.79	4 350.78	2 284.60	3 802.69	285.22	109.18	3 565.39
2 875.65	3 346.56	1 573.02	3 058.56	252.71	94.15	2 841.55
2 930.70	2 790.93	1 578.43	3 104.20	253.18	86.56	2 866.03
1 598.70	1 966.57	865.43	1 652.52	150.19	50.73	1 526.44
1 919.34	2 977.60	1 462.90	2 058.81	128.08	61.98	1 975.06
84.64	120.06	54.63	88.33	1.68	2.99	88.96
8.98	40.90	21.31	29.41	2.57	1.13	28.40
6 420.77	**7 415.26**	**3 700.77**	**6 782.36**	**516.40**	**196.45**	**6 336.17**
104.09	88.10	38.95	122.79	6.09	2.08	117.79
250.48	307.15	202.92	250.03	19.11	18.69	232.69
30.51	45.71	26.55	46.49	3.20	4.61	41.80
20.84	9.23	5.22	20.85	3.25	14.41	6.00
68.30	61.11	28.96	75.62	4.63	2.84	71.33
91.87	88.51	45.62	94.65	1.03	2.41	94.08
25.82	21.73	13.05	25.62	0.45	0.57	25.18
19.47	20.95	10.69	17.84	1.19	0.72	16.48

表 13.14 续表 continued

类别	Types	单位数（个）Quantity of Enterprises (unit)	从业人员（万人）Employees (10 000 persons)
家具制造业	Furniture Manufacturing	20	1.01
造纸和纸制品业	Paper-making and Paper Products Manufacturing	15	0.62
印刷和记录媒介复制业	Printing and Record Duplicating	16	0.72
文教、工美、体育和娱乐用品制造业	Culture, Education, Industrial Arts, Sports and Entertainment Goods Manufacturing	17	0.77
石油加工、炼焦和核燃料加工业	Oil Processing, Coking and Nuclear Fuel Processing	1	0.05
化学原料和化学制品制造业	Raw Chemical Materials and Chemical Products Manufacturing	64	3.12
医药制造业	Medicine Manufacturing	41	2.09
化学纤维制造业	Chemical Fiber Manufacturing	1	0.03
橡胶和塑料制品业	Rubber and Plastic Products Manufacturing	73	3.54
非金属矿物制品业	Non-metallic Mineral Products Manufacturing	31	1.58
黑色金属冶炼和压延加工业	Ferrous Metal Smelting and Rolling Processing Industry	7	0.32
有色金属冶炼和压延加工业	Nonferrous Metal Smelting and Rolling Processing Industry	19	0.92
金属制品业	Metal Products Manufacturing	75	3.90
通用设备制造业	General Equipment Manufacturing	116	6.10
专用设备制造业	Special Purpose Equipment Manufacturing	82	4.07
汽车制造业	The Automotive Manufacturing	137	7.37
铁路、船舶、航空航天和其他运输设备制造业	The Railroad, Marine, Aerospace and Other Transportation Equipment Manufacturing	15	0.78
电气机械和器材制造业	Electric Machinery Equipments and Manufacturing	146	7.26
计算机、通信和其他电子设备制造业	Computer, Communications and Other Electronic Equipment Manufacturing	135	8.02
仪器仪表制造业	Instrumentation Manufacturing	27	1.34
其他制造业	Other Manufacturing	7	0.44
金属制品、机械和设备修理业	Metal Products, Machinery and Equipment Repair Industry	8	0.67
电力、热力、燃气及水生产和供应业	**Electricity, Heat, Gas and Water Production and Supply Industry**	**13**	**0.81**
电力、热力生产和供应业	Production and Supply of Electricity and Thermal Power	5	0.33
燃气生产和供应业	Production and Supply of Gas	2	0.16
水的生产和供应业	Production and Supply of Water	6	0.31

工业总产值（亿元）Gross Output Value of Industry (100 million yuan)	工业销售产值（亿元）Sales Value of Industry Products (100 million yuan)	年末资产总计（亿元）Total Assets (year-end) (100 million yuan)	年末负债合计（亿元）Total Liabilities (year-end) (100 million yuan)	主营业务收入（亿元）Prime Operation Revenue (100 million yuan)	利润总额（亿元）Total Pre-tax Profits (100 million yuan)	税金总额（亿元）Total Tax and Duties (100 million yuan)	成本费用总额（亿元）Total Costs and Expenses (100 million yuan)
89.50	89.86	77.16	45.21	88.35	10.90	2.09	77.66
47.71	47.67	71.59	36.34	51.60	2.18	0.32	50.57
46.28	45.54	63.88	23.11	50.97	7.48	2.38	49.06
247.09	253.54	112.92	66.75	349.67	18.94	3.62	338.61
3.35	3.34	1.45	0.95	3.35	0.04	0.11	3.31
549.52	**553.19**	**581.83**	**259.29**	**587.55**	**46.44**	**22.72**	**544.84**
221.70	213.14	444.51	115.87	214.06	49.12	15.26	181.03
0.84	0.82	6.80	0.21	0.83	0.20	0.03	1.05
239.44	237.11	250.56	81.14	245.20	29.42	7.42	219.91
141.79	144.83	193.27	105.78	148.89	5.59	3.17	141.56
147.40	146.21	96.60	39.10	148.21	2.96	1.95	145.28
142.97	136.59	137.83	67.81	133.68	5.76	0.14	130.15
259.25	259.44	311.05	145.79	264.09	18.56	6.80	250.85
672.25	670.74	737.96	362.74	701.24	58.81	19.59	644.89
370.53	369.44	638.46	341.24	386.79	35.04	11.86	355.63
1 014.93	1 011.07	967.83	564.44	1 092.83	104.33	27.61	1 007.01
48.95	48.41	78.39	46.17	52.01	-4.11	1.27	51.67
818.55	825.00	938.68	501.48	837.29	52.15	17.11	792.01
604.70	603.53	703.91	352.62	621.44	17.94	1.39	608.85
112.82	112.52	140.67	52.09	113.23	16.48	3.38	98.56
11.45	11.68	12.96	4.67	11.51	0.44	0.67	11.14
24.06	25.72	204.50	115.98	25.67	-1.23	1.24	27.16
122.43	**121.59**	**480.81**	**281.93**	**150.91**	**19.30**	**6.93**	**148.72**
84.99	84.99	353.00	197.97	105.77	19.28	5.59	102.03
25.18	25.18	42.13	30.45	28.53	0.49	0.58	28.63
12.27	11.43	85.67	53.51	16.60	-0.46	0.76	18.06

表 13.15 小型工业企业主要指标(2015)
MAJOR INDICATORS OF SMALL SIZED INDUSTRIAL ENTERPRISES

类 别	Types	单位数（个）Quantity of Enterprises (unit)	从业人员（万人）Employees (10 000 persons)	工业总产值（亿元）Gross Output Value of Industry (100 million yuan)
总 计	**Total**	**7 474**	**79.14**	**8 030.37**
按隶属关系分	**Grouped by Subordination**			
中央工业	Central Government	79	0.96	270.94
地方工业	Local Government	7 395	78.18	7 759.43
按从业人员分	**Grouped by Number of Employees**			
200 人及以上	200 persons and above	917	22.27	2 083.54
100 ~ 199 人	100 ~ 199 persons	2 417	34.03	3 180.43
100 人以下	Below 100 persons	4 140	22.85	2 766.40
按工业总产值分	**Grouped by Gross Output Value of Industry**			
5 亿元及以上	500 million yuan and above	180	3.10	2 193.87
1 ~ 4.99 亿元	100 ~ 499 million yuan	1 710	25.94	3 276.37
5 000 ~ 9 999 万元	50 ~ 99.99 million yuan	2 090	24.32	1 467.26
5 000 万元以下	Below 50 million yuan	3 494	25.78	1 092.87
按工业行业分	**Grouped by Sectors**			
采矿业	**Mining Industry**	**1**	**0.02**	**6.56**
石油和天然气开采业	Petroleum and Natural Gas Exploiting	1	0.02	6.56
制造业	**Manufacture Industry**	**7 419**	**78.49**	**7 505.04**
农副食品加工业	Farm and Sideline Products Processing	116	1.11	206.28
食品制造业	Food Manufacturing	165	2.10	155.03
酒、饮料和精制茶制造业	Wine, Beverage and Refined Tea Manufacturing	26	0.27	41.39
纺织业	Textile	165	1.62	107.86
纺织服装、服饰业	Textiles and Clothing Industry	289	3.34	170.07
皮革、毛皮、羽毛及其制品和制鞋业	Leather, Fur, Wool Products and Shoes Manufacturing	96	1.09	43.35
木材加工和木、竹、藤、棕、草制品业	Timber Processing and Timber, Bamboo, Rattan, Coir and Straw Products Manufacturing	63	0.58	47.73

工业销售产值（亿元）Sales Value of Industry Products (100 million yuan)	年末资产总计（亿元）Total Assets (year-end) (100 million yuan)	年末负债合计（亿元）Total Liabilities (year-end) (100 million yuan)	主营业务收入（亿元）Prime Operation Revenue (100 million yuan)	利润总额（亿元）Total Pre-tax Profits (100 million yuan)	税金总额（亿元）Total Tax and Duties (100 million yuan)	成本费用总额（亿元）Total Costs and Expenses (100 million yuan)
7 997.18	**9 412.93**	**4 852.01**	**8 462.21**	**435.64**	**243.77**	**8 116.03**
262.45	354.11	189.64	312.35	28.63	13.06	285.18
7 734.73	9 058.81	4 662.37	8 149.85	407.01	230.71	7 830.85
2 069.13	2 454.10	1 209.33	2 175.61	165.88	74.08	2 038.70
3 171.39	3 729.61	1 829.62	3 335.38	174.52	91.00	3 195.63
2 756.66	3 229.21	1 813.05	2 951.22	95.23	78.69	2 881.70
2 185.84	1 958.84	1 021.48	2 349.10	142.70	54.60	2 229.17
3 254.24	3 833.57	1 880.02	3 398.71	230.10	96.09	3 204.36
1 459.02	1 818.87	950.06	1 512.23	48.87	49.33	1 476.42
1 098.09	1 801.65	1 000.45	1 202.16	13.97	43.74	1 206.08
6.42	**34.24**	**7.70**	**6.42**	**-1.96**	**0.71**	**8.39**
6.42	34.24	7.70	6.42	-1.96	0.71	8.39
7 470.20	**8 590.68**	**4 503.60**	**7 922.09**	**379.95**	**224.81**	**7 624.42**
210.44	163.09	90.55	236.10	5.68	4.39	237.70
155.76	161.15	87.61	164.31	7.67	7.25	156.75
41.22	40.31	21.98	43.20	9.23	3.20	37.24
107.21	108.31	53.67	112.46	3.16	2.09	110.28
169.92	149.55	94.52	197.35	4.22	3.24	199.54
44.38	37.64	21.30	45.01	0.33	1.24	44.81
49.94	55.38	31.66	54.55	0.45	1.46	54.11

表 13.15 续表 continued

类 别	Types	单位数（个）Quantity of Enterprises (unit)	从业人员（万人）Employees (10 000 persons)
家具制造业	Furniture Manufacturing	144	1.73
造纸和纸制品业	Paper-making and Paper Products Manufacturing	171	1.72
印刷和记录媒介复制业	Printing and Record Duplicating	145	1.73
文教、工美、体育和娱乐用品制造业	Culture, Education, Industrial Arts, Sports and Entertainment Goods Manufacturing	106	1.33
石油加工、炼焦和核燃料加工业	Oil Processing, Coking and Nuclear Fuel Processing	34	0.22
化学原料和化学制品制造业	**Raw Chemical Materials and Chemical Products Manufacturing**	**657**	**5.76**
医药制造业	Medicine Manufacturing	148	2.09
化学纤维制造业	Chemical Fiber Manufacturing	26	0.31
橡胶和塑料制品业	Rubber and Plastic Products Manufacturing	632	6.45
非金属矿物制品业	Non-metallic Mineral Products Manufacturing	345	3.03
黑色金属冶炼和压延加工业	Ferrous Metal Smelting and Rolling Processing Industry	97	0.87
有色金属冶炼和压延加工业	Nonferrous Metal Smelting and Rolling Processing Industry	110	0.92
金属制品业	Metal Products Manufacturing	649	7.05
通用设备制造业	General Equipment Manufacturing	1 034	10.70
专用设备制造业	Special Purpose Equipment Manufacturing	530	5.61
汽车制造业	The Automotive Manufacturing	349	4.65
铁路、船舶、航空航天和其他运输设备制造业	The Railroad, Marine, Aerospace and Other Transportation Equipment Manufacturing	96	1.14
电气机械和器材制造业	Electric Machinery Equipments and Manufacturing	688	7.15
计算机、通信和其他电子设备制造业	Computer, Communications and Other Electronic Equipment Manufacturing	282	3.34
仪器仪表制造业	Instrumentation Manufacturing	167	1.75
其他制造业	Other Manufacturing	34	0.35
废弃资源综合利用业	Comprehensive Utilization of Waste Resources	27	0.16
金属制品、机械和设备修理业	Metal Products, Machinery and Equipment Repair Industry	28	0.33
电力、热力、燃气及水生产和供应业	**Electricity, Heat, Gas and Water Production and Supply Industry**	**54**	**0.63**
电力、热力生产和供应业	Production and Supply of Electricity and Thermal Power	30	0.33
燃气生产和供应业	Production and Supply of Gas	9	0.12
水的生产和供应业	Production and Supply of Water	15	0.18

工业总产值 (亿元) Gross Output Value of Industry (100 million yuan)	工业销售产值 (亿元) Sales Value of Industry Products (100 million yuan)	年末资产总计 (亿元) Total Assets (year-end) (100 million yuan)	年末负债合计 (亿元) Total Liabilities (year-end) (100 million yuan)	主营业务收　入 (亿元) Prime Operation Revenue (100 million yuan)	利润总额 (亿元) Total Pre-tax Profits (100 million yuan)	税金总额 (亿元) Total Tax and Duties (100 million yuan)	成本费用总额 (亿元) Total Costs and Expenses (100 million yuan)
111.15	111.01	96.72	62.85	114.57	4.19	3.29	110.54
146.95	146.07	146.68	85.56	146.91	0.07	3.87	146.18
108.34	106.39	130.56	62.20	109.29	9.39	4.54	101.41
86.64	84.56	79.08	41.91	89.41	4.87	1.64	87.46
85.98	73.11	45.17	18.46	92.41	9.14	4.25	82.82
1 112.37	**1 113.11**	**1 224.56**	**565.49**	**1 174.47**	**64.17**	**35.92**	**1 125.26**
211.48	204.53	295.48	106.23	208.66	34.76	13.76	176.31
31.07	30.21	41.68	20.96	31.22	0.58	0.41	31.77
483.98	482.31	591.77	305.89	499.77	20.84	13.57	484.59
315.66	314.21	429.51	250.76	332.45	10.88	10.79	326.41
114.84	117.78	161.94	117.60	154.56	-0.01	2.80	156.01
218.92	215.74	137.99	85.99	235.71	1.09	1.17	234.64
495.89	490.34	545.56	303.81	512.82	12.19	15.97	501.25
833.00	825.08	1 094.02	545.04	866.03	41.26	28.74	832.75
442.20	440.61	676.90	350.02	457.86	25.71	13.33	436.66
581.60	584.72	481.80	284.28	601.38	27.63	14.00	579.28
108.88	107.76	140.71	68.87	110.05	6.41	3.35	105.11
686.22	685.58	888.93	496.16	732.87	35.88	16.83	700.64
326.31	326.46	405.00	206.45	355.38	18.50	5.91	338.59
133.39	133.69	165.42	70.93	143.97	13.54	4.61	133.32
22.92	22.68	25.36	15.73	23.46	0.44	0.67	23.08
25.67	26.22	29.49	14.64	25.48	2.27	0.82	24.49
49.89	49.16	40.90	22.49	50.41	5.41	1.70	45.43
518.77	**520.57**	**788.00**	**340.71**	**533.70**	**57.64**	**18.24**	**483.22**
224.37	227.30	439.48	208.01	227.38	46.42	16.15	183.13
275.84	275.83	251.90	88.31	286.20	6.71	1.03	282.57
18.57	17.45	96.62	44.39	20.12	4.51	1.06	17.52

表 13.16 国家级、市级工业园区主要经济指标(2015)
MAJOR ECONOMIC INDICATORS OF MUNICIPAL AND NATIONAL INDUSTRIAL ZONE

指标	Indicators	国家级开发区 National Level Develop Zone	其中 of which 上海张江高新技术产业开发区 Zhangjiang High and New Technical Industrial Development Zone	其中 of which 中国(上海)自由贸易试验区 China (Shanghai) Test Area of Free Trade
单位数(个)	Quantity of Enterprises (unit)	1 193	160	122
从业人员(万人)	Employees (10 000 persons)	52.64	8.52	4.13
工业总产值(亿元)	Gross Output Value of Industry(100 million yuan)	8 987.90	1 126.98	526.40
出口交货值(亿元)	Delivery Value of Industry Exports(100 million yuan)	3 258.16	353.15	205.75
年末资产总计(亿元)	Total Assets (year-end)(100 million yuan)	11 700.86	3 233.03	540.66
流动资产合计(亿元)	Total Current Assets(100 million yuan)	6 056.38	1 449.85	442.25
年末负债合计(亿元)	Total Liabilities (year-end)(100 million yuan)	5 217.59	960.14	349.79
年末所有者权益(亿元)	Owners'Equity (year-end)(100 million yuan)	6 476.87	2 272.45	190.24
主营业务收入(亿元)	Prime Operating Revenue(100 million yuan)	10 650.30	1 305.19	721.61
利润总额(亿元)	Total Pre-tax Profits(100 million yuan)	860.13	313.26	27.53
税金总额(亿元)	Total Tax and Duties(100 million yuan)	270.79	25.34	19.43
亏损总额(亿元)	Total Loss(100 million yuan)	101.26	20.28	4.35

表 13.16 续表 1 continued

指标	Indicators	其中 of which 松江出口加工区 Songjiang Export Processing Zone	其中 of which 闵行出口加工区 Minhang Export Processing Zone	其中 of which 青浦出口加工区 Qingpu Export Processing Zone
单位数(个)	Qiantity of Enterprises (unit)	37	9	8
从业人员(万人)	Employees (10 000 persons)	6.75	0.55	0.28
工业总产值(亿元)	Gross Output Value of Industry(100 million yuan)	1 583.28	78.21	49.12
出口交货值(亿元)	Delivery Value of Industry Exports(100 million yuan)	1 502.95	62.15	46.63
年末资产总计(亿元)	Total Assets (year-end)(100 million yuan)	554.31	49.86	40.88
流动资产合计(亿元)	Total Current Assets(100 million yuan)	467.63	36.75	23.67
年末负债合计(亿元)	Total Liabilities (year-end)(100 million yuan)	414.71	36.41	22.67
年末所有者权益(亿元)	Owners'Equity (year-end)(100 million yuan)	139.60	13.45	18.22
主营业务收入(亿元)	Prime Operating Revenue(100 million yuan)	1 553.63	82.61	48.40
利润总额(亿元)	Total Pre-tax Profits(100 million yuan)	5.27	2.39	2.48
税金总额(亿元)	Total Tax and Duties(100 million yuan)		0.11	0.01
亏损总额(亿元)	Total Loss(100 million yuan)	3.24	0.66	0.08

其　中 of which							
虹桥经济技术开发区 Hongqiao Economic and Technological Development Zone	闵行经济技术开发区 Minhang Hi-tec Park	漕河泾出口加工区 Caohejing Export Processing Zone	上海紫竹高新技术产业开发区 Zizhu High and New Technical Industrial Development Zone	嘉定出口加工区 Jiading Export Processing Zone	陆家嘴金融贸易区 Lujiazui Financial Trade Zone	金桥经济技术开发区 Jinqiao Economic and Technological Development Zone	金桥经济技术开发区南区 Jinqiao Economic and Technological Development Zone South Area
3	56	9	6	1	10	142	37
0.07	3.21	1.76	0.46	0.21	1.95	8.36	1.12
216.71	1.90	517.09	271.89	129.53	8.17	910.64	1 606.86
0 .50	65.86	249.40	27.96	8.81	5.71	254.01	48.19
5.29	532.82	142.36	194.10	8.31	2 161.58	1 838.22	164.08
4.05	433.53	113.61	143.90	6.87	354.63	1 259.80	119.00
3.16	316.19	105.74	106.20	2.65	713.07	999.95	68.14
2.13	215.62	36.62	87.90	5.66	1 448.51	838.22	95.92
2.01	540.52	271.77	160.78	8.79	977.33	2 682.61	212.62
0.17	53.92	2.13	18.48	0.22	37.98	257.43	21.83
0.09	24.57		7.52		34.25	98.57	6.64
	3.65	1.14	0.35		0.80	12.27	1.56

其　中 of which			市级开发区 Municipal Level Development Zone	其　中 of which		
上海化学工业经济技术开发区 Chemical Industry Economic and Technological Development Zone	上海松江经济技术开发区 Songjiang Economic and Technological Development Zone	漕河泾开发区浦江高科技园 Pujiang Hi-Tech Park of Caohejing Development Zone		上海新杨工业园区 Xinyang Industrial Psrk	上海未来岛高新技术产业园区 Weilai Island High and New Technical Industrial Park	上海市市北高新技术服务园区 Shibei Hi-Tech Park
32	534	27	2 874	8	12	16
0.95	13.66	0.67	63.21	0.19	0.25	0.34
710.03	1 192.37	58.69	6 482.36	18.70	29.54	28.22
69.45	346.85	10.79	1 173.31	0.46	4.42	3.36
800.69	1 363.99	70.67	7 535.10	42.43	26.76	54.88
228.50	932.14	40.21	4 944.84	17.22	18.59	42.28
463.30	612.11	43.37	3 832.49	18.85	14.12	39.59
337.38	747.65	27.30	3 665.88	23.58	12.64	15.15
758.59	1 259.07	64.76	6 820.97	20.50	29.97	33.46
23.11	88.93	5.00	509.17	1.62	5.24	-1.25
21.77	29.45	3.03	184.26	0.79	1.68	1.95
36.08	14.70	2.09	78.76	0.02	0.32	3.46

表 13.16 续表 2 continued

指标	Indicators	其中 of which 上海市莘庄工业园区 Xinzhuang Industrial Paek	上海宝山工业园区 Haibaoshan Industrial Park	上海月杨工业园区 Yueyang Industrial Park
单位数(个)	Quantity of Enterprises (unit)	250	209	90
从业人员(万人)	Employees (10 000 persons)	7.32	4.05	1.75
工业总产值(亿元)	Gross Output Value of Industry(100 million yuan)	947.39	324.52	210.04
出口交货值(亿元)	Delivery Value of Industry Exports(100 million yuan)	228.49	56.94	7.52
年末资产总计(亿元)	Total Assets (year-end)(100 million yuan)	1 179.93	497.08	253.40
流动资产合计(亿元)	Total Current Assets(100 million yuan)	837.65	306.34	154.85
年末负债合计(亿元)	Total Liabilities (year-end)(100 million yuan)	606.25	242.93	140.69
年末所有者权益(亿元)	Owners'Equity (year-end)(100 million yuan)	565.48	253.50	112.33
主营业务收入(亿元)	Prime Operating Revenue(100 million yuan)	1 010.28	357.26	243.68
利润总额(亿元)	Total Pre-tax Profits(100 million yuan)	99.29	18.80	17.67
税金总额(亿元)	Total Tax and Duties(100 million yuan)	26.71	13.45	6.24
亏损总额(亿元)	Total Loss(100 million yuan)	9.15	5.66	1.79

表 13.16 续表 3 continued

指标	Indicators	其中 of which 上海松江经济开发区 Songjiang Economic Development Zone	上海青浦工业园区 Qingpu Industrial Park	上海西郊工业园区 Xijiao Economic Development Zone
单位数(个)	Qiantity of Enterprises (unit)	110	378	118
从业人员(万人)	Employees (10 000 persons)	1.67	8.23	2.72
工业总产值(亿元)	Gross Output Value of Industry(100 million yuan)	117.91	837.93	204.06
出口交货值(亿元)	Delivery Value of Industry Exports(100 million yuan)	25.68	161.35	63.49
年末资产总计(亿元)	Total Assets (year-end)(100 million yuan)	129.10	925.42	227.84
流动资产合计(亿元)	Total Current Assets(100 million yuan)	88.68	637.83	153.89
年末负债合计(亿元)	Total Liabilities (year-end)(100 million yuan)	61.07	408.53	110.22
年末所有者权益(亿元)	Owners'Equity (year-end)(100 million yuan)	67.66	504.77	117.59
主营业务收入(亿元)	Prime Operating Revenue(100 million yuan)	121.68	853.45	210.36
利润总额(亿元)	Total Pre-tax Profits(100 million yuan)	7.96	64.00	10.35
税金总额(亿元)	Total Tax and Duties(100 million yuan)	3.39	31.90	6.40
亏损总额(亿元)	Total Loss(100 million yuan)	0.93	10.89	1.17

其　中 of which						
上海嘉定工业园区 Jiading Industrial Park	上海嘉定汽车产业园区 Jiading Automobile Industrial Park	上海浦东空港工业园区 Pudong Konggang Industrial Park	上海浦东合庆工业园区 Pudong Heqing Industrial Park	上海朱泾工业园区 Zhujing Industrial Park	上海枫泾工业园区 Fengjing Industrial Park	上海金山工业园区 Jinshan Industrial Park
419	205	119	56	74	110	308
9.93	6.49	3.00	1.51	1.07	1.62	4.83
1 156.40	**845.40**	**205.15**	**118.35**	**57.19**	**119.52**	**510.09**
199.79	64.96	50.19	41.87	10.86	10.40	78.87
1 249.28	670.52	209.68	168.00	76.24	176.92	612.00
828.86	474.12	130.30	94.09	44.37	124.37	326.87
639.56	373.60	104.83	78.87	49.00	80.61	337.89
607.98	287.08	105.02	89.13	27.24	94.31	271.24
1 220.25	881.13	202.29	124.85	55.98	119.55	518.92
109.50	**77.28**	**11.99**	**9.37**	**1.27**	**8.52**	**13.97**
31.71	20.58	3.39	2.48	0.65	3.71	7.02
11.86	2.29	3.41	0.43	0.74	0.80	14.06

其　中 of which						
上海浦东康桥工业园区 Pudong Kangqiao Industial Park	上海南汇工业园区 Nanhui Industrial Park	上海奉城工业园区 Fengcheng Industrial Park	上海星火工业园区 Xinghuo Industrial Park	上海奉贤经济开发区 Fengxian Economic Development Zone	上海崇明工业园区 Congming Industrial Park	上海富盛经济开发区 Fusheng Economic Development Zone
49	74	56	43	153	14	3
0.57	1.63	0.80	1.07	3.96	0.20	0.03
31.12	**125.15**	**60.93**	**152.15**	**370.59**	**10.42**	**1.58**
7.06	32.56	8.04	35.73	80.14	0.75	0.37
34.86	147.23	54.54	184.42	598.08	14.55	1.95
24.55	107.50	37.39	95.91	388.63	9.43	1.13
17.17	90.69	29.69	104.50	275.44	7.54	0.87
17.69	57.47	24.85	79.93	323.16	7.01	1.08
37.10	129.96	60.21	157.00	421.04	10.26	1.82
3.01	**2.73**	**3.29**	**0.64**	**43.30**	**0.53**	**0.11**
1.43	2.25	1.58	0.72	15.72	0.45	0.06
0.14	2.71	0.47	6.65	1.76	0.07	

上/海/统/计/年/鉴

主要统计指标解释

工 业

指从事自然资源的开采，对采掘品和农产品进行加工和再加工的物质生产部门。具体包括：(1)对自然资源的开采，如采矿、晒盐等(但不包括禽兽捕猎和水产捕捞)；(2)对农副产品的加工、再加工，如粮油加工、食品加工、缫丝、纺织、制革等；(3)对采掘品的加工、再加工，如炼铁、炼钢、化工生产、石油加工、机器制造、木材加工等，以及电力、自来水、煤气的生产和供应等；(4)对工业品的修理、翻新，如机器设备的修理、交通运输工具(不包括汽车)的修理等。

工业统计调查单位为独立核算法人工业企业。

独立核算法人工业企业指从事工业生产经营活动的单位。独立核算法人工业企业应同时具备以下条件：①依法成立，有自己的名称、组织机构和场所，能够承担民事责任；②独立拥有和使用资产，承担负债，有权与其他单位签订合同；③独立核算盈亏，并能够编制资产负债表。

工业总产值

(1)定义：工业总产值是以货币形式表现的，工业企业在一定时期内生产的工业最终产品或提供工业性劳务活动的总价值量。它反映一定时间内工业生产的总规模和总水平。

(2)计算原则：

工业生产的原则，即凡是企业在报告期生产的经检验合格的产品，不管是否在报告期销售，均包括在内。

最终产品的原则，即凡是计入工业总产值的产品，必须是本企业生产的经检验合格的，不需要再进行任何加工的最终产品。如果企业有中间产品(半成品)对外销售，则对外销售的中间产品应视为企业的最终产品。

工厂法原则，即工业总产值是以工业企业作为基本计算(核算)单位，即按企业的最终产品计算工业总产值。按这种方法计算的工业总产值，不允许同一产品价值在企业内部重复计算，不能把企业内部各个车间(分厂)生产的成果相加，但允许企业间的重复计算。

(3)内容及计算方法：

1995年全国工业普查对工业总产值(原规定)的内容及计算原则和方法做了某些修订，修订后的工业总产值(新规定)包括三项内容：即本期生产成品价值、对外加工费收入、在制品半成品期末期初差额价值三部分。

本期生产成品价值：指企业本期生产，并在报告期内不再进行加工，经检验、包装入库的全部工业成品(半产品)价值合计，包括企业生产的自制设备及提供给本企业在建工程、其他非工业部门和福利部门等单位使用的成品价值。本期生产成品价值为按自备原材料生产的产品的数量乘以本期不含增值税(销项税额)的产品实际销售平均单价计算；会计核算中按成本价格转帐的自制设备和自产自用的成品，按成本价格计算生产成品价值。生产成品价值中不包括用定货者来料加工的成品 (半产品)价值。

对外加工费收入：指企业在报告期内完成的对外承接的工业品加工(包括用定货者来料加工产品)的加工费收入和对外工业修理作业所取得的加工费收入。对外加工费收入按不含增值税(销项税额)的价格计算，可根据会计“产品销售收入”科目的有关资料取得。

对于本企业对内非工业部门提供的加工修理、设备安装的劳务收入，如果企业会计核算基础较好，能取得这部分资料，而且这部分价值所占比重较大，应包括在对外加工费收入中。

自制半成品在制品期末期初差额价值：指企业报告期在制品期末减期初的差额价值，本指标一般可以从会计核算资料中取得。如果会计产品成本核算中不计算半成品、在制品的成本，则总产值中也不包括这部分价值，反之则包括。

(4)工业总产值统计范围变化和计算方法修订情况：

1984年以前工业总产值不包括村办工业，村办工业总产值划归农业。1984年以后工业总产值包括村办工业。

1995年工业普查对工业总产值计算方法做了修订，即从1995年始按新修订(新规定)方法计算工业总产值。新规定与原规定的区别如下：

全价与加工费的计算原则不同：新规定为凡自备原材料，不论其生产繁简程度如何，一律按全价计算工业总产值；凡来料加工，允许按加工费计算工业总产值。原规定则视生产加工的繁简程度不同，规定哪些行业按全价，哪些行业按加工费计算工业总产值。

自制半成品、在产品期末期初差额价值的计算原则不同：新规定要求，凡会计产品成本核算时计算了成本的差额价值，总产值中就应包括，否则可不包括；原规定则

主要统计指标解释

按生产周期六个月的界限区分，凡生产周期六个月以上的企业，总产值计算中应包括这部分差额价值，否则可不包括。

计算价格不同：新规定按不含增值税(销项税额)的价格计算；原规定则按含增值税(销项税额)的价格计算。

工业大、中、小、微型企业

大中小微型企业划分标准：自 2011 年年报起，大中小型企业划分标准执行“关于印发中小企业划型标准规定的通知”(工信部联企业〔2012〕300 号)。即对于工业企业来说，大型企业必须同时达到从业人员≥1000 人、营业收入≥40000 万元；中型企业必须同时达到 1000 人>从业人员≥300 人、40000 万元>营业收入≥2000 万元；小型企业必须同时达到 300 人>从业人员≥20 人、2000 万元>营业收入≥300 万元；其余的均为微型企业。

资产总计

指企业过去的交易或者事项形成的、由企业拥有或者控制的、预期会给企业带来经济利益的资源。资产一般按流动性(资产的变现或耗用时间长短)分为流动资产和非流动资产。其中流动资产可分为货币资金、交易性金融资产、应收票据、应收帐款、预付款项、其他应收款、存货等；非流动资产可分为长期股权投资、固定资产、无形资产及其它非流动资产等。

流动资产

资产满足以下条件之一应归为流动资产：(1)预计在一个正常营业周期中变现、出售或耗用，主要包括存货、应收帐款等；(2)主要为交易目的而持有；(3)预计在资产负债表日起一年内(含一年)变现；(4)自资产负债日起一年内，交换其他资产或清偿负债的能力不受限制的现金或现金等价物。包括货币资金、应收票据、应收帐款、存货等项目。

负债合计

指企业过去的交易或者事项形成的，预期会导致经济利益流出企业的现时义务。负债一般按偿还期长短分为流动负债和非流动负债。

所有者权益

指企业投资人对企业净资产的所有权。企业净资产等于企业全部资产减去全部负债后的余额，包括企业投资人对企业的最初投入的实际到位的资产及资本公积金、盈余公积金和未分配利润。所有者权益合计数小于零，表示企业资不抵债。

总资产贡献率

反映企业全部资产的获利能力，是企业经营业绩和管理水平的集中体现，是评价和考核企业盈利能力的核心指标。计算公式为：

总资产贡献率(%)=(利润总额 + 税金总额 + 利息净支出)/ 平均资金总额×100%

公式中：税金总额为主营业务税金及附加与应缴增值税之和；平均资产总额为期初期末资产之和的算术平均值。

资产负债率

该指标既反映企业经营风险的大小，也反映企业利用债权人提供的资金从事经营活动的能力。计算公式为：

资产负债率(%)= 负债合计 / 资产总计×100%

资产与负债均为报告期期末数。

流动资产周转次数

指一定时期内流动资产完成的周转次数，反映投入工业企业流动资金的周转速度。计算公式为：

流动资产周转次数 = 主营业务收入 / 全部流动资产平均余额

公式中：全部流动资产平均余额为期初和期末的流动资产之和的算术平均值。

成本费用利润率

反映企业投入的生产成本及费用的经济效益，同时也反映企业降低成本所取得的经济效益。计算公式为：

成本费用利润率 (%)= 利润总额 / 成本费用总额×100%

公式中：成本费用总额为主营业务成本、销售费用、管理费用、财务费用之和。

产品销售率

该指标反映工业产品已实现销售的程度，是分析工业产销衔接情况、研究工业产品满足社会需求的指标。计算公式为：

产品销售率 (%)= 工业销售产值 / 工业总产值 (现价)×100%

主要统计指标解释

资本保值增值率

该指标反映企业净资产的变动状况，是企业发展能力的集中体现。计算公式为：

资本保值增值率(%)＝报告期期末所有者权益／上年同期期末所有者权益×100%

所有者权益等于资产总计减负债合计。

EXPLANATORY NOTES TO MAJOR STATISTICAL INDICATORS

□ Industry

Industry refers to the material production sector which is engaged in extraction of natural resources and processing and reprocessing of minerals and agricultural products, including (1) extraction of natural resources, such as mining, salt production (but not including hunting and fishing); (2) processing and reprocessing of farm and sideline produces, such as rice husking, flour milling, wine making, oil pressing, silk reeling, spinning and weaving, and leather making; (3) manufacture of industrial products, such as steel making, iron smelting, chemicals manufacturing, petroleum processing, machine building, timber processing; water and gas production and electricity generation and supply; (4)repairing of industrial products such as the repairing of machinery and means of transport (cars) are not included.

Units of industrial statistics survey corporate industrial enterprises with independent accounting system.

Corporate industrial enterprises with independent accounting system refer to enterprises engaging in industrial production activities, which meet the following requirements: ①They are established legally, having their own names, organizations, location, able to take civil liability; ②They possess and use their assets independently, assume liabilities, and are entitled to sign contracts with other units; ③They are financially independent and compile their own balance sheets.

□ Gross Output Value of Industry

(1) Definition: Gross industrial output value is the total volume of final industrial products produced and industrial services provided during a given period. It reflects the total achievements and overall scale of industrial production during a given period.

(2) Principles for calculation:

Statistics on industrial production follow the principle that all products produced by the enterprises and accepted during the reference period are to be included no matter whether they are sold or not during the reference period.

Determination of final products follow the principle that all products that are included in the calculation of grow industrial output value are the final products of the enterprise which have been accepted through quality check and require no further processing. If an enterprise has intermediate (semi-finished) products to sell, these intermediate products are considered as the final products of the enterprise.

Gross industrial output value is calculated following the principle of factory approach, i.e. industrial enterprise is used as the basic accounting unit in calculating the gross industrial output value. By this approach, value of the same product is not to be double counted, and the output value of different workshops (branch factories) should not be added. However, this approach does not exclude the possibility of double counting between enterprises.

(3) Content and calculation method:

The old definition of gross industrial output value was modified during the national industrial census in 1995. The revised (new) definition of gross industrial output value consists of 3 components: value of the finished products during the reference period, income from external processing, and value of change in semi-finished products at the end and at the beginning of the reference period.

Value of the finished products during the reference period: refers to the value of all finished (semi-finished) industrial products that are produced during the reference period without the need for further processing, checked for acceptance, packed and put into the warehouse of the enterprise, including the value of own-produced equipment and the value of products provided to the projects under construction of the enterprise, and to other non-industrial or welfare units. Value of finished products during the reference period is calculated by the quantity of products produced using own materials multiplied by the average unit prices at which products are sold (excluding value-added tax). Own-produced equipment and products produced for own use are value at cost prices as in the case of enterprise accounting. Value of finished products does not include the value of finished products (semi-finished products) that are produced using the materials from the clients who make the orders.

Income from external processing: refers to income from contracted external processing of industrial products (including processing of industrial products using materials from the clients), and the income from industrial repairing work provided to other units. Income from external processing is calculated using information from the item "products sales income" in the enterprise

EXPLANATORY NOTES TO MAJOR STATISTICAL INDICATORS

accounting at the prices excluding value-added tax.

For income from services such as processing, repairing and installation of equipment provided to non-industrial units within the enterprise, if the accounting work of the enterprise is good enough to separate it from other records, and the share of such services is significant, it should also be included in the income from external processing.

Value of change in semi-finished products at the end and at the beginning of the reference period: refers to the value of change in semi-finished products at the end and at the beginning of the reference period, which generally can be obtained from accounting records of enterprises. If the enterprise accounting excludes the cost of semi-finished products, then it should not be included in the gross industrial output value, and vice versa.

(4) Changes in the coverage and method of calculation of gross industrial output value

Prior to 1984, the value of rural industry run by villages was classified into agriculture instead of industry. Since 1984, it has been included in the gross industrial output value.

Method of calculation for the gross industrial output value was modified in the industrial census in 1995. The difference in the new method as compared with the old one is outlined below:

Principle in using full value vs. processing fee: The new method stipulates that all products produced using own materials are to be calculated with full value in reporting the gross industrial output value irrespective of sophistication of production, and for external processing, it allows calculation using processing fee. In the old method, however, the use of full value or processing fee was determined by the degree of sophistication of production in different branches of industries.

Principle in determining the value of change in semi-finished products: The new method requires that value of the change in semi-finished products should be included in the gross industrial output value if it is included in the accounting record of the enterprise, otherwise it should not be included. By the old method, it is determined by the type of enterprises in terms of production cycle. If the production cycle is over 6 months, the value of change in semi-finished products is included in the gross industrial output value, otherwise it is excluded.

Difference in prices: The new method uses prices excluding value-added tax in the calculation of gross industrial output value, while the old method used prices including value-added tax.

□ Large, Medium, Small and Micro Industrial Enterprises

Large, Medium, Small and Micro Industrial Enterprises division criteria: Since 2011 annual report, criteria for classifying Large, Medium and Small Enterprises follow the Notice On the issuance of small and medium enterprises designated standards (MIIT Joint on Enterprise, [2012] No.300). Under the new classification criteria, an industrial enterprise could be entitled Large Enterprise only when it has more than 1000 employees, its operating revenue exceeds 400 million yuan, simultaneously. An enterprise could be entitled Medium Enterprise only when its employee number ranges from 300 to 1000, its operating revenue ranges from 20 million and 400 million yuan, simultaneously. An enterprise could be entitled Small Enterprise only when its employee number ranges from 20 to 300, its operating revenue ranges from 3 million and 200 million yuan, simultaneously. All other enterprises should be entitled Micro Enterprise.

□ Total Assets

Total Assets refer to economic resources which are gained from past transactions or events by enterprise, owned or controlled by enterprise, and are expected to bring economic benefits to enterprise.

According to liquidity (length of time that assets are realized of consumed), assets are generally divided into current assets and non current assets. Current assets can by divided into monetary funds, financial trading assets, notes receivable, accounts receivable, prepayments, other receivables and inventories, etc. Non curren assets can be divided into longterm equity investments, fixed assets, intangible assets and other non current assets, etc.

□ Current Assets

Assets which meet one of the following conditions can be classed as current assets: (1)expected to be realized, sold or consumed in a normal operating cycle; (2)held for trading purposes; (3) expected to be realized within one year (including one year) from the balance sheet; (4)cash or cash equivalents of which the ability to exchange other assets or to repay debts is not restricted within one year from the date of balance sheet. Current Assets include monetary funds, notes receivable, accounts receivable, inventory and other projects.

□ Total Liabilities

Total Liabilities refer to the current obligations which are

EXPLANATORY NOTES TO MAJOR STATISTICAL INDICATORS

created from business transactions or events in the past and expected to result in an outflow of economic benefits from the enterprise. Liabilities are generally divided into current liabilities and non current liabilities according to the length of repayment period.

□ Creditors' Equity

Creditors' Equity refers to investors ownership of net assets of the enterprise, which is equal to the total assets of the enterprise minus its total liabilities, including the primary input actually received at the enterprise from investors, capital accumulation fund, surplus accumulation fund and undistributed profit. When the total of creditors' equity is less than zero, that indicates the liability of the enterprise is larger that its assets.

□ Ratio of Profits, Taxes and Interests to Average Assets

Ratio of Profits, Taxes and Interests to Average Assets reflects the profit-making capability of all assets of the enterprise and is a key indicator manifesting the performance and management and evaluating the profit-making potential of the enterprise. It is calculated as follows:

Ratio of Profits, Taxes and Interests to Average Assets (%) = [(total profits + total taxes +net interest payment) / average assets] × 100%

In the above formula, total taxes is the sum of tax and extra charges of prime operating and value-added tax payable; and average assets is the arithmetic mean of the sum of beginning assets and ending assets.

□ Ratio of Debts to Assets

Ratio of Debts to Assets reflect both the operation risk and the capability of the enterprise in making use of the capital from the creditors. It is calculated as follows:

Ratio of Debts to Assets (%) = (total debts / total assets) × 100%

Both assets and debts are figures at the end of the reference period.

□ Turnover of Working Capital

Turnover of Working Capital refers to the number of times of turnover of working capital in a given period of time, which reflects the speed of the turnover of working capital of industrial enterprises, and is calculated as follows:

Turnover of Working Capital= (prime operating revenue) / (average balance of total working capital)

In the above formula, average balance of total working capital refers to the arithmetic mean of the sum of working capital at the beginning and at the end of the reference period.

□ Ratio of Profits to Total Industrial Costs

Ratio of Profits to Total Industrial Costs refers to the ratio of profits realized in a given period to the total costs in the same period, which reflects the economic efficiency of input cost and is calculated as follows:

Ratio of Profits to Total Industrial Cost(%)=(total profits/ total costs) × 100%

Total costs in the above formula is the sum of prime operating costs, marketing cost, management cost and financial cost.

□ Ratio of Sales to Gross Output Value

Ratio of Sales to Gross Output Value reflects the degree at which industrial products are sold. It helps to analyze the linkage between production and sales and the extent of the needs of the society that has been met by the supply of industrial products. It is calculated as follows:

Ratio of Sales to Gross Output Value(%)=(industrial sales / gross industrial output value at current prices) × 100%

□ Capital Maintenance and Appreciation Rate

Capital Maintenance and Appreciation Rate reflects the changes of an enterprise's net assets. It epitomizes the growth capability of an enterprise. Its calculating formula is:

Capital Maintenance and Appreciation Rate (%)=(ownership equity at the end of the reporting period/ownership equity at the same period of the previous year) × 100%.

Ownership equity is the result of total assets minus total liabilities.

第十四篇

CHAPTER 14

建筑业

CONSTRUCTION

简要说明

一、本章资料的主要内容

本篇资料反映上海市建筑业概况和发展情况。包括建筑业企业基本情况和生产经营情况。主要指标有企业个数、从业人员数、建筑业签订的合同额、建筑业总产值、房屋建筑面积和劳动生产率指标等。此外,还包括本市各区县主要建筑业指标完成情况。

二、本篇资料的统计范围

根据建筑业发展的实际情况,建筑业统计范围从2002年年报起由原具有建筑业资质等级四级及四级以上的独立核算的建筑业企业调整为具有建筑业资质的独立核算建筑业企业。

三、本篇的资料来源及统计调查方法

本篇建筑业企业统计数据是根据国家统计局制定的《建筑业统计报表制度》整理汇总的。建筑业统计报表是上海市统计局根据企业实际情况采取全面调查的方法布置、收集,由各资质内建筑业企业通过联网直报上报的全面报表。

BRIEF INTRODUCTION

I. Main Contents

Data in this chapter show a general situation and development of the construction industry in Shanghai. They cover the situation of production and management of the construction enterprises, including the number of enterprises; number of employed persons; construction contracts signed; gross output value of construction industry; floor space of buildings under construction and labor productivity etc. They also cover the performance of main construction indicators in districts and counties.

II. Scope of Statistics

In view of the development of the construction industry, since 2002, the scope of construction statistics has been adjusted to include all the construction enterprises of various types of ownership with qualification certificates and independent accounting systems, replacing the previous criteria that required construction enterprises of various types of ownership to have qualification certificates at or above Class 4 with independent accounting systems.

III. Sources of Data and Methods of Survey

Data on construction enterprises are collected in accordance with the Reporting Form System of Construction Statistics stipulated by the NBS. The annual reporting forms on construction statistics are designed by the Shanghai Municipal Statistics Bureau in accordance with local situations for comprehensive collection by the qualified construction enterprises through the comprehensive network straight report.

表 14.1 建筑业主要指标(1978～2015)
MAJOR INDICATORS OF CONSTRUCTION INDUSTRY

年 份 Year	年末从业人员（万人） Year-end Employees (10 000 persons)	总产值（亿元） Output Value (100 million yuan)	房屋竣工面积（万平方米） Floor Space of Building Completed (10 000 sq. m)	人均房屋竣工面积（平方米/人） Area of Completed Building Per Employee (sq. m/person)	全员劳动生产率（按总产值计算）（元/人） Overall Labor Productivity (In Term of Output Value) (yuan/person)
1978	10.07	5.55	234.03	26.32	6 005
1979	23.35	13.98	564.62	26.10	6 226
1980	27.27	17.07	607.91	24.13	6 513
1981	30.21	18.03	649.93	22.28	5 941
1982	30.73	21.56	684.61	22.90	6 928
1983	33.35	24.64	736.34	22.46	7 189
1984	32.94	30.62	799.40	23.10	8 402
1985	33.35	36.73	819.24	23.78	10 070
1986	35.53	49.91	867.08	22.87	12 147
1987	35.83	59.45	872.25	22.66	14 455
1988	36.70	68.83	836.73	21.26	16 251
1989	34.43	74.75	758.34	19.70	18 053
1990	34.01	75.62	747.88	20.01	18 569
1991	34.62	84.30	775.63	20.14	21 022
1992	36.33	117.68	860.49	19.92	26 221
1993	36.90	193.00	1 144.16	26.10	44 020
1994	39.95	309.68	1 557.87	29.33	58 305
1995	41.10	391.42	1 485.87	25.44	67 023
1996	36.19	450.41	1 514.58	26.95	80 161
1997	37.40	564.37	1 777.41	29.60	93 995
1998	40.88	593.11	1 913.55	33.08	102 531
1999	39.01	573.06	1 950.76	33.86	99 473
2000	35.91	631.64	1 909.11	33.02	109 244
2001	35.52	730.33	2 434.73	39.55	118 641
2002	41.97	822.27	2 596.95	42.23	133 698
2003	50.52	1 195.80	3 609.20	71.44	153 910
2004	74.26	1 724.40	4 672.53	62.92	168 719
2005	72.23	1 889.25	5 648.85	78.21	182 299
2006	73.44	2 285.38	6 506.41	88.59	208 368
2007	69.33	2 524.18	6 090.22	87.84	228 710
2008	80.79	3 245.77	5 723.90	70.85	293 520
2009	88.88	3 830.53	5 719.93	64.36	312 360
2010	96.09	4 300.19	6 217.15	64.70	344 720
2011	96.86	4 586.28	5 984.74	61.79	359 232
2012	88.08	4 843.44	6 476.07	73.52	451 564
2013	81.54	5 102.84	6 274.25	76.95	417 313
2014	77.65	5 499.94	7 580.77	97.63	416 002
2015	69.19	5 652.47	7 258.69	104.91	445 768

表 14.2 建筑业主要指标（2015）
MAJOR INDICATORS OF CONSTRUCTION INDUSTRY

类别	Types	企业数（个）Quantity of Enterprises (unit)	年末从业人员（万人）Year-end Employees (10 000 persons)	竣工产值（亿元）Output Value of Construction Completed (100 million yuan)
总　计	**Total**	**3 065**	**69.19**	**3 121.47**
按登记注册类型分	**By Registration Categories**			
内　资	Domestic Funded	2 937	67.53	3 024.95
#国　有	State-owned	28	0.55	47.18
集　体	Collective Owned	29	0.87	19.51
股份合作	Stock-holding Cooperative	14	0.20	2.94
联　营	Joint Owned	5	0.05	4.98
有限责任公司	Limited Liability Companies	604	21.89	1 514.90
股份有限公司	Stock-holding Companies Ltd.	57	3.50	507.91
私　营	Private	2 200	40.47	927.54
港澳台商投资	Hong Kong, Macao and Taiwan Funded	69	0.92	34.99
外商投资	Foreign Funded	59	0.74	61.53
按行业分	**By Sectors**			
房屋建筑业	Housing Construction Industry	929	44.45	2 085.53
土木工程建筑业	Civil Engineering Industry	603	9.93	482.51
建筑安装业	Construction and Installation Industry	726	7.82	308.08
建筑装饰和其他建筑业	Construction and Decoration Industry and Other Construction Industry	807	6.99	245.36
按资质标准分	**By Qualification Standard**			
施工总承包	Chief Construction Contract	1 439	55.43	2 646.98
专业承包	Professional Contract	1 626	13.76	474.49

表 14.2 续表 1 continued

类别	Types	总产值（亿元） Output Value (100 million yuan)	其中 of which #建筑工程 Construction	安装工程 Installation
总计	**Total**	**5 652.47**	**4 762.36**	**778.27**
按登记注册类型分	**By Registration Categories**			
内资	Domestic Funded	5 470.00	4 630.16	734.52
#国有	State-owned	66.13	29.50	33.29
集体	Collective Owned	25.63	20.31	5.00
股份合作	Stock-holding Cooperation	3.24	1.61	1.63
联营	Joint Owned	5.40	4.99	0.11
有限责任公司	Limited Liability Companies	3 215.51	2 838.61	314.41
股份有限公司	Stock-holding Companies Ltd.	577.52	437.96	137.61
私营	Private	1 576.57	1 297.18	242.47
港澳台商投资	Hong Kong, Macao and Taiwan Funded	87.58	62.03	25.37
外商投资	Foreign Funded	94.89	70.17	18.38
按行业分	**By Sectors**			
房屋建筑业	Housing Construction Industry	3 104.19	2 844.96	202.24
土木工程建筑业	Civil Engineering Industry	1 495.37	1 310.71	156.97
建筑安装业	Construction and Installation Industry	514.63	110.93	384.47
建筑装饰和其他建筑业	Construction and Decoration Industry and Other Construction Industry	538.28	495.76	34.60
按资质标准分	**By Qualification Standard**			
施工总承包	Chief Construction Contract	4 720.16	4 112.33	519.80
专业承包	Professional Contract	932.31	650.03	258.47

表 14.2 续表 2 continued

类别	Types	房屋建筑面积(万平方米) Floor Space of Buildings (10 000 sq. m) 施工面积 Under Construction	竣工面积 Completed
总计	**Total**	**36 659.77**	**7 258.69**
按登记注册类型分	**By Registration Categories**		
内资	Domestic Investment	36 397.00	7 186.45
#国有	State-owned	21.87	3.95
集体	Collective Owned	121.85	106.77
股份合作	Stock-holding Cooperation	0.95	
联营	Joint Owned	14.70	
有限责任公司	Limited Liability Companies	23 710.88	3 712.08
股份有限公司	Stock-holding Companies Ltd.	4 995.94	1 305.26
私营	Private	7 530.82	2 058.40
港澳台商投资	Hong Kong, Macao and Taiwan Funded	98.80	
外商投资	Foreign Funded	163.97	72.24
按行业分	**By Sectors**		
房屋建筑业	Housing Construction Industry	36 028.51	7 149.56
土木工程建筑业	Civil Engineering Industry	525.73	87.50
建筑安装业	Construction and Installation Industry	91.81	19.13
建筑装饰和其他建筑业	Construction and Decoration Industry and Other Construction Industry	13.72	2.49
按资质标准分	**By Qualification Standard**		
施工总承包	Chief Construction Contract	36 364.70	7 196.27
专业承包	Professional Contract	295.07	62.43

表 14.3 各区、县建筑业主要指标(2015)
MAIN CONSTRUCTION INDICATORS OF DISTRICTS AND COUNTIES

地 区	District	企业数(个) Quantity of Enterprises (unit)	年末从业人员(万人) Year-end Employees (10 000 persons)	总产值(亿元) Output Value (100 million yuan)
总 计	**Total**	**3 065**	**69.19**	**5 652.47**
浦东新区	Pudong New Area	568	14.19	1 347.88
黄 浦 区	Huangpu	148	2.61	260.83
徐 汇 区	Xuhui	214	4.50	484.38
长 宁 区	Changning	149	4.13	233.60
静 安 区	Jing'an	75	1.12	52.37
普 陀 区	Putuo	238	5.31	391.36
闸 北 区	Zhabei	119	4.05	479.09
虹 口 区	Hongkou	161	3.64	404.57
杨 浦 区	Yangpu	246	5.22	333.90
闵 行 区	Minhang	167	5.49	351.99
宝 山 区	Baoshan	236	6.36	643.08
嘉 定 区	Jiading	168	2.36	140.24
金 山 区	Jinshan	133	2.34	105.65
松 江 区	Songjiang	133	2.81	171.43
青 浦 区	Qingpu	75	1.56	97.07
奉 贤 区	Fengxian	177	2.86	126.10
崇 明 县	Chongming	58	0.64	28.95

表 14.3 续表 Continued

地 区 District		房屋施工面积（万平方米）Floor Space of Buildings Under Construction (10 000 sq. m)	房屋竣工面积（万平方米）Floor Space of Buildings Completed (10 000 sq. m)	其中 of which #住宅房屋 Residence
总 计	**Total**	**36 659.77**	**7 258.69**	**3 476.12**
浦东新区	Pudong New Area	12 610.85	2 145.31	990.24
黄 浦 区	Huangpu	393.74	65.92	35.03
徐 汇 区	Xuhui	807.33	154.43	122.00
长 宁 区	Changning	2 223.68	468.20	203.40
静 安 区	Jing'an	172.15	…	…
普 陀 区	Putuo	2 540.44	751.49	450.18
闸 北 区	Zhabei	995.07	271.95	157.33
虹 口 区	Hongkou	3 013.78	609.79	297.53
杨 浦 区	Yangpu	792.17	196.91	152.59
闵 行 区	Minhang	4 851.74	543.42	316.80
宝 山 区	Baoshan	4 661.96	902.95	237.49
嘉 定 区	Jiading	904.67	224.25	161.50
金 山 区	Jinshan	166.24	60.92	24.37
松 江 区	Songjiang	1 061.65	404.94	82.33
青 浦 区	Qingpu	538.98	243.34	157.83
奉 贤 区	Fengxian	867.34	172.38	76.82
崇 明 县	Chongming	57.96	42.48	10.67

表 14.4 建筑业主要财务指标(2015)
MAJOR ACCOUNTING INDICATORS OF CONSTRUCTION ENTERPRISES

指 标	Indicators	合 计 Total	内 资 Domestic Investment
施工企业单位数（个）	Quantity of Construction Enterprises (unit)	3 065	2 937
固定资产原价（亿元）	Fixed Assets (Original Value) (100 million yuan)	702.07	676.83
固定资产净值（亿元）	Fixed Assets (Net Value) (100 million yuan)	350.29	332.52
总产值（亿元）	Output Value(100 million yuan)	5 652.47	5 470.00
资产合计（亿元）	**Assets at Year-end (100 million yuan)**	**8 818.56**	**8 462.11**
#流动资产	Current Assets	7 479.89	7 151.50
固定资产	Fixed Assets	424.56	406.00
无形资产	Intangible Assets	39.02	38.68
负债合计（亿元）	**Total Liabilities at Year-end (100 million yuan)**	**6 794.06**	**6 519.73**
流动负债	Current Liabilities	6 386.57	6 116.82
非流动负债	Non-current Liabilities	223.74	222.67
所有者权益（亿元）	Total Owners Equity (100 million yuan)	2 021.72	1 939.61
企业总收入（亿元）	Total Revenue of Enterprises (100 million yuan)	7 374.38	7 074.05
主营业务收入	Prime Operating Revenue	7 322.21	7 028.59
其他业务收入	Other Revenue	52.18	45.47
房屋施工面积（万平方米）	Floor Space of Building Under Construction (10 000 sq. m)	36 659.77	36 397.00
房屋竣工面积（万平方米）	Floor Space of Building Completed (10 000 sq. m)	7 258.69	7 186.45
利润总额（亿元）	Total Profits (100 million yuan)	199.16	179.78
全员劳动生产率（元/人）（按总产值计算）	Overall Labor Productivity (yuan/person) (In Term of Output Value)	445 768	445 399
房屋建筑面积竣工率（%）	Rate of Buiding Completed (%)	19.8	19.7
产值利润率（%）	Ratio of Profit/Gross Output Value (%)	3.5	3.3
产值利税率（%）	Ratio of Profit and Taxes/Gross Output Value (%)	3.4	3.4

其中 of which					
#国有 State-owned	集体 Collective Owned	股份合作 Stock-holding Cooperation	联营 Joint Owned	有限责任公司 Companies With Limited Liabilition	股份有限公司 Stock-holding Companies Liabilities
28	29	14	5	604	57
11.73	12.86	0.46	0.15	395.37	74.87
4.90	8.84	0.19	0.12	192.06	34.10
66.13	25.63	3.24	5.40	3 215.51	577.52
89.84	**95.94**	**4.97**	**1.22**	**5 332.79**	**793.62**
79.57	76.36	4.63	1.02	4 475.61	634.89
6.68	8.89	0.21	0.12	238.80	40.81
1.26	0.12			21.79	3.37
76.48	64.61	3.47	0.52	4 375.54	594.73
76.08	63.75	3.47	0.50	4 164.83	579.90
0.40	0.27			182.35	6.96
13.30	31.33	1.49	0.70	956.24	198.89
91.73	61.88	7.10	2.44	4 105.55	877.60
89.96	61.78	7.02	2.42	4 086.68	873.01
1.77	0.10	0.08	0.02	18.87	4.59
21.87	121.85	0.95	14.70	23 710.88	4 995.94
3.95	106.77			3 712.08	1 305.26
1.81	1.13	0.12	0.09	123.41	18.62
519 720	210 951	156 942	281 344	575 934	463 270
18.1	87.6			15.7	26.1
2.7	4.4	3.7	1.7	3.8	3.2
3.4	8.2	6.8	2.0	3.4	2.8

表 14.4 续表 Continued

指标	Indicators	其中 of which 私营 Private	港澳台商投资 Hong Kong, Macao and Taiwan Funded	外商投资 Foreign Funded
施工企业单位数（个）	Quantity of Construction Enterprises (unit)	2 200	69	59
固定资产原价（亿元）	Fixed Assets (Original Value) (100 million yuan)	181.33	20.80	4.44
固定资产净值（亿元）	Fixed Assets (Net Value) (100 million yuan)	92.29	16.29	1.48
总产值（亿元）	Output Value(100 million yuan)	1 576.57	87.58	94.89
资产合计（亿元）	**Assets at Year-end (100 million yuan)**	**2 143.63**	**185.69**	**170.76**
#流动资产	Current Assets	1 879.33	162.93	165.46
固定资产	Fixed Assets	110.48	17.05	1.51
无形资产	Intangible Assets	12.14	0.20	0.14
负债合计（亿元）	**Total Liabilities at Year-end (100 million yuan)**	**1 404.36**	**141.68**	**132.65**
流动负债	Current Liabilities	1 228.26	137.88	131.87
非流动负债	Non-current Liabilities	32.68	0.88	0.19
所有者权益（亿元）	Total Owners Equity (100 million yuan)	737.57	44.00	38.11
企业总收入（亿元）	Total Revenue of Enterprises (100 million yuan)	1 927.55	149.97	150.36
主营业务收入	Prime Operating Revenue	1 907.50	145.58	148.04
其他业务收入	Other Revenue	20.05	4.39	2.32
房屋施工面积（万平方米）	Floor Space of Building Under Construction (10 000 sq. m)	7 530.82	98.80	163.97
房屋竣工面积（万平方米）	Floor Space of Building Completed (10 000 sq. m)	2 058.40		72.24
利润总额（亿元）	Total Profits (100 million yuan)	34.61	10.82	8.56
全员劳动生产率（元/人）（按总产值计算）	Overall Labor Productivity (yuan/person) (In Term of Output Value)	305 371	413 003	507 108
房屋建筑面积竣工率（%）	Rate of Buiding Completed (%)	27.3		44.1
产值利润率（%）	Ratio of Profit/Gross Output Value (%)	2.2	12.4	9.0
产值利税率（%）	Ratio of Profit and Taxes/Gross Output Value (%)	3.7	3.7	3.2

表 14.5 建筑业签订合同情况(2015)
SITUATION OF CONSTRUCTION CONTRACTS

单位:亿元(100 million yuan)

类 别	Types	签订合同额 Signed Contract Value	上年结转合同额 Value from Contracts Signed in 2014	本年新签合同额 Value from New Contracts Signed in 2015
总 计	**Total**	**15 938.38**	**8 135.22**	**7 803.17**
按经济类型分	**Grouped by Registration Categories**			
内 资	Domestic Funded	15 561.98	7 932.38	7 629.60
#国 有	State-owned	167.61	91.84	75.77
集 体	Collective Owned	33.19	11.48	21.71
股份合作	Stock-holding Cooperation	3.94	1.79	2.14
联 营	Joint Owned	11.64	4.58	7.05
有限责任公司	Limited Liability Companies	10 043.31	5 008.22	5 035.10
股份有限公司	Stock-holding Companies Ltd.	2 425.96	1 414.84	1 011.12
私 营	Private	2 876.34	1 399.63	1 476.71
港澳台商投资	Hong Kong, Macao and Taiwan Funded	163.28	94.94	68.33
外商投资	Foreign Funded	213.13	107.90	105.23
按隶属关系分	**Grouped by Subordination**			
#中央属	Central Government	6 577.01	3 110.03	3 466.99
市 属	Municipality	3 696.30	2 061.71	1 634.59
区(县)属	District and County	764.52	395.02	369.50
按资质等级分	**Grouped by Quarlification Level**			
#特 级	Special Grade	7 102.04	3 745.11	3 356.93
一 级	First Grade	6 481.57	3 403.60	3 077.96
二 级	Second Grade	1 540.31	686.53	853.77
三 级	Third Grade	754.63	266.37	488.26
按行业类别分	**Grouped by Sector**			
房屋建筑业	Housing Construction Industry	10 080.16	5 480.70	4 599.47
土木工程建筑业	Civil Engineering Industry	4 156.22	2 041.77	2 114.45
建筑安装业	Construction and Installation Industry	868.53	283.22	585.32
建筑装饰和其他建筑业	Construction and Decoration Industry and Other Construction Industry	833.47	329.53	503.93
按资质标准分	**Grouped by Qualification**			
施工总承包	Chief Construction Contract	14 543.95	7 643.32	6 900.63
专业承包	Professional Contract	1 394.43	491.90	902.53

表 14.6 建筑业承包工程完成情况(2015)
COMPLETION OF CONTRACTED PROJECTS BY CONSTRUCTION ENTERPRISES

单位:亿元(100 million yuan)

类别	Types	直接从建设单位承揽工程完成产值 Completed Output Value of Projects Contracted Directly form Investors	其中 of Which 自行完成施工产值 Own-completed Output Value	分包出去工程的产值 Output Value of Out-sourced Projects	从建设单位外承揽工程完成产值 Completed Output Value of Projects Contracted from Non-investors
总计	**Total**	**5 849.45**	**5 031.19**	**818.26**	**621.28**
按经济类型分	**Grouped by Registration Categories**				
内资	Domestic Funded	5 646.78	4 878.68	768.09	591.32
#国有	State-owned	68.03	54.71	13.32	11.42
集体	Collective Owned	24.15	24.12	0.03	1.51
股份合作	Stock-holding Cooperation	3.10	3.09	0.01	0.15
联营	Joint Owned	5.45	5.06	0.39	0.34
有限责任公司	Limited Liability Companies	3 286.96	2 949.00	337.96	266.51
股份有限公司	Stock-holding Companies Ltd.	792.76	433.55	359.20	143.97
私营	Private	1 466.32	1 409.14	57.18	167.43
港澳台商投资	Hong Kong, Macao and Taiwan Funded	85.92	75.10	10.82	12.49
外商投资	Foreign Funded	116.75	77.41	39.35	17.48
按隶属关系分	**Grouped by Subordination**				
#中央属	Central Government	1 921.43	1 835.41	86.02	52.02
市属	Municipality	1 311.48	783.42	528.05	193.57
区(县)属	District and County	356.28	306.77	49.51	26.00
按资质等级分	**Grouped by Quarlification Level**				
#特级	Special Grade	1 944.66	1 467.53	477.13	155.22
一级	First Grade	2 537.37	2 302.28	235.08	318.36
二级	Second Grade	916.31	846.62	69.69	93.37
三级	Third Grade	428.89	393.38	35.51	53.77
按行业类别分	**Grouped by Sector**				
房屋建筑业	Housing Construction Industry	3 385.46	2 743.98	641.48	360.21
土木工程建筑业	Civil Engineering Industry	1 535.22	1 401.52	133.70	93.85
建筑安装业	Construction and Installation Industry	481.73	448.31	33.41	66.31
建筑装饰和其他建筑业	Construction and Decoration Industry and Other Construction Industry	447.04	437.37	9.68	100.91
按资质标准分	**Grouped by Qualification**				
施工总承包	Chief Construction Contract	5 077.16	4 282.23	794.93	437.93
专业承包	Professional Contract	772.28	748.96	23.33	183.35

上/海/统/计/年/鉴

主要统计指标解释

建筑业总产值

建筑业总产值是以货币表现的建筑业企业在一定时期内生产的建筑业产品和服务的总和。建筑业总产值包括:

(1)建筑工程产值: 指列入建筑工程预算内的各种工程价值。

(2)安装工程产值: 指设备安装工程价值,不包括被安装设备本身价值。

(3)其他产值:建筑业总产值中除建筑工程、安装工程以外的产值。包括房屋构筑物修理产值、非标准设备制造产值、总包企业向分包企业收取的管理费以及不能明确划分的施工活动所完成的产值。

a.房屋构筑物修理产值:指房屋和构筑物修理所完成的产值,但不包括被修理房屋、构筑物本身价值和生产设备的修理产值。

b.非标准设备制造产值:指加工制造没有定型的非标准生产设备的加工费和原材料价值(如化工厂、炼油厂用的各种罐、槽,矿井生产统一使用的各种漏斗、三角槽、阀门等) 以及附属加工厂为本企业承建工程制作的非标准设备的价值。

按建筑业总产值计算的全员劳动生产率

即平均每个从事建筑业生产活动的人员的建筑业总产值,计算公式为:

按建筑业总产值计算的全员劳动生产率 = 建筑业总产值 / 计算建筑业劳动生产率的平均人数

计算建筑业劳动生产率的平均人数指建筑业企业报告期实际拥有的、与建筑施工活动有关的人员的平均人数,包括参加本企业建筑施工活动的非本企业人员,但不包括企业内部社会服务性机构的人员以及由本企业支付工资但所从事的工作与本企业生产基本无关的人员。

房屋建筑面积

指房屋全部平面面积的总和。它从房屋的外墙线算起,包括可供使用的有效面积和墙柱等结构占用面积。多层房屋按各层(包括地下室)面积总和计算。旧房加层或改造,只计算增加的建筑面积;旧房拆除重建,计算其全部面积;临时房屋不计算建筑面积。

房屋施工面积

指报告期内施工的全部房屋建筑面积, 包括本期新开工的房屋面积、上期跨入本期继续施工的房屋面积、上期停缓建在本期恢复施工的房屋面积、本期竣工的房屋面积及本期施工后又停缓建的房屋面积。

房屋竣工面积

指在报告期内房屋建筑按照设计要求已全部完工,达到了使用条件,经检查验收鉴定合格,正式移交使用单位的房屋建筑面积。

SHANGHAI STATISTICAL YEARBOOK

EXPLANATORY NOTES TO MAJOR STATISTICAL INDICATORS

□ Gross Output Value of Construction

Gross Output Value of Construction refers to total of construction products and services, expressed in money terms, produced of rendered by construction and installation enterprises during a given period of time. It includes:

(1) Output value of construction projects: the value of projects covered by the project budgets;

(2) Output value of installation projects: the value of the installation of equipments, (excluding the value of the equipment to be installed);

(3) Other output values: the output value of construction industry apart from that of construction projects and installation projects. It includes: output value of repair of buildings and structures; output value of non-standard equipment manufacturing; overhead expenses received by contracted enterprises from the sub-contracted enterprises and the complete output value of construction activities for which there is no clear definition.

Output value of repair of buildings and structures: the value created through the repair of buildings and structures. It doesn't include the value of buildings or structures being repaired and the value of the repair of production equipment;

b. Output value of manufactured non-standard equipment: the value of non-standard production equipment, including raw materials and manufacturing cost, made for the project (i.e., chemical plant; kettles or tanks used by refineries; various fillers, triangle tanks, valves used by mines). It also includes the output value of equipment manufactured by subsidiary workshops.

□ All-personnel Labor Productivity Calculated by Gross Output Value of Construction Industry

All-personnel labor productivity calculated by gross output value of construction industry refers to the average gross output value of construction industry by every personnel engaged in production activities in the construction industry.

All-personnel labor Productivity Calculated by Gross Output Value of Construction Industry = Gross Output Value of Construction Industry / Average Number of Construction Industry

Average Number of Construction Industry refers to average number of persons that construction enterprises actually have and related to construction activities, includes those engaged in the construction activities of the enterprises but belong to other enterprises, and excludes those work for the social service institutions inside the enterprise and those paid by the enterprise but whose work has nothing to do with the construction.

□ Floor Space of Buildings

Floor Space of Buildings under Construction refers to total floor space of the horizontal section of outer walls above the plinth of the building, including the effective area and the area occupied by the structure. Multi-storey building refers to the sum of each storey, including the basement. The old buildings with storey added or rebuild only calculate the floor space added. The old buildings after dismantling and reconstruction calculate the total floor space. The tabernacle calculates no floor space.

□ Floor Space of Buildings Under Construction

Floor Space of Buildings under Construction refers to floor space of buildings under construction during the reference period, including newly started buildings, buildings started earlier and continued during the reference period, and buildings suspended earlier but restarted during the reference period, buildings completed during the reference period, and buildings under construction and then suspended during the reference period.

□ Floor Space of Buildings Completed

Floor Space of Buildings Completed refers to the floor space of buildings that are completed in the reference period in accordance with the requirements of the design, up to the standard for putting them into use, and have been checked and accepted by concerned departments as qualified ones.

第十五篇

CHAPTER 15

2016上海统计年鉴 SHANGHAI STATISTICAL YEARBOOK

交通运输、邮政和信息传输

TRANSPORTATION, POSTS AND INFORMATION TRANSMISSION

简要说明

一、本章资料的主要内容

本篇资料反映上海市交通运输、仓储和邮政业及信息传输业发展的基本状况。

交通运输、仓储和邮政业资料主要包括:运输线路长度、旅客发送量、旅客周转量、货物运输量、货物周转量、港口码头情况、港口货物吞吐量、集装箱吞吐量、邮轮经济、经营性停车场、民用车辆拥有量、邮政业务主要指标等内容。

信息传输业资料主要包括:电信业务开展情况、邮电通信水平、信息化基础设施情况、信息服务业经营情况、信息技术应用等方面资料。

二、本篇资料的统计范围和统计方式

1. 铁路资料:包括国家铁路(含控股合资)、地方铁路和非控股合资铁路运营情况,不含军用铁路及由厂矿企事业单位自建的铁路专用线和专用铁道。

2. 公路、水路、港口资料:(1)公路、水路运输量统计包括全面调查和非全面调查两种方式,统计范围为在上海市交通运输主管部门登记注册的从事公路、水路客、货运输的营业性的车辆和船舶所完成的运输量;(2)港口统计采用全面调查方式,统计范围为上海市全部沿海港口和内河港口。

3. 民用车辆拥有量资料:民用车辆拥有量由民用汽车拥有量和民用拖拉机拥有量组成。

4. 民航运输资料:统计范围为在上海市注册从事民用航空运输飞行和通用飞行的航空运输企业和定期航班通航机场,不包括在上海市从事运输飞行的外省市和外国航空公司。

5. 邮电业务量按业务种类分为邮政业务量和电信业务量:邮政业务量统计范围是上海市邮政业企业和取得快递业务经营许可的快递企业及其备案分支机构;邮政业基础设施资料统计范围是上海市境内提供国家邮政服务的机构和设施。

三、本篇的资料来源

本篇资料中的交通运输、仓储和邮政业资料由上海市统计局工业交通处负责整理、编辑。有关交通运输资料分别来源于上海市铁路局、上海市交通委员会、上海机场(集团)有限公司、上海市公安局车辆管理所、上海市农业机械化管理办公室、上海市邮政公司、上海市邮政管理局。

本篇资料中的信息传输资料由上海市统计局社会与科技统计处负责采集、整理和编辑。相关电信业务资料由上海市通信管理局提供,信息化基础设施、信息服务业、信息技术应用等方面资料由上海市经济和信息化委员会提供。

BRIEF INTRODUCTION

I. Main Contents

Data in this chapter reflect the basic conditions of transportation warehousing, postal services and telecommunications industries in Shanghai.

Data on the transportation, warehousing and postal services industries cover mainly the length of the traffic lines, passenger departing volume, turnover volume of passenger traffic, freight traffic volume, turnover volume of freight traffic, conditions of ports, port freight throughput, container throughput, yacht economy, parking lots operation, civil motor vehicles, and postal services.

Data on the telecommunications industry cover mainly conditions of telecommunications services, telecommunications level, infrastructure of informatization, operation of information service industry, and application of information technology.

II. Scope and Methodology of Statistics

(1)Data on railway transportation: They include the operation and management of the national (including state-controlled joint ventures), local and non state-controlled joint-venture railways but exclude railways for military purpose, lines built by industrial and mining enterprises and special railways.

(2) Data on highways, waterways and ports: (a) Data on highway and waterway transportation are collected through both comprehensive reporting system and non-comprehensive reporting system. The statistical scope encompasses all the vehicles and ships registered with the transportation authorities in Shanghai and engaged in highway or waterway freight or passenger transportation business. (b) Data on ports are collected through comprehensive reporting system. The statistical scope encompasses all ports along the sea and the rivers.

(3) Data on civil motor vehicles: They include the numbers of civil automobiles and tractors.

(4) Data on civil aviation transportation: The targets of statistical collection are enterprises registered in Shanghai for engagement in civil aviation transportation flights and flights for general purposes and general aviation airports with scheduled flights. They exclude foreign companies and companies registered in other provinces and cities, which operate flights within the Shanghai territory.

(5)By types of business, the business volumes of postal and telecommunications sectors are divided into those of postal services and telecommunication services: Data on postal businesses include postal enterprises and express delivery companies and its filing branches with express business license. Data on postal infrastructure include institutions and facilities in Shanghai that provide state postal services.

III. Sources of Data

Data on transportation, warehousing and postal services in this chapter are collected, processed and compiled by the Department of Industry and Transportations, Shanghai Municipal Statistics Bureau. Data on transportation are from the Shanghai Railway Bureau, Shanghai Municipal Transportation Commission, Shanghai Airport Group, Shanghai City Public Security Bureau vehicle management, Shanghai Civil Agricultural Mechanization Management Office, Shanghai Post Corporation and Shanghai Municipal Postal Administration.

Data on information transmission in this chapter are collected, processed and complied by Department of Society and Technology, Shanghai Municipal Statistics Bureau. Data on telecommunication businesses are provided by Shanghai Communications Administration. Data on infrastructure of informatization, information service industry, and application of information technology are provided by Shanghai Municipal Economic and Informatization Commission.

表 15.1 主要年份运输线路长度
LENGTHS OF TRAFFIC LINES IN MAIN YEARS

指 标	Indicators	2000	2010	2014	2015
铁路运输	**Railway**				
运营里程(公里)	Operation Mileage (km)	257	414	456	456
正线延展里程(公里)	Mainline Railway Length Extended (km)	397	697	825	825
公路运输	**Highway**				
通车里程(公里)	Operation Mileage(km)	5 970	11 974	12 945	13 195
#高速公路	High Speed Highways	98	775	825	825
内河航道	**Navigable Inland Waterways**				
航道里程(公里)	Length of Navigable Inland Waterways (km)	2 100	2 110	2 073	2 058

表 15.2 主要年份交通运输主要指标
MAJOR INDICATORS OF TRANSPORTATION IN MAIN YEARS

指 标	Indicators	2000	2010	2014	2015
公路运输	**Highway Transportation**				
营运汽车拥有量(辆)	Operating Vehicles (vehicle)	155 860	185 531	237 646	238 957
载客汽车	Passenger Vehicles	30 757	20 386	22 659	27 156
载货汽车	Freight Trucks	125 103	165 145	214 987	211 801
载客汽车客位数(客位)	Seat of Passenger Vehicles(seat)	309 834	523 564	527 153	567 416
载货汽车吨位数(万吨)	Tonnage of Freight Trucks(10 000 tons)	48.36	132.59	216.91	228.21
港 口	**Harbor**				
船舶平均在港停泊时间(天)	Average Days of Vessel Berthed at Harbor (day)	0.90	0.40	0.46	0.43
机 场	**Aviation**				
起降航班数(万架次)	Aircraft Movements(10 000 sortie-times)		55.11	65.54	70.58
进出港旅客人次(万人次)	Passenger Turnover(10 000 person-times)		7 187.74	8 965.90	9 918.90
#国内航线	Domestic Flight		5 106.96	6 073.58	6 643.88
国际及地区航线	International and Regional Flight		2 080.78	2 892.32	3 275.02

表 15.3 主要年份旅客发送量
PASSENGER DEPARTING IN MAIN YEARS

单位:万人次(10 000 person-times)

年 份 Year	旅客发送量 Passenger Departures	其中 of which 铁 路 Railway	公 路 Highway	港 口 Harbor	民用航空 Civil Aviation
1990	3 835	2 476	605	555	199
1995	5 265	2 929	1 257	512	567
2000	6 893	2 980	2 482	539	892
2001	6 324	3 231	1 508	543	1 042
2002	7 326	3 518	2 046	526	1 236
2003	7 212	3 391	2 052	528	1 241
2004	8 968	4 076	2 465	621	1 806
2005	9 487	4 313	2 468	626	2 080
2006	9 619	4 458	2 784	68	2 309
2007	10 371	4 795	2 872	95	2 609
2008	10 927	5 343	2 934	89	2 565
2009	11 136	5 161	2 995	90	2 890
2010	13 456	6 095	3 634	85	3 642
2011	13 519	6 198	3 477	78	3 766
2012	14 547	6 758	3 748	66	3 974
2013	15 933	7 972	3 720	68	4 173
2014	17 560	9 194	3 754	90	4 522
2015	18 571	9 692	3 766	113	5 000

①2000 年前旅客发送量是专业运输部门的数字，2001 年开始改为跨省市旅客运输的行业统计数字。
②港口旅客发送量从 2006 年起口径不包含海港到内河部分。
❶The passenger departures volume before 2000 is based on the figures for special traffic departments and the volume since 2001 is based on the figures for the inter-provincial passenger transport industries.
❷The Volume of Passenger Departures excludes those from seaports to freshwater since 2006.

表 15.4 主要年份旅客周转量
TURNOVER VOLUME OF PASSENGER TRAFFIC IN MAIN YEARS

单位:亿人·公里 (100 million persons·km)

年 份 Year	旅客周转量 Turnover Volume of Passenger Traffic	其中 of which 铁 路 Railway	公 路 Highway	水 运 Waterway	民用航空 Civil Aviation
1990	113.94	26.85	8.42	40.84	37.84
1995	170.98	34.18	8.23	31.71	96.86
2000	234.72	35.40	16.44	6.77	176.11
2001	286.93	37.81	42.31	5.48	201.30
2002	332.12	39.48	50.43	4.41	237.80
2003	353.62	38.10	58.00	4.65	252.88
2004	599.62	46.35	72.09	4.49	476.70
2005	663.93	48.86	75.06	4.52	535.48
2006	742.87	51.23	86.85	4.52	600.28
2007	883.25	51.34	94.02	6.10	731.79
2008	869.07	53.22	94.07	6.73	715.09
2009	1 002.59	51.12	99.57	6.38	845.52
2010	1 214.25	60.16	115.44	3.69	1 034.96
2011	1 307.56	63.11	106.74	1.02	1 136.69
2012	1 223.05	68.38	112.72	0.99	1 040.97
2013	1 343.73	75.26	108.71	0.82	1 158.95
2014	1 427.10	84.46	124.34	1.04	1 217.26
2015	1 661.03	88.95	125.45	0.81	1 445.81

表 15.5 主要年份货物运输量
FREIGHT TRAFFIC VOLUME IN MAIN YEARS

单位:万吨(10 000 tons)

年 份 Year	货物运输量 Freight Traffic Volume	其 中 of which				
		铁 路 Railway	公 路 Highway	水 运 Waterway	其 中 of which #远洋运输 Ocean Shipping	民用航空 Civil Aviation
1990	22 848	1 257	8 714	12 864	2 246	13
1995	22 531	1 376	6 273	14 845	2 778	37
2000	47 954	1 055	28 369	18 442	7 022	88
2001	49 545	1 080	28 869	19 496	7 129	100
2002	54 196	1 131	29 759	23 174	7 210	132
2003	58 669	1 208	30 678	26 621	7 832	162
2004	63 180	1 284	31 554	30 148	8 603	194
2005	68 741	1 278	32 684	34 557	10 091	222
2006	72 617	1 223	33 799	37 342	11 766	253
2007	78 108	1 143	35 634	41 041	12 575	290
2008	84 347	1 012	40 328	42 729	12 197	305
2009	76 967	941	37 745	37 983	11 916	298
2010	81 023	959	40 890	38 803	15 172	371
2011	93 318	888	42 685	49 389	16 044	356
2012	94 376	825	42 911	50 302	17 491	338
2013	91 535	694	43 809	46 697	15 255	335
2014	90 341	549	42 848	46 583	16 541	361
2015	91 239	471	40 627	49 770	18 145	371

①2005 年起，民航货物吞吐量不包括旅客行李。
②2008 年，公路货运量为交通部公路运输专项调查数据。
❶The Freight Traffic Volume of Civil Aviation in 2005 doesn't include the freight transportation volume.
❷The Highway Freight Traffic Volume of 2008 refers to the result of highway transportation special investigation hold by Ministry of Communications.

表 15.6 主要年份货物周转量
TURNOVER VOLUME OF FREIGHT TRAFFIC IN MAIN YEARS

单位:亿吨·公里(100 million tons·km)

年 份 Year	货物周转量 Turnover Volume of Freight Traffic	其 中 of which				
		铁 路 Railway	公 路 Highway	水 运 Waterway	其 中 of which #远洋运输 Ocean Shipping	民用航空 Civil Aviation
1990	3 359	111	11	3 236	1 957	1
1995	4 187	143	9	4 030	2 259	5
2000	6 620	122	56	6 430	5 285	12
2001	6 992	113	60	6 808	5 511	11
2002	7 472	100	65	7 295	5 674	12
2003	8 587	118	69	8 385	6 376	15
2004	10 036	42	71	9 899	7 486	24
2005	12 132	47	73	11 986	9 285	27
2006	13 837	55	80	13 683	10 817	19
2007	15 949	35	85	15 789	12 039	40
2008	16 031	29	253	15 712	11 529	37
2009	14 436	25	244	14 118	10 596	49
2010	16 173	26	266	15 818	14 535	63
2011	20 367	21	284	20 005	15 654	57
2012	20 427	18	288	20 067	16 086	54
2013	17 868	14	299	17 497	13 562	57
2014	18 691	12	301	18 320	14 487	57
2015	19 553	11	290	19 196	15 150	57

①2004 年起，上海铁路分局改为上海铁路局，货物周转量数据有所调整。
②2006 年民航货物周转量未包括中国货运航空公司的数据。
③2008 年，公路货物周转量为交通部公路运输专项调查数据。
❶Since 2004, Shanghai Railway Branch Bureau has been change into Shanghai Railway Bureau ,the Turnover Volume of Freight has been adjusted accordingly.
❷In 2006,the date of China Cargo Airlines wasn't included in the Turnover Volume of Freight of Aviation .
❸The Highway Freight Turnover Volume of 2008 refers to the result of highway transportation special investigation hold by Ministry of Communications.

表 15.7 主要年份港口码头情况
PORTS IN MAIN YEARS

年份 Year	沿海码头长度（万米） Length of Harbor (10 000 m)	沿海泊位（个） Berths (unit)	其中 of which #万吨级 10 000 Tonnage	其中 of which #集装箱泊位 Container Berths
1990	1.77	122	64	7
1995	1.90	140	68	12
2000	7.64	1 098	111	18
2001	7.67	1 087	112	18
2002	7.92	1 096	115	20
2003	8.76	1 202	125	24
2004	8.90	1 198	123	24
2005	8.95	1 181	124	28
2006	9.16	1 140	131	32
2007	10.15	1 155	133	37
2008	11.49	1 203	137	42
2009	11.68	1 145	153	38
2010	11.92	1 218	157	45
2011	11.97	1 226	160	43
2012	12.29	1 245	162	43
2013	12.40	1 253	170	43
2014	12.60	1 282	170	42
2015	12.69	1 300	174	42

注：1997 年以前，沿海码头长度、沿海泊位为原港务局数据，从 1998 年后，为全港数据。
Note: Before 1997, the figures of length of harbor and berths were from the ports belonged to Port Administration Bureau, and after 1998, data have been collected from all types of ports.

表 15.8 主要年份港口货物吞吐量
PORT FREIGHT THROUGHPUT IN MAIN YEARS

单位：万吨（10 000 tons）

年份 Year	港口货物吞吐量 Port freight Throughput	其中 of which 内贸 Internal Trade	其中 of which 外贸 Foreign Trade	进港 Arrival	其中 of which 内贸 Internal Trade	其中 of which 外贸 Foreign Trade	出港 Departure	其中 of which 内贸 Internal Trade	其中 of which 外贸 Foreign Trade
1990	13 959	11 366	2 593	9 461	7 592	1 869	4 498	3 774	724
1995	16 567	12 481	4 086	12 097	9 492	2 605	4 470	2 989	1 481
2000	20 440	12 807	7 633	13 791	9 242	4 549	6 649	3 565	3 084
2001	22 099	13 446	8 653	14 922	9 706	5 216	7 177	3 740	3 437
2002	26 384	15 776	10 609	17 444	11 096	6 349	8 940	4 680	4 260
2003	31 621	18 653	12 968	20 606	12 999	7 607	11 015	5 654	5 361
2004	37 897	22 061	15 836	24 113	15 022	9 091	13 784	7 039	6 745
2005	44 317	25 825	18 492	27 539	17 441	10 098	16 778	8 384	8 394
2006	53 748	32 480	21 268	34 600	23 613	10 987	19 148	8 867	10 281
2007	56 144	30 574	25 570	35 479	22 619	12 860	20 665	7 956	12 709
2008	58 170	30 793	27 377	36 481	22 782	13 699	21 689	8 012	13 677
2009	59 205	33 394	25 811	39 000	24 920	14 080	20 205	8 474	11 731
2010	65 339	35 114	30 225	41 549	25 083	16 466	23 791	10 032	13 759
2011	72 758	38 980	33 778	45 525	27 173	18 352	27 233	11 807	15 426
2012	73 559	37 734	35 825	45 151	25 233	19 918	28 408	12 501	15 907
2013	77 575	39 869	37 706	46 978	25 657	21 321	30 597	14 213	16 384
2014	75 529	37 297	38 232	44 663	23 654	21 009	30 866	13 643	17 223
2015	71 740	33 943	37 797	41 907	21 447	20 460	29 833	12 495	17 337

表 15.9 主要年份国际集装箱吞吐量(按进出港分)
INTERNATIONAL CONTAINERS AND CARGO THROUGHPUT OF FOREIGN TRADE IN MAIN YEARS

年份 Year	国际标准集装箱吞吐量重量(万吨) Weight of International Containers (10 000 tons)	国际标准集装箱吞吐量(万 TEU) International Containers (10 000 TEU)	其中 of which	
			进港 Input	出港 Output
1990	446	45.6	22.4	23.2
1995	1 389	152.6	69.3	83.3
1996	1 785	197.1	92.4	104.7
1997	2 304	252.8	114.7	138.1
1998	2 766	306.6	141.1	165.5
1999	3 949	421.6	196.7	224.9
2000	5 170	561.2	266.1	295.1
2001	5 911	634.0	305.4	328.6
2002	7 822	861.2	414.1	447.1
2003	10 225	1 128.3	544.4	583.8
2004	13 294	1 455.4	699.6	755.8
2005	16 250	1 808.4	887.2	921.3
2006	19 595	2 171.9	1 064.4	1 107.5
2007	23 850	2 615.2	1 276.3	1 338.9
2008	25 992	2 800.6	1 397.8	1 402.8
2009	24 619	2 500.2	1 222.9	1 277.3
2010	27 992	2 906.9	1 436.1	1 470.8
2011	31 220	3 173.9	1 555.1	1 618.9
2012	32 480	3 252.9	1 605.1	1 647.9
2013	34 243	3 361.7	1 652.2	1 709.5
2014	35 335	3 528.5	1 732.3	1 796.2
2015	35 850	3 653.7	1 818.7	1 835.0

注：TEU 是"折合 20 英尺标准箱"英文缩写语。
Note: TEU is the abbreviation, which refers to 20-foot equivalent unit.

表 15.10 邮轮经济发展情况(2012~2015)
CRUISE ECONOMIC DEVELOPMENT

指标	Indicators	2012	2013	2014	2015
邮轮靠泊次数(次)	Cruise Berthing Times (time)	180	197	269	341
# 以上海为母港靠泊次数	Homeport in Shanghai	128	167	240	317
邮轮旅客吞吐量(万人)	Cruise Passenger Throughput (10 000 persons)	35.03	75.66	121.52	164.26
# 以上海为母港吞吐量	Homeport in Shanghai	25.58	69.79	115.11	159.53

表 15.11 经营性停车场(库)营运情况(2012~2015)
STATISTICS OF PARKING LOTS (GARAGES) OPERATION

指 标	Indicators	2012	2013	2014	2015
计时停放(万辆次)	Time Parking (10 000 vehicletimes)	11 259.06	13 004.48	14 837.51	16 969.32
包月停放(万辆次)	Monthly Parking (10 000 vehicletimes)	4 340.44	5 120.81	5 669.41	6 237.96
车辆停放车次合计(万辆次)	Quantity of Parking Times (10 000 vehicletimes)	17 231.21	20 638.73	23 814.56	27 715.88
经营车辆停放收入(亿元)	Revenue of Parking Lots (100 million yuan)	14.92	17.83	21.05	23.17

表 15.12 民用车辆拥有量(2012~2015)
CIVIL MOTOR VEHICLES

单位:万辆(10 000 vehicles)

指 标	Indicators	2012	2013	2014	2015
总 计	**Total**	**260.90**	**282.46**	**304.45**	**332.35**
#汽 车	Civil Automobile	212.86	235.10	255.19	282.32
载客汽车	Passenger Vehicles	185.71	207.99	228.58	256.26
#轿 车	Cars	140.20	155.82	170.26	187.28
载货汽车	Freight Trucks	20.73	20.14	19.56	19.49
其他汽车	Other Automobile	6.41	6.97	7.05	6.57
摩托车	Motorcycle	42.53	41.48	42.52	42.90
拖拉机	Tractors	1.09	1.05	1.05	1.05

①本表不包括军用车辆和码头、机场等专用特种车辆。
②从 2012 年起，民用车辆拥有量的数据不含强制报废量(下表同)。
❶This table doesn't include the quantity of military vehicles and special vehicles for port and airport.
❷Since 2012, the civil vehicle ownership data does not contain mandatory retirement amount (the same as the following table).

表 15.13 个人民用车辆拥有量(2012~2015)
INDIVIDUAL CIVIL MOTOR VEHICLES

单位:万辆(10 000 vehicles)

指 标	Indicators	2012	2013	2014	2015
总 计	**Total**	**182.57**	**203.64**	**224.75**	**250.51**
#汽 车	Civil Automobile	141.32	163.38	183.43	208.71
载客汽车	Passenger Vehicles	140.84	162.88	182.81	208.22
#轿 车	Cars	114.58	130.46	144.98	161.98
载货汽车	Freight Trucks	0.25	0.21	0.28	0.25
其它汽车	Other Automobile	0.23	0.29	0.34	0.24
摩托车	Motorcycle	41.23	40.23	41.27	41.74

表 15.14 邮政电信主要指标(2012 ~2015)
MAIN INDICATORS OF POST AND TELECOMMUNICATION

指 标	Indicators	2012	2013	2014	2015
邮电局、所(个)	Post Office (unit)	541	544	537	537
报刊图书销售点(个)	Publications Sales Outlet (unit)	1 659	1 606	1 476	1 428
邮政信筒信箱(个)	Mail Boxe (unit)	3 363	3 210	3 169	2 997
集邮品销售点(个)	Stamps Sales Outlet (unit)	195	226	199	220
邮政储蓄网点(个)	Postal Savings Office (unit)	370	370	372	378
邮路条数(条)	Number of Mail Route (route)	685	604	589	496
邮路总长度(万公里)	Total Length of Mail Routes (10 000 km)	6.39	7.13	7.73	6.01
农村投递路线总长度(万公里)	Length of Rural Delivery Routes (10 000 km)	2.27	2.24	1.72	0.11
长途业务电路(2M)	Long-distance Line (2M)	3 884 451	5 077 494	5 979 616	6 476 603

注：由于邮政速递物流公司成立，邮政公司的部分基础设施被拨出。
Note: The part of post infrastructure are transferred from Shanghai Post Corporation to newly established Shanghai Post Express and Logistics Corporation.

表 15.15 主要年份邮政业务主要指标
MAJOR INDICATORS OF POSTAL BUSINESS IN MAIN YEARS

指 标	Indicators	2000	2010	2014	2015
邮政业务总量(亿元)	Volume of Postal Business (100 million yuan)	22.40	49.48	310.53	385.75
函 件(亿件)	Mails (100 million units)	4.61	11.66	11.03	9.07
国内特快专递(万件)	Domestic Express Mails (10 000 pieces)	709.90	25 708.85	123 575.38	165 778.25
国际及港澳台特快专递(万件)	International and Hong Kong、Macao and Taiwan Express Mails (10 000 pieces)	52.10	3 088.01	4 790.72	4 999.71
邮政储蓄期末余额(亿元)	Postal Saving Deposit Balance (100 million yuan)	153.50	545.64	850.10	812.25
报纸、杂志累计订销数(亿份)	Total Copies of Newspapers and Magazines Subscribed and Sold (100 million pieces)	11.30	11.99	10.17	9.77
集邮业务(万枚)	Stamp Collection Business (10 000 stamps)	9 467	5 156	6 559	7 684

注：2012 年起，"邮政业务总量"包括国家邮政业务总量和非国家邮政业务总量。
Note: Since 2012, Volume of Postal Business Contains Volume of National Postal business and Volume of Non-national Postal-business.

表 15.16 主要年份电信业务主要指标
MAJOR INDICATORS OF TELECOM BUSINESS IN MAIN YEARS

指标	Indicators	2005	2010	2014	2015
电信业务总量(亿元)	Volume of Telecom Business (100 million yuan)	375.77	966.96	596.99	780.32
年末固定电话用户（万户）	Year-end Installed Telephones (10 000 households)	966.70	935.91	840.18	797.29
#住宅电话	Household Phones Installed	685.00	574.52	484.17	461.52
移动电话用户（万户）	Mobile Phone Subscribers Users (10 000 households)	1 444.20	2 361.55	3 292.74	3 259.93
#3G 及 4G 移动电话用户	3G and 4G Mobile Phone Users		197.32	1 664.15	2 211.28
长途通话时长（亿分钟）	Long-distance Call Lasting Time (100 million minutes)	110.10	205.77	254.65	243.95
固定电话长途通话时长	Installed Telephone Domestic Long-distance Call Lasting Time	31.20	38.84	43.88	39.83
国内长途电话通话时长	Domestic Trunk Calls	29.90	36.67	41.26	37.82
国际及港澳台电话通话时长	Overseas Calls	1.30	2.17	2.62	2.01
移动电话长途通话时长	Mobile Telephone Long-distance Call Lasting Time	19.60	37.37	210.77	204.12
国内长途电话通话时长	Domestic Trunk Calls	18.70	36.00	208.19	202.25
国际及港澳台电话通话时长	Overseas Calls	0.90	1.37	2.58	1.87
固定电话通话时长(亿分钟)	Installed Telephone Call Lasting Time	541.75	340.05	223.08	193.36
移动电话通话时长（亿分钟）	Mobile Calls (100 million minutes)	290.10	1 012.39	1 286.81	1 238.20
移动短信业务量(亿条)	Volume of Mobile Short Messages (100 million pieces)	180.60	371.54	221.93	211.86
局用交换机容量（含接入网设备容量）（万门）	Capacity of Office Telephone Exchanges(Including Access Network Capacity) (10 000 units)	1 357.00	1 338.61	1 225.56	1 200.47
移动电话交换机容量(万户)	Mobile Phone Exchange Capacity (10 000 households)	1 991	3 995	4 228	4 424
互联网网民数(万人)	Internet Netizen(10 000 persons)	463	1 239	1 716	1 773
互联网普及率(%)	Popularization Rate of Internet(%)	26.6	64.5	71.1	73.1
固定互联网宽带接入用户(万户)	Fixed Broadband Internet Access Users (10 000 households)	224.4	545.0	672.3	695.3
移动互联网用户(万户)	Mobile Internet Users (10 000 households)	503.6	1 355.0	2 562.7	2 569.3
移动互联网接入流量(万 G)	Mobile Internet Access Traffic (10 000G)		1 115.1	5 829.1	10 684.0

注：2010 年起，固定互联网宽带接入用户的统计口径从基础电信企业的用户调整为所有宽带驻地网企业的用户。
Note: The Indicator Fixed Broadband Internet Access Users was calculated by all local business users since 2010.

表 15.17 主要年份邮电通信水平
POSTAL AND TELECOM LEVEL IN MAIN YEARS

指标	Indicators	2005	2010	2014	2015
固定电话普及率（%）	Popularity Rate of Telephone Line (%)	51.1	40.6	34.6	33.0
住宅电话普及率（%）	Popularity Rate of Household Telephone (%)	137.9	110.6	90.9	86.0
移动电话普及率(%)	Popularity Rate of Mobile Telephone (%)	76.4	102.6	135.7	135.0
平均每一邮政局所服务面积（平方公里）	Average Area Served by One Post Office (sq. km)	10.00	10.69	11.81	11.81
平均每一邮政局所服务人口(万人)	Average Population Served by Every Post Office (10 000 persons)	2.99	3.86	4.52	4.50
人均每年发函件数(件)	Average Number of Letters Mailed (piece)	52.00	50.89	45.47	37.56
人均每年购报刊数(份)	Average Number of Newspaper and Magazine Purchased (piece)	65.00	50.50	41.93	40.46

注：固定电话普及率及移动电话普及率为根据第六次人口普查调整后的数据。
Note: Data of Popularity Rate of Telephone Line and Popularity Rate of Mobile Telephone have been adjusted according to the sixth census.

表 15.18 主要年份信息化基础设施情况
INFRASTRUCTURE OF INFORMATIZATION IN MAIN YEARS

指标	Indicators	2005	2010	2014	2015
信息通信管线长度（沟公里）	Length of Information Communication Pielines (channel km)	1 621	5 821	8 860	9 975
家庭宽带接入用户(万户)	Household Users of broadband access (10 000 households)	223	440	600	620
家庭宽带接入用户普及率(%)	Household Users of broadband access per hundred household (%)	31.8	51.6	69.7	75.2
IPTV 用户(万户)	IPTV Users (10 000 households)		130	200	177
有线数字电视用户(万户)	Digital Cable TV Users (10 000 households)		220	604	662

①互联网用户普及率和家庭宽带接入用户普及率为根据第六次人口普查调整后的数据。
②2013 年起，家庭宽带接入用户及普及率的统计口径从基础电信企业的用户调整为所有宽带驻地网企业的用户。
❶Data of Users of Internet per Thousand People and Household Users of Broadband Access per Hundred Household have been adjusted according to the sixth census.
❷The Indicator "Household Users of broadband access per hundred household" was calculated by all local business users since 2013.

表 15.19 主要年份信息服务业经营情况
OPERATION OF INFORMATION SERVICE INDUSTRY IN MAIN YEARS

指 标	Indicators	2005	2010	2014	2015
信息服务业经营收入(亿元)	Operating Revenue of Information Service Industry (100 million yuan)	905.06	1 978.51	3 726.03	4 069.00
#软件和信息技术服务业	Computer Service & Software Industry	390.09	1 145.10	2 501.45	2 775.73
信息服务业从业人员(万人)	Employees of Information Service Industry (10 000 persons)	18.81	31.20	49.14	49.70
#软件和信息技术服务业	Computer Service & Software Industry	12.70	23.25	38.39	39.33

注：2012 年起，软件和信息技术服务业为根据国民经济行业分类(GB/T 4754 - 2011)统计的行业数据。 表中其他年份根据国民经济行业分类(GB/T 4754 - 2002)统计。

Note: Since 2012, industry data on software and information technology services are according to National industry classification (GB/T 4754-2011), data before 2012 are according to National industry classification (GB/T 4754-2002).

表 15.20 信息技术应用(2012 ~2015)
APPLICATION OF INFORMATION TECHNOLOGY

指 标	Indicators	2012	2013	2014	2015
社会公共服务领域信息化	**Informatization of Public Service**				
"市民信箱"累计注册用户(万人)	Accumulative Registered Users of Citizen Mail Box(10 000 persons)	416.76	427.00	452.40	483.10
交通卡销售额(亿元)	All-year Sales Value of Traffic Card (100 million yuan)	14.39	13.09	11.33	8.49
银行卡累计发卡量(万张)	Accumulative Volum of Bank Card (10 000 pieces)	14 207.38	16 556.26	17 932.02	18 741.58
银行卡交易额(亿元)	All-year Exchange Value of Bank Card (100 million yuan)	16 608.12	21 403.08	24 217.35	28 754.00
#持卡消费金额	Consumption Value with Bank Card	8 843.11	12 072.26	23 300.00	20 102.00

上/海/统/计/年/鉴

主要统计指标解释

铁路运营里程

铁路运营里程又称营业长度(包括正式营业和临时营业里程),指办理客货运输业务的铁路正线总长度。凡是全线或部分建成双线及以上的线路,以第一线的实际长度计算;复线、站线、段管线、岔线和特殊用途线以及不计算运费的联络线都不计算营业里程。铁路营业里程是反映铁路运输业基础设施发展水平的重要指标,也是计算客货周转量、运输密度和机车车辆运用效率等指标的基础资料。

内河航道里程

内河航道里程也称内河通航里程,指在一定时期内,能通航运输船舶及排筏的天然河流、湖泊水库、运河及通航渠道的长度。包括全年季节性通航累计三个月以上的航道,不包括仅供零散流放竹、木排的河道。该指标可以反映内河水运网的规模、水平和发展情况。

货物(旅客)周转量

指在一定时期内,由各种运输工具运送的货物(旅客)数量与其相应运输距离的乘积之总和,是反映运输业生产总成果的重要指标,也是编制和检查运输生产计划,计算运输效益、劳动生产率以及核算运输单位成本的主要基础资料。通常以吨公里和人公里为计算单位。计算货物周转量通常按发出站与到达站之间的最短距离,也就是计费距离计算。

货(客)运量

指在一定时期内,各种运输工具实际运送的货物(旅客)数量。它是反映运输业为国民经济和人民生活服务的数量指标,也是制定和检查运输生产计划、研究运输发展规模和速度的重要指标。货运按吨计算,客运按人计算。货物不论运输距离长短、货物类别,均按实际重量统计。旅客不论行程远近或票价多少,均按一人一次客运量统计;半价票、小孩票也按一人统计。

港口货物吞吐量

指经由水路进出港区范围,并经过装卸的货物数量。按货物流向分为进港吞吐量和出港吞吐量,按货物贸易性质分为内贸和外贸吞吐量。按货物的类别分,可根据现行的交通行业标准《运输货物分类和代码》分类。

国际标准集装箱吞吐量

凡经过水运进出港区范围,并经过装卸的集装箱箱数和重量(含集装箱自重),通常是按进港和出港分别统计。

TEU 是"折合 20 英尺标准箱"的英文缩写。它是指各种尺寸的国际标准集装箱的自然箱数,按各自的换算比例,折算为 20 英尺标准箱的换算箱数。其换算比例为:40 英尺箱 1∶2;35 英尺箱 1∶1.75;20 英尺箱 1∶1;10 英尺箱 1∶0.5。

民用车辆拥有量

指报告期末,在公安交通管理部门按照《机动车注册登记工作规范》,已注册登记领有民用车辆牌照的全部汽车数量。汽车拥有量统计的主要分类:根据汽车结构分为载客汽车、载货汽车及其他汽车;根据汽车所有者不同分为个人(私人)汽车、单位汽车;根据汽车的使用性质分为营运汽车、非营运汽车和特种汽车;根据汽车大小规格不同载客汽车分为大型、中型、小型和微型,载货汽车分为重型、中型、轻型和微型。

邮政业务总量

指以货币表现的邮政部门用于邮政服务的总数量。它综合反映了一定时期邮政工作的总成果,是研究邮政业务量构成和发展趋势的重要指标。它用各种邮政分类业务量,如函件件数、电报份数、订销报刊累计份数等,分别乘以相应的平均单位(不变价),加总后再加上其他业务收入求得。

住宅电话用户

指安装在居民住宅或农民家里并按照住宅电话用户登记注册和收费的电话用户。包括私人付费、单位付费和按规定免费安装的住宅电话用户。

主要统计指标解释

移动电话用户

指通过移动电话交换机进入移动电话网、占用移动电话号码的电话用户。用户数量以报告期末在移动电话营业部门实际办理登记手续进入移动电话网的户数进行计算,一部移动电话统计为一户。

局用交换机容量

指安装在电信企业用于接续本地固定电话的电话交换机容量。

电信业务总量

是指以货币形式表示的电信企业为社会提供的各类电信服务的总数量。包括固定话音业务总量、固定数据及互联网业务总量、固定增值及其他业务总量、移动话音业务总量、移动数据及互联网业务总量、移动增值及其他业务总量。

长途业务电路

是指报告期末固定电话网、移动电话网和各类数据通信网内为疏通长途业务开放使用的长途电路。

SHANGHAI STATISTICAL YEARBOOK

EXPLANATORY NOTES TO MAJOR STATISTICAL INDICATORS

□ Operation Mileage of Railways

Operation Mileage of Railways refers to the total length of the trunk line under passenger and freight transportation (including both full operation and temporary operation). The calculation is based on the actual length of the first line even if this line has a full or partial double track or more tracks, excluding double tracks, station sidings, tracks under the charge of stations, branch lines, special-purpose lines and the non-payable connecting lines. The length of railways in operation is an important indicator to show the development of the infrastructure for the railway transport, and also the essential data to calculate volume of passenger freight transport, traffic density and utilization efficiency of the locomotives and carriages.

□ Length of Navigable Inland Waterways

Length of Navigable Inland Waterways it is an indicator reflecting the size and development of inland water network, it refers to the length of the natural rivers, lakes, reservoirs, canals, and ditches open to navigation during a given period, which enables the transport by ships and rafts. It includes the channels open to navigation for over an accumulative 3 months in a year, yet this does not include the river courses, which are only used to float odd logs and bamboo rafts. This indicator can reflect the scale, level and development situation of the inland waterway network.

□ Freight (Passenger) Turnover Volume

Freight (Passenger) Turnover Volume refers to the total of the product of the physical volume of transported cargo (passenger) by the transport distance, usually using ton/kilometer and person/kilometer as calculating units. Normally, the shortest distance between the departure point and the destination is the basis to calculate the freight turnover volume, that is to say, the payable distance. This is an important indicator to show the total results of the transport industry, to prepare and examine the transport plan and to measure the efficiency, the labor productivity and the unit cost of transport.

□ Freight (Passenger) Traffic

Freight (Passenger) Traffic refers to the volume of freight (passenger) transported with various means. The freight (passenger) traffic provides a quantitative measure to show how the transport industry serves the national economy and people, and is also an important indicator for planning the transport industry and for studying the development scale and speed of the transport industry. Freight transport is calculated in tons and passenger traffic is calculated in the number of persons. Despite the type of freight and travelling distance, the freight transport is calculated in the actual weight of the goods: and despite the travelling distance and ticket price, the passenger traffic is calculated by the principle that one person can be counted only once in one travel. The passenger who travels with a half price ticket or a child ticket is also calculated as one person.

□ Volume of Freight Handled in Ports

Volume of Freight Handled in Ports refers to the volume of cargo passing in and out of the harbour area of the major coastal ports and having been loaded and unloaded. The volume of freight handled may be classified by direction of flow as freight for import and freight for export, or by nature of cargo as freight for domestic trade and freight for foreign trade. The volume of freight handled maybe classified by the classification of cargo, or the current transport standard of The Classification and Code of Cargo Type.

□ International Container Throughput Capacity

International Container Throughput Capacity refers to number and weight of containers which are loaded or unloaded within port area via water carriage. It is often calculated by entering and leaving port, respectively. TEU was the abbreviation of twenty foot equivalent unit, which refers to converted number of all kinds of containers. The conversion method is based on respective conversion ratio and the number of all kinds of container is converted to the standard number of twenty foot equivalent unit. The conversion ratio is: 40 feet container 1 ∶ 2, 35 feet container 1 ∶ 1.75, 20 feet container 1 ∶ 1, 10 feet container 1 ∶ 0.5.

□ Individual Civil Motor Vehicles

Individual Civil Motor Vehicles refers to the total numbers of vehicles that are registered and received vehicles' license tags according to the Work Standard for Motor Vehicles Registration formulated by transport management office under department of

EXPLANATORY NOTES TO MAJOR STATISTICAL INDICATORS

public security at the end of reference period. They are divided into following categories according to the structure of motor vehicles: passenger vehicles, trucks and others; and private vehicles and vehicles for units use according to ownerships; working vehicles, non-working vehicles and special motor vehicles according to kind of usage; large passenger vehicles, medium passenger vehicles and small passenger vehicles, heavy trucks, light -heavy trucks and light trucks according to sizes of vehicles.

□ Volume of Post Business

Volume of Post Business refers to the total amount of post services provided by the post department, which reflects the total achievements by the post departments during a given period of time in a comprehensive way, and is an important indicator to study the composition and development of the post business. It is arrived by first multiplying the business volume of different types, such as number of letters, telegrams and accumulated number of newspaper and journals subscribed and sold, etc. by their respective average unit price (fixed price) and then adding these products together, plus the income from other business revenues.

□ Household Telephone Subscribers

Household Telephone Subscribers refer to telephone sets installed in the dwelling units of urban or rural residents, and registered as residence subscribers for payment, including 3 types of payment for the service: private payment, public payment and free service.

□ Mobile Phone Subscribers

Mobile Phone Subscribers refer to the persons who own mobile telephone numbers and are connected with the mobile telephone communication network through the mobile telephone switchboards. The number of subscribers is calculated by the subscribers who have completed registration at mobile communication business centers and entered into the mobile telephone network. One mobile telephone is taken as a user.

□ Capacity of Office Telephone Exchanges

Capacity of Office Telephone Exchanges refers to the capacity of telephone exchanges installed in the office of telecommunication service providers for communication between fixed telephones.

□ Total Amount of Telecommunication Services

Total Amount of Telecommunication Services refers to the total amount of various types of telecommunications services in the form of money provided by telecommunications companies for society. It includes the total amount of fixed voice services, fixed data and Internet services, fixed value-added business and other services, mobile voice services, mobile data and internet services, mobile value-added business and other services.

□ Long-distance Service Circuit

Long-distance Service Circuit refers to the long-distance circuit within fixed telephone networks, mobile telephone networks and all kinds of data communication networks, which is available for dredging long-distance business at the end of reporting period.

第十六篇
CHAPTER 16

批发、零售和住宿、餐饮
WHOLESALE AND RETAIL, HOTELS AND CATERING SERVICES

简要说明

一、本章资料的主要内容

本篇资料主要反映上海市批发和零售业、住宿和餐饮业的发展与经营状况，同时反映国内商品流通、商品消费、市场运行态势。主要内容包括:限额以上批发和零售业产业活动单位和从业人员、商品流转情况、财务状况;限额以上住宿餐饮业产业活动单位和从业人员、经营状况、财务状况;连锁经营情况;商品交易市场成交情况;社会消费品零售总额;商品销售总额等。

二、本篇资料的统计范围

批发和零售业、住宿和餐饮业的法人企业、产业活动单位、个体户,零售业、住宿和餐饮业连锁集团,商品交易市场。

三、本篇的资料来源

本篇资料是根据《批发和零售业统计报表制度》、《住宿和餐饮业统计报表制度》进行搜集和加工整理而得。

四、本篇的统计调查方法

本篇资料中限额以上批发和零售业、住宿和餐饮业法人企业、个体户、其他行业附营的限额以上批发和零售业、住宿和餐饮业产业活动单位资料,以及零售业、住宿和餐饮业连锁集团,商品交易市场采用全面调查的方法;限额以下企业及个体户等资料采用抽样调查方法推算。

BRIEF INTRODUCTION

I. Main Contents

Data in this chapter reflect the development and operation of Shanghai's wholesale and retail trade, hotels and catering service. Data also reflect domestic commodity circulation, consumption, and market operation. Main contents include the basic conditions, employment, circulation of commodities, and financial status of wholesale and retail trades above the set scale; basic conditions, employment, business situation, and financial status of hotels and catering services above the set scale; chain business conditions, transactions of commodities market, retail sales of main consumer goods, and total sales of consumer goods.

II. Scope of Statistics

Included in this chapter are the registered enterprises and self–employed individuals of wholesale and retail trade, hotels and catering service; chain enterprises in retail, hotels, and catering businesses; and commodities markets.

III. Sources of Data

Data in this chapter are collected and processed in accordance with The Statistical Reporting Form System on Wholesale and Retail Trades and The Statistical Reporting Form System on Hotel and Catering.

IV. Survey Methodology

Data on basic conditions for all corporate enterprises and self–employed individuals above the set scale of whole–sale and retail trades, hotel, and catering businesses; affiliating establishments above the set scale of other industries involved in the wholesale and retail trades, hotels and catering businesses; chain enterprises of wholesale and retail trades; and commodities markets data are collected through comprehensive reporting system. Data on enterprises and self–employed individuals below the set scale are collected by sample surveys.

表 16.1 批发和零售业、住宿和餐饮业从业人员(1978～2015)
EMPLOYEES OF WHOLESALE AND RETAIL, HOTELS AND CATERING SERVICES

单位:万人(10 000 persons)

年 份 Year	从业人员 Employees	其 中 of which				
		批发零售贸易业 Wholesale and Retail	其 中 of which		餐饮业 Catering	住宿业 Hotels
			批发业 Wholesale	零售业 Retail		
1978	39.62	30.70	5.46	25.24	5.57	
1979	44.70	32.94	7.87	25.07	5.82	
1980	45.78	33.94	7.91	26.03	5.66	
1981	48.47	35.31	8.41	26.90	6.25	
1982	50.24	36.70	9.05	27.65	6.51	
1983	51.30	37.64	8.86	28.78	6.51	
1984	55.24	40.57	8.81	31.76	6.86	
1985	62.64	45.41	8.99	36.42	7.66	
1986	63.76	44.98	8.96	36.02	7.97	
1987	66.13	45.98	8.85	37.13	8.18	
1988	72.80	50.89	9.42	41.47	8.67	
1989	77.31	52.20	9.67	42.53	9.35	
1990	74.75	50.48	8.19	42.29	9.33	
1991	75.41	52.47	8.53	43.94	10.71	
1992	87.27	63.71	13.74	49.97	10.98	
1993	109.98	98.44	29.68	68.76	11.54	
1994	88.51	77.49	27.58	49.91	11.02	
1995	111.24	94.78	34.31	60.47	16.46	
1996	145.67	122.21	50.79	71.42	23.46	
1997	149.97	125.64	53.68	71.96	24.33	
1998	150.96	126.56	53.67	72.89	24.40	
1999	153.90	128.18	53.93	74.25	25.72	
2000	154.32	128.41	53.79	74.62	25.91	
2001	165.68	138.73	56.33	82.40	26.95	
2002	179.34	152.19	65.40	86.79	27.15	
2003	174.93	147.91	59.31	88.60	27.02	
2004	181.25	156.21	74.77	81.44	25.04	
2005	195.92	169.60	84.71	84.89	26.32	
2006	203.51	174.49	86.32	88.17	29.02	
2007	204.46	175.50	86.23	89.27	28.96	
2008	202.84	172.72	87.98	84.74	30.12	
2009	205.49	175.32	90.36	84.96	30.17	
2010	207.94	176.69	91.58	85.21	31.25	
2011	215.57	184.61	96.96	87.65	30.96	
2012	226.70	194.28	104.33	89.95	32.42	
2013	230.26	194.91	106.98	87.93	35.35	
2014	286.99	235.52				51.47
2015	290.22	238.31				51.91

注：本表从业人员是指本行业的全部从业人员，包含个体户及非正规就业等。由于统计制度方法调整，2014 年起本表从业人员由批发零售业、住宿餐饮业两部分组成。

Note: Employees in this table refer to all the employees in the sector, including self-employed and informal employees. Because of the adjustment of statistical method for statistics, since 2014, employees in this table include the employees in the sector of whole and retail, commodation and catering.

表 16.2 限额以上批发贸易业产业活动单位和从业人员（2015）
QUANTITY OF BUSINESS UNITS AND EMPLOYEES OF WHOLESALE TRADE ABOVE THE SET SCALE

类 别	Types	法人企业（个）Quantity of Corporations (unit)	产业活动单位数（个）Quantity of Business Units (unit)	从业人员（人）Quantity of Employees (person)
总 计	**Total**	**3 853**	**7 333**	**450 960**
按登记注册类型分	**Grouped by Registration Categories**			
内 资	Domestic Enterprises	2 467	4 102	164 475
国 有	State-owned	54	94	3 573
集 体	Collective-owned	11	22	396
股份合作	Share Holding Cooperative Enterprises	4	4	76
联 营	Joint-Owned Enterprises	4	4	739
有限责任公司	Companies with Limited Liabilities	758	1 461	68 798
股份有限公司	Share Holding Companies with Limited Liabilities	75	645	20 410
私 营	Private	1 556	1 866	70 248
其 他	Others	5	6	235
港澳台商投资	Hong Kong, Macao and Taiwan Funded	465	1 121	115 769
外商投资	Foreign Funded	921	2 110	170 716
按行业分	**Grouped By Sectors**			
农、林、牧产品批发	Agriculture, Forestry and Animal Husbandry Products	46	60	2 078
食品、饮料及烟草制品批发	Food, Beverage and Tabacco	289	1 219	54 336
# 米、面制品及食用油批发	Rice, Flour and Cooking Oil	54	110	9 319
烟草制品批发	Tabacco	24	415	6 329
纺织、服装及日用品批发	Textile Products, Garments and Commodity	559	1 385	142 781
# 服装批发	Garments	194	598	55 533
文化、体育用品及器材批发	Culture & Sports Articles and Equipments	122	190	15 009
医药及医疗器材批发	Medicines and Special Appliances of Medicines	179	360	49 689
矿产品、建材及化工产品批发	Mineral Products, Materials of Construction and Chemical Products	1 492	2 279	60 677
# 煤炭及制品批发	Coal	58	61	1 659
石油及制品批发	Petroleum	150	636	12 564
金属及金属矿批发	Metal Products and Metal Minerals	633	720	15 841
建材批发	Building Materials	101	131	3 595
机械设备、五金交电及电子产品批发	Mechinery Equipments, Hardwares, Electric Appliances and Eletronic Products	870	1 415	103 236
# 汽车批发	Automobiles	38	58	10 022
汽车零配件批发	Spare and Component Parts for Automobiles	92	124	9 027
电气设备批发	Electrical Equipment	59	86	8 165
计算机、软件及辅助设备批发	Computers, Softwares and Accessorial Equipments	75	95	8 307
贸易经纪与代理	Trade Broker and Agent	134	177	8 564
其他批发	Others	162	248	14 590

表 16.3 限额以上零售贸易业产业活动单位和从业人员（2015）
QUANTITY OF BUSINESS UNITS AND EMPLOYEES OF RETAIL TRADE ABOVE THE SET SCALE

类 别	Types	法人企业（个）Quantity of Corporations (unit)	产业活动单位数（个）Quantity of Business Units (unit)	从业人员（人）Quantity of Employees (person)
总 计	**Total**	**1 943**	**12 279**	**367 084**
按登记注册类型分	**Grouped by Registration Categories**			
内 资	Domestic Funded	1 662	8 882	205 741
国 有	State-owned	59	144	3 942
集 体	Collective-owned	32	102	1 434
股份合作	Share Holding Cooperative Enterprises	12	62	232
联 营	Joint-Owned Enterprises	25	27	360
有限责任公司	Companies with Limited Liabilities	667	5 253	109 030
股份有限公司	Share Holding Companies with Limited Liabilities	42	692	18 110
私 营	Private	816	2 569	71 948
其 他	Others	9	33	685
港澳台商投资	Hong Kong, Macao and Taiwan Funded	158	1 187	67 621
外商投资	Foreign Funded	123	2 210	93 722
按行业分	**Grouped By Sectors**			
综合零售	Comprehensive Retail Sale	267	5 162	123 297
#百货零售	Articles For Daily Use	123	274	26 459
超级市场零售	Retail Sale of Supermarket	105	1 303	75 013
食品、饮料及烟草制品专门零售	Food, Beverage and Tabacco	130	1 840	22 167
纺织、服装及日用品专门零售	Textile, Garments and Articles for Daily Use	279	2 201	114 660
#服装零售	Garments	165	1 516	93 268
文化、体育用品及器材专门零售	Culture & Sports Articles and Equipments	132	384	11 194
#体育用品及器材零售	Sporting Goods and Equipment	9	24	1 993
图书、报刊零售	Books, Newspapers and Periodicals	18	129	3 224
医药及医疗器材专门零售	Medicines and Special Appliances of Medicines	108	1 138	12 484
#药品零售	Medicine	93	1 047	11 489
汽车、摩托车、燃料及零配件专门零售	Automobiles, Motocycles, Fuels and Their Parts	718	846	42 034
#汽车零售	Automobiles	499	530	36 404
家用电器及电子产品专门零售	Household Electrical Appliances and Electronic Products	107	376	13 853
#家用视听设备零售	Home Audio-visual Equipment	7	39	1 919
日用家电设备零售	Household Appliances	30	148	4 526
计算机、软件及辅助设备零售	Computers, Softwares and Accessorial Equipments	38	58	1 636
通信设备零售	Telecommunication Appliances	14	44	2 829
五金、家具及室内装修材料专门零售	Hardwares, Furnitures and Materials of Decoration	98	135	7 368
货摊、无店铺及其他零售业	Stall, Non-store and Other Retailing	104	197	20 027
#互联网零售	Internet	48	58	15 581
邮购及电视、电话零售	Mail Order and TV, Telephone Sales	6	6	494

表 16.4 社会消费品零售总额(1978～2015)
TOTAL RETAIL SALES OF CONSUMER GOODS

单位:亿元(100 million yuan)

年 份 Year	社会消费品零售总额 Total Retail Sales of Consumer Goods	按商品用途分 by Use			
		食品类 Foods	衣着类 Clothing	用品类 Articles	燃料类 Fuels
1978	54.10	26.51	11.60	15.16	0.83
1979	68.28	30.05	16.07	21.28	0.88
1980	80.43	34.30	19.75	25.44	0.94
1981	88.73	38.78	21.27	27.73	0.95
1982	89.80	40.72	19.57	28.52	0.99
1983	100.68	44.20	22.31	33.18	0.99
1984	123.72	50.18	27.71	44.81	1.02
1985	173.39	64.08	35.51	72.70	1.10
1986	196.84	76.99	39.38	79.31	1.16
1987	225.25	91.01	42.52	90.41	1.31
1988	295.83	119.36	53.66	121.17	1.64
1989	331.38	140.03	51.95	137.70	1.70
1990	333.86	142.15	52.33	137.23	2.15
1991	382.06	162.82	52.91	163.30	3.03
1992	464.82	190.70	67.04	202.83	4.25
1993	675.92	259.93	101.30	309.26	5.43
1994	834.76	325.44	123.89	378.86	6.57
1995	1 050.96	407.44	153.74	481.96	7.82
1996	1 258.00	490.97	178.80	579.12	9.11
1997	1 435.38	564.62	200.62	659.61	10.53
1998	1 593.27	640.84	212.85	728.22	11.36
1999	1 722.33	694.03	228.18	787.62	12.50
2000	1 865.28	743.31	248.94	858.33	14.70
2001	2 016.37	802.53	266.31	931.02	16.51
2002	2 203.89	874.76	289.43	1 021.84	17.85
2003	2 404.45	939.29	309.70	1 135.27	20.19
2004	2 656.91	1 043.26	341.28	1 247.39	24.98
2005	2 979.50	1 026.70	335.30	1 563.15	54.35
2006	3 375.20	1 119.77	379.83	1 770.75	104.85
2007	3 873.30	1 204.70	435.88	2 032.07	200.65
2008	4 577.23	1 383.63	515.09	2 401.39	277.12
2009	5 213.11	1 408.84	715.94	2 689.51	398.82
2010	6 186.58	1 602.90	843.81	3 210.30	529.57
2011	7 185.83	1 782.84	935.01	3 831.11	636.87
2012	7 840.40	1 844.96	1 060.76	4 261.50	673.18
2013	8 556.96	1 962.39	1 147.71	4 752.34	694.52
2014	9 303.49	2 065.56	1 313.05	5 210.09	714.79
2015	10 131.50	2 248.70	1 531.97	5 769.28	581.55

注：2005 年起社会消费品零售总额及分组依相应年份经普数据，按国家统计局规定进行了修订。
Note: The Total Value of Retail Sales of Cosumer Goods are from Economic Census, and have been revised according to the regulations of NBS since 2005.

表 16.4 续表 1　continued

单位:亿元(100 million yuan)

年　份 Year	按经济类型分　by Type of Ownership 国有经济 State-owned	集体经济 Collective-owned	私营经济 Private-owned	个　体 Individual	其　他 Others
1978	39.50	14.41		0.19	
1979	46.47	21.32		0.20	0.29
1980	54.01	25.31		0.24	0.87
1981	56.57	30.28	0.04	0.29	1.55
1982	56.48	31.39	0.03	0.32	1.58
1983	63.17	34.55	0.02	0.70	2.24
1984	75.63	43.80	0.02	1.68	2.59
1985	102.59	59.49	0.18	6.42	4.71
1986	111.73	69.06	0.67	8.47	6.91
1987	123.05	80.38	0.88	11.46	9.48
1988	161.65	103.84	1.72	14.56	14.06
1989	176.07	119.97	1.76	16.16	17.42
1990	179.37	115.59	2.05	16.17	20.68
1991	200.25	135.30	2.72	18.70	25.09
1992	247.68	157.56	5.75	22.88	30.95
1993	250.97	202.05	0.51	41.45	180.94
1994	249.27	198.56	0.64	65.00	321.29
1995	247.10	193.03	0.86	76.44	533.54
1996	238.54	183.50	30.10	92.64	713.22
1997	225.35	173.85	21.83	114.88	899.47
1998	210.92	161.70	59.48	126.94	1 034.23
1999	180.33	141.83	62.77	141.16	1 196.24
2000	150.09	118.26	496.86	153.57	946.50
2001	135.69	105.90	596.21	172.66	1 005.91
2002	131.91	102.19	699.75	190.66	1 079.38
2003	133.36	102.68	803.74	208.45	1 156.22
2004	134.44	102.78	935.44	233.01	1 251.24
2005	157.98	51.63	814.31	443.31	1 512.28
2006	178.96	58.48	922.46	502.18	1 713.12
2007	205.37	67.11	1 058.59	576.29	1 965.93
2008	242.69	79.31	1 250.98	681.03	2 323.22
2009	389.15	28.97	1 267.85	731.77	2 795.37
2010	450.57	32.69	1 521.58	868.42	3 313.32
2011	442.79	35.51	1 652.05	1 008.69	4 046.79
2012	471.36	45.85	1 749.08	1 100.57	4 473.54
2013	470.28	38.82	1 745.91	1 201.15	5 100.80
2014	504.34	37.24	1 869.29	1 305.94	5 586.68
2015	542.82	35.01	2 028.24	1 388.59	6 136.83

注：1997 年以前私营经济为合营。
Note：The figures of Private Owned before 1997 refer to these of Joint Owned.

表 16.4 续表 2 continued

单位：亿元(100 million yuan)

年 份 Year	社会消费品零售总额 Total Retail Sales of Consumer Goods	按行业分 by Sectors			
		批发零售贸易业 Wholesale and Retail Trade	住宿餐饮业 Hotels and Catering Trade	制造业 Manufacturing	其他行业 Others
1978	54.10	47.55	2.39	1.65	2.51
1979	68.28	59.02	2.82	2.54	3.90
1980	80.43	70.28	3.41	4.24	2.50
1981	88.73	77.53	3.68	4.61	2.91
1982	89.80	77.31	3.76	5.44	3.29
1983	100.68	84.93	4.26	7.72	3.77
1984	123.72	103.27	4.90	10.60	4.95
1985	173.39	150.03	7.58	8.41	7.37
1986	196.84	170.12	9.54	8.79	8.39
1987	225.25	193.50	11.09	10.47	10.19
1988	295.83	254.99	14.48	11.90	14.46
1989	331.38	265.87	15.66	16.84	33.01
1990	333.86	265.67	17.08	15.15	35.96
1991	382.06	300.26	20.91	17.70	43.19
1992	464.82	362.03	25.92	20.25	56.62
1993	675.92	559.56	35.47	29.24	51.65
1994	834.76	684.81	42.74	32.75	74.46
1995	1 050.96	864.01	52.61	38.05	96.29
1996	1 258.00	1 032.78	78.50	39.84	106.88
1997	1 435.38	1 173.94	93.49	44.38	123.57
1998	1 593.27	1 298.40	96.58	45.41	152.88
1999	1 722.33	1 391.08	114.93	47.22	169.10
2000	1 865.28	1 493.13	134.12	49.16	188.87
2001	2 016.37	1 619.13	148.88	50.78	197.58
2002	2 203.89	1 756.77	193.68	52.66	200.78
2003	2 404.45	1 920.20	225.83	53.87	204.55
2004	2 656.91	2 108.59	279.44	56.29	212.59
2005	2 979.50	2 637.29	342.21		
2006	3 375.20	2 987.54	387.66		
2007	3 873.30	3 428.43	444.87		
2008	4 577.23	4 051.51	525.72		
2009	5 213.11	4 610.76	602.35		
2010	6 186.58	5 494.69	691.89		
2011	7 185.83	6 446.61	739.22		
2012	7 840.40	7 039.16	801.24		
2013	8 556.96	7 714.96	842.00		
2014	9 303.49	8 414.81	888.68		
2015	10 131.50	9 116.93	1 014.57		

表 16.5 主要年份批发零售贸易业销售、库存总额
PURCHASE, SALES AND INVENTORY OF WHOLESALE AND RETAIL TRADE IN MAIN YEARS

单位：亿元(100 million yuan)

指标	Indicators	2000	2010	2014	2015
商品销售总额	**Sales of Commodities**	**7 474.81**	**48 659.55**	**87 829.31**	**93 406.57**
零售	Retail	1 723.31	5 090.26	8 305.94	9 045.17
批发	Wholesale	5 751.50	43 569.29	79 523.37	84 361.40
年末库存总额	**Year-end Inventory**	**262.50**	**1 913.49**	**5 071.99**	**4 367.59**

注：本表为国内批发零售贸易业、物资供销业、对外贸易业统计口径。
Note: The figures in this table are based on the scope of wholesale and retail trade, purchase and sales of commodities and foreign trade.

表 16.6 批发零售贸易业商品销售、库存总额(2015)
PURCHASE, SALES AND INVENTORY OF WHOLESALE AND RETAIL TRADE

单位：亿元(100 million yuan)

类别	Types	商品销售总额 Sales of Commodities	商品库存总额 Year-end Inventory
总计	**Total**	**93 406.57**	**4 367.59**
限额以上单位	Above the Set Scale	70 322.22	4 090.57
限额以下单位	Below the Set Scale	23 084.35	277.02

表 16.7 住宿餐饮业营业额(2015)
TURNOVER OF HOTELS AND CATERING SERVICES

单位：亿元(100 million yuan)

类别	Types	总计 Total	其中 of which	
			限额以上单位 Above the set scale	限额以下单位 Below the Set Scale
营业额	**Turnover**	**1 237.13**	**832.32**	**404.81**
客房收入	Room Revenue	185.49	140.95	44.54
餐费收入	Catering Service Revenue	969.70	628.26	341.44
商品销售额	Commodity Sales	15.85	11.38	4.47
其他收入	Other Revenue	66.09	51.73	14.36

表 16.8 汽车交易情况(2012～2015)
DISTRIBUTION OF AUTOMOBILE

单位：万辆(10 000 vehicles)

类别	Types	2012	2013	2014	2015
国产小型客车(本市上牌量)	Domestic Small Passenger Cars (Number of New Car Licences)	27.18	25.60	24.79	32.57
#国产轿车	Domestic Cars	21.34	18.90	16.87	19.66
进口小型客车(含轿车)	Small Passenger Cars Imported(including cars)	4.43	4.26	4.87	5.29
二手车交易量	Dealing Number of Secondhand Cars	37.91	38.68	43.06	39.38
#轿车	Saloon Cars	22.53	23.62	26.54	26.09

表16.9 限额以上批发贸易业商品购、销、存总额(2015)
PURCHASE, SALES AND INVENTORY OF WHOLESALE TRADE ABOVE THE SET SCALE

单位:亿元(100 million yuan)

类别	Types	商品购进总额 Purchase of Commodities	商品销售总额 Sales of Commodities	商品库存总额 Year-end Inventory
总计	**Total**	**57 528.34**	**64 035.09**	**3 281.72**
按登记注册类型分	**Grouped by Type of Registration**			
内资	Domestic Funded	34 442.80	36 419.38	1 295.09
国有	State-Owned Enterprises	2 593.89	2 703.32	52.62
集体	Collective-Owned Enterprises	16.11	16.68	3.05
股份合作	Share Holding Cooperative Enterprises	116.27	116.26	0.16
联营	Joint-Owned Enterprises	24.30	19.96	6.82
有限责任公司	Companies with Limited Liabilities	16 327.30	16 908.31	694.61
股份有限公司	Share Holding Companies with Limited Liabilities	2 099.60	2 204.66	110.45
私营	Private Enterprises	13 197.82	14 378.77	425.37
其他	Others	67.51	71.42	2.01
港澳台商投资	Hong Kong, Macao and Taiwan Funded Enterprises	6 111.77	7 622.95	690.96
外商投资	Foreign Funded Enterprises	16 973.77	19 992.76	1 295.67
按行业分	**Grouped by Sector**			
农、林、牧产品批发	Agriculture, Forestry and Animal Husbandry products	394.70	412.21	31.51
食品、饮料及烟草制品批发	Food, Beverage and Tabacco	3 142.77	3 699.70	254.38
#米、面制品及食用油批发	Rice, Flour and Cooking Oil	1 132.21	1 305.77	55.20
烟草制品批发	Tabacco	498.71	568.57	15.51

表 16.9 续表 continued

单位:亿元(100 million yuan)

类别	Types	商品购进总额 Purchase of Commodities	商品销售总额 Sales of Commodities	商品库存总额 Year-end Inventory
纺织、服装及家庭用品批发	Textile, Clothing and Household Goods	3 072.10	4 442.93	560.16
#服装批发	Garments	848.50	1 341.02	242.82
文化、体育用品及器材批发	Culture & Sports Articles and Equipments	1 064.65	1 160.41	130.16
医药及医疗器材批发	Medicines and Special Appliances of Medicines	1 910.36	2 355.07	311.98
矿产品、建材及化工产品批发	Mineral Products, Materials of Construction and Chemical Products	31 483.86	32 971.72	828.48
#煤炭及制品批发	Coal	1 271.90	1 307.37	36.60
石油及制品批发	Petroleum	5 813.47	6 006.83	104.82
金属及金属矿批发	Metal Products and Metal Minerals	19 585.65	20 470.63	386.64
建材批发	Building Materials	610.51	635.16	63.90
化肥批发	Chemical Fertilizer	36.99	40.21	2.72
机械设备、五金交电及电子产品批发	Mechinery Equipments, Hardwares, Electric Appliances and Eletronic Products	14 473.84	16 615.58	982.04
#汽车批发	Automobiles	5 768.79	6 750.54	393.04
汽车零配件批发	Spare and Component Parts for Automobiles	719.49	942.09	55.08
电气设备批发	Electrical Equipment	286.14	333.59	37.48
计算机、软件及辅助设备批发	Computers, Softwares and Accessorial Equipments	1 037.29	1 085.70	86.99
贸易经纪与代理	Trade Broker and Agent	991.94	1 112.00	86.07
其他批发	Others	994.12	1 265.47	96.94

表 16.10 限额以上零售贸易业商品购、销、存总额(2015)
PURCHASE, SALES AND INVENTORY OF RETAIL TRADE ABOVE THE SET SCALE

单位:亿元(100 million yuan)

类别	Types	商品购进总额 Purchase of Commodities	商品销售总额 Sales of Commodities	商品库存总额 Year-end Inventory
总计	**Total**	**5 153.07**	**6 287.13**	**808.85**
按登记注册类型分	**Grouped by Type of Registration**			
内资	Domestic Funded	3 546.92	4 119.16	442.71
国有	State-Owned Enterprises	32.38	55.14	5.65
集体	Collective-Owned Enterprises	9.93	10.88	1.09
股份合作	Share Holding Cooperative Enterprises	3.42	3.76	0.19
联营	Joint-Owned Enterprises	14.09	15.63	0.22
有限责任公司	Companies with Limited Liabilities	1 895.80	2 277.37	181.66
股份有限公司	Share Holding Companies with Limited Liabilities	361.64	391.89	65.52
私营	Private Enterprises	1 220.80	1 352.86	187.16
其他	Others	8.86	11.63	1.22
港澳台商投资	Hong Kong, Macao and Taiwan Funded	759.45	972.14	219.64
外商投资	Foreign Funded Enterprises	846.70	1 195.83	146.50
按行业分	Grouped by Sector			
#综合零售	Comprehensive Retail Sale	1 247.96	1 585.99	156.24
食品、饮料及烟草制品专门零售	Food, Beverage and Tabacco	103.78	132.06	8.64
纺织、服装及日用品专门零售	Textile Products, Gaments and Commodity	625.08	1 039.11	308.54
文化、体育用品及器材专门零售	Culture & Sports Articles and Equipments	149.94	184.52	62.20
医药及医疗器材专门零售	Medicines and Special Appliances of Medicines	191.93	225.28	17.90
汽车、摩托车、燃料及零配件专门零售	Automobiles, Motocycles, Fuels and Their Parts	1 636.44	1 745.53	178.02
家用电器及电子产品专门零售	Household Electrical Appliances and Electronic Products	336.06	398.46	37.15
五金、家具及室内装修材料专门零售	Hardwares, Furnitures and Materials of Decoration	52.04	85.57	12.30

表 16.11 主要年份限额以上批发零售贸易业主要生产资料销售量
SALES OF MAJOR PRODUCT MATERIAL OF WHOLESALE AND RETAIL SALES TRADE ABOVE THE SET SCALE IN MAIN YEARS

单位:万吨(10 000 tons)

生产资料名称	Names of Product Material	2005	2010	2014	2015
钢材	Steels	1 807.99	5 579.00	7 522.92	10 086.20
铜	Cuprum	57.38	162.95	1 691.33	1 682.39
铝	Aluminium	21.34	152.32	862.54	1 489.29
水泥	Concrete	118.73	362.00	807.38	789.88

表 16.12 限额以上批发零售贸易业主要商品分类销售额(2015)
TOTAL SALES OF ENTERPRISES ABOVE THE SET SCALE IN WHOLESALE AND RETAIL TRADE BY CATEGORY OF MAIN COMMODITIES

单位:亿元(100 million yuan)

类 别	Types	合 计 Total	批发额 Wholesale	零售额 Retail
粮油、食品类	Grain and Oil, and Food	3 106.17	2 460.78	645.39
#粮油类	Grain and Oil	1 508.03	1 340.26	167.77
肉禽蛋类	Meat, Poultry and Eggs	235.94	156.13	79.81
饮料类	Beverages	221.33	160.24	61.09
烟酒类	Tobacco and Liquor	1 100.76	885.23	215.53
服装、鞋帽、针纺织品类	Clothing, Shoes, Hats and Textiles	3 183.05	2 098.35	1 084.70
#服装类	Clothing	2 109.53	1 188.64	920.89
鞋帽类	Shoes and Hat	481.47	356.12	125.35
针、纺织品类	Knitwear and Textiles	592.06	553.60	38.46
化妆品类	Cosmetics	771.81	520.02	251.79
金银珠宝类	Gold, Silver and Jewelry	701.68	491.54	210.14
日用品类	Articles for Daily Use	1 541.63	1 185.42	356.21
#儿童玩具类	Toys for Children	58.02	27.76	30.26
五金、电料类	Hardware and Electrical Materials	507.00	494.17	12.83
体育、娱乐用品类	Sports and Recreation Articles	75.91	49.57	26.34
书报杂志类	Newspapers and Magazines	52.70	27.57	25.13
电子出版物及音像制品类	E-journal and Video Products	3.83	2.65	1.18
家用电器和音像器材类	Household Appliances and Video Appliances	820.19	359.64	460.55
中西药品类	Traditional Chinese and Western Medicines	1 454.39	1 116.61	337.78
#西药类	Western Medicines	1 225.44	949.43	276.01
中草药及中成药类	Traditional Chinese Medicines	146.06	91.58	54.48
文化办公用品类	Cultural and Official Goods	1 931.05	1 676.37	254.68
家具类	Furniture	131.34	70.00	61.34
通讯器材类	Communication Appliances	3 489.28	3 262.14	227.14
煤炭及制品类	Coal and Related Product	1 097.73	1 097.27	0.46
木材及制品类	Lumber and Related Product	112.55	112.55	
石油及制品类	Oil and Related Product	6 603.74	6 191.81	411.93
化工材料及制品类	Chemical Material and Related Product	4 062.03	4 062.03	
#化肥类	Fertilizer	127.74	127.74	
金属材料类	Metal Material	18 541.28	18 541.28	
建筑及装潢材料类	Building and Decoration Materials	359.42	305.26	54.16
机电产品及设备类	Mechanical and Electrical Products	3 609.79	3 593.39	16.40
#农机类	Agriculture Machinery	32.38	32.38	
汽车类	Automobile	8 934.70	7 511.13	1 423.57
种子饲料类	Seed and Feedstuff	178.93	178.93	
棉麻类	Cotton and Hemp	37.66	37.53	0.13
其他类	Others	3 655.29	3 542.95	112.34

表 16.13 商品交易市场成交情况(2015)
DEALS IN MERCHANDISE EXCHANGE MARKET

分类	Types	年末出租摊位数(个) Quantity of Year-end Booth Lent (unit)	成交额(亿元) Transaction Volume (100 million yuan)
总计	**Total**	**148 247**	**9 318.51**
#粮油、食品、饮料、烟酒类	Grain and Oil, Foodstuff, Beverage, Tobacco and Liquor	63 192	1 025.12
服装、鞋帽、针纺织品类	Garments, Shoes and Hats, Textile Products	23 367	97.05
化妆品类	Cosmetics	268	1.06
金银珠宝类	Jewelry	246	1.12
日用品类	Articles for Daily Use	4 245	200.15
五金、电料类	Hardware and Electrical Appliances	4 909	28.82
体育、娱乐用品类	Recreation and Sports Articles	351	4.68
书报杂志类	Books, Newspapers and Magazines	94	0.38
电子出版物及音像制品类	Electronic Publications and Audio-video Products	159	0.79
家用电器和音像器材类	Household Appliances and Audio-video Equipments	985	4.65
中西药品类	Medicines	227	4.31
文化办公用品类	Culture and Office Articles	1 388	11.68
家具类	Furnitures	3 890	25.88
通讯器材类	Telecommunication Appliances	1 608	2.78
木材及制品类	Woods and Woods Product	1 810	79.87
石油及制品类	Oil and Oil Product	591	1 140.35
化工材料及制品类	Chemical Material and Chemical Product	788	132.88
金属材料类	Mental and Mental Product	3 563	5 959.77
建筑及装潢材料类	Construct and Decorate Material	18 208	266.16
机电产品及设备类	Mechanical and Electrical Product and Equipments	734	10.61
汽车类	Automobile	4 208	251.54

表16.14 主要年份限额以上批发零售贸易业主要财务指标
MAIN FINANCIAL INDICATORS OF WHOLESALE AND RETAIL SALES ABOVE THE SET SCALE IN MAIN YEARS

单位:亿元(100 million yuan)

指　标	Indicators	2005	2010	2014	2015
流动资产	Current Assets	2 929.27	7 608.03	17 986.27	18 831.64
#存　货	Inventory	722.78	1 655.36	3 646.24	4 484.58
固定资产原价	Fixed Assets Original Value	546.78	790.06	1 537.57	1 595.54
累计折旧	Accumulative Depreciation	169.94	291.58	655.29	700.05
#本年折旧	Depreciation	31.20	55.82	126.33	131.06
资产总计	Total Assets	3 926.22	9 608.53	22 501.49	23 843.32
负债合计	Total Liabilities	2 727.25	6 710.76	16 625.80	17 274.47
所有者权益合计	Total Owner's Equities	1 198.97	2 897.78	5 875.65	6 568.87
实收资本	Paid-up Capital	862.49	1 464.26	3 933.80	4 098.65
#国家资本	State Capital	132.19	379.67	559.34	516.03
港澳台资本	Hong Kong, Macao and Taiwan Capital	38.17	137.69	459.22	518.11
外商资本	Foreign Capital	242.71	376.04	728.81	798.17
主营业务收入	Prime Operating Revenues	11 236.19	26 372.58	64 891.00	62 098.50
主营业务成本	Operating Costs	9 874.12	24 300.03	60 043.19	57 228.78
营业费用	Operating Expenses	501.98	1 135.41	2 851.62	2 966.65
主营业务税金及附加	Sales Taxes and Extra Charges	10.10	40.73	95.36	111.30
管理费用	Management Expenses	243.12	475.41	1 083.47	1 131.59
财务费用	Financial Expenses	24.09	47.93	148.99	220.05
营业利润	Operating Profits	248.71	535.95	997.20	876.70
利润总额	Total Profits	223.35	640.19	1 018.65	1 011.58
主营业务应付工资总额	Total Payable Salaries Involved in Major Business	130.25	258.66	864.93	1 001.40
主营业务应付福利费总额	Total Payable Welfare Involved in Major Business	21.89	17.63		

表 16.15 主要年份限额以上餐饮业主要财务指标
MAIN FINANCIAL INDICATORS OF CATERING SECTOR ABOVE THE SET SCALE IN MAIN YEARS

单位：亿元(100 million yuan)

指 标	Indicators	2005	2010	2014	2015
流动资产	Current Assets	43.60	114.24	226.63	226.17
#存 货	Inventory	5.10	8.28	22.42	23.63
固定资产原价	Fixed Assets Original Value	44.76	81.97	121.42	74.40
累计折旧	Accumulative Depreciation	15.65	31.64	52.34	56.34
#本年折旧	Depreciation	3.83	6.63	8.74	8.85
资产总计	Total Assets	94.49	214.43	395.20	403.13
负债合计	Total Liabilities	64.13	156.19	306.97	305.59
所有者权益合计	Total Owner's Equities	30.36	58.25	88.23	97.54
实收资本	Paid-up Capital	31.05	62.42	131.57	152.31
#国家资本	State Capital	0.78	5.28	7.15	8.14
港澳台资本	Hong Kong, Macao and Taiwan Capital	6.95	13.36	20.67	27.97
外商资本	Foreign Capital	6.66	17.62	28.05	33.53
主营业务收入	Prime Operating Revenues	157.66	335.96	578.31	612.14
主营业务成本	Operating Costs	72.03	145.44	256.45	262.62
营业费用	Operating Expenses	53.86	123.32	214.76	236.70
主营业务税金及附加	Sales Taxes and Extra Charges	8.14	17.34	30.83	32.79
管理费用	Management Expenses	19.42	37.25	67.69	68.57
财务费用	Financial Expenses	1.15	3.47	5.63	6.16
营业利润	Operating Profits	5.49	10.96	7.81	10.41
利润总额	Total Profits	5.49	15.12	11.67	13.23
主营业务应付工资总额	Total Payable Salaries Involved in Major Business	17.54	41.08	90.80	105.86
主营业务应付福利费总额	Total Payable Welfare Involved in Major Business	2.26	2.51		

表 16.16 主要年份限额以上连锁批发和零售业、住宿和餐饮业经营情况
BASIC STATISTICS OF CHAIN RETAIL, HOTELS AND CATERING SERVICES ABOVE THE SET SCALE IN MAIN YEARS

指 标	Indicators	2005	2010	2014	2015
门店总数(个)	Quantity of Stores(unit)	15 775	20 977	21 193	21 503
营业面积(万平方米)	Operational Area(10 000 sq. m)	809.16	938.35	1 149.30	1 178.87
从业人数(万人)	Number of Persons Employed(10 000 person)	24.47	36.68	35.27	34.20
批发和零售业商品购进总额(亿元)	Purchase of Commodities(100 million yuan)	1 222.94	2 249.57	2 303.75	2 275.62
批发和零售业商品销售总额(亿元)	Sales of Commodities (100 million yuan)	1 815.32	3 071.67	3 390.42	3 361.41
#零售额	Retail Sales	1 201.03	2 241.97	2 546.90	2 581.26
住宿和餐饮业营业收入(亿元)	Total Operating Revenue (100 million yuan)	35.69	106.81	171.33	191.44

表 16.17 限额以上批发零售贸易业主要财务指标 (2015)
MAIN FINANCIAL INDICATORS OF WHOLESALE AND RETAIL ENTERPRISES ABOVE THE SET SCALE

类别	Types	流动资产 Current Assets	固定资产原价 Fixed Assets Original Value	资产总计 Total Assets
总计	**Total**	**18 831.64**	**1 595.54**	**23 843.32**
按登记注册类型分	**Grouped by Type of Registration**			
批发贸易业	**Wholesale Trade**	**16 612.11**	**905.88**	**20 751.14**
内资	Domestic Funded Enterprises	8 223.20	451.08	10 918.13
国有	State-Owned Enterprises	228.21	58.15	312.78
集体	Collective-Owned Enterprises	9.71	0.29	12.04
股份合作	Share Holding Cooperative Enterprises	5.01	0.35	5.60
联营	Joint-Owned Enterprises	15.77	0.16	15.85
有限责任公司	Companies with Limited Liabilities	4 020.04	166.88	5 368.62
股份有限公司	Share Holding Companies with Limited Liabilities	564.36	82.42	956.46
私营	Private Enterprises	3 371.84	142.77	4 233.48
其他	Others	8.25	0.05	13.31
港澳台商投资	Hong Kong, Macao and Taiwan Funded Enterprises	2 764.06	159.90	3 248.78
外商投资	Foreign Funded Enterprises	5 624.84	294.90	6 584.23
零售贸易业	**Retail Trade**	**2 219.53**	**689.66**	**3 092.18**
内资	Domestic Funded Enterprises	1 416.64	380.81	1 944.14
国有	State-Owned Enterprises	19.20	4.97	33.10
集体	Collective-Owned Enterprises	4.39	2.42	6.64
股份合作	Share Holding Cooperative Enterprises	1.34	0.16	1.49
联营	Joint-Owned Enterprises	2.04	0.71	2.30
有限责任公司	Responsibility Co. Ltd.	691.81	244.36	995.90
股份有限公司	Share Holding Co. Ltd.	206.99	65.78	313.83
私营	Private Enterprises	482.46	62.10	582.09
其他	Others	8.41	0.31	8.79
港澳台商投资	Hong Kong, Macao and Taiwan Funded Enterprises	386.62	126.08	535.54
外商投资	Foreign Funded Enterprises	416.27	182.76	612.49

单位:亿元(100 million yuan)

负债合计 Total Liabilities	所有者权益合计 Total Owner's Equity	实收资本 Paid-up Capital	主营业务收入 Prime Operating Revenues	主营业务成本 Prime Operating Costs	利润总额 Total Profits
17 274.47	**6 568.87**	**4 098.65**	**62 098.50**	**57 228.78**	**1 011.58**
14 912.83	**5 838.32**	**3 315.55**	**56 624.52**	**52 717.81**	**948.43**
8 119.15	2 798.98	2 222.01	31 848.51	31 000.14	292.39
255.50	57.28	40.55	2 640.90	2 564.08	41.89
8.51	3.53	1.48	15.17	14.57	0.34
4.11	1.49	1.29	98.61	98.40	-0.02
14.29	1.55	1.03	17.05	14.67	0.15
3 904.69	1 463.93	757.47	14 893.17	14 524.97	143.30
512.44	444.01	687.52	1 422.05	1 311.02	53.85
3 408.77	824.71	730.39	12 700.46	12 412.83	52.81
10.84	2.47	2.27	61.10	59.61	0.06
2 154.36	1 094.43	418.84	6 698.77	5 760.47	225.07
4 639.32	1 944.91	674.70	18 077.26	15 957.20	430.95
2 361.64	**730.55**	**783.10**	**5 473.98**	**4 510.97**	**63.15**
1 460.38	483.76	391.90	3 541.92	3 122.54	50.43
20.16	12.94	6.76	49.75	41.75	0.41
3.93	2.71	1.07	10.09	8.25	0.40
0.65	0.84	0.18	3.39	3.02	0.21
0.64	1.67	0.29	13.60	12.14	0.86
781.50	214.40	212.45	1 932.81	1 716.86	16.95
162.91	150.91	42.89	326.19	276.69	26.56
482.93	99.16	126.72	1 194.83	1 055.19	4.08
7.66	1.13	1.54	11.26	8.64	0.95
409.90	125.63	176.60	857.21	604.83	-0.65
491.33	121.16	214.60	1 074.87	783.58	13.38

表16.17 续表 continued

类别	Types	流动资产 Current Assets	固定资产原价 Fixed Assets Original Value	资产总计 Total Assets
按行业分	**Grouped by Sector**			
批发贸易业	**Wholesale Trade**	**16 612.11**	**905.88**	**20 751.14**
农、林、牧产品批发	Agriculture, Forestry and Animal Husbandry Products	152.81	26.48	259.18
食品、饮料及烟草制品批发	Food, Beverage and Tabacco	1 323.46	100.75	1 829.60
纺织、服装及家庭用品批发	Textile, Clothing and Household Goods	1 888.11	172.75	2 402.97
文化、体育用品及器材批发	Culture & Sports Articles and Equipments	387.22	19.42	460.22
医药及医疗器材批发	Medicines and Special Appliances of Medicines	972.87	153.24	1 201.93
矿产品、建材及化工产品批发	Mineral Products, Materials of Construction and Chemical Products	6 465.69	249.89	8 202.34
机械设备、五金交电及电子产品批发	Mechinery Equipments, Hardwares, Electric Appliances and Eletronic Products	4 592.28	137.70	5 421.96
贸易经纪与代理	Trade Broker and Agent	338.03	17.54	384.60
其他批发	Others	491.64	28.11	588.34
零售贸易业	**Retail Trade**	**2 219.53**	**689.66**	**3 092.18**
综合零售	Comprehensive Retail Sale	570.53	362.73	963.74
食品、饮料及烟草制品专门零售	Food, Beverage and Tabacco	40.10	14.37	55.18
纺织、服装及日用品专门零售	Textile Products, Garments and Commodity	497.78	124.28	690.41
文化、体育用品及器材专门零售	Culture & Sports Articles and Equipments	96.45	25.11	122.62
医药及医疗器材专门零售	Medicines and Special Appliances of Medicines	77.74	5.94	85.34
汽车、摩托车、燃料及零配件专门零售	Automobiles, Motocycles, Fuels and Their Parts	486.02	78.87	606.31
家用电器及电子产品专门零售	Household Electrical Appliances and Electronic Products	174.46	6.46	198.34
五金、家具及室内装修材料专门零售	Hardwares, Furnitures and Materials of Decoration	41.91	43.80	105.28
货摊、无店铺及其他零售业	Stall, Non-store and Other Retailing	234.54	28.10	264.96

单位:亿元(100 million yuan)

负债合计 Total Liabilities	所有者权益合计 Total Owner's Equity	实收资本 Paid-up Capital	主营业务收入 Prime Operating Revenues	主营业务成本 Prime Operating Costs	利润总额 Total Profits
14 912.83	**5 838.32**	**3 315.55**	**56 624.52**	**52 717.81**	**948.43**
136.26	122.92	33.79	377.97	371.26	1.99
1 240.30	589.30	211.87	3 295.60	2 842.25	125.81
1 545.33	857.65	326.50	3 935.21	2 902.68	188.89
289.54	170.68	94.10	1 038.35	931.54	26.35
796.82	405.11	140.26	2 132.69	1 743.04	90.22
6 327.79	1 874.55	1 727.39	28 728.10	28 213.81	143.10
3 904.48	1 517.48	650.62	14 984.10	13 772.21	323.06
264.77	119.83	51.75	999.69	929.75	17.01
407.54	180.80	79.27	1 132.81	1 011.27	32.00
2 361.64	**730.55**	**783.10**	**5 473.98**	**4 510.97**	**63.15**
707.19	256.55	301.32	1 351.16	1 107.29	20.20
44.21	10.97	16.20	119.51	92.50	-3.69
514.90	175.51	153.87	913.04	513.53	23.57
81.16	41.46	43.31	155.07	112.45	0.99
70.84	14.50	55.63	190.35	165.57	6.39
459.15	147.16	97.48	1 557.30	1 464.50	22.14
124.52	73.82	27.00	350.36	305.78	16.21
84.94	20.34	28.28	69.52	48.44	1.47
274.73	-9.76	60.01	767.67	700.91	-24.13

表 16.18 限额以上住宿餐饮业主要财务指标(2015)
MAIN FINANCIAL INDICATORS OF HOTELS AND CATERING ENTERPRISES ABOVE THE SET SCALE

类 别	Types	流动资产 Current Assets	固定资产原价 Fixed Assets Original Value	资产总计 Total Assets
总 计	**Total**	**534.96**	**670.31**	**1 212.89**
按登记注册类型分	**Grouped by Type of Registration**			
住宿业	**Accommodation**	**308.78**	**543.53**	**809.76**
内 资	**Domestic Enterprises**	**212.40**	**351.11**	**525.84**
国 有	State-Owned Enterprises	33.04	88.20	93.13
集 体	Collective-Owned Enterprises	0.85	4.95	3.90
股份合作	Share Holding Cooperative Enterprises			
联 营	Joint-Owned Enterprises	0.38	2.03	1.62
有限责任公司	Companies with Limited Liabilities	93.90	203.62	268.29
股份有限公司	Share Holding Companies with Limited Liabilities	1.27	2.79	2.88
私 营	Private Enterprises	81.29	47.65	153.68
其 他	Others	1.67	1.87	2.34
港澳台商投资	Hong Kong, Macao and Taiwan Funded	78.29	158.73	239.79
外商投资	Foreign Funded Enterprises	18.09	33.69	44.13
餐饮业	**Catering**	**226.18**	**126.78**	**403.13**
内 资	**Domestic Enterprises**	**141.50**	**68.34**	**229.93**
国 有	State-Owned Enterprises	1.17	0.18	1.36
集 体	Collective-Owned Enterprises	1.19	1.23	2.28
股份合作	Share Holding Cooperative Enterprises	0.40	0.18	0.56
联 营	Joint-Owned Enterprises	0.01	0.22	0.22
有限责任公司	Responsibility Co. Ltd.	34.82	16.23	54.66
股份有限公司	Share Holding Co. Ltd.	11.63	1.02	22.41
私 营	Private Enterprises	91.60	48.70	147.28
其 他	Others	0.68	0.58	1.16
港澳台商投资	Hong Kong, Macao and Taiwan Funded	47.69	31.00	84.57
外商投资	Foreign Funded Enterprises	36.99	27.44	88.63

单位:亿元(100 million yuan)

负债合计 Total Liabilities	所有者权益合计 Total Owner's Equity	实收资本 Paid-up Capital	主营业务收入 Prime Operating Revenues	主营业务成本 Prime Operating Costs	利润总额 Total Profits
773.73	**439.12**	**438.38**	**872.96**	**342.05**	**25.78**
468.15	**341.58**	**286.08**	**260.81**	**79.43**	**12.56**
291.40	234.41	197.74	193.63	57.79	7.03
32.00	61.12	26.27	29.46	6.96	1.09
1.97	1.92	0.62	1.91	0.89	-0.44
-0.48	2.10	2.99	0.64	0.13	-0.22
134.26	134.03	132.64	93.44	28.09	6.12
1.81	1.07	1.19	2.08	0.60	0.26
119.77	33.91	33.93	62.20	19.84	-0.69
2.07	0.26	0.10	3.90	1.28	0.91
145.40	94.39	62.63	52.06	19.56	6.12
31.35	12.78	25.71	15.12	2.08	-0.59
305.58	**97.54**	**152.30**	**612.15**	**262.62**	**13.22**
184.63	45.30	75.21	285.30	137.33	1.97
0.92	0.44	0.23	2.64	1.59	0.08
1.02	1.27	0.18	2.49	1.16	0.21
0.23	0.32	0.05	0.55	0.23	0.01
0.08	0.14	0.15	0.05	0.03	
43.20	11.46	12.80	53.77	22.21	2.75
13.51	8.90	1.98	6.57	3.53	0.92
124.69	22.59	59.71	217.52	107.59	-2.03
0.98	0.18	0.11	1.71	0.99	0.03
56.53	28.04	32.61	136.72	51.71	4.52
64.42	24.20	44.48	190.13	73.58	6.73

表 16.18 续表 continued

类别	Types	流动资产 Current Assets	固定资产原价 Fixed Assets Original Value	资产总计 Total Assets
按行业分	**Grouped by Sector**			
批发贸易业	**Wholesale Trade**	**16 612.11**	**905.88**	**20 751.14**
农、林、牧产品批发	Agriculture, Forestry and Animal Husbandry Products	152.81	26.48	259.18
食品、饮料及烟草制品批发	Food, Beverage and Tabacco	1 323.46	100.75	1 829.60
纺织、服装及家庭用品批发	Textile, Clothing and Household Goods	1 888.11	172.75	2 402.97
文化、体育用品及器材批发	Culture & Sports Articles and Equipments	387.22	19.42	460.22
医药及医疗器材批发	Medicines and Special Appliances of Medicines	972.87	153.24	1 201.93
矿产品、建材及化工产品批发	Mineral Products, Materials of Construction and Chemical Products	6 465.69	249.89	8 202.34
机械设备、五金交电及电子产品批发	Mechinery Equipments, Hardwares, Electric Appliances and Eletronic Products	4 592.28	137.70	5 421.96
贸易经纪与代理	Trade Broker and Agent	338.03	17.54	384.60
其他批发	Others	491.64	28.11	588.34
零售贸易业	**Retail Trade**	**2 219.53**	**689.66**	**3 092.18**
综合零售	Comprehensive Retail Sale	570.53	362.73	963.74
食品、饮料及烟草制品专门零售	Food, Beverage and Tabacco	40.10	14.37	55.18
纺织、服装及日用品专门零售	Textile Products, Garments and Commodity	497.78	124.28	690.41
文化、体育用品及器材专门零售	Culture & Sports Articles and Equipments	96.45	25.11	122.62
医药及医疗器材专门零售	Medicines and Special Appliances of Medicines	77.74	5.94	85.34
汽车、摩托车、燃料及零配件专门零售	Automobiles, Motocycles, Fuels and Their Parts	486.02	78.87	606.31
家用电器及电子产品专门零售	Household Electrical Appliances and Electronic Products	174.46	6.46	198.34
五金、家具及室内装修材料专门零售	Hardwares, Furnitures and Materials of Decoration	41.91	43.80	105.28
货摊、无店铺及其他零售业	Stall, Non-store and Other Retailing	234.54	28.10	264.96

单位:亿元(100 million yuan)

负债合计 Total Liabilities	所有者权益合计 Total Owner's Equity	实收资本 Paid-up Capital	主营业务收入 Prime Operating Revenues	主营业务成本 Prime Operating Costs	利润总额 Total Profits
14 912.83	**5 838.32**	**3 315.55**	**56 624.52**	**52 717.81**	**948.43**
136.26	122.92	33.79	377.97	371.26	1.99
1 240.30	589.30	211.87	3 295.60	2 842.25	125.81
1 545.33	857.65	326.50	3 935.21	2 902.68	188.89
289.54	170.68	94.10	1 038.35	931.54	26.35
796.82	405.11	140.26	2 132.69	1 743.04	90.22
6 327.79	1 874.55	1 727.39	28 728.10	28 213.81	143.10
3 904.48	1 517.48	650.62	14 984.10	13 772.21	323.06
264.77	119.83	51.75	999.69	929.75	17.01
407.54	180.80	79.27	1 132.81	1 011.27	32.00
2 361.64	**730.55**	**783.10**	**5 473.98**	**4 510.97**	**63.15**
707.19	256.55	301.32	1 351.16	1 107.29	20.20
44.21	10.97	16.20	119.51	92.50	-3.69
514.90	175.51	153.87	913.04	513.53	23.57
81.16	41.46	43.31	155.07	112.45	0.99
70.84	14.50	55.63	190.35	165.57	6.39
459.15	147.16	97.48	1 557.30	1 464.50	22.14
124.52	73.82	27.00	350.36	305.78	16.21
84.94	20.34	28.28	69.52	48.44	1.47
274.73	-9.76	60.01	767.67	700.91	-24.13

表 16.19　限额以上住宿和餐饮业经营情况(2015)

OPERATING CONDITIONS OF HOTELS AND CATERING INDUSTRY ABOVE THE SET SCALE

单位:亿元(100 million yuan)

类　别	Types	营业额 Turnover	其中 of which: 客房收入 Room Revenue	餐费收入 Catering Service Revenue	商品销售额 Commodity Sales	其他收入 Other Revenue
总　计	**Total**	**889.43**	**148.48**	**674.85**	**11.18**	**54.92**
住宿业	**Accommodation**	**263.86**	**141.02**	**70.37**	**3.21**	**49.26**
按登记注册类型分	**Grouped by Type of Registration**					
内资企业	Domestic Funded Enterprises	196.41	111.26	50.48	2.96	31.72
国有企业	State-Owned Enterprises	30.30	14.25	8.99	0.73	6.33
集体企业	Collective-Owned Enterprises	1.95	0.61	1.07		0.27
联营企业	Joint-Owned Enterprises	0.71	0.28	0.31		0.11
有限责任公司	Companies with Limited Liabilities	94.48	46.25	26.99	1.29	19.94
股份有限公司	Share Holding Companies with Limited Liabilities	2.27	1.62	0.35	0.01	0.29
私营企业	Private Enterprises	62.79	45.68	11.68	0.92	4.51
其他企业	Others	3.92	2.57	1.08		0.27
港、澳、台商投资企业	Hong Kong, Macao and Taiwan Funded Enterprises	52.40	23.15	14.80	0.09	14.37
外商投资企业	Foreign Funded Enterprises	15.05	6.61	5.10	0.17	3.18
按星级分组	**Grouped by Star Level**					
五　星	Five-Star	112.13	50.62	38.93	1.46	21.12
四　星	Four-Star	42.72	19.09	11.80	0.48	11.35
三　星	Three-Star	18.62	7.72	4.35	0.16	6.40
二　星	Two-Star	2.56	1.50	0.63	0.06	0.37
一　星	One-Star	0.14	0.14			
其　他	Others	87.68	61.94	14.66	1.06	10.01
餐饮业	**Catering**	**625.57**	**7.46**	**604.48**	**7.97**	**5.66**
按登记注册类型分	**Grouped by Type of Registration**					
内资企业	Domestic Funded Enterprises	293.12	7.13	274.94	7.33	3.71
国有企业	State-Owned Enterprises	2.74	0.10	2.33	0.04	0.27
集体企业	Collective-Owned Enterprises	2.54	0.07	2.34		0.12
股份合作企业	Share Holding Cooperative Enterprises	0.57	0.01	0.54	0.01	0.01
联营企业	Joint-Owned Enterprises	0.05		0.04		
有限责任公司	Companies with Limited Liabilities	55.09	2.37	50.21	0.47	2.05
股份有限公司	Share Holding Companies with Limited Liabilities	11.00	0.14	8.31	2.53	0.02
私营企业	Private Enterprises	219.41	4.34	209.70	4.22	1.15
其他企业	Others	1.72	0.10	1.47	0.07	0.08
港、澳、台商投资企业	Hong Kong, Macao and Taiwan Funded Enterprises	137.10	0.22	135.14	0.55	1.19
外商投资企业	Foreign Funded Enterprises	195.35	0.11	194.40	0.09	0.75
按餐饮行业小类分组	**Grouped by Catering Categories**					
正餐服务	Restaurant	420.48	7.02	401.62	7.37	4.47
快餐服务	Fast Food	95.00	0.22	94.36	0.04	0.38
饮料及冷饮服务	Beverages and Cold Drinks	79.61		79.56	0.04	0.01
茶馆服务	Teahouse	0.44		0.44		
咖啡馆服务	Café	65.12		65.08	0.04	0.01
酒吧服务	Bar	0.49		0.49		
其他饮料及冷饮服务	Others	13.56		13.55	0.01	
其他餐饮业	Others	30.47	0.22	28.94	0.53	0.79
小吃服务	Refreshment	7.90		7.85	0.01	0.04
餐饮配送服务	Food Distribution	14.68		14.19	0.42	0.06
其他未列明餐饮业	Others	7.90	0.22	6.90	0.09	0.69

上 / 海 / 统 / 计 / 年 / 鉴

主要统计指标解释

社会消费品零售总额

指批发和零售业、餐饮业、新闻出版业、邮政业和其他服务业等，售予城乡居民用于生活消费的商品和社会集团用于公共消费的商品之总量。社会消费品零售总额包括：

一、批发和零售业企业(单位)：

1.售予城乡居民的各种生活消费品。

2.售予入境旅游的外国人、华侨、港澳台同胞的各类商品。

3.售予行政事业单位、社会团体、军队和武警等机构的商品，以及以零售方式售予各类企业的商品。具体包括：用于非生产和社会交往的办公用品，如通讯设备、计算器具和设备、电讯网络设备、文印设备、音像视听器材和设备、纸张、本册、文具及装订文印材料、家具、日用电器、针纺织品、清洁卫生用品、文体用品、奖品、纪念品、礼品等；供内部人员乘坐的交通工具和燃料；用于办公设施修缮的各类配件、材料、工具等；用于取暖和防暑降温的设备、燃料、材料及食品等；专用于教学的用品和设备；非营利医疗机构的中、西药品、中药材和医疗设备器材；非专用的劳动保护用品；不对外营业的内部食堂用的餐具、炊具、设备、清洁卫生工具和食品、燃料等；军队、武警用于其人员生活的衣着品和个人用品；其他各类非生产性设备和用品。

二、餐饮业出售的主食、菜肴、烟酒饮料和其他商品。

三、新闻出版业、邮政业售予城乡居民、企事业单位、军队和武警等机构的书报杂志、音像制品、邮品等。

四、其他服务业出售的食品、烟酒饮料、服装鞋帽、日常生活用品、医药保健用品、艺术品、工艺美术品、玩具、殡葬用品以及其他消费品。

商品购进总额

指从本企业(单位)以外的单位和个人购进(包括从境外直接进口)作为转卖或加工后转卖的商品总额。它反映批发零售贸易业从国内、国外市场上购进商品的总量。商品购进总额包括：(1) 从工农业生产者购进的商品；(2)从出版社、报社的出版发行部门购进的图书、杂志和报纸；(3)从各种登记注册类型的批发零售贸易企业(单位)购进的商品；(4)从其他单位购进的商品，如从机关、团体、企业等单位购进的剩余物资，从餐饮业、服务业购进的商品，从海关、市场管理部门购进的缉私和没收的商品，从居民手中收购的废旧商品等；(5)从国(境)外直接进口的商品。不包括企业(单位)为自身经营用和未通过买卖行为而收入的商品以及销售退回、商品升溢等。

商品销售总额

指对本企业以外的单位和个人出售(包括对国(境)外直接出口)的商品。这个指标反映批发零售贸易业在上海市场以及上海以外市场上销售商品的总量。商品销售总额包括：(1) 售给城乡居民和社会集团消费用的商品；(2) 售给工业、农业、建筑业、运输邮电业、批发零售贸易业、餐饮业、服务业等作为生产、经营使用的商品；(3) 售给批发零售贸易业作为转卖或加工后转卖的商品；(4) 对国(境)外直接出口的商品。不包括：出售本企业自用的废旧包装用品，未通过买卖行为付出的商品，经本单位介绍，由买卖双方直接结算，本单位只收取手续费的业务，购货退出的商品以及商品损耗和损失等。

主营业务收入

指企业在销售商品、提供劳务等日常活动中所产生的收入总额。

主营业务成本

指企业已销商品应负担的进货原价和商品进价成本。

营业费用

指批发零售贸易企业在购、销、存过程中发生的各项经营费用。包括运输费、装卸费、包装费、保险费、展览费、差旅费、广告费、商品损耗、进出口商品累计佣金、经营人员的工资及福利费等。

营业额

指住宿和餐饮业单位在经营活动中因提供服务或销售商品等取得的全部收入，包括：客房收入、餐费收入、商品销售额(含增值税)和其他收入。不包括法人企业附营的其他行业产业活动单位的餐费收入、商品销售收入等各项收入。

SHANGHAI STATISTICAL YEARBOOK

EXPLANATORY NOTES TO MAJOR STATISTICAL INDICATORS

□ Total Retail Sales of Consumer Goods

Total Retail Sales of Consumer Goods refer to the sum of retail sales of commodities sold by wholesale, retail, catering, publishing, post and telecommunications and other service industries to urban and rural households for private consumption and to social institutions for public consumption. Retail sales of consumer goods include:

Sales by wholesale and retail units:

of consumer goods sold to urban and rural households

of commodities sold to foreigners, overseas Chinese and Chinese compatriots from Hong Kong, Macau and Taiwan visiting in China

of commodities sold to government agencies, institutions, social organizations, military and armed police units, and commodities sold to enterprises in the form of retail sales. More specifically, they include: office facilities and articles for non-production purposes such as communications equipment, computing equipment and instruments, TV and network equipment, printing and copying equipment, audio-visual equipment and instruments, paper, notebooks, stationeries, furniture, electric appliances, knitwear, sanitation and cleaning articles, cultural and sport articles, articles for prizes, souvenirs, etc.; transport vehicles and fuels for employees; materials, spare parts and tools for the maintenance of office facilities; equipment, fuels, materials and food for winter heating or summer cooling purposes; articles and equipment for teaching purpose; Chinese and western medicines and medical equipment and facilities purchased by non profit-making medical institutes; non-specialized work safety articles; cooking utensils, tableware, equipment, cleaning articles, food and fuels purchased by internal cafeterias; clothes and personal articles purchased by military or armed police units for their officials and soldiers; and other equipment and articles for non-production purposes.

Sales of stable food, cooked dishes, beverages, tobaccos and other articles by catering units.

Sales of books, newspapers, magazines, audio-visual products and post products by publishing, post and telecommunications departments to urban and rural households and to enterprises, institutions, military and armed police units.

Sales of food, beverages, tobaccos, clothing, hats, footwear, articles for daily use, medicines, medical and health articles, work of art, handicrafts, toys, funeral articles and other articles by other service industries.

□ Total Purchase of Commodities

Purchase, Sales and Stock of Commodities by Wholesale and Retail Trades refer to the total volume of commodities purchased, total volume of sales and exports, and the stock of commodities by wholesale and retail enterprises (establishments) of different status of registration from domestic and overseas markets. This indictor reflects the relationship among purchase, sales and stock of commodities in the circulation of goods and reveals the existing problems.

□ Total Sales of Commodities

Total Sales of Commodities refer to the selling of commodities to other establishments and individuals (including direct export). Reflecting the total value of sales of commodities at Shanghai markets and out-of-Shanghai markets, this indicator includes: (1) commodities sold to urban and rural households and institutions for their consumption; (2) commodities sold to establishments in industry, agriculture, construction, transportation, post and telecommunications, wholesale and retail trade, catering and service trade and public utility for their production and operation; (3)commodities sold to wholesale and retail establishments for re-selling, with or without further processing; and (4) commodities for direct export to other countries. Excluded are selling of waste packaging materials used by enterprises themselves commodities transferred without buying or selling procedures, commission income from brokerage in transactions whose settlement is directly handled by buyers and sellers, rejected commodities in the purchase, loss in commodities, etc.

□ Prime Operating Revenue

Prime Operating Revenue refers to the earnings a corporation receives in daily activity such as selling goods and offering labor service.

SHANGHAI STATISTICAL YEARBOOK

□ Operating Cost

Operating Cost refers to the cost a corporation paid to buy and deliver the commodities.

□ Operating Expenses

Operating Expenses refer to the spendings that a wholesaler or retailer pays in buying, selling or stocking goods. It includes fees incurred in transport, loading and unloading, packaging, insurance, exhibition, business trip, advertisement, commodity wastage, commissions in import and export, salaries and bonus paid to workers involved.

□ Turnover

Turnover refers to the all revenue of hotels and catering units for providing services or selling goods in business activities, including: room income, meals income, merchandise sales (including VAT) and other income. And all income as meals income and merchandise sales from industrial activity unit of other trade affiliated with incorporated enterprise are excluded.

第十七篇
CHAPTER 17

金融业
FINANCE

简要说明

本篇反映上海市金融业发展情况。由以下四部分组成：一是保费收支情况，数据由中国保险监督管理委员会上海监管局提供；二是金融机构存贷款余额及利率调整情况，数据由中国人民银行上海总部和上海公积金管理中心提供；三是金融业单位数，数据由中国银行业监督管理委员会上海监管局、中国保险监督管理委员会上海监管局、中国证券监督管理委员会上海监管局等部门提供；四是金融市场运行情况，数据由上海证券交易所、上海期货交易所、中国金融期货交易所、全国银行间同业拆借中心和上海黄金交易所提供。

BRIEF INTRODUCTION

Data in this chapter reflect the development of Shanghai's financial industries. The data consit of four parts: (1) Premium of primary insurance and payment. Data are provided by the China Insurance Regulatory Commission Shanghai Bureau. (2) The situations regarding the changes of deposit and loan balance, and adjustment of interest rates. Data are provided by the Shanghai Headquarters of People's Bank of China and the Shanghai Provident Fund Administration Center. (3) Quantity of financial institutions. Statistics are provided by the China Banking Regulatory Commission Shanghai Bureau, the China Insurance Regulatory Commission Shanghai Bureau, and the China Securities Regulatory Commission Shanghai Bureau. (4) Data on the activities of financial institutions. Data are provided by the Shanghai Stock Exchange, the Shanghai Futures Exchange, the China Financial Futures Exchange, the National Interbank Funding Center, and the Shanghai Gold Exchange.

表 17.1 原保险保费收入和赔付支出(1978～2015)
PREMIUM OF PRIMARY INSURANCE AND PAYMENT

单位:亿元(100 million yuan)

年 份 Year	原保险保费收入 Premium of Primary Insurance	其 中 of which 人身保险 Liability Insurance	财产保险 Property Insurance	原保险赔付支出 Payment of Primary Insurance	其 中 of which 人身保险 Liability Insurance	财产保险 Property Insurance
1978	0.17			0.17		
1979	0.16			0.07		
1980	0.70			0.13		
1981	0.95			0.32		
1982	1.11			0.21		
1983	1.33			0.45		
1984	1.76			0.36		
1985	2.27			0.54		
1986	3.04			0.68		
1987	4.03			0.92		
1988	5.38			1.55		
1989	7.37			1.89		
1990	8.99			2.22		
1991	11.16			4.47		
1992	18.20			4.23		
1993	25.91			5.89		
1994	39.48			11.91		
1995	44.04	17.08	26.96	12.75		
1996	58.10	28.64	29.46	15.00		
1997	87.72	58.13	29.59	19.10		
1998	102.92	70.50	32.42	28.67		
1999	115.28	81.53	33.75	39.46		
2000	127.23	92.14	35.09	36.44	20.56	15.88
2001	180.25	140.30	39.95	38.82	19.61	19.21
2002	237.61	193.30	44.31	49.97	28.38	21.59
2003	289.93	232.50	57.43	61.97	34.87	27.10
2004	307.11	231.30	75.81	70.86	36.79	34.07
2005	333.62	245.76	87.86	87.46	40.20	47.26
2006	407.04	305.72	101.33	91.31	46.14	45.17
2007	482.64	363.22	119.43	139.82	86.79	53.03
2008	600.06	468.27	131.79	184.09	104.57	79.52
2009	665.03	513.22	151.81	176.74	98.24	78.50
2010	883.86	686.68	197.18	194.54	110.28	84.26
2011	753.11	519.71	233.39	260.71	156.39	104.32
2012	820.64	564.26	256.38	255.79	117.16	138.63
2013	821.43	536.18	285.25	301.95	139.62	162.33
2014	986.75	666.39	320.36	378.66	201.42	177.24
2015	1 125.16	769.77	355.40	473.59	282.22	191.38

注：2010 年原保险保费收入为按财产险公司和寿险公司分类。
Note: Data of Premium of Primary Insurance of 2010 are classified by Property Insurance Company and Liability Insurance Company.

表 17.2 金融机构存贷款年末余额（2013～2015）
DEPOSIT AND LOAN BALANCE OF FINANCIAL INSTITUTIONS AT YEAR-END

单位：亿元（100 million yuan）

指标	Indicators	2013	2014	2015
金融机构存款余额	**Saving Deposit Balance of Financial Institutions**	**69 256.32**	**73 882.45**	**103 760.60**
中资金融机构	Chinese Financial Institutions	63 346.88	67 813.15	96 929.66
人民币	RMB	60 321.03	64 659.94	92 710.97
外汇（折人民币）	Foreign Currencies(Converting into RMB)	3 025.85	3 153.21	4 218.69
外资金融机构	Foreign-funded Financial Institutions	5 909.44	6 069.30	6 881.30
外汇（折人民币）	Foreign Currencies (Converting into RMB)	1 193.00	1 180.10	1 282.65
人民币	RMB	4 716.44	4 889.20	5 598.65
金融机构贷款余额	**Loan Balance of Financial Institutions**	**44 357.88**	**47 915.81**	**53 387.21**
中资金融机构	Chinese Financial Institutions	39 992.48	43 386.58	48 578.51
人民币	RMB	37 033.88	40 375.78	45 150.28
外汇（折人民币）	Foreign Currencies (Converting into RMB)	2 958.60	3 010.80	3 428.23
外资金融机构	Foreign-funded Financial Institutions	4 365.40	4 529.23	5 655.17
外汇（折人民币）	Foreign Currencies (Converting into RMB)	1 650.73	1 677.68	2 094.05
人民币	RMB	2 714.67	2 851.55	3 561.12

表 17.3 金融机构存款年末余额（2015）
DEPOSITS OF FINANCIAL INSTITUTIONS AT YEAR-END

单位：亿元（100 million yuan）

指标	Indicators	2015	比 2015 年初增加 Increase from the Beginning of 2015
各项存款余额	**All Deposits**	**103 760.60**	**13 328.75**
境内存款	Domestic Deposits	100 191.05	15 140.92
住户存款	Household Deposits	23 384.73	645.70
活期存款	Current Deposits	8 184.76	1 246.84
定期及其他存款	Time Deposits and Other Deposits	15 199.97	-601.14
非金融企业存款	Non Financial Enterprise Deposits	38 041.95	4 327.99
活期存款	Current Deposits	12 518.99	3 018.60
定期及其他存款	Time Deposits and Other Deposits	25 522.96	1 309.39
广义政府存款	General Government Deposits	13 398.86	999.31
财政性存款	Fiscal Deposits	3 062.91	488.93
机关团体存款	Deposits of Non-profit Institutions	10 335.94	510.38
非银行业金融机构存款	Deposits of Non Banking Financial Institutions	25 365.51	9 167.92
境外存款	Foreign Deposits	3 569.55	-1 812.16

注：自 2015 年起，各项存款包括非银行业金融机构存款。
Note: Since year 2015, deposits has included deposits of non banking financial institutions.

表 17.4 中资金融机构人民币贷款年末余额(2015)
LOAN BALANCE OF FINANCIAL INSTITUTIONS AT YEAR-END

单位:亿元(100 million yuan)

指标	Indicators	2015	比 2015 年初增加 Increase from the Beginning of 2015
各项贷款余额	**All Loans**	**53 387.21**	**4 880.58**
境内贷款	Domestic Loans	51 354.02	4 178.23
住户贷款	Household Loans	11 717.97	2 011.65
短期贷款	Short-term Loans	1 220.49	141.47
中长期贷款	Mid and Long-term Loans	10 497.47	1 870.19
非金融企业及机关团体贷款	Loans of Non Financial Enterprise and Non-profit Institutions	39 330.98	1 971.10
#短期贷款	Short-term Loans	12 961.85	611.29
中长期贷款	Mid and Long-term Loans	19 919.31	113.07
票据融资	Notes Finacing	3 467.18	907.99
非银行业金融机构贷款	Loans of Non Banking Financial Institutions	305.08	195.48
境外贷款	Foreign Loans	2 033.18	702.34

表 17.5 个人消费贷款及公积金贷款年末余额(2013~2015)
PERSONAL CONSUMPTION LOAN AND ACCUMULATION FUND LOAN AT YEAR-END

指标	Indicators	2013	2014	2015
金融机构人民币个人消费贷款余额(亿元)	**Personal Consumption Loan from Domestic Funded Commercial Banks(100 million yuan)**	**7 700.47**	**8 753.46**	**10 751.60**
#个人住房贷款	Housing Mortgage Loan	5 686.28	6 258.86	7 765.81
汽车消费贷款	Car Consumption Loan	1 278.30	1 524.11	1 869.75
个人住房贷款占金融机构人民币个人消费贷款额比重(%)	**Housing Mortgage Loan Percentage of Personal Consumption Loan**	**73.8**	**71.5**	**72.2**
公积金贷款余额(亿元)	**Accumulation Fund Loan(100 million yuan)**	**1 788.31**	**2 012.00**	**2 770.08**

表 17.6 年末金融业单位数(2013～2015)
QUANTITY OF FINANCIAL INSTITUTIONS

单位:家(unit)

指 标	Indicators	2013	2014	2015
金融业单位数	Financial Institutions	1 240	1 336	1 430
#货币金融	Monetary and Financial	564	601	618
资本市场	Capital Markets	252	292	350
保险业	Insurance Institutions	347	363	382
#外资金融单位数	Foreign Financial Institutions Operating in Shanghai	215	216	230

表 17.7 主要金融市场成交额(2013～2015)
TURNOVER OF MAIN FANANCIAL MARKET

单位:亿元(100 million yuan)

指 标	Indicators	2013	2014	2015
上海证券交易所成交额	Turnover of Shanghai Stock Exchange	865 098.34	1 281 497.98	2 663 690.84
上海期货交易所成交额	Turnover of Shanghai Future Exchange	1 208 335.46	1 264 706.51	635 552.63
中国金融期货交易所成交额	Turnover of China Financial Futures Exchange	1 410 066.21	1 640 169.72	4 177 604.71
银行间市场成交额	Turnover of Interbank Market	2 847 442.95	3 615 067.75	7 042 637.12
上海黄金交易所成交额	Turnover of Shanghai Gold Exchange	52 242.22	65 139.91	107 841.61

注：自 2013 年起,银行间市场成交额包括银行间本币市场和外汇市场成交额。本表数据中上海黄金交易所成交额和 2013 年、2014 年上海期货交易所成交额按双向计算,其他成交额数据均按单向计算。

Note: Since 2013, the turnover of Interbank Market has included turnover of Interbank RMB market and turnover of foreign exchange trading market. The turnover data in the table are calculated by buy or sell, except Shanghai Gold Exchange turnover and Shanghai Futures Exchange(year 2013 and year 2014) are calculated by buy and sell.

表 17.8 金融机构人民币存款基准利率(1990 ~2015)
BENCHMARK INTEREST RATE OF RMB DEPOSIT FOR FINANCIAL INSTITUTIONS

单位:年利率% (annual interest rate)

调整时间 Adjust Time	活期 Checking Deposit	定期 fixed deposit					
		3个月 3 Months	6个月 6 Months	1年 1 Year	2年 2 Years	3年 3 Years	5年 5 Years
1990.04.15	2.88	6.30	7.74	10.08	10.98	11.88	13.68
1990.08.21	2.16	4.32	6.48	8.64	9.36	10.08	11.52
1991.04.21	1.80	3.24	5.40	7.56	7.92	8.28	9.00
1993.05.15	2.16	4.86	7.20	9.18	9.90	10.80	12.06
1993.07.11	3.15	6.66	9.00	10.98	11.70	12.24	13.86
1996.05.01	2.97	4.86	7.20	9.18	9.90	10.80	12.06
1996.08.23	1.98	3.33	5.40	7.47	7.92	8.28	9.00
1997.10.23	1.71	2.88	4.14	5.67	5.94	6.21	6.66
1998.03.25	1.71	2.88	4.14	5.22	5.58	6.21	6.66
1998.07.01	1.44	2.79	3.96	4.77	4.86	4.95	5.22
1998.12.07	1.44	2.79	3.33	3.78	3.96	4.14	4.50
1999.06.10	0.99	1.98	2.16	2.25	2.43	2.70	2.88
2002.02.21	0.72	1.71	1.89	1.98	2.25	2.52	2.79
2004.10.29	0.72	1.71	2.07	2.25	2.70	3.24	3.60
2006.08.19	0.72	1.80	2.25	2.52	3.06	3.69	4.14
2007.03.18	0.72	1.98	2.43	2.79	3.33	3.96	4.41
2007.05.19	0.72	2.07	2.61	3.06	3.69	4.41	4.95
2007.07.21	0.81	2.34	2.88	3.33	3.96	4.68	5.22
2007.08.22	0.81	2.61	3.15	3.60	4.23	4.95	5.49
2007.09.15	0.81	2.88	3.42	3.87	4.50	5.22	5.76
2007.12.21	0.72	3.33	3.78	4.14	4.68	5.40	5.85
2008.10.09	0.72	3.15	3.51	3.87	4.41	5.13	5.58
2008.10.30	0.72	2.88	3.24	3.60	4.14	4.77	5.13
2008.11.27	0.36	1.98	2.25	2.52	3.06	3.60	3.87
2008.12.23	0.36	1.71	1.98	2.25	2.79	3.33	3.60
2010.10.20	0.36	1.91	2.20	2.50	3.25	3.85	4.20
2010.12.26	0.36	2.25	2.50	2.75	3.55	4.15	4.55
2011.02.09	0.40	2.60	2.80	3.00	3.90	4.50	5.00
2011.04.06	0.50	2.85	3.05	3.25	4.15	4.75	5.25
2011.07.07	0.50	3.10	3.30	3.50	4.40	5.00	5.50
2012.06.08	0.40	2.85	3.05	3.25	4.10	4.65	5.10
2012.07.06	0.35	2.60	2.80	3.00	3.75	4.25	4.75
2014.11.22	0.35	2.35	2.55	2.75	3.35	4.00	-
2015.03.01	0.35	2.10	2.30	2.50	3.10	3.75	-
2015.05.11	0.35	1.85	2.05	2.25	2.85	3.50	-
2015.06.28	0.35	1.60	1.80	2.00	2.60	3.25	-
2015.08.26	0.35	1.35	1.55	1.75	2.35	3.00	-
2015.10.24	0.35	1.10	1.30	1.50	2.10	2.75	-

注:本表数据摘自中国人民银行网站。自2014年11月22日起,人民银行不再公布金融机构人民币五年期定期存款基准利率。

Note: Data in the table are from the web of People's Bank of China . Since 22 November, 2014, People's Bank of China has stopped announcing five-year benchmark interest rate of RMB deposit .

表 17.9 金融机构人民币贷款基准利率(1991 ~2015)
BENCHMARK INTEREST RATE OF RMB LOAN FOR FINANCIAL INSTITUTIONS

单位:年利率%(annual interest rate)

调整时间 Adjust Time	6个月 6 Months	1年 1 Year	1~3年(含) 1~3 Years	3~5年(含) 3~5 Years	5年以上 Above 5 Years
1991.04.21	8.10	8.64	9.00	9.54	9.72
1993.05.15	8.82	9.36	10.80	12.06	12.24
1993.07.11	9.00	10.98	12.24	13.86	14.04
1995.01.01	9.00	10.98	12.96	14.58	14.76
1995.07.01	10.08	12.06	13.50	15.12	15.30
1996.05.01	9.72	10.98	13.14	14.94	15.12
1996.08.23	9.18	10.08	10.98	11.70	12.42
1997.10.23	7.65	8.64	9.36	9.90	10.53
1998.03.25	7.02	7.92	9.00	9.72	10.35
1998.07.01	6.57	6.93	7.11	7.65	8.01
1998.12.07	6.12	6.39	6.66	7.20	7.56
1999.06.10	5.58	5.85	5.94	6.03	6.21
2002.02.21	5.04	5.31	5.49	5.58	5.76
2004.10.29	5.22	5.58	5.76	5.85	6.12
2006.04.28	5.40	5.85	6.03	6.12	6.39
2006.08.19	5.58	6.12	6.30	6.48	6.84
2007.03.18	5.67	6.39	6.57	6.75	7.11
2007.05.19	5.85	6.57	6.75	6.93	7.20
2007.07.21	6.03	6.84	7.02	7.20	7.38
2007.08.22	6.21	7.02	7.20	7.38	7.56
2007.09.15	6.48	7.29	7.47	7.65	7.83
2007.12.21	6.57	7.47	7.56	7.74	7.83
2008.09.13	6.21	7.20	7.29	7.56	7.74
2008.10.09	6.12	6.93	7.02	7.29	7.47
2008.10.30	6.03	6.66	6.75	7.02	7.20
2008.11.27	5.04	5.58	5.67	5.94	6.12
2008.12.23	4.86	5.31	5.40	5.76	5.94
2010.10.20	5.10	5.56	5.60	5.96	6.14
2010.12.26	5.35	5.81	5.85	6.22	6.40
2011.02.09	5.60	6.06	6.10	6.45	6.60
2011.04.06	5.85	6.31	6.40	6.65	6.80
2011.07.07	6.10	6.56	6.65	6.90	7.05
2012.06.08	5.85	6.31	6.40	6.65	6.80
2012.07.06	5.60	6.00	6.15	6.40	6.55
2014.11.22	5.60		6.00		6.15
2015.03.01	5.35		5.75		5.90
2015.05.11	5.10		5.50		5.65
2015.06.28	4.85		5.25		5.40
2015.08.26	4.60		5.00		5.15
2015.10.24	4.35		4.75		4.90

注:本表数据摘自中国人民银行网站。自2014年11月22日起,金融机构人民币贷款基准利率期限档次简并为一年以内(含一年)、一至五年(含五年)和五年以上三个档次。

Note: Data in the table are from the web of People's Bank of China . Since 22 November, 2014, period of benchmark lending rates has been adjusted into three grades: within one year (including one year), one to five years (including five years), and more than five years.

表 17.10 上海证券交易所上市公司股本结构(2013～2015)
CAPITAL STOCK STRUCTURE OF PUBLIC COMPANIES IN SHANGHAI STOCK EXCHANGE

单位:亿元(100 million yuan)

指 标	Indicators	2013	2014	2015
发行总股本	**Total**	**32 414.37**	**33 801.57**	**37 102.33**
尚未流通股份	Non-circulation Shares	2 020.56	2 170.58	2 817.13
国家拥有股份	State Shares	1 164.30	1 079.59	1 175.90
境内法人持有股份	Domestic Sponsoring Corporate Shares	322.93	339.38	619.58
外资法人持有股份	Foreign Corporate Shares	24.74	55.50	48.77
个人发起人股	Personal Sponsor Shares	91.59	83.94	117.35
募集法人股	Raised Corporate	1.26	1.04	1.04
机构配售	Agencies placing	47.86	54.64	45.33
其 他	Others	367.87	556.49	809.16
已流通股份	Circulation Shares	30 393.81	31 630.99	34 285.20
境内上市的人民币普通股	A Shares	23 584.87	24 763.56	27 272.05
境内上市外资股	B Shares	146.66	151.03	146.36
境外上市外资股	H Shares	6 662.68	6 716.39	6 866.80

表 17.11 上海证券交易所市场概况(2013～2015)
SHANGHAI STOCK EXCHANGE MARKET

指 标	Indicators	2013	2014	2015
上市公司数(个)	Quantity of Public Company (unit)	953	995	1 081
上市证券数(个)	Quantity of Negotiable Securities(unit)	2 786	3 758	5 914
上市股票数(个)	Quantity of Listed Stock(unit)	997	1 039	1 125
股票发行股数(亿股)	Shares of Stocks Issued (100 million shares)	25 751.69	27 085.17	30 235.54
A 股	A Shares	25 605.03	26 934.14	30 089.18
B 股	B Shares	146.66	151.03	146.36
股票市价总值(亿元)	Aggregate Value of Stocks in Market Price (100 million yuan)	151 165.27	243 974.02	295 194.20
A 股	A Shares	150 406.94	243 102.74	293 946.10
B 股	B Shares	758.33	871.28	1 248.10
流通股数(亿股)	Shares in Circulation (100 million shares)	23 731.13	24 914.59	27 418.41
A 股	A Shares	23 584.47	24 763.56	27 272.05
B 股	B Shares	146.66	151.03	146.36
流通市值(亿元)	Value in Circulation (100 million yuan)	136 526.37	220 495.87	254 127.85
A 股	A Shares	135 768.04	219 624.59	252 879.75
B 股	B Shares	758.33	871.28	1 248.10
市场筹资额(亿元)	Funds Raised from Market (100 million yuan)	5 646.14	7 947.79	28 085.63
普通股	Common shares	2 515.72	3 962.59	8 712.96
首次发行	IPO		311.77	1 086.90
再次发行	Additional Issued	2 515.72	3 650.82	7 626.06
优先股	Preferred shares		1 030.00	1 959.00
债 券	Bond	3 130.42	2 955.20	17 413.67

表 17.12 主要年份上证综合指数
THE SHANGHAI COMPOSITE INDEX IN MAIN YEARS

年份 Year	开盘 Open	最高 High	日期 Date		最低 Low	日期 Date		收盘 Close
1990	96.05	127.61	12月31日	31,Dec	95.79	12月19日	19,Dec	127.61
1995	637.72	926.41	5月22日	22,May	524.43	2月7日	7,Feb	555.29
1996	550.26	1 258.69	12月11日	11,Dec	512.83	1月19日	19,Jan	917.02
1997	914.06	1 510.18	5月12日	12,May	870.80	2月20日	20,Feb	1 194.10
1998	1 200.95	1 422.95	6月4日	4,June	1 043.02	8月18日	18,Aug	1 146.70
1999	1 144.89	1 756.18	6月30日	30,June	1 047.83	5月17日	17,May	1 366.58
2000	1 368.69	2 125.72	11月23日	23,Nov	1 361.21	1月4日	4,Jan	2 073.48
2001	2 077.08	2 245.44	6月14日	14,June	1 514.86	10月22日	22,Oct	1 645.97
2002	1 643.49	1 748.89	6月25日	25,June	1 339.20	1月29日	29,Jan	1 357.65
2003	1 347.43	1 649.60	4月16日	16,Apr	1 307.40	11月13日	13,Nov	1 497.04
2004	1 492.72	1 777.52	4月6日	6,Apr	1 260.32	9月13日	13,Sep	1 266.50
2005	1 260.78	1 318.27	3月8日	8, Mar	1 011.50	7月11日	11, July	1 161.06
2006	1 163.88	2 698.90	12月29日	29,Dec	1 161.91	1月4日	4,Jan	2 675.47
2007	2 728.19	6 124.04	10月16日	16,Oct	2 541.53	2月6日	6,Feb	5 261.56
2008	5 265.00	5 522.78	1月14日	14,Jan	1 664.93	10月28日	28,Oct	1 820.81
2009	1 849.02	3 478.01	8月4日	4,Aug	1 844.09	1月5日	5,Jan	3 277.14
2010	3 289.75	3 282.18	1月5日	5,Jan	2 363.95	7月5日	5,July	2 808.08
2011	2 825.33	3 057.33	4月18日	18,Apr	2 166.21	12月27日	27,Dec	2 199.42
2012	2 212.00	2 478.38	2月27日	27,Feb	1 949.46	12月4日	4,Dec	2 269.13
2013	2 289.51	2 444.80	2月18日	18,Feb	1 849.65	6月25日	25,jun	2 115.98
2014	2 112.13	3 239.36	12月31日	31,Dec	1 974.38	3月12日	12,Mar	3 234.68
2015	3 258.63	5 178.19	6月12日	12,June	2 850.71	8月26日	26,Aug	3 539.18

表 17.13 上证各类指数概况(2015)
ALL KINDS OF INDEX OF SHANGHAI

指标	Indicators	最高 High	日期 Date		最低 Low	日期 Date		收盘 Close
上证综指	SSE Composite Index	5 178.19	6月12日	12,June	2 850.71	8月26日	26,Aug	3 539.18
上证180	SSE 180 Index	11 815.51	6月9日	9,June	6 360.08	8月26日	26,Aug	7 995.77
上证50	SSE 50 Index	3 494.82	6月9日	9,June	1 874.22	8月26日	26,Aug	2 420.80
上证380	SSE 380 Index	10 307.63	6月12日	12,June	4 659.07	1月19日	19,Jan	6 712.76
红利指数	Dividend Index	4 195.21	6月15日	15,June	2 254.62	8月26日	26,Aug	2 784.95
治理指数	Governance Index	1 615.72	6月9日	9,June	861.68	8月26日	26,Aug	1 073.87
A股指数	A-Share Index	5 423.25	6月12日	12,June	2 986.40	8月26日	26,Aug	3 704.30
B股指数	B-Share Index	539.69	6月5日	5,June	272.20	8月26日	26,Aug	426.41
基金指数	Fund Index	7 670.68	6月8日	8,June	5 114.16	8月26日	26,Aug	5 904.92
国债指数	T-Bond Index	154.67	12月31日	31,Dec	145.75	1月5日	5,Jan	154.54
企业债指数	C-Bond Index	197.18	12月31日	31,Dec	181.24	1月5日	5,Jan	197.12

表 17.14 上海证券交易所有价证券成交总额(2012 ~2015)
TOTAL VOLUME OF PRICED SECURITIES TRADING IN SHANGHAI STOCK EXCHANGE

单位:亿元 (100 million yuan)

指　标	Indicators	2012	2013	2014	2015
总　计	**Total**	**547 535**	**865 098**	**1 281 498**	**2 663 691**
股　票	Shocks	164 545	230 266	377 162	1 330 992
#A　股	A Shares	164 047	228 919	375 150	1 323 231
B　股	B Shares	413	690	484	2 357
债　券	Bond	379 819	625 839	866 849	1 228 534
基　金(含 ETF)	Fund	3 171	8 989	37 479	103 814

表 17.15 上海证券交易所股票账户开户情况(2012 ~2015)
ACCOUNT-OPENING BY INVESTORS IN SHANGHAI STOCK EXCHANGE

单位:万户(10 000 households)

指　标	Indicators	2012	2013	2014	2015
累计总户数	**Total Accounts Accumulated**				
总　数	Total	8 996.40	9 253.44	9 737.52	13 751.31
个　人	Private	8 954.88	9 210.14	9 691.47	13 698.94
机　构	Institution	41.52	43.30	46.05	52.37
A 股累计户数	**A Shares Accounts Accumulated**				
总　数	Total	8 841.56	9 097.68	9 580.73	13 586.32
个　人	Private	8 802.09	9 056.53	9 536.94	13 536.32
机　构	Institution	39.47	41.15	43.79	50.00
B 股累计户数	**B Shares Accounts Accumulated**				
总　数	Total	154.84	155.76	156.79	164.99
个　人	Private	152.79	153.61	154.53	162.62
机　构	Institution	2.05	2.15	2.26	2.37
当年新开户总数	**Newly Opened Accounts During the Year**				
总　数	Total	291.38	257.04	484.08	4 013.79
个　人	Private	289.95	255.26	481.33	4 007.47
机　构	Institution	1.43	1.78	2.75	6.32
A 股新开户数	**Newly Opened Accounts of A Shares**				
总　数	Total	290.71	256.12	484.08	4 013.79
个　人	Private	289.38	254.44	480.41	3 999.38
机　构	Institution	1.33	1.68	2.64	6.21
B 股新开户数	**Newly Opened Accounts of B Shares**				
总　数	Total	0.67	0.92	1.04	8.20
个　人	Private	0.57	0.82	0.92	8.09
机　构	Institution	0.10	0.10	0.12	0.10

上/海/统/计/年/鉴

主要统计指标解释

存　款

机构或个人在保留资金或货币所有权的条件下，以不可流通的存款凭证为依据，暂时让渡或接受资金使用权所形成的债权或债务。

贷　款

机构或个人在保留资金或货币所有权的条件下，以不可流通的借款凭证或类似凭证为依据，暂时让渡或接受资金使用权所形成的债权或债务。

上证综合指数

以在上海证券交易所上市的全部股票(A 股和 B 股)作为样本计算的股票价格指数。

市场筹资额

企业在上海证券交易所通过发行股票和债券所筹集的资金总额。

原保险保费收入

指保险人与投保人之间直接签订的原保险合同中确认的保费收入，不包括再保险保费收入。

原保险赔付支出

指保险企业根据保险人与投保人之间直接签订的原保险合同中确认的赔付款项，不包括再保险赔付支出。

SHANGHAI STATISTICAL YEARBOOK

EXPLANATORY NOTES TO MAJOR STATISTICAL INDICATORS

□ Deposit

Deposit refers to the creditor's rights or debt formed by temporary lending or receiving funds in condition of institutions or individuals to retain the ownership of funds or monetary and based on the non-negotiable certificates of deposits.

□ Loan

Loan refers to the creditor's rights or debt formed by temporary lending or receiving funds in condition of institutions or individuals to retain the ownership of funds or monetary and based on the non-negotiable certificates of loan or similar certificates.

□ SSE Composite Index

SSE Composite Index is a stock price index, which is calculated by the price of all stocks (including A stocks and B stocks) in Shanghai Stock Exchange.

□ Market Financing

Market Financing refers to the total amount of fund which enterprises raise by issuing shares or bonds in Shanghai Stock Exchange.

□ Premium of Primary Insurance

Premium of Primary Insurance includes the insurance premium which is entered into the original insurance contract signed directly between the insurer and the insured, and reinsurance premium is excluded.

□ Payment of Primary Insurance

Payment of Primary Insurance includes the insurance payment which is entered into the original insurance contract signed directly between the insurer and the insured, and reinsurance payment is excluded.

第十八篇

CHAPTER 18

房地产业

REAL ESTATE

简要说明

一、本篇资料的主要内容

本篇资料反映上海市房地产业生产经营和发展情况。主要指标有房地产开发投资额、房屋施工面积、商品房销售面积、房屋征收(拆迁)户数、存量房买卖登记面积等。

二、本篇的资料来源

本篇中房地产开发投资和到位资金情况、房屋建筑面积、商品房销售和出租情况根据上海市统计局制定的《房地产开发、经营统计报表制度》调查汇总提供。

本篇中房屋征收(拆迁)情况、存量房买卖登记情况由上海市住房和城乡建设管理委员会提供。

本篇中土地使用权出让情况由上海市规划和国土资源管理局提供。

三、本篇资料的统计调查方法

本篇中涉及房地产开发经营统计资料采用全面调查的方法，由全市房地产开发经营法人企业通过联网直报的方式上报取得。

BRIEF INTRODUCTION

I. Main Contents

Data in this chapter reflect business operation and development of real estate industry in Shanghai. Main indicators include investment in real estate development, floor area of construction, sold area of commodity, quantity of expropriation (resettlements), and registration areas traded of second–hand houses.

II. Sources of statistics

Data on real estate development investment and capital in place, construction area, commodity housing sold and leased are compiled in accordance with Statistical Reporting System on Real Estate Development and Operation made by Shanghai Municipal Statistics Bureau.

Data on buildings resettlement and the registration of second–hand houses transaction are provided by Shanghai Municipal Housing and Urban and Rural Construction Management Committee

Data on lease of land plot tenure are provided by Shanghai Municipal Bureau of Planning and Land Resources.

Ⅲ. Survey Methodology

Data on development and operation of real estate adopt comprehensive reporting system, being collected from data directly reported by the city's real estate development and operation enterprises with legal person status through the Internet.

表 18.1 主要年份房地产开发投资和到位资金情况
INVESTMENT IN REAL ESTATE DEVELOPMENT AND AVAILABILITIES OF CAPITALS IN MAIN YEARS

单位:亿元(100 million yuan)

指标	Indicators	2000	2010	2014	2015
房地产开发投资额	**Total Investment**	**566.17**	**1 980.68**	**3 206.48**	**3 468.94**
按开发用途分	By use				
住　宅	Residence	408.82	1 229.83	1 724.65	1 813.32
#别墅、高档公寓	Villas and Apartment	40.72	373.67	360.01	381.48
办公楼	Office Building	57.47	224.46	534.77	654.54
商业营业用房	Commercial Building	51.51	244.70	457.92	467.67
其　他	Others	48.38	281.69	489.14	533.41
本年新增固定资产	**Newly Increased Fixed Assets This Year**	**477.39**	**964.27**	**1 583.93**	**1 890.67**
本年实际到位资金合计	**Total Capital in Place This Year**	**778.16**	**4 443.85**	**7 422.19**	**7 483.72**
上年末结余资金	Balance at End of Previous Year	113.48	1 214.56	2 152.29	1 951.86
本年实际到位资金小计	Capital in Place This Year	664.68	3 229.29	5 269.90	5 531.86
国内贷款	Domestic Loans	155.37	819.57	1 638.84	1 516.59
利用外资	Foreign Capital Utilized	28.11	96.05	69.61	33.92
#外商直接投资	Foreign Direct Investment	16.24	65.52	67.73	32.36
自筹资金	Self-Financed Capital	211.86	1 070.88	1 560.83	1 519.99
其他资金	Other Capital	269.34	1 242.78	2 000.62	2 461.36

表 18.2 主要年份房地产开发企业房屋建筑面积
CONSTRUCTION AREA DEVELOPED BY REAL ESTATE COMPANIES IN MAIN YEARS

指 标	Indicators	2000	2010	2014	2015
房屋施工面积（万平方米）	**Floor Area of Construction (10 000 sq. m)**	**5 523.23**	**11 295.03**	**14 690.18**	**15 095.33**
住 宅	Residence	4 263.50	7 313.85	8 525.85	8 372.12
#别墅、高档公寓	Villas and Apartment	254.11	1 584.11	1 575.97	1 647.69
办公楼	Office Building	515.10	1 103.18	1 779.04	1 978.49
商业营业用房	Commercial Building	438.47	1 292.96	1 751.99	1 944.02
其 他	Others	306.16	1 585.04	2 633.30	2 800.70
房屋新开工面积（万平方米）	**Floor Space of Newly-started Buildings (10 000 sq. m)**	**1 992.31**	**3 030.59**	**2 782.02**	**2 605.08**
住 宅	Residence	1 781.64	2 111.11	1 547.29	1 560.28
#别墅、高档公寓	Villas and Apartment	120.54	389.84	276.90	208.55
办公楼	Office Building	18.89	147.39	365.25	304.87
商业营业用房	Commercial Building	91.21	298.10	388.03	307.57
其 他	Others	100.57	473.99	481.45	432.36
房屋竣工面积（万平方米）	**Floor Area Completed (10 000 sq. m)**	**1 643.62**	**1 941.25**	**2 313.29**	**2 647.18**
住 宅	Residence	1 388.01	1 396.05	1 535.55	1 588.95
#别墅、高档公寓	Villas and Apartment	66.38	328.00	180.10	340.65
办公楼	Office Building	95.93	150.69	165.03	219.23
商业营业用房	Commercial Building	100.16	176.41	208.36	306.45
其 他	Others	59.52	218.09	404.35	532.55
房屋竣工价值(亿元)	**Value of Building Completed (100 million yuan)**	**355.79**	**779.93**	**1 058.42**	**1 488.32**
住 宅	Residence	270.29	536.66	644.47	881.17
#别墅、高档公寓	Villas and Apartment	20.66	178.27	106.73	285.39
办公楼	Office Building	45.41	74.23	133.96	174.90
商业营业用房	Commercial Building	24.29	87.13	123.62	176.58
其 他	Others	15.80	81.91	156.37	255.67

表 18.3 主要年份商品房销售和出租情况
COMMODITY HOUSING SOLD AND LEASED IN MAIN YEARS

指标	Indicators	2000	2010	2014	2015
商品房销售面积（万平方米）	**Sold Area of Commodity Housing (10 000 sq. m)**	**1 557.87**	**2 055.53**	**2 084.66**	**2 431.36**
住　宅	Residence	1 445.87	1 685.35	1 780.91	2 009.17
#别墅、高档公寓	Villas and Apartment	53.44	341.71	257.24	390.97
办公楼	Office Building	47.76	162.89	120.28	197.41
商业营业用房	Commercial Building	54.54	125.56	102.86	113.70
其　他	Others	9.70	81.72	80.61	111.08
商品房销售额（亿元）	**Sales Volume of Commodity Housing (100 million yuan)**	**555.45**	**2 959.94**	**3 499.53**	**5 093.55**
住　宅	Residence	480.97	2 395.35	2 923.44	4 319.93
#别墅、高档公寓	Villas and Apartment	32.65	852.62	859.54	1 462.81
办公楼	Office Building	44.05	307.67	300.43	488.68
商业营业用房	Commercial Building	27.87	197.57	226.44	227.89
其　他	Others	2.56	59.34	49.22	57.05
商品房出租面积（万平方米）	**Commodity Housing Leased (10 000 Sq. m)**	**358.38**	**1 262.47**	**1 142.46**	**1 202.42**
住　宅	Residence	59.29	85.72	72.16	120.59
#别墅、高档公寓	Villas and Apartment	37.43	76.18	60.39	66.26
办公楼	Office Building	156.15	516.18	502.65	501.86
商业营业用房	Commercial Building	62.04	373.34	373.99	367.02
其　他	Others	80.91	287.23	193.66	212.95

表 18.4 房屋征收(拆迁)情况(1995～2015)
BUILDINGS EXPROPRIATION(RESETTLEMENT)

年 份 Year	征收(拆迁)户数 (户) Quantity of Expropriation (Resettlements) (unit)	其 中 of which #居民住宅 Residence	征收(拆迁)面积 (万平方米) Floor Area Expropriated (Resettled)(10 000 sq. m)	其 中 of which #居民住宅 Residence
1995	75 777	73 695	322.77	253.90
1996	89 132	86 481	342.95	258.86
1997	79 857	77 388	479.67	363.16
1998	78 205	75 157	452.22	343.94
1999	75 185	73 709	342.50	248.17
2000	70 606	68 293	365.77	288.35
2001	73 728	71 909	515.65	386.66
2002	101 097	98 714	644.53	485.00
2003	80 858	79 077	584.93	475.47
2004	42 415	41 552	308.40	232.52
2005	75 857	74 483	1 222.53	851.85
2006	81 126	76 874	1 516.85	848.35
2007	51 354	49 092	825.00	690.00
2008	53 583	51 288	1 028.53	753.71
2009	68 286	65 439	927.63	612.56
2010	39 721	38 441	585.70	389.87
2011	23 112	22 349	333.83	182.83
2012	21 910	21 262	219.42	127.27
2013	30 921	30 322	159.57	123.18
2014	26 799	26 334	118.58	95.81
2015	23 062	22 801	78.52	69.83

表 18.5 各区房屋征收(拆迁)情况(2015)
BUILDINGS EXPROPRIATION(RESETTLEMENT) IN DIFFERENT DISTRICTS

地 区	District	征收(拆迁)户数 (户) Quantity of Expropriation (Resettlements)(unit)	其 中 of which #居民住宅 Residence	征收(拆迁)面积 (万平方米) Floor Area Expropriated (Resettld) (10 000 sq. m)	其 中 of which #居民住宅 Residence
总 计	**Total**	**23 062**	**22 801**	**78.52**	**69.83**
#浦东新区	Pudong New Area	114	104	1.02	0.80
黄 浦 区	Huangpu	3 766	3 766	11.76	11.76
徐 汇 区	Xuhui	1		0.15	
长 宁 区	Changning	108	100	0.72	0.62
静 安 区	Jing'an	224	170	0.88	0.50
普 陀 区	Putuo	3 309	3 309	10.22	10.22
闸 北 区	Zhabei	6 356	6 356	19.29	19.28
虹 口 区	Hongkou	4 607	4 607	15.63	15.63
杨 浦 区	Yangpu	4 571	4 389	14.53	11.01
闵 行 区	Minhang	6		4.32	

表 18.6 土地使用权出让情况(2015)
LEASE OF LAND PLOT TENURE

指 标	Indicators	出让地块(幅) Leased Plot (piece)	出让面积(万平方米) Leased Area (10 000 sq. m)
总 计	**Total**	**246**	**1 188.83**
商业服务	Commercial Service	54	193.81
住 宅	Residence	126	658.54
工业仓储	Storage of Industry	61	317.40
公共建筑	Public Buildings	5	19.08

表 18.7 存量房买卖登记情况(1994 ~2015)
REGISTRATION OF EXCHANGE OF SECOND-HAND HOUSES

年 份 Year	买卖登记套数(套) Houses Traded (set)	买卖登记面积(万平方米) Areas Traded (10 000 sq. m.)	其 中 of which		
			#住 宅 Residence	办公楼 Office	商业营业用房 Commerce
1994	2 821	31.76	10.59		
1995	4 176	60.87	19.70		
1996	4 689	82.29	25.09		
1997	9 180	162.40	87.68	23.95	14.95
1998	24 501	315.23	197.56	21.49	18.28
1999	44 234	510.84	336.69	37.63	14.61
2000	96 348	778.52	648.23	39.48	21.65
2001	164 598	1 422.43	1 031.48	56.99	57.24
2002	204 239	1 790.50	1 341.60	65.70	91.80
2003	263 297	2 306.28	1 807.57	105.14	114.28
2004	303 291	2 726.70	2 222.24	117.12	121.39
2005	189 896	1 971.50	1 608.20	88.10	78.00
2006	184 194	1 706.81	1 375.22	67.35	46.53
2007	213 733	1 992.59	1 715.05	49.73	36.34
2008	142 224	1 413.41	1 107.17	40.61	42.04
2009	312 857	2 809.45	2 490.58	48.19	43.59
2010	202 511	1 966.86	1 522.21	68.31	70.61
2011	146 151	1 398.67	1 058.71	62.87	51.21
2012	157 585	1 446.77	1 136.17	57.34	46.71
2013	291 176	2 575.70	2 228.02	65.59	47.18
2014	177 083	1 586.14	1 324.18	52.61	40.90
2015	303 414	2 647.83	2 351.30	52.27	41.62

上 / 海 / 统 / 计 / 年 / 鉴

主要统计指标解释

房地产开发投资

指报告期内房地产开发企业完成的全部用于房屋建设工程、土地开发工程的投资额以及公益性建筑和土地购置费等的投资。

施工面积

指报告期内房地产开发企业施工的全部房屋建筑面积。包括本期新开工的面积和上期开工跨入本期继续施工的房屋面积，以及上期已停建在本期恢复施工的房屋面积。本期竣工和本期施工后又停缓建的房屋，其建筑面积仍计入本期房屋施工面积中。

新开工面积

指报告期内房地产开发企业新开工建设的房屋建筑面积，以单位工程为核算对象。不包括在上期开工跨入报告期继续施工的房屋建筑面积和上期停缓建而在本期复工的建筑面积。房屋的开工以房屋正式开始破土刨槽（地基处理或打永久桩）的日期为准。

竣工面积

指在报告期内房屋建筑按照设计要求已经全部完工，达到住人和使用条件，经验收鉴定合格(或达到竣工验收标准)，可正式移交使用的各栋房屋建筑面积的总和。

指房地产开发企业本年按照设计要求已全部完工，达到住人和使用条件，经验收鉴定合格或达到竣工验收标准，可正式移交使用的各栋房屋建筑面积的总和。

商品房销售面积

指报告期内房地产开发企业出售新建商品房屋的合同总面积（即双方签署的正式买卖合同中所确认的建筑面积）。

商品房销售额

指报告期内房地产开发企业出售新建商品房屋的合同总价款（即双方签署的正式买卖合同中所确认的合同总价）。该指标与商品房销售面积同口径。

指房地产开发企业本年出售商品房屋的合同总价款(即双方签署的正式买卖合同中所确定的合同总价)。该指标与商品房销售面积同口径。

商品房出租面积

指在报告期末房地产开发企业出租的商品房屋的全部面积。

SHANGHAI STATISTICAL YEARBOOK

EXPLANATORY NOTES TO MAJOR STATISTICAL INDICATORS

□ Investment in Real Estate Development

Investment in Real Estate Development refers to investment entirely used for building construction project and land development project by real estate development enterprises, and investment in public buildings and purchase costs of land.

□ Floor Area of Construction

Floor Area of Construction refers to total floor space of all buildings constructing by real estate development enterprises during the reference period, including floor space of newly started buildings during the reference period, floor space of construction extended from the previous period to the current period, and floor space of construction suspended during the previous period and resumed in the current period. Floor space of construction completed in the current period, and floor space of construction started and then suspended in the current period are also included in the floor space under construction of the current year.

□ Floor Area of Newly-started Buildings

Floor Area of Newly-started Buildings refers to the floor space of buildings newly started to construct by real estate development enterprises during the reference period, one unit project was considered as a calculating unit. Excluding the floor space of buildings started in last period or stopped or delayed in last period and restarted in this period. The date of start construction refers to the beginning of breaking gouging (foundation treatment or permanent pile).

□ Floor Area Completed

Floor Area Completed refers to the floor space of all buildings completed in the reference period, which have been appraised and accepted (or come up to the designed standards) and have been transferred to the owners for use.

□ Sold Area of Commodity Housing

Sold Area of Commodity Housing refers to the total area of new commodity housing sold by real estate development enterprises in the reference period (the construction area confirmed by formal contracts).

□ Sales Volume of Commodity Housing

Sales Volume of Commodity Housing refers to the total sales volume of new commodity housing sold by real estate development enterprises in the reference period (the sales volume confirmed by formal contracts). The caliber of this index is same to Sold Area of Commodity Housing.

□ Commodity Housing Leased

Commodity Housing Leased refers to the total area of com-Commodity Housing Leased refers to the total area of commodity housing leased by real estate development enterprises at the end of the reference period.

第十九篇
CHAPTER 19

科学技术
SCIENCE AND TECHNOLOGY

简要说明

一、本篇资料的主要内容

科技统计资料主要内容包括：全社会以及工业企业、政府部门属研究机构、高校的研究与试验发展(R&D)活动情况；技术市场交易情况；科技成果情况；科技型企业情况；科协系统科技活动情况；专利申请和授权情况等。

二、本篇资料的统计范围

科技活动统计资料范围为全社会有研究与试验发展(R&D)活动的企事业单位，具体包括工业企业、政府部门属研究机构、普通高等学校以及研究与试验发展(R&D)活动相对密集行业(包括农、林、牧、渔业，建筑业，交通运输、仓储和邮政业，信息传输、软件和信息技术服务业，金融业，租赁和商务服务业，科学研究和技术服务业，水利、环境和公共设施管理业，卫生和社会工作，文化、体育和娱乐业等)中从事研究与试验发展(R&D)活动的企事业单位。

三、本篇的资料来源

全市综合资料、企业及有关行业企事业单位的研究与试验发展(R&D)活动情况资料由上海统计局调查提供；政府部门属研究机构资料由上海市科学技术委员会、上海市经济和信息化委员会调查提供；科学研究、技术服务和地质勘查业企事业的研究与试验发展(R&D)活动情况资料，以及技术市场资料、科技成果、科技型企业状况由上海市科学技术委员会调查提供；高校资料由上海市教育委员会调查提供；科协系统科技活动资料由上海市科学技术协会调查提供；专利资料由上海市知识产权局调查提供。

四、本篇的调查方法

研究与试验发展(R&D)活动情况采用全面调查取得；科协、专利资料采用抽样等多种调查方法取得。

五、统计资料口径变化

2000年以前科技活动统计资料只包括大中型工业企业、政府部门属研究机构、普通高等学校，2000年及以后年份扩大到了全社会范围。

BRIEF INTRODUCTION

I. Main Contents

Data on science and technology mainly include: data on scientific and technological activities, R&D activities all over the country, including industrial enterprises, scientific and technological institutions under government departments, universities and colleges; data on technological markets; data on science and technology achievements; data on scientific and technology enterprises; data on the scientific and technological activities in the system of associations for science and technology; patents application accepted and granted.

II. Statistical Range

Data on science and technology include research and development (R&D) activities of enterprises and institutions all over the country, mainly including industrial enterprises, scientific and technological institutions under government departments, universities, colleges and relatively R&D-intensive industries (such as agriculture, forestry, animal husbandry, fisher, construction, transport, storage and post, information transmission, software industry and information technology service, financial intermediation, leasing and business services, scientific research and technical service, management of water conservancy, environment and public facilities, health and social work, culture, sports and entertainment).

III. Data Sources

Data on citywide aggregates and R&D activities of various enterprises and institutions are from Shanghai Municipal Statistics Bureau; data on scientific and technological institutions under government departments are from Science and Technology Commission of Shanghai Municipality、Shanghai Municipal Commission of Economy and Informatization; data on R&D activities of scientific research、technical service、geologic prospecting, and technological markets, scientific and technical payoffs, scientific and technology enterprises are from Science and Technology Commission of Shanghai Municipality; data on scientific and technological activities in universities and colleges are from Shanghai Municipal Education Commission; data on the scientific and technological activities of associations for science and technology are from Science and Technology Commission of Shanghai Municipality; Shanghai Intellectual Property Administration provides data on patents.

IV. Statistical Methodology

Data on R&D activities are collected through complete surveys. Data on scientific and technological associations and patent applications are through sample surveys and other surveys.

V. Changes of the statistical coverage of data

Before 2000, data only included large and medium-sized industrial enterprises, scientific research institutions under government departments, and universities and colleges. Since 2000 (inclusive), data have covered all industries.

表 19.1 主要年份科技活动主要指标
MAIN INDICATORS OF SCIENTIFIC AND TECHNOLOGICAL ACTIVITIES IN MAIN YEARS

年 份 Year	科技活动人员(万人) Personnel Engaged in Scientific and Technological Activities (10 000 persons)	研究与试验发展(R&D)人员全时当量(万人年) Full-time Equivalent of R&D Personnel (10 000 person-years)	研究与试验发展(R&D)经费内部支出(亿元) Expenditures on R&D (100 million yuan)	研究与试验发展经费支出相当于上海市生产总值比例(%) R&D as Percentage of Gross Domestic Product (%)	地方财政科技经费支出(亿元) Local Fiscal Expenditures on Scientific and Technological Research (100 million yuan)	科技经费支出占地方财政支出比重(%) Percentage of Expenditures on Scientific and Technological Research in Local Fiscal (%)
1990	19.34		10.13	1.30	2.44	3.2
1995	18.25		32.60	1.30	5.12	2.0
2000	20.17	6.31	76.73	1.61	10.08	1.6
2001	17.57	5.20	88.08	1.69	12.39	1.7
2002	17.89	5.02	102.36	1.78	15.25	1.7
2003	17.59	5.62	128.92	1.93	19.84	1.8
2004	18.25	5.73	170.28	2.11	39.32	2.8
2005	19.67	7.07	213.77	2.31	79.34	4.8
2006	20.07	8.01	258.84	2.45	94.89	5.2
2007	22.79	9.03	307.50	2.46	105.77	4.9
2008	23.08	9.75	362.30	2.58	120.27	4.6
2009	33.90	13.29	423.38	2.81	215.31	7.2
2010	33.46	13.50	481.70	2.81	202.03	6.1
2011	37.53	14.85	597.71	3.11	218.50	5.6
2012	38.91	15.34	679.46	3.37	245.43	5.9
2013	43.16	16.58	776.78	3.60	257.66	5.7
2014	45.10	16.82	861.95	3.66	262.29	5.3
2015	44.81	17.18	936.14	3.73	271.85	4.4

注：本表部分数据由上海市财政局等部门提供。
Note: Data in this table are mainly provided by Shanghai Municipal Finance Bureau.

表 19.2 主要年份研究与试验发展(R&D)经费内部支出按执行部门分类
EXPENDITURES ON R&D GROUPED BY EXECUTIVE DEPARTMENT IN MAIN YEARS

单位:亿元(100 million yuan)

指 标	Indicators	2000	2010	2014	2015
总 计	**Total**	**76.73**	**481.70**	**861.95**	**936.14**
科研机构	Research Institutions	25.58	105.35	232.23	264.70
高等院校	Institutions of Higher Education	7.43	45.80	71.60	86.65
企 业	Enterprises	41.44	321.31	546.46	569.31
#工业企业	Industrial Enterprises	34.78	274.05	449.22	474.24
#大中型工业企业	Large and Medium Industrial Enterprises	30.98	237.75	379.12	402.75
其 他	Others	2.28	9.25	11.66	15.48

表 19.3 主要年份研究与试验发展(R&D)活动情况
BASIC STATISTICS OF RESEARCH AND DEVELOPMENT(R&D)ACTIVITIES IN MAIN YEARS

指 标	Indicators	2000	2010	2014	2015
有 R&D 活动单位数(个)	**Quantity of Science and Technology Institutions (unit)**	**1 070**	**1 782**	**2 469**	**2 547**
#科研机构	Research Institutions	125	113	112	111
高等院校	Institutions of Higher Education	41	68	68	114
企 业	Enterprises	820	1 453	2 156	2 188
其 他	Others	84	148	133	134
R&D 人员投入情况	**Personnel Investment on R&D**				
R&D 人员(万人)	R&D Personnel(10 000 persons)		17.75	23.68	24.27
R&D 人员全时当量(万人年)	Full-time Equivalent of R&D Personnel(10 000 person-year)	6.31	13.50	16.82	17.18
基础研究	Basic Research	0.60	1.42	1.82	1.96
应用研究	Applied Research	1.92	2.29	2.34	2.52
试验发展	Experimental Development	3.79	9.79	12.66	12.70
R&D 经费投入情况	**Expenditure on R&D**				
R&D 经费内部支出(亿元)	Intramural Expenditure on R&D (100 million yuan)	76.73	481.70	861.95	936.14
#基础研究	Basic Research	4.98	31.05	61.20	76.95
应用研究	Applied Research	18.18	68.99	104.43	127.84
试验发展	Experimental Development	53.57	381.67	696.32	731.35
#政府资金	Government Funds	24.22	142.78	292.36	340.80
企业资金	Self-raised Funds by Enterprises	33.76	318.28	513.15	540.88
境外资金	Offshore Funds	4.79	6.80	16.03	15.12
其 他	Others	13.96	13.83	40.41	39.33
R&D 项目(课题)情况	**R&D project**				
项目(课题)数 (万项)	Quantity of Projects (10 000 item)	2.07	5.56	7.58	7.56
项目(课题)参加人员(万人年)	Personnel Engaged in Projects (10 000 persons year)	5.42	11.89	15.57	15.58
项目(课题)经费内部支出(亿元)	Inner Expenditure on Projects (100 million yuan)	54.31	379.37	711.27	805.55
科技活动产出情况	**Output of Science and Technic Activities**				
新产品产值(亿元)	Production Value of New Product(100 million yuan)	1 401.62	5 870.02	7 407.99	7 312.24
新产品销售收入(亿元)	Sales Revenue of New Product(100 million yuan)	1 398.54	6 543.07	8 446.96	7 470.93
专利申请数(件)	Patent Applications(piece)	11 337	71 196	81 664	38 266
#发明专利	Invention Patents	4 713	26 165	39 133	23 452
专利授权数(件)	Patents Granted(piece)	4 050	48 215	50 488	8 756
#发明专利	Invention Patents	304	6 867	11 614	6 207
有效发明专利数(件)	Effective Invention Patents(piece)		23 843	56 515	55 577
发表科技论文数(篇)	Quantity of Science and Technic Papers Published(case)	37 216	87 971	94 187	98 035
出版科技著作(种)	Science and Technic Works Published(piece)	2 614	3 329	3 031	3 208
商标申请注册数(万件)	Register Applications for Trade Marks (case)	0.95	6.02	13.76	20.7
商标核准注册数(万件)	Registration approved for Trade Marks (case)	0.62	7.04	7.64	13.2
科技成果登记数(项)	Quantity of Achievements Registered in Scientific and Technological Activities(item)	1 102	2 318	2 384	2 356

注：本表部分数据由市知识产权局、市工商局和市科学技术委员会提供。
Note: Data in this table are partly provided by Shanhgai? Intellectual Property Service Center, Shanghai Administration of Industry and Commerce and Shanghai Municipal Science and Technology Commission.

表 19.4 国有企事业单位专业技术人员基本情况(2015)
PROFESSIONAL AND TECHNICAL PERSONNEL IN STATE-OWNED ENTERPRISES AND INSTITUTIONS

单位:万人(10 000 persons)

类别	Types	合计 Total	其中 of which	按学历分 by Education Background		
			#女性 Female	大学本专科以上 College and University above	中等专业 Specialized Secondary School	高中及以下 Senior Middle School and below
总计	**Total**	**96.83**	**48.01**	**89.20**	**4.51**	**3.12**
高级岗位	Senior	10.64	4.14	10.56	0.05	0.02
中级岗位	Medium	29.22	15.52	28.44	0.57	0.21
初级岗位	Junior	29.61	16.00	26.48	2.38	0.75
未聘人员	Not Appointed	27.36	12.35	23.72	1.51	2.14

表 19.4 续表 continued

单位:万人(10 000 persons)

类别	Types	合计 Total	其中 of which	按学历分 by Education Background		
			#女性 Female	大学本专科以上 College and University above	中等专业 Specialized Secondary School	高中及以下 Senior Middle School and below
总计	**Total**	**96.83**	**48.01**	**89.20**	**4.51**	**3.12**
工程技术人员	Engineering	27.39	6.01	25.14	1.20	1.05
农业技术人员	Agriculture	0.36	0.11	0.30	0.04	0.02
科学研究人员	Scientific Research	2.61	0.93	2.58	0.02	0.01
卫生技术人员	Medical Professionals	11.57	8.55	10.39	1.12	0.07
教学人员	Teaching	18.69	13.42	18.53	0.13	0.04
经济人员	Economic	24.19	11.89	21.40	1.31	1.48
财会人员	Financial Accounting	7.03	4.62	6.34	0.44	0.25
统计人员	Statistical	0.87	0.49	0.79	0.04	0.04
翻译人员	Translator	0.11	0.06	0.10	…	…
新闻出版、播音人员	Media, Publishing & Announcer	0.87	0.48	0.84	0.01	0.01
艺术人员	Culture&Art	0.65	0.28	0.52	0.08	0.05
其他专业人员	Others	2.50	1.15	2.28	0.11	0.11

注:本页数据由市委组织部提供。
Note: Data on this page are provide by Shanghai Municipal Party Committee Organization Department.

表 19.5 主要年份各类技术合同项目
VARIOUS TECHNOLOGICAL CONTRACTS IN MAIN YEARS

单位：项（item）

年 份 Year	项 目 Item	其中 of which 技术开发 Technological Development	技术转让 Technological Transfer	技术咨询 Technological Consulting	技术服务 Technological Service
1991	25 023	3 038	1 992	3 203	16 790
1995	21 213	1 915	775	3 672	14 851
1996	20 074	1 841	823	3 821	13 589
1997	18 863	1 643	1 037	3 569	12 614
1998	18 364	1 206	919	3 235	13 004
1999	19 721	1 158	937	3 993	13 633
2000	20 974	1 561	888	3 905	14 620
2001	23 816	2 385	1 294	5 012	15 125
2002	26 010	2 984	1 156	4 983	16 887
2003	27 292	3 512	2 112	5 306	16 362
2004	27 327	4 398	2 453	4 814	15 662
2005	30 290	5 256	2 444	4 753	17 837
2006	28 191	6 165	2 172	3 592	16 262
2007	27 742	6 425	2 133	3 086	16 098
2008	28 713	7 154	1 749	3 873	15 937
2009	27 109	8 071	1 549	3 034	14 455
2010	26 185	8 894	1 370	2 685	13 236
2011	29 332	10 771	1 317	3 277	13 967
2012	27 998	10 974	1 170	3 026	12 828
2013	26 297	10 057	1 102	3 094	12 044
2014	25 238	10 187	1 201	2 876	10 974
2015	22 513	9 579	1 050	2 458	9 426

表 19.6 主要年份各类技术合同成交金额
TOTAL CONTRACTED VALUE IN VARIOUS TECHNOLOGICAL CONTRACTS IN MAIN YEARS

单位：亿元（100 million yuan）

年 份 Year	成交金额 Contracted Value	其中 of which 技术开发 Technological Development	技术转让 Technological Transfer	技术咨询 Technological Consulting	技术服务 Technological Service
1991	9.33	2.15	1.90	0.55	4.72
1995	23.04	4.14	1.57	2.12	15.21
1996	25.65	4.38	1.50	2.81	16.97
1997	28.76	5.72	2.14	3.28	17.61
1998	31.41	4.55	2.58	2.44	21.85
1999	36.63	3.68	3.50	3.24	26.21
2000	73.90	9.96	36.44	3.51	23.99
2001	106.16	28.24	50.71	4.63	22.58
2002	120.22	45.40	46.18	4.63	24.01
2003	142.78	50.96	50.79	6.11	34.92
2004	171.70	61.31	42.32	6.00	62.07
2005	231.73	87.47	110.08	6.42	27.76
2006	344.43	142.79	165.18	7.60	28.86
2007	432.64	181.50	212.49	5.50	33.15
2008	485.75	213.24	229.53	6.41	36.57
2009	489.86	266.30	174.34	5.39	43.83
2010	525.45	264.68	213.86	4.93	41.98
2011	550.32	328.25	164.49	5.40	52.18
2012	588.52	297.14	223.48	5.17	62.73
2013	620.87	267.33	230.15	7.40	115.99
2014	667.99	299.83	221.99	5.95	140.22
2015	707.99	321.49	296.99	5.32	84.20

注：本页数据由市技术市场管理办公室提供。
Note: Data on this page are provided by Shanghai Technology Market Administrative Office.

表 19.7 科技成果（2000～2015）
ACHIEVEMENTS IN SCIENTIFIC AND TECHNICAL RESEARCH

单位：项（item）

年 份 Year	科技成果 Achievements in Science and Technology	按成果水平分 By Level of Achievements			
		#国际领先 Being First Created in the World	国际先进 Attaining Advanced World Levels	国内领先 Being First Created in China	国内先进 Attaining Advanced Domestic Levels
2000	1 102	45	462	452	117
2001	1 338	78	542	444	116
2002	1 418	65	603	463	106
2003	1 508	71	532	481	155
2004	1 629	147	669	480	155
2005	1 701	123	629	588	189
2006	1 953	250	675	655	191
2007	2 396	180	761	938	254
2008	1 866	125	664	663	226
2009	2 166	260	651	831	247
2010	2 318	188	698	724	202
2011	2 388	211	598	568	158
2012	2 415	177	572	596	142
2013	2 490	125	462	548	164
2014	2 384	108	423	531	149
2015	2 356	125	367	467	155

表 19.7 续表 continued

单位：项（item）

年 份 Year	按成果分 By Type of Achievements				
	基础理论成果 Fundamental Theory Research Results	应用技术成果 Application of Technological Achievements	其 中 of which		软科学成果 Soft Scientific Achievements
			已推广应用 Been Populized	未应用 Not Been Populized	
2000	79	953	809	144	70
2001	81	1 196	940	256	61
2002	110	1 250	961	289	58
2003	97	1 281	1 045	236	130
2004	70	1 488	1 204	284	71
2005	61	1 555	1 261	294	85
2006	52	1 799	1 506	293	102
2007	139	2 162	1 724	438	95
2008	115	1 695	1 337	358	56
2009	94	2 009	1 747	262	63
2010	152	2 104	1 824	280	62
2011	182	2 137	1 943	194	69
2012	218	2 112	1 914	198	85
2013	248	2 152	1 872	280	90
2014	263	2 023	1 798	225	98
2015	239	2 040	1 764	276	77

表 19.8 主要年份科研机构研究与试验发展(R&D)活动情况
BASIC STATISTICS OF RESEARCH AND DEVELOPMENT(R&D)ACTIVITIES OF SCIENTIFIC RESEARCH INSTITUTIONS IN MAIN YEARS

指 标	Indicators	2000	2010	2014	2015
有 R&D 活动单位数(个)	**Quantity of Science and Technology Institutions (unit)**	**125**	**113**	**112**	**111**
R&D 人员投入情况	**Personnel Investment on R&D**				
R&D 人员(人)	R&D Personnel(person)		26 550	32 972	33 943
R&D 人员全时当量(人年)	Ful-time Equivalent of R&D Personnel(person-year)	19 802	23 241	29 343	29 432
#基础研究	Basic Research	2 675	3 781	6 471	6 453
应用研究	Applied Research	8 873	8 771	10 196	10 092
试验发展	Experimental Development	8 254	10 689	12 676	12 887
R&D 经费投入情况	**Expenditure on R&D**				
R&D 经费内部支出(亿元)	Intramural Expenditure on R&D (100 million yuan)	25.58	105.35	232.23	264.70
#基础研究	Basic Research	3.06	13.87	33.78	36.78
应用研究	Applied Research	9.84	34.51	57.64	63.99
试验发展	Experimental Development	12.68	56.97	140.81	163.93
#政府资金	Government Funds	18.89	88.98	200.24	238.40
企业资金	Self-raised Funds by Enterprises	1.09	6.61	6.29	5.31
境外资金	Offshore Funds	0.69	0.54	0.83	1.29
R&D 项目(课题)情况	**R&D project**				
R&D 项目(课题)数(项)	Quantity of Projects (10 000 item)	3 190	5 933	8 401	8 785
R&D 项目(课题)人员全时当量(人年)	Personnel Engaged in Projects (10 000 person-years)	14 015	18 799	26 651	19 289
R&D 项目(课题)经费内部支出(亿元)	Inner Expenditure on Projects (100 million yuan)	8.56	58.99	166.38	95.20
科技产出及成果情况	**Output of Science and Technic Activities**				
发表科技论文数(篇)	Quantity of Science and Technic Papers Published(case)	6 831	7 896	9 910	10 107
出版科技著作(种)	Works of Science and Technology Published(kind)	187	197	220	218
专利申请受理数(件)	Number of Patents Applications(piece)	425	1 864	3 841	4 095
#发明专利	Inventions	275	1 593	3 066	3 364
专利申请授权数(件)	Number of Patents Application Granted(piece)		817	2 194	2 401
#发明专利	Inventions		502	1 451	1 715
有效发明专利数(件)	Effective Invention Patents(piece)	779	2 732	5 667	7 143

表 19.9 主要年份获得科技成果奖励情况
ACHIEVEMENTS AWARDED IN SCIENTIFIC AND TECHNOLOGICAL RESEARCH IN MAIN YEARS

单位：项(item)

指标	Indicators	2000	2010	2014	2015
科技成果获奖总数	**Quantity of Achievements Awarded**	**287**	**298**	**341**	**355**
获国家科技成果奖	**National Award**	**21**	**58**	**54**	**42**
#国家最高科学技术奖(人)	State Supreme Science Award		1		
国家自然科学奖	Natural Science Award	3	6	7	5
国家技术发明奖	Technological Invention Award	1	4	8	6
国家科学技术进步奖	Science and Technology Progress Award	17	46	39	31
获上海科技进步奖	**Shanghai Award**	**266**	**240**	**287**	**313**
#国际科学技术合作奖(人)	International Science and Technology Cooperation Award		1	3	5

表 19.10 主要年份自然科学研究与技术开发机构课题情况
PROJECTS OF NATURAL SCIENCE RESEARCH AND TECHNOLOGICAL DEVELOPMENT INSTITUTIONS IN MAIN YEARS

年份 Year	机构数 (个) Quantity of Institutions (unit)	课题数 (项) Quantity of Projects (item)	投入人力 (人年) Manpower Input (person-year)	投入经费 (万元) Funds Invested (10 000 yuan)
1990	229	8 339	23 279	33 061
1995	230	6 544	17 531	80 957
1996	233	5 538	17 434	90 504
1997	232	5 481	17 507	117 199
1998	230	5 554	16 713	122 513
1999	225	5 135	16 396	125 620
2000	229	4 879	17 104	148 846
2001	221	4 468	16 972	210 910
2002	218	4 393	15 523	251 837
2003	216	4 473	17 058	282 865
2004	212	4 540	17 299	330 063
2005	206	4 416	18 924	425 266
2006	202	4 585	19 008	494 657
2007	199	5 534	20 443	542 601
2008	194	6 006	21 111	719 082
2009	195	6 653	23 773	698 690
2010	191	7 141	26 080	992 896
2011	182	7 356	26 643	1 215 674
2012	180	8 031	29 745	1 324 384
2013	179	8 462	30 969	1 622 659
2014	180	9 564	33 587	1 866 208
2015	180	10 225	34 475	1 965 410

表 19.11　自然科学研究与技术开发机构课题情况(2015)
STATISTICS OF PROJECTS OF NATURAL SCIENCE RESEARCH AND DEVELOPMENT INSTITUTIONS

类　别	Types	机构数（个）Number of Institutions (unit)	课题数（项）Number of Projects (item)	投入人力（人年）Manpower Input (person-year)	投入经费（万元）Funds Invested (10 000 yuan)
总　计	**Total**	**180**	**10 225**	**34 475**	**1 965 410**
按学科分	**By Subject**				
自然科学	Natural Science	17	4 192	3 370	251 471
农业科学	Agriculture Science	19	927	1 144	42 975
医学科学	Medical Science	18	1 267	1 815	88 883
工程科学与技术	Engineering Science and Technology	122	3 692	27 980	1 579 646
社会与人文科学	Social Science and Humanities	4	147	166	2 435
按行业分	**By Sector**				
# 制造业	Manufacturing	85	1 734	19 107	1 211 167
建筑业	Construction	4	159	475	20 430
交通运输、仓储和邮政业	Transportation, Warehousing and Post	5	26	342	10 070
科学研究和技术服务业	Scientific Research and Technical Service	45	6 641	11 716	651 388
水利、环境和公共设施管理业	Water Conservancy, Environment and Public Facility Management	8	270	547	8 978
卫生和社会工作	Health and Social Work	13	477	958	16 008

表 19.12　自然科学研究与技术开发机构论文与著作情况(2015)
PAPERS AND WORKS OF NATURAL SCIENCE RESEARCH AND TECHNOLOGICAL DEVELOPMENT INSTITUTIONS

类　别	Types	论　文（篇）Papers (piece)	其中 of which # 国外发表 Issued Abroad	科技著作（种）Scientific and Technological Works (sort)
总　计	**Total**	**10 961**	**4 370**	**134**
按学科领域分	**By Subject**			
自然科学	Natural Science	2 920	1 881	29
农业科学	Agriculture Science	875	237	12
医学科学	Medical Science	2 042	1 067	50
工程科学与技术	Engineering Science and Technology	5 099	1 184	39
社会与人文科学	Social and Humanities Science	25	1	4
按行业分	**By Sector**			
# 农、林、牧、渔业	Farming, Forestry, Animal Husbandry and Fishery	760	209	12
制造业	Manufacturing	2 796	546	28
建筑业	Construction	400	17	
科学研究和技术服务业	Scientific Research and Technical Service	5 841	3 095	66
卫生和社会工作	Health and Social Work	845	430	23

表 19.13 区县级以上国有单位独立研究与开发机构人员(2015) PERSONNEL OF STATE-OWNED INDEPENDENT RESEARCH AND DEVELOPMENT INSTITUTIONS ABOVE DISTRICT AND COUNTY LEVEL

单位:人(person)

类 别	Types	从事科技活动人员 Personnel Engaged in Scientific and Technological Activities	其中 of which # R&D 人员 R&D Personnel	# 高中级技术职称人员 Personnel with High and Medium Technic Titles	# 研究生 Post-graduates	# 大学 University and College
总 计	**Total**	**49 952**	**46 130**	**32 308**	**23 425**	**18 387**
按隶属关系分	**By Subordination**					
中 央	Central	36 036	37 671	24 118	17 549	12 466
# 中国科学院	The Chinese Academy of Science	8 465	14 076	6 641	5 372	1 928
地 方	Local	13 916	8 459	8 190	5 876	5 921
按领域分	**By Subject**					
自然科学	Natural Science	47 696	45 418	30 735	22 316	17 542
社会与人文科学	Social Sciences and Humanities	1 148	710	859	801	252
科技信息文献	Scientific & Technological Information & Documents	1 108	2	714	308	593

表 19.14 主要年份区县级属研究与开发机构状况 RESEARCH AND DEVELOPMENT INSTITUTIONS AT DISTRICT AND COUNTY LEVEL IN MAIN YEARS

指 标	Indicators	2000	2010	2014	2015
机构数(个)	Quantity of Institutions (unit)	35	18	17	16
从业人员(人)	Quantity of Employees (person)	1 261	1 015	907	890
# 从事科技活动人员	Personnel Engaged in Science and Technic Activities	736	764	736	765
科技活动经费内部支出(万元)	Inner Expenditures on Science and Technic Activities (10 000 yuan)	7 343	15 482	21 933	19 378

表 19.15 主要年份高等学校研究与试验发展(R&D)活动情况
RESERCH AND DEVELOPMENT(R&D) ACTIVITIES OF HIGHER EDUCATION IN MAIN YEARS

	指 标 Indicators	2000	2010	2014	2015
有 R&D 活动单位数(个)	**Quantity of Science and Technology Institutions (unit)**	**41**	**68**	**68**	**114**
#理工农医	Science, Engineering, Agriculture and Medicine		38	38	57
人文社科	Humanity and Social Science		30	30	57
R&D 人员投入情况	**Personnel Investment on R&D**				
R&D 人员(人)	R&D Personnel(person)		38 175	40 381	43 574
R&D 人员全时当量(人年)	Full-time Equivalent of R&D Personnel (person-year)	10 816	21 565	22 198	23 282
#基础研究	Basic Research	3 015	9 026	10 353	11 724
应用研究	Applied Research	6 378	10 387	9 659	10 197
试验发展	Experimental Development	1 423	2 152	2 186	1 362
R&D 经费投入情况	**Expenditure on R&D**				
R&D 经费内部支出(亿元)	Intramural Expenditure on R&D (100 million yuan)	7.43	45.80	71.60	86.65
#基础研究	Basic Research	1.44	15.19	25.17	37.87
应用研究	Applied Research	4.50	24.71	35.35	41.65
试验发展	Experimental Development	1.49	5.90	11.08	7.13
#政府资金	Government Funds	3.26	27.33	42.51	55.35
企业资金	Self-raised Funds by Enterprises	3.38	15.47	25.85	27.26
境外资金	Offshore Funds	0.31	0.67	0.48	0.37
R&D 课题情况	**R&D Projects**				
R&D 课题数(项)	Quantity of Projects(item)	12 525	36 656	50 323	52 167
R&D 课题人员全时当量(人年)	Full-time Equivalent of Personnel in Projects(person-year)	15 945	21 541	22 186	23 268
R&D 课题经费内部支出(亿元)	Inner Expenditure on Projects(100 million yuan)	7.28	32.96	56.03	63.61
科技产出及成果情况	**Output of Science and Technic Activities**				
发表科技论文(篇)	Quantity of Science and Technic Papers Published (case)	25 896	70 290	74 108	78 275
出版科技著作(种)	Works of Science and Technology Published(sort)	2 206	3 020	2 690	2 877
专利申请数(件)	Number of Patents Applications(piece)	527	6 828	9 503	9 507
#发明专利	Inventions	385	4 834	7 367	7 695
专利授权数(件)	Number of Patents Application Granted(piece)		4 035	5 453	6 177
#发明专利	Inventions		2 169	3 189	4 393
有效发明专利数(件)	Effective Invention Patents(piece)		11 558	14 234	15 445

表 19.16 高等学校科技活动人员（2015）
SCIENTIFIC AND TECHNOLOGICAL PERSONNEL OF INSTITUTIONS OF HIGHER EDUCATION

单位：人(person)

指标	Indicators	合计 Total	其中 of which 自然科学 Natural Science	工程与技术 Engineering and Technology	医学科学 Medical Science	农业科学 Agriculture Science	其他 Others
总计	**Total**	**46 752**	**5 092**	**14 710**	**22 685**	**333**	**3 932**
#科学家和工程师	Scientists and Engineers	45 196	5 004	14 453	21 718	333	3 688
按职称分	**By Professional Title**						
高级	Senior	16 292	2 933	6 858	5 526	178	797
中级	Medium	17 922	1 791	6 189	7 765	120	2 057
初级	Junior	10 982	280	1 406	8 427	35	834

表 19.17 高等学校研究机构和课题情况（2015）
RESEARCH INSTITUTIONS AND PROJECT OF HIGHER EDUCATION

指标	Indicators	合计 Total	其中 of which #自然科学 Natural Science	工程与技术 Engineering and Technology	医学科学 Medical Science	农业科学 Agriculture Science
研究机构数（个）	Research Institutions(unit)	288	63	121	84	5
机构 R&D 人员（人）	Institutions Personnel of R&D(person)	7 533	1 772	3 230	2 318	85
机构 R&D 经费支出(亿元)	R&D expenditure of Institutions (100 million yuan)	11.7	3.5	5.9	2.0	0.2
课题数（个）	Quantity of Projects of R&D (unit)	35 115	5 401	17 988	10 859	867
课题投入人员（人年）	Project Personnel(person-year)	20 404.3	2 613.8	8 259.7	9 071.2	459.6
课题投入经费(亿元)	Project Funding(100 million yuan)	92.94	14.27	59.93	16.94	1.79
课题经费支出（亿元）	Project Expenditure(100 million yuan)	76.30	11.32	50.23	13.59	1.16

注：本页统计范围是指高等学校中理工农医类口径。
Note: Figures of this page refer to those of science, engineering, agriculture and medicine of higher education.

表 19.18 主要年份专利申请量和授权量
PATENT APPLICATIONS AND CERTIFIED IN MAIN YEARS

单位:件(item)

指 标	Indicators	2000	2010	2014	2015
专利申请量	**Patent Applications**	**11 337**	**71 196**	**81 664**	**100 006**
#发 明	Inventions	4 713	26 165	39 133	46 976
专利授权量	**Patent Certified**	**4 050**	**48 215**	**50 488**	**60 623**
#发 明	Inventions	304	6 867	11 614	17 601
有效发明专利	Effective Invention Patents		23 843	56 515	69 982
PCT 国际专利受理	PCT International Patent Application Accepted		735	1 038	1 060

表 19.19 科协系统出版物和科技服务情况(2015)
PUBLICATIONS AND CONSULTATIVE ACTIVITIES OF SCIENCE AND TECHNOLOGY ASSOCIATIONS

指 标	Indicators	合 计 Total	其 中 of which: 市级科协 Municipal Level Associations	区(县)级科协 District and County Level Associations	市级学会 Municipal Level Societies
出版物	**Publications**				
主办科技期刊(种)	Scientific Journals (sort)	81	1	2	78
科技期刊总印数(万册)	Total Printed (10 000 copies)	492	24		468
编著科技图书(种)	Science and Technology Books (sort)	253	218		35
科技图书总印数(万册)	Total Printed of Science and Technology Books (10 000 copies)	80	51		30
主办科技报纸(种)	Technology Newspaper (sort)	6	2	2	2
科技报纸总印数(万份)	Total Printed of Technology Newspaper (10 000 copies)	678	672	1	5
咨 询	**Consultation**				
提供决策咨询报告(篇)	Decision Consultation Reports (sheet)	322	26	61	235
#获上级领导批示报告(篇)	Marking by Superiors (sheet)	162	5	20	137
举办决策咨询活动(次)	Decision Consultation Activities (time)	381	44	80	257
参加决策咨询活动专家数(人次)	Experts Participating in Decision Consultation Activities (person-time)	2 743	455	567	1 721

表 19.20 科协系统科普活动和科技培训情况（2015）
PROMOTING SCIENCE ACTIVITIES AND TRAINING PROGRAM ORGANIZED BY SCIENCE AND TECHNOLOGY ASSOCIATIONS

指 标	Indicators	合 计 Total	其中 of which 市级科协 Municipal level Associations	区(县)级科协 District and County Level Associations	市级学会 Municipal Level Societies
举办科普宣讲活动(次)	Science Propaganda Activities (time)	10 656	306	8 964	1 386
科普宣讲活动参加人次（万人次）	Participants in Science Propaganda Activities (10 000 person-times)	525.55	36.68	325.05	163.82
举办实用技术培训(次)	Practical Technical Training (time)	4 099	58	3 306	735
实用技术培训参加人数（万人次）	Trainees of Practical Technical Training (10 000 person-times)	25.45	0.24	19.44	5.80
举办青少年科技竞赛(次)	Youth Science Competition (time)	1 060	5	991	64
青少年科技竞赛参加人数（万人次）	Competitors of Youth Science Competition (10 000 person-times)	93.36	37.01	44.94	11.41
青少年科技竞赛获奖人数（人次）	Winners of Youth Science Competition (person-time)	39 979	6 038	27 405	6 536
青少年参加国际及港澳台科技交流活动(次)	International and Hong Kong, Macao and Taiwan Technology Exchange Activities (time)	45	11	29	5
青少年参加国际及港澳台科技交流活动人数(人次)	Participants in International and Hong Kong, Macao and Taiwan Technology Exchange Activities(person-time)	1 362	510	781	71
举办青少年科学营(次)	Youth Science Camp (time)	237	2	184	51
青少年科学营参加人数(人次)	Participants in Youth Science Camp(person-time)	131 034	2 200	117 227	11 607
举办青少年科技教育培训(次)	Youth Science and Technology Education and Training (time)	2 539	453	1 692	394
青少年科技教育培训参加人数（万人次）	Trainees of Youth Science and Technology Education and Training(10 000 person-times)	41.52	14.04	26.16	1.33

表 19.21 各级科协机构和人员（2015）
INSTITUTIONS AND PERSONNEL OF SCIENCE AND TECHNOLOGY ASSOCIATIONS AT VARIOUS LEVELS

指 标	Indicators	市级科协 Municipal Level Associations	区级科协 District Level Associations	县级科协 County Level Associations
机构数（个）	Institutions(unit)	1	16	1
人 员（人）	Personnel(person)	64	211	5
各级学会在册个数（个）	All Levels Societies Registered(unit)	195	432	27

表 19.21 续表 continued

指 标	Indicators	机构数(个) Quantity of Institutions (unit)	个人会员（万人） Individual Members (10 000 persons)	团体会员数(个) Organization Members (unit)	所属分科学会(个) Attached Associations (unit)
市级学会	Prefectural Societies	195	25.6	15 907	1 068

表19.22 科协系统学术交流情况（2015）
ACADEMIC EXCHANGES OF SCIENCE AND TECHNOLOGY ASSOCIATIONS

指标	Indicators	合计 Total	其中 of which #市级科协 Municipal Level Associations	市级学会 Municipal Level Academies
国内学术会议	**Domestic Academic Conferences**			
举办次数(次数)	Times(time)	2 373	25	2 046
参加人数(人次)	Participants (person-times)	309 790	15 000	249 303
交流论文(篇)	Papers Exchanged (piece)	37 767	1 500	34 428
境内国际学术会议	**International Academic Conferences**			
举办次数(次数)	Times(time)	145	2	126
参加人数(人次)	Participants (person-times)	68 263	450	63 143
交流论文(篇)	Papers Exchanged (piece)	6 164	6	5 771
港澳台地区学术会议	**Quantity of Academic Meeting Related with Hong Kong, Macao and Taiwan**			
举办次数(次数)	Times(time)	11		11
参加人数(人次)	Participants (person-times)	1 029		1 029
交流论文(篇)	Papers Exchanged (piece)	244		244
参加国外科技活动人数(人次)	**Participants in Foreign Scientific and Technological Activities (person-time)**	**663**	**23**	**625**
参加港澳台地区科技活动人数(人次)	**Participants in Hong Kong, Macao and Taiwan Scientific and Technological Activities (person-time)**	**301**	**75**	**226**
接待国外专家学者(人次)	**Reception of Foreign Experts and Scholars (person-time)**	**1 541**	**135**	**1 400**
接待港澳台地区专家学者(人次)	**Reception of Hong Kong, Macao and Taiwan Experts and Scholars (person-time)**	**374**	**92**	**282**

表 19.23 主要年份科技型企业状况
SCIENTIFIC AND TECHNOLOGICAL ENTERPRISES IN MAIN YEARS

指标	Indicators	2000	2010	2014	2015
机构数（个）	**Number of Institutions（unit）**	**12 316**	**18 008**	**14 147**	**14 869**
从业人员（万人）	**Employment（10 000 persons）**	**26.33**	**94.25**	**160.47**	**160.95**
#从事科技活动人员	Scientific & Technological Personnel	12.95	21.69	60.04	59.27
#高中级技术职称人员	Personnel with Medium and Senior Titles	8.90	12.12	22.79	21.99
资产总额(亿元)	Total Assets(100 million yuan)	1 064.07	9 070.91	27 808.05	28 591.29
总收入(亿元)	Revenue(100 million yuan)	811.35	8 462.57	21 441.43	19 509.61
企业内部用于科技活动的经费支出(亿元)	Inner Expenditure on Scientific and Technological Activities（100 million yuan）		473.32	1 357.44	1 370.09
当年形成用于科技活动的固定资产(亿元)	Annual Fixed Assets Formation on Scientific and Technological Activities（100 million yuan）		78.17	169.59	144.99
使用来自政府部门的科技活动资金(亿元)	Government Funds on Scientific and Technological Activities（100 million yuan）		69.80	99.03	114.11
委托外单位开展科技活动的经费支出(亿元)	External Expenditure on Scientific and Technological Activities（100 million yuan）		14.52	145.65	132.45
工业总产值(亿元)	Gross Output Value(100 million yuan)	311.22	5 687.91	16 265.30	12 776.97
利润总额(亿元)	Total Pre-tax Profits(100 million yuan)	47.58	601.59	1 773.57	1 620.27
税金总额(亿元)	Total Tax and Duties(100 million yuan)	28.64	417.57	1 025.00	961.99
出口创汇(亿美元)	Foreign Exchange Income(100 million USD)	2.83	647.36	541.01	454.51
专利申请量(件)	Patent Applications(piece)	452	31 997	54 173	55 214
#发明专利	Inventions		11 259	26 723	26 708
专利授权量(件)	Patent Certified(piece)	1 169	15 052	37 094	36 508
#发明专利	Inventions		3 912	10 088	11 636

注：本表统计范围是符合《上海市科技企业界定参考标准》(沪科〔2015〕70 号)的本市科技型企业。

Note: The statistical range of the data in this table is science and technology enterprises complied with <The reference definition standard of Shanghai science and technology enterprises>(Shanghai Science (2015) No. 70).

表 19.24 主要年份规模以上工业企业研究与试验发展(R&D)活动情况
BASIC STATISTICS OF SCIENTIFIC AND TECHNOLOGICAL ACTIVITIES IN MAIN YEARS

指标	Indicators	2000	2010	2014	2015
有 R&D 活动单位数(个)	**Quantity of Science and Technology Institutions (unit)**	**327**	**1 193**	**1 839**	**1 866**
R&D 人员投入情况	**Personnel Investment on R&D**				
R&D 人员(人)	R&D Personnel(person)	26 253	82 095	124 334	124 753
R&D 人员全时当量(人年)	Full-time Equivalent of R&D Personnel (person-year)	20 576	69 077	93 868	94 981
#基础研究	Basic Research			55	27
应用研究	Applied Research	764	244	307	1 133
试验发展	Experimental Development	19 812	68 833	93 507	93 821
R&D 经费投入情况	**Expenditure on R&D**				
R&D 经费内部支出(亿元)	Intramural Expenditure on R&D (100 million yuan)	31.15	274.05	449.22	474.24
#基础研究	Basic Research			0.17	0.07
应用研究	Applied Research	1.33	2.00	2.33	4.47
试验发展	Experimental Development	29.82	272.05	446.71	469.71
#政府资金	Government Funds	31.15	16.77	37.16	29.38
企业资金	Self-raised Funds by Enterprises	0.37	253.75	407.53	441.53
境外资金	Offshore Funds	20.19	2.37	2.74	2.17
R&D 项目(课题)情况	**R&D project**				
R&D 项目(课题)数(项)	Quantity of Projects (item)	2 412	9 240	13 821	11 089
R&D 项目(课题)人员全时当量(人年)	Personnell Engaged in Projects (person-year)		60 232	87 007	85 158
R&D 项目(课题)经费内部支出(亿元)	Inner Expenditure on Projects (100 million yuan)	28.14	247.29	401.33	451.95
科技产出及成果情况	**Output of Science and Technic Activities**				
新产品产值(亿元)	Output Value of New Products (100 millon yuan)	1 355.19	5 870.20	7 407.99	7 312.24
新产品销售收入(亿元)	Sales Revenue of New Products (100 millon yuan)	1 351.69	6 543.07	8 446.96	7 470.93
发表科技论文数(篇)	Quantity of Science and Technic Papers Published(case)		2 846	3 395	2 975
形成国家或行业标准数(项)	Becoming The Formation of National or Industry Standards (item)		630	680	589
专利申请受理数(件)	Number of Patents Applications Accepted(piece)	1 455	14 967	26 848	21 725
#发明专利	Inventions	221	6 474	12 524	10 740
有效发明专利数(件)	Effective Invention Patents(piece)	468	9 822	27 540	30 815

注：本表 2000 年数据统计范围为大中型工业企业。
Note: Statistics range of data of 2000 is large and medium-sized industrial enterprises.

表 19.25 规模以上工业企业科技活动人员情况（2015）
PERSONNEL FOR SCIENCE AND TECHNIC ACTIVITY IN INDUSTRIAL ENTERPRISES ABOVE THE SET SCALE

单位：万人（10 000 persons）

类 别	Types	从事科技活动人员数 Technological Development Personnel	其中 of which #R&D 人员 R&D Personnel	#本科毕业及以上人员 Personnel with Bachelor Degree and above
总 计	**Total**	**21.26**	**12.48**	**13.96**
按隶属关系分	**By Subordination**			
中央单位	Central Units	3.08	1.77	2.47
地方单位	Local Units	18.18	10.71	11.49
按登记注册类型分	**By Registration Categories**			
内 资	Domestic Funded	11.28	6.62	7.18
#国 有	State-owned	0.41	0.18	0.31
有限责任公司	Companies with Limited Liabilities	3.81	2.21	2.55
股份有限公司	Share-holding Companies with Limited Liabilities	1.97	1.28	1.39
港澳台商投资	Hong Kong, Macao and Taiwan Funded	2.48	1.44	1.42
外商投资	Foreign Funded	7.50	4.42	5.36
按企业规模分	**By Size**			
#大型企业	Large	9.16	5.86	6.89
中型企业	Medium	6.46	3.59	3.87
小型企业	Small	5.49	3.01	3.07
按行业分	**By Sectors**			
#高技术产业	**High Technology Industry**	**5.77**	**3.43**	**4.17**
信息化学品制造	Information Chemical Product Manufacturing	0.03	0.02	0.03
医药制造业	Medicine Manufacturing	0.94	0.57	0.63
航空航天器制造	Aviation and Aircraft Manufacturing	0.42	0.28	0.36
电子及通信设备制造业	Electronic and Communicantion Equipment Manufacturing	3.09	1.90	2.12
电子计算机及办公设备制造业	Electronic Computer and Office Equipment Manufacturing	0.36	0.11	0.30
医疗设备及仪器仪表制造业	Medical Machinery amd Measuring Instrument Manufacturing	0.93	0.55	0.73
#六个重点发展工业行业	**Six Key Industries**	**15.85**	**9.59**	**10.96**
电子信息产品制造业	Electronic Information Product Manufacturing	4.69	2.68	3.15
汽车制造业	Automobile Manufacturing	3.57	2.17	2.64
石油化工及精细化工制造业	Petrochemical and Fine Chemical Products Manufacturing	1.18	0.76	0.74
精品钢材制造业	Fine Steel Manufacturing	0.50	0.38	0.36
成套设备制造业	Equipment Complex Manufacturing	4.43	2.66	3.04
生物医药制造业	Bio-medicine Manufacturing	1.49	0.94	1.02

表 19.26 规模以上工业企业科技项目数与科技经费支出情况（2015）
SCIENCE AND TECHNICAL PROJECTS AND EXPENDITURES OF INDUSTRIAL ENTERPRISES ABOVE THE SET SCALE

类别	Types	科技项目数（项）Quantity of Science and Tehnic Project (item)	科技活动经费内部支出（亿元）Inner Expenditures on Science and Technic Activity (100 million yuan)	其中 of which #新产品开发经费支出 on New Products Development
总计	**Total**	**18 194**	**634.76**	**571.62**
按隶属关系分	**By Subordination**			
中央单位	Central Units	2 022	119.01	103.01
地方单位	Local Units	16 172	515.75	468.62
按登记注册类型分	**By Registration Categories**			
内资	Domestic Funded	10 504	303.11	264.85
#国有	State-owned	363	7.17	4.70
有限责任公司	Companies with Limited Liabilities	3 500	110.06	92.08
股份有限公司	Share-holding Companies with Limited Liabilities	1 348	73.31	74.51
港澳台商投资	Hong Kong, Macao and Taiwan Funded	2 202	61.42	51.95
外商投资	Foreign Funded	5 488	270.23	254.82
按企业规模分	**By Size**			
#大型企业	Large	4 449	364.91	347.38
中型企业	Medium	5 446	153.61	135.03
小型企业	Small	8 231	107.64	88.07
按行业分	**By Sectors**			
#高技术产业	**High Technology Industry**	**3 968**	**178.35**	**162.07**
信息化学品制造	Information Chemical Product Manufacturing	34	0.77	0.47
医药制造业	Medicine Manufacturing	1 114	23.22	21.25
航空航天器制造	Aviation and Aircraft Manufacturing	116	20.48	14.06
电子及通信设备制造业	Electronic and Communication Equipment Manufacturing	1 575	101.57	95.45
电子计算机及办公设备制造业	Electronic Computer and Office Equipment Manufacturing	169	9.03	9.09
医疗设备及仪器仪表制造业	Medical Machinery amd Measuring Instrument Manufacturing	960	23.28	21.76
#六个重点发展工业行业	**Six Key Industries**	**12 472**	**518.32**	**480.96**
电子信息产品制造业	Electronic Information Product Manufacturing	2 728	133.41	124.86
汽车制造业	Automobile Manufacturing	2 402	161.71	158.74
石油化工及精细化工制造业	Petrochemical and Fine Chemical Products Manufacturing	1 496	31.34	27.96
精品钢材制造业	Fine Steel Manufacturing	464	28.45	29.16
成套设备制造业	Equipment Complex Manufacturing	3 725	126.53	106.09
生物医药制造业	Bio-medicine Manufacturing	1 657	36.89	34.15

表 19.27 规模以上工业企业 R&D 经费内部支出来源构成(2015)
STRUCTURE OF R&D INNER EXPENDITURE SOURCE IN INDUSTRIAL ENTERPRISES ABOVE THE SET SCALE

单位:亿元(100 million yuan)

类别	Types	R&D经费内部支出合计 Total of R&D Inner Expenditure	其中 of which: #政府资金 Government Funds	企业资金 Enterprise Funds	境外资金 Foreign Funds
总计	**Total**	**474.24**	**29.38**	**441.53**	**2.17**
按隶属关系分	**By Subordination**				
中央单位	Central Units	81.57	15.20	65.98	0.01
地方单位	Local Units	392.68	14.17	375.55	2.16
按登记注册类型分	**By Registration Categories**				
内资	Domestic Funded	224.70	25.89	197.86	0.17
#国有	State-owned	4.93	0.81	4.11	0.01
有限责任公司	Companies with Limited Liabilities	76	8.96	66.48	0.01
股份有限公司	Share-holding Companies with Limited Liabilities	63.90	1.58	62.24	0.02
港澳台商投资	Hong Kong, Macao and Taiwan Funded	44.56	0.95	43.19	0.19
外商投资	Foreign Funded	204.98	2.54	200.48	1.81
按企业规模分	**By Size**				
#大型企业	Large	293.94	19.90	274.02	0.49
中型企业	Medium	108.81	7.28	99.67	0.73
小型企业	Small	70.61	2.20	66.95	0.95
按行业分	**By Sectors**				
#高技术产业	**High Technology Industry**	**125.37**	**20.97**	**103.07**	**0.84**
信息化学品制造	Information Chemical Product Manufacturing	0.67	…	0.66	
医药制造业	Medicine Manufacturing	19.98	0.68	19.25	
航空航天器制造	Aviation and Aircraft Manufacturing	14.51	10.33	3.81	
电子及通信设备制造业	Electronic and Communication Equipment Manufacturing	69.66	9.27	59.81	0.55
电子计算机及办公设备制造业	Electronic Computer and Office Equipment Manufacturing	3.79	0.04	3.73	0.02
医疗设备及仪器仪表制造业	Medical Machinery amd Measuring Instrument Manufacturing	16.77	0.67	15.82	0.26
#六个重点发展工业行业	**Six Key Industries**	**391.62**	**28.37**	**360.45**	**1.94**
电子信息产品制造业	Electronic Information Product Manufacturing	87.91	9.63	77.33	0.77
汽车制造业	Automobile Manufacturing	134.60	1.27	132.70	0.55
石油化工及精细化工制造业	Petrochemical and Fine Chemical Products Manufacturing	24.62	0.58	23.68	0.34
精品钢材制造业	Fine Steel Manufacturing	25.16	0.36	24.79	
成套设备制造业	Equipment Complex Manufacturing	88.75	15.48	72.77	0.05
生物医药制造业	Bio-medicine Manufacturing	30.57	1.04	29.18	0.23

表 19.28 规模以上工业企业办科技机构情况(2015)
SCIENCE AND TECHNIC RESEARCH INSTITUTIONS FUNDED BY INDUSTRIAL ENTERPRISES ABOVE THE SET SCALE

类别	Types	科技机构数(个) Technological Development Institutions (unit)	机构人员数(万人) Quantity of Personnel (10 000 persons)	机构经费支出(亿元) Expenditure of Institutions (100 million yuan)	机构仪器设备原价(亿元) Original Value of Equipment (100 million yuan)
总计	**Total**	**738**	**7.39**	**328.22**	**310.86**
按隶属关系分	**By Subordination**				
中央单位	Central Units	35	1.47	72.27	67.41
地方单位	Local Units	703	5.91	255.95	243.46
按登记注册类型分	**By Registration Categories**				
内资	Domestic Funded	435	3.72	134.67	100.27
#国有	State-owned	12	0.14	4.72	8.64
有限责任公司	Companies with Limited Liabilities	141	1.34	43.73	32.36
股份有限公司	Share-holding Companies with Limited Liabilities	49	0.86	49.23	32.03
港澳台商投资	Hong Kong, Macao and Taiwan Funded	88	0.69	23.05	29.50
外商投资	Foreign Funded	215	2.98	170.51	181.09
按企业规模分	**By Size**				
#大型企业	Large	118	4.39	253.75	220.49
中型企业	Medium	241	1.91	50.31	69.46
小型企业	Small	373	1.06	23.81	20.59
按行业分	**By Sectors**				
#高技术产业	High Technology Industry	177	2.17	86.13	117.18
#医药制造业	Medicine Manufacturing	58	0.30	10.47	7.98
航空航天器制造	Aviation and Aircraft Manufacturing	3	0.15	3.86	9.76
电子及通信设备制造业	Electronic and Communication Equipment Manufacturing	71	1.34	58.14	95.20
电子计算机及办公设备制造业	Electronic Computer and Office Equipment Manufacturing	11	0.03	1.49	0.28
医疗设备及仪器仪表制造业	Medical Machinery amd Measuring Instrument Manufacturing	34	0.35	12.15	3.96
#六个重点发展工业行业	**Six Key Industries**	**496**	**6.08**	**283.44**	**247.72**
电子信息产品制造业	Electronic Information Product Manufacturing	106	1.60	64.82	100.22
汽车制造业	Automobile Manufacturing	71	1.77	116.34	70.81
石油化工及精细化工制造业	Petrochemical and Fine Chemical Products Manufacturing	85	0.37	11.82	11.47
精品钢材制造业	Fine Steel Manufacturing	2	0.08	14.04	14.20
成套设备制造业	Equipment Complex Manufacturing	149	1.74	58.35	40.14
生物医药制造业	Bio-medicine Manufacturing	83	0.51	18.06	10.88

表 19.29 规模以上工业企业其他技术活动费用支出情况(2015)
SPECIAL TECHNICAL PROJECT FUNDS OF INDUSTRIAL ENTERPRISES ABOVE THE SET SCALE

单位:亿元 (100 million yuan)

类 别	Types	技术改造经费支出 Expenditures of Technical Transformation	技术引进经费支出 Expenditures of Technical Introduction	购买国内技术支出 Expenditures of Buying Domestic Technology
总 计	**Total**	**122.06**	**50.44**	**26.04**
按隶属关系分	**By Subordination**			
中央单位	Central Units	52.41	11.17	21.69
地方单位	Local Units	69.65	39.26	4.35
按登记注册类型分	**By Registration Categories**			
内 资	Domestic Funded	63.72	12.55	23.99
#国 有	State-owned	1.39		
有限责任公司	Companies with Limited Liabilities	14.74	3.11	2.54
股份有限公司	Share-holding Companies with Limited Liabilities	41.36	7.33	19.52
港澳台商投资	Hong Kong, Macao and Taiwan Funded	2.72	1.14	0.04
外商投资	Foreign Funded	55.62	36.75	2.01
按企业规模分	**By Size**			
#大型企业	Large	103.55	44.32	23.74
中型企业	Medium	12.01	5.50	1.82
小型企业	Small	6.49	0.61	0.48
按行业分	**By Sectors**			
#高技术产业	**High Technology Industry**	**4.60**	**1.82**	**2.40**
信息化学品制造	Information Chemical Product Manufacturing			
医药制造业	Medicine Manufacturing	0.80		0.41
航空航天器制造	Aviation and Aircraft Manufacturing			
电子及通信设备制造业	Electronic and Communicantion Equipment Manufacturing	3.33	0.69	1.39
电子计算机及办公设备制造业	Electronic Computer and Office Equipment Manufacturing			
医疗设备及仪器仪表制造业	Medical Machinery amd Measuring Instrument Manufacturing	0.47	1.13	0.60
#六个重点发展工业行业	**Six Key Industries**	**105.35**	**48.11**	**25.13**
电子信息产品制造业	Electronic Information Product Manufacturing	3.65	1.80	1.40
汽车制造业	Automobile Manufacturing	51.93	32.4	1.59
石油化工及精细化工制造业	Petrochemical and Fine Chemical Products Manufacturing	6.87	0.66	0.38
精品钢材制造业	Fine Steel Manufacturing	35.78	5.23	19.56
成套设备制造业	Equipment Complex Manufacturing	5.95	7.97	1.79
生物医药制造业	Bio-medicine Manufacturing	1.19	0.05	0.41

表 19.30 规模以上工业企业新产品产出情况（2015）
OUTPUT OF NEW PRODUCTS OF INDUSTRIAL ENTERPRISES ABOVE THE SET SCALE

单位：亿元（100 million yuan）

类别	Types	新产品产值 Output Value of New Products	新产品销售收入 Sales Revenue of New Products	其中 of which #新产品出口 Exports of New Products
总计	**Total**	**7 312.24**	**7 470.94**	**1 079.84**
按隶属关系分	**By Subordination**			
中央单位	Central Units	1 550.67	1 550.94	330.43
地方单位	Local Units	5 761.56	5 920.00	749.41
按登记注册类型分	**By Registration Categories**			
内资	Domestic Funded	2 916.10	3 045.64	374.86
#国有	State-owned	24.59	25.28	0.53
有限责任公司	Companies with Limited Liabilities	1 313.06	1 375.24	150.99
股份有限公司	Share-holding Companies with Limited Liabilities	441.63	421.82	28.88
港澳台商投资	Hong Kong, Macao and Taiwan Funded	510.45	523.01	196.62
外商投资	Foreign Funded	3 885.69	3 902.28	508.36
按企业规模分	**By Size**			
#大型企业	Large	5 207.55	5 294.18	797.72
中型企业	Medium	1 365.09	1 425.47	202.75
小型企业	Small	698.17	704.70	79.29
按行业分	**By Sectors**			
#高技术产业	**High Technology Industry**	**985.28**	**981.04**	**455.85**
信息化学品制造	Information Chemical Product Manufacturing	10.66	10.46	7.15
医药制造业	Medicine Manufacturing	205.89	187.74	8.79
航空航天器制造	Aviation and Aircraft Manufacturing	38.88	42.04	
电子及通信设备制造业	Electronic and Communicantion Equipment Manufacturing	629.47	633.53	400.91
电子计算机及办公设备制造业	Electronic Computer and Office Equipment Manufacturing	40.57	39.10	29.34
医疗设备及仪器仪表制造业	Medical Machinery amd Measuring Instrument Manufacturing	59.82	68.16	9.68
#六个重点发展工业行业	**Six Key Industries**	**5 696.64**	**5 812.26**	**892.56**
电子信息产品制造业	Electronic Information Product Manufacturing	936.10	951.55	432.80
汽车制造业	Automobile Manufacturing	2 524.92	2 651.35	30.37
石油化工及精细化工制造业	Petrochemical and Fine Chemical Products Manufacturing	241.38	291.37	11.41
精品钢材制造业	Fine Steel Manufacturing	221.52	206.23	22.03
成套设备制造业	Equipment Complex Manufacturing	1 541.26	1 494.48	384.00
生物医药制造业	Bio-medicine Manufacturing	231.46	217.28	11.95

注：新产品既包括经政府有关部门认定并在有效期内的新产品，也包括企业自行研制开发，未经政府有关部门认定，从投产之日起一年之内的新产品。

Note: New Products include new products certified by relevant government agencies within the period of certification, as well as new products designed and produced by enterprices within a year without certification by government agencies.

表 19.31 主要年份大中型工业企业科技活动情况
SCIENCE AND TECHNIC ACTIVITIES OF LARGE AND MEDIUM INDUSTRIAL ENTERPRISES IN MAIN YEARS

指 标	Indicators	2000	2010	2014	2015
企业办科技机构数（个）	**Science and Technic Institutions Funded by Enterprises (unit)**	**264**	**638**	**419**	**359**
从事科技活动人员数（万人）	**Personnel Engaged in Science and Technic Activities (10 000 persons)**	**7.48**	**11.96**	**16.6**	**15.73**
#R&D 人员	R&D Personnel	2.63	6.64	9.21	9.45
#本科毕业及以上人员	Personnel with High and Medium Technic Titles				10.85
科技活动经费支出情况	**Expenditures on Science and Technic Activities**				
内部经费支出(亿元)	Inner Expenditures(100 million yuan)	91.63	356.24	580.36	567.40
#R&D 经费支出	R&D Expenditures	30.98	237.75	379.12	402.75
#新产品开发经费支出	Expenditures on New Products Development	47.56	302.45	496.10	482.41
外部经费支出(亿元)	External Expenditures(100 million yuan)	9.15	33.12	53.07	72.46
其他技术活动费用支出(亿元)	**Other Expenditures on Technic Activities (100 million yuan)**	**117.47**	**235.63**	**265.88**	**216.83**
技术改造经费支出	Expenditures on Technological Transformation	75.31	123.21	141.62	115.56
技术引进经费支出	Expenditures on Technological Introduction	39.00	61.09	65.95	49.82
用于消化吸收的经费	Expenditures on Technological Digesting and Absorbing	2.41	28.68	26.66	25.88
购买国内技术支出	Expenditures on Buying Domestic Technology	0.75	22.65	31.65	25.56
科技项目情况	**Science and Technic Project**				
项目数（项）	Quantity of Projects (item)	5 140	11 384	14 684	9 898
项目人员（人）	Personnel of Project Groups (person)	45 254	94 165	143 028	126 721
项目经费内部支出(亿元)	Intramural Expenditure on Projects(100 million yuan)	63.72	309.75	492.18	525.68
科技活动产出情况	**Output of Science and Technic Activities**				
新产品产值(亿元)	Output Value of New Products (100 million yuan)	1 355.19	5 504.38	6 670.49	6 594.43
新产品销售收入(亿元)	New Products Sales Revenue (100 million yuan)	1 351.69	6 180.81	7 686.25	6 741.45
#新产品出口	New Products Exported	197.41	1 023.11	962.56	1 000.46

上 / 海 / 统 / 计 / 年 / 鉴

主要统计指标解释

科技活动

指在自然科学、农业科学、医药科学、工程与技术科学、人文与社会科学领域(简称科学技术领域)中,与科技知识的产生、发展、传播和应用密切相关的有组织的活动。可分为研究与试验发展(R&D)、研究与试验发展成果应用及相关的科技服务三类活动。

R&D

R&D 是"科学研究与试验发展"的英文缩写。指在科学技术领域,为增加知识总量,以及运用这些知识去创造新的应用进行的系统的创造性的活动。R&D 包括基础研究、应用研究、试验发展三类活动。

基础研究

指为了获得关于现象和可观察事实的基本原理的新知识(揭示客观事物的本质、运动规律,获得新发现、新学说)而进行的实验性或理论性研究,它不以任何专门或特定的应用或使用为目的。其成果以科学论文和科学著作为主要形式。用来反映知识的原始创新能力。

应用研究

指为获得新知识而进行的创造性研究,主要针对某一特定的目的或目标。应用研究是为了确定基础研究成果可能的用途,或是为达到预定的目标探索应采取的新方法(原理性)或新途径。其成果形式以科学论文、专著、原理性模型或发明专利为主。

试验发展

指利用从基础研究、应用研究和实际经验所获得的现有知识,为产生新的产品、材料和装置,建立新的工艺、系统和服务,以及对已产生和建立的上述各项作实质性的改进而进行的系统性工作。其成果形式主要是专利、专有技术、具有新产品基本特征的产品原型或具有新装置基本特征的原始样机等。在社会科学领域,试验发展是指把通过基础研究、应用研究获得的知识转变成可以实施的计划(包括为进行检验和评估实施示范项目)的过程。人文科学领域没有对应的试验发展活动。

科技活动人员

指直接从事科技活动、以及专门从事科技活动管理和为科技活动提供直接服务,累计从事科技活动的时间占全年制度工作时间 10%及以上的人员。(1)直接从事科技活动的人员,包括:在独立核算的科学研究与技术开发机构、高等学校、各类企业及其他事业单位内设的研究室、实验室、技术开发中心及中试车间(基地)等机构中从事科技活动的研究人员、工程技术人员、技术工人及其它人员;虽不在上述机构工作,但编入科技活动项目(课题)组的人员;科技信息与文献机构中的专业技术人员;从事论文设计的研究生等。(2)专门从事科技活动管理和为科技活动提供直接服务的人员包括:独立核算的科学研究与技术开发机构、科技信息与文献机构、高等学校、各类企业及其他事业单位主管科技工作的负责人,专门从事科技活动的计划、行政、人事、财务、物资供应、设备维护、图书资料管理等工作的各类人员,但不包括保卫、医疗保健人员、司机、食堂人员、茶炉工、水暖工、清洁工等为科技活动提供间接服务的人员。

R&D 人员

R&D 人员一般用折合全时当量来表示。即参加 R&D 项目人员的全时当量及应分摊在 R&D 项目的管理和直接服务人员的全时当量两部分相加计算。一个折合全时当量是一人年。例如,一个人在 R&D 活动上花费了 30%的正常工作时间而 70%的时间用于其他工作,则其折合全时当量为 0.3。

科技活动经费支出

指企事业单位实际支出的全部科技活动费用,包括来自科研渠道的经费、教育事业费、基本建设投资、技术改造投资等实际用于科技活动支出的费用。科技活动经费支出分为内部支出和外部支出。

R&D 经费内部支出

指企事业单位用于内部开展 R&D 活动(包括基础研究、应用研究、试验发展)的实际支出。包括用于 R&D 项目(课题)活动的直接支出,以及间接用于 R&D 活动的管理费、服务费、与有关的基本建设支出以及外协加工费等。不包括生产性活动支出、归还贷款支出以

主要统计指标解释

及与外单位合作或委托外单位进行 R&D 活动而转拨给对方的经费支出。

专　利

是专利权的简称，是对发明人的发明创造经审查合格后，由专利局依据专利法授予发明人和设计人对该项发明创造享有的专有权。专利包括发明、实用新型和外观设计三种类型。

发　明

指对产品、方法或者其改进所提出的新的技术方案。是国际通行的反映拥有自主知识产权技术的核心指标。

实用新型

指对产品的形状、构造或者其结合所提出的适于实用的新的技术方案。反映具有一定技术含量的技术成果情况。

外观设计

指对产品的形状、图案、色彩或者其结合所作出的富有美感并适于工业上应用的新设计。反映拥有自主知识产权的外观设计成果情况。

新产品

指采用新技术原理、新设计构思研制、生产的全新产品，或在结构、材质、工艺等某一方面比原有产品有明显改进，从而显著提高了产品性能或扩大了使用功能的产品。新产品既包括政府有关部门认定并在有效期内的新产品，也包括企业自行研制开发，未经政府有关部门认定，从投产之日起一年之内的新产品。

独立研究与开发机构

指有明确的任务和研究方向，有一定学术水平的业务骨干和一定数量的研究人员，具有研究、开发、开展学术工作的基本条件，主要进行科学研究与技术开发活动，并且在行政上有独立的组织形式，财务上独立核算盈亏，有权与其他单位签订合同，在银行有单独户头的单位。

SHANGHAI STATISTICAL YEARBOOK

EXPLANATORY NOTES TO MAJOR STATISTICAL INDICATORS

□ Scientific and Technological Activities (S&T Activities)

Scientific and Technological Activities (S&T Activities) refer to organized activities which are closely related with the creation, development, dissemination and application of the scientific and technical knowledge in the fields of natural sciences, agricultural sciences, medical sciences, engineering and technological sciences, humanities and social sciences (referred to as scientific and technological fields). S&T activities can be classified into 3 categories: research and development (R&D) activities, application of R&D results, and related S&T services.

□ R&D

R&D is an abbreviation which stands for 'Science Research and Experimental Development', which means systematic and creative endeavors aimed at expanding the overall volume of knowledge and applying the knowledge in systematic creation. R&D includes basic studies, application research and experimental development.

□ Basic Research

Basic Research refers to empirical or theoretical research aiming at obtaining new knowledge on the fundamental principles of phenomena of observable facts to reveal the nature and law of movement of objects and to acquire new discoveries or new theories. Basic research takes no specific or designated application as the aim of the research. Results of basic research are mainly released or disseminated in the form of scientific papers or monographs. This indicator reflects the original innovation capacity of knowledge.

□ Applied Research

Applied Research refers to creative research aiming at obtaining new knowledge on a specific objective or target. Purpose of the applied research is to identify the possible use of results from basic research, or to explore new (fundamental) methods or new approaches. Results of applied research are expressed in the form of scientific papers, monographs, fundamental models or invention patents.

□ Experimental Development

Experimental Development refer to systematic activities aiming at using the knowledge from basic and applied researches or from practical experience to develop new products, materials and equipment, to establish new production process, systems and services, or to make substantial improvement on the existing products, process or services. Results of experiment and development activities are embodied in patents, exclusive technology, and monotype of new products or equipment. In social sciences, experiment and development activities refer to the process of converting the knowledge from basic or applied researches into feasible programmes (including conduct of demonstration projects for assessment and evaluation). There are no experiment and development activities in the science of humanities.

□ Personnel Engaged in S&T Activities

Personnel Engaged in S&T Activities refer to personnel directly engaged in S&T activities, in the management of S&T activities, and in providing direct service to S&T activities, who spend over 10% of the total working hours in a year in S&T activities. (1) Personnel directly engaged in S&T activities include researchers, engineers, technicians and other related personnel engaged in S&T activities in independent-accounting R&D institutions, institutions of higher learning, and in research institutes, laboratories, technology development centers and central experiment workshops under enterprises and institutions. Also included are people working in S&T information archiving institutes, and graduate students working on the design of their thesis. (2) Personnel engaged in the management of S&T activities and in providing direct service to S&T activities include senior management people responsible for S&T activities in independent-accounting R&D institutions, S&T information archiving institutes, institutions of higher learning, and in enterprises and institutions where S&T activities are undertaken. Also included are people responsible for the planning, administration, personnel management, financial management, logistics supply, equipment maintenance, information and library management that are related with S&T activities. People providing indirect services are excluded, such as security, medical service, drivers, plumbers, cleaners and those providing catering and related service.

EXPLANATORY NOTES TO MAJOR STATISTICAL INDICATORS

□ R&D Personnel

R&D Personnel generally amount to the full-time equivalent. It equals the full-time equivalent of personnel engaged in the R&D projects plus the full-time equivalent of personnel directly manage and service the allocated R&D projects. A full-time equivalent refers to a person year. For example, a person spent thirty percent of common working time on R&D activities and seventy percent on other jobs, then the full-time equivalent is 0.3.

□ Expenditures on Science and Technical Activities

Expenditures on Science and Technical Activities refers to the total expenditures that the enterprises actually spent on science and technical activities. It includes expenditures on scientific research, education expenses, basic construction investment, investment on technical transformation. It is divided into internal expenditure and external expenditure.

□ Internal Expenditure on R&D

Internal Expenditure on R&D refers to the actually expense on R&D activities inside enterprises. It includes the direct expense on R&D projects, and indirect expense, such as management fees, service fees, basic construction investment and processing fees, on R&D activities. But it does not include the expenditures for productive activities, expenditures on repay the loans and the expenditures pay for the R&D activities entrusted to other enterprises.

□ Patent

Patent is an abbreviation for the patent right and refers to the exclusive right of ownership by the inventors or designers for the creation or inventions, given from the patent offices after due process of assessment and approval in accordance with the Patent Law. Patents are granted for inventions, utility models and designs.

□ Invention

Inventions refer to the new technical proposals to the products or methods or their modifications. This is universal core indicator reflecting the technologies with independent intellectual property.

□ Utility Models

Utility Models refer to the practical and new technical proposals on the shape and structure of the product or the combination of both. This indicator reflects the condition of technological results with certain technical content.

□ Exterior Designs

Exterior Designs refer to the aesthetics and industrially applicable new designs for the shape, pattern and color of the product, or their combinations. This indicator reflects the appearance design achievements with independent intellectual property.

□ New Products

New Products refer to new products produced with new technology and new design, or products that represent noticeable improvement in terms of structure, material, or production process so as to improve significantly the character or function of the older versions. They include new products certified by relevant government agencies within the period of certification, as well as new products that are not certified by relevant government agencies and are designed and produced by enterprises within one year since they are put into production.

□ Independent Research and Development Institutions

Independent Research and Development Institutions refer to the state-owned institutions which have direct mission and research purpose, a certain research level and quantities of personnel, favorable conditions for R&D and engaging in scientific research and technological development. The institutions also have their own independent organization, accounting system authority to sign contract with other units, and their own accounts in banks.

第二十篇
CHAPTER 20

2016上海统计年鉴 SHANGHAI STATISTICAL YEARBOOK

教　育
EDUCATION

简要说明

一、本篇资料的主要内容

教育统计资料包括公办教育和民办教育、学历教育和非学历教育。具体有高等教育(研究生教育、普通高等教育和成人高等教育)、中等教育(高中阶段教育、初中阶段教育和成人中等教育)、初等教育(小学)、学前教育(幼儿园)、特殊教育(特殊教育学校和工读学校等)和留学生教育等资料。主要指标包括学校数、在校学生数、招生数、毕业生数、教职工数和专任教师数等。

二、本篇资料的来源

教育统计资料由上海市教育委员会提供。

BRIEF INTRODUCTION

I. Main Contents

Data on education cover the situations on education funded by government and non-government agencies, and the education with and without academic credentials including higher education (education of postgraduates, general higher education and adult education), secondary education (senior and junior high schools), elementary education (primary schools), preschool education, special education (special education schools and reformatory schools) and overseas education. The main indicators include the number of schools, the number of students enrolled, the number of new students enrolled, the number of graduates, the number of staff and workers, the number of full-time teachers.

II. Sources of Data

Data on education are provided by Shanghai Municipal Education Commission.

表 20.1 主要年份教育事业基本情况
BASIC STATISTICS OF EDUCATION IN MAIN YEARS

指 标	Indicators	2000	2010	2014	2015
学校数（所）	**Quantity of Schools（unit）**	**2 225**	**1 730**	**1 724**	**1 748**
普通高等学校	Regular Institutions of Higher Education	37	66	68	67
普通中等学校	Secondary Schools	1 133	869	870	888
中等专业学校	Specialized Secondary Schools	84	65	54	51
职业中学	Vocational Secondary Schools	60	26	28	27
技工学校	Technical Schools	115	10	7	7
普通中学	Regular Secondary Schools	861	755	768	790
工读学校	Reformatory	13	13	13	13
普通小学	Primary Schools	1 021	766	757	764
特殊教育学校	Special Education Schools	34	29	29	29
教职工数(万人)	**Quantity of Teachers and Staff（10 000 persons）**	**22.73**	**21.42**	**21.75**	**21.88**
普通高等学校	Regular Institutions of Higher Education	6.01	7.42	7.34	7.36
普通中等学校	Secondary Schools	10.43	8.26	8.29	8.33
中等专业学校	Specialized Secondary Schools	1.27	0.91	0.80	0.78
职业中学	Vocational Secondary Schools	0.66	0.43	0.39	0.38
技工学校	Technical Worker Schools	0.77	0.13	0.10	0.10
普通中学	Regular Secondary Schools	7.66	6.73	6.95	7.02
工读学校	Reformatory	0.07	0.06	0.05	0.05
普通小学	Primary Schools	6.13	5.58	5.96	6.03
特殊教育学校	Special Education Schools	0.16	0.16	0.16	0.16
专任教师(万人)	**Quantity of Full-time Teachers（10 000 persons）**	**12.83**	**14.52**	**15.59**	**15.87**
普通高等学校	Regular Institutions of Higher Education	2.05	3.92	4.06	4.16
普通中等学校	Secondary Schools	6.26	5.97	6.26	6.36
中等专业学校	Specialized Secondary Schools	0.53	0.50	0.48	0.48
职业中学	Vocational Secondary Schools	0.39	0.29	0.28	0.28
技工学校	Technical Worker Schools	0.30	0.07	0.05	0.06
普通中学	Regular Secondary Schools	5.01	5.07	5.41	5.50
高 中	Senior Secondary Schools	1.42	1.67	1.70	1.74
初 中	Junior Secondary Schools	3.59	3.40	3.71	3.76
工读学校	Reformatory	0.03	0.04	0.04	0.04
普通小学	Primary Schools	4.43	4.52	5.15	5.23
特殊教育学校	Special Education Schools	0.09	0.11	0.12	0.12

注：普通中学学校数中，完全中学 93 所高级中学 141 所，初级中学 362 所，九年一贯制学校 175 所，十二年一贯制学校 19 所。

Note: In regular secondary schools there are 93 whole secondary schools 141 senior high schools 362 junior high schools, 175 system schools of 9 years and 19 system schools of 12 years.

表20.1 续表 continued

指 标	Indicators	2000	2010	2014	2015
毕业生数(万人)	**Graduates (10 000 persons)**	**55.67**	**47.14**	**45.71**	**44.07**
普通高等学校	Regular Institutions of Higher Education	4.09	13.37	13.24	12.87
普通中等学校	Secondary Schools	32.76	21.24	19.27	18.33
中等专业学校	Specialized Secondary Schools	3.86	3.34	3.55	2.49
职业中学	Vocational Secondary Schools	3.99	1.38	1.05	0.97
技工学校	Technical Worker Schools	1.86	0.31	0.29	0.25
普通中学	Regular Secondary Schools	22.92	16.13	14.32	14.55
高 中	Senior Secondary Schools	7.18	6.24	5.10	5.12
初 中	Junior Secondary Schools	15.74	9.89	9.22	9.43
工读学校	Reformatory	0.13	0.08	0.06	0.07
普通小学	Primary Schools	18.73	12.44	13.12	13.79
特殊教育学校	Special Education Schools	0.09	0.09	0.08	0.08
招生数(万人)	**New Student Enrollment (10 000 persons)**	**52.23**	**50.66**	**50.48**	**49.82**
普通高等学校	Regular Institutions of Higher Education	8.13	14.46	14.19	14.07
普通中等学校	Secondary Schools	33.71	21.07	19.89	20.11
中等专业学校	Specialized Secondary Schools	3.00	2.99	2.25	2.22
职业中学	Vocational Secondary Schools	2.44	1.23	0.79	0.66
技工学校	Technical Worker Schools	1.68	0.42	0.29	0.32
普通中学	Regular Secondary Schools	26.46	16.33	16.51	16.87
高 中	Senior Secondary Schools	7.84	5.39	5.29	5.34
初 中	Junior Secondary Schools	18.62	10.94	11.22	11.53
工读学校	Reformatory	0.13	0.10	0.05	0.04
普通小学	Primary Schools	10.28	15.05	16.34	15.58
特殊教育学校	Special Education Schools	0.11	0.08	0.06	0.06
在校学生(万人)	**Student Enrollment (10 000 persons)**	**207.61**	**197.70**	**201.23**	**198.97**
普通高等学校	Regular Institutions of Higher Education	22.68	51.57	50.66	51.16
普通中等学校	Secondary Schools	105.53	75.47	69.81	67.49
中等专业学校	Specialized Secondary Schools	11.89	10.91	7.74	7.24
职业中学	Vocational Secondary Schools	8.48	3.77	2.72	2.32
技工学校	Technical Worker Schools	5.37	1.08	0.79	0.78
普通中学	Regular Secondary Schools	79.54	59.44	58.42	57.05
高 中	Senior Secondary Schools	23.94	16.89	15.74	15.82
初 中	Junior Secondary Schools	55.60	42.55	42.68	41.23
工读学校	Reformatory	0.25	0.27	0.14	0.10
普通小学	Primary Schools	78.86	70.16	80.30	79.87
特殊教育学校	Special Education Schools	0.54	0.50	0.46	0.45

表 20.2 每万人口在校学生数、每个教师负担学生数(1978～2015)
STUDENTS ENROLLMENT PER 10 000 PERSONS AND STUDENTS TAUGHT BY EACH TEACHER

单位:人(person)

年 份 Year	平均每万人口在校学生数 Students Enrollment per 10 000 Persons				平均每个教师负担学生数 Students Taught by Each Teacher		
	大学生 Colleges and Universities	中专生 Speciallized Secondary Schools	中学生 Secondary Schools	小学生 Primary Schools	普通高等学校 Institutions of Higher Education	普通中等学校 Regular Secondary Schools	普通小学 Primary Schools
1978	46	14	908	789	3	17	18
1979	60	21	719	774	4	16	19
1980	67	24	544	742	4	13	18
1981	78	25	427	713	5	11	17
1982	71	28	451	665	4	12	16
1983	66	30	433	665	4	10	16
1984	74	37	404	686	4	11	17
1985	88	48	391	683	4	12	17
1986	94	55	387	693	5	11	17
1987	97	55	381	706	5	11	17
1988	100	51	355	764	5	11	18
1989	96	49	351	809	5	11	19
1990	90	46	362	826	5	11	19
1991	87	45	379	825	5	12	19
1992	88	47	401	830	5	13	22
1993	95	54	417	845	6	14	21
1994	100	66	468	815	6	15	21
1995	101	76	512	776	7	16	20
1996	102	68	525	734	7	16	20
1997	103	75	500	688	8	16	20
1998	108	81	483	630	8	17	19
1999	119	83	489	556	9	17	19
2000	141	74	494	490	11	17	18
2001	168	73	481	433	13	16	17
2002	194	74	461	393	14	17	17
2003	214	78	427	367	16	16	17
2004	227	77	451	293	15	17	14
2005	234	72	407	283	14	16	14
2006	237	70	362	272	14	15	14
2007	235	62	318	258	14	14	14
2008	235	56	289	276	14	13	14
2009	232	52	273	304	13	13	15
2010	224	47	258	305	13	13	16
2011	218	44	252	311	13	12	16
2012	213	42	248	319	13	12	16
2013	209	38	246	328	13	12	16
2014	209	32	241	331	12	11	16
2015	212	30	246	331	12	11	15

表 20.3 各级各类学校在校学生数(1978 ~ 2015)
STUDENTS ENROLLMENT BY VARIOUS SCHOOLS

单位:万人 (10 000 persons)

年份 Year	普通高等学校 Institutions of Higher Education	普通中等学校 Secondary Schools	其中 of which: 中等专业学校 Specialized Secondary Schools	普通中学 Regular Secondary Schools	职业学校 Secondary Vocational Schools	技工学校 Technical Worker Schools	普通小学 Primary Schools	特殊教育学校 Special Education Schools
1978	5.06	101.81	1.55	100.26			87.06	0.18
1979	6.74	90.80	2.42	81.72		6.66	88.00	0.18
1980	7.67	71.68	2.81	62.71	0.29	5.87	85.47	0.18
1981	9.11	58.82	2.94	49.93	0.45	5.50	83.22	0.16
1982	8.39	61.69	3.30	53.53	0.85	4.01	78.88	0.16
1983	7.87	60.53	3.61	52.04	1.71	3.17	79.82	0.23
1984	8.99	61.01	4.48	49.18	3.07	4.28	83.47	0.21
1985	10.79	63.50	5.92	48.23	4.69	4.66	84.18	0.23
1986	11.77	64.82	6.86	48.31	4.71	4.94	86.56	0.25
1987	12.25	64.50	7.03	48.21	4.08	5.18	89.35	0.28
1988	12.82	61.20	6.52	45.68	3.69	5.31	98.39	0.30
1989	12.61	61.01	6.45	46.10	3.54	4.92	106.02	0.32
1990	12.13	62.59	6.17	48.31	3.66	4.45	110.19	0.33
1991	11.69	65.92	6.01	51.24	3.97	4.70	111.38	0.35
1992	11.95	70.84	6.41	54.77	4.90	4.76	113.37	0.38
1993	13.10	76.54	7.58	57.69	6.39	4.88	116.70	0.44
1994	14.04	87.23	9.23	65.56	7.54	4.90	113.98	0.52
1995	14.41	96.38	10.85	72.40	8.64	4.49	109.78	0.57
1996	14.79	99.97	9.95	76.23	9.12	4.67	106.46	0.62
1997	15.38	100.81	11.10	74.43	10.29	4.99	102.44	0.63
1998	16.51	102.53	12.38	73.85	10.72	5.58	96.14	0.52
1999	18.63	105.66	13.06	76.69	10.21	5.70	87.16	0.53
2000	22.68	105.28	11.89	79.54	8.48	5.37	78.86	0.54
2001	28.00	104.37	12.12	80.23	7.48	4.54	72.28	0.48
2002	33.16	103.59	12.66	78.97	7.56	4.40	67.24	0.55
2003	37.85	100.71	13.69	75.47	7.04	4.51	64.83	0.55
2004	41.57	106.94	14.05	82.78	6.43	3.68	53.74	0.54
2005	44.26	99.24	13.67	77.02	5.76	2.79	53.50	0.52
2006	46.63	92.25	13.70	71.17	5.33	2.05	53.37	0.50
2007	48.49	85.17	12.81	65.60	5.20	1.56	53.33	0.50
2008	50.29	79.97	12.08	61.77	4.80	1.32	59.06	0.51
2009	51.28	77.07	11.50	60.37	4.14	1.06	67.12	0.50
2010	51.57	75.20	10.91	59.44	3.77	1.08	70.16	0.50
2011	51.13	73.96	10.22	59.17	3.52	1.05	73.11	0.49
2012	50.66	73.45	9.88	59.04	3.55	0.98	76.04	0.49
2013	50.48	72.63	9.23	59.35	3.24	0.81	79.25	0.47
2014	50.66	69.67	7.74	58.42	2.72	0.79	80.30	0.46
2015	51.16	67.39	7.24	57.05	2.32	0.78	79.87	0.45

注：本表中普通中等学校在校学生数中不包括工读学校在校学生。
Note: Quantity of students enrollment of secondary schools in this table doesn't include those of reformatory schools.

表 20.4 主要年份各阶段教育实施情况
BASIC STATISTICS OF VARIOUS PHASES EDUCATION IN MAIN YEARS

单位:%

指 标	Indicators	2000	2010	2014	2015
小 学	**Primary Schools**				
小学学龄儿童净入学率	Enrollment Rate of Schoolage Children	99.9	99.9	99.9	99.9
初 中	**Junior Schools**				
初中学生净入学率	Enrollment Rate of Students in Junior Secondary School Phase	99.9	99.9	99.9	99.9
高 中	**Senior Schools**				
高中阶段新生入学率	Enrollment Rate ofStudents in Senior Secondary School Phase	97.0	96.5	97.0	97.0
普通高中招生比例	Recruit Students Rate of Regular Senior Secondary Schools	51	51	56	57
高 校	**Institutions of Higher Education**				
普通高等学校录取率	Admission Rate of Students in Regular Institution of Higher Education	67.4	85.1	89.0	89.0

表 20.5 主要年份各级民办学校基本情况
BASIC STATISTICS OF CIVIL SCHOOLS IN MAIN YEARS

类 别	Types	2000	2010	2014	2015
民办高等学校	**Civil Institutions of Higher Education**				
学校数(所)	Schools (unit)	3	20	20	20
在校学生(万人)	Students Enrollment(10 000 persons)	0.67	9.37	9.22	10.01
专任教师(人)	Full-time Teachers(person)	304	3 906	4 041	4 461
民办中等专业学校	**Civil Specialized Secondary Schools**				
学校数(所)	Schools (unit)	3	3	2	2
在校学生(万人)	Students Enrollment(10 000 persons)	0.14	0.13	0.12	0.13
专任教师(人)	Full-time Teachers(person)	98	45	49	51
民办职业高中学校	**Civil Vocational Schools**				
学校数(所)	Schools (unit)	1	2	3	3
在校学生(万人)	Students Enrollment(10 000 persons)	0.08	0.11	0.14	0.11
专任教师(人)	Full-time Teachers(person)	30	25	41	41
民办中学	**Civil Secondary Schools**				
学校数(所)	Schools (unit)	155	109	107	117
班级数(个)	Classes(unit)	1 842	2 103	2 113	2 150
在校学生(万人)	Students Enrollment(10 000 persons)	8.48	7.87	7.44	7.39
高 中	Senior	4.54	1.68	1.36	1.42
初 中	Junior	3.94	6.19	6.08	5.97
专任教师(人)	Full-time Teachers(person)	2 400	4 583	6 016	6 246
民办小学	**Civil Primary Schools**				
学校数(所)	Schools (unit)	35	184	174	173
班级数(个)	Classes(unit)	987	3 747	3 776	3 512
在校学生(万人)	Students Enrollment(10 000 persons)	3.95	16.42	15.60	13.94
专任教师(人)	Full-time Teachers(person)	831	7 181	8 176	7 661
民办幼儿园	**Civil Kindergarten**				
学校数(所)	Schools (unit)	92	396	532	562
班级数(个)	Classes(unit)	636	3 584	5 077	5 592
在校学生(万人)	Students Enrollment(10 000 persons)	1.77	9.91	15.00	16.83
专任教师(人)	Full-time Teachers(person)	1 056	7 161	9 689	10 353

表 20.6 民办学校(园)基本情况(2015)
BASIC STATISTICS OF CIVIL SCHOOLS

单位：人(person)

指 标	Indicators	学校数(所) Schools (unit)	毕业生数 Graduates	招生数 Students Recruited	在校生数 Students Enrollment	专任教师数 Full-time Teachers
普通高等学校	Institutions of Higher Education	20	22 633	32 052	100 105	4 461
普通中等专业学校	Specialized Secondary Schools	2	403	335	1 118	51
职业高中学校	Secondary Vocational Schools	3	497	325	1 094	41
普通中学	Regular Secondary Schools	117	18 637	21 068	73 885	6 246
高 中	Senior Schools	55	4 199	5 147	14 222	1 613
初 中	Junior Schools	62	14 438	15 921	59 663	4 633
普通小学	Primary Schools	173	29 265	23 690	139 437	7 661
幼儿园	Kindergartens	562	50 468	58 886	168 348	10 353

注：根据《民办教育促进法》的新规定，民办中、小学统计口径中扣除了公立转制学校。
Note: According to new provision of Civil Education Advance Law, the scope of civil secondary and primary school excluded public schools transformed School excluded public schools transformed.

表 20.7 主要年份外国留学生情况
STATISTICS OF FOREIGN STUDENT IN MAIN YEARS

指 标	Indicators	2005	2010	2014	2015
外国留学生人数(人)	**Quantity of Foreign Students(person)**	**13 691**	**17 340**	**23 702**	**29 242**
按费用来源分	By Tuition Resource				
中国政府资助	Chinese Government Sustentation	934	2 585	4 555	6 040
本国政府资助	Homeland Government Sustentation	15	347	193	156
国际组织资助	International Organization Sustentation			1	
学校间交换	Inter-school Communion	463	1 570	3 070	4 862
自 费	Commoners	12 279	12 838	15 883	18 184
按地区来源分	By District				
亚 洲	Aisa	10 490	11 689	13 463	15 348
非 洲	Africa	289	969	1 641	1 958
欧 洲	Europe	1 927	3 023	5 718	7 727
北美洲	North America	766	983	2 075	3 227
南美洲	South America	129	477	525	613
大洋洲	Oceania	90	199	280	369

表 20.8 主要年份研究生人数
QUANTITY OF GRADUATE STUDENTS IN MAIN YEARS

单位：人(person)

年 份 Year	获博士学位人数 Quantity of Doctor's Degrees Obtained	获硕士学位人数 Quantity of Master's Degrees Obtained	研究生 Postgraduates					
			毕业生数 Graduates		招生数 New Students Enrollment		在读人数 Students Enrollment	
			普通高等学校 Institutions of Higher Education	研究所(院) Research Institutions (Academies)	普通高等学校 Institutions of Higher Education	研究所(院) Research Institutions (Academies)	普通高等学校 Institutions of Higher Education	研究所(院) Research Institutions (Academies)
1978			9		1 072		1 253	
1980			6		410		2 696	
1985	57	1 371	1 543	37	4 264	83	8 163	170
1990	300	2 746	2 953	369	2 803	324	8 533	1 035
1991	342	2 739	2 936	320	2 717	302	8 020	949
1992	343	2 124	2 262	264	3 323	345	8 858	997
1993	368	2 489	2 569	315	3 919	363	10 037	1 008
1994	442	2 363	2 608	251	4 665	465	11 905	1 185
1995	606	2 742	3 038	317	4 776	525	13 378	1 335
1996	627	3 233	3 537	323	5 915	592	15 307	1 528
1997	890	3 585	4 117	358	6 163	562	16 841	1 619
1998	1 090	3 552	4 253	389	7 281	593	19 499	1 663
1999	1 323	4 288	5 196	415	8 758	655	22 656	1 764
2000	1 307	4 546	5 435	433	11 796	856	28 582	2 032
2001	1 487	5 330	6 380	437	14 751	1 075	36 528	2 515
2002	1 655	6 067	7 481	445	17 848	1 363	45 713	3 183
2003	1 994	7 683	9 501	578	20 767	1 757	55 092	3 998
2004	2 678	10 580	12 788	681	23 545	1 789	64 747	4 690
2005	3 119	13 245	15 857	884	25 845	1 847	73 557	5 171
2006	3 772	15 957	18 833	1 098	28 250	1 849	81 487	5 419
2007	4 355	19 250	22 691	1 235	28 748	1 862	86 177	5 586
2008	4 483	20 734	24 431	1 322	30 195	1 947	89 778	5 720
2009	4 661	23 622	26 949	1 342	35 418	2 007	97 639	5 853
2010	4 749	23 458	26 843	1 364	36 619	2 024	105 711	6 006
2011	4 610	25 568	29 431	1 385	37 971	2 109	112 902	6 115
2012	4 913	29 270	33 189	1 417	41 899	2 330	120 503	6 511
2013	5 077	30 311	34 148	1 521	43 659	2 564	127 803	6 996
2014	4 516	32 056	36 013	559	43 353	577	131 806	1 748
2015	4 490	33 378	37 289	579	45 400	605	136 539	1 748

①2001 年前的获博士学位和获硕士学位的人数为当年毕业生人数。
②2014 学年起，中科院、煤炭院所属科研机构不纳入本市研究生培养机构统计。
❶Quantity of Doctor's and Master's Degrees obtained refer to Quantity of graduates in this year before 2001.
❷Since 2014 school year, subsidiary institutions of Chinese Academy of Science and Coal Research Institute are not included in the statistics of postgraduage training mechanism.

表20.9 普通高等学校基本情况（2015）
BASIC STATISTICS OF INSTITUTIONS OF HIGHER EDUCATION

类别 Types		学校（所）Institutions (unit)	毕业生数（人）Graduates (person)	招生数（人）New Students Enrollment (person)	在校学生人数（人）Students Enrollment (person)	教职员工（人）Staff and Workers (person)	其中 of which #专任教师 Full-time Teacher	其中 of which #正、副高级 Senior and Associate Title
总计	Total	67	128 711	140 709	511 623	73 578	41 570	21 082
综合大学	Comprehensive Universities	4	17 528	15 979	68 810	25 013	10 982	7 437
理工院校	Science and Engineering	25	47 731	54 564	192 667	20 703	12 900	5 734
农林院校	Agriculture and Forestry	2	4 186	4 360	15 532	1 474	1 034	466
医药院校	Medical	3	5 203	3 648	16 575	2 169	1 324	484
师范院校	Teacher Training	2	8 847	8 614	35 241	6 823	3 942	2 426
语文院校	Linguistics and Literacy	3	4 652	5 934	19 001	2 078	1 336	487
财经院校	Economics and Finance	18	29 248	36 693	122 902	9 705	6 412	2 602
政法院校	Politics and Law	3	6 524	5 980	22 762	2 535	1 769	660
体育院校	Physical Culture	2	1 122	1 117	4 422	1 203	647	321
艺术院校	Art Schools	5	3 670	3 820	13 711	1 875	1 224	465

注：学生数中未包括在读研究生人数，在分类院校学生数中未包括成人高等学校中的普通本专科学生。

Note: Post-graduates are not included in the students enrollment. Undergraduates and junior college students in adult education schools are not included in the students enrollment by types of colleges.

表20.10 普通高等学校分科专任教师数（2015）
FULL-TIME TEACHERS IN INSTITUTIONS OF HIGHER EDUCATION BY SUBJECTS

单位：人（person）

类别 Types		专任教师数 Full-time Teachers	其中 of which 正高级 Senior Title	副高级 Associate Title	中级 Junior Title	初级 Primary Title	无职称 Non-Title
总计	Total	41 570	7 541	13 541	16 358	2 743	1 387
哲学	Philosophy	980	175	281	385	88	51
经济学	Economics	2 323	400	870	873	82	98
法学	Law	2 918	478	823	1 228	230	159
教育学	Education	3 579	296	894	1 747	506	136
文学	Literature	6 505	735	1 795	3 191	445	339
历史学	History	479	160	135	149	11	24
理学	Science	4 249	1 255	1 598	1 223	80	93
工学	Engineering	11 708	2 608	4 421	4 064	437	178
农学	Agriculture	294	76	106	76	33	3
医学	Medical	2 226	470	685	850	187	34
管理学	Administration	3 611	566	1 224	1 430	256	135
艺术学	Art	2 698	322	709	1 142	388	137

表 20.11 普通高等学校本科分科学生数(2015)
UNDERGRADUATE STUDENTS IN INSTITUTIONS OF HIGHER EDUCATION BY SUBJECTS

单位:人 (person)

类 别	Types	毕业生人数 Graduates	招生人数 New Students Enrollment	在校学生人数 Students Enrollment
总 计	**Total**	**85 435**	**91 984**	**367 233**
哲 学	Philosophy	112	106	525
经济学	Economics	8 205	9 198	34 927
法 学	Law	5 918	5 548	22 123
教育学	Education	2 213	2 321	9 117
文 学	Literature	8 824	9 406	37 278
历史学	History	209	199	855
理 学	Science	4 908	5 443	21 729
工 学	Engineering	29 406	31 262	125 840
农 学	Agriculture	520	466	1 886
医 学	Medical	2 231	2 854	11 594
管理学	Administration	16 631	18 018	73 146
艺术学	Art	6 258	7 163	28 213

表 20.12 中等专业学校基本情况(2015)
BASIC STATISTICS OF SPECIALIZED SECONDARY SCHOOLS

单位:人 (person)

类 别	Types	毕业生数 Graduates	招生数 New Students Enrollment	在校学生 Students Enrollment	专业课专任教师 Full-time Teachers in Professional Course	其中 of which: #正副高级 Senior and Associate Title	中 级 Junior Title
总 计	**Total**	**24 944**	**22 176**	**72 405**	**2 806**	**751**	**1 360**
#土木水利工程	Construction and Water Conservancy Engineering	1 834	1 827	6 043	145	46	54
加工制造	Machining and Manufacture	4 085	3 337	11 829	404	126	187
交通运输	Transport	2 745	2 437	7 836	174	32	100
信息技术	Information Technology	2 825	2 387	7 844	336	75	188
医药卫生	Health	2 843	2 541	8 151	250	91	113
财经商贸	Trade and Tour	5 970	5 170	15 923	458	94	243
旅游服务	Finance and Economics	732	707	2 080	69	15	37
文化艺术	Culture and Art	1 329	1 286	4 745	316	84	160
体育与健身	Sports and Fitness	240	248	691	204	63	87
公共管理与服务	Society Commonality Business	203	223	797	24	9	6

表 20.13 各区、县普通中学基本情况(2015)
BASIC STATISTICS OF REGULAR SECONDARY SCHOOLS BY DISTRICTS AND COUNTIES

地 区	District	学 校 (所) Schools (unit)	毕业生数 (人) Graduates (person)	招生数 (人) New Students Enrollment (person)	在校学生 (人) Students Enrollment (person)	教职员工 (人) Staff and Workers (person)	其中 of which #专任教师 Full-time Teachers
总 计	**Total**	**790**	**145 501**	**168 717**	**570 546**	**70 231**	**54 962**
浦东新区	Pudong New Area	160	33 704	41 541	136 173	14 449	12 078
黄 浦 区	Huangpu	36	6 530	6 898	23 285	3 532	2 664
徐 汇 区	Xuhui	39	9 578	10 556	35 472	4 316	3 438
长 宁 区	Changning	26	5 048	4 760	17 157	2 865	2 004
静 安 区	Jing'an	15	3 164	3 338	11 645	1 659	1 186
普 陀 区	Putuo	46	7 130	7 585	26 633	3 724	2 773
闸 北 区	Zhabei	37	6 396	6 278	22 828	3 145	2 301
虹 口 区	Hongkou	39	6 387	6 143	21 895	3 207	2 613
杨 浦 区	Yangpu	50	8 823	8 531	30 063	3 987	3 191
闵 行 区	Minhang	68	11 225	14 449	47 884	5 954	4 613
宝 山 区	Baoshan	58	10 675	12 912	43 091	4 346	3 712
嘉 定 区	Jiading	39	6 293	8 624	29 015	3 146	2 528
金 山 区	Jinshan	32	5 733	7 246	24 091	2 908	2 289
松 江 区	Songjiang	36	7 827	10 475	34 132	3 903	2 819
青 浦 区	Qingpu	29	5 535	6 623	22 465	2 786	2 203
奉 贤 区	Fengxian	44	6 479	7 903	27 621	3 240	2 428
崇 明 县	Chongming	36	4 974	4 855	17 096	3 064	2 122

表20.14　各区、县普通中学初、高中学生基本情况(2015)
BASIC STATISTICS OF REGULAR JUNIOR AND SENIOR SCHOOLS' STUDENTS BY DISTRICTS AND COUNTIES

单位:人 (person)

地　区 District		毕业生数 Graduates		招生数 New Students Enrollment		在校学生 Students Enrollment	
		初　中 Junior	高　中 Senior	初　中 Junior	高　中 Senior	初　中 Junior	高　中 Senior
总　计	**Total**	**94 274**	**51 227**	**115 278**	**53 439**	**412 345**	**158 201**
浦东新区	Pudong New Area	22 580	11 124	29 573	11 968	100 900	35 273
黄 浦 区	Huangpu	3 458	3 072	3 517	3 381	13 349	9 936
徐 汇 区	Xuhui	5 974	3 604	6 278	4 278	23 685	11 787
长 宁 区	Changning	3 285	1 763	3 095	1 665	12 163	4 994
静 安 区	Jing'an	1 902	1 262	1 830	1 508	7 289	4 356
普 陀 区	Putuo	4 486	2 644	4 912	2 673	18 491	8 142
闸 北 区	Zhabei	4 030	2 366	4 016	2 262	15 911	6 917
虹 口 区	Hongkou	3 858	2 529	3 876	2 267	14 875	7 020
杨 浦 区	Yangpu	5 149	3 674	4 854	3 677	19 074	10 989
闵 行 区	Minhang	7 602	3 623	10 534	3 915	36 417	11 467
宝 山 区	Baoshan	7 276	3 399	9 519	3 393	32 783	10 308
嘉 定 区	Jiading	4 318	1 975	6 375	2 249	22 527	6 488
金 山 区	Jinshan	3 763	1 970	5 210	2 036	18 005	6 086
松 江 区	Songjiang	5 473	2 354	7 902	2 573	26 660	7 472
青 浦 区	Qingpu	3 603	1 932	4 745	1 878	16 782	5 683
奉 贤 区	Fengxian	4 564	1 915	5 850	2 053	21 685	5 936
崇 明 县	Chongming	2 953	2 021	3 192	1 663	11 749	5 347

表 20.15 各区、县普通小学基本情况(2015)
BASIC STATISTICS OF REGULAR PRIMARY SCHOOLS BY DISTRICTS AND COUNTIES

地 区	District	学 校(所) Schools (unit)	毕业生数(人) Graduates (person)	招生数(人) New Students Enrollment (person)	在校学生(人) Students Enrollment (person)	教职员工(人) Staff and Workers (person)	其中 of which #专任教师 Full-time Teachers
总 计	**Total**	**764**	**137 911**	**155 792**	**798 686**	**60 293**	**52 321**
浦东新区	Pudong New Area	167	33 303	38 506	201 482	13 185	12 118
黄 浦 区	Huangpu	29	3 249	4 125	20 274	2 137	1 718
徐 汇 区	Xuhui	44	5 973	8 811	39 514	2 866	2 472
长 宁 区	Changning	23	3 399	4 263	21 484	1 890	1 564
静 安 区	Jing'an	12	1 678	1 929	10 163	1 033	752
普 陀 区	Putuo	25	5 286	7 895	36 310	2 727	2 538
闸 北 区	Zhabei	33	3 957	4 890	24 257	2 083	1 649
虹 口 区	Hongkou	33	3 809	4 442	22 877	2 084	1 853
杨 浦 区	Yangpu	43	4 956	7 322	32 268	2 702	2 420
闵 行 区	Minhang	65	14 171	18 424	91 028	6 234	5 285
宝 山 区	Baoshan	73	11 194	12 999	65 294	4 942	4 567
嘉 定 区	Jiading	41	7 970	9 310	47 473	3 162	2 677
金 山 区	Jinshan	31	5 468	4 754	26 395	2 283	1 935
松 江 区	Songjiang	35	12 184	12 174	61 741	4 104	3 527
青 浦 区	Qingpu	46	9 637	5 873	40 208	3 361	2 819
奉 贤 区	Fengxian	35	8 276	7 134	40 728	3 023	2 602
崇 明 县	Chongming	29	3 401	2 941	17 190	2 477	1 825

表 20.16 主要年份实验性示范性中学基本情况
BASIC STATISTICS OF SECONDARY CAMPUS SCHOOL IN MAIN YEARS

指 标	Indicators	2000	2010	2014	2015
学校(所)	Schools (unit)	84	128	143	147
班级数(个)	Classes (unit)	2 584	4 063	4 318	4 356
在校学生(万人)	Students Enrollment(10 000 persons)	12.10	14.67	15.09	15.16
教职员工(万人)	Staff and Workers (10 000 persons)	1.40	1.88	1.99	2.03
#专任教师	Full-time Teachers	0.88	1.42	1.58	1.61

注：实验性示范性中学包括重点中学和寄宿制高级中学。
Note: Secondary campus school includs important secondary school and boarding high school.

表 20.17 主要年份幼儿园基本情况
BASIC STATISTICS OF KINDERGARTENS IN MAIN YEARS

指 标	Indicators	2000	2010	2014	2015
幼儿园(所)	Kindergartens (unit)	958	1 252	1 462	1 510
幼儿数(万人)	Children Enrollment (10 000 persons)	24.12	40.03	50.29	53.59
教职员工(万人)	Staff and Workers(10 000 persons)	2.52	4.09	5.34	5.62
#教 师	Teachers	1.50	2.67	3.49	3.66

表 20.18 主要年份特殊教育基本情况
BASIC STATISTICS OF SPECIAL EDUCATION IN MAIN YEARS

指 标	Indicators	2000	2010	2014	2015
学校(所)	Schools (unit)	34	29	29	29
毕业生数(人)	Graduates(person)	868	918	844	754
招生数(人)	New Students Enrollment(person)	1 141	776	621	529
在校学生(人)	Students Enrollment(person)	5 407	5 036	4 603	4 334
教职员工(人)	Staff and Workers(person)	1 584	1 596	1 587	1 590
#专任教师	Full-time Teachers	943	1 143	1 228	1 239

表20.19 网络教育本科学生情况(2015)
BASIC STATISTICS OF UNDERGRADUATE STUDENTS OF NETWORK EDUCATION BY SUBJECT

单位:人(person)

类 别	Types	毕业生人数 Graduates	招生人数 New Students Enrollment	在校学生人数 Students Enrollment
总 计	**Total**	**15 192**	**13 978**	**32 599**
#经济学	Economics	529	366	933
法 学	Law	320	176	423
教育学	Education	2 205	1 888	3 780
文 学	Literature	758	492	1 087
理 学	Science	368	374	745
工 学	Engineering	2 172	1 875	4 899
医 学	Medical	1 442	1 732	3 489
管理学	Administration	7 273	6 862	16 785
艺术学	Art	124	213	458

表20.20 各级各类成人学校基本情况(2015)
BASIC STATISTICS OF ADULT SCHOOLS AT VARIOUS LEVELS

类 别	Types	学校数(所) Schools (unit)	毕业生人数(人) Graduates (person)	招生数(人) New Students Enrollment (person)	在校学生人数(人) Students Enrollment (person)	教职员工人数(人) Staff and Workers (person)	其中 of which #专任教师 Full-time Teachers
成人高等教育	**Adult Higher Education**	**14**	**49 683**	**47 850**	**158 012**	**1 473**	**764**
广播电视大学	Broadcasting and TV Universities	1				293	121
职工高等学校	Staff Higher Education Schools	10	2 637	1 709	5 873	850	517
管理干部学院	Institutes for Administrative Officials	3	338	359	971	330	126
普通高等学校办	Run by Regular High Education Institutions	(50)	49 341	47 568	157 099		
#函 授	Correspondence Programs	(9)	2 554	2 051	7 364		
业 余	Spare Time	(41)	46 787	45 517	149 735		
成人网络本、专科	**Adult Network Education**		**47 701**	**44 175**	**113 564**		
成人中等教育	**Adult Secondary Education**	**13**	**7 110**	**6 905**	**16 364**	**379**	**175**
#成人中等专业学校	Specialized Secondary Schools	13	7 110	6 905	16 364	379	175
成人职业技术学校	**Adult Technical Secondary Schools**	**636**	**1 646 437**		**1 656 630**	**16 991**	**8 362**

①"( )"指高等院校举办的各类成人教学点数据。成人中学学校在校学生数为在校注册学生数。
②成人职业技术学校毕业生及在校学生数为培训半年以上人次数。
❶The figures with"( )" refer to the number of the adult education places conducted by higher education institutions. Students enrollment of adult spare-time secondary schools refers to accumulative total number of students registered at schools who has been trained more than half a year.
❷Graduates and Students Enrollment of adult technical secondary schools refers to accumulative total number of students registered at schools who has been trained more than half a year.

上 / 海 / 统 / 计 / 年 / 鉴

主要统计指标解释

学 校

指按国家规定的设置标准和审批程序批准设立的，招收适龄人口实施各级各类教育活动的教育机构。

普通高等学校

指按照国家规定的设置标准和审批程序批准举办的，通过全国普通高等学校统一招生考试，招收高中毕业生为主要培养对象，实施高等教育的全日制大学、独立设置的学院和高等专科学校、高等职业学校和其他机构。

大学、独立设置的学院主要实施本科层次以上教育，高等专科学校、高等职业学校实施专科层次教育，其他机构是承担国家普通招生计划任务不计校数的机构。包括普通高等学校分校和批准筹建的普通高等学校等。

成人高等学校

指按国家规定的设置标准和审批程序举办的，通过全国成人高等教育统一招生考试，招收高中毕业或同等学历的人员为主要培养对象，利用函授、业余、脱产的多种形式对其实施高等学历教育的学校。包括：职工高等学校、农民高等学校、管理干部学院、教育学院、独立函授学院、广播电视大学、其他机构等。

中等专业学校

指经县或县以上教育行政部门批准设立，招收初中毕业生实施中等专业课程教育的教学机构。

职业中学（职业高中、职业初中）

指经县或县以上教育行政部门批准设立，招收小学或初中毕业生实施中等职业技术教育的教学机构。按学校性质类别可分为：独立设置的职业中学（包括：职业初中、职业高中、职业初高中合设学校）；附设有普通中学班的职业中学。

普通中学（普通高中、普通初中）

普通中学分为普通高级中学和普通初级中学两个阶段。普通初级中学是指独立设置的招收小学毕业的适龄人口进行初级中等基础教育的机构；普通高级中学是指独立设置的招收初中毕业的适龄人口进行高级中等基础教育的机构；完全中学是指普通初、高中合设的教育机构；一贯制学校是指在一所学校连续实施中小学教育的机构。其中包括实施九年义务教育的九年一贯制学校和实施高中教育的十二年一贯制学校。（说明：一贯制学校的办学条件如能划分为小学、初中、高中，则分开填报；如不能划分清楚，可按就高不就低的方法填入初中、高中报表中，不能重复填写。）

普通小学

指由区或区以上教育行政部门批准，招收学龄儿童实施初等教育的教学机构。

幼儿园

指招收三周岁以上（含三周岁）学龄前幼儿，对其进行保育和教育的单位。

特殊教育学校

指本市独立设置的招收盲聋哑和智残儿童，以及其他特殊需要的儿童、青少年进行普通或职业初、中等教育的教学机构。

小学学龄儿童净入学率

小学学龄人口中正在接受小学教育人数所占比重。

初中学生净入学率

是指初中阶段教育（接受普通初中教育和职业初中教育）在校学生总数占初中阶段教育学龄人口数的比重。

SHANGHAI STATISTICAL YEARBOOK

EXPLANATORY NOTES TO MAJOR STATISTICAL INDICATORS

□ School Institutions

School Institutions refer to education establishments set up according to the government evaluation and approval procedures, enrolling population of the right age, providing various phase education activity.

□ Regular Institutions of Higher Education

Regular Institutions of Higher Education refer to educational establishments set up according to the government evaluation and approval procedures, enrolling graduates from senior secondary schools and providing higher education courses and training for senior professionals. They include full-time universities, colleges, high professional schools, high professional vocational schools and others.

Universities and colleges are mainly providing undergraduate courses; those high professional schools and high professional vocational schools are mainly providing professional trainings; and others refer to educational establishments, which are responsible for enrolling students but not covered in the total number of schools, including: branch schools of universities and colleges, and universities and colleges that have been proved and prepared to construct.

□ Institutions of Higher Education for Adults

Institutions of Higher Education for Adults refer to educational establishments, set up in line with relevant rules approved by the government, enrolling personnel with senior secondary schools or equivalent education, and providing higher education courses in many forms of correspondence, spare time, or full time for adults. Institutions of higher schools for adults include schools of higher educations for staff and workers, schools of higher education for peasants, colleges for management cadres, pedagogical colleges, independent correspondence colleges, Radio and TV universities and other educational establishments, etc.

□ Specialized Secondary Schools

Specialized Secondary schools refer to educational establishments set up according to approval and permission by educational administration department of district and above government, enrolling graduates from junior secondary schools and providing secondary professional education courses.

□ Vocational Secondary Schools (senior secondary schools and junior secondary schools)

Vocational Secondary Schools (senior secondary schools and junior secondary schools) refer to educational establishments set up according to approval and permission by educational administration department of district and above government, enrolling graduates from primary schools and junior secondary schools and providing secondary vocational education courses.

□ Regular Secondary Schools (senior secondary schools and junior secondary schools)

Regular Secondary Schools (senior secondary schools and junior secondary schools) are classified as senior secondary schools and junior secondary schools. Junior Secondary Schools refer to educational establishments enrolling graduates from primary schools and providing junior secondary educational courses. Senior Secondary Schools refer to educational establishments enrolling graduates from junior secondary schools and providing higher secondary educational courses.

□ Regular Primary Schools

Regular Primary Schools refer to educational establishments set up according to approval and permission by educational administration department of district and above government, enrolling graduates from children of school age and providing primary educational courses.

□ Kindergartens

Kindergartens refer to nursery and education establishments, enrolling children in 3 years old and above.

□ Special Education Schools

Special Education Schools refer to educational establishments set up independently, enrolling blind, deaf, dumb, amentia or other special children, and educational establishment, providing regular or vocational junior and senior secondary education for hobbledehoy.

EXPLANATORY NOTES TO MAJOR STATISTICAL INDICATORS

□ Enrollment Rate of School-age Children

Enrollment Rate of School-age Children refers to the proportion of school age children enrolled at schools to the total number of school age children both in and outside schools.

□ Enrollment Rate of Students in Junior Secondary School Phase

It refers to the proportion of total quantity of student in junior secondary school to the population of junior school age.

第二十一篇
CHAPTER 21

卫生、社会保障和社会福利业
HEALTH, SOCIAL SECURITY AND SOCIAL WELFARE

简要说明

一、本篇资料的主要内容

本篇主要反映卫生、社会保障和社会福利的发展情况。

卫生部分主要包括卫生机构、卫生技术人员、卫生机构床位、医疗机构诊疗入院、疾病死亡原因、婴儿死亡原因、三大死亡率、防病工作、家庭病床、妇幼卫生工作、公民献血用血、卫生总费用等情况。

社会保障部分主要包括城镇基本养老保险、城镇职工基本医疗保险、城镇居民基本医疗保险、城镇职工失业保险、城镇职工生育保险、城镇职工工伤保险、农村合作医疗、少儿住院基金等参保人数情况。

社会福利部分主要包括社会保障标准、社会福利事业机构、民间组织、养老服务、医疗服务和红十字会等情况。

二、本篇资料的来源

卫生部分资料由上海市卫生和计划生育委员会提供。社会保障资料由上海市人力资源和社会保障局提供。社会福利资料中,社会保障标准、社会福利事业机构、民间组织、养老服务资料由上海市民政局提供;医疗服务资料由上海市卫生和计划生育委员会提供;红十字会资料由上海市红十字会提供。

BRIEF INTRODUCTION

I. Main Contents

Data in this chapter mainly reflect the development of public health, social security, and social welfare.

Data on public health include mainly the number of medical and healthcare institutions, medical personnel, beds available at such institutions, in-patients medical treatment and death-causing diseases, infant death-causing diseases and composition, top three death-causing diseases, disease prevention, family sickbeds, work of gynecology and pediatrics, blood offered and used by citizens, total expenditure on health.

Data on social security include mainly the numbers of participants in urban basic pension insurance, urban employee basic medical care insurance, urban basic medical care insurance, unemployment insurance, maternity insurance, work injury insurance, rural social medical care insurance, and medical fund of children.

Data on social welfare include social security standards, social welfare institutions, civil organizations, services for aged people, medical services and basic statistics about the Red Cross Society of China Shanghai Municipal Branch.

II. Sources of data

Data on public health are provided by Shanghai Municipal Health and Family Planning Commission. Data on social security are provided by Shanghai Municipal Human Resources and Social Security Bureau. Of data on social welfare, data on social security standards, social welfare institutions, civil organizations, and services for aged people are provided by Shanghai Civil Affairs Bureau; data on medical services are provided by Shanghai Health and Family Planning Commission; data on Red Cross are provided by the Red Cross Society of China Shanghai Municipal Branch.

表21.1 卫生事业基本情况(1978~2015)
BASIC STATISTICS OF PUBLIC HEALTH

年 份 Year	卫生机构数(个) Health Care Institutions (unit)	其中 of which #医 生 Doctors	卫 生 技术人员(万人) Medical Professionals (10 000 persons)	其中 of which #执 业(助理)医师 Licensed (Assistant) Doctors	卫生机构床位数(万张) Beds in Health Care Institutions (10 000 beds)	其中 of which #医 院 Hospitals	每万人口医生数(人) Doctors per 10 000 Persons (person)	每万人口医院床位数(张) Hospital Beds per 10 000 Persons (bed)
1978	4 823	388	8.50	3.35	5.47	4.68	30	42
1979	5 627	394	8.88	3.58	5.56	4.78	31	42
1980	6 067	399	9.41	3.92	5.80	4.94	34	43
1981	6 337	403	9.57	4.37	5.84	4.99	37	43
1982	6 445	408	9.88	4.72	5.93	5.11	40	43
1983	6 451	415	10.09	4.87	6.00	5.20	41	43
1984	6 318	420	10.24	4.84	6.16	5.34	40	44
1985	7 245	405	10.42	4.85	6.02	5.32	39	43
1986	7 306	419	10.71	4.91	6.22	5.47	39	44
1987	7 330	431	11.00	5.05	6.38	5.60	40	44
1988	7 471	444	11.46	5.40	6.79	5.89	42	46
1989	7 550	460	11.65	5.73	6.87	6.04	44	46
1990	7 690	462	11.84	5.82	6.96	6.21	44	47
1991	7 554	463	11.92	5.89	7.01	6.31	44	47
1992	7 363	454	11.82	5.88	7.07	6.42	43	47
1993	6 077	486	11.53	5.75	7.12	6.75	42	49
1994	5 606	497	11.20	5.52	7.20	6.81	39	49
1995	5 286	485	11.06	5.37	7.10	6.69	38	47
1996	5 200	477	10.95	5.24	7.00	6.73	36	46
1997	5 028	474	10.89	5.13	7.00	6.78	34	46
1998	4 637	473	10.84	5.03	7.02	6.83	33	45
1999	4 620	465	10.81	5.06	7.24	7.06	32	45
2000	4 400	459	10.71	4.99	7.53	7.31	31	45
2001	3 813	432	10.51	4.85	7.88	7.63	30	47
2002	2 422	436	10.16	4.38	8.15	8.13	27	50
2003	2 319	452	10.22	4.41	8.44	8.11	26	47
2004	2 577	489	10.17	4.38	8.64	8.50	25	49
2005	2 527	487	10.35	4.40	9.08	8.93	25	50
2006	2 519	505	10.90	4.55	9.44	9.28	25	51
2007	2 646	288	12.24	4.88	9.59	7.54	26	41
2008	2 809	301	12.77	5.12	9.78	7.78	27	41
2009	3 013	296	13.09	5.11	9.97	7.95	27	41
2010	3 270	306	13.54	5.13	10.51	8.48	22	37
2011	3 358	308	13.91	5.21	10.71	8.75	22	37
2012	3 465	317	14.61	5.42	10.96	9.00	23	38
2013	4 929	328	15.64	5.81	11.43	9.47	24	39
2014	4 987	332	16.40	6.13	11.75	9.83	25	41
2015	5 016	338	17.02	6.31	12.28	10.35	26	42

①2002 年开始，卫生指标按照新的《中国卫生统计调查制度》统计。
②2007 年开始，医院统计范围按照新的《2007 国家卫生统计调查制度》统计，不再包括社区卫生服务中心、妇幼保健院和专科防治院。
③2013 年开始，卫生机构，卫生技术人员和床位数中包含村卫生室相关数据。
❶Since 2002, statistics of health care has been based on "China Health Care Statistical Investigation System ".
❷Since 2007, statistics of hospital has been based on "2007 National Health Care Statistical Investigation System", not including the community health care service center, maternity and child care hospital and special disease hospital.
❸Since 2013, data of health institutions, health technology personnel and beds contain the related data of village health rooms.

表21.2 各类卫生机构、床位及人员数(2015)
VARIOUS HEALTH CARE INSTITUTIONS,BEDS AND PERSONNEL

机构类别	Type of Institutions	机构数(个) Health Care Institutions (unit)	床位数(张) Beds (bed)	从业人员数(人) Personnel (person)
总　计	**Total**	**5 016**	**122 813**	**208 624**
#医　院	Hospitals	338	103 526	140 943
综合医院	Comprehensive Hospitals	181	60 838	96 783
中医医院	Hospitals of Traditional Chinese Medicine	18	5 966	9 511
中西医结合医院	Hospitals of Traditional Chinese and Western Medicine	8	3 502	5 516
专科医院	Special Diseases Hospitals	106	26 575	26 745
护理院	Nursing Homes	25	6 645	2 388
基层医疗卫生机构	Basic Medical and Health Institutions	4 480	17 099	52 918
社区卫生服务中心(站)	Community Health Care Centers	1 035	17 099	34 551
村卫生室	Village Health Rooms	1 271		2 405
门诊部	Policlinics	633		10 578
诊所、卫生所、医务室、护理站	Clinics, Health Centers and Infirmaries	1 541		5 384
专业公共卫生机构	Professional Medical and Health Institutions	116	1 465	11 909
疾病预防控制中心	Disease Prevention and Control Centers	19		3 051
专科疾病防治院(所、站)	Special Disease Hospitals and Institutions	21	148	1 384
健康教育所(站、中心)	Health Education Institutions	1		100
妇幼保健院(所、站)	Maternity and Child Care Hospitals and Institutions	21	1 317	3 170
急救中心(站)	First-aid Centers	11		2 235
采供血机构	Blood Collection and Supply Institutions	8		599
卫生监督所(中心)	Health Supervision Centers	18		1 215
计划生育技术服务机构	The Family Planning Technical Service Institutions	17		155
其他卫生机构	Other Health Care Institutions	82	723	2 854
疗养院	Sanatoriums	4	723	507
卫生监督检验(监测、检测)所(站)	Health Supervision and Inspection Institutions	1		269
医学科学研究机构	Institutions of Medical Science	9		453
医学在职培训机构	Medical In-service Training Institutions	10		240
临床检验中心(所、站)	Clinical Test Centers	7		522
其　他	Others	51		863

表21.2 续表 continued

机构类别	Type of Institutions	#卫生技术人员 Medical Professionals	#执业(助理)医师 Licensed (Assistant) Doctors	注册护士 Registered Nurses
		其中 of which		
			其中 of which	
总　计	**Total**	**170 189**	**63 118**	**75 438**
#医　院	Hospitals	117 209	38 559	57 911
综合医院	Comprehensive Hospitals	81 626	27 523	40 321
中医医院	Hospitals of Traditional Chinese Medicine	7 964	2 991	3 320
中西医结合医院	Hospitals of Traditional Chinese and Western Medicine	4 705	1 691	2 215
专科医院	Special Diseases Hospitals	21 079	5 986	11 094
护理院	Nursing Homes	1 835	368	593
基层医疗卫生机构	Basic Medical and Health Institutions	43 399	20 814	15 153
社区卫生服务中心(站)	Community Health Care Centers	28 498	12 021	10 376
村卫生室	Village Health Rooms	1 520	1 505	15
门诊部	Policlinics	8 310	4 056	3 262
诊所、卫生所、医务室、护理站	Clinics, Health Centers and Infirmaries	5 071	3 232	1 500
专业公共卫生机构	Professional Medical and Health Institutions	8 256	3 309	2 086
疾病预防控制中心	Disease Prevention and Control Centers	2 211	1 264	47
专科疾病防治院(所、站)	Special Disease Hospitals and Institutions	1 107	564	374
健康教育所(站、中心)	Health Education Institutions	42	32	
妇幼保健院(所、站)	Maternity and Child Care Hospitals and Institutions	2 695	1 039	1 280
急救中心(站)	First-aid Centers	774	377	154
采供血机构	Blood Collection and Supply Institutions	440	25	229
卫生监督所(中心)	Health Supervision Centers	973		
计划生育技术服务机构	The Family Planning Technical Service Institutions	14	8	2
其他卫生机构	Other Health Care Institutions	1 325	436	288
疗养院	Sanatoriums	338	134	125
卫生监督检验(监测、检测)所(站)	Health Supervision and Inspection Institutions	77	77	
医学科学研究机构	Institutions of Medical Science	265	90	6
医学在职培训机构	Medical In-service Training Institutions	34	15	13
临床检验中心(所、站)	Clinical Test Centers	214	33	1
其　他	Others	397	87	143

表21.3 各区、县卫生机构基本情况(2015)
STATISTICS OF HEALTH CARE INSTITUTIONS BY DISTRICTS AND COUNTIES

地 区 District		机构数(个) Health Care Institutions(unit)	床位数(张) Hospital Beds (bed)	卫生技术人员(人) Medical Professionals (person)	其中 of which # 执业(助理)医师 Licensed (Assistant) Doctors	注册护士 Registered Nurses
总 计	**Total**	**5 016**	**122 813**	**170 189**	**63 118**	**75 438**
浦东新区	Pudong New Area	952	17 818	25 188	9 800	10 546
黄 浦 区	Huangpu	216	11 147	17 163	6 119	7 892
徐 汇 区	Xuhui	326	15 146	21 031	7 518	9 416
长 宁 区	Changning	241	4 857	8 546	3 282	3 708
静 安 区	Jing'an	126	6 767	10 048	3 521	4 784
普 陀 区	Putuo	176	6 776	8 589	3 171	3 843
闸 北 区	Zhabei	139	6 456	7 698	2 516	3 482
虹 口 区	Hongkou	168	6 844	10 011	3 629	4 595
杨 浦 区	Yangpu	189	8 194	10 412	3 609	5 070
闵 行 区	Minhang	404	7 616	10 622	3 979	4 768
宝 山 区	Baoshan	288	6 655	9 038	3 363	4 125
嘉 定 区	Jiading	293	4 202	6 728	2 768	2 817
金 山 区	Jinshan	267	4 057	5 342	1 980	2 267
松 江 区	Songjiang	278	4 436	5 780	2 298	2 361
青 浦 区	Qingpu	339	3 410	4 679	1 765	1 995
奉 贤 区	Fengxian	262	5 306	5 161	2 039	2 129
崇 明 县	Chongming	352	3 126	4 153	1 761	1 640

表21.4 医疗机构病床使用情况(2015)
STATISTICS OF HOSPITAL BED USAGE IN MEDICAL TREATMENT INSTITUTION

机构类别	Types	平均开放床位数(张) Average Beds Opened(bed)	病床周转次数(次) Turnover Times of Beds(time)	病床使用率(%) Usage Rate of Beds(%)	出院者平均住院日(日) Average Days to Inpatient in Hospital(day)
总 计	**Total**	**127 384.79**	**28.42**	**93.66**	**11.36**
卫生部门	Medical Institutions	100 801.74	30.68	96.21	10.91
#医 院	Hospital	82 197.82	34.89	98.67	9.81
#综合医院	Comprehensive Hospitals	50 810.92	40.00	98.70	9.01
中(西)医医院	Hospitals of Chinese (Western) Medicine	9 324.11	34.87	95.81	10.08
护理院	Nursing Hospitals	907.56	3.10	96.16	128.15
社区卫生服务中心	Community Health Care Centers	16 871.38	4.97	86.02	60.47
其他部门	Other Departments	26 583.05	19.86	84.02	14.03

表21.5 医疗机构诊疗人次和入院人数(2015)
PATIENTS TREATED AND INPATIENTS IN MEDICAL TREATMENT INSTITUTION

机构类别	Types	诊疗人次(万人次) Total Patients Treated(10 000 person-times)	其中 of which #门、急诊 Outpatients and Emergency Patients	入院人数(万人) Inpatients (10 000 persons)	每百诊次的入院人数(人) Inpatients per 100 Patient-times (person)
总 计	**Total**	**26 522.32**	**24 748.83**	**362.33**	**1.37**
医 院	Hospitals	15 361.11	15 297.94	339.67	2.21
综合医院	Comprehensive Hospitals	11 119.12	11 062.35	241.91	2.18
中(西)医医院	Hospitals of Chinese(Western) Medicine	2 251.92	2 251.10	32.55	1.45
传染病医院	Infectious Diseases Hospitals	57.92	57.92	2.13	3.68
精神病医院	Mental Hospitals	164.86	163.43	1.18	0.72
结核病医院	Tuberculosis Hospitals	101.50	101.50	7.09	6.99
肿瘤医院	Tumor Hospitals	129.77	129.77	6.64	5.12
儿童医院	Children's Hospitals	589.49	589.49	10.24	1.74
其他专科医院	Other Specialized Hospitals	907.23	903.08	35.38	3.90
护理院	Nurse Hospitals	39.30	39.30	2.55	6.49
社区卫生服务中心(站)	Community Health-care Service Centers (Stations)	8 674.01	8 451.50	8.38	0.10
妇幼保健院(所、站)	Maternity and Child Care Hospital	244.00	236.10	7.22	2.96
其他医疗机构	Other Medical Facilities	2 243.20	763.29	7.06	0.31

表21.6 前十位疾病死亡原因和构成(2015)
THE TOP 10 DEATH-CAUSING DISEASES AND COMPOSITION

死亡原因	Cause of Death	死亡专率(1/10万) Death Rate(1/100 000)	占死亡总数(%) Percentage of Total Death(%)
循环系病	Circulation Diseases	338.69	39.32
肿　瘤	Tumor	264.30	30.69
呼吸系病	Respiratory System Diseases	81.53	9.47
内分泌营养代谢病	Endocrine-Immunity-Metabolic Diseases	43.29	5.03
损伤中毒	Damnification and Poisoning	40.52	4.70
消化系病	Digestive System Diseases	19.80	2.30
神经系病	Nervous System Disease	11.80	1.37
传染病及寄生虫病	Infectious & Parasitic Diseases	9.27	1.08
精神病	Mental System Diseases	9.26	1.07
泌尿生殖系病	Genitourinary Diseases	7.10	0.82

表21.7 婴儿前五位疾病死亡原因和构成(2015)
THE TOP 5 INFANT DEATH-CAUSING DISEASES AND COMPOSITION

死亡原因	Cause of Death	死亡专率(1/10万) Death Rate(1/100 000)	占死亡总数(%) Percentage of Total Death(%)
先天异常	Congenital Anomaly	98.77	40.08
围生期疾病(新生儿病)	Neonatal Disease	94.61	38.40
损伤中毒	Damnification and Poisoning	12.48	5.06
内分泌营养代谢病	Endocrine-Immunity-Metabolic Diseases	10.40	4.22
神经系病	Nervous System Disease	9.36	3.80

表21.8 婴儿死亡率、新生儿死亡率、孕产妇死亡率(2012～2015)
DEATH RATE OF INFANT,NEW BORN,PREGNANT AND LYING-IN WOMAN

指　标	Indicators	2012	2013	2014	2015
婴儿死亡率(‰)	Death Rate of Infant(‰)	5.04	5.73	4.83	4.58
新生儿死亡率(‰)	Death Rate of New Born(‰)	2.58	2.85	2.58	2.27
孕产妇死亡率(1/10万)	Death Rate of Pregnant and Lying-in Woman(1/100 000)	7.10	7.08	6.74	6.66

表21.9 主要年份防病工作情况
BASIC STATISTICS OF DISEASE PREVENTION IN MAIN YEARS

指标	Indicators	2000	2010	2014	2015
传染病发病总例数（甲、乙）(万例)	**Cases of Contagious Diseases Reported (A,B)(10 000 cases)**	**3.58**	**2.22**	**2.26**	**2.52**
发病率(1/10万)	Disease Rate(1/100 000)	271.66	161.17	158.38	176.13
传染病死亡总人数(人)	Quantity of Deaths Caused by Contagious Diseases (person)	179	127	112	93
死亡率(1/10万)	Death Rate (1/100 000)	1.36	0.92	0.79	0.65
结核病登记病人数(千例)	T. B. Patients Registered (1 000 cases)	3.09	3.26	3.51	3.46
登记患病率(‰)	Registered Disease Rate(‰)	0.23	0.23	0.24	0.24
结核病新发病人数(千例)	Newly Reported T. B. Cases(1 000 cases)	5.18	3.76	4.05	3.82
登记新发病率(1/万)	Registered Newly Diseased Rate (1/10 000)	3.94	2.67	2.82	2.65
结核病死亡人数(人)	Quantity of Deaths Caused By T. B (person)	293	112	108	99
死亡率(1/10万)	Death Rate (1/100 000)	2.22	0.80	0.75	0.69
牙病受检人数(万人)	Quantity of People Undergoing Tooth Disease Check (10 000 persons)	51.89	54.85	62.03	63.95
龋牙患病率(%)	Rate of Caries Patients (%)	28.3	38.6	36.9	36.32
小学生视力不良率(%)	Nearsight Rate of Students in Primary School (%)	26.0	36.1	34.6	35.4
初中生视力不良率(%)	Nearsight Rate of Students in Junior High School (%)	55.0	70.0	69.8	70.2
高中生视力不良率(%)	Nearsight Rate of Students in Senior High School (%)	78.5	85.7	83.1	86.4
免疫规划疫苗常规免疫接种率(%)	Conventional Vaccines of Vaccine Immunization Programmes Recipients Rate	99.7	99.8	99.9	99.9
乙肝疫苗全程接种率(%)	Hepatitis-B Inoculation Rate(%)	99.9	99.8	99.9	99.9

表21.10 家庭病床情况(2015)
FAMILY SICKBEDS

机构类别	Types	开展工作机构数(个) Running Institutions (unit)	上门诊疗总次数(次) Total Times of Family Call (time)	年底实有病床数(张) Year-end Sickbeds (bed)	年内开设总病床数(张) Sickbeds Set up in 2015 (bed)
总 计	**Total**	**220**	**1 160 631**	**24 249**	**52 309**
医 院	Hospitals	9	35 003	709	1 107
社区卫生服务中心	Community Health-care Centers	215	1 125 628	23 540	51 202

表21.11 主要年份妇幼卫生工作情况
BASIC STATISTICS OF GYNAECOLOGY AND PAEDIATRICS IN MAIN YEARS

指标	Indicators	2000	2010	2014	2015
妇女病普查人数(万人)	**Quantity of People Surveyed for Female Diseases (10 000 persons)**	**40.27**	**86.54**	**84.01**	**67.7**
患病率(%)	Sufferers Rate(%)	35.0	33.3	29.9	33.2
治疗率(%)	Patients Treated Rate(%)	91.1	98.7	94.1	96.3
胎儿娩出顺产数(万人)	Quantity of Smooth Delivery (10 000 persons)	4.05	8.81	12.11	10.03
顺产率(%)	Smooth Delivery Rate(%)	47.5	45.1	51.9	52.4
出生低体重儿(人)	Quantity of Low-weight Newborns (person)	2 567	6 961	8 857	8 268
占活产总数(%)	Proportion in All Deliveries (%)	3.0	3.6	3.8	4.3
出生缺陷人数(人)	Quantity of Newborns with Innate Problems (person)	764	2 496	2 250	2 357
出生缺陷率(‰)	Disabled Among All Deliveries Rate (‰)	8.96	12.80	9.70	1.23
0~6岁儿童保健管理率(%)	Children of 0-6 Years Old under Health Programm Rate(%)	94.3	97.0	99.5	99.2
婚前检查人数(万人)	Quantity of People Undergoing Pre-marriage Checkup (10 000 persons)	17.36	8.53	6.22	5.38
婚检率(%)	Pre-marriage Checkup Recipients Rate(%)	98.4	35.4	23.9	22.2

表21.12 主要年份公民献血、用血情况
BASIC STATISTICS OF BLOOD DONATION AND USE IN MAIN YEARS

指标	Indicators	2000	2010	2014	2015
无偿(义务)献血(万人份)	Volunteer or Compulsory Blood Offer (10 000 person unit)	35.19	46.27	45.70	45.70
临床用血量(万人份)	Clinic Blood Use Volum (10 000 person unit)	34.70	42.02	43.50	40.30

表 21.13 主要年份社会保险参保人数
QUANTITY OF PARTICIPANTS IN SOCIAL INSURANCE IN MAIN YEARS

单位:万人(10 000 persons)

指标	Indicators	2000	2010	2014	2015
城镇基本养老保险	**Urban Basic Pension Insurance**				
城镇职工	Urban Staff and Workers	431.27	522.44	936.99	961.05
个体工商户和自由职业人员	Individual Businessmen	9.82	20.43	32.31	34.58
领取养老金的离退休人员	Retired Veteran Cadres and Retired Staff and Workers with Pensions	234.23	352.02	404.07	415.81
城镇职工基本医疗保险	**Basic Medical Insurance for Urban Staff and Workers**				
城镇职工	Urban Staff and Workers	364.59	608.41	967.64	980.54
享受医保的离退休人员	Retired Veteran Cadres and Retired Staff and Workers with Medicare	202.14	391.33	453.21	465.83
城镇居民基本医疗保险	**Basic Medical Insurance for Urban Residents**		**259.17**	**257.66**	**272.87**
城镇职工失业保险	Unemployment Insurance of Urban Staff and Workers	434.86	556.20	634.08	641.77
城镇职工生育保险	Generational Insurance of Urban Staff and Workers		657.30	717.54	735.41
城镇职工工伤保险	Injured Insurance of Urban Staff and Workers		555.36	920.49	932.87
农村合作医疗	Cooperartion Medicare Insurance in Country		148.95	98.74	95.98
少儿住院基金	Medicare Fund of Children	212.47	197.19	218.20	220.11

注：根据《中华人民共和国保险法》，2011 年对社会保险政策进行了调整。原参加"小城镇社会保险"和"来沪从业人员综合保险"的从业人员被纳入城镇职工保险范围内，并对养老、医疗、工伤、失业、生育保险的相关政策作出了调整。

Note: According to Insurance Law of the People's Republic of China, the social insurance policy has been adjusted since 2011. Employees, who have participated in Town Social Insurance and General Insurance of Employment of Migratory Population before, are now within the range of insurance for urban staff and workers. Relative policies of pension, medical, injured, unemployment and generational insurances have also been adjusted.

表 21.14 主要年份社会保障标准
SOCIAL SECURITY STANDARD IN MAIN YEARS

单位:元/月(yuan/month)

指标	Indicators	2000	2010	2014	2015
职工工资最低标准	Minimum Standard of Wages of Staff and Workers	445	1 120	1 820	2 020
城镇基本养老金最低标准	Minimum Standard of Urban Basic Pension Insurance	460	460	460	460
城镇居民生活保障最低标准	Minimum Standard of Urban Living Security	280	450	710	790

表21.15　社会福利院、儿童福利院、社会福利医院和收养性老年福利机构情况(1980～2015)

INSTITUTIONS OF SOCIAL WELFARE, CHILDREN WELFARE, SOCIAL WELFARE HOSPITALS AND ADOPTIVE SENIORS WELFARE INSTITUTIONS

年份 Year	社会福利院 Social Welfare Institutions			儿童福利院 Children Welfare Homes		
	单位(个) Units (unit)	床位数(张) Beds (bed)	年末在院人数(人) Year-end Population Housed(person)	单位(个) Units (unit)	床位数(张) Beds (bed)	年末在院人数(人) Year-end Population Housed(person)
1980	9	1 555	1 337	2	600	559
1981	9	1 621	1 313	2	650	634
1982	9	1 525	1 495	2	650	672
1983	9	1 644	1 491	2	600	676
1984	10	1 948	1 635	2	600	633
1985	10	1 727	1 630	2	580	625
1986	10	1 697	1 648	2	550	612
1987	10	1 991	1 770	2	378	449
1988	13	2 189	1 790	2	387	458
1989	14	2 418	2 012	2	538	481
1990	15	2 679	2 019	2	589	586
1991	14	2 687	2 138	2	611	592
1992	14	2 776	2 431	2	665	651
1993	14	2 874	2 554	2	708	690
1994	15	2 931	2 648	2	878	862
1995	15	3 006	2 722	2	988	919
1996	17	3 294	2 866	2	988	943
1997	21	4 012	3 441	2	988	946
1998	24	4 596	3 678	2	1004	984
1999	20	4 215	3 498	2	981	958
2000	23	4 884	4 137	2	1 100	1 092
2001	26	5 570	4 410	2	1 221	1 221
2002	27	5 590	4 760	3	1 491	1 429
2003	26	5 818	4 779	2	1 087	1 512
2004	26	5 876	4 848	6	1 300	1 893
2005	23	5 999	4 809	6	2 016	1 986
2006	25	6 583	5 024	6	1 252	2 142
2007	24	6 499	5 068	6	1 252	2 341
2008	26	6 864	5 215	6	2 490	2 454
2009	26	7 686	5 351	6	2 584	2 552
2010	25	7 944	5 774	6	2 454	2 423
2011	29	8 297	6 013	6	2 427	2 336
2012	30	8 703	6 200	6	2 455	2 289
2013	23	7 028	5 556	7	2 499	2 261
2014	23	7 434	4 937	3	2 133	2 053
2015	22	6 915	4 651	2	1 921	1 863

表21.15 续表 continued

年份 Year	社会福利医院 Social Welfare hospitals			收养性老年福利机构 Adoptive Seniors Welfare Institutions			
	单位(个) Units (unit)	床位数(张) Beds (bed)	年末在院人数(人) Year-end Population Housed(person)	机构(个) Institutions (unit)	床位数(张) Beds (bed)	年末在院人数(人) Year-end Population Housed(person)	其中 of which #老人 Elders
1980	3	1 475	1 424	42		630	
1981	3	1 460	1 430	53		762	
1982	3	1 490	1 422	58		1 022	
1983	3	1 490	1 432	90		1 402	
1984	3	1 460	1 380	135		2 328	
1985	3	1 480	1 360	199	3 870	3 038	2 786
1986	3	1 510	1 354	249	4 655	3 446	3 100
1987	3	1 497	1 342	277	5 520	4 262	3 893
1988	3	1 497	1 313	322	5 969	4 754	4 429
1989	3	1 433	1 324	349	6 281	5 129	4 835
1990	3	1 497	1 298	332	6 275	5 031	4 452
1991	3	1 391	1 285	341	6 731	5 763	5 642
1992	3	1 510	1 404	351	7 002	6 035	5 655
1993	3	1 510	1 394	331	7 143	6 365	5 934
1994	3	1 510	1 392	333	7 533	6 838	6 541
1995	3	1 510	1 409	330	8 576	7 405	6 633
1996	3	1 510	1 429	333	10 270	8 361	7 867
1997	3	1 500	1 452	323	11 253	9 295	8 647
1998	3	1 500	1 455	339	13 958	11 122	10 826
1999	3	1 710	1 703	331	16 526	12 698	12 013
2000	3	1 840	1 779	398	22 244	16 988	16 541
2001	3	1 894	1 894	378	23 627	17 363	16 923
2002	3	1 917	1 901	417	33 413	20 900	20 309
2003	3	1 680	1 881	422	36 791	23 451	22 682
2004	3	1 780	1 829	414	33 891	26 993	25 902
2005	3	1 811	1 811	450	43 131	31 301	30 181
2006	3	1 860	1 796	479	52 427	35 946	34 447
2007	3	1 852	1 806	536	64 115	42 665	40 731
2008	3	1 851	1 809	556	72 365	46 107	44 226
2009	3	1 842	1 808	589	84 714	51 974	49 789
2010	3	1 835	1 800	600	89 897	56 860	55 118
2011	3	1 821	1 776	602	93 599	58 660	57 597
2012	3	1 802	1 753	601	96 512	61 268	59 383
2013	3	1 783	1 734	609	102 097	65 030	63 152
2014	3	1 800	1 717	637	107 473	66 614	64 549
2015	3	1 800	1 680	607	105 284	69 280	67 286

表21.16 主要年份社会福利事业机构数和职工人数
QUANTITY OF SOCIAL WELFARE INSTITUTIONS AND STAFF AND WORKERS IN MAIN YEARS

	指 标 Indicators	2000	2010	2014	2015
机构数(个)	**Total Institutions (unit)**				
收养性福利单位	Adopting Social Welfare Institutions	427	635	667	705
优抚类	Subsidy	1	1	1	1
福利类	Welfare	426	634	666	704
社会福利企业	Social Welfare Enterprises	3 352	1 375	928	776
优抚安置单位	Subsidy and Arrangement Institutions	45	41	26	35
救助类单位	Salvation Institutions	16	22	7	7
婚姻登记服务单位	Marriage Register Service Institutions		16	18	18
殡仪服务单位	Funeral and Interment Service Institutions	68	79	75	74
福利彩票发行单位	Issue Institutions of Welfare Lottery	16	19	18	18
职工人数(人)	Staff and Workers (person)				
收养性福利单位	Adopting Social Welfare Institutions	7 793	19 966	23 084	23 924
优抚类	Subsidy	35	47	44	43
福利类	Welfare	7 758	19 919	23 040	23 881
社会福利企业	Social Welfare Enterprises	177 260	92 351	74 486	60 395
优抚安置单位	Subsidy and Arrangement Institutions	745	714	498	650
救助类单位	Salvation Institutions	472	403	76	92
婚姻登记服务单位	Marriage Register Service Institutions		110	149	156
殡仪服务单位	Funeral and Interment Service Institutions	2 577	3 201	3 080	3 390
福利彩票发行单位	Issue Institutions of Welfare Lottery	86	87	196	222

表21.17 主要年份民间组织情况
STATISTICS OF CIVIL ORGANIZATIONS AND CHARITY IN MAIN YEARS

	指 标 Indicators	2005	2010	2014	2015
民间组织数(个)	**Quantity of Civil Organizations (unit)**	**7 556**	**10 104**	**12 365**	**13 355**
社会团体	Social Organizations	2 952	3 634	3 909	4 003
民办非企业	Civil Non-Enterprises	4 537	6 353	8 257	9 082
基金会	Foundations	67	117	199	270

表21.18 主要年份养老服务
ENDOWMENT SERVICE IN MAIN YEARS

指 标	Indicators	2005	2010	2014	2015
机构养老服务	**Endowment Service of Institutions**				
机构数(家)	Quantity of Institutions (unit)	474	625	660	699
床位数(万张)	Quantity of Beds (10 000 beds)	4.96	9.78	11.49	12.60
#新增养老床位	Newly Added Endowmet Beds	1.01	1.08	0.58	1.10
养老床位占60周岁及以上老年人口比例(%)	Ratio of Endowment Bed in Population above 60 (%)	1.9	3.1	2.8	2.9
居家养老服务	**Household Endowment Service**				
社区老年人日间服务机构机构数(家)	Community Daytime Service Institutions for Aged People Quantity of Institutions (unit)	83	303	381	442
日托老年人数(万人)	Population of Daytime Service Aged People (10 000 persons)	0.21	0.90	1.40	1.50
社区助老服务社(个)	Community Service Center for Assisting Aged People (unit)	233	233	224	202
社区居家养老服务月服务人数(万人)	Monthly Population of Community Household Endowment Service (10 000 persons)	5.48	25.20	29.50	30.55
获得政府补贴的老年人(万人)	Population of Aged People Gained Governmental Subsidy (10 000 persons)	3.94	13.00	113.00	13.18

表21.19 主要年份老年医疗服务
MEDICARE SERVICE FOR AGED PEOPLE IN MAIN YEARS

指 标	Indicators	2005	2010	2014	2015
老年护理院	**Nursing Home for Aged People**				
独立老年护理院	Independent Nursing Home for Aged People				
机构数(所)	Quantity of Institutions (unit)	13	14	21	24
建筑面积(平方米)	Structure Area (sq. m)	59 742	101 048	226 938	243 159
床位数(张)	Beds (bed)	2 353	3 285	5 415	6 645
住院人次(人次)	Person-time in Hospital (person-time)	4 346	10 322	15 336	25 105
老年医院	**Hospital for Aged People**				
机构数(所)	Quantity of Institutions(unit)	3	4	5	4
住院人次(人次)	Person-time in Hospital (person-time)	9 124	15 520	15 356	5 704
家庭病床总数(张)	**Total Quantity of bed in home (bed)**	**40 745**	**43 880**	**52 447**	**52 731**

表21.20 主要年份红十字会基本情况
BASIC STATISICS ON RED CROSS SOCIETY OF CHINA SHANGHAI MUNICIPAL BRANCH IN MAIN YEARS

指标	Indicators	2005	2010	2014	2015
红十字会组织机构	**Institutions**				
红十字会各级组织机构(个)	Organizing Instituntions(unit)	2 934	3 042	4 048	3 217
红十字会医疗机构(个)	Medical Institutions(unit)	67	72	64	64
红十字会会员人数(万人)	**Quantity of Members(10 000 persons)**	**62**	**87**	**112**	**91**
#青少年会员(万人)	Hobbledehoy Members(10 000 persons)	37	59	60	36
红十字会团体会员单位(个)	Team Members(unit)	970	969	1 278	953
社区公益服务站点(个)	**Community Commonweal Service Stations (unit)**	**1 589**	**3 077**	**4 727**	**4 991**
组织各种宣传活动	**Times of Publicizing Activity**				
在报刊登载宣传文章(篇)	Articles on Newspaper and Periodical (piece)	831	609	326	260
电视台播报宣传节目(条/次)	Programs on Television (piece/time)	459	200	96	40
参加普及宣传无偿献血活动人次数(万人次)	Person-time Attended Publicizing Volunteer Blood Donation Activiies (10 000 person-times)		23.76	21.79	26.66
卫生救护工作	**Sanitation Rescue**				
救护普及培训(万人次)	Rescue Popularization Training (10 000 person-time)	24.72	37.35	50.08	49.15
造血干细胞捐献工作	**Contributing Trunk Cell**				
当年参加造血干细胞捐献库人数(万人)	Quantity of Subscribers (10 000 persons)	5.60	10.42	13.70	0.69
遗体捐献工作	**Contributing Reliquiae**				
遗体捐献登记站(个)	Register Centers(unit)	27	25	25	22
遗体捐献接收站(个)	Accepting Centers(unit)	8	7	8	6
全年接受捐献遗体登记(人)	Quantity of Contributing Reliquiae(Person)	1 284	1 170	1 753	1 725
全年接受角膜捐献登记(人)	Quantity of Contributing Cornea(Person)	133	73	746	741
社会救灾和社区救助工作	**Working on Social Relieving**				
救灾投入(万元)	Relieve Devotion (10 000 yuan)	10 635.36	19 267.76	2 424.23	1 146.02
社区救助款物投入(万元)	Community Salvation Devotion (10 000 yuan)	1 538.12	4 780.71	1 776.27	1 562.66
受益人次(万人次)	Quantity of Beneficiaries (10 000 persons-times)	2.87	4.11	10.23	1.79

①社区救助受益人次不包含外省市受益人次。
②2013年起,"参加普及宣传无偿献血活动人次数"口径调整为红十字会主办活动人次数。
❶Persons benefited from commuruity salvation devotion do not contain people from other provinces and cities.
❷The statistical caliber of Person-time Attended Publicizing Volunteer Blood Donation Activities was adjusted to Person-time of participating in the activities organized by the Red Cross Since 2013.

表21.21 全市残疾人各残疾类别人数情况(2015)
THE NUMBER OF CASES OF EACH TYPE OF DISABILITY

单位:人(person)

地区	District	总计 Total	视力 Vision	听力 Hearing	言语 Speech	肢体 Limb	智力 Intelligence	精神 Spirit	多重 Multiple
全市	**Total**	**423 520**	**76 945**	**42 733**	**4 258**	**190 806**	**56 168**	**46 743**	**5 867**
浦东新区	Pudong New Area	78 552	15 243	9 706	823	30 656	12 202	8 955	967
黄浦	Huangpu	27 968	8 320	3 397	223	9 346	2 686	3 568	428
徐汇	Xuhui	19 766	4 789	1 675	149	7 400	2 460	2 932	361
长宁	Changning	17 349	3 001	1 614	171	8 668	1 374	2 059	462
静安	Jing'an	8 923	1 948	1 117	58	3 477	820	1 327	176
普陀	Putuo	27 484	4 515	2 281	238	14 042	2 638	3 043	727
闸北	Zhabei	23 295	4 782	2 612	202	10 776	2 016	2 631	276
虹口	Hongkou	19 383	4 315	2 048	133	7 885	2 037	2 715	250
杨浦	Yangpu	32 517	5 783	2 917	226	17 024	2 785	3 277	505
闵行	Minhang	24 340	4 498	2 585	183	10 530	3 451	2 809	284
宝山	Baoshan	23 764	4 320	2 071	224	10 634	3 436	2 875	204
嘉定	Jiading	18 493	2 035	1 654	178	9 490	2 908	1 963	265
金山	Jinshan	15 387	1 963	808	643	6 784	3 271	1 782	136
松江	Songjiang	19 767	2 716	1 450	169	10 938	3 092	1 330	72
青浦	Qingpu	19 236	1 893	1 793	135	11 313	1 864	2 156	82
奉贤	Fengxian	15 969	1 428	1 255	326	7 611	3 527	1 617	205
崇明	Chongming	31 327	5 396	3 750	177	14 232	5 601	1 704	467

注：本表数据由市残疾人联合会提供。
Note：Date in this table are provided by Shanghai Disabled Persons' Federation.

表21.22 卫生总费用(2001～2014)
TOTAL HEALTH EXPENDITURE

年份 Year	卫生总费用(亿元) Total Health Expenditure	其中 of which			比重(%)			人均卫生费用(元) Per Capita Health Expenditure
		政府卫生支出 Government Health Expenditure	社会卫生支出 Social Health Expenditure	个人卫生支出 Personal Health Expenditure	政府卫生支出 Government Health Expenditure	社会卫生支出 Social Health Expenditure	个人卫生支出 Personal Health Expenditure	
2001	202.63	45.70	98.01	58.93	22.6	48.4	29.0	1 233
2002	220.31	40.65	121.14	58.52	18.5	55.0	26.5	1 356
2003	266.19	51.30	151.60	63.29	19.3	56.9	23.8	1 556
2004	315.48	59.54	170.14	85.80	18.9	53.9	27.2	1 811
2005	362.13	70.30	199.44	92.39	19.4	55.1	25.5	2 036
2006	401.46	77.13	226.39	97.94	19.2	56.4	24.4	2 212
2007	485.67	99.39	278.50	107.79	20.5	57.3	22.2	2 614
2008	559.83	135.82	314.97	109.04	24.2	56.3	19.5	2 965
2009	656.66	141.30	366.90	148.45	21.5	55.9	22.6	3 418
2010	751.99	177.20	419.82	154.96	23.6	55.8	20.6	3 266
2011	931.00	215.70	521.62	193.68	23.2	56.0	20.8	3 966
2012	1 092.35	232.49	646.51	213.35	21.3	59.2	19.5	4 589
2013	1 248.68	250.82	740.42	257.44	20.1	59.3	20.6	5 170
2014	1 347.79	275.29	792.51	279.99	20.4	58.8	20.8	5 556

表21.23 卫生总费用构成(2001～2014)
THE STRUCTURE OF TOTAL HEALTH EXPENDITURE

单位:%

年份 Year	卫生总费用 Total Health Expenditure	医院 Hospitals	基层医疗卫生机构 Basic Medical and Health Institutions	药品零售机构 Drug Retailers	公共卫生机构 Public Health Institutions	卫生行政管理机构 Health Administrative Organization	其他 Others
2001	100	62.9	18.3	10.1	5.3	0.3	3.1
2002	100	65.9	15.7	8.9	5.2	0.3	4.0
2003	100	65.6	13.7	8.1	5.1	0.4	7.1
2004	100	65.1	14.1	8.4	5.8	0.5	6.1
2005	100	63.6	14.6	8.4	5.8	0.5	7.1
2006	100	65.3	14.8	8.4	6.1	0.3	5.1
2007	100	66.5	14.8	7.5	5.2	1.7	4.3
2008	100	62.5	17.8	10.0	6.2	1.2	2.3
2009	100	64.9	17.3	8.1	6.3	1.1	2.3
2010	100	65.8	14.6	8.0	5.6	1.6	4.4
2011	100	68.1	13.0	7.4	3.2	1.9	6.4
2012	100	69.8	12.9	7.2	3.2	2.3	4.6
2013	100	70.7	13.1	7.2	3.5	2.6	2.9
2014	100	71.7	12.9	7.3	3.1	2.8	2.2

上/海/统/计/年/鉴

主要统计指标解释

卫生机构

是指从卫生行政部门取得《医疗机构执业许可证》，或从民政、工商行政、机构编制管理部门取得法人单位登记证书，为社会提供医疗保健、疾病控制、卫生监督服务或从事医学研究和医学在职培训等工作的单位。

医疗机构

指从卫生行政部门取得《医疗机构执业许可证》的机构，包括医院、疗养院、社区卫生服务中心（站）、卫生院、门诊部、诊所（卫生所、医务室）、妇幼保健院（所、站）、专科疾病防治院（所、站）、急救中心（站）和临床检验中心，但不包括村卫生室（单纯统计）。

医　院

包括综合医院、中医医院、中西医结合医院、民族医院、各类专科医院和护理院，不包括专科疾病防治院、妇幼保健院和疗养院

卫生技术人员

包括执业医师、执业助理医师、注册护士、药师（士）、检验技师、影像技师（士）、卫生监督员和见习医（药、护、技）师（士）等卫生专业人员。不包括从事管理工作的卫生技术人员（如院长、副院长、党委书记等）。

执业（助理）医师

一律按领取医师执业证书且实际从事临床工作的人数统计，不包括从事管理工作的医师。

优抚对象

优抚指政府对革命烈士家庭、病故残疾工作人员以及参战负伤致残的民兵、民工的抚恤和人民群众对其的优待。优抚对象包括革命烈士家属、因公牺牲和病故军人家属、革命伤残人员、现役军属、退伍红军老战士、红军失散人员、复员军人、退伍军人、在职退役军人、在乡退役军人、带病回乡退伍军人、复退军人精神病员、孤老优抚对象等。

社会福利事业单位

指集中收养社会孤老、残、幼的机构。包括由民政部门管理的社会福利院、儿童福利院、精神病人福利院和城镇集体办的福利院，以及农村集体办的敬老院。

基本养老保险

1.（参保）职工人数：指报告期末按照国家法律、法规和有关政策规定参加基本养老保险并在社保经办机构已建立缴费记录档案的职工人数，包括中断缴费但未终止养老保险关系的职工人数，不包括只登记未建立缴费记录档案的人数。

2.（参保）离退休人员人数：指报告期末参加基本养老保险的离休、退休和退职人员的人数。

3.基本养老保险基金收入：指根据国家有关规定，由纳入基本养老保险范围的缴费单位和个人按国家规定的缴费基数和缴费比例缴纳的养老保险基金，以及通过其他方式取得的形成基金来源的收入。包括单位和职工个人缴纳的基本养老保险费、基本养老保险基金利息收入、上级补助收入、下级上解收入、转移收入、财政补贴和其他收入。

4.基本养老保险基金支出：指按照国家政策规定的开支范围和开支标准从养老保险基金中支付给参加基本养老保险的离休、通休、退职人员个人的养老金、丧葬抚恤补助，以及由于保险关系转移、上下级之间调剂资金等原因而发生的支出。包括离休金、退休金、退职金、各种补贴、医疗费、死亡丧葬补助费、抚恤救济费、社会保险经办机构管理费、补助下级支出、上解上级支出、转移支出、其他支出等。

5.基本养老保险基金累计结余：指截止报告期末基本养老保险基金收支相抵后的累计余额。

基本医疗保险

1. 参保人数：指报告期末按国家有关规定参加基本医疗保险的人数。包括参加保险的职工人数和退休人员人数。

2.基金收入：指根据国家有关规定，由纳入基本医疗保险范围的缴费单位和个人，按国家规定的缴费基数和缴费比例缴纳的基金，以及通过其他方式取得的形成基金来源的款项，包括：单位缴纳的社会统筹基金收入、个人缴纳的个人账户基金收入、财政补贴收入、利息收入、其他收入。

主要统计指标解释

3.基金支出：指按照国家政策规定的开支范围和开支标准从社会统筹基金中支付给参加基本医疗保险的职工和退休人员的医疗保险待遇支出，和从个人帐户基金中支付给参加基本医疗保险的职工和退休人员的医疗费用支出，以及其他支出。包括：住院医疗费用支出、门急诊医疗费用支出、个人账户基金支出、其他支出。

4.基金累计结余：指截止报告期末基本医疗保险的社会统筹和个人帐户基金累计结余金额。包括银行存款、财政专户、债券投资和其他。

失业保险

1. 参保人数：指报告期末按照国家法律、法规和有关政策规定参加了失业保险的城镇企业事业单位的职工及地方政府规定参加失业保险的其他人员的人数。

2.失业保险基金收入：指按照规定从企业、事业及其他单位筹集的失业保险费及其他并入失业保险基金收入的总额。包括单位和个人缴纳的失业保险费、失业保险基金利息收入、上级补助收入、下级上解收入、转移收入、财政补贴和其他收入。

3.失业保险基金支出：指报告期内为保障失业人员和下岗职工基本生活、促进其再就业等支出的基金总额。包括失业救济金、医疗费、死亡丧葬补助费、抚恤救济费、转业训练费支出、失业保险经办机构管理费、补助下级支出、上解上级支出、转移支出和其他支出。

4.基金累计结余：指截止报告期末失业保险基金收支相抵后的累计余额。

工伤保险

1.参加保险人数: 指报告期末依据国家有关规定参加工伤保险的职工人数。

2.享受保险待遇人数: 指劳动者因工负伤致残、死亡或因患职业病致残，根据有关规定享受工伤保险待遇职工或供养直系亲属人数。包括伤残人数、职业病人数、因工死亡人数、供养直系亲属人数。

3.基金收入: 指根据国家有关规定，由参加工伤保险的单位按国家规定的缴费基数和缴费比例缴纳的工伤保险基金，以及通过其他形式取得的形成基金来源的款项。包括：单位缴纳的社会统筹基金收入、财政补贴收入、利息收入、其他收入。

4.基金支出: 指按照国家政策规定的开支范围和开支标准从工伤保险基金中支付给参加工伤保险的人员及供养直系亲属工伤保险待遇支出及其他支出。包括工伤医疗费、伤残补助金、工亡补助金、护理费、丧葬补助费、工伤预防费用、职业康复费用和其他支出。

5.基金累计结余: 指截止报告期末工伤保险基金累计结余金额。包括银行存款、财政专户、债券投资和其他。

生育保险

1.参保人数: 指报告期末依据有关规定参加生育保险的职工人数。

2.基金收入: 指根据国家有关规定，由参加生育保险的单位按照国家规定的缴费基数和缴费比例缴纳的生育保险基金，以及通过其他方式取得的形成基金来源的款项，包括：单位缴纳的基金收入、利息收入和其他收入。

3.基金支出: 指按照国家政策规定的开支范围和开支标准，从生育保险基金中支付给参加生育保险的职工，因妊娠、分娩和计划生育手术而享受的待遇及其他支出。包括：生育津贴、医疗费用支出及其他支出。

4.基金累计结余: 指截止报告期末生育保险基金累计结余金额。包括银行存款、财政专户、债券投资和其他。

SHANGHAI STATISTICAL YEARBOOK

EXPLANATORY NOTES TO MAJOR STATISTICAL INDICATORS

□ Health Care Institutions

Health Care Institutions refer to the units which have been qualified the Certification of Health Care Institution by the administration of public health, or qualified the Certification of Corporate Unit by the civil affairs, administration for industry and commerce, commission office for public sector reform, and engaging in medical care, disease prevention and control, health supervision and inspection, medicine research and health professional education, etc.

□ Medical Organizations

Medical Organizations refer to the institutions which have been qualified the Certification of Health Care Institution by the administration of public health, including: hospitals, health centers, community health service centers (stations), health centers, clinics (health stations and infirmaries), women and children care agencies (centers and stations), special disease prevention and curing agencies (centers and stations), first-aid centers (stations) and clinic inspection centers, but excluding village health care rooms.

□ Hospitals

Hospitals includes comprehensive hospitals, traditional Chinese medicine hospitals, traditional Chinese and western medicine hospitals, ethnic minority medicine hospitals, various special disease hospitals and nursing homes, but excludes special disease prevention and curing agencies, women and children care agencies and health centers.

□ Medical Technical Personnel

Medical Technical Personnel includes licensed doctors, licensed assistant doctors, pharmacists (assistant pharmacists), inspection technicians, image technicians (assistant image technicians), health care inspectors and practice doctors (pharmacists, nurses, and technicians), excludes medical technical personnel engaging in administrative jobs.

□ Licensed Doctors (Assistant Doctors)

It refers to the medical workers who have obtained the license of qualified doctors (assistant doctors) and are employed by medical institutions, but excludes the doctors engaging in administrative jobs.

□ Special Care

Special Care is offered by the government to the family member of the martyrs, disabled or demobilized servicemen or laborers who were injured on duty. Entitled to the special care are family members of the revolutionary martyrs, family members of servicemen who dies on duty or died of an illness, disabled servicemen, family members of servicemen on active service, retired veteran Red Army soldiers, scattered Red Army soldiers, demobilized servicemen, ex-servicemen, servicemen who were demobilized while on duty, ex-servicemen back to their rural homes, ex-servicemen who were demobilized because of an illness and have gone back to their rural homes, ex-servicemen who suffer from mental illness and elderly persons with no family.

□ Social Welfare Institutions

Social Welfare Institutions refer to institutions taking care of old people without children, handicapped people and orphans. They include social welfare institutions run by civil affairs departments, children's welfare institutions, welfare institutions for mental patients, and collectively-run old people's homes in rural areas.

□ Basic Pension Insurance

1.Number of staff and workers covered refer to staff and workers participating in basic pension insurance programme in line with national laws, regulations and related policies by the end of reference period, who have already had payment records in social security management agencies, including those who interrupt payment without terminating the insurance programme. Those who have registered in the programme with no payment records are not included.

2. Number of retirees participating in basic pension insurance programme refer to number of retirees participating in basic pension insurance programme by the end of reference period.

3. Revenue of basic pension insurance refer to payments made by employers and individuals participating in pension insurance programs in accordance with the basis and proportion

EXPLANATORY NOTES TO MAJOR STATISTICAL INDICATORS

stipulated in state regulations, and income from other sources that become source of pension insurance fund, including the premium paid by employers and individuals, interest income, subsidies from higher level agencies, income as transfer from subordinate agencies, transferred income, government financial subsidies and other income.

4. Expenses of basic pension insurance refer to payment made to those retired and resigned people covered in pension insurance program in terms of pension or compensation within the scope and standards of expenditure according to related national policies, and expenditure occurred due to shift of the insurance relationship or adjustment of funds among agencies, including pension for resigned people, pension for retired people, pension for people quitting jobs, various subsidies, medical fees, funeral subsidies, compensation pension, management fees for social security agencies, expenses on subsidies to lower subordinates, expenses as transfer to agencies at higher level, transferred expenditure and other expenditure.

5. Balance of basic pension insurance refers to the balance of basic pension insurance at the end of the reference period after deducting expenses from revenue.

□ Basic Medical Care Insurance

1.Number of people participating in the insurance programme refers to people participating in the basic medical care insurance programme according to related regulations by the end of reference period, including number of staff and workers and retirees participating in this insurance programme.

2. Revenues of insurance programme refer to payments made by employers and individuals participating in medical care insurance programs in accordance with the basis and proportion stipulated in state regulations, and income from other sources that become source of medical insurance fund, including income of social comprehensive funds paid by employers, income from individual accounts, government financial subsidies, interest income and other income.

3. Expenses of insurance programme refer to payments made from social comprehensive funds to those retired and resigned people covered in basic medical care insurance within the scope and standards of expenditure according to related national policies, and medical care payment made from individual accounts to staff and workers and retirees, and other expenses, including medical expenses of hospital inpatients, medical expenses for outpatients and emergency patients, payment from individual accounts and other expenditure.

4. Balance of basic medical care insurance refer to the balance of medical care insurance of social comprehensive funds and individual accounts at the end of the reference period, including bank savings, special fiscal accounts, investment in bonds and others.

□ Unemployment Insurance

1. Number of people covered refers to staff and workers in urban enterprises or institutions who have participated in unemployment insurance programme in line relevant policies and regulations, and other people who have participated according to local government regulations, by the end of reference period.

2. Revenue of unemployment insurance refer to payments made by employers and individuals participating in unemployment insurance programme in accordance with relevant regulations and other income contributed to this programme, including unemployment insurance premium made by employers and individuals, interest income, subsidies from higher level agencies, income as transfer from subordinate agencies, transferred income, government financial subsidies and other income.

3. Expenses of unemployment insurance refers to total expenses during the reference period to guarantee the basic livelihood of unemployed people and laid-off staff and workers and to encourage their re-employment. Included are unemployment relief, medical fees, funeral subsidies, compensation pension, training expenses, management fees for unemployment insurance agencies, subsidies to lower level agencies, expenses as transfer to higher level agencies, transferred expenditure and other expenditure.

4. Balance of unemployment insurance refer to the balance of unemployment revenue deducting unemployment expenses at the end of the reference period.

□ Work Injury Insurance

1. Number of people covered refers to staff and workers who have participated in work injury insurance programme in line with relevant national regulations.

2. Number of beneficiaries refers to staff and workers and their direct dependents who can, in line with relevant regulations, benefit from work injury insurance, as a result of work injury leading to disability or death of the staff/worker, or occupational disease leading to disability. Included in this category are number of injured and disabled people, number of people with occupa-

EXPLANATORY NOTES TO MAJOR STATISTICAL INDICATORS

tional diseases, number of deaths at work places, and number of direct dependents.

3. Revenues of work injury insurance refer to payments made by employers participating in work injury insurance programs in accordance with the basis and proportion stipulated in state regulations, and income from other sources that become source of work injury insurance fund, including income of social comprehensive funds paid by employers, government financial subsidies, interest income and other income.

4. Expenses of work injury insurance refer to payments made from work injury insurance funds to those who participated in the work injury insurance programme and their direct dependents within the scope and standards of expenditure according to related national policies, and other expenditure, including medical fees for work injury, injury and disability subsidies, death subsidies, nursing fees, funeral subsidies, injury prevention fees, rehabilitation fees for occupational diseases and other expenditure.

5. Balance of work injury insurance refers to the balance of the work injury funds at the end of the reference period, including bank savings, special fiscal account, investment in bonds and others.

□ Maternity Insurance

1. Number of people covered refers to staff and workers who have participated in maternity insurance programme according to relevant regulation at the end of the reporting period.

2. Revenues of maternity insurance refer to payments made by employers participating in maternity insurance programs in accordance with the basis and proportion stipulated in state regulations, and income from other sources that become source of maternity insurance fund, including income of funds paid by employers, interest income and other income.

3. Expenses of maternity insurance refer to payments made from maternity insurance funds to staff and workers who participated in maternity insurance programme within the scope and standards of expenditure according to related national policies, expenses paid for pregnancy, child delivery or surgeries related to family planning, and other expenditure, including allowance for child bearing, medical fees and other expenditure.

4. Balance of the maternity insurance refers to the balance of the maternity insurance funds at the end of reference period, including bank savings, special fiscal account, investment in funds and others.

第二十二篇
CHAPTER 22

文化和体育
CULTURE AND SPORTS

简要说明

一、本篇资料的主要内容

本篇主要反映文化、文物、广电、新闻出版、档案、体育事业发展情况。

内容包括全市艺术表演团体、艺术表演场馆、群众文化活动机构、文物机构、文化娱乐机构、公共图书馆、新闻出版机构、档案机构等单位的机构、人员、经费和业务活动情况；全市广播电视机构设施、制作播出节目时间情况；全市电影摄制、译制和发行反映情况；全市图书、期刊、报纸、音像电子出版数量情况；全市优秀运动员、教练员、体育系统职工、群众体育健身活动场所情况。

二、本篇资料的来源

文化、广电资料由上海市文化广播影视管理局提供；文物资料由上海市文物局提供；新闻出版资料由上海市新闻出版局提供；档案机构资料由上海市档案局提供；体育资料由上海市体育局提供。

BRIEF INTRODUCTION

I. Main Contents

Data mainly reflect the development of culture; cultural relics; radio broadcasting, films and television; news and publication; archives and sports undertakings.

Data mainly include: data on institutions and employed persons, funds and activities of art troupes, art venues, mass cultural institutions, heritage institutions, cultural entertainment institutions, public libraries, press and publications, archival institutions, etc; data and playing hours of television stations and broadcasting stations, data on production, dubbing and showing of films, data on books, periodicals, newspaper, electronic audio and video products published, data on excellent athletes, coaches, staff and workers in sports sectors, mass physical activities.

II. Sources of data

Data on culture, television and broadcasting are from Shanghai Municipal Administration of Culture Radio Film& TV; data on historical relics are from Shanghai Municipal Administration of Cultural Heritage; data on news and publishing are from Shanghai Municipal Press and Publication Bureau; data on archive institutions are from Shanghai Municipal Archives; data on sports are from Shanghai Municipal Sports Bureau.

表22.1　主要年份文化机构数
QUANTITY OF CULTURAL INSTITUTIONS IN MAIN YEARS

单位：个（unit）

年份 Year	图书馆 Libraries	群众文化活动机构 Mass Culture	艺术教育机构 Art Education	文艺科研机构 Research	文物机构 Agency of Historic Relics	档案机构 Archives Institutions
1978	23	364	3		7	
1980	21	367	2	2	8	
1985	46	369	3	2	9	
1986	49	403	3	2	11	
1987	50	407	3	2	13	127
1988	54	416	3	2	16	125
1989	52	405	3	2	19	134
1990	51	410	3	2	18	137
1991	31	397	3	2	18	671
1992	31	394	3	2	20	745
1993	31	376	3	2	21	720
1994	31	371	3	2	23	
1995	31	332	3	2	23	768
1996	32	348	4	2	24	674
1997	32	352	4	2	24	681
1998	32	355	4	2	23	643
1999	32	349	4	2	24	994
2000	31	340	4	2	24	792
2001	32	276	3	2	23	614
2002	32	270	1	2	26	652
2003	35	261	1	2	26	656
2004	28	251	1	2	99	513
2005	28	248	1	2	106	545
2006	28	250	1	2	106	439
2007	30	247	1	2	111	524
2008	29	245	1	2	111	524
2009	29	242	1	2	112	533
2010	28	240	1	2	115	707
2011	25	241	1	2	125	677
2012	25	240	1	2	115	734
2013	25	239	1	2	112	743
2014	25	238	1	2	114	818
2015	25	237	1	2	110	760

注：自2004年起文物保护机构中包括系统外的机构数。
Note: From 2004, Agency of Historic Relics Preservation refers to total quantity of Agency Bureau.

表 22.2 影剧院、艺术表演场馆、艺术表演团体数(1978 ~ 2015)
QUANTITY OF CINEMAS, THEATRES AND ART PERFORMANCE TROUPES

单位:个(unit)

年 份 Year	电影放映单位 Film Projection Units	其中 of which #影、剧院 Cinemas and Theatres	艺术表演场馆 Art Performance Places	其中 of which #剧 院 Theatres	书 场 Storytelling Places	艺术表演团体 Art Performance Troupes
1978	803	109	31	26	4	17
1979	799	115	46	32	5	45
1980	770	119	47	43	6	48
1981	804	127	60	56	6	49
1982	815	134	31	48	6	46
1983	822	140	54	49	8	46
1984	815	146	54	48	8	44
1985	847	156	52	47	8	44
1986	859	169	53	49	9	42
1987	890	199	51	48	8	42
1988	734	215	53	50	8	40
1989	579	213	52	49	8	37
1990	577	211	49	46	8	38
1991	548	229	51	47	9	38
1992	530	249	51	47	9	37
1993	462	254	49	40	9	34
1994	462	254	47	39	8	35
1995	452	249	43	35	7	31
1996	488	280	45	38	7	31
1997	466	263	45	38	7	31
1998	445	242	44	39	5	29
1999	445	242	44	41	4	29
2000	445	242	44	39	5	29
2001	370	273	41	35	3	28
2002	370	273	37	31		28
2003	328	238	180	174	4	72
2004	311	225	177	163	7	75
2005	236	193	160	150	5	85
2006	245	186	148	137	2	97
2007	233	175	150	140	6	103
2008	235	172	139	134	5	107
2009	226	169	104	100	0	77
2010	152	136	97	86	2	89
2011	161	146	103	90	4	102
2012	153	140	111	99	3	138
2013	169	151	127	116	3	148
2014	189	172	93	81	4	158
2015	209	202	50	34	1	180

注：自 2003 年起文化统计范围扩大到全行业。
Note: The scope of statistics to culture expands to total sectors since 2003.

表22.3 主要年份主要文化机构从业人员数
QUANTITY OF EMPLOYEES IN MAJOR CULTURAL INSTITUTIONS IN MAIN YAERS

单位：人(person)

机构类别	Category of Institution	2000	2010	2014	2015
总　计	**Total**	**217 572**	**274 267**	**255 337**	**257 758**
艺术机构	Art	4 759	9 482	7 536	8 036
图书馆	Libraries	2 513	2 180	2 104	2 113
档案机构	Archives Institutions	2 330	3 822	4 315	4 283
群众文化活动机构	Mass Culture	3 874	4 702	4 958	4 835
文物机构	History Relic	1 136	2 558	3 367	3 315
文化市场经营机构	Cultural Market Operation Institutions	63 297	60 358	30 037	53 486
新闻出版机构	Institutions Engaged in News and Publishing	138 492	185 620	200 005	179 362
其他文化机构	Other Cultural Institutions	1 171	5 545	3 015	2 328

表22.4 主要文化机构和人员数(2015)
MAJOR CULTURAL INSTITUTIONS AND PERSONNEL

机构类别	Category of Institution	机构数(个) Institutions(unit)	从业人数(人) Employees(person)
艺术机构	**Art**	**233**	**8 150**
艺术表演团体	Art Performance Troupes	180	6 106
艺术表演场馆	Art Centers	50	1 930
艺术教育机构	Art Education	1	74
文艺科研机构	Literaturde and Art Research	2	40
图书馆	**Libraries**	**25**	**2 113**
# 少儿图书馆	Libraries for Children	4	81
档案机构	**Archives Institution**	**760**	**4 283**
群众文化活动机构	**Mass Culture**	**237**	**4 835**
群众艺术馆	Mass Art Centers	1	65
文化馆	Cultural Centers	24	882
文化站	Cultural Stations	212	3 888
文物机构	**Historical Relic**	**110**	**3 315**
文物保护管理机构	Heritage management agencies	6	75
博物馆	Museums	99	3 117
文物商店	Cultural Relic Shops	1	66
其他文物机构	Other Historical Relic	4	57
文化市场经营机构	**Cultural Market Operation Institutions**	**3 890**	**53 486**
新闻出版机构	**Institutions Engaged in News and Publishing**	**9 761**	**179 362**
其他文化机构	**Other Cultural Institutions**	**76**	**2 328**

表22.5 群众艺术馆和文化馆(站)情况（2015）
MASS ART AND CULTURAL CENTERS

指 标	Indicators	合 计 Total	群众艺术馆 Mass Art Centers	文化馆 Cultural Centers	文化站 Cultural Stations
单位数（个）	Quantity of Units（unit）	237	1	24	212
从业人员(人)	Employees（person）	4 835	65	882	3 888
组织活动	Organizing Activity				
文艺活动（次）	Literary Activity(time)	64 393		7 968	56 425
理论研讨和讲座（次）	Theoretics Conference and Chair(time)	760	240	520	
举办训练班(次)	Conducting Training Courses(time)	51 408		7 971	43 437
举办展览个数（个）	Exhibitions Conducted（unit）	3 259	35	387	2 837
藏书(万册)	Collection of Books(10 000 copies)	1 025.78		31.60	994.18
场地面积(万平方米)	Floor Space(10 000 sq. m)	137.12	1.90	18.90	116.31

表22.6 艺术表演团体情况（2015）
BASIC STATISTICS OF ART TROUPES

类 别	Types	剧团数（个） Troupes（unit）	从业人员（人） Employees（person）	国内演出场次(场) Times of Domestic Performance（time）	观众人数（万人次） Spectators（10 000 person-times）
总 计	**Total**	**180**	**6 106**	**28 730**	**863**
按隶属关系分	**By Administrative Relationship**				
市 级	Perfectural level	18	3 167	10 290	365
区、县级	District and County level	162	2 939	18 440	498
按剧种分	**By Type of Drama**				
话剧、儿童剧、滑稽剧团	Drama, Children's Play & Comedy Troupes	57	1 958	9 650	268
歌剧、舞剧、歌舞剧团	Opera, Dance Drama, Opera and Dance Troupes	48	1 808	4 820	156
歌舞团、轻音乐团	Song and Dances Troupeand Light Music Orchestras	5	504	650	33
乐团、合唱团	Orchestras and Chorus	26	944	8 850	232
戏剧团	Drama Troupes	7	330	1 510	84
曲艺、杂技、木偶、皮影团	Quyi, Acrobatics, Puppet, and Shadow Play Troupes	9	223	960	35
综合艺术表演团体	Comprehensive Art Performance Groups	28	339	2 290	55

表 22.7 博物馆、纪念馆情况（2015）
STATISTICS OF MUSEUMS AND MEMORIALS

类 别 Types		机构数（个） Quantity of Institutions (unit)	馆内藏品实际数量 Real Quantity of Collections		展览活动（个） Exhibit Activity (unit)	参观人次（万人次） Visiting Person-times (10 000 person-times)
			（万件） (10 000 pieces)	# 一至三级藏品 Collections of Class One to Three		
总 计	**Total**	**124**	**215.26**	**24.72**	**407**	**1 935.12**
综合性	Comprehensive	12	5.01	0.74	67	330.68
历史类	Historical	40	56.20	8.58	176	706.30
艺术类	Art	7	102.09	14.33	61	239.77
科学技术类	Science and Technology	3	28.73	0.46	4	389.69
其 他	Others	62	23.22	0.61	99	268.68

表 22.8 主要年份文物保护维修情况
PRESERVATION AND MAINTAIN OF HISTORICAL RELICS IN MAIN YEARS

指 标	Indicators	2005	2010	2014	2015
保护维修项目数（个）	Items of Preservation and Maintaining (item)	44	45	30	30
# 国家级	National	4	10	4	2
市 级	Municipal	18	6	12	12
维修面积（万平方米）	Area of Maintaining (10 000 sq. m.)	2.30	13.51	6.20	4.10
项目总预算（万元）	Aggregate Budget of Items (10 000 yuan)	19 650	20 555	7 900	8 200
# 专项补助	Special Assistance	934	8 463	2 572	1 166
已拨入专项补助（万元）	Special Assistance Appropriated (10 000 yuan)	1 209	8 463	2 100	1 166
当年保护维修支出（万元）	Expend on Preservation and Maintaining (10 000 yuan)	19 571	20 554	5 670	5 700

表 22.9 主要年份广播电台、电视台情况
TELEVISION STATIONS AND BROADCASTING STATIONS IN MAIN YEARS

类别	Types	2005	2010	2014	2015
广播电台	**Broadcasting Stations**				
中、短波发射台(座)	**Relaying Stations of Medium and Short Wave Broadcast (uint)**	**4**	**4**	**3**	**3**
发射功率(千瓦)	Transmited Power (kw)	390	240	240	227
公共广播节目套数(套)	Public Radio Programs (set)	21	21	21	21
付费广播节目套数(套)	Pay Radio Programs(set)	1	1	1	1
日均播音时间(小时)	Broadcasting Time a day (hour)	347	360	377	373
全年制作节目时间(小时)	Length of Programs Produced (hours)	83 665	85 262	84 673	85 966
电视台	**Television Stations**				
发射台(座)	Realying Stations (uint)	11	11	11	22
发射功率(千瓦)	Transmitted Power (kw)	170	172	100	100
公共电视节目套数(套)	Public TV Programs (set)	25	25	25	25
付费电视节目套数(套)	Pay TV Programs (set)	15	16	16	15
周均播放时间(小时)	Broadcast Time a week (hour)	2 871	3 361	3 434	3 422
全年制作节目时间(小时)	Length of Programs Produced (hours)	62 819	49 507	60 664	73 455
广播电视卫星地球站(座)	Satellite Earth Station of Radio and TV Programs (uint)	1	1	1	1

注：2015 年起，电视发射台与调频发射台合并统计，不再单独统计。
Note: Since 2015,the statistics of television transmitting station have merged with FM transmitting station, and are no longer separate.

表 22.10 电视和广播公共节目播出时间（2015）
PLAYING HOURS OF TELEVISION AND BROADCASTING PUBLIC PROGRAMS

单位：小时(hour)

类别	Types	电视台 Television Stations 合计 Total	市级 Municipal Level	区县级 District Level	广播电台 Broadcasting Stations 合计 Total	市级 Municipal Level	区县级 District Level
总计	**Total**	**178 409**	**126 818**	**51 591**	**136 049**	**81 606**	**54 443**
新闻资讯类节目	News Program	31 649	24 808	6 841	39 041	27 657	11 384
专题服务类节目	Subject Service Program	41 097	29 468	11 629	29 067	19 176	9 891
综艺类节目	Recreational and Artistic Program	10 756	9 539	1 217	47 213	26 029	21 184
影视剧类节目	Film and TV Program	60 284	36 745	23 539			
广播剧类节目	Broadcasting Drama Program				8 259	365	7 894
广告类节目	Advertising Program	15 566	9 752	5 814	10 287	8 379	1 908
其他类节目	Others	19 057	16 506	2 551	2 182		2 182

表 22.11 主要年份有线电视基本情况
BASIC STATISTICS ON CABLE TELEVISION IN MAIN YEARS

指标	Indicators	2000	2010	2014	2015
有线电视总用户数(万户)	Quantity of Cable TV Users (10 000 households)	303.0	573.0	687.8	745.5
#数字电视用户	Digital TV Users		235.6	554.7	670.7
有线电视入户率(%)	Popularity of Cable TV (%)	64.50	112.36	130.40	139.98
有线广播电视传输网络干线总长(公里)	Lines Total Length (kilometer)	604	36 211	44 092	55 035

表22.12 电影摄制、译制和放映情况(1978~2015)
PRODUCTION, DUBBING AND SHOWING OF FILMS

年 份 Year	摄制和译制电影片 Production and Dubbing		电影放映 Film Showing			
	故事片 (部) Feature Films (film)	动画电影 (本) Animated Film(reel)	放映场次 (万场) Showing (10 000 times)	其 中 of which #影、剧院 Cinemas and Theatres	观众人次 (万人次) Spectators (10 000 person-times)	其 中 of which #影、剧院 Cinemas and Theatres
1978	10	24	35	17	27 405	15 291
1979	14	25	40	20	32 763	29 743
1980	17	30	39	20	29 304	18 039
1981	17	32	38	19	26 823	16 203
1982	19	35	38	20	25 828	15 586
1983	19	34	37	20	25 204	15 124
1984	19	40	36	21	24 149	15 539
1985	15	43	34	21	21 885	14 748
1986	19	38	36	24	23 220	16 720
1987	17	38	37	28	21 985	17 067
1988	13	29	38	30	20 461	16 742
1989	17	29	37	32	20 776	18 216
1990	16	47	38	33	19 351	17 021
1991	17	37	36	31	15 766	13 615
1992	17	42	29	25	9 145	8 089
1993	16	35	16	14	3 862	3 332
1994	14	13	22	20	4 001	3 617
1995	17	37	23	20	4 419	3 913
1996	10	58	27	25	4 420	3 783
1997	11	17	25	23	3 670	3 023
1998	4	16	23	21	2 924	2 451
1999	17	10	20	19	2 055	1 678
2000	10	20	18	17	1 794	1 452
2001	12	2	18	17	1 553	1 315
2002	10	2	20	17	1 198	921
2003	9	10	20	19	971	870
2004	12	1	24	23	1 364	1 183
2005	13		28	26	1 509	1 323
2006	9		27	26	1 254	1 173
2007	9		33	32	1 385	1 277
2008	17	8	35	34	1 456	1 381
2009	11		44	43	1 938	1 844
2010	19	2	55	54	2 288	2 174
2011	25		76	75	2 792	2 668
2012	22	6	96	95	3 154	3 074
2013	27		132	120	3 793	3 618
2014	28	8	158	149	4 678	4 621
2015	34	10	190	190	6 810	6 797

注：2012年起，译制片的统计口径发生变化，单位由过去的“本”改为“部”。
Note: Since 2012, the statistical calibre of dubbed films has been changed from reel to set.

表22.13 主要年份电影发行放映情况
BASIC STATISTICS OF FILM DISTRIBUTION AND PROJECTION IN MAIN YEARS

指 标	Indicators	2005	2010	2014	2015
电影放映机构(个)	**Movie Projection Agencies**		**117**	**189**	**209**
电影院	Cinema		69	145	175
影剧院	Theater		42	27	27
开放礼堂、俱乐部	Open Auditorium and Clubs		2	15	7
放映队和对内俱乐部	Projection Team and Inside Club		4	2	
放映场次(万场)	**Projection Times (10 000 times)**	**27.60**	**54.63**	**157.70**	**190.15**
# 电影院	Cinema	22.20	51.72	145.80	186.50
影剧院	Theater	3.90	2.19	2.90	3.16
开放礼堂、俱乐部	Open Auditorium and Clubs	1.16	0.68	1.50	0.49
观众人次数(万人次)	**Quantity of Audience (10 000 person-times)**	**1 509.31**	**2 287.84**	**4 677.50**	**6 809.77**
# 电影院	Cinema	893.92	2 052.62	4 500.50	6 659.60
影剧院	Theater	428.63	121.33	120.10	137.50
开放礼堂、俱乐部	Open Auditorium and Clubs	36.24	55.99	56.90	12.67
放映收入(万元)	**Projection Revenue (10 000 yuan)**	**27 192.03**	**93 875.11**	**204 462.50**	**293 967.66**
# 电影院	Cinema	23 591.47	89 302.91	199 076.50	289 123.00
影剧院	Theater	2 389.52	2 697.84	3 783.00	4 408.90
开放礼堂、俱乐部	Open Auditorium and Clubs	1 009.58	1 807.88	1 603.00	435.76
平均每一放映场次	**Average on per Projection Time**				
观众人数(人)	Quantity of Audience (Person)	54.69	41.88	29.66	35.81
放映收入(元)	Returns (yuan)	985.22	1 718.38	1 296.53	1 545.98
日均放映场次(场)	**Projection Time a Day (time)**	**756**	**1 497**	**4 321**	**5 210**
日均观众人次(万人次)	**Average Audience a Day (10 000 person-times)**	**4.14**	**6.27**	**12.82**	**18.66**

注：电影放映机构数为正在活动的单位数。
Note: The number of movie projection agencies is the number fo units being active.

表22.14 文化娱乐机构基本情况(2015)
BASIC STATISTICS OF CULTURE AND ENTERTAINMENT INSTITUTIONS

类别	Types	机构数(个)	从业人员(人) Employees (person)	主营业务收入(万元) Major Business Revenue (10 000 yuan)	主营业务利润(万元) Major Business Profits (10 000 yuan)	房屋建筑面积(万平方米) Floor Space of Buildings (10 000 sq. m)
总 计	**Total**	**3 679**	**51 075**	**2 732 887**	**330 586**	**65**
歌舞娱乐场所	Singing & Dancing Rooms	1 262	15 766	219 840	32 102	
游戏电子游艺经营场所	Gaming Rooms	749	3 766	78 256	41 796	
网 吧	Internet Bar	1 336	6 510	56 194	9 496	45
经营性互联网文化单位	Internet-Culturel Business Unit	278	24 306	2 370 509	245 688	20

表22.15 公共图书馆情况(2015)
PUBLIC LIBRARIES

指标	Indicators	合计 Total	市级 Municipal Level	区、县级 District and County Level
机构数(个)	Institutions (unit)	25	2	23
从业人员(人)	Employees (person)	2 133	773	1 340
总藏量(万册、件)	Collection (10 000 copies)	7 568.18	5 645.40	1 922.78
#图 书	Books	3 295.80	1 523.20	1 772.60
报 刊	Newspaper and Magzines	385.95	348.40	37.56
本年新购藏量(万册、件)	Publications Newly Bought (10 000 copies)	241.72	52.57	189.15
建筑面积(万平方米)	Floor Space of Buildings (10 000 sq. m)	41.83	13.05	28.78
#书 库	Stack Room	9.28	6.07	3.22
阅览室	Reading Room	10.48	1.36	9.12
阅览座位(个)	Seats in Reading Room (unit)	22 037	2 316	19 721
书刊文献外借情况	Books Lending			
人 次(万人次)	Readers (10 000 person-times)	1 922.34	1 408.33	514.01
册 数(万册次)	Books (10 000 copy-times)	8 681.37	6 580.06	2 101.31
信息化装备	Information Equipment			
计算机(台)	Computer(unit)	6 545	2 779	3 766
#电子阅览室终端数	E-reading Room Terminals	2 348	362	1 986
为读者举办各种活动	Activities Held for Readers			
组织各类讲座次数(次)	All Kinds of Lectures (time)	2 853	260	2 593
参加人次(万人次)	Participants (10 000 person-times)	28.33	4.71	23.63

表22.16 图书出版数量(1978～2015)
BOOKS PUBLISHED

年份 Year	种数 (种) Quantity of Publications (type)	其中 of which #新出版 Newly Published	总印数 (亿册) Total Printed (100 million copies)	总印张数 (亿印张) Total Printed Signatures (100 million signatures)
1978	1 666	1 332	3.92	12.19
1979	2 040	1 563	4.58	15.54
1980	2 338	1 804	5.62	17.73
1981	2 801	1 949	6.01	22.89
1982	3 395	2 057	6.07	21.76
1983	3 653	2 254	4.65	21.31
1984	3 848	2 328	5.37	25.58
1985	4 176	2 634	4.96	23.95
1986	4 531	3 045	3.66	17.81
1987	5 103	3 151	4.26	19.84
1988	5 538	3 658	4.33	19.04
1989	6 765	4 960	3.28	14.52
1990	7 767	4 887	2.98	14.66
1991	8 141	4 756	3.11	17.30
1992	8 095	4 179	2.75	17.19
1993	7 721	4 272	2.26	15.34
1994	7 812	4 382	2.35	17.01
1995	8 338	4 185	2.44	17.92
1996	9 234	4 445	2.79	20.10
1997	9 928	4 844	2.70	18.00
1998	10 718	5 083	2.83	18.69
1999	11 381	5 880	2.68	18.69
2000	12 682	6 936	2.54	19.05
2001	14 000	7 947	2.68	21.24
2002	14 537	8 156	2.59	21.38
2003	15 636	8 726	2.74	23.27
2004	16 449	9 391	2.67	23.54
2005	16 504	9 286	2.59	23.65
2006	17 283	9 338	2.54	24.86
2007	16 958	9 085	2.40	24.05
2008	17 780	9 945	2.64	24.97
2009	18 873	10 615	2.74	25.46
2010	19 519	11 241	2.89	26.34
2011	22 056	12 542	2.89	27.37
2012	23 792	13 142	3.35	31.35
2013	24 969	13 665	3.37	32.09
2014	24 676	13 193	3.26	30.47
2015	25 954	13 626	3.53	33.83

表22.17 期刊出版数量(1978~2015)
PERIODICALS PUBLISHED

年 份 Year	种 数 (种) Quantity of Publications (type)	每期平均印数 (万册、份) Average Publications Issued (10 000 copies)	总印数 (亿册) Total Printed (100 million copies)	总印张数 (亿印张) Total Printed Signatures (100 million signatures)
1978	42	459	0.47	1.12
1979	90	721	0.73	2.08
1980	126	1 061	1.22	3.37
1981	266	1 873	2.03	5.95
1982	308	2 203	2.31	6.37
1983	349	2 572	2.51	7.07
1984	402	3 502	3.10	8.56
1985	491	3 424	3.45	9.21
1986	541	3 073	3.03	8.17
1987	546	3 058	3.13	8.05
1988	535	2 624	2.66	6.63
1989	527	1 793	1.86	4.58
1990	522	1 735	1.73	4.24
1991	504	1 749	1.79	4.44
1992	527	1 794	1.84	4.59
1993	535	1 668	1.82	4.95
1994	556	1 569	1.72	4.87
1995	565	1 583	1.78	5.30
1996	582	1 530	1.66	5.14
1997	587	1 513	1.66	5.35
1998	591	1 503	1.65	5.81
1999	606	1 493	1.78	6.87
2000	613	1 489	1.85	7.38
2001	616	1 413	1.85	7.58
2002	621	1 332	1.80	7.77
2003	626	1 335	1.83	8.51
2004	612	1 184	1.93	8.94
2005	612	1 130	1.90	8.96
2006	616	1 125	1.83	8.76
2007	624	1 117	1.83	8.75
2008	623	1 105	1.90	9.27
2009	621	1 039	1.79	9.02
2010	632	1 019	1.78	9.04
2011	632	1 023	1.82	9.42
2012	626	938	1.76	9.67
2013	625	875	1.62	9.00
2014	627	804	1.45	8.10
2015	628	715	1.28	7.23

表22.18 报纸出版数量(1978～2015)
NEWSPAPER PUBLISHED

年 份 Year	种 数 (种) Quantity of Publications (type)	每期平均印数 (万份) Average Publication Issued (10 000 copies)	总印数 (亿份) Total Printed (100 million copies)	总印张数 (亿印张) Total Printed Signatures (100 million signatures)
1978	5	257	6.41	6.20
1979	8	349	7.32	7.08
1980	12	464	8.55	8.20
1981	15	640	10.28	9.77
1982	31	936	14.93	13.13
1983	34	1 185	18.13	15.49
1984	41	1 429	19.63	16.57
1985	89	1 656	19.54	17.07
1986	93	1 750	19.94	18.37
1987	90	2 003	22.45	20.49
1988	83	1 958	21.38	22.07
1989	81	1 477	15.85	16.25
1990	81	1 510	16.16	16.76
1991	75	1 506	18.48	19.16
1992	77	1 506	24.76	24.76
1993	81	1 506	32.27	32.27
1994	87	1 369	30.43	30.43
1995	86	1 358	19.04	34.00
1996	87	1 357	18.93	36.96
1997	87	1 397	19.34	43.19
1998	80	1 441	19.73	49.84
1999	75	1 311	18.42	46.26
2000	103	1 135	16.77	44.57
2001	101	1 060	16.98	47.67
2002	101	983	16.46	51.42
2003	101	886	17.05	66.13
2004	103	939	19.71	83.66
2005	102	903	19.06	89.94
2006	101	850	17.89	87.33
2007	101	815	17.04	86.75
2008	100	787	17.24	88.29
2009	100	741	16.33	77.94
2010	100	752	15.90	78.65
2011	100	734	15.61	79.38
2012	100	686	14.54	68.03
2013	101	605	13.16	58.86
2014	100	537	11.45	48.96
2015	98	505	10.80	44.59

表22.19 主要年份新闻出版机构和人员数
NUMBER OF INSTITUTIONS AND EMPLOYEES ENGAGED IN NEWS AND PUBLISHING IN MAIN YEARS

	指 标 Indicators	2000	2010	2014	2015
图书出版机构	**Publishing Houses**				
机构数（个）	Institutions (unit)	37	40	40	40
从业人员（人）	Employee (person)	3 666	3 949	3 732	3 558
书刊印刷机构	**Printing Houses**				
机构数（个）	Institutions (unit)	4 543	4 606	4 403	4 235
从业人员（万人）	Employee (10 000 persons)	11.54	16.02	16.72	14.99
发行机构	**Issuing Houses**				
机构数（个）	Institutions (unit)	6 743	9 327	7 785	5 486
从业人员（万人）	Employee (10 000 persons)	1.94	2.14	2.90	2.59

注：发行机构数中包括发行网点数。
Note: Issuing Houses include quantity of net places.

表22.20 图书出版数量(2015)
BOOKS PUBLISHED

类 别	types	种 数（种）Number of Publications (type)	其中 of which #新出版 Newly Published	总印数（万册）Total Printed (10 000 copies)	总印张数（万印张）Total Printed Signatures (10 000 signatures)
总 计	**Total**	**25 954**	**13 626**	**35 303.57**	**338 329.62**
书 籍	**Books**	**19 627**	**11 272**	**21 129.41**	**214 701.10**
社科人文类	Humanities and Social Sciences	17 525	9 762	20 387.79	202 760.65
科学技术类	Science and Technology	1 943	1 393	680.52	10 083.14
综合类	Complex	159	117	61.10	1 857.31
课 本	**Textbooks**	**6 305**	**2 332**	**14 164.10**	**123 547.84**
大专及以上课本	University and College	3 707	1 419	3 239.96	50 462.62
中专技校教材	Specialized Secondary and Technical Worker School	694	164	5 725.99	42 321.02
中学课本	Secondary School	455	91	4 409.55	20 187.73
小学课本	Primary School	403	272	193.13	2 506.83
业余教育课本	Spare-time Education	281	134	421.99	5 634.06
教学用书	Teaching References	765	252	173.48	2 435.57
图 片	**Pictures**	**22**	**22**	**10.06**	**80.68**

表 22.21 期刊出版数量(2015)
PERIODICALS PUBLISHED

类 别	Types	种 数（种）Quantity of Publications (type)	出版期数（期）Quantity of Issue (issue)	总印数（万册）Total Printed (10 000 copies)	总印张数（万印张）Total Printed Signatures (10 000 signatures)
总 计	**Total**	**628**	**6 087**	**12 842.61**	**72 286.72**
综 合	Comprehensive	14	144	506.48	2 393.21
哲学、社会科学	Philosophy and Social Science	141	1 669	4 740.92	25 914.48
自然科学、科技	Natural Science and Technology	356	2 995	2 270.39	19 147.34
文化教育	Culture and Education	79	793	1 540.83	9 004.32
文学艺术	Literature and Art	38	486	3 783.98	15 827.37

表 22.22 报纸出版数量(2015)
NEWSPAPER PUBLISHED

类 别	Types	种 数（种）Quantity of Publications (type)	期 数（期）Issue (issue)	每期平均印数（万份）Average Publication Per Issue (10 000 copies)	总印数（万份）Total Printed (10 000 copies)	总印张数（万印张）Total Printed Signatures (10 000 signatures)
总 计	**Total**	**98**	**9 662**	**505.10**	**108 044.38**	**445 886.79**
综合报	Comprehensive	12	3 066	178.25	63 830.59	324 916.30
专业报	Specialized	86	6 596	326.85	44 213.79	120 970.49

表 22.23 音像电子出版数量 (2015)
AUDIO, VIDEO AND ELECTRON PUBLISHED

类 别	Types	种 数（种）Quantity of Publications (type)	出版数量（万张、万盒）Quantity of Publications (10 000 piece box)	发行数量（万张、万盒）Quantity of Issued (10 000 piece box)	发行总金额（万元）Total Values (10 000 yuan)
总 计	**Total**	**5 611**	**5 347.16**	**4 596.10**	**21 102.54**
电子出版物	Electronic Publication	783	1 420.33	853.07	3 133.64
数码激光视盘	DVD	486	127.65	128.62	406.89
高密度激光视盘	EVD	434	752.08	710.96	2 317.26
激光唱盘	CD	2 742	942.27	928.18	6 253.58
录音带	Tape	278	1 512.54	1 533.36	7 460.91
其 他	Others	888	592.29	441.91	1 530.26

表22.24 档案机构基本情况(2015)
BASIC STATISTICS OF ARCHIVE INSTITUTIONS

指 标	Indicators	合 计 Total	档案行政管理部门 Archival Administrative Department	档案馆 Archives Library	档案室(处、科) Archives
机构数(个)	**Quantity of Institutions(unit)**	**760**	**18**	**48**	**694**
从业人员(人)	**Employees(person)**	**4 283**	**241**	**891**	**3 151**
专 职	Full-time	2 138	241	891	1 006
兼 职	Part-time	2 145			2 145
馆藏档案	**Archives Collected**				
全 宗(个)	Overall Rolls(unit)	8 008		6 126	1 882
案 卷(万卷)	Rolls(10 000 rolls)	3 567.97		1 461.43	2 106.54
以件为保管单位档案(万件)	Archives(10 000 pieces)	1 371.08		437.93	933.16
录音、录像、影片档案(万盘)	Recprd,Video and Film(10 000 disks)	14.33		4.43	9.91
照片档案(万张)	Photo Records(10 000 pieces)	262.59		160.30	102.29
底 图(万张)	Base Maps(10 000 pieces)	1 784.07		61.14	1 722.93
微缩胶片	Microfilm				
平 片(万张)	Flat Film(10 000 pieces)	14.90		13.39	1.51
开窗卡(万张)	Open Window Card(10 000 pieces)	22.06			22.06
卷 片(万幅)	Roll Film(10 000 meters)	2 843.90		2 843.00	0.90
档案利用	**Records Utilized**				
已开放档案	Records Opened				
案 卷(万卷)	Rolls(10 000 rolls)	171.94		171.94	
案 件(万件)	Cases(10 000 cases)	1.43		1.43	
开放档案目录(万条)	Catalog of Records Opened(10 000 pieces)				
案卷级	Roll Grade	129.12		129.12	
文件级	Document Grade	543.35		543.35	
本年利用档案	Records Utilized during the Year				
卷 次(万卷次)	Roll-times(10 000 roll-times)	165.71		40.69	125.02
件 次(万件次)	Piece-times(10 000 piece-times)	91.08		46.82	44.26
人 次(万人次)	Person-times(10 000 person-times)	58.90		35.81	23.09

表22.25 主要年份优秀运动员、教练员情况
BASIC STATISTICS ON EXCELLENT ATHLETES AND COACHES IN MAIN YEARS

单位:人（person）

指　标	Indicators	2000	2010	2014	2015
等级裁判员(人)	Certified Referees(person)	880	559	623	416
优秀运动员(人)	Excellent Athletes(person)	899	771	766	766
# 女运动员	Women	402	371	431	249
优秀运动队专职教练员(人)	Full-time Coaches(person)	196	73	265	289
# 女专职教练员	Women	30	22	78	114

表22.26 体育系统职工人数(2015)
STAFF AND WORKERS IN SPORTS SECTORS

单位:人（person）

指　标	Indicators	总　计 Total	其中 of which: # 优秀运动队 Excellent Sports Teams	体育运动学校 Physical Education and Sports Schools	普通业余体校 Popular Sparetime Sports School	公共体育场(馆) Public Stadiums and Gymnasiums
总　计	**Total**	**4 591**	**1 199**	**325**	**828**	**1 303**
# 专职教练员	Full-time Coaches	859	265	54	498	57
运动员	Athletes	766	718	10		
管理干部	Administraive Staff	1 229	81	87	156	601
专职教师	Full-time Teachers	120		88	24	8
科技人员	Scientific and Technical Personnel	92	4	2	8	20
医务人员	Medical Personnel	27	4	12	2	7

表22.27 群众体育健身活动场所情况(2012～2015)
PLACES OF MASS PHYSICAL ACTIVITIES

指　标	Indicators	2012	2013	2014	2015
社区体育健身设施数(个)	Quantity of Community Fitness Facilities (unit)	6 429	6 562	13 529	12 000
# 健身点	Fitness Centers	4 586	4 586	11 091	9 905
社区健身场地面积(万平方米)	Area of Community Fitness Space (10 000 sq. m)	427	435	449	452
社区公共运动场(个)	Quantity of Community Public Playground(unit)	324	324	355	390
社区公共运动场面积(万平方米)	Area of Community Public Playground (10 000 sq. m)	46.7	46.7	49.8	53.2

上 / 海 / 统 / 计 / 年 / 鉴

主要统计指标解释

文化机构

是指专门从事文化工作具有法人资格，独立核算的事业、企业单位，以及单独核算，附属于事业单位的经营性专业文化活动单位。包括从事艺术、图书馆、档案馆、群众文化、文物保护、艺术教育、艺术研究、文化娱乐、新闻出版等机构，以及其他文化机构。

电影放映单位

指具有放映机器设备、固定或不固定的放映场所与专职或兼职的放映技术人员，经有关部门登记批准，经常为一定的观众对象放映电影的机构。包括电影院、影剧院、开放礼堂、俱乐部、放映队、对内礼堂俱乐部。

艺术表演团体

指从事戏曲、音乐、舞蹈、杂技等专业艺术表演，有独立账户的单位，不包括半工半艺、半农半艺和民间职业剧团。该指标主要反映上海专业艺术表演团体发展规模水平。

艺术表演观众人次

指售票、包场演出或民族地区免费演出的艺术表演观众人次数，不包括彩排审查和内部观摩演出的观看人次数。该指标主要反映上海观看专业艺术表演团体演出的效益规模。

等级运动员人数

指经考核正式批准授予等级运动员称号的人数。运动员等级分为国际级运动健将、运动健将、一级运动员、二级运动员、三级运动员、少年级运动员。该指标主要反映运动员队伍的技术质量水平。

等级裁判员人数

指经考核正式批准授予等级裁判员称号的人数。裁判员等级分为国际裁判、国家级裁判、一级裁判、二级裁判、三级裁判。该指标主要反映裁判员队伍的技术质量水平。

SHANGHAI STATISTICAL YEARBOOK

EXPLANATORY NOTES TO MAJOR STATISTICAL INDICATORS

□ Cultural Institutions

Cultural Institution refers to undertaking and business institutions which specialize in cultural work and have legal personality and independent accounting system, and those professional cultural institutions attached to undertaking institutions and have independent accounting system. It includes institutions specialize in art, library, archives, mass culture, historical relic protection, art education, art research, entertainment, news and publication and other cultural institutions.

□ Film Projection Units

Film Projection Units refer to units with film projection equipments, full or part-time projectionists, permanent or non-permanent places, approved by related administrative departments to show films regularly for certain groups of audience, including cinemas, theaters, public auditoriums, clubs, film projection teams, and interior auditorium clubs.

□ Art Troupe

Art Troupe refers to the troupe which is engaged in drama, opera, music, dance, acrobatics or other art performance, opens independent accounts with banks and has self-supporting accounting system; excluding the troupes which are engaged partly in industrial or agricultural activities, partly in art performance and the professional troupes organized by the people. This indicator reflects the development of Shanghai's professional art troupes.

□ Quantity of Spectators at Art Performance

Number of Spectators at Art Performance refers to the number of attendants at commercial shows, completely booked shows or free shows given in minority national areas, and does not include the number of spectators at rehearsals for examination and internal shows for study. This indicator reflects beneficial results of spectators at Professional Art Performance.

□ Quantity of Athletes in Grades

Number of Athletes in Grades refers to the number of athletes who have been given titles through examination. The titles of athletes include international masters of sports, masters of sports, first-grade, second-grade and third-grade sportsmen and young athletes. This indicator reflects skill of the athletes.

□ Quantity of Referees in Grades

Number of Referees in Grades refers to the number of referees who have been given titles after examination. They are classified as international referees, national referees and referees of the first, second and third grades. This indicator reflects the skill of referees.

第二十三篇
CHAPTER 23

法律、公证和其他
LAWS, NOTARY AND OTHERS

简要说明

一、本篇资料的主要内容

本篇主要包括公检法司的情况。

内容主要包括律师机构、公证机构、人民调解委员会的机构、人员、主要业务活动情况；公安机立案的刑事案件及查处的治安案件情况；交通事故和火灾事故的次数、伤亡人数和损失折款情况；检察院直接立案侦查案件、民事行政案件办理、申诉案件处理情况；法院各类案件办理、执行案件和各类案件结案情况。

二、本篇资料的来源

律师、公证和人民调解等资料由上海市司法局提供；刑事案件、治安案件、交通火灾事故等资料由上海市公安局提供；检察院相关案件资料由上海市检察院提供；法院相关案件资料由上海市高级人民法院提供。

BRIEF INTRODUCTION

I. Main Contents

Data in this chapter reflect statistics on public security,procuratorial,legal and judicial affairs.

Data include mainly general information, personnel, and main activities of law firms, notarizations and meditations; criminal cases registered and offense cases handled by the public security agencies; casualties, and losses in traffic or fire accidents, cases under direct investigation by procurator's office, civil cases, administrative cases and appeals handled by procurator's offices; cases handled, executed, and closed by courts.

II. Sources of Data

Data on law firms, notarizations, and meditations are provided by Shanghai Municipal Bureau of Justice; data on criminal cases, offense cases, and traffic and fire accidents are provided by Shanghai Municipal Public Security Bureau; Data on procurators are provided by Shanghai Municipal People's Procurator's Offices; data on courts are provided by Shanghai Municipal Senior People's Court.

表 23.1 主要年份律师、公证及调解工作基本情况
BASIC STATISTICS OF LAWYERS, NOTARIZATIONS AND MEDIATIONS IN MAIN YEARS

指 标	Indicators	2000	2010	2014	2015
律师工作	**Lawyers**				
法律律师事务所（个）	Law Offices (unit)	415	1 064	1 321	1 409
律师人数（人）	Lawyers (person)	4 642	13 027	16 900	18 360
# 专职律师	Ful-time Lawyers	3 522	11 749	16 246	17 693
兼职律师	Part-time Lawyers	731	549	654	667
全年办理	Total Transacted				
民事案件诉讼代理（万件）	Civil Lawsuit(10 000 cases)	7.05	7.69	11.27	12.38
刑事诉讼辩护及代理（万件）	Criminal Lawsuit and Vindication(10 000 cases)	1.13	1.49	1.94	1.84
非诉讼法律事务（万件）	Non-litigation Action(10 000 cases)	2.65	3.32	4.75	5.49
解答法律询问(万人次)	Legal Advisory Services (10 000 person times)	10.36	13.09	14.64	12.19
代写法律事务文书（万件）	Legal Documents Written on Behalf of Clients(10 000 cases)	1.92	2.67	3.96	2.06
公证工作	**Notarizations**				
公证处（个）	Notarial Offices (unit)	22	22	21	21
公证人员（人）	Notarial Personnel (person)	366	821	1 059	1 113
# 公证员	Notaries	243	359	458	462
办理公证文书（万件）	Documents Notarized (10 000 cases)	47.72	40.76	57.17	59.22
国内公证	Domestic	12.79	18.54	27.57	29.44
涉外公证	Foreign	19.93	20.98	28.48	28.77
涉港澳台公证	Hong Kong, Macao and Taiwan		1.24	1.12	1.01
公证费收入（亿元）	Revenue of Notarial Fees (100 million yuan)	1.13	4.70	6.10	7.33
人民调解工作	**People's Mediation**				
专职司法助理员（人）	Full-time Judicial Assistants (person)	416	734	782	777
人民调解委员会（万个）	People's Mediation Committees(10 000 units)	0.89	0.63	0.64	0.68
调解人员（万人）	Mediators (10 000 persons)	3.55	3.41	3.38	3.33
调解民间纠纷（万件）	Civil Disputes Mediated (10 000 cases)	6.37	23.24	30.36	33.10
# 调解成功	Successfully Mediated		22.81	28.92	31.24
# 婚姻家庭	Family Disputes	1.97	3.63	4.13	3.81
邻 里	Neighbor Disputes	2.51	5.12	6.23	5.93
赔 偿	Compensation	0.25	3.02	6.17	5.98
房屋宅基地	Housing and Housing Sites	1.04	1.29	2.02	1.76

注：办理公证文件中包括涉及港、澳、台公证文件。
Note: The number of notarized documents handled included Hong Kong, Macao and Taiwan's.

表23.2 主要年份国内和涉外公证文书分类情况
DOMESTIC AND FOREIGN NOTARIAL DOCUMENTS BY TYPE IN MAIN YEARS

单位:件(case)

指标	Indicators	2000	2010	2014	2015
国内公证	**Domestic Notarized**	**277 949**	**185 425**	**275 722**	**294 402**
# 贷款合同	Loans Contracts	80 980	24 100	23 008	24 041
招标、投标	Bidding	55	82	6	12
劳务合同	Labour Contracts	4 982	9	1	1
财产租赁	Property Leases	22	711	479	374
法人资格	Legal Person Identification	109	116	23	
继承权	Rights of Inheritance	5 217	17 482	29 021	33 073
遗　嘱	Testaments	1 709	4 468	12 825	7 405
委托书	Certificate of Entrustment	4 520	48 788	71 467	78 298
赠与书	Presentation Documents	5 196	1 062	1 051	708
申明书	Declarations	10 424	5 404	8 101	8 116
涉外公证	**Foreign Notarized**	**199 323**	**209 813**	**284 834**	**287 737**
# 出　生	Births	28 535	28 627	34 305	33 995
学　历	Schooling	21 644	2 107	941	604
亲属关系	Kinship	22 488	19 286	27 665	28 841
婚姻状况	Marriages	20 274	7 246	5 434	4 486
有无违法犯罪记录	Criminal Records & Uncriminal Records	20 669	22 850	27 442	25 059
文本相符	Confirmation of Copies and Photo-offset Copies to Originals	23 645	58 999	102 410	66 210

表23.3 主要年份公安机关立案刑事案件情况
CRIMINAL CASES REGISTERED IN PUBLIC SECURITY ORGANS IN MAIN YEARS

单位:起(time)

类别	Types	2000	2010	2014	2015
总 计	**Total**	**104 946**	**119 691**	**139 999**	**205 186**
杀 人	Homicide	252	174	144	131
伤 害	Injury	1 553	2 545	2 565	2 719
抢 劫	Robbery	3 033	1 558	692	592
强 奸	Rape	396	448	484	412
诈 骗	Fraud	8 425	16 598	21 465	36 715
盗 窃	Larceny	77 912	78 322	84 639	132 720
其 他	Others	13 375	20 046	30 010	31 897

表23.4 主要年份公安机关查处治安案件情况
OFFENSE CASES AGAINST PUBLIC ORDER HANDLED BY PUBLIC SECURITY ORGANS IN MAIN YEARS

单位:起(time)

类别	Types	2000	2010	2014	2015
总 计	**Total**	**194 141**	**566 607**	**778 779**	**748 791**
#扰乱公共秩序	Disturbing Work and Public Order	23 568	25 787	37 273	27 500
寻衅滋事	Gang Fighting or Picking Quarrels and Making Trouble	3 373	3 315	2 028	1 941
阻碍执行职务	Obstructing the Government Workers to Perform Their Duty	1 029	658	809	1 772
殴打他人	Beating Other Body	16 973	59 876	52 171	51 798
诈骗、抢夺、敲诈勒索财物	Defrauding, Snatching or Extoring and Racketeering Valuables	2 936	24 510	61 826	70 807
伪造、变造、倒卖有价票证、凭证	Forging and Fraudulently Selling Bills or Certificates	5 551	524	30	59
卖淫、嫖娼	Prostitution or Going Whoring	4 631	7 281	12 104	11 410
赌 博	Gambling	17 464	21 760	64 028	72 057

表23.5 交通事故和火灾情况(1980～2015)
BASIC STATISTICS OF TRAFFIC ACCIDENTS AND FIRES

年 份 Year	交通事故 Traffic Accidents 次 数(万次) Times (10 000 times)	死亡人数(人) Death (person)	受伤人数(万人) Injuries (10 000 persons)	损失折款(万元) Losses Converted -into Cash (10 000 yuan)	火 灾 Fires 次 数(万次) Times (10 000 times)	死亡人数(人) Death (person)	受伤人数(人) Injuries (person)	损失折款(万元) Losses Converted -into Cash (10 000 yuan)
1980	1.10	445	1.01	96	0.08	17	126	457
1981	1.18	507	1.06	119	0.09	33	81	202
1982	0.83	434	0.77	98	0.07	33	76	255
1983	0.73	443	0.70	99	0.06	24	67	533
1984	0.83	503	0.75	123	0.05	21	71	177
1985	0.71	687	0.57	318	0.05	30	74	374
1986	0.84	678	0.62	576	0.06	25	54	790
1987	1.01	811	0.67	959	0.06	51	56	575
1988	0.84	707	0.56	1 117	0.06	58	53	460
1989	0.75	652	0.49	1 137	0.03	30	30	394
1990	0.76	608	0.47	1 345	0.21	45	137	1 868
1991	0.75	594	0.45	1 530	0.17	38	112	937
1992	0.45	591	0.18	2 029	0.17	40	57	2 742
1993	0.81	699	0.29	4 652	0.14	73	128	2 252
1994	1.26	722	0.33	8 337	0.11	51	95	2 378
1995	1.67	788	0.38	12 077	0.11	47	86	2 100
1996	2.01	783	0.44	13 462	0.09	87	96	2 206
1997	2.16	780	0.58	13 682	0.74	51	138	2 639
1998	2.40	781	0.65	15 186	0.72	42	114	2 205
1999	2.61	726	0.78	15 924	0.66	43	90	1 487
2000	4.13	1 492	1.61	20 391	0.52	40	57	1 919
2001	4.21	1 503	1.57	23 883	0.32	31	65	966
2002	4.71	1 400	1.57	30 052	0.60	39	58	1 313
2003	5.42	1 406	1.12	39 721	0.58	47	85	1 724
2004	2.71	1 543	1.13	19 149	0.51	30	47	1 681
2005	0.92	1 393	0.88	7 961	0.43	54	84	1 731
2006	0.66	1 231	0.67	3 292	0.45	45	54	2 292
2007	0.40	1 171	0.38	1 943	0.42	50	45	2 650
2008	0.27	1 100	0.26	1 469	0.35	50	57	14 523
2009	0.28	1 042	0.27	1 226	0.61	63	41	3 990
2010	0.22	1 011	0.19	967	0.57	101	125	22 949
2011	0.21	944	0.18	1 349	0.58	43	46	11 000
2012	0.23	916	0.21	1 488	0.45	39	45	6 924
2013	0.20	914	0.15	988	0.96	73	79	12 417
2014	0.12	902	0.06	463	0.58	59	55	7 428
2015	0.10	868	0.05	470	0.46	52	41	14 000

表23.6 交通事故情况(2015)
BASIC STATISTICS OF TRAFFIC ACCIDENTS

类别	Types	发生数(起) Number (case)	死亡人数(人) Death (person)	受伤人数(人) Injuries (person)	损失折款(万元) Losses Converted -into Cash (10 000 yuan)
总计	**Total**	**1 044**	**868**	**455**	**469.60**
#死亡事故	Death Accident	832	868	182	387.00
伤人事故	Injury Accident	206		273	73.00
#机动车	Motor-driven Vehicles	792	684	336	424.00
#汽车	Automobiles	715	615	310	400.00
摩托车	Motorcycles	60	52	21	21.00
非机动车	Non-motor-driven Vehicles	194	140	95	36.00
#自行车	Bicycles	26	25	3	4.00
行人乘车人	Pedestrians and Passengers	50	36	20	9.00
其他	Other	1	1		0.60

表23.7 火灾事故情况(2015)
BASIC STATISTICS OF FIRES

指标	Indicators	发生数(起) Number (case)	死亡人数(人) Death (person)	受伤人数(人) Injuries (person)	损失折款(万元) Losses Converted -into Cash (10 000 yuan)
总计	**Total**	**4 606**	**52**	**41**	**14 000.00**
电气火灾	Electrical Fire	1 720	21	15	11 315.80
生产作业类火灾	Production Operations	156		2	673.12
生活用火不慎	Careless Use of Fire	788	6	8	360.26
吸烟	Smoking	146	10		105.22
玩火	Play with Fire	55	2	2	117.54
自燃	Spontaneous Combustion	75			126.19
雷击	Lightning	4			1.43
静电	Static Electricity	2			0.75
不明确原因	Unexplained	47	1	1	12.37
放火	Set Fire	60	9	4	121.19
其他	Others	1 553	3	9	1 166.14

表23.8 检察院直接立案侦查案件情况(2015)
CASES UNDER DIRECT INVESTIGATION BY PROCURATOR'S OFFICES

类别	Types	受案(件) Cases Accepted (case)	立案件数(件) Quantity of Cases Registered (case)	立案人数(人) Person of Cases Registered (person)	侦查终结件数(件) Quantity of Cases Settled (case)	侦查终结人数(人) Person of Cases Settled (person)
总计	**Total**	**1 044**	**401**	**476**	**363**	**439**
贪污贿赂案件	Quantity of Cases on Corruption and Bribery	946	363	428	325	394
贪污	Corruption	334	70	88	68	93
贿赂	Bribery	560	272	317	222	264
挪用公款	Misappropriation of Public Funds	30	18	18	27	29
集体私分	Collective Illegal Possession of Public Funds	6	3	5	2	2
巨额财产来源不明	Huge Amount of Property from Unidentified Sources	15				
其他	Others	1			6	6
渎职侵权案件	**Quantity of Cases on Abuse and Dereliction of Duty**	**98**	**38**	**48**	**38**	**45**
滥用职权	Abuse of Power	58	22	28	26	32
玩忽职守	Dereliction of Duty	14	5	6	6	7
徇私舞弊	Fraudulent Practice	13	5	8	2	2
侵犯公民权利	Infringement of Civil Right	2				
其他	Others	11	6	6	4	4

表23.9 检察院民事、行政案件办理情况(2015)
CIVIL CASES AND ADMINISTRATIVE CASES HANDLED BY PROCURATOR'S OFFICES

单位:件(case)

类别	Types	受案 Cases Accepted	审查处理 Cases Investigated	其中 of which: 本院处理 Settled by Such Procurator Office	结案处理 Cases Settled	其中 of which: 提出抗诉 Appeals Rejected
总计	**Total**	**1 579**	**1 060**	**1 057**	**1 292**	**51**
民事案	**Civil Cases**	**1 334**	**934**	**931**	**1 046**	**49**
婚姻家庭	Marriages Disputes	59	37	37	48	2
继承纠纷	Inheritance Disputes	59	37	37	57	5
物权保护	Property Rights Protection	94	59	59	72	4
所有权争议	Ownership Disputes	76	46	46	61	1
合同纠纷	Contract Disputes	642	469	467	493	24
劳动人事争议	Labor and Personnel Disputes	159	117	117	133	6
其他	Others	245	169	168	182	7
行政案	**Administrative Cases**	**245**	**126**	**126**	**246**	**2**

表23.10 检察院申诉案件处理情况(2015)
APPEALS HANDLED BY PROCURATOR'S OFFICES

单位:件(case)

类别 Types		受案 Cases Accepted	审查处理 Cases Investigated	其中 of which 分送本院其他部门 Dilivering to Other Department of Such Procurator's Offices
总计	**Total**	**1 852**	**1 291**	**634**
#首次申诉	**Appeals First Time**	**1 811**	**1 254**	**613**
#不服不起诉	Appeals Against Non-prosecution	17	18	12
不服不立案	Appeals Against Rejection of the Case	263	266	207
不服逮捕	Appeals Against Arrest	8	8	4
不服刑事判决	Appeals Against Judgment of Criminal Case	253	247	80
不服民事行政裁决	Appeals Against Adminnistration Arbitrament of Civil Case	1 009	464	180

表23.10 续表 continued

单位:件(case)

类别 Types		其中 of which 移送其他检察院 Removing to Other Procurator's Offices	移送公安机关 Removing to Public Security Organs	移送其他机关 Removing to Other Organs	直接答复 Direct Reply
总计	**Total**	**300**	**21**	**3**	**262**
#首次申诉	**Appeals First Time**	**296**	**20**	**3**	**255**
#不服不起诉	Appeals Against Non-prosecution	2			2
不服不立案	Appeals Against Rejection of the Case	47	4		5
不服逮捕	Appeals Against Arrest	3			
不服刑事判决	Appeals Against Judgment of Criminal Case	101		1	41
不服民事行政裁决	Appeals Against Adminnistration Arbitrament of Civil Case	93			170

表23.11 法院各类案件办理情况(2015)
CASES HANDLED BY COURTS

单位:件(case)

类别	Types	收案 Cases Accepted	结案 Cases Settled	其中 of which 判决 Judgement	裁定 Arbitration	调解 Mediation
一审刑事案件	**First Trial Criminal Cases**	**32 842**	**32 741**	**32 619**	**119**	**3**
# 侵犯公民人身权利、民主权利罪	Offences Against Citizens' Personal and Democratic Rights	3 104	3 090	3 037	51	2
侵犯财产罪	Offences Against Properties	9 958	9 940	9 907	32	1
妨碍社会管理秩序罪	Offences Against Social Management of Order	9 661	9 699	9 677	22	
一审民事案件	**First Trial Civil Cases**	**412 678**	**406 667**	**109 146**	**210 463**	**87 058**
婚姻家庭、继承案件	Marriages and Inheritance Cases	34 009	33 777	9 807	8 027	15 943
婚姻家庭案件	Marriages and Fimily Cases	25 699	25 599	8 545	6 841	10 213
继承案件	Inheritance Cases	8 310	8 178	1 264	1 184	5 730
合同纠纷案件	Contract Disputes Cases	288 337	283 941	67 944	180 384	35 613
# 买卖合同纠纷	Trade Contracts	22 367	21 485	8 840	7 345	5 300
房地产开发经营合同纠纷	Real Estate Development Contracts	5 176	5 273	2 856	1 823	594
借款合同纠纷	Loan Contracts	42 582	41 005	19 856	14 140	7 009
租赁合同纠纷	Lease Contracts	12 311	11 170	5 227	3 732	2 211
劳动争议	Labor Disputes	14 341	14 353	7 554	3 264	3 535
劳务合同	Labor Contracts	2 094	1 928	792	565	571
权属、侵犯纠纷及其他民事案件	Disputes of Right Infringement of Right and Other Civil Affairs	90 332	88 949	31 395	22 052	35 502
# 所有权及与所有权相关权力纠纷	Ownership and Related Rights	12 936	12 686	4 862	4 398	3 426
人身权纠纷	Personal Rights	55 651	55 307	19 210	5 925	30 172
一审行政案件	**First Trial Administrative Cases**	**5 714**	**5 382**	**2 625**	**2 757**	

表23.12 法院执行案件情况(2015) CASES EXECUTED BY COURTS

单位:件(case)

类别 Types		收案 Cases Accepted	结案 Cases Settled	其中 of which 自动履行 Automatic Performance	和解 Mediation	强制执行 Compellent Execution
总计	**Total**	**122 755**	**121 634**	**47 540**	**1 538**	**18 096**
刑事	Criminal Cases	4 905	4 762	237	6	127
民事	Civil Cases	98 290	97 455	39 277	1 304	13 952
行政	Administrative Cases	169	167	77		15
行政非诉审查与执行	Non-litigious Investigation and Execution of Administration	2 341	2 359	846	4	276
仲裁	Arbitration	15 459	15 307	7 020	193	3 551
公证债权文书	Notary Creditor's Rights	1 435	1 426	80	30	143
其他	Others	156	158	3	1	32

表23.13 主要年份法院各类案件结案情况 CASES ENDED BY COURTS IN MAIN YEARS

单位:起(time)

类别 Types		2005	2010	2013	2014	2015
总计	**Total**	**283 230**	**406 582**	**464 950**	**534 928**	**614 484**
刑事案件	Criminal Cases	17 353	22 137	30 880	35 957	36 928
婚姻家庭、继承案件	Marriages and Inheritance Cases	28 563	31 114	32 668	33 886	35 527
合同纠纷案件	Contract Disputes Cases	128 118	180 459	199 569	249 160	302 667
权属、侵犯纠纷及其他民事案件	Disputes of Right Infringement of Right and Other Civil Affairs	31 153	64 395	83 353	88 257	85 704
行政案件	Administrative Cases	3 016	2 135	3 933	4 984	8 015
申诉、申请再审	Second Trial on Appeals and Requisition	4 023	4 120	4 100	4 233	4 675
司法赔偿	Justice Compensation	6	1	10	22	46
执行案件	Executed Cases	70 998	102 221	110 437	118 429	121 632

上/海/统/计/年/鉴

主要统计指标解释

律　师

指依法取得律师执业证书,担任法律顾问,民事(刑事、行政)案件代理人、刑事案件辩护人、办理非诉讼业务,解答法律询问,代写法律事务文书等,为社会提供法律服务的人员。

公证人员

指在国家机关依法办理公证事务的司法人员。包括公证员、助理公证员和在公证处工作的其他人员。

公证文书

指公证处根据当事人申请,依照事实和法律,按照法定程序制作的,具有法律效力的司法证明文书。根据公证书用途和使用地,公证书分为国内公证书、国内经济公证书、涉外民事公证书、涉外经济公证书四类。

调解民间纠纷

指调解委员会按照法律规定,根据自愿原则,用说服教育的方法调解民间发生的有关民事权利和义务争执的件数,包括调解成功数和调解未成功数。该指标主要反映人民调解委员会的工作量。

立　案

指人民检察院对受理的报案、控告、举报或自首及自行发现的犯罪线索、犯罪嫌疑人进行初步调查后,认为存在职务犯罪事实和应追究刑事责任,并决定作为刑事案件进行侦查的诉讼活动,是追究犯罪的开始。该指标主要反映人民检察院依法将职务犯罪线索作为刑事案件进行侦查的诉讼活动。

申　诉

指经检察机关信访部门审查处理后,移送到检察机关申诉部门的申诉案件,包括不服检察机关处理决定和不服法院刑事判决和裁定的申诉的案件。

SHANGHAI STATISTICAL YEARBOOK

EXPLANATORY NOTES TO MAJOR STATISTICAL INDICATORS

□ Lawyers

Lawyers are certified legal workers according to law, and who are employed by legal counseling firms to act as legal advisers, agents in criminal or civil lawsuits, or defenders in criminal lawsuits, or to handle non–litigious legal affairs, to advise on matters of law or to write legal papers for others, and provide service to the public.

□ Notary Personnel

Notary Personnel are judicial workers of the state notary organs handling notarization work according to law. They include notaries, assistant notaries, and other people working in notary firms.

□ Notary Documents

Notary Documents refer to the judicatory notary documents drawn up by the request of the party and are in accordance with facts and laws and following certain legal proceedings. According to usage and locality, the notary documents are divided into following 4 types: domestic notary documents, domestic economic notary documents, foreign–related civil notary documents and foreign–related economic notary documents.

□ Mediation of Civil Disputes

Mediation of Civil Disputes refers to number of cases made by mediation committees in mediating in civil disputes concerning civil rights and duties through persuasion and education in accordance with the provisions of law on a voluntary basis, so as to solve disputes by helping the parties involved come to an agreement and understanding, including those unsuccessful ones. This indicator reflects the workload of the mediation committees.

□ Acceptance of Case

Acceptance of Case refers to the decision made by the people's procuratorate office on reported cases, prosecution, impeachment, surrender, self–found criminal clues or suspects after initial investigation to confirm the act of crime and to start legal proceedings of the case as criminal case.

□ Appeals

Appeals refer to cases transferred to the appeal departments of procurator's offices after initial review by departments dealing with complaint letters and calls of the public. Included are appeals against decisions made by procurator's offices and appeals against court rules and verdicts.

图书在版编目(CIP)数据

上海统计年鉴. 2016：汉英对照 / 上海市统计局，国家统计局上海调查总队编
——北京：中国统计出版社，2016.7
ISBN 978-7-5037-7849-0

Ⅰ. ① 上…
Ⅱ. ① 上… ② 国…
Ⅲ. ① 统计资料－上海市－2016－年鉴－汉、英
Ⅳ. ① C832.51-54

中国版本图书馆CIP数据核字(2016)第159400号

上海统计年鉴—2016

作　　者 / 上海市统计局　国家统计局上海调查总队
责任编辑 / 佘竞雄　熊威
出版发行 / 中国统计出版社
地　　址 / 北京市丰台区西三环南路甲6号
邮政编码 / 100073
电　　话 / 邮购 (010) 63376909　书店 (010) 68783171
网　　址 / http://www.zgtjcbs.com
印　　刷 / 上海万卷印刷股份有限公司
经　　销 / 新华书店
开　　本 / 890mm × 1240 mm　1/16
字　　数 / 132 万字
印　　张 / 31.625
版　　别 / 2016年10月第1版
版　　次 / 2016年10月第1次印刷
定　　价 / 480.00元

本书附同版本CD-ROM一张，光盘内容以书面文字为准。
如有印装错误，由本社发行部调换。